Linear Algebra and Geometry

SMP Further Mathematics Series

Linear Algebra and Geometry

DAVID SMART

The right of the University of Cambridge to print and sell all manner of books was granted by Henry VIII in 1534. The University has printed and published continuously since 1584.

CAMBRIDGE UNIVERSITY PRESS

Cambridge
New York New Rochelle
Melbourne Sydney

Published by the Press Syndicate of the University of Cambridge
The Pitt Building, Trumpington Street, Cambridge CB2 1RP
32 East 57th Street, New York, NY 10022, USA
10 Stamford Road, Oakleigh, Melbourne 3166, Australia

First published 1988

Printed in Great Britain at the University Press, Cambridge

British Library cataloguing in publication data

Smart, David
Linear algebra and geometry.—(SMP
further mathematics series).
1. Algebras, Linear
I. Title II. Series
512′.5 QA184

ISBN 0 521 33616 3

MP

Contents

Preface

Although this book has been written to cater for the 'Linear Algebra and Geometry' section of the SMP Further Mathematics examination, much of the ground covered is common to other further mathematics and higher education courses and should therefore equally well meet their requirements.

The book divides naturally into four sections, each terminating with a revision exercise. The first section (Chapters 1–4), which builds on O-level or GCSE knowledge of matrices, is a two-dimensional geometric approach to linear transformations and their applications. Important work on eigenvalues and eigenvectors is introduced. In the second section (Chapters 5–9), the ideas of the first four chapters are extended to three dimensions. The concept of a vector space is central to the third section (Chapters 10–14). Examples are drawn from a variety of areas of mathematics and not just geometry. Some of the work becomes more 'abstract' and a number of general results about linear transformations are proved. The fourth section (Chapters 15–19) deals with several other algebraic structures; namely, groups, rings, fields and equivalence relations. 'What is its use?' is a question often asked. The final chapter gives a number of examples, drawn from a variety of branches of mathematics, where the ideas and techniques introduced in this book are applied. Throughout the book I have tried to introduce new ideas within a familiar mathematical context (hence the reliance on geometry in the first half of the book) so that the student can get a 'feel' of what is happening before meeting the ideas in the 'abstract'.

It is recognised that some students will be working on this course in parallel with their single-subject A-level studies, perhaps in small groups with limited teacher help. So I have tried to write a text which can be read by the student and begun early in the sixth-form course. This book builds on elementary knowledge of matrices and the first two sections are suitable for study in the first year of a two-year sixth-form course. Very little single-subject A-level knowledge is assumed.

Each chapter is divided into sections which contain exposition, worked examples and questions in the text (numbered consecutively Q.1, Q.2, ... throughout a chapter); these questions are an essential part of the teaching material, so solutions of them are given at the end of the book. Each chapter also contains exercises which test the theory covered in the previous section(s). The miscellaneous exercise which appears at the end of each chapter includes more difficult questions on the ideas of the chapter as well as questions which extend these ideas further. The revision exercises contain two types of question: the 'A' questions test the basic techniques and ideas of the chapter, while the 'B' questions are less straightforward problems. There are also three exercises of examination questions. Thanks are due to the University of Cambridge Local Examinations Syndicate, the Oxford Delegacy of Local Examinations, the University of London School Examination Board, the Oxford and Cambridge Schools Examination Board (which also provides examinations for MEI and SMP), the University of Cambridge, the University of Oxford and the Mathematical Association for permission to use examination questions in the text.

In planning and writing this book I have had invaluable support and advice from the Advisory Group set up by SMP: Simon Baxter, Douglas Bridges, Peter Fale, Timothy Lewis, Timothy Vessey and John Hersee, formerly Executive Director of SMP. This group hammered out the shape of the book in a series of meetings and made many constructive comments and criticisms about the draft text and exercises. The first draft was duplicated and distributed by SMP to a number of schools, and I am very grateful to the teachers and students who tried it out in the classroom and sent me some very helpful feedback.

David Smart

1

Linear transformations

1.1 GENERAL TRANSFORMATIONS

We begin this chapter with two questions on transformations. As you answer them try to think of any assumptions which you are making.

Q.1 Describe the transformation represented by the matrix $\begin{bmatrix} 2 & -1 \\ 1 & 2 \end{bmatrix}$.

Q.2 Under a transformation the image of the point (1, 0) is (3, 1) and the image of the point (0, 1) is (2, 2). Find the image of (*a*) (2, 0), (*b*) (1, 1) under this transformation.

Discussion of Q.1
You probably began by considering the image of the unit square

$$\begin{bmatrix} 2 & -1 \\ 1 & 2 \end{bmatrix}\begin{bmatrix} 0 & 1 & 1 & 0 \\ 0 & 0 & 1 & 1 \end{bmatrix} = \begin{bmatrix} 0 & 2 & 1 & -1 \\ 0 & 1 & 3 & 2 \end{bmatrix}$$

and then drew a diagram (Fig. 1).

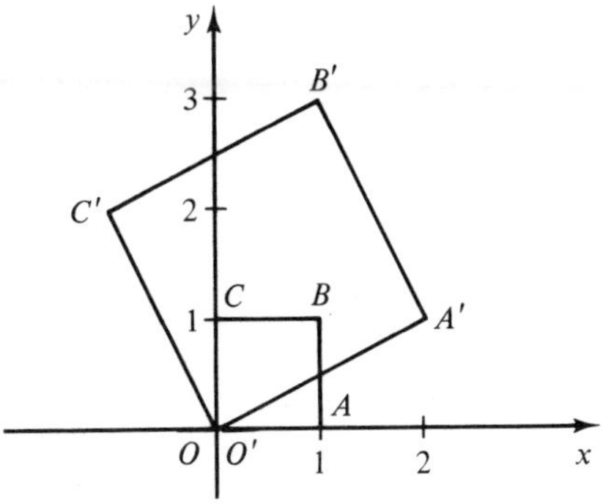

Figure 1

From Fig. 1 we see that the transformation is a combination of a rotation about O and an enlargement. The angle of rotation is 26.6° (the angle between OA and $O'A'$ is 26.6°) and the scale factor of the enlargement is $\sqrt{5}$ ($O'A'$ is of length $\sqrt{5}$).

Several questions arise from this approach:

(1) Would we have come to the same conclusion if we had started with another figure and not the unit square?

Q.3 Try the triangle with vertices (1, 1), (0, 2), (−1, 1) or any other figure of your choice.

(2) In Fig. 1 AB is a straight line. We found the image of A and the image of B and assumed that $A'B'$ is also a straight line. Is this valid?

Q.4 Choose several points on the line AB and find their images. Are these images on the line $A'B'$? Are they in the same order?

(3) What happens to the original grid under this transformation?

Q.5 Draw the images of the lines $x = -2, -1, 0, 1, 2$ and $y = -2, -1, 0, 1, 2$ under this transformation. Verify that the answers are as in Fig. 2.

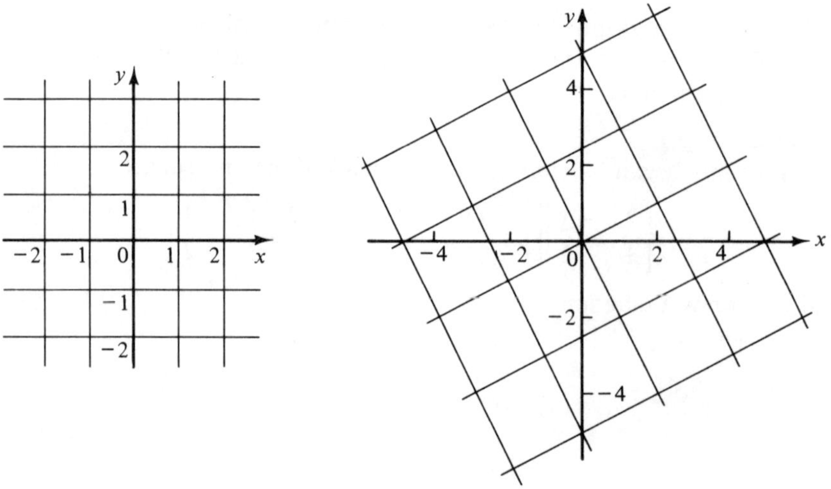

Figure 2

From (1) we guess that the description of the transformation is independent of the object being transformed and its position. From (2) we guess that lines are transformed into lines, and from (3), although we have only drawn part of the xy-plane, we guess that the transformation applies to the *whole* plane.

In the discussion so far we have used two different but equivalent ways of representing a point: coordinates and position vector. For example, if the point A has coordinates (1, 1), the position vector of A is $\mathbf{a} = \begin{bmatrix} 1 \\ 1 \end{bmatrix}$.

Discussion of Q.2

There are three possible approaches:

(1) You may have assumed that the transformation could be represented by the

matrix $\begin{bmatrix} a & b \\ c & d \end{bmatrix}$, so $\begin{bmatrix} a & b \\ c & d \end{bmatrix}\begin{bmatrix} 1 \\ 0 \end{bmatrix} = \begin{bmatrix} 3 \\ 1 \end{bmatrix}$ and $\begin{bmatrix} a & b \\ c & d \end{bmatrix}\begin{bmatrix} 0 \\ 1 \end{bmatrix} = \begin{bmatrix} 2 \\ 2 \end{bmatrix}$.

$$\begin{bmatrix} a \\ c \end{bmatrix} = \begin{bmatrix} 3 \\ 1 \end{bmatrix} \quad \text{and} \quad \begin{bmatrix} b \\ d \end{bmatrix} = \begin{bmatrix} 2 \\ 2 \end{bmatrix}.$$

So the matrix is $\begin{bmatrix} 3 & 2 \\ 1 & 2 \end{bmatrix}$.

(*a*) The image of the point (2,0) is found from

$$\begin{bmatrix} 3 & 2 \\ 1 & 2 \end{bmatrix}\begin{bmatrix} 2 \\ 0 \end{bmatrix} = \begin{bmatrix} 6 \\ 2 \end{bmatrix}, \quad \text{that is, the point } (6, 2).$$

(*b*) The image of the point (1, 1) is found from

$$\begin{bmatrix} 3 & 2 \\ 1 & 2 \end{bmatrix}\begin{bmatrix} 1 \\ 1 \end{bmatrix} = \begin{bmatrix} 5 \\ 3 \end{bmatrix}, \quad \text{that is, the point } (5, 3).$$

(2) You may have spotted that the translation vector $\begin{bmatrix} 2 \\ 1 \end{bmatrix}$ takes the point (1,0) to (3, 1) and the point (0, 1) to (2, 2), so under this translation

(*a*) the image of (2,0) is (4, 1), and

(*b*) the image of (1, 1) is (3, 2).

In this case we are making the assumption that the tıansformation is a translation (Fig. 3).

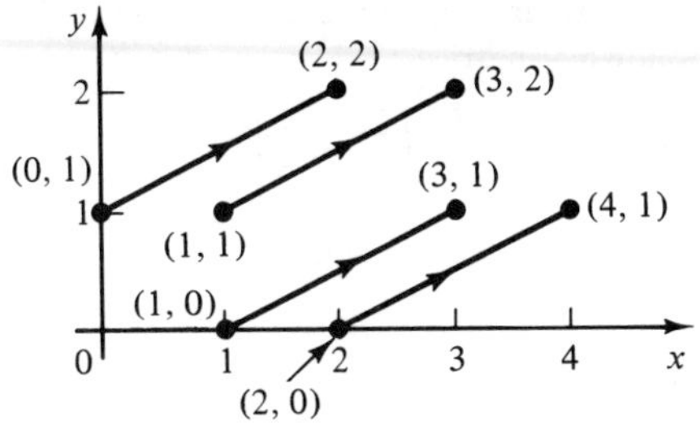

Figure 3

(3) You may have recognised that the position vector of the point (1,0), that is $\begin{bmatrix} 1 \\ 0 \end{bmatrix}$, is the base vector **i** and the position vector of (0, 1), that is $\begin{bmatrix} 0 \\ 1 \end{bmatrix}$, is the base vector **j** and noticed that $\begin{bmatrix} 2 \\ 0 \end{bmatrix} = 2\mathbf{i}$ and $\begin{bmatrix} 1 \\ 1 \end{bmatrix} = \mathbf{i} + \mathbf{j}$.

You may have assumed that the same sort of relationship holds for the *images* under the transformation.

So (*a*) the position vector of the image of the point (2, 0)

$$= 2 \text{ (position vector of the image of } \mathbf{i})$$

$$= 2\begin{bmatrix} 3 \\ 1 \end{bmatrix}$$

$$= \begin{bmatrix} 6 \\ 2 \end{bmatrix};$$

and (*b*) the position vector of the image of the point (1, 1)

$$= \text{(position vector of the image of } \mathbf{i}$$

$$+ \text{ position vector of the image of } \mathbf{j})$$

$$= \begin{bmatrix} 3 \\ 1 \end{bmatrix} + \begin{bmatrix} 2 \\ 2 \end{bmatrix}$$

$$= \begin{bmatrix} 5 \\ 3 \end{bmatrix}.$$

These are the same answers as in (1).

Q.6 Methods (1) and (3) gave the same answers for the points (2, 0) and (1, 1). Would they have agreed if we had chosen other points? Investigate what happens with the points (−4, 5) and (p, q).

Exercise 1A

1 Draw, on graph paper, the unit square and its image under the transformations represented by the following matrices:

(*a*) $\begin{bmatrix} 1 & 3 \\ 0 & 1 \end{bmatrix}$ (*b*) $\begin{bmatrix} 1 & 0 \\ 0 & 1\frac{1}{2} \end{bmatrix}$ (*c*) $\begin{bmatrix} 2 & -1 \\ 1 & 0 \end{bmatrix}$

Describe fully each of these transformations.

2 $\mathbf{T}$ is the translation $\begin{bmatrix} 2 \\ 1 \end{bmatrix}$.

(*a*) Is it true that $\mathbf{T}\left(k\begin{bmatrix} 4 \\ 7 \end{bmatrix}\right) = k\mathbf{T}\begin{bmatrix} 4 \\ 7 \end{bmatrix}$, where k is a real number? If your answer is 'yes', for which value(s) of k is it true?

(*b*) Is it true that $\mathbf{T}\left(\begin{bmatrix} 4 \\ 7 \end{bmatrix} + \begin{bmatrix} -1 \\ 5 \end{bmatrix}\right) = \mathbf{T}\begin{bmatrix} 4 \\ 7 \end{bmatrix} + \mathbf{T}\begin{bmatrix} -1 \\ 5 \end{bmatrix}$?

(*c*) Is it true that $\mathbf{T}\begin{bmatrix} 0 \\ 0 \end{bmatrix} = \begin{bmatrix} 0 \\ 0 \end{bmatrix}$?

3 The transformation $\mathbf{S}$ is an enlargement, centre (0, 0), scale factor 3.

(*a*) Is it true that $\mathbf{S}\left(k\begin{bmatrix} 4 \\ -3 \end{bmatrix}\right) = k\mathbf{S}\begin{bmatrix} 4 \\ -3 \end{bmatrix}$ where k is a real number? If your answer is 'yes', for which value(s) of k is it true?

(*b*) Is it true that $\mathbf{S}\left(\begin{bmatrix} 2 \\ -1 \end{bmatrix} + \begin{bmatrix} -1 \\ 3 \end{bmatrix}\right) = \mathbf{S}\begin{bmatrix} 2 \\ -1 \end{bmatrix} + \mathbf{S}\begin{bmatrix} -1 \\ 3 \end{bmatrix}$?

(*c*) Is it true that $\mathbf{S}\begin{bmatrix} 0 \\ 0 \end{bmatrix} = \begin{bmatrix} 0 \\ 0 \end{bmatrix}$?

4 Repeat question 3 for the transformation **R**, which is an enlargement, centre (1,0), scale factor 2.

5 The points A, B, C and D have coordinates $(0, 1), (\frac{1}{2}, 0), (0, -5)$ and $(5, 0)$ respectively. Find the coordinates of the point K, where the lines AB and CD meet. The images of the A, B, C and D under the transformation represented by the matrix $\begin{bmatrix} 2 & -1 \\ 1 & 0 \end{bmatrix}$ are A', B', C' and D'. Find the coordinates of K', the point where the lines $A'B'$ and $C'D'$ meet. Is it true that K' is the image of K under this transformation? Did you notice anything about the lines CD and $C'D'$?

6 Write down the coordinates of any two points A and B on the line $y = x + 3$ and of any two points C and D on the parallel line $y = x - 4$. Find the images A', B', C' and D' of these four points under the transformation represented by the matrix $\begin{bmatrix} 1 & 1 \\ 1 & 2 \end{bmatrix}$. Are the lines $A'B'$ and $C'D'$ parallel?

1.2 PROPERTIES OF LINEAR TRANSFORMATIONS

In the discussion of Q.2 we saw that we arrived at the same answer using either method (1) or method (2). This is an example of a type of transformation that is very important in mathematics and which is known as a *linear transformation*. The properties which must hold are:

$$\mathbf{T}(k\mathbf{a}) = k\mathbf{T}(\mathbf{a}) \qquad (A)$$

and

$$\mathbf{T}(\mathbf{a} + \mathbf{b}) = \mathbf{T}(\mathbf{a}) + \mathbf{T}(\mathbf{b}) \qquad (B)$$

where **T** is the transformation, **a** and **b** are any vectors in the plane, and k is a real number.

Consequences of the definition of a linear transformation

Starting from the definition of a linear transformation, we can deduce a number of important results which we shall be able to use later.

Result 1
A transformation **T** represented by a 2×2 matrix **M** is linear.

Q.7 If $\mathbf{T} = \begin{bmatrix} p & q \\ r & s \end{bmatrix}$, $\mathbf{a} = \begin{bmatrix} e \\ f \end{bmatrix}$, $\mathbf{b} = \begin{bmatrix} g \\ h \end{bmatrix}$ and k is a scalar, use matrix multiplication to show that (*a*) $\mathbf{T}(k\mathbf{a}) = k\mathbf{T}(\mathbf{a})$, (*b*) $\mathbf{T}(\mathbf{a} + \mathbf{b}) = \mathbf{T}(\mathbf{a}) + \mathbf{T}(\mathbf{b})$, where $\mathbf{T}(\mathbf{a}) = \mathbf{M}\mathbf{a}$.

Result 2
In general, lines are mapped onto lines.

We begin by revising the method of finding the vector equation of a line (Fig. 4).

The vector **AB** = **b** − **a**.

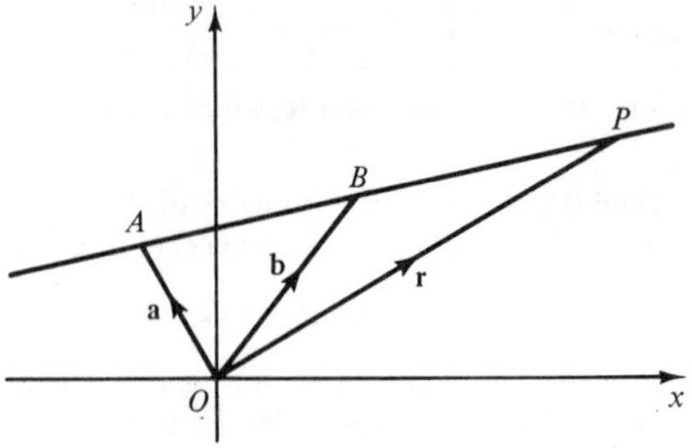

Figure 4

If P is a point with position vector $\mathbf{r} = \begin{bmatrix} x \\ y \end{bmatrix}$ on the line AB, then $\mathbf{AP} = t(\mathbf{AB})$ where t is a real number.

Now $$\mathbf{OP} = \mathbf{OA} + \mathbf{AP}$$

$$\Rightarrow \quad \mathbf{r} = \mathbf{a} + t(\mathbf{b} - \mathbf{a}), \quad \text{where } t \text{ is a real number.}$$

Example 1

Find the vector equation of the line through the points A and B whose position vectors are $\mathbf{a} = \begin{bmatrix} 1 \\ 3 \end{bmatrix}$ and $\mathbf{b} = \begin{bmatrix} 5 \\ -1 \end{bmatrix}$. Where does the line AB meet the line CD, which has vector equation $\mathbf{r} = \begin{bmatrix} 2 \\ -1 \end{bmatrix} + s\begin{bmatrix} 1 \\ 2 \end{bmatrix}$?

Solution

Substituting the values of **a** and **b**, the vector equation of the line AB is

$$\mathbf{r} = \begin{bmatrix} 1 \\ 3 \end{bmatrix} + t\begin{bmatrix} 4 \\ -4 \end{bmatrix}.$$

If the lines AB and CD meet at the point P with position vector **p**, then

$$\mathbf{p} = \begin{bmatrix} 1 \\ 3 \end{bmatrix} + t\begin{bmatrix} 4 \\ -4 \end{bmatrix} \quad \text{for some number } t \text{ since } P \text{ lies on } AB$$

and $$\mathbf{p} = \begin{bmatrix} 2 \\ -1 \end{bmatrix} + s\begin{bmatrix} 1 \\ 2 \end{bmatrix} \quad \text{for some number } s \text{ since } P \text{ lies on } CD$$

so $$\begin{bmatrix} 1 \\ 3 \end{bmatrix} + t\begin{bmatrix} 4 \\ -4 \end{bmatrix} = \begin{bmatrix} 2 \\ -1 \end{bmatrix} + s\begin{bmatrix} 1 \\ 2 \end{bmatrix}.$$

Equating components: $$1 + 4t = 2 + s$$

$$3 - 4t = -1 + 2s.$$

Solving for s and t gives $\quad s = 1 \quad$ and $\quad t = \frac{1}{2}$.

Substituting back gives
$$\mathbf{p} = \begin{bmatrix} 1 \\ 3 \end{bmatrix} + \tfrac{1}{2}\begin{bmatrix} 4 \\ -4 \end{bmatrix}$$
$$= \begin{bmatrix} 3 \\ 1 \end{bmatrix}. \quad \left(\begin{bmatrix} 2 \\ -1 \end{bmatrix} + 1\begin{bmatrix} 1 \\ 2 \end{bmatrix} = \begin{bmatrix} 3 \\ 1 \end{bmatrix}\right)$$

So the lines AB and CD meet at the point with position vector $\begin{bmatrix} 3 \\ 1 \end{bmatrix}$. □

Q.8 Find the vector equation of the line joining the points A and B, whose position vectors are

(*a*) $\begin{bmatrix} 4 \\ -1 \end{bmatrix}$ and $\begin{bmatrix} 2 \\ 6 \end{bmatrix}$ (*b*) $\begin{bmatrix} 0 \\ 3 \end{bmatrix}$ and $\begin{bmatrix} 2 \\ 0 \end{bmatrix}$

(*c*) $\begin{bmatrix} 3 \\ -1 \end{bmatrix}$ and $\begin{bmatrix} 2 \\ \frac{1}{2} \end{bmatrix}$ (*d*) $\begin{bmatrix} -1 \\ -2 \end{bmatrix}$ and $\begin{bmatrix} 2 \\ 4 \end{bmatrix}$

Q.9 Find the position vector of the points where the following pairs of lines meet:

(*a*) $\mathbf{r} = \begin{bmatrix} 1 \\ 3 \end{bmatrix} + t\begin{bmatrix} -1 \\ 4 \end{bmatrix}$ and $\mathbf{r} = \begin{bmatrix} 2 \\ -1 \end{bmatrix} + s\begin{bmatrix} 3 \\ -1 \end{bmatrix}$

(*b*) $\mathbf{r} = \begin{bmatrix} 0 \\ -4 \end{bmatrix} + t\begin{bmatrix} -1 \\ -1 \end{bmatrix}$ and $\mathbf{r} = \begin{bmatrix} 1 \\ -2 \end{bmatrix} + s\begin{bmatrix} 2 \\ 6 \end{bmatrix}$

Example 2

Find the image of the line through the points A and B, whose position vectors are $\mathbf{a} = \begin{bmatrix} -1 \\ 2 \end{bmatrix}$ and $\mathbf{b} = \begin{bmatrix} 2 \\ 3 \end{bmatrix}$, under the linear transformation represented by the matrix $\begin{bmatrix} 3 & 1 \\ -2 & 4 \end{bmatrix}$.

Solution

The vector equation of the line AB is
$$\mathbf{r} = \begin{bmatrix} -1 \\ 2 \end{bmatrix} + t\left(\begin{bmatrix} 2 \\ 3 \end{bmatrix} - \begin{bmatrix} -1 \\ 2 \end{bmatrix}\right);$$

that is,
$$\begin{bmatrix} x \\ y \end{bmatrix} = \begin{bmatrix} -1 \\ 2 \end{bmatrix} + t\begin{bmatrix} 3 \\ 1 \end{bmatrix}.$$

So
$$\mathbf{T}\begin{bmatrix} x \\ y \end{bmatrix} = \mathbf{T}\left(\begin{bmatrix} -1 \\ 2 \end{bmatrix} + t\begin{bmatrix} 3 \\ 1 \end{bmatrix}\right)$$
$$= \mathbf{T}\begin{bmatrix} -1 \\ 2 \end{bmatrix} + \mathbf{T}\left(t\begin{bmatrix} 3 \\ 1 \end{bmatrix}\right), \quad \text{using property } (B)$$
$$= \mathbf{T}\begin{bmatrix} -1 \\ 2 \end{bmatrix} + t\mathbf{T}\begin{bmatrix} 3 \\ 1 \end{bmatrix}, \quad \text{using property } (A).$$

Now **T** is represented by the matrix $\begin{bmatrix} 3 & 1 \\ -2 & 4 \end{bmatrix}$

and $$\begin{bmatrix} 3 & 1 \\ -2 & 4 \end{bmatrix}\begin{bmatrix} -1 \\ 2 \end{bmatrix} = \begin{bmatrix} -1 \\ 10 \end{bmatrix}, \quad \begin{bmatrix} 3 & 1 \\ -2 & 4 \end{bmatrix}\begin{bmatrix} 3 \\ 1 \end{bmatrix} = \begin{bmatrix} 10 \\ -2 \end{bmatrix}.$$

Therefore, $$\mathbf{T}\begin{bmatrix} x \\ y \end{bmatrix} = \begin{bmatrix} -1 \\ 10 \end{bmatrix} + t\begin{bmatrix} 10 \\ -2 \end{bmatrix}.$$

That is, the image has vector equation

$$\mathbf{r} = \begin{bmatrix} -1 \\ 10 \end{bmatrix} + t\begin{bmatrix} 10 \\ -2 \end{bmatrix}$$

where t is a real number. This is the equation of the line through the point $(-1, 10)$ with direction $\begin{bmatrix} 10 \\ -2 \end{bmatrix}$ (Fig. 5).

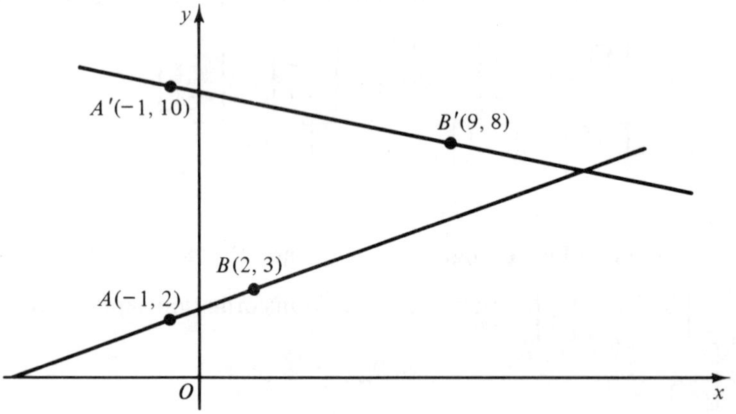

Figure 5

Notice how the properties of a linear transformation were used in this particular example in showing that the image of AB is a line. We did not simply find the images of A and B and assume that the image of the line AB is a straight line through A' and B'. □

Q.10 If $\mathbf{M} = \begin{bmatrix} 6 & -3 \\ 2 & -1 \end{bmatrix}$, find the image of the line joining the points whose position vectors are **a** and **b** where:

(*a*) $\mathbf{a} = \begin{bmatrix} 4 \\ -4 \end{bmatrix}$, $\mathbf{b} = \begin{bmatrix} 3 \\ 5 \end{bmatrix}$

(*b*) $\mathbf{a} = \begin{bmatrix} 4 \\ 3 \end{bmatrix}$, $\mathbf{b} = \begin{bmatrix} 6 \\ 7 \end{bmatrix}$

Can you see why the words ‘in general’ were included in Result 2?

Result 3

For a linear transformation, $\mathbf{T}(\mathbf{0}) = \mathbf{0}$, where $\mathbf{0} = \begin{bmatrix} 0 \\ 0 \end{bmatrix}$.

Q.11 From the properties, prove that $\mathbf{T}(\mathbf{0}) = \mathbf{0}$.

Q.12 Why is a translation not a linear transformation?

Result 4
For a linear transformation,

$$\mathbf{T}(\lambda\mathbf{a} + \mu\mathbf{b}) = \lambda\mathbf{T}(\mathbf{a}) + \mu\mathbf{T}(\mathbf{b}).$$

Q.13 Prove that $\mathbf{T}(\lambda\mathbf{a} + \mu\mathbf{b}) = \lambda\mathbf{T}(\mathbf{a}) + \mu\mathbf{T}(\mathbf{b})$.

Result 5
If we know the images of two points in a plane (whose position vectors are not in the same direction), we can find the image of any point in the plane.

Example 3
Under a linear transformation the image of the point (1,0) is (−2,3) and the image of the point (0, 1) is (3, −2); find the image of the point (4, −5).

Solution
The vectors $\mathbf{i} = \begin{bmatrix} 1 \\ 0 \end{bmatrix}$ and $\mathbf{j} = \begin{bmatrix} 0 \\ 1 \end{bmatrix}$ are known as base vectors, and the position vector of any point on the plane can be expressed in terms of **i** and **j**, for example

$$\begin{bmatrix} 4 \\ -5 \end{bmatrix} = 4\mathbf{i} - 5\mathbf{j}.$$

$$\Rightarrow \quad \mathbf{T}\begin{bmatrix} 4 \\ -5 \end{bmatrix} = \mathbf{T}(4\mathbf{i} - 5\mathbf{j})$$

$$= 4\mathbf{T}(\mathbf{i}) - 5\mathbf{T}(\mathbf{j}) \qquad \text{(using Result 4)}$$

$$= 4\begin{bmatrix} -2 \\ 3 \end{bmatrix} - 5\begin{bmatrix} 3 \\ -2 \end{bmatrix} \qquad \left(\text{as we are given that } \mathbf{T}(\mathbf{i}) = \begin{bmatrix} -2 \\ 3 \end{bmatrix} \text{ and } \mathbf{T}(\mathbf{j}) = \begin{bmatrix} 3 \\ -2 \end{bmatrix}\right)$$

$$= \begin{bmatrix} -23 \\ 22 \end{bmatrix}.$$

□

Vectors other than **i** and **j** can be used as *base vectors* (provided they are not in the same direction); for example we could choose $\mathbf{a} = \begin{bmatrix} 1 \\ -3 \end{bmatrix}$ and $\mathbf{b} = \begin{bmatrix} 4 \\ -2 \end{bmatrix}$ as our base vectors since *every* point in the plane can be expressed in the form $\lambda\mathbf{a} + \mu\mathbf{b}$. This is known as a *linear combination* of **a** and **b**.

Example 4

If the image of the point $(1, -3)$ is $(4, 1)$ and the image of the point $(4, -2)$ is $(-3, 2)$ under a linear transformation, find the image of the point $(5, 5)$.

Solution

We begin by expressing $\begin{bmatrix} 5 \\ 5 \end{bmatrix}$ as a linear combination of $\begin{bmatrix} 1 \\ -3 \end{bmatrix}$ and $\begin{bmatrix} 4 \\ -2 \end{bmatrix}$.

That is,
$$\begin{bmatrix} 5 \\ 5 \end{bmatrix} = p\begin{bmatrix} 1 \\ -3 \end{bmatrix} + q\begin{bmatrix} 4 \\ -2 \end{bmatrix}.$$

So
$$\left.\begin{aligned} 5 &= p + 4q \\ 5 &= -3p - 2q \end{aligned}\right\}$$
and

Solving these equations gives $p = -3$ and $q = 2$.

That is, $\begin{bmatrix} 5 \\ 5 \end{bmatrix} = -3\begin{bmatrix} 1 \\ -3 \end{bmatrix} + 2\begin{bmatrix} 4 \\ -2 \end{bmatrix}$ $(= -3\mathbf{a} + 2\mathbf{b}$, see Fig. 6).

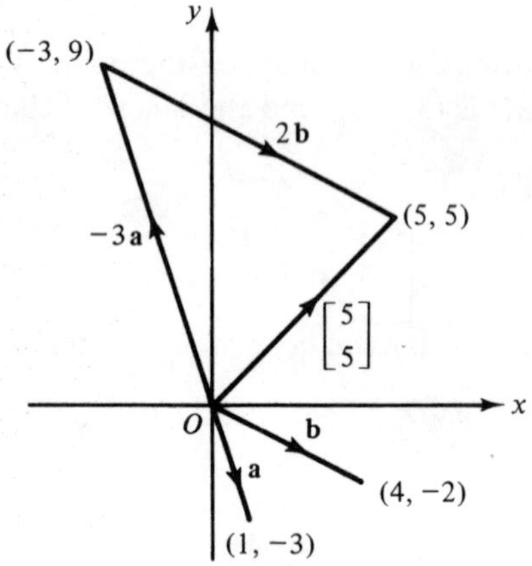

Figure 6

$$\mathbf{T}\begin{bmatrix} 5 \\ 5 \end{bmatrix} = \mathbf{T}\left(-3\begin{bmatrix} 1 \\ -3 \end{bmatrix} + 2\begin{bmatrix} 4 \\ -2 \end{bmatrix}\right)$$

$$= -3\mathbf{T}\begin{bmatrix} 1 \\ -3 \end{bmatrix} + 2\mathbf{T}\begin{bmatrix} 4 \\ -2 \end{bmatrix} \quad \text{(using Result 4)}$$

$$= -3\begin{bmatrix} 4 \\ 1 \end{bmatrix} + 2\begin{bmatrix} -3 \\ 2 \end{bmatrix}$$

(as we are given that $\mathbf{T}\begin{bmatrix} 1 \\ -3 \end{bmatrix} = \begin{bmatrix} 4 \\ 1 \end{bmatrix}$ and $\mathbf{T}\begin{bmatrix} 4 \\ -2 \end{bmatrix} = \begin{bmatrix} -3 \\ 2 \end{bmatrix}$)

$$= \begin{bmatrix} -18 \\ 1 \end{bmatrix}.$$

□

Q.14 Write the vector $\begin{bmatrix}2\\5\end{bmatrix}$ as a linear combination of the following vectors:

(*a*) $\begin{bmatrix}4\\6\end{bmatrix}$ and $\begin{bmatrix}-2\\1\end{bmatrix}$ (*b*) $\begin{bmatrix}1\\2\end{bmatrix}$ and $\begin{bmatrix}0\\1\end{bmatrix}$ (*c*) $\begin{bmatrix}1\\3\end{bmatrix}$ and $\begin{bmatrix}2\\7\end{bmatrix}$

Q.15 Why is it important to choose base vectors that are not in the same direction?

Result 6
The image of the unit square is a parallelogram under a linear transformation.

Q.16 Draw the image of the unit square under the transformations represented by each of the following matrices:

(*a*) $\begin{bmatrix}4 & 1\\2 & 3\end{bmatrix}$ (*b*) $\begin{bmatrix}-3 & 4\\-1 & -5\end{bmatrix}$ (*c*) $\begin{bmatrix}a & b\\c & d\end{bmatrix}$

Verify that the image is a parallelogram in each case.

Exercise 1B

1 Find the vector equation of the line joining the points A and B whose position vectors are

(*a*) $\begin{bmatrix}5\\7\end{bmatrix}$ and $\begin{bmatrix}7\\12\end{bmatrix}$ (*b*) $\begin{bmatrix}1\\3\end{bmatrix}$ and $\begin{bmatrix}-1\\11\end{bmatrix}$

(*c*) $\begin{bmatrix}5\\-2\end{bmatrix}$ and $\begin{bmatrix}-1\\0\end{bmatrix}$ (*d*) $\begin{bmatrix}2\\-2\end{bmatrix}$ and $\begin{bmatrix}-3\\-7\end{bmatrix}$

2 Find the position vector of the points where the following pairs of lines meet:

(*a*) $\mathbf{r} = \begin{bmatrix}7\\2\end{bmatrix} + t\begin{bmatrix}3\\4\end{bmatrix}$ and $\mathbf{r} = \begin{bmatrix}12\\7\end{bmatrix} + s\begin{bmatrix}-2\\-1\end{bmatrix}$

(*b*) $\mathbf{r} = \begin{bmatrix}-2\\-3\end{bmatrix} + t\begin{bmatrix}5\\3\end{bmatrix}$ and $\mathbf{r} = \begin{bmatrix}-3\\-4\end{bmatrix} + s\begin{bmatrix}-2\\-1\end{bmatrix}$

(*c*) $\mathbf{r} = \begin{bmatrix}4\\1\end{bmatrix} + t\begin{bmatrix}-2\\4\end{bmatrix}$ and $\mathbf{r} = \begin{bmatrix}-1\\22\end{bmatrix} + s\begin{bmatrix}-5\\-1\end{bmatrix}$

(*d*) $\mathbf{r} = \begin{bmatrix}2\\0\end{bmatrix} + t\begin{bmatrix}7\\-4\end{bmatrix}$ and $\mathbf{r} = \begin{bmatrix}3\\-7\end{bmatrix} + s\begin{bmatrix}-2\\-3\end{bmatrix}$

(*e*) $\mathbf{r} = \begin{bmatrix}-3\\2\end{bmatrix} + t\begin{bmatrix}2\\5\end{bmatrix}$ and $\mathbf{r} = \begin{bmatrix}1\\-3\end{bmatrix} + s\begin{bmatrix}-3\\-2\end{bmatrix}$

3 Write down the vector $\begin{bmatrix}6\\4\end{bmatrix}$ as a linear combination of the following vectors:

(*a*) $\begin{bmatrix}3\\-1\end{bmatrix}$ and $\begin{bmatrix}2\\3\end{bmatrix}$ (*b*) $\begin{bmatrix}-1\\-\frac{2}{3}\end{bmatrix}$ and $\begin{bmatrix}1\\1\end{bmatrix}$ (*c*) $\begin{bmatrix}4\\3\end{bmatrix}$ and $\begin{bmatrix}-1\\2\end{bmatrix}$.

4 Find the image of the line $\mathbf{r} = \begin{bmatrix}4\\-1\end{bmatrix} + t\begin{bmatrix}2\\-3\end{bmatrix}$ under the linear transformation

represented by the matrix $\begin{bmatrix} 2 & -3 \\ 4 & 1 \end{bmatrix}$. Where does this image line meet the x-axis and the y-axis?

5 The three lines $\mathbf{r} = \begin{bmatrix} 5 \\ 7 \end{bmatrix} + s\begin{bmatrix} 3 \\ 4 \end{bmatrix}$, $\mathbf{r} = \begin{bmatrix} 0 \\ -3 \end{bmatrix} + t\begin{bmatrix} 1 \\ -2 \end{bmatrix}$ and $\mathbf{r} = \begin{bmatrix} 2 \\ 3 \end{bmatrix} + u\begin{bmatrix} 4 \\ 2 \end{bmatrix}$ form the sides of the triangle ABC. Find the vertices of the image triangle $A'B'C'$ under the transformation represented by the matrix $\begin{bmatrix} 1 & -3 \\ 6 & 5 \end{bmatrix}$.

6 If the image of the point $(3, -1)$ is $(9, 14)$ and the image of the point $(-2, 5)$ is $(-19, -5)$ under a linear transformation, find the image of the point $(5, 7)$.

7 Find the image of the line $3x - 2y = 6$ under the transformation represented by the matrix $\begin{bmatrix} -3 & 1 \\ 1 & 2 \end{bmatrix}$.

8 Repeat question 7 for the line $3y = 1 - 4x$ and the matrix $\begin{bmatrix} 1 & 0 \\ 5 & 3 \end{bmatrix}$.

1.3 TESTING FOR LINEARITY

In the SMP New Numbered Books course, transformations of the plane are defined as mappings on ordered pairs of real numbers. For example,

$$\mathbf{S}: \begin{bmatrix} x \\ y \end{bmatrix} \mapsto \begin{bmatrix} x - 3y \\ 2x + y \end{bmatrix}$$

or

$$\mathbf{T}: \begin{bmatrix} x \\ y \end{bmatrix} \mapsto \begin{bmatrix} x + 3 \\ y - 4 \end{bmatrix}$$

Example 5
Prove that **S** is a linear transformation.

Solution
Let $\mathbf{a} = \begin{bmatrix} p \\ q \end{bmatrix}$ and $\mathbf{b} = \begin{bmatrix} r \\ s \end{bmatrix}$.

$$\mathbf{a} + \mathbf{b} = \begin{bmatrix} p + r \\ q + s \end{bmatrix} \quad \text{and} \quad k\mathbf{a} = \begin{bmatrix} kp \\ kq \end{bmatrix}, \quad \text{where } k \text{ is a real number.}$$

$$\begin{aligned} \mathbf{S}(\mathbf{a} + \mathbf{b}) = \mathbf{S}\begin{bmatrix} p + r \\ q + s \end{bmatrix} &= \begin{bmatrix} p + r - 3(q + s) \\ 2(p + r) + (q + s) \end{bmatrix} \\ &= \begin{bmatrix} p - 3q \\ 2p + q \end{bmatrix} + \begin{bmatrix} r - 3s \\ 2r + s \end{bmatrix} \\ &= \mathbf{S}(\mathbf{a}) + \mathbf{S}(\mathbf{b}), \end{aligned}$$

so property (B) is satisfied (see §1.2).

$$\mathbf{S}(k\mathbf{a}) = \mathbf{S}\begin{bmatrix} kp \\ kq \end{bmatrix} = \begin{bmatrix} kp - 3kq \\ 2kp + kq \end{bmatrix}$$

$$= k\begin{bmatrix} p - 3q \\ 2p + q \end{bmatrix}$$

$$= k\mathbf{S}(\mathbf{a}),$$

so property (A) is also satisfied.

As **a**, **b** and k are arbitrary, we have shown that **S** is a linear transformation. □

Example 6

Show that **T** is not a linear transformation.

Solution

Using the same notation as in Example 5,

$$\mathbf{T}(\mathbf{a} + \mathbf{b}) = \mathbf{T}\begin{bmatrix} p + r \\ q + s \end{bmatrix} = \begin{bmatrix} p + r + 3 \\ q + s - 4 \end{bmatrix}.$$

Now $$\mathbf{T}(\mathbf{a}) + \mathbf{T}(\mathbf{b}) = \mathbf{T}\begin{bmatrix} p \\ q \end{bmatrix} + \mathbf{T}\begin{bmatrix} r \\ s \end{bmatrix} = \begin{bmatrix} p + 3 \\ q - 4 \end{bmatrix} + \begin{bmatrix} r + 3 \\ s - 4 \end{bmatrix}$$

$$= \begin{bmatrix} p + r + 6 \\ q + s - 8 \end{bmatrix}$$

so $$\mathbf{T}(\mathbf{a} + \mathbf{b}) \neq \mathbf{T}(\mathbf{a}) + \mathbf{T}(\mathbf{b}).$$

$$\mathbf{T}(k\mathbf{a}) = \mathbf{T}\begin{bmatrix} kp \\ kq \end{bmatrix} = \begin{bmatrix} kp + 3 \\ kq - 4 \end{bmatrix}.$$

$$k\mathbf{T}(\mathbf{a}) = k\mathbf{T}\begin{bmatrix} p \\ q \end{bmatrix} = k\begin{bmatrix} p + 3 \\ q - 4 \end{bmatrix} = \begin{bmatrix} kp + 3k \\ kq - 4k \end{bmatrix}$$

so $$\mathbf{T}(k\mathbf{a}) \neq k\mathbf{T}(\mathbf{a}) \quad (\text{unless } k = 1).$$

As neither property (A) nor property (B) is satisfied, **T** is not a linear transformation.

We did not need to check both conditions: once we have found that one condition does not hold we can say that **T** is *not* a linear transformation. □

Q.17 An alternative way to show that a property does not hold is to produce a 'counter-example'; that is, a specific case which does not satisfy the definition. Use this method to show that **T** is not a linear transformation.

The transformation **S** can be written as

$$\mathbf{S}: \begin{bmatrix} x \\ y \end{bmatrix} \mapsto \begin{bmatrix} 1 & -3 \\ 2 & 1 \end{bmatrix}\begin{bmatrix} x \\ y \end{bmatrix}$$

and this has the advantage that it separates out the numbers which determine the transformation (namely $\begin{bmatrix} 1 & -3 \\ 2 & 1 \end{bmatrix}$), from the position vector of the object point (that is $\begin{bmatrix} x \\ y \end{bmatrix}$). We have seen this already and referred to the matrix of the transformation.

S was a linear transformation and we have been able to express it in matrix form. We may be tempted to assume that any linear transformation can therefore be written in matrix form. This is in fact a true result, but we will not be able to prove it until Chapter 12. It was the converse of this result which we proved earlier in this chapter (Result 1); that is, a transformation which can be represented by a matrix is a linear transformation.

Sometimes there is confusion between a transformation and the matrix which represents the transformation, as the same letter is often used to represent them both. It is important to realise that they are not the same; one is a transformation and the other is a matrix, yet there is a connection between them.

Exercise 1C

1 Determine which of the following mappings are linear. If they are linear write out a proof as in Example 5. If they are not linear, give a counter-example.

(*a*) $\begin{bmatrix} x \\ y \end{bmatrix} \mapsto \begin{bmatrix} y \\ x \end{bmatrix}$ (*b*) $\begin{bmatrix} x \\ y \end{bmatrix} \mapsto \begin{bmatrix} 2 \\ 3 \end{bmatrix}$ (*c*) $\begin{bmatrix} x \\ y \end{bmatrix} \mapsto \begin{bmatrix} x + y \\ x - y \end{bmatrix}$

(*d*) $\begin{bmatrix} x \\ y \end{bmatrix} \mapsto \begin{bmatrix} x \\ x^2 \end{bmatrix}$ (*e*) $\begin{bmatrix} x \\ y \end{bmatrix} \mapsto \begin{bmatrix} y \\ 3y \end{bmatrix}$ (*f*) $\begin{bmatrix} x \\ y \end{bmatrix} \mapsto \begin{bmatrix} x - 3y \\ y \end{bmatrix}$

(*g*) $\begin{bmatrix} x \\ y \end{bmatrix} \mapsto \begin{bmatrix} \sin x \\ \sin y \end{bmatrix}$ (*h*) $\begin{bmatrix} x \\ y \end{bmatrix} \mapsto \begin{bmatrix} |x| \\ |y| \end{bmatrix}$

2 If possible, express the mappings in question 1 in matrix form.

3 Under a linear transformation, the image of $(3, 2)$ is $(11, -5)$ and the image of $(2, -1)$ is $(-2, -8)$. What is the matrix which represents this transformation?

In this chapter we have relied heavily on the use of matrices in the development of our work on transformations. The British mathematician Cayley was one of the first to study matrices. This work was developed in a paper he wrote in about 1850 on the theory of transformations. We have been particularly interested in the class of transformations known as *linear transformations*. The idea of linearity is a very important concept in mathematics and there is a branch of mathematics known as 'linear mathematics' which has applications in many areas. We shall study some of these applications in later chapters.

Miscellaneous exercise 1

1 Write the vector $\begin{bmatrix} 7 \\ 3 \end{bmatrix}$ as a linear combination of the three vectors $\begin{bmatrix} 1 \\ 3 \end{bmatrix}$, $\begin{bmatrix} -2 \\ 3 \end{bmatrix}$ and $\begin{bmatrix} 4 \\ -1 \end{bmatrix}$ in two different ways. Why is your answer not unique?

2 The triangle ABC has vertices $(2, 0)$, $(2, 5)$ and $(3, 5)$. Choose a point L *inside* the

triangle. Find the image $A'B'C'$ of the triangle ABC and the image L' of L under the following transformations and in each case determine whether L' is inside or outside the triangle $A'B'C'$:

(a) $\begin{bmatrix} 1 & -2 \\ 3 & 1 \end{bmatrix}$ (b) $\begin{bmatrix} 2 & 1 \\ 1 & \frac{1}{2} \end{bmatrix}$ (c) $\begin{bmatrix} 1 & -1 \\ 0 & 4 \end{bmatrix}$

What general theorem can you deduce from your answer?

3 A parabola has the equation $y = x^2$. This says that the y-coordinate is the square of the x-coordinate. Hence points $(1, 1)$, $(2, 4)$, (a, a^2) lie on the curve. What are their images under the transformations represented by the following matrices?

(a) $\begin{bmatrix} 3 & 0 \\ 0 & 1 \end{bmatrix}$ (b) $\begin{bmatrix} 0 & -1 \\ 1 & 0 \end{bmatrix}$ (c) $\begin{bmatrix} 1 & 0 \\ 0 & -1 \end{bmatrix}$

In each case write down the equation of the curve on which all the image points lie.

4 Find the images of the circle $x^2 + y^2 = 1$ under the transformations represented by the following matrices:

(a) $\begin{bmatrix} 2 & 0 \\ 0 & 2 \end{bmatrix}$ (b) $\begin{bmatrix} 1 & -1 \\ 1 & 1 \end{bmatrix}$ (c) $\begin{bmatrix} 2 & 3 \\ 1 & 2 \end{bmatrix}$

5 Two lines p and q meet at a point H. Under a certain transformation $\mathbf{M}$, $\mathbf{M}(p) = p'$ and $\mathbf{M}(q) = q'$, where p' and q' are lines. If $\mathbf{M}(H) = H'$, show that H' is the point of intersection of p' and q'.

6 Prove that in general the image of the line joining the points (a, b) and (c, d) under the transformation represented by the matrix $\begin{bmatrix} p & q \\ r & s \end{bmatrix}$ is another straight line. When is the image a point?

SUMMARY

Definitions

(1) If $\mathbf{T}$ is a transformation, $\mathbf{a}$ and $\mathbf{b}$ are any vectors in the plane and k is a real number, then $\mathbf{T}$ is a *linear transformation* if

$$\mathbf{T}(k\mathbf{a}) = k\mathbf{T}(\mathbf{a})$$

and

$$\mathbf{T}(\mathbf{a} + \mathbf{b}) = \mathbf{T}(\mathbf{a}) + \mathbf{T}(\mathbf{b}).$$

(2) If $\mathbf{a}$ and $\mathbf{b}$ are vectors in the plane and λ are μ real numbers, then $\lambda\mathbf{a} + \mu\mathbf{b}$ is said to be a *linear combination* of $\mathbf{a}$ and $\mathbf{b}$.

Results

Consequences of the definition of a linear transformation:

(1) Transformations represented by a matrix are linear.

(2) In general, lines are mapped onto lines.

(3) For a linear transformation, $\mathbf{T}(\mathbf{0}) = \mathbf{0}$.

(4) For a linear transformation, $\mathbf{T}(\lambda\mathbf{a} + \mu\mathbf{b}) = \lambda\mathbf{T}(\mathbf{a}) + \mu\mathbf{T}(\mathbf{b})$.

(5) If we know the image of two points in the plane (whose position vectors are not in the same direction), we can find the image of every point in the plane.

(6) Under a linear transformation, the image of the unit square is a parallelogram.

2

Linear equations and transformations

In the first part of this chapter we bring together a number of the different ways of thinking about simultaneous linear equations and then solving them. Some of this work may seem rather trivial but many of the ideas are important and will be developed later in more complicated situations.

2.1 GEOMETRICAL INTERPRETATION OF LINEAR EQUATIONS

In two-dimensional space an equation of the form $ax + by = r$ represents a straight line provided that a and b are not both zero. So the problem of solving two linear equations in two unknowns, for example

$$\left.\begin{aligned} ax + by &= r \\ cx + dy &= s \end{aligned}\right\}$$

can be reduced to finding where two straight lines intersect in the plane. In general, the diagram is something like Fig. 1, and the coordinates of the point P give the solution.

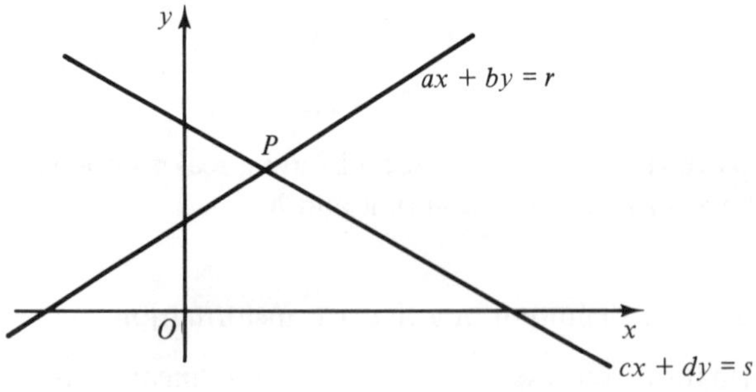

Figure 1

We look at two special cases which can arise:

(1) *The two lines are parallel* (Fig. 2).
The lines do not intersect and so the solution is the empty set, i.e. there is no pair (x, y) which satisfies this pair of linear equations.

As the lines are parallel, the gradients of the two lines are the same; so c and d are the same multiple of a and b respectively, that is $c = ka$ and $d = kb$.

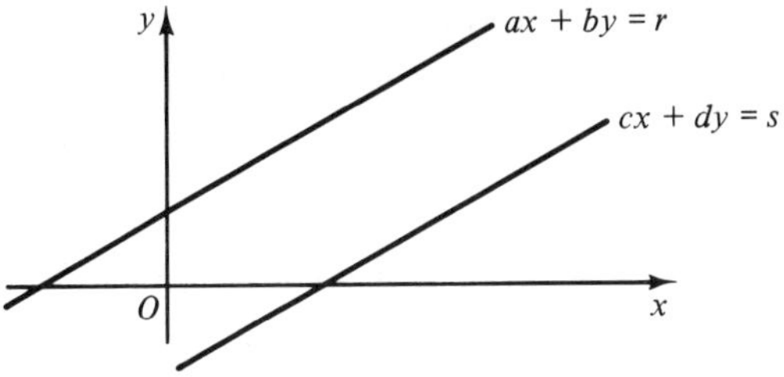

Figure 2

(2) *The two lines are coincident* (Fig. 3).

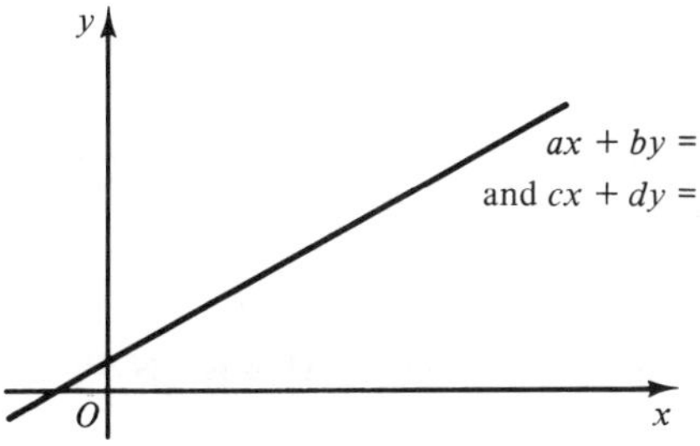

Figure 3

This is the special case of parallel lines in which $s = kr$ as well. This time there are an infinite number of solutions.

2.2 MATRIX METHOD FOR SOLVING LINEAR EQUATIONS

Simultaneous linear equations can be written in matrix form and solved by finding the inverse of the matrix if it exists. We illustrate the method by an example.

Example 1
Solve the equations
$$\left.\begin{aligned} 3x - y &= 10 \\ x + 2y &= 1 \end{aligned}\right\}$$

Solution
Written in matrix form this is

$$\begin{bmatrix} 3 & -1 \\ 1 & 2 \end{bmatrix}\begin{bmatrix} x \\ y \end{bmatrix} = \begin{bmatrix} 10 \\ 1 \end{bmatrix}.$$

The determinant of $\begin{bmatrix} 3 & -1 \\ 1 & 2 \end{bmatrix}$ is $(3) \times (2) - (-1) \times (1) = 7$ so the inverse is $\frac{1}{7}\begin{bmatrix} 2 & 1 \\ -1 & 3 \end{bmatrix}$.

Multiplying through by the inverse we get

$$\frac{1}{7}\begin{bmatrix} 2 & 1 \\ -1 & 3 \end{bmatrix}\begin{bmatrix} 3 & -1 \\ 1 & 2 \end{bmatrix}\begin{bmatrix} x \\ y \end{bmatrix} = \frac{1}{7}\begin{bmatrix} 2 & 1 \\ -1 & 3 \end{bmatrix}\begin{bmatrix} 10 \\ 1 \end{bmatrix}$$

$$\Rightarrow \qquad \begin{bmatrix} 1 & 0 \\ 0 & 1 \end{bmatrix}\begin{bmatrix} x \\ y \end{bmatrix} = \frac{1}{7}\begin{bmatrix} 21 \\ -7 \end{bmatrix}$$

$$\Rightarrow \qquad \begin{bmatrix} x \\ y \end{bmatrix} = \begin{bmatrix} 3 \\ -1 \end{bmatrix};$$

that is, $x = 3$ and $y = -1$. □

It is important to realise that this method will only work provided that the determinant of the matrix is not zero (for the inverse to exist).

A matrix with a non-zero determinant is called *non-singular*. A *singular* matrix has determinant equal to zero.

2.3 LINEAR EQUATIONS AND TRANSFORMATIONS

The linear equations

$$\left.\begin{aligned} 3x + 4y &= 12 \\ x + 3y &= 6 \end{aligned}\right\}$$

can be written in matrix form as

$$\begin{bmatrix} 3 & 4 \\ 1 & 3 \end{bmatrix}\begin{bmatrix} x \\ y \end{bmatrix} = \begin{bmatrix} 12 \\ 6 \end{bmatrix}.$$

We saw in Chapter 1 that the matrix $\begin{bmatrix} 3 & 4 \\ 1 & 3 \end{bmatrix}$ can be thought of as the matrix of a transformation of the plane. This leads us to two other ways of looking at the solution of linear equations:

(1) Let us consider the transformation represented by the matrix $\begin{bmatrix} 3 & 4 \\ 1 & 3 \end{bmatrix}$.

We can find the images of a few points; for example,

$$\begin{bmatrix} 3 & 4 \\ 1 & 3 \end{bmatrix}\begin{bmatrix} 0 \\ 2 \end{bmatrix} = \begin{bmatrix} 8 \\ 6 \end{bmatrix} \qquad \text{so } (0,2)\mapsto(8,6);$$

$$\begin{bmatrix} 3 & 4 \\ 1 & 3 \end{bmatrix}\begin{bmatrix} -2 \\ 3 \end{bmatrix} = \begin{bmatrix} 6 \\ 7 \end{bmatrix} \qquad \text{so } (-2,3)\mapsto(6,7);$$

$$\begin{bmatrix} 3 & 4 \\ 1 & 3 \end{bmatrix}\begin{bmatrix} -4 \\ 1 \end{bmatrix} = \begin{bmatrix} -8 \\ -1 \end{bmatrix} \qquad \text{so } (-4,1)\mapsto(-8,-1).$$

This can be represented by a diagram as in Fig. 4, so the problem is equivalent to asking which point P in the plane on the left maps onto the point (12, 6) in the plane on the right.

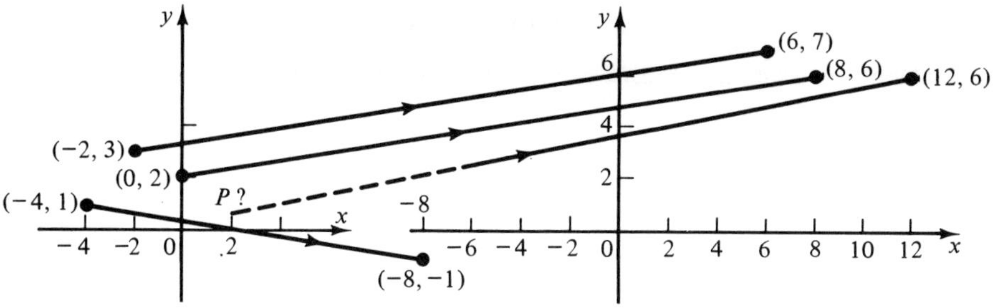

Figure 4

(2) In Q.5 of Chapter 1 we drew the image of a grid under a transformation. Fig. 5 shows the original grid and the image grid for the matrix $\begin{bmatrix} 3 & 4 \\ 1 & 3 \end{bmatrix}$.

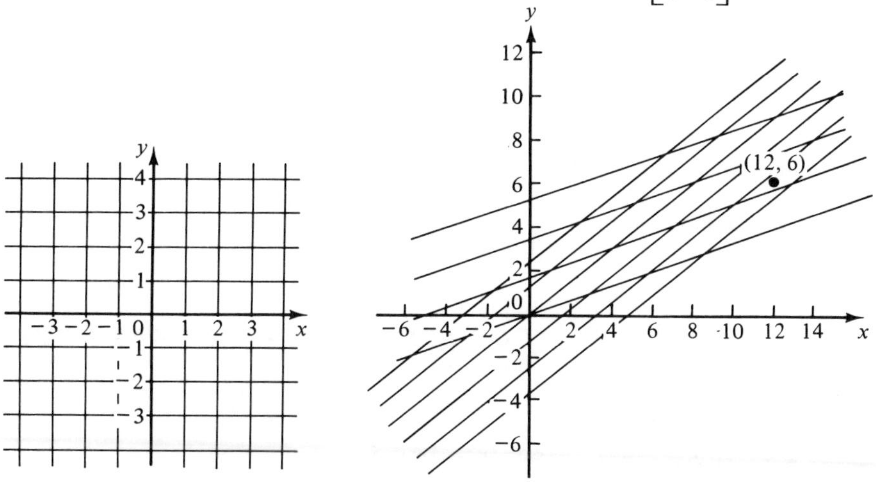

Figure 5

As the image of $\begin{bmatrix} 1 \\ 0 \end{bmatrix}$ is $\begin{bmatrix} 3 \\ 1 \end{bmatrix}$ and the image of $\begin{bmatrix} 0 \\ 1 \end{bmatrix}$ is $\begin{bmatrix} 4 \\ 3 \end{bmatrix}$, the problem reduces to expressing the vector $\begin{bmatrix} 12 \\ 6 \end{bmatrix}$ as a linear combination of the vectors $\begin{bmatrix} 3 \\ 1 \end{bmatrix}$ and $\begin{bmatrix} 4 \\ 3 \end{bmatrix}$. We can check on Fig. 5 that

$$2.4\begin{bmatrix} 3 \\ 1 \end{bmatrix} + 1.2\begin{bmatrix} 4 \\ 3 \end{bmatrix} = \begin{bmatrix} 12 \\ 6 \end{bmatrix},$$

so under this transformation $\begin{bmatrix} 2.4 \\ 1.2 \end{bmatrix}$ maps onto $\begin{bmatrix} 12 \\ 6 \end{bmatrix}$; that is, the solution of

$$\begin{bmatrix} 3 & 4 \\ 1 & 3 \end{bmatrix}\begin{bmatrix} x \\ y \end{bmatrix} = \begin{bmatrix} 12 \\ 6 \end{bmatrix}$$

is

$$\begin{bmatrix} x \\ y \end{bmatrix} = \begin{bmatrix} 2.4 \\ 1.2 \end{bmatrix}.$$

Exercise 2A

1 Draw, on graph paper, each of the following pairs of straight lines and hence find where they meet:

(*a*) $\left.\begin{aligned} 3x - y &= -1 \\ x + 2y &= 9 \end{aligned}\right\}$ (*b*) $\left.\begin{aligned} 5x + 2y &= 4 \\ 4x - y &= 11 \end{aligned}\right\}$

(*c*) $\left.\begin{aligned} 3x - 2y &= 4 \\ -5x + 4y &= -8 \end{aligned}\right\}$ (*d*) $\left.\begin{aligned} x - 4y &= 1 \\ -3x + 12y &= 2 \end{aligned}\right\}$

2 Use the matrix method to solve the linear equations:

(*a*) $\left.\begin{aligned} x + 2y &= 3 \\ 3x - y &= -1 \end{aligned}\right\}$ (*b*) $\left.\begin{aligned} \tfrac{1}{2}x + \tfrac{1}{3}y &= 4 \\ x - 2y &= -\tfrac{1}{2} \end{aligned}\right\}$ (*c*) $\left.\begin{aligned} 2x - 3y &= 5 \\ -6x + 9y &= 7 \end{aligned}\right\}$

3 (*a*) Draw, on graph paper, the image of the grid formed by the lines $x = 0, 1, 2, 3$ and $y = 0, 1, 2, 3$ under the transformation represented by the matrix $\mathbf{M} = \begin{bmatrix} 2 & 1 \\ 1 & 3 \end{bmatrix}$. Mark the point $(3, 2)$ on your diagram and hence write down a solution for $\begin{bmatrix} 2 & 1 \\ 1 & 3 \end{bmatrix}\begin{bmatrix} x \\ y \end{bmatrix} = \begin{bmatrix} 3 \\ 2 \end{bmatrix}$.

(*b*) Solve the equation by an exact method.

4 Repeat question 3 with $\mathbf{M} = \begin{bmatrix} 2 & 1 \\ -1 & 1 \end{bmatrix}$ and $\mathbf{M}\begin{bmatrix} x \\ y \end{bmatrix} = \begin{bmatrix} 4 \\ -1 \end{bmatrix}$.

2.4 ELIMINATION METHOD AND ELEMENTARY MATRICES

Example 2

Solve the equations $\left.\begin{aligned} 2x + 3y &= 2 \\ x - 2y &= 5 \end{aligned}\right\}$

Solution

The simplest and quickest way is by systematic elimination. To eliminate x we take twice the second equation from the first to give

$$7y = -8$$

so $$y = -\tfrac{8}{7}.$$

Substituting this value for y in the second equation gives

$$x - 2(-\tfrac{8}{7}) = 5$$

so $$x = \tfrac{19}{7}.$$ □

This method relies on being able to 'spot' a way of eliminating one of the variables. Today, computers are often used to find the solution of routine questions and so must rely on a method which does not have any subjective element. We can modify this method so that the elimination is done systematically as shown in the following example. It may be longer, but produces a 'recipe' which is applicable in all cases.

Example 3

Solve the equations

$$\left.\begin{aligned} 2x + 3y &= 2 \\ x - 2y &= 5 \end{aligned}\right\} \qquad \begin{matrix} (A) \\ (B) \end{matrix}$$

Solution — *In matrix form*

Stage 1 (A) $\quad 2x + 3y = 2$ $\qquad \begin{bmatrix} 2 & 3 \\ 1 & -2 \end{bmatrix}\begin{bmatrix} x \\ y \end{bmatrix} = \begin{bmatrix} 2 \\ 5 \end{bmatrix}$

(B) $\quad x - 2y = 5$

Stage 2 $(C) = \frac{1}{2} \times (A)$ $\quad x + \frac{3}{2}y = 1$ $\qquad \begin{bmatrix} 1 & \frac{3}{2} \\ 1 & -2 \end{bmatrix}\begin{bmatrix} x \\ y \end{bmatrix} = \begin{bmatrix} 1 \\ 5 \end{bmatrix}$

$(D) = (B)$ $\quad x - 2y = 5$

Stage 3 $(E) = (C)$ $\quad x + \frac{3}{2}y = 1$ $\qquad \begin{bmatrix} 1 & \frac{3}{2} \\ 0 & -\frac{7}{2} \end{bmatrix}\begin{bmatrix} x \\ y \end{bmatrix} = \begin{bmatrix} 1 \\ 4 \end{bmatrix}$

$(F) = (D) - (C)$ $\quad -\frac{7}{2}y = 4$

Stage 4 $(G) = (E)$ $\quad x + \frac{3}{2}y = 1$ $\qquad \begin{bmatrix} 1 & \frac{3}{2} \\ 0 & 1 \end{bmatrix}\begin{bmatrix} x \\ y \end{bmatrix} = \begin{bmatrix} 1 \\ -\frac{8}{7} \end{bmatrix}$

$(H) = -\frac{2}{7} \times (F)$ $\quad y = -\frac{8}{7}$

Stage 5 $(I) = (G) - \frac{3}{2} \times (H)$ $\quad x = \frac{19}{7}$ $\qquad \begin{bmatrix} 1 & 0 \\ 0 & 1 \end{bmatrix}\begin{bmatrix} x \\ y \end{bmatrix} = \begin{bmatrix} \frac{19}{7} \\ -\frac{8}{7} \end{bmatrix}$

$(J) = (H)$ $\quad y = -\frac{8}{7}$

We see more clearly what is happening if we look at the equations written in matrix form. Our aim was to reduce the matrix $\begin{bmatrix} 2 & 3 \\ 1 & -2 \end{bmatrix}$ to the matrix $\begin{bmatrix} 1 & 0 \\ 0 & 1 \end{bmatrix}$ in a systematic manner. □

Q.1 Describe in words the various stages in the reduction of the matrix $\begin{bmatrix} 2 & 3 \\ 1 & -2 \end{bmatrix}$ to $\begin{bmatrix} 1 & 0 \\ 0 & 1 \end{bmatrix}$. (For example, stage 2 was to get a '1' in the top left corner of the matrix.)

Elementary matrices

If we start with the matrix $\mathbf{A} = \begin{bmatrix} a & b \\ c & d \end{bmatrix}$ and premultiply by $\begin{bmatrix} 1 & -2 \\ 0 & 1 \end{bmatrix}$ we get

$$\begin{bmatrix} 1 & -2 \\ 0 & 1 \end{bmatrix}\begin{bmatrix} a & b \\ c & d \end{bmatrix} = \begin{bmatrix} a - 2c & b - 2d \\ c & d \end{bmatrix}.$$

So the effect of premultiplying by $\begin{bmatrix} 1 & -2 \\ 0 & 1 \end{bmatrix}$ is to produce a new first row which is equal to (the first row of $\mathbf{A}$ $- 2 \times$ the second row of $\mathbf{A}$), while the second row remains unchanged.

Q.2 Describe the effect of premultiplying the matrix $\mathbf{A} = \begin{bmatrix} a & b \\ c & d \end{bmatrix}$ by each of the following matrices:

(*a*) $\begin{bmatrix} 6 & 0 \\ 0 & 1 \end{bmatrix}$ (*b*) $\begin{bmatrix} 1 & 0 \\ 0 & -\frac{1}{2} \end{bmatrix}$ (*c*) $\begin{bmatrix} 1 & 0 \\ 4 & 1 \end{bmatrix}$ (*d*) $\begin{bmatrix} 0 & 1 \\ 1 & 0 \end{bmatrix}$

Each of the matrices in Q.2 is an example of an *elementary matrix*.

For 2 × 2 matrices there are three types of *elementary matrix*:

(1) $\begin{bmatrix} k & 0 \\ 0 & 1 \end{bmatrix}$ or $\begin{bmatrix} 1 & 0 \\ 0 & l \end{bmatrix}$, which multiplies one of the rows by a constant $(k, l \neq 0)$.

(2) $\begin{bmatrix} 1 & k \\ 0 & 1 \end{bmatrix}$ or $\begin{bmatrix} 1 & 0 \\ l & 1 \end{bmatrix}$, which adds a multiple of one row to the other.

(3) $\begin{bmatrix} 0 & 1 \\ 1 & 0 \end{bmatrix}$, which interchanges the two rows.

We now refer back to Example 3 and see how elementary matrices are useful in describing the transition from one stage to the next.

The transition from Stage 1 to Stage 2,

$$\left.\begin{aligned} (C) &= \tfrac{1}{2} \times (A) \\ (D) &= (B) \end{aligned}\right\}$$

is equivalent to multiplying the first row by $\frac{1}{2}$ and leaving the second row the same, which is represented by the elementary matrix

$$\mathbf{E}_1 = \begin{bmatrix} \frac{1}{2} & 0 \\ 0 & 1 \end{bmatrix}.$$

Check that

$$\begin{bmatrix} \frac{1}{2} & 0 \\ 0 & 1 \end{bmatrix}\begin{bmatrix} 2 & 3 \\ 1 & -2 \end{bmatrix} = \begin{bmatrix} 1 & \frac{3}{2} \\ 1 & -2 \end{bmatrix} \quad \text{and} \quad \begin{bmatrix} \frac{1}{2} & 0 \\ 0 & 1 \end{bmatrix}\begin{bmatrix} 2 \\ 5 \end{bmatrix} = \begin{bmatrix} 1 \\ 5 \end{bmatrix}.$$

Q.3 Verify that the other elementary matrices which would be used in Example 3 are:

Stage 2 → Stage 3 $\quad \mathbf{E}_2 = \begin{bmatrix} 1 & 0 \\ -1 & 1 \end{bmatrix}$

Stage 3 → Stage 4 $\quad \mathbf{E}_3 = \begin{bmatrix} 1 & 0 \\ 0 & -\frac{2}{7} \end{bmatrix}$

Stage 4 → Stage 5 $\quad \mathbf{E}_4 = \begin{bmatrix} 1 & -\frac{3}{2} \\ 0 & 1 \end{bmatrix}$

Q.4 Evaluate $\mathbf{E}_4\mathbf{E}_3\mathbf{E}_2\mathbf{E}_1$ for the matrices given in Q.3. How is your answer related to the inverse of the matrix $\begin{bmatrix} 2 & 3 \\ 1 & -2 \end{bmatrix}$?

Example 4

Solve the equations

$$\left.\begin{aligned} 2x - y &= -3 \\ 4x + 3y &= 7 \end{aligned}\right\}$$

using elementary matrices to reduce the matrix $\mathbf{M} = \begin{bmatrix} 2 & -1 \\ 4 & 3 \end{bmatrix}$ to $\begin{bmatrix} 1 & 0 \\ 0 & 1 \end{bmatrix}$.

Solution

	Matrix		*Elementary matrix involved*
	$\begin{bmatrix} 2 & -1 \\ 4 & 3 \end{bmatrix}$	$\begin{bmatrix} -3 \\ 7 \end{bmatrix}$	
Subtracting 2 × row 1 from row 2:	$\begin{bmatrix} 2 & -1 \\ 0 & 5 \end{bmatrix}$	$\begin{bmatrix} -3 \\ 13 \end{bmatrix}$	$\mathbf{E}_1 = \begin{bmatrix} 1 & 0 \\ -2 & 1 \end{bmatrix}$
Multiplying row 1 by $\frac{1}{2}$:	$\begin{bmatrix} 1 & -\frac{1}{2} \\ 0 & 5 \end{bmatrix}$	$\begin{bmatrix} -\frac{3}{2} \\ 13 \end{bmatrix}$	$\mathbf{E}_2 = \begin{bmatrix} \frac{1}{2} & 0 \\ 0 & 1 \end{bmatrix}$
Adding $\frac{1}{10}$ × row 2 to row 1:	$\begin{bmatrix} 1 & 0 \\ 0 & 5 \end{bmatrix}$	$\begin{bmatrix} -0.2 \\ 13 \end{bmatrix}$	$\mathbf{E}_3 = \begin{bmatrix} 1 & \frac{1}{10} \\ 0 & 1 \end{bmatrix}$
Multiplying row 2 by $\frac{1}{5}$:	$\begin{bmatrix} 1 & 0 \\ 0 & 1 \end{bmatrix}$	$\begin{bmatrix} -0.2 \\ 2.6 \end{bmatrix}$	$\mathbf{E}_3 = \begin{bmatrix} 1 & 0 \\ 0 & \frac{1}{5} \end{bmatrix}$

So $\qquad x = -0.2 \quad \text{and} \quad y = 2.6.$ □

Exercise 2B

1 If $\mathbf{M} = \begin{bmatrix} 1 & 3 \\ -1 & 2 \end{bmatrix}$, find the elementary matrix such that $\mathbf{EM} = \mathbf{A}$ where $\mathbf{A}$ is

(*a*) $\begin{bmatrix} 1 & 3 \\ -2 & 4 \end{bmatrix}$ (*b*) $\begin{bmatrix} 2 & 1 \\ -1 & 2 \end{bmatrix}$ (*c*) $\begin{bmatrix} -1 & 2 \\ 1 & 3 \end{bmatrix}$ (*d*) $\begin{bmatrix} 1 & 3 \\ 0 & 5 \end{bmatrix}$

2 (*a*) If $\mathbf{M} = \begin{bmatrix} 4 & 2 \\ 5 & 3 \end{bmatrix}$, find elementary matrices $\mathbf{E}_1$, $\mathbf{E}_2$, $\mathbf{E}_3$ and $\mathbf{E}_4$ such that $\mathbf{E}_4\mathbf{E}_3\mathbf{E}_2\mathbf{E}_1\mathbf{M} = \mathbf{I}$.

(*b*) What is the matrix product $\mathbf{E}_4\mathbf{E}_3\mathbf{E}_2\mathbf{E}_1$?

(*c*) Write down the inverses of the matrices $\mathbf{E}_1$, $\mathbf{E}_2$, $\mathbf{E}_3$, $\mathbf{E}_4$ and verify that $\mathbf{E}_1^{-1}\mathbf{E}_2^{-1}\mathbf{E}_3^{-1}\mathbf{E}_4^{-1} = \mathbf{M}$.

3 Draw the parallelogram *ABCD*, where *A* is (0, 0), *B* is (4, 5), *C* is (6, 8) and *D* is (2, 3). Sketch the positions of this parallelogram when the transformations corresponding to $\mathbf{E}_1$, $\mathbf{E}_2$, $\mathbf{E}_3$, $\mathbf{E}_4$ of question 2 are applied successively to the position vectors of its vertices, and show that they transform *ABCD* ultimately to the unit square.

4 Use elementary matrices to find the inverses of the following matrices:

(*a*) $\begin{bmatrix} 3 & -1 \\ 1 & \frac{1}{2} \end{bmatrix}$ (*b*) $\begin{bmatrix} 3 & -6 \\ -2 & 4 \end{bmatrix}$ (*c*) $\begin{bmatrix} 7 & -6 \\ -10 & 9 \end{bmatrix}$

5 Is the inverse of an elementary matrix an elementary matrix? Give reasons for your answer.

2.5 SOME BASIC TRANSFORMATIONS

We first recall that, in a matrix transformation $\begin{bmatrix} a & b \\ c & d \end{bmatrix}$, the image of $\begin{bmatrix} 1 \\ 0 \end{bmatrix}$ is the first column of the matrix, i.e. $\begin{bmatrix} a \\ c \end{bmatrix}$, and the image of $\begin{bmatrix} 0 \\ 1 \end{bmatrix}$ is the second column, i.e. $\begin{bmatrix} b \\ d \end{bmatrix}$.

Thus if we wish to find the matrix of a given linear transformation, we need only find the images of the base vectors $\begin{bmatrix} 1 \\ 0 \end{bmatrix}$ and $\begin{bmatrix} 0 \\ 1 \end{bmatrix}$.

Example 5

Find the matrix of the transformation which is a reflection in the line $y = -x$.

Solution

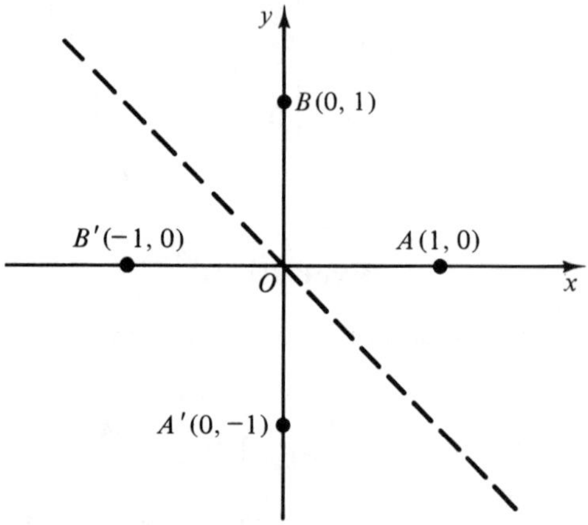

Figure 6

From Fig. 6 we see that

$$\begin{bmatrix} 1 \\ 0 \end{bmatrix} \mapsto \begin{bmatrix} 0 \\ -1 \end{bmatrix}, \quad \text{so the first column of the matrix is } \begin{matrix} 0 \\ -1 \end{matrix}$$

and $$\begin{bmatrix} 0 \\ 1 \end{bmatrix} \mapsto \begin{bmatrix} -1 \\ 0 \end{bmatrix}, \quad \text{so the second column of the matrix is } \begin{matrix} -1 \\ 0 \end{matrix}.$$

So the matrix is $\begin{bmatrix} 0 & -1 \\ -1 & 0 \end{bmatrix}$.

Exercise 2C

1 Find the matrices corresponding to the following transformations:

(*a*) reflection in the x-axis

(*b*) rotation about $(0, 0)$ through $60°$

(*c*) shear with invariant line Ox in which $(2, 1) \mapsto (-1, 1)$

(*d*) one-way stretch parallel to Oy of factor 3

(*e*) enlargement, centre $(0, 0)$, scale factor 5

(*f*) rotation about $(0, 0)$ through $210°$

(*g*) projection parallel to the x-axis on to the y-axis
(*h*) reflection in the line $y = 2x$.

2 Find the matrices corresponding to the following transformations:
(*a*) rotation about (0,0) through $\theta°$
(*b*) reflection in the line $y = (\tan\theta)x$

3 Describe the geometrical effect of the transformations represented by the following matrices:

(*a*) $\begin{bmatrix} 1 & 0 \\ -2 & 1 \end{bmatrix}$ (*b*) $\begin{bmatrix} 3 & 0 \\ 0 & 2 \end{bmatrix}$ (*c*) $\begin{bmatrix} 0 & 1 \\ 1 & 0 \end{bmatrix}$ (*d*) $\begin{bmatrix} 0.8 & 0.6 \\ -0.6 & 0.8 \end{bmatrix}$

(*e*) $\begin{bmatrix} -3 & 0 \\ 0 & -3 \end{bmatrix}$ (*f*) $\begin{bmatrix} 1 & 0 \\ 0 & 0 \end{bmatrix}$ (*g*) $\begin{bmatrix} 0 & 1 \\ -1 & 0 \end{bmatrix}$ (*h*) $\begin{bmatrix} -1 & 0 \\ 0 & 1 \end{bmatrix}$

In the summary at the end of this chapter there is a list of some of the basic transformations and their geometrical effects. You may wish to use it as a reference table when you are studying some of the other sections in this and subsequent chapters.

2.6 GEOMETRICAL DESCRIPTION OF A TRANSFORMATION

In this section we shall link together the ideas of §2.4 and §2.5, to help us give a geometrical description of a transformation in terms of basic transformations.

Example 6

Express the transformation given by $\mathbf{M} = \begin{bmatrix} 2 & 6 \\ -2 & -7 \end{bmatrix}$ as a sequence of basic transformations.

Solution

$$\mathbf{M} = \begin{bmatrix} 2 & 6 \\ -2 & -7 \end{bmatrix}$$

Adding row 1 to row 2, using $\mathbf{E}_1 = \begin{bmatrix} 1 & 0 \\ 1 & 1 \end{bmatrix}$: $\mathbf{E}_1\mathbf{M} = \begin{bmatrix} 2 & 6 \\ 0 & -1 \end{bmatrix}$

Dividing row 1 by 2, using $\mathbf{E}_2 = \begin{bmatrix} \frac{1}{2} & 0 \\ 0 & 1 \end{bmatrix}$: $\mathbf{E}_2\mathbf{E}_1\mathbf{M} = \begin{bmatrix} 1 & 3 \\ 0 & -1 \end{bmatrix}$

Adding $3 \times$ row 2 to row 1, using $\mathbf{E}_3 = \begin{bmatrix} 1 & 3 \\ 0 & 1 \end{bmatrix}$: $\mathbf{E}_3\mathbf{E}_2\mathbf{E}_1\mathbf{M} = \begin{bmatrix} 1 & 0 \\ 0 & -1 \end{bmatrix}$

Multiplying row 2 by -1, using $\mathbf{E}_4 = \begin{bmatrix} 1 & 0 \\ 0 & -1 \end{bmatrix}$: $\mathbf{E}_4\mathbf{E}_3\mathbf{E}_2\mathbf{E}_1\mathbf{M} = \begin{bmatrix} 1 & 0 \\ 0 & 1 \end{bmatrix}$

Thus we have $\mathbf{E}_4\mathbf{E}_3\mathbf{E}_2\mathbf{E}_1\mathbf{M} = \mathbf{I}$.
Premultiplying both sides by $\mathbf{E}_4^{-1}$: $\mathbf{E}_4^{-1}\mathbf{E}_4\mathbf{E}_3\mathbf{E}_2\mathbf{E}_1\mathbf{M} = \mathbf{E}_4^{-1}\mathbf{I}$
that is $\mathbf{E}_3\mathbf{E}_2\mathbf{E}_1\mathbf{M} = \mathbf{E}_4^{-1}\mathbf{I}$;
Premultiplying both sides by $\mathbf{E}_3^{-1}$: $\mathbf{E}_2\mathbf{E}_1\mathbf{M} = \mathbf{E}_3^{-1}\mathbf{E}_4^{-1}\mathbf{I}$;
Premultiplying both sides by $\mathbf{E}_2^{-1}$: $\mathbf{E}_1\mathbf{M} = \mathbf{E}_2^{-1}\mathbf{E}_3^{-1}\mathbf{E}_4^{-1}\mathbf{I}$;

Premultiplying both sides by $\mathbf{E}_1^{-1}$: $\mathbf{M} = \mathbf{E}_1^{-1}\mathbf{E}_2^{-1}\mathbf{E}_3^{-1}\mathbf{E}_4^{-1}\mathbf{I}$;
that is, $\mathbf{M} = \mathbf{E}_1^{-1}\mathbf{E}_2^{-1}\mathbf{E}_3^{-1}\mathbf{E}_4^{-1}$.

Hence $$\begin{bmatrix} 2 & 6 \\ -2 & -7 \end{bmatrix} = \begin{bmatrix} 1 & 0 \\ -1 & 1 \end{bmatrix}\begin{bmatrix} 2 & 0 \\ 0 & 1 \end{bmatrix}\begin{bmatrix} 1 & -3 \\ 0 & 1 \end{bmatrix}\begin{bmatrix} 1 & 0 \\ 0 & -1 \end{bmatrix}$$

So **M** can be described as a reflection in the x-axis ($\mathbf{E}_4^{-1}$), followed by a shear with invariant line the x-axis, factor -3 ($\mathbf{E}_3^{-1}$), followed by a one-way stretch with invariant line the y-axis, factor 2 ($\mathbf{E}_2^{-1}$), followed by a shear with invariant line the y-axis, factor -1 ($\mathbf{E}_1^{-1}$).

Notice that the order is $\mathbf{E}_4^{-1}$, then $\mathbf{E}_3^{-1}$, etc.

We can show this sequence of transformations applied to the unit square (Fig. 7, opposite). □

Q.5 What happens when you try the above technique to describe the transformation represented by the matrix $\begin{bmatrix} 2 & 3 \\ 4 & 6 \end{bmatrix}$?

In trying to simplify the matrix $\mathbf{M} = \begin{bmatrix} 2 & 3 \\ 4 & 6 \end{bmatrix}$ in Q.5, you should have found a matrix of the form $\begin{bmatrix} a & b \\ 0 & 0 \end{bmatrix}$ which can only be simplified as far as $\begin{bmatrix} 1 & b/a \\ 0 & 0 \end{bmatrix}$ by the methods of §2.4.

Q.6 Verify that $$\begin{bmatrix} 1 & c \\ 0 & 0 \end{bmatrix} = \begin{bmatrix} 1 & 0 \\ 0 & 0 \end{bmatrix}\begin{bmatrix} 1 & c \\ 0 & 1 \end{bmatrix}.$$

Discussion of Q.5

We are now in a position to continue with Q.5.

Simplifying **M** by using elementary matrices:

$$\mathbf{M} = \begin{bmatrix} 2 & 3 \\ 4 & 6 \end{bmatrix}$$

Subtracting 2 × row 1 from row 2 using $\mathbf{E}_1 = \begin{bmatrix} 1 & 0 \\ -2 & 1 \end{bmatrix}$: $$\mathbf{E}_1\mathbf{M} = \begin{bmatrix} 2 & 3 \\ 0 & 0 \end{bmatrix}.$$

Dividing row 1 by 2 using $\mathbf{E}_2 = \begin{bmatrix} \frac{1}{2} & 0 \\ 0 & 1 \end{bmatrix}$: $$\mathbf{E}_2\mathbf{E}_1\mathbf{M} = \begin{bmatrix} 1 & \frac{3}{2} \\ 0 & 0 \end{bmatrix} = \mathbf{A}, \text{ say.}$$

So $\mathbf{E}_2\mathbf{E}_1\mathbf{M} = \mathbf{A}$.

Premultiplying by $\mathbf{E}_2^{-1}$: $\mathbf{E}_1\mathbf{M} = \mathbf{E}_2^{-1}\mathbf{A}$.

Premultiplying by $\mathbf{E}_1^{-1}$: $\mathbf{M} = \mathbf{E}_1^{-1}\mathbf{E}_2^{-1}\mathbf{A}$,

So $$\mathbf{M} = \begin{bmatrix} 1 & 0 \\ 2 & 1 \end{bmatrix}\begin{bmatrix} 2 & 0 \\ 0 & 1 \end{bmatrix}\begin{bmatrix} 1 & \frac{3}{2} \\ 0 & 0 \end{bmatrix}.$$

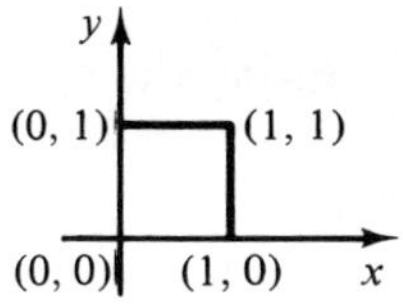

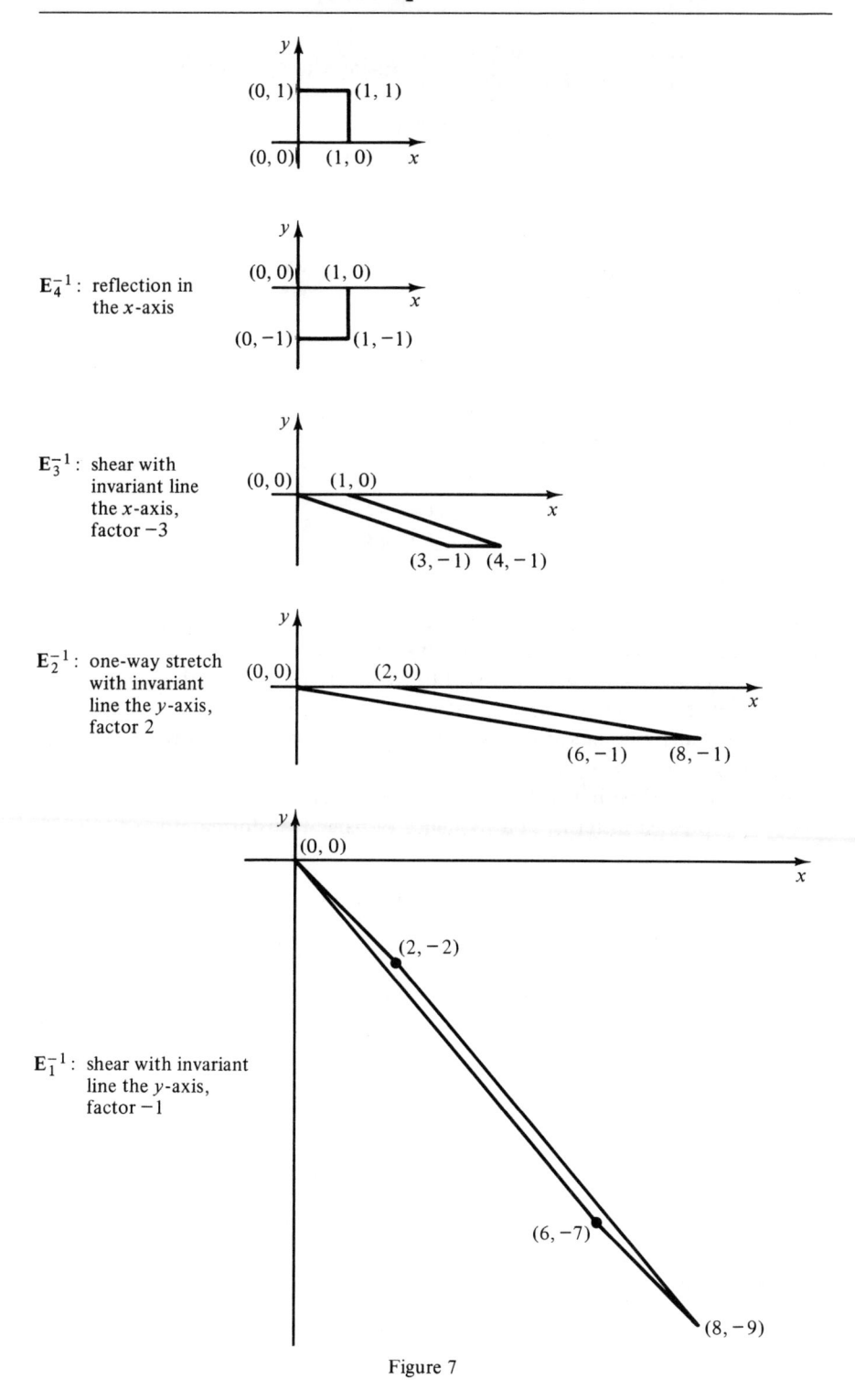

$\mathbf{E}_4^{-1}$: reflection in the x-axis

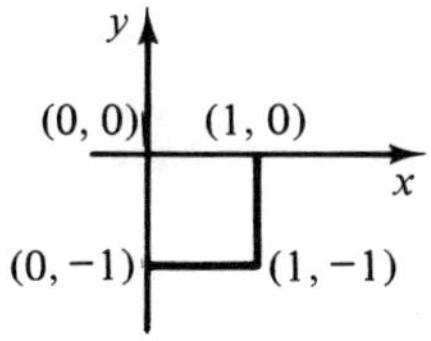

$\mathbf{E}_3^{-1}$: shear with invariant line the x-axis, factor −3

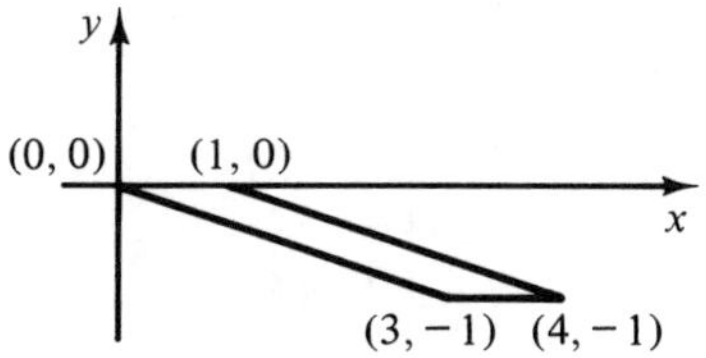

$\mathbf{E}_2^{-1}$: one-way stretch with invariant line the y-axis, factor 2

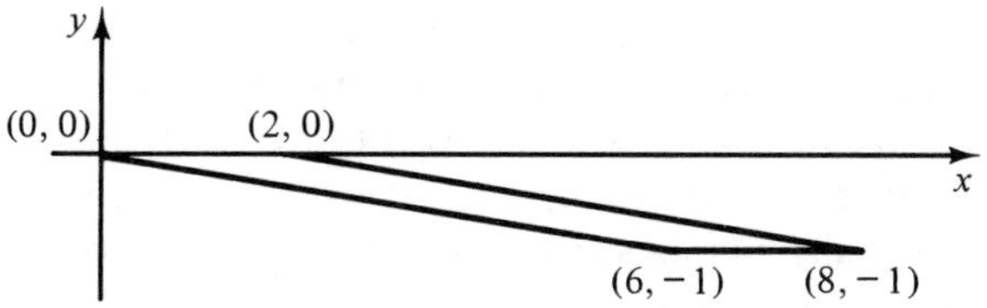

$\mathbf{E}_1^{-1}$: shear with invariant line the y-axis, factor −1

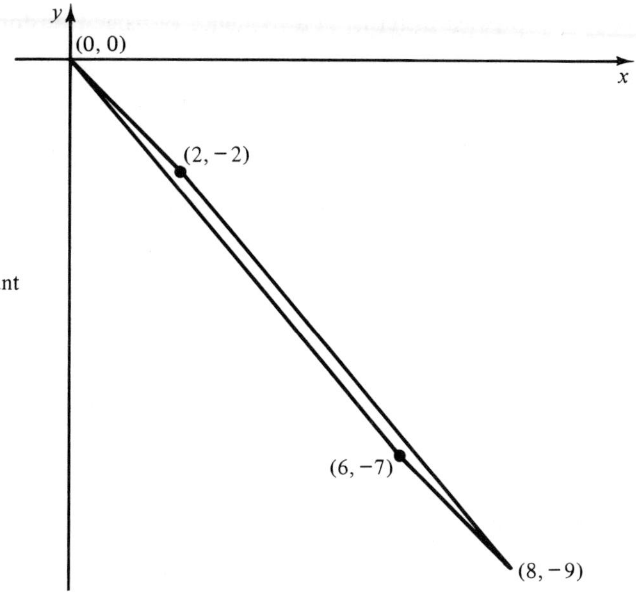

Figure 7

But $\begin{bmatrix} 1 & \frac{3}{2} \\ 0 & 0 \end{bmatrix} = \begin{bmatrix} 1 & 0 \\ 0 & 0 \end{bmatrix}\begin{bmatrix} 1 & \frac{3}{2} \\ 0 & 1 \end{bmatrix}$ (using the result of Q.6)

$$\Rightarrow \qquad \mathbf{M} = \begin{bmatrix} 1 & 0 \\ 2 & 1 \end{bmatrix}\begin{bmatrix} 2 & 0 \\ 0 & 1 \end{bmatrix}\begin{bmatrix} 1 & 0 \\ 0 & 0 \end{bmatrix}\begin{bmatrix} 1 & \frac{3}{2} \\ 0 & 1 \end{bmatrix}.$$

So **M** can be described as a shear with invariant line the x-axis, factor $\frac{3}{2}$, followed by a projection parallel to the the y-axis on to the x-axis, followed by a one-way stretch, invariant line the y-axis, factor 2, followed by a shear with invariant line the y-axis, factor 2.

Exercise 2D

Describe the following matrix transformations as a sequence of basic transformations:

1 $\begin{bmatrix} 2 & 1 \\ 4 & 3 \end{bmatrix}$ **2** $\begin{bmatrix} 3 & -2 \\ 2 & -1 \end{bmatrix}$ **3** $\begin{bmatrix} 1 & 3 \\ 5 & 12 \end{bmatrix}$ **4** $\begin{bmatrix} 3 & 0 \\ 4 & 2 \end{bmatrix}$

5 $\begin{bmatrix} 1 & -2 \\ -3 & 6 \end{bmatrix}$ **6** $\begin{bmatrix} -2 & 2 \\ 5 & -5 \end{bmatrix}$ **7** $\begin{bmatrix} 0 & 3 \\ 2 & 4 \end{bmatrix}$ **8** $\begin{bmatrix} 0 & 3 \\ 0 & 4 \end{bmatrix}$ **9** $\begin{bmatrix} 0 & 2 \\ 0 & 0 \end{bmatrix}$

There have been two strands in this chapter. We have looked at a number of ways of interpreting linear equations and trying to solve them. For two linear equations in two unknowns, the straightforward elimination method is often the best. However, with more complicated systems of linear equations, extensions of some of the other methods are useful and they also help us to discover quickly the nature of the solution. We shall meet these methods again in later chapters. The chapter concluded with a section in which it was shown how a transformation could be expressed in terms of a sequence of basic transformations.

Miscellaneous exercise 2

1 (*a*) For what values of p and q are the lines $3x + 2y = 5$ and $px - y = q$ (i) parallel, (ii) coincident?

(*b*) For what value(s) of p do the following three lines meet in a point?

$$\left.\begin{aligned} x + 2y &= 4 \\ px - \ \ y &= 5 \\ 2x + \ \ y &= 7 \end{aligned}\right\}$$

2 Solve the equations $\left.\begin{aligned} x - y &= 1 \\ \alpha x - y &= -1 \end{aligned}\right\}$, where $\alpha \neq 1$.

What is the locus of the point of intersection as α varies?

3 (*a*) The lines whose equations are $x - y + 1 = 0$ and $x + y - 5 = 0$ intersect at the point P. Find P and show that the line whose equation is

$$(x - y + 1) + 2(x + y - 5) = 0$$

also passes through P.

(*b*) Show that for different values of λ and μ, the line with equation

$$\lambda(x - y + 1) + \mu(x + y - 5) = 0$$

will also pass through P. Hence find the equation of the line joining P to the point $(4, 3)$.

(*c*) Prove that if three equations in two unknowns have a solution, then one equation is a linear combination of the other two.

4 Evaluate the matrix product

$$\begin{bmatrix} a & 0 \\ 0 & 1 \end{bmatrix}\begin{bmatrix} 1 & 0 \\ c & 0 \end{bmatrix}\begin{bmatrix} 1 & 0 \\ 0 & (ad - bc)/a \end{bmatrix}\begin{bmatrix} 1 & b/a \\ 0 & 1 \end{bmatrix}\begin{bmatrix} 1 & 0 \\ 0 & 1 \end{bmatrix}.$$

Describe geometrically a series of one-way stretches and shears which will transform the unit square into the parallelogram determined by the position vectors $\begin{bmatrix} a \\ c \end{bmatrix}, \begin{bmatrix} b \\ d \end{bmatrix}$. What happens if (*a*) $a = 0$, (*b*) $ad - bc = 0$?

5 The simultaneous equations

$$\left.\begin{aligned} x + 2y &= 4 \\ 2x - y &= 0 \\ 3x + y &= 5 \end{aligned}\right\}$$

may be written in matrix form as

$$\begin{bmatrix} 1 & 2 \\ 2 & -1 \\ 3 & 1 \end{bmatrix}\begin{bmatrix} x \\ y \end{bmatrix} = \begin{bmatrix} 4 \\ 0 \\ 5 \end{bmatrix} \quad \text{or} \quad \mathbf{AX} = \mathbf{B}.$$

If $\mathbf{A}^{\mathrm{T}} = \begin{bmatrix} 1 & 2 & 3 \\ 2 & -1 & 1 \end{bmatrix}$, carry out numerically the procedure of the following three steps:

(*a*) $\mathbf{A}^{\mathrm{T}}\mathbf{AX} = \mathbf{A}^{\mathrm{T}}\mathbf{B}$, that is, premultiplying by $\mathbf{A}^{\mathrm{T}}$

(*b*) $(\mathbf{A}^{\mathrm{T}}\mathbf{A})^{-1}(\mathbf{A}^{\mathrm{T}}\mathbf{A})\mathbf{X} = (\mathbf{A}^{\mathrm{T}}\mathbf{A})^{-1}\mathbf{A}^{\mathrm{T}}\mathbf{B}$, that is premultiplying by the inverse of $(\mathbf{A}^{\mathrm{T}}\mathbf{A})$

(*c*) $\mathbf{IX} = \begin{bmatrix} x \\ y \end{bmatrix} = (\mathbf{A}^{\mathrm{T}}\mathbf{A})^{-1}\mathbf{A}^{\mathrm{T}}\mathbf{B}$

Verify that the values of x, y so found do not satisfy all the original three equations. Suggest a reason for this. [SMP, adapted]

SUMMARY

(1) A *singular* matrix has its determinant equal to zero.
A *non-singular* matrix has a non-zero determinant.

(2) *Elementary matrices*: For 2×2 matrices there are three types of elementary matrix:

(*a*) $\begin{bmatrix} k & 0 \\ 0 & 1 \end{bmatrix}$ or $\begin{bmatrix} 1 & 0 \\ 0 & l \end{bmatrix}$ $(k, l \neq 0)$

(*b*) $\begin{bmatrix} 1 & k \\ 0 & 1 \end{bmatrix}$ or $\begin{bmatrix} 1 & 0 \\ l & 1 \end{bmatrix}$

(c) $\begin{bmatrix} 0 & 1 \\ 1 & 0 \end{bmatrix}$

(3) Some basic transformations:

Transformation	Image of the unit square	Matrix of the transformation	Inverse of the matrix	Determinant of the matrix
Reflection in the x-axis	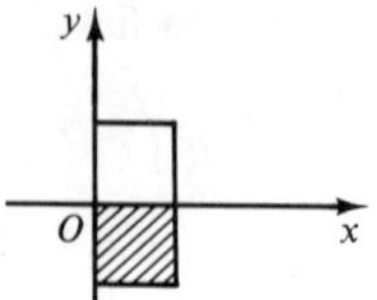	$\begin{bmatrix} 1 & 0 \\ 0 & -1 \end{bmatrix}$	$\begin{bmatrix} 1 & 0 \\ 0 & -1 \end{bmatrix}$	-1
Reflection in the y-axis	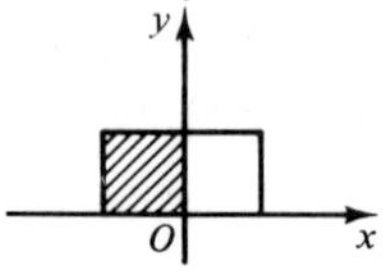	$\begin{bmatrix} -1 & 0 \\ 0 & 1 \end{bmatrix}$	$\begin{bmatrix} -1 & 0 \\ 0 & 1 \end{bmatrix}$	-1
Reflection in the line $y = x$	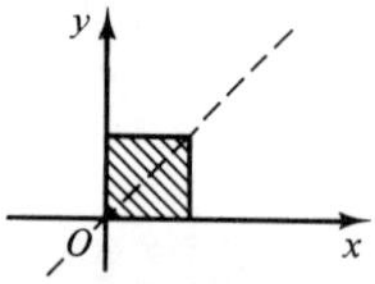	$\begin{bmatrix} 0 & 1 \\ 1 & 0 \end{bmatrix}$	$\begin{bmatrix} 0 & 1 \\ 1 & 0 \end{bmatrix}$	-1
Reflection in the line $y = -x$	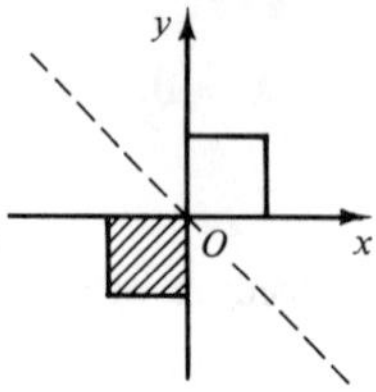	$\begin{bmatrix} 0 & -1 \\ -1 & 0 \end{bmatrix}$	$\begin{bmatrix} 0 & -1 \\ -1 & 0 \end{bmatrix}$	-1
Reflection in the line $y = (\tan\theta)x$	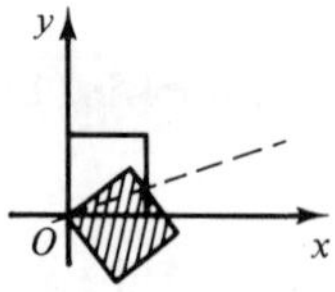	$\begin{bmatrix} \cos 2\theta & \sin 2\theta \\ \sin 2\theta & -\cos 2\theta \end{bmatrix}$	$\begin{bmatrix} \cos 2\theta & \sin 2\theta \\ \sin 2\theta & -\cos 2\theta \end{bmatrix}$	-1
Rotation about the origin through an angle of $\theta°$	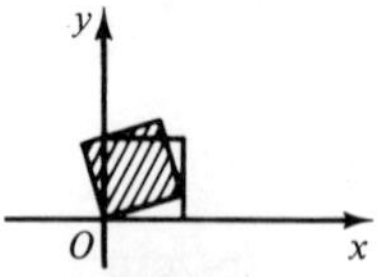	$\begin{bmatrix} \cos\theta & -\sin\theta \\ \sin\theta & \cos\theta \end{bmatrix}$	$\begin{bmatrix} \cos\theta & \sin\theta \\ -\sin\theta & \cos\theta \end{bmatrix}$	$+1$
Enlargement, centre the origin, scale factor k	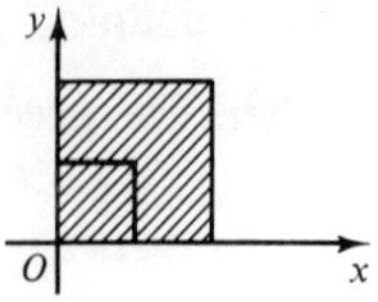	$\begin{bmatrix} k & 0 \\ 0 & k \end{bmatrix}$	$\begin{bmatrix} 1/k & 0 \\ 0 & 1/k \end{bmatrix}$	k^2
Shear with x-axis invariant, factor k	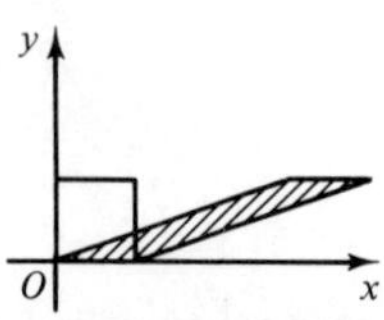	$\begin{bmatrix} 1 & k \\ 0 & 1 \end{bmatrix}$	$\begin{bmatrix} 1 & -k \\ 0 & 1 \end{bmatrix}$	$+1$

Transformation	Image of the unit square	Matrix of the transformation	Inverse of the matrix	Determinant of the matrix
Shear with y-axis invariant, factor k	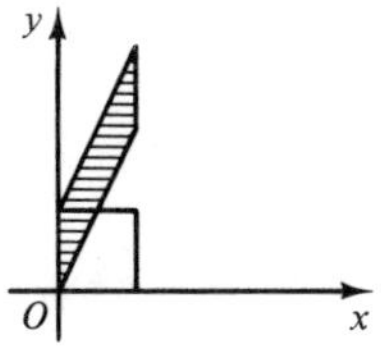	$\begin{bmatrix} 1 & 0 \\ k & 1 \end{bmatrix}$	$\begin{bmatrix} 1 & 0 \\ -k & 1 \end{bmatrix}$	$+1$
A two-way stretch, factors a and b in the directions of the x- and y-axes, respectively	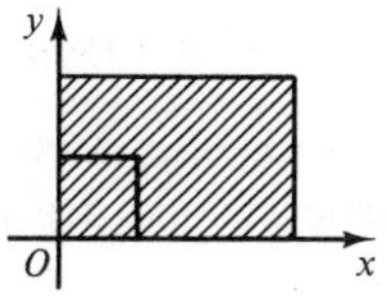	$\begin{bmatrix} a & 0 \\ 0 & b \end{bmatrix}$	$\begin{bmatrix} 1/a & 0 \\ 0 & 1/b \end{bmatrix}$	ab
A projection parallel to the y-axis onto the x-axis	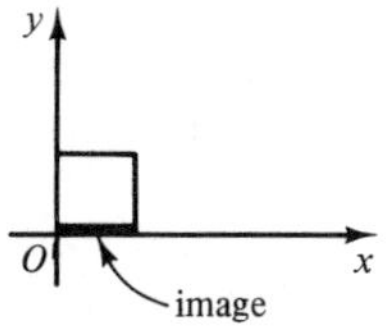	$\begin{bmatrix} 1 & 0 \\ 0 & 0 \end{bmatrix}$	does not exist	0
A projection parallel to the x-axis onto the y-axis	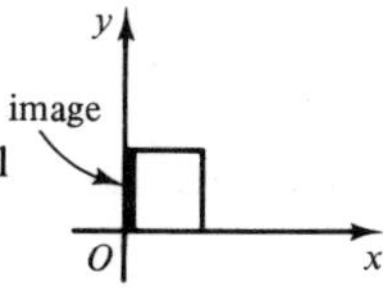	$\begin{bmatrix} 0 & 0 \\ 0 & 1 \end{bmatrix}$	does not exist	0

3

Invariant properties of a linear transformation

3.1 INVARIANT PROPERTIES

With geometrical transformations we are often interested in those properties which remain unchanged; that is, properties which are *invariant* under the transformation.

Q.1 What properties can you think of which are invariant under (*a*) a rotation, (*b*) a reflection, (*c*) a shear, (*d*) an enlargement, (*e*) a two-way stretch, (*f*) a projection?

We shall look especially at two properties which we can use to help us to identify a transformation.

(a) Which points are invariant?

Example 1

Which points are invariant under the linear transformation represented by the matrix $\begin{bmatrix} -1 & 2 \\ -2 & 3 \end{bmatrix}$?

Solution

If $\begin{bmatrix} x \\ y \end{bmatrix}$ remains unchanged, then

$$\begin{bmatrix} -1 & 2 \\ -2 & 3 \end{bmatrix}\begin{bmatrix} x \\ y \end{bmatrix} = \begin{bmatrix} x \\ y \end{bmatrix}$$

so

$$\begin{bmatrix} -x+2y \\ -2x+3y \end{bmatrix} = \begin{bmatrix} x \\ y \end{bmatrix};$$

that is,

$$-x + 2y = x \qquad (A)$$

and

$$-2x + 3y = y. \qquad (B)$$

Both (A) and (B) lead to the same equation, $y = x$, so all points on the line $y = x$ are invariant under the transformation represented by the matrix $\begin{bmatrix} -1 & 2 \\ -2 & 3 \end{bmatrix}$. We can therefore say that this transformation is *not* a rotation, an enlargement or a two-way stretch. *Why*? □

Example 2

Which points are invariant under the linear transformation represented by the matrix $\begin{bmatrix} -0.6 & -0.8 \\ 0.8 & -0.6 \end{bmatrix}$?

Solution

If $\begin{bmatrix} x \\ y \end{bmatrix}$ remains unchanged, then

$$\begin{bmatrix} -0.6 & -0.8 \\ 0.8 & -0.6 \end{bmatrix}\begin{bmatrix} x \\ y \end{bmatrix} = \begin{bmatrix} x \\ y \end{bmatrix},$$

so
$$\begin{bmatrix} -0.6x - 0.8y \\ 0.8x - 0.6y \end{bmatrix} = \begin{bmatrix} x \\ y \end{bmatrix};$$

that is,
$$-1.6x - 0.8y = 0 \qquad (C)$$

and
$$0.8x - 1.6y = 0. \qquad (D)$$

Solving (C) and (D) we get $x = 0,\ y = 0$.

So the *only* point which remains unchanged is the origin. We can therefore say that this transformation is *not* a reflection, a shear or a projection. □

Q.2 If we have a transformation which is represented by a matrix, is the origin always an invariant point?

Let us now look at the second property.

(b) When does the area remain the same?

We saw in Result 6 of Chapter 1 that under $\begin{bmatrix} a & b \\ c & d \end{bmatrix}$ the image of the unit square is a parallelogram. One possible diagram is shown in Fig. 1.

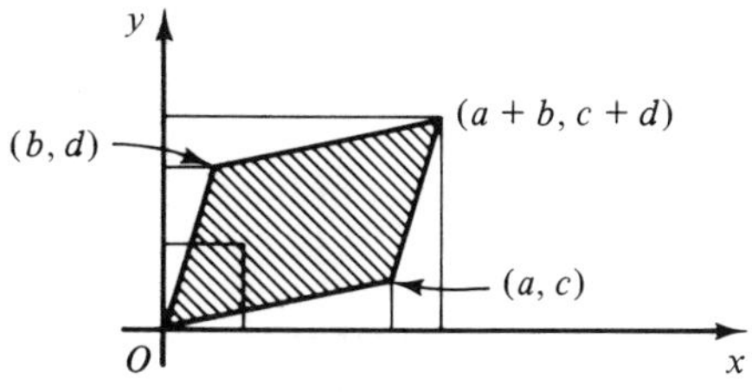

Figure 1

We can calculate its area by calculating the area of the rectangle and subtracting the areas of the triangles and trapezia:

$$\text{This area} = (a+b)(c+d) - \tfrac{1}{2}ac - \tfrac{1}{2}bd - \tfrac{1}{2}b(2c+d) - \tfrac{1}{2}c(2b+a)$$

$$= ad - bc.$$

So $$\frac{\text{area of the image}}{\text{area of the object}} = ad - bc.$$

You may recognise that this expression $(ad - bc)$ is the *determinant* of the matrix $\begin{bmatrix} a & b \\ c & d \end{bmatrix}$.

Q.3 Another possible figure for the parallelogram is shown in Fig. 2. Show that in this case the area is $(bc - ad)$.

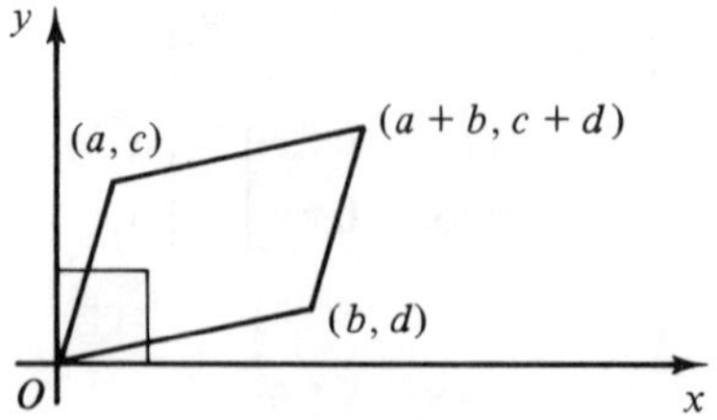

Figure 2

As area is a positive quantity, the expression for this figure is $(bc - ad)$ and not $(ad - bc)$. So it is the magnitude of the determinant which measures the area scale factor of the transformation.

Q.4 If we had not chosen the unit square, but had chosen a different figure, would the ratio above have remained the same? Try another figure.

Q.5 What is the ratio $\dfrac{\text{area of the image}}{\text{area of the object}}$ for the following transformations?
(*a*) a rotation (*b*) a reflection (*c*) a shear (*d*) an enlargement
(*e*) a one-way stretch (*f*) a two-way stretch (*g*) a projection
If the transformation can be represented by a matrix, what would you expect the determinant of the matrix to be in each case?

We see that if the magnitude of the area remains unchanged, the determinant of the matrix $= \pm 1$ and the transformation could possibly be a rotation, reflection, shear or a two-way stretch (if the matrix of the two-way stretch is $\begin{bmatrix} a & 0 \\ 0 & b \end{bmatrix}$ then $ab = \pm 1$).

In Example 1 the determinant of the matrix is $(-1)(3) - (-2)(2) = +1$, so the transformation is not a reflection and might be a rotation, a shear or a two-way stretch. As there is an invariant line ($y = x$), the transformation might be a shear.

In Example 2 the determinant of the matrix is $(-0.6)(-0.6) - (-0.8)(0.8) = +1$ so again the transformation is not a reflection and might be a rotation, a shear or a two-way stretch. In this case the origin is the only fixed point and so the transformation is not a shear. From a diagram it appears therefore that the transformation is a rotation.

Q.6 If Example 2 is a rotation, what is the angle of rotation?

Exercise 3A

For each of the following matrices:

(*a*) Find the invariant points of the transformation represented by the matrix.

(*b*) Calculate the area scale factor.

(*c*) Let O, A, B, C be $(0,0)$, $(1,0)$, $(1,1)$, $(0,1)$. The points $OABC$ form an anticlockwise circuit. Draw the images of $OABC$ and investigate its 'sense'. Compare your answers with your answers to part (*b*). What do you notice?

(*d*) Describe the geometrical effect of the transformation represented by the matrix. Show that your answer to this part is consistent with your answers to parts (*a*), (*b*) and (*c*).

1 $\begin{bmatrix}1 & -2\\0 & 1\end{bmatrix}$ **2** $\begin{bmatrix}1 & 0\\0 & -1\end{bmatrix}$ **3** $\begin{bmatrix}\frac{5}{13} & -\frac{12}{13}\\\frac{12}{13} & \frac{5}{13}\end{bmatrix}$ **4** $\begin{bmatrix}3 & 0\\0 & -\frac{1}{3}\end{bmatrix}$

5 $\begin{bmatrix}1 & 0\\0 & 0\end{bmatrix}$ **6** $\begin{bmatrix}2 & 0\\0 & -3\end{bmatrix}$ **7** $\begin{bmatrix}3 & 1\\-2 & 0\end{bmatrix}$ **8** $\begin{bmatrix}0 & -1\\1 & 2\end{bmatrix}$

3.2 MORE ABOUT TRANSFORMATIONS

In the last chapter we found the matrix representing a transformation by finding the image of $\begin{bmatrix}1\\0\end{bmatrix}$ and $\begin{bmatrix}0\\1\end{bmatrix}$. The next two examples illustrate an alternative method for finding the matrix when we are given the transformation.

Example 3

Find the matrix **M** which represents a reflection in the line $y = 3x$.

Solution

We can easily write down the matrix which rotates the x-axis through any angle we choose. So let **R** be the rotation which takes the x-axis to the line $y = 3x$, that is an anti-clockwise rotation of $\theta°$ about the origin (Fig. 3).

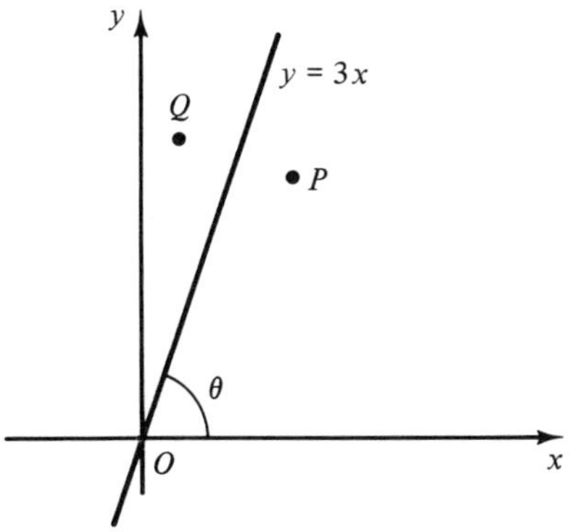

Figure 3

Starting position

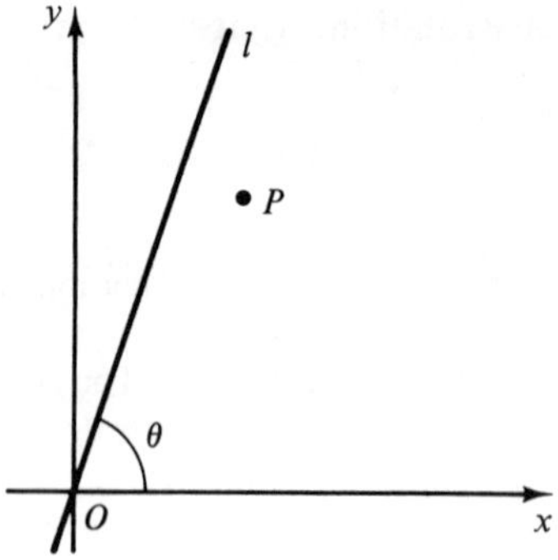

Rotate the plane clockwise through $\theta°$ so that the line $y = 3x$ (line ℓ in the diagram) coincides with x-axis (to become the line ℓ'); also $P \to P'$.

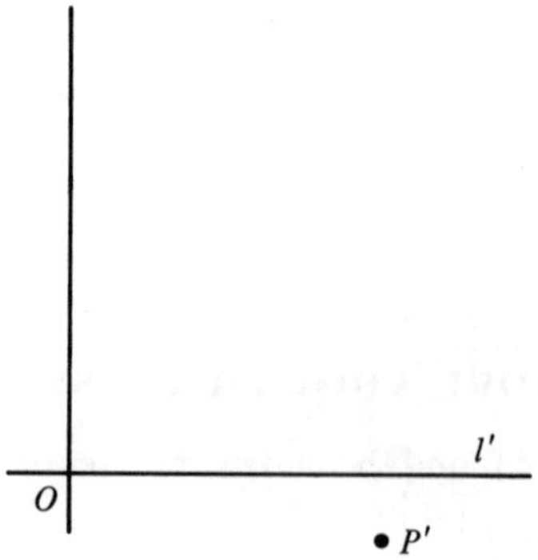

Transformation $\mathbf{R}^{-1}$

Reflect the plane in the x-axis; $P' \to P''$.

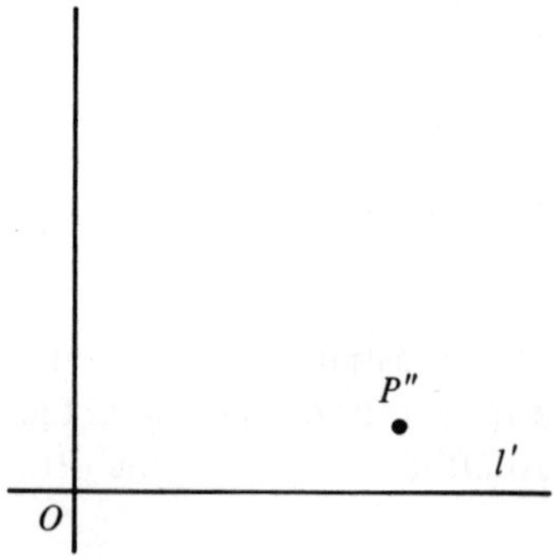

Transformation **S** (reflection in the x-axis)

Rotate the plane anti-clockwise through $\theta°$. The x-axis is then rotated to become the line $y = 3x$; also $P'' \to P'''$(that is, Q)

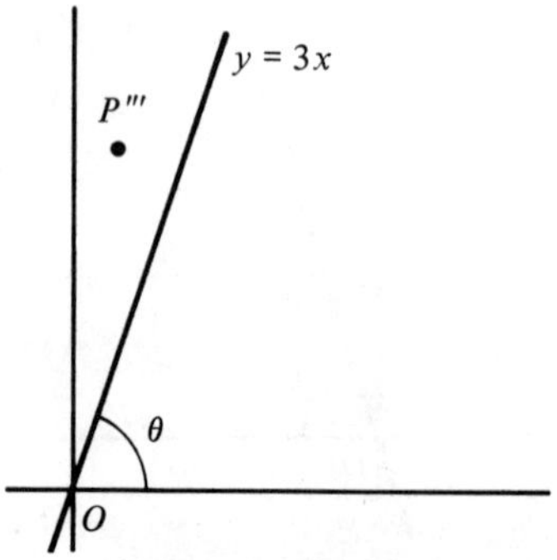

Transformation **R**

Figure 4

Q.7 Use tracing paper to check that a reflection in $y = 3x$ can be accomplished using the sequence of transformations in Fig. 4.

So $\mathbf{M} = \mathbf{RSR}^{-1}$. (Notice the order in which these transformations are written.)

As $\tan\theta = \dfrac{3}{1}$, $\sin\theta = \dfrac{3}{\sqrt{10}}$ and $\cos\theta = \dfrac{1}{\sqrt{10}}$.

(Consider the triangle 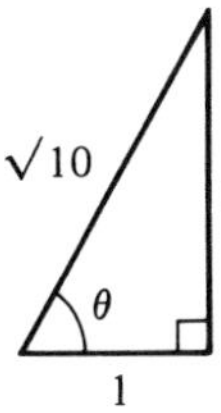)

So $$\mathbf{R} = \begin{bmatrix} \cos\theta & -\sin\theta \\ \sin\theta & \cos\theta \end{bmatrix} = \begin{bmatrix} \dfrac{1}{\sqrt{10}} & -\dfrac{3}{\sqrt{10}} \\ \dfrac{3}{\sqrt{10}} & \dfrac{1}{\sqrt{10}} \end{bmatrix}.$$

Also $$\mathbf{S} = \begin{bmatrix} 1 & 0 \\ 0 & -1 \end{bmatrix}$$

and $$\mathbf{R}^{-1} = \begin{bmatrix} \dfrac{1}{\sqrt{10}} & \dfrac{3}{\sqrt{10}} \\ -\dfrac{3}{\sqrt{10}} & \dfrac{1}{\sqrt{10}} \end{bmatrix}.$$

Now $$\mathbf{M} = \mathbf{RSR}^{-1}$$

$$= \begin{bmatrix} \dfrac{1}{\sqrt{10}} & -\dfrac{3}{\sqrt{10}} \\ \dfrac{3}{\sqrt{10}} & \dfrac{1}{\sqrt{10}} \end{bmatrix} \begin{bmatrix} 1 & 0 \\ 0 & -1 \end{bmatrix} \begin{bmatrix} \dfrac{1}{\sqrt{10}} & \dfrac{3}{\sqrt{10}} \\ -\dfrac{3}{\sqrt{10}} & \dfrac{1}{\sqrt{10}} \end{bmatrix}$$

So $$\mathbf{M} = \begin{bmatrix} \dfrac{1}{\sqrt{10}} & \dfrac{3}{\sqrt{10}} \\ \dfrac{3}{\sqrt{10}} & -\dfrac{1}{\sqrt{10}} \end{bmatrix} \begin{bmatrix} \dfrac{1}{\sqrt{10}} & \dfrac{3}{\sqrt{10}} \\ -\dfrac{3}{\sqrt{10}} & \dfrac{1}{\sqrt{10}} \end{bmatrix}$$

that is $$\mathbf{M} = \begin{bmatrix} -\frac{8}{10} & \frac{6}{10} \\ \frac{6}{10} & \frac{8}{10} \end{bmatrix}.$$ □

Example 4

Find the matrix **M** which represents a stretch with invariant line $y = \frac{1}{3}x$ parallel to $y = -3x$ of factor 2.

Solution
Using diagrams similar to those in Fig. 4, it can be seen that

$$\mathbf{M} = \mathbf{RSR}^{-1}$$

where, this time, **R** is the rotation which takes the x-axis to the line $y = -3x$ (Fig. 5) and **S** is a stretch parallel to the x-axis of factor 2.

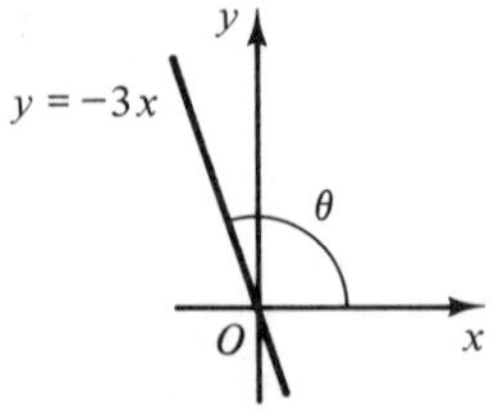

Figure 5

As $\tan\theta = -3$, $\sin\theta = \dfrac{3}{\sqrt{10}}$ and $\cos\theta = -\dfrac{1}{\sqrt{10}}$.

So $$\mathbf{R} = \begin{bmatrix} \cos\theta & -\sin\theta \\ \sin\theta & \cos\theta \end{bmatrix} = \begin{bmatrix} -\dfrac{1}{\sqrt{10}} & -\dfrac{3}{\sqrt{10}} \\ \dfrac{3}{\sqrt{10}} & -\dfrac{1}{\sqrt{10}} \end{bmatrix}$$

and $$\mathbf{S} = \begin{bmatrix} 2 & 0 \\ 0 & 1 \end{bmatrix}.$$

Now $$\mathbf{M} = \mathbf{RSR}^{-1}$$

$$= \begin{bmatrix} -\dfrac{1}{\sqrt{10}} & \dfrac{3}{\sqrt{10}} \\ -\dfrac{3}{\sqrt{10}} & -\dfrac{1}{\sqrt{10}} \end{bmatrix} \begin{bmatrix} 2 & 0 \\ 0 & 1 \end{bmatrix} \begin{bmatrix} -\dfrac{1}{\sqrt{10}} & \dfrac{3}{\sqrt{10}} \\ -\dfrac{3}{\sqrt{10}} & -\dfrac{1}{\sqrt{10}} \end{bmatrix}$$

So $$\mathbf{M} = \begin{bmatrix} \frac{11}{10} & -\frac{3}{10} \\ -\frac{3}{10} & \frac{19}{10} \end{bmatrix}.$$

Alternatively, for this question we could have rotated the x-axis to the line $y = \frac{1}{3}x$, in which case the stretch would have been parallel to the y-axis. □

Rearranging $\mathbf{M} = \mathbf{RSR}^{-1}$

we get $\mathbf{R}^{-1}\mathbf{M} = \mathbf{SR}^{-1}$ (premultiplying both sides by **R**)

and $\mathbf{R}^{-1}\mathbf{MR} = \mathbf{S}$ (postmultiplying both sides by **R**).

This new form of the equation may be useful in helping us to describe the geometrical effect of a transformation.

Example 5

Describe fully the transformation which is represented by the matrix $\begin{bmatrix} -1 & 2 \\ -2 & 3 \end{bmatrix}$.

Solution

We know from Example 1 that the line $y = x$ is invariant. We therefore choose **R** so that the x-axis is rotated onto this invariant line.

$$\mathbf{R} = \begin{bmatrix} \frac{1}{\sqrt{2}} & -\frac{1}{\sqrt{2}} \\ \frac{1}{\sqrt{2}} & \frac{1}{\sqrt{2}} \end{bmatrix} \quad \text{and so} \quad \mathbf{R}^{-1} = \begin{bmatrix} \frac{1}{\sqrt{2}} & \frac{1}{\sqrt{2}} \\ -\frac{1}{\sqrt{2}} & \frac{1}{\sqrt{2}} \end{bmatrix}.$$

We are given

$$\mathbf{M} = \begin{bmatrix} -1 & 2 \\ -2 & 3 \end{bmatrix}.$$

Now $\qquad \mathbf{S} = \mathbf{R}^{-1}\mathbf{M}\mathbf{R}$

$$\Rightarrow \quad \mathbf{S} = \begin{bmatrix} \frac{1}{\sqrt{2}} & \frac{1}{\sqrt{2}} \\ -\frac{1}{\sqrt{2}} & \frac{1}{\sqrt{2}} \end{bmatrix} \begin{bmatrix} -1 & 2 \\ -2 & 3 \end{bmatrix} \begin{bmatrix} \frac{1}{\sqrt{2}} & -\frac{1}{\sqrt{2}} \\ \frac{1}{\sqrt{2}} & \frac{1}{\sqrt{2}} \end{bmatrix}$$

$$= \begin{bmatrix} -\frac{3}{\sqrt{2}} & \frac{5}{\sqrt{2}} \\ -\frac{1}{\sqrt{2}} & \frac{1}{\sqrt{2}} \end{bmatrix} \begin{bmatrix} \frac{1}{\sqrt{2}} & -\frac{1}{\sqrt{2}} \\ \frac{1}{\sqrt{2}} & \frac{1}{\sqrt{2}} \end{bmatrix}$$

$$= \begin{bmatrix} 1 & 4 \\ 0 & 1 \end{bmatrix}.$$

This is a shear with invariant line the x-axis and factor 4. Therefore $\begin{bmatrix} -1 & 2 \\ -2 & 3 \end{bmatrix}$ is a shear with invariant line $y = x$ and factor 4. □

Note that by 'a shear with invariant line l and factor k' we mean: 'Rotate *clockwise* until l coincides with the x-axis, then shear with the invariant line the x-axis and factor k, then rotate *anticlockwise* until the x-axis coincides with the original position of l.'

Matrices **M** and **S** both represent shears with factor 4 and are examples of *similar matrices*.

Definition

Matrices **A** and **B** are said to be *similar* if there is a non-singular matrix **P** for which $\mathbf{B} = \mathbf{P}^{-1}\mathbf{A}\mathbf{P}$.

Exercise 3B

1 Find the matrices for the following transformations:

(*a*) a reflection in the line $y = 3x$

(*b*) a shear with invariant line $y = x$ of factor 2

(*c*) a one-way stretch parallel to $y = -x$ of factor 3 with invariant line $y = x$

(*d*) a projection parallel to $y = -2x$ onto $2y = x$

(*e*) a reflection in the line $y = -\frac{1}{2}x$

For each part, use the matrix to find the invariant points and check that these are consistent with the transformation.

2 Using the method of Example 5, describe fully the geometrical effect of each of the following transformations:

(*a*) $\begin{bmatrix} \frac{3}{5} & \frac{4}{5} \\ \frac{4}{5} & -\frac{3}{5} \end{bmatrix}$ (*b*) $\begin{bmatrix} 2 & 1 \\ -1 & 0 \end{bmatrix}$ (*c*) $\begin{bmatrix} 10 & 3 \\ 3 & 2 \end{bmatrix}$

(*d*) $\frac{1}{13}\begin{bmatrix} 4 & 6 \\ 6 & 9 \end{bmatrix}$ (*e*) $\begin{bmatrix} -\frac{4}{5} & -\frac{3}{5} \\ -\frac{3}{5} & \frac{4}{5} \end{bmatrix}$

3.3 REFLECTIONS

If $\mathbf{M}$ is the matrix of a linear transformation, we can find the invariant points by solving $\mathbf{M}\begin{bmatrix} x \\ y \end{bmatrix} = \begin{bmatrix} x \\ y \end{bmatrix}$. If $\mathbf{M}$ is a reflection, we shall have a line of invariant points which is the axis of reflection.

Q.8 In §3.2, we found that the matrix for reflection in the line $y = 3x$ is

$$\mathbf{M} = \begin{bmatrix} -0.8 & 0.6 \\ 0.6 & 0.8 \end{bmatrix}.$$

(*a*) Verify that $\mathbf{M}\begin{bmatrix} k \\ 3k \end{bmatrix} = \begin{bmatrix} k \\ 3k \end{bmatrix}$.

(*b*) Also solve $\mathbf{M}\begin{bmatrix} x \\ y \end{bmatrix} = -\begin{bmatrix} x \\ y \end{bmatrix}$. How is your answer related to the line $y = 3x$?

Q.9 Why is it always true that there is a line of solutions to $\mathbf{M}\begin{bmatrix} x \\ y \end{bmatrix} = -\begin{bmatrix} x \\ y \end{bmatrix}$ if $\mathbf{M}$ is a reflection?

In Chapter 1 our approach to identifying a transformation was to draw the image of the unit square and see if we could recognise the result. Our aim in this chapter has been to introduce a more analytical approach through looking at invariant points and the area scale factor.

Miscellaneous exercise 3

1 Show that $\begin{bmatrix} 4 & -1 \\ 3 & 5 \end{bmatrix}$ and $\begin{bmatrix} 13 & -5 \\ 15 & -4 \end{bmatrix}$ are similar matrices. (*Hint*: write $\mathbf{B} = \mathbf{P}^{-1}\mathbf{AP}$ as $\mathbf{PB} = \mathbf{AP}$.)

2 Prove that the matrix representing a reflection in the line $y = (\tan\theta)x$ is $\begin{bmatrix} \cos 2\theta & \sin 2\theta \\ \sin 2\theta & -\cos 2\theta \end{bmatrix}$.

3 Show that the matrix $\mathbf{M} = \begin{bmatrix} a & b \\ c & d \end{bmatrix}$ with $a + d = 0$ and $\det(\mathbf{M}) = -1$ is self-inverse. Hence describe geometrically the transformation represented by the matrix $\begin{bmatrix} 3 & 2 \\ -4 & -3 \end{bmatrix}$.

4 Find the matrix for a two-way stretch of factor 3 parallel to $x = y$ and of factor 4 parallel to $x = -y$. Show that the lines $x = y$ and $x = -y$ are invariant as a whole under this transformation.

5 If $\mathbf{M} = \begin{bmatrix} a & b \\ c & d \end{bmatrix}$, where a, b, c, d are all positive and $a + c = b + d = 1$, show that it is always possible to find a non-zero vector $\mathbf{x}$ such that $\mathbf{Mx} = \mathbf{x}$.

6 Show, by using matrix algebra, that the combination of two reflections in intersecting mirror lines is equivalent to a rotation through twice the angle between them.

SUMMARY

(1) Properties which remain unchanged under a transformation are known as *invariant* properties; for example, invariant points are found by solving $\mathbf{M}\begin{bmatrix} x \\ y \end{bmatrix} = \begin{bmatrix} x \\ y \end{bmatrix}$.

(2) The *determinant* of the matrix $\begin{bmatrix} a & b \\ c & d \end{bmatrix}$ is $(ad - bc)$. Its magnitude measures the area scale factor of the transformation.

(3) Matrices $\mathbf{A}$ and $\mathbf{B}$ are said to be *similar* if there is a non-singular matrix $\mathbf{P}$ for which $\mathbf{B} = \mathbf{P}^{-1}\mathbf{AP}$.

4

Eigenvalues and eigenvectors

4.1 THE FIXED DIRECTIONS OF A LINEAR MAPPING

If we consider the effect of the matrix $\mathbf{M} = \begin{bmatrix} 1 & 1 \\ -2 & 4 \end{bmatrix}$ on the vectors $\begin{bmatrix} 3 \\ 3 \end{bmatrix}$ and $\begin{bmatrix} 2 \\ 4 \end{bmatrix}$, we find that

$$\begin{bmatrix} 1 & 1 \\ -2 & 4 \end{bmatrix}\begin{bmatrix} 3 \\ 3 \end{bmatrix} = \begin{bmatrix} 6 \\ 6 \end{bmatrix} = 2\begin{bmatrix} 3 \\ 3 \end{bmatrix}$$

and

$$\begin{bmatrix} 1 & 1 \\ -2 & 4 \end{bmatrix}\begin{bmatrix} 2 \\ 4 \end{bmatrix} = \begin{bmatrix} 6 \\ 12 \end{bmatrix} = 3\begin{bmatrix} 2 \\ 4 \end{bmatrix}.$$

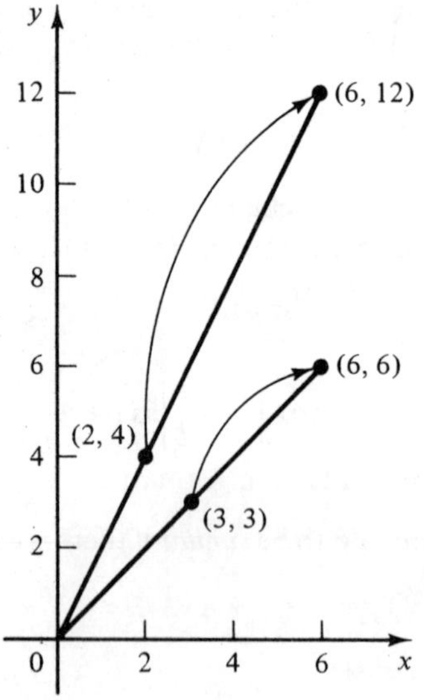

Figure 1

The points $(3, 3)$ and $(6, 6)$ both lie on the line $y = x$, and $(6, 6)$ is twice as far away from the origin as $(3, 3)$ (Fig. 1). Also, the points $(2, 4)$ and $(6, 12)$ both lie on the line $y = 2x$, and $(6, 12)$ is three times as far away from the origin as $(2, 4)$. What happens to other points on the lines $y = x$ and $y = 2x$?

For the point (k, k) on the line $y = x$, we have $\begin{bmatrix} 1 & 1 \\ -2 & 4 \end{bmatrix}\begin{bmatrix} k \\ k \end{bmatrix} = 2\begin{bmatrix} k \\ k \end{bmatrix}$, so the image of a point on the line $y = x$ stays on the line, but is twice as far away from the origin as it was before. If we think of the images of all the points on this line, we get the line itself again. We say that the line $y = x$ is invariant *as a whole* under this linear transformation, though it is *not pointwise* invariant. By 'pointwise invariant', we mean that each point maps onto itself (as we considered in §3.1 of Chapter 3).

Q.1 Show that the line $y = 2x$ is also invariant.

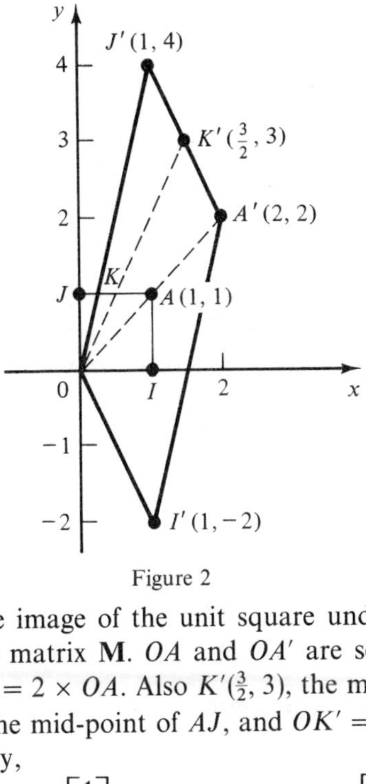

Figure 2

Fig. 2 shows the image of the unit square under the transformation represented by the matrix **M**. OA and OA' are seen to be in the same direction with $OA' = 2 \times OA$. Also $K'(\frac{3}{2}, 3)$, the mid-point of $A'J'$, is the image of $K(\frac{1}{2}, 1)$, the mid-point of AJ, and $OK' = 3 \times OK$.

Expressed another way,

$$\text{the vector } \mathbf{OA} = \begin{bmatrix} 1 \\ 1 \end{bmatrix} \mapsto \text{the vector } \mathbf{OA}' = \begin{bmatrix} 2 \\ 2 \end{bmatrix} = 2\begin{bmatrix} 1 \\ 1 \end{bmatrix},$$

and

$$\text{the vector } \mathbf{OK} = \begin{bmatrix} \frac{1}{2} \\ 1 \end{bmatrix} \mapsto \text{the vector } \mathbf{OK}' = \begin{bmatrix} \frac{3}{2} \\ 3 \end{bmatrix} = 3\begin{bmatrix} \frac{1}{2} \\ 1 \end{bmatrix}.$$

The values 2 and 3 are called the *eigenvalues* of the matrix **M** and the corresponding vectors $\begin{bmatrix} 1 \\ 1 \end{bmatrix}$ and $\begin{bmatrix} \frac{1}{2} \\ 1 \end{bmatrix}$ (or any non-zero scalar multiples of them) are called the *eigenvectors*.

Definition
An *eigenvector of* **M** is a non-zero vector **x** such that $\mathbf{Mx} = \lambda\mathbf{x}$; λ is the corresponding *eigenvalue*.*

* The word 'eigenvalue' is a combination of the German word 'eigen', meaning 'own' or 'belonging to', and the English word 'value'.

There are three important points to note from this definition:

(1) $\mathbf{x}$ is a non-zero vector by definition.

(2) $\lambda = 0$ is a possible eigenvalue.

(3) For a given eigenvalue, there is not a unique eigenvector. Once one eigenvector has been found, any non-zero scalar multiple of that vector is also an eigenvector.

Finding eigenvalues and eigenvectors

To find the eigenvalues and eigenvectors of a matrix $\mathbf{M}$ we start with the definition $\mathbf{Mx} = \lambda\mathbf{x}$, where $\mathbf{x}$ is a non-zero vector. So for the example above we have

$$\begin{bmatrix} 1 & 1 \\ -2 & 4 \end{bmatrix}\begin{bmatrix} x \\ y \end{bmatrix} = \lambda\begin{bmatrix} x \\ y \end{bmatrix};$$

that is,
$$\begin{bmatrix} x + y \\ -2x + 4y \end{bmatrix} = \begin{bmatrix} \lambda x \\ \lambda y \end{bmatrix},$$

so
$$(1 - \lambda)x + y = 0 \tag{A}$$

and
$$-2x + (4 - \lambda)y = 0 \,. \tag{B}$$

$2 \times (A) + (1 - \lambda) \times (B)$ gives $[2 + (1 - \lambda)(4 - \lambda)]y = 0$,

so either $\quad y = 0 \quad$ or $\quad 2 + (1 - \lambda)(4 - \lambda) = 0$.

Alternatively, eliminating y:
$(4 - \lambda) \times (A) - (B)$ gives $\quad [(4 - \lambda)(1 - \lambda) + 2]x = 0$,

so either $\quad x = 0 \quad$ or $\quad (4 - \lambda)(1 - \lambda) + 2 = 0$.

Now we are looking for a non-zero vector $\mathbf{x}$, so we cannot have both x and y equal to zero.

Therefore $(4 - \lambda)(1 - \lambda) + 2 = 0$;

that is, $\quad \lambda^2 - 5\lambda + 6 = 0$:

this equation is known as the *characteristic equation.*

Factorising, $\quad (\lambda - 2)(\lambda - 3) = 0$.

So $\quad \lambda = 2 \quad$ or $\quad 3$: these are the *eigenvalues.*

If $\lambda = 2$, Equations (A) and (B) become

$$\left.\begin{aligned} -\ x + \ y &= 0 \\ -2x + 2y &= 0 \end{aligned}\right\}$$

These two equations give the same line, which is an invariant line under the transformation $\mathbf{M}$. The position vector of any point on this line is an eigenvector corresponding to the eigenvalue $\lambda = 2$, for example $\begin{bmatrix} 1 \\ 1 \end{bmatrix}$.

If $\lambda = 3$, Equations (A) and (B) become

$$\left.\begin{aligned} -2x + y &= 0 \\ -2x + y &= 0 \end{aligned}\right\}$$

So the second invariant line is $y = 2x$. $\begin{bmatrix} 1 \\ 2 \end{bmatrix}$ is the position vector of a point on this line, and so is an eigenvector corresponding to the eigenvalue $\lambda = 3$.

Q.2 Find the characteristic equation, and hence the eigenvalues and eigenvectors of $\begin{bmatrix} 1 & 2 \\ 3 & 2 \end{bmatrix}$.

4.2 THE GENERAL CASE FOR FINDING EIGENVALUES AND EIGENVECTORS

If $\mathbf{M} = \begin{bmatrix} a & b \\ c & d \end{bmatrix}$ we find the eigenvalues and eigenvectors by solving the equation

$$\mathbf{Mx} = \lambda\mathbf{x}, \quad \text{where} \quad \mathbf{x} \neq \mathbf{0}$$

$$\Rightarrow \qquad \mathbf{Mx} = \lambda\mathbf{Ix}, \quad \text{where } \mathbf{I} \text{ is the identity matrix}$$

$$\Rightarrow \qquad \mathbf{Mx} - \lambda\mathbf{Ix} = \mathbf{0}$$

$$\Rightarrow \qquad (\mathbf{M} - \lambda\mathbf{I})\mathbf{x} = \mathbf{0}$$

$$\Rightarrow \begin{bmatrix} a - \lambda & b \\ c & d - \lambda \end{bmatrix}\begin{bmatrix} x \\ y \end{bmatrix} = \begin{bmatrix} 0 \\ 0 \end{bmatrix};$$

that is, $\qquad (a - \lambda)x + by = 0 \qquad (A)$

and $\qquad cx + (d - \lambda)y = 0. \qquad (B)$

$(d - \lambda) \times (A) - b \times (B)$ gives $[(a - \lambda)(d - \lambda) - dc]x = 0$,

so either $\qquad x = 0 \quad \text{or} \quad (a - \lambda)(d - \lambda) - bc = 0.$

Also, $c \times (A) - (a - \lambda) \times (B)$ gives $[bc - (a - \lambda)(d - \lambda)]y = 0$,

so either $\qquad y = 0 \quad \text{or} \quad bc - (a - \lambda)(d - \lambda) = 0$

Now we are looking for a non-zero vector $\mathbf{x}$, so we cannot have both x and y equal to zero,

therefore $\qquad (a - \lambda)(d - \lambda) - bc = 0; \qquad (C)$

that is, $\qquad \lambda^2 - (a + d)\lambda + (ad - bc) = 0. \qquad (D)$

You may recognise that (C) is the *determinant* of the 2×2 matrix $(\mathbf{M} - \lambda\mathbf{I})$. Equation (D) is known as the *characteristic equation* for the matrix $\mathbf{M}$, and the roots of this equation are the *eigenvalues*. The *eigenvectors* corresponding to each eigenvalue are then found from equation (A) or (B).

In practice, we often go straight to the characteristic equation by writing down

$$\det(\mathbf{M} - \lambda\mathbf{I}) = 0.$$

The solution of this equation gives the eigenvalues, and the eigenvectors are then found from the equation $(\mathbf{M} - \lambda\mathbf{I})\mathbf{x} = \mathbf{0}$.

Example 1
Find the characteristic equation, and the eigenvalues and eigenvectors of the matrix $\mathbf{M} = \begin{bmatrix} 4 & -5 \\ 1 & -2 \end{bmatrix}$.

Solution

$$\mathbf{M} - \lambda\mathbf{I} = \begin{bmatrix} 4-\lambda & -5 \\ 1 & -2-\lambda \end{bmatrix}$$

so
$$\det(\mathbf{M} - \lambda\mathbf{I}) = (4-\lambda)(-2-\lambda) + 5.$$

The characteristic equation is

$$\lambda^2 - 2\lambda - 3 = 0$$

$$\Rightarrow \quad (\lambda - 3)(\lambda + 1) = 0$$

so the eigenvalues are 3 and -1.

If $\lambda = 3$, $(\mathbf{M} - \lambda\mathbf{I})\mathbf{x} = \mathbf{0}$ becomes $\begin{bmatrix} 1 & -5 \\ 1 & -5 \end{bmatrix}\begin{bmatrix} x \\ y \end{bmatrix} = \begin{bmatrix} 0 \\ 0 \end{bmatrix}$

so an eigenvector is $\begin{bmatrix} 5 \\ 1 \end{bmatrix}$ (or any non-zero scalar multiple).

If $\lambda = -1$ we get $\begin{bmatrix} 5 & -5 \\ 1 & -1 \end{bmatrix}\begin{bmatrix} x \\ y \end{bmatrix} = \begin{bmatrix} 0 \\ 0 \end{bmatrix}$;

that is,
$$\left.\begin{aligned} 5x - 5y &= 0 \\ x - y &= 0 \end{aligned}\right\}$$

so an eigenvector is $\begin{bmatrix} 1 \\ 1 \end{bmatrix}$ (or any non-zero scalar multiple). □

For a 2×2 matrix, the characteristic equation is a quadratic equation which can have:

(1) two distinct real roots, for example $\begin{bmatrix} 1 & 1 \\ -2 & 4 \end{bmatrix}$, or

(2) two equal real roots, for example $\begin{bmatrix} 1 & 1 \\ 0 & 1 \end{bmatrix}$ or $\begin{bmatrix} 3 & 0 \\ 0 & 3 \end{bmatrix}$, or

(3) no real roots, for example $\begin{bmatrix} 1 & -1 \\ 1 & 1 \end{bmatrix}$.

In (2), the matrix $\begin{bmatrix} 1 & 1 \\ 0 & 1 \end{bmatrix}$ has eigenvector $\begin{bmatrix} 1 \\ 0 \end{bmatrix}$, corresponding to eigenvalue 1, whereas any vector of the form $\begin{bmatrix} a \\ b \end{bmatrix}$ (where a, b are real numbers) is an eigenvector corresponding to eigenvalue 3 for the matrix $\begin{bmatrix} 3 & 0 \\ 0 & 3 \end{bmatrix}$.

Exercise 4A

Find the characteristic equation, and the eigenvalue and eigenvectors of the following matrices. (You will need your answers to questions 1–4 in Exercise 4B.)

1 $\begin{bmatrix} 2 & 1 \\ 4 & -1 \end{bmatrix}$ **2** $\begin{bmatrix} 3 & 2 \\ 1 & 2 \end{bmatrix}$ **3** $\begin{bmatrix} 1 & 3 \\ 2 & -4 \end{bmatrix}$

4 $\begin{bmatrix} -2 & 2 \\ -1 & -5 \end{bmatrix}$ **5** $\begin{bmatrix} 1 & 6 \\ 6 & 1 \end{bmatrix}$ **6** $\begin{bmatrix} 2 & -3 \\ -4 & 6 \end{bmatrix}$

7 $\begin{bmatrix} 1 & -1 \\ \frac{1}{3} & -\frac{1}{6} \end{bmatrix}$ **8** $\begin{bmatrix} \frac{3}{4} & -\frac{1}{2} \\ \frac{1}{2} & -\frac{1}{2} \end{bmatrix}$ **9** $\begin{bmatrix} \frac{1}{2} & \frac{5}{4} \\ \frac{1}{2} & -\frac{1}{4} \end{bmatrix}$

4.3 $\mathbf{U \Lambda U^{-1}}$

In the next two sections we will only be considering matrices which have two real distinct eigenvalues.

(a) A geometrical approach

We have seen that for the matrix $\mathbf{M} = \begin{bmatrix} 1 & 1 \\ -2 & 4 \end{bmatrix}$ the lines $y = x$ and $y = 2x$ are invariant with a stretch factor 2 in the direction $y = x$ and a stretch factor 3 in the direction $y = 2x$. So we can describe the transformation represented by the matrix **M** as *a two-way stretch in oblique directions* $y = x$ *and* $y = 2x$ *with factors 2 and 3.*

The transformation represented by the matrix **M** can be broken down into the steps shown in Fig. 3 (overleaf).

We are familiar with the matrix for Step 2, which is $\mathbf{S} = \begin{bmatrix} 2 & 0 \\ 0 & 3 \end{bmatrix}$.

Also, Steps 1 and 3 are inverses. To find the matrix for Step 3, choose a point on each of the lines $y = x$ and $y = 2x$, for example $(1, 1)$ on $y = x$ and $(1, 2)$ on $y = 2x$.

The linear transformation which maps $\begin{bmatrix} 1 \\ 0 \end{bmatrix}$ to $\begin{bmatrix} 1 \\ 1 \end{bmatrix}$ and $\begin{bmatrix} 0 \\ 1 \end{bmatrix}$ to $\begin{bmatrix} 1 \\ 2 \end{bmatrix}$ will map the x-axis onto the line $y = x$ and the y-axis onto the line $y = 2x$ (Fig. 4, on page 49). So the matrix for Step 3 is

$$\mathbf{R} = \begin{bmatrix} 1 & 1 \\ 1 & 2 \end{bmatrix}$$

and the matrix for Step 1 is $\mathbf{R}^{-1} = \begin{bmatrix} 2 & -1 \\ -1 & 1 \end{bmatrix}$.

Starting position

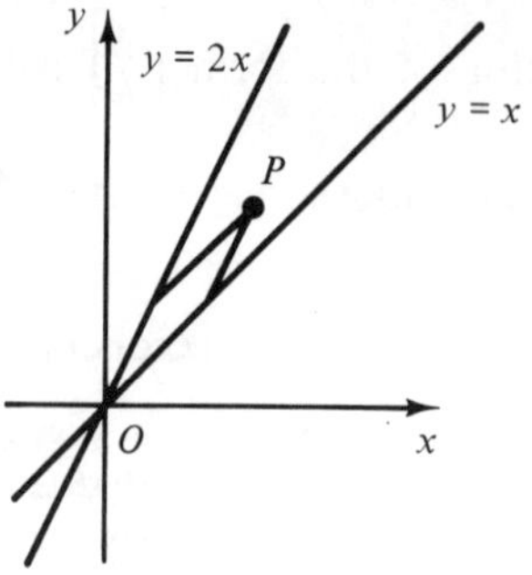

Step 1 Transform the lines $y = x$ and $y = 2x$ onto the x- and y-axes respectively.

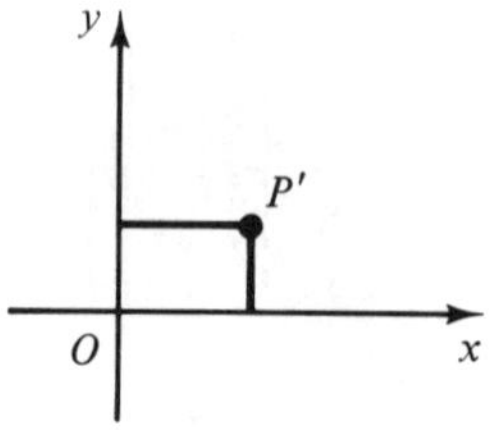

Step 2 A two-way stretch, factors 2 and 3 in the directions of x- and y-axes respectively.

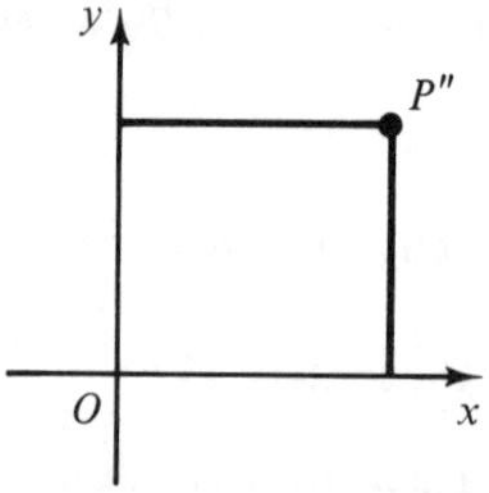

Step 3 Transform the x- and y-axes back to the lines $y = x$ and $y = 2x$ respectively.

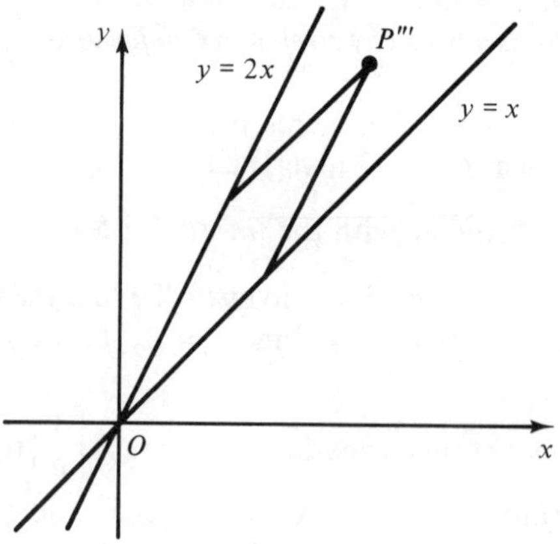

Figure 3

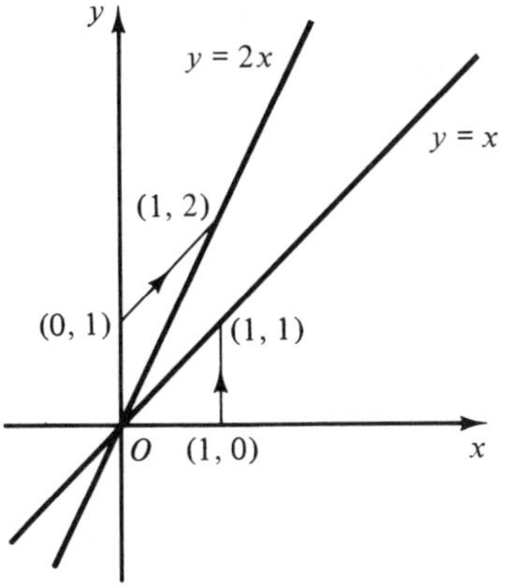

Figure 4

Therefore $$\mathbf{M} = \mathbf{RSR}^{-1} \text{ – note the order.}$$

Q.3 Verify using matrix multiplication that $\mathbf{M} = \mathbf{RSR}^{-1}$.

Rearranging $$\mathbf{M} = \mathbf{RSR}^{-1}$$

we get $$\mathbf{S} = \mathbf{R}^{-1}\mathbf{MR};$$

that is, **M** and **S** are *similar* matrices – they both represent two-way stretches with factors 2 and 3, but with respect to different axes.

Change of notation
As matrices **R** and **S** arise from the eigenvalues and eigenvectors of the matrix **M** we shall use different names for these two matrices.

Instead of **S** we shall define $\mathbf{\Lambda}$ as the diagonal matrix whose entries are the eigenvalues of **M**, and instead of **R** we shall define **U** as the matrix whose columns are the corresponding eigenvectors of **M**.

So $$\mathbf{M} = \mathbf{U\Lambda U}^{-1}.$$

Q.4 In Q.2 we found the eigenvalues and eigenvectors of $\mathbf{M} = \begin{bmatrix} 1 & 2 \\ 3 & 2 \end{bmatrix}$.

Express **M** in the form $\mathbf{U\Lambda U}^{-1}$ and verify your answers by matrix multiplication.

Conversely, if we have a two-way stretch in oblique directions we can now find the matrix of the transformation.

Example 2
A transformation is a two-way stretch in oblique directions $y = -3x$ and $y = x$ with factors 2 and $\frac{1}{3}$ respectively. Find the matrix **T** of this transformation.

Solution

The eigenvalues and eigenvectors of $\mathbf{M}$ are therefore

Eigenvalue	*Eigenvector*
2	$\begin{bmatrix} 1 \\ -3 \end{bmatrix}$
$\frac{1}{3}$	$\begin{bmatrix} 1 \\ 1 \end{bmatrix}$

So we can calculate $\mathbf{M}$ from $\mathbf{U\Lambda U}^{-1}$,

where
$$\mathbf{U} = \begin{bmatrix} 1 & 1 \\ -3 & 1 \end{bmatrix} \text{ and } \mathbf{\Lambda} = \begin{bmatrix} 2 & 0 \\ 0 & \frac{1}{3} \end{bmatrix}.$$

Therefore
$$\mathbf{M} = \mathbf{U\Lambda U}^{-1}$$
$$\Rightarrow \mathbf{M} = \begin{bmatrix} 1 & 1 \\ -3 & 1 \end{bmatrix}\begin{bmatrix} 2 & 0 \\ 0 & \frac{1}{3} \end{bmatrix}\left(\frac{1}{4}\begin{bmatrix} 1 & -1 \\ 3 & 1 \end{bmatrix}\right)$$
$$\Rightarrow \mathbf{M} = \frac{1}{4}\begin{bmatrix} 2 & \frac{1}{3} \\ -6 & \frac{1}{3} \end{bmatrix}\begin{bmatrix} 1 & -1 \\ 3 & 1 \end{bmatrix}$$
$$\Rightarrow \mathbf{M} = \frac{1}{4}\begin{bmatrix} 3 & 1\frac{2}{3} \\ -5 & 6\frac{1}{3} \end{bmatrix}$$
$$\Rightarrow \mathbf{M} = \begin{bmatrix} \frac{3}{4} & -\frac{5}{12} \\ -\frac{5}{4} & \frac{19}{12} \end{bmatrix}.$$
□

Q.5 In Example 2 we chose eigenvectors $\begin{bmatrix} 1 \\ -3 \end{bmatrix}$ and $\begin{bmatrix} 1 \\ 1 \end{bmatrix}$. Choose other eigenvectors, thus giving a different matrix $\mathbf{U}$, and verify that $\mathbf{U\Lambda U}^{-1}$ still gives the same matrix $\mathbf{M}$.

Q.6 A transformation is a two-way stretch in oblique directions $y = \frac{1}{2}x$ and $y = -x$ with factors 3 and 2 respectively. Find the matrix $\mathbf{M}$ of this transformation.

(b) An algebraic approach

The eigenvalues of the matrix $\mathbf{M}$ are λ_1 and λ_1 and the corresponding eigenvectors are $\begin{bmatrix} u_1 \\ v_1 \end{bmatrix}$ and $\begin{bmatrix} u_2 \\ v_2 \end{bmatrix}$ respectively;

that is,
$$\mathbf{M}\begin{bmatrix} u_1 \\ v_1 \end{bmatrix} = \lambda_1\begin{bmatrix} u_1 \\ v_1 \end{bmatrix} = \begin{bmatrix} \lambda_1 u_1 \\ \lambda_1 v_1 \end{bmatrix} \qquad (A)$$

and
$$\mathbf{M}\begin{bmatrix} u_2 \\ v_2 \end{bmatrix} = \lambda_2\begin{bmatrix} u_2 \\ v_2 \end{bmatrix} = \begin{bmatrix} \lambda_2 u_2 \\ \lambda_2 v_2 \end{bmatrix}. \qquad (B)$$

Now $\mathbf{U} = \begin{bmatrix} u_1 & u_2 \\ v_1 & v_2 \end{bmatrix}$ (the columns of this matrix **U** are the eigenvectors of **M**)

and $\mathbf{\Lambda} = \begin{bmatrix} \lambda_1 & 0 \\ 0 & \lambda_2 \end{bmatrix}$ (the diagonal contains the corresponding eigenvalues of **M**).

We can combine Equations (A) and (B) to give

$$\mathbf{M}\begin{bmatrix} u_1 & u_2 \\ v_1 & v_2 \end{bmatrix} = \begin{bmatrix} \lambda_1 u_1 & \lambda_2 u_2 \\ \lambda_1 v_1 & \lambda_2 v_2 \end{bmatrix}$$

$$\Rightarrow \quad \mathbf{M}\begin{bmatrix} u_1 & u_2 \\ v_1 & v_2 \end{bmatrix} = \begin{bmatrix} u_1 & u_2 \\ v_1 & v_2 \end{bmatrix}\begin{bmatrix} \lambda_1 & 0 \\ 0 & \lambda_2 \end{bmatrix}$$

$$\Rightarrow \quad \mathbf{MU} = \mathbf{U\Lambda}$$

$$\Rightarrow \quad \mathbf{M} = \mathbf{U\Lambda U}^{-1}$$

(postmultiplying both sides by $\mathbf{U}^{-1}$, which does exist, as the eigenvectors of **M** are in different directions since $\lambda_1 \neq \lambda_2$.)

So we have expressed in the required form a matrix **M** which has real distinct eigenvalues and eigenvectors.

4.4 FURTHER APPLICATIONS OF EIGENVALUES AND EIGENVECTORS

(a) To find powers of M

If $\quad \mathbf{M} = \mathbf{U\Lambda U}^{-1}$

then $\quad \mathbf{M}^2 = (\mathbf{U\Lambda U}^{-1})(\mathbf{U\Lambda U}^{-1}) = \mathbf{U\Lambda}^2\mathbf{U}^{-1}$

and $\quad \mathbf{M}^3 = (\mathbf{U\Lambda}^2\mathbf{U}^{-1})(\mathbf{U\Lambda U}^{-1}) = \mathbf{U\Lambda}^3\mathbf{U}^{-1}$,

and so on, giving $\quad \mathbf{M}^n = \mathbf{U\Lambda}^n\mathbf{U}^{-1}$, where n is a positive integer.

Example 3

Find $\begin{bmatrix} 4 & -5 \\ 1 & -2 \end{bmatrix}^4$.

Solution

From Example 1, we can write down

$$\mathbf{U} = \begin{bmatrix} 5 & 1 \\ 1 & 1 \end{bmatrix} \quad \text{and} \quad \mathbf{\Lambda} = \begin{bmatrix} 3 & 0 \\ 0 & -1 \end{bmatrix}.$$

Therefore

$$\begin{bmatrix} 4 & -5 \\ 1 & -2 \end{bmatrix}^4 = \begin{bmatrix} 5 & 1 \\ 1 & 1 \end{bmatrix}\begin{bmatrix} 3 & 0 \\ 0 & -1 \end{bmatrix}^4\begin{bmatrix} 5 & 1 \\ 1 & 1 \end{bmatrix}^{-1}$$

$$= \begin{bmatrix} 5 & 1 \\ 1 & 1 \end{bmatrix}\begin{bmatrix} 81 & 0 \\ 0 & 1 \end{bmatrix}\left(\tfrac{1}{4}\begin{bmatrix} 1 & -1 \\ -1 & 5 \end{bmatrix}\right)$$

$$= \tfrac{1}{4}\begin{bmatrix} 405 & 1 \\ 81 & 1 \end{bmatrix}\begin{bmatrix} 1 & -1 \\ -1 & 5 \end{bmatrix}$$

$$= \tfrac{1}{4}\begin{bmatrix} 404 & -400 \\ 80 & -76 \end{bmatrix}$$

$$= \begin{bmatrix} 101 & -100 \\ 20 & -19 \end{bmatrix}. \qquad \square$$

(b) The Cayley–Hamilton theorem*

A square matrix satisfies its own characteristic equation.

Example 4

Verify the Cayley–Hamilton theorem for the matrix $\mathbf{M} = \begin{bmatrix} 4 & -5 \\ 1 & -2 \end{bmatrix}$. (See Example 1.)

Solution

The characteristic equation is

$$\lambda^2 - 2\lambda - 3 = 0,$$

therefore we want to show that $\mathbf{M}^2 - 2\mathbf{M} - 3\mathbf{I} = \mathbf{0}$.

$$\mathbf{M}^2 = \begin{bmatrix} 4 & -5 \\ 1 & -2 \end{bmatrix}\begin{bmatrix} 4 & -5 \\ 1 & -2 \end{bmatrix} = \begin{bmatrix} 11 & -10 \\ 2 & -1 \end{bmatrix}$$

so $$\mathbf{M}^2 - 2\mathbf{M} - 3\mathbf{I} = \begin{bmatrix} 11 & -10 \\ 2 & -1 \end{bmatrix} - 2\begin{bmatrix} 4 & -5 \\ 1 & -2 \end{bmatrix} - 3\begin{bmatrix} 1 & 0 \\ 0 & 1 \end{bmatrix}$$

$$= \begin{bmatrix} 0 & 0 \\ 0 & 0 \end{bmatrix}. \qquad \square$$

The Cayley–Hamilton theorem is true for all square matrices. For a 2×2 matrix which has real, distinct eigenvalues we can prove the theorem using the results of §4.2 and §4.3(a).

If $\mathbf{M} = \begin{bmatrix} a & b \\ c & d \end{bmatrix}$, $\mathbf{U} = \begin{bmatrix} u_1 & u_2 \\ v_1 & v_2 \end{bmatrix}$ and $\mathbf{\Lambda} = \begin{bmatrix} \lambda_1 & 0 \\ 0 & \lambda_2 \end{bmatrix}$, $\mathbf{M}$ has characteristic equation

$$\lambda^2 - (a + d)\lambda + (ad - bc) = 0.$$

Now $$\mathbf{M}^2 = \mathbf{U}\mathbf{\Lambda}^2\mathbf{U}^{-1} = \mathbf{U}\begin{bmatrix} \lambda_1{}^2 & 0 \\ 0 & \lambda_2{}^2 \end{bmatrix}\mathbf{U}^{-1},$$

$$(a + d)\mathbf{M} = \mathbf{U}\begin{bmatrix} (a + d)\lambda_1 & 0 \\ 0 & (a + d)\lambda_2 \end{bmatrix}\mathbf{U}^{-1},$$

* Named after Sir William Rowan Hamilton (1805–1865) and Arthur Cayley (1821–1895).

and $$(ad - bc)\mathbf{I} = \mathbf{U}\begin{bmatrix}(ad - bc) & 0 \\ 0 & (ad - bc)\end{bmatrix}\mathbf{U}^{-1}.$$

Therefore $\mathbf{M}^2 - (a + d)\mathbf{M} + (ad - bc)\mathbf{I}$

$$= \mathbf{U}\left(\begin{bmatrix}\lambda_1{}^2 & 0 \\ 0 & \lambda_2{}^2\end{bmatrix} - \begin{bmatrix}(a + d)\lambda_1 & 0 \\ 0 & (a + d)\lambda_2\end{bmatrix} + \begin{bmatrix}(ad - bc) & 0 \\ 0 & (ad - bc)\end{bmatrix}\right)\mathbf{U}^{-1}$$

$$= \mathbf{U}\begin{bmatrix}0 & 0 \\ 0 & 0\end{bmatrix}\mathbf{U}^{-1}$$ (since λ_1 and λ_2 are roots of the characteristic equation)

$$= \begin{bmatrix}0 & 0 \\ 0 & 0\end{bmatrix}.$$

(c) Consequences of the Cayley–Hamilton theorem

If the characteristic equation for a matrix **M** is

$$\lambda^2 - a\lambda - b = 0$$

then, by the Cayley–Hamilton theorem,

$$\mathbf{M}^2 - a\mathbf{M} - b\mathbf{I} = \mathbf{0}; \qquad (A)$$

that is, $$\mathbf{M}^2 = a\mathbf{M} + b\mathbf{I}.$$

Multiplying through by **M**: $$\mathbf{M}^3 = a\mathbf{M}^2 + b\mathbf{M}.$$

But $$\mathbf{M}^2 = a\mathbf{M} + b\mathbf{I}$$

so $$\mathbf{M}^3 = a(a\mathbf{M} + b\mathbf{I}) + b\mathbf{M};$$

that is, $$\mathbf{M}^3 = (a^2 + b)\mathbf{M} + ab\mathbf{I}.$$

Continuing in this way, we can calculate successive powers of **M** as a linear combination of **M** and **I**.

Now multiply Equation (A) by $\mathbf{M}^{-1}$:

$$\mathbf{M} - a\mathbf{I} - b\mathbf{M}^{-1} = \mathbf{0}$$

therefore $$\mathbf{M}^{-1} = \frac{1}{b}(\mathbf{M} - a\mathbf{I}) \quad (\text{provided } b \neq 0).$$

So $\mathbf{M}^{-1}$ can also be written as a linear combination of **M** and **I**. (Notice that the condition for $\mathbf{M}^{-1}$ to exist is that $b \neq 0$.)

Exercise 4B

1 For each of the matrices **M** below:
(i) write **M** in the form $\mathbf{U\Lambda U}^{-1}$;
(ii) give a geometrical description of the transformation represented by **M**;
(iii) calculate $\mathbf{M}^5$;

(iv) use the Cayley–Hamilton theorem to calculate $\mathbf{M}^{-1}$;
(v) use the Cayley–Hamilton theorem to express $\mathbf{M}^4$ as a linear combination of **M** and **I**.

(*a*) $\begin{bmatrix} 2 & 1 \\ 4 & -1 \end{bmatrix}$ (*b*) $\begin{bmatrix} 3 & 2 \\ 1 & 2 \end{bmatrix}$ (*c*) $\begin{bmatrix} 1 & 3 \\ 2 & -4 \end{bmatrix}$ (*d*) $\begin{bmatrix} -2 & 2 \\ -1 & -5 \end{bmatrix}$

2 Show that the eigenvalues of the matrix $\mathbf{P} = \begin{bmatrix} 4 & 2 \\ -1 & 1 \end{bmatrix}$ are 2 and 3.

Deduce a matrix **A** such that $\mathbf{PA} = \mathbf{A\Lambda}$, where $\mathbf{\Lambda} = \begin{bmatrix} 3 & 0 \\ 0 & 2 \end{bmatrix}$.

3 A linear transformation is a two-way stretch in the oblique directions $y = 3x$ and $2y = -x$ with stretch factors $\frac{1}{3}$ and 2. Find the matrix which represents this transformation.

4 The eigenvalues of the matrix $\mathbf{M} = \begin{bmatrix} 2 & -6 \\ -1 & 1 \end{bmatrix}$ are p and q. Find p and q. Show that the eigenvalues of the matrix $(\mathbf{M} - 3\mathbf{I})$ are $(p - 3)$ and $(q - 3)$.

How are the eigenvectors of the matrices **M** and $(\mathbf{M} - 3\mathbf{I})$ related?

4.5 MORE ABOUT VECTORS

In the chapters so far we have examined in detail the effect of multiplying a vector such as $\begin{bmatrix} 2 \\ 1 \end{bmatrix}$ by a 2×2 matrix.

Since you first met the idea of a matrix in earlier work, we have referred to objects like $\begin{bmatrix} 2 \\ 1 \end{bmatrix}$ as vectors, position vectors, column matrices, price matrices, order matrices, translations and so on. In fact, it appears that we can expect the numbers in the expression $\begin{bmatrix} 2 \\ 1 \end{bmatrix}$ to represent a variety of things.

We have found it convenient (by appealing strongly to the idea that a geometrical translation can be represented by, say, $\begin{bmatrix} 2 \\ 1 \end{bmatrix}$) to assume that the answer to $\begin{bmatrix} a \\ b \end{bmatrix} + \begin{bmatrix} c \\ d \end{bmatrix}$ is $\begin{bmatrix} a + c \\ b + d \end{bmatrix}$.

The essential idea in the expression $\begin{bmatrix} 2 \\ 1 \end{bmatrix}$ has been that the '2' and '1' refer to separate, independent and necessary parts of the description of the object. For example:

(1) A translation $\begin{bmatrix} 2 \\ 1 \end{bmatrix}$: '2' means 2 units in a given direction and '1' means 1 unit in a perpendicular direction.

(2) An order matrix $\begin{bmatrix} 2 \\ 1 \end{bmatrix}$ could mean an order for 2 oranges and 1 apple.

(3) $\begin{bmatrix} 5 \\ 8 \end{bmatrix}$ could mean a force of 5 newtons in one direction and 8 newtons in a perpendicular direction.

In each of these three examples (and there are many others) we have used a *unit* of some kind, and not necessarily the same unit for both numbers – see example (2). Therefore when we 'add' these vectors together, we must carry the units with us. For example, an order of $\begin{bmatrix} 2 \\ 1 \end{bmatrix}$ plus an order of $\begin{bmatrix} 5 \\ 3 \end{bmatrix}$ for oranges and apples is clearly a total order for $\begin{bmatrix} 2+5 \\ 1+3 \end{bmatrix}$ oranges and apples.

Does this mean that any object that requires two pieces of information to describe it (the information being given as a number with an appropriate unit) can be described by the form $\begin{bmatrix} a \\ b \end{bmatrix}$?

Let us try two more examples:

(1) A velocity of 10 m s^{-1} due North and a velocity of 5 m s^{-1} on a bearing of 045° may be represented by the vectors $\begin{bmatrix} 10 \\ 0 \end{bmatrix}$ and $\begin{bmatrix} \frac{5}{2}\sqrt{2} \\ \frac{5}{2}\sqrt{2} \end{bmatrix}$ respectively. Does a particle with *both* velocities have a velocity $\begin{bmatrix} 10 \\ 0 \end{bmatrix} + \begin{bmatrix} \frac{5}{2}\sqrt{2} \\ \frac{5}{2}\sqrt{2} \end{bmatrix}$, that is $\begin{bmatrix} 10 + \frac{5}{2}\sqrt{2} \\ \frac{5}{2}\sqrt{2} \end{bmatrix}$? Yes, this is the correct answer.

(2) Now suppose we describe the velocities in (1) by the expressions $\begin{bmatrix} 10 \\ 0 \end{bmatrix}$ and $\begin{bmatrix} 5 \\ 45 \end{bmatrix}$, where the 'top' number is the speed and the 'lower' number is the bearing. These descriptions are certainly correct.

But $\begin{bmatrix} 10 \\ 0 \end{bmatrix} + \begin{bmatrix} 5 \\ 45 \end{bmatrix} = \begin{bmatrix} 15 \\ 45 \end{bmatrix}$ produces an answer which is clearly wrong, in the sense that the two velocities together are not equal to a velocity of 15 m s^{-1} on a bearing of 45°.

The above examples lead us to define an object or quantity as a vector or vector quantity if it can be expressed in the form $\begin{bmatrix} a_1 \\ a_2 \end{bmatrix}$ *and* if the sum of any two such quantities can be found correctly by adding their vector descriptions according to the rule

$$\begin{bmatrix} a_1 \\ b_1 \end{bmatrix} + \begin{bmatrix} a_2 \\ b_2 \end{bmatrix} = \begin{bmatrix} a_1 + a_2 \\ b_1 + b_2 \end{bmatrix}$$

and

$$\lambda \begin{bmatrix} a \\ b \end{bmatrix} = \begin{bmatrix} \lambda a \\ \lambda b \end{bmatrix}.$$

In this chapter we have continued the theme of Chapter 3 by looking at invariant properties. But this time the lines are invariant as a whole and not necessarily pointwise invariant, which has led to the ideas of eigenvectors and eigenvalues.

Miscellaneous exercise 4

1 If $\mathbf{M} = \begin{bmatrix} \frac{1}{2} & \frac{1}{4} \\ \frac{1}{2} & \frac{3}{4} \end{bmatrix}$, find $\mathbf{U}$ and $\mathbf{\Lambda}$ (using the notation of this chapter). Hence find $\mathbf{M}^2$, $\mathbf{M}^3$ and $\mathbf{M}^n$. Find the limit of $\mathbf{M}^n$ as $n \to \infty$.

2 If $\mathbf{M} = \begin{bmatrix} a & b \\ c & d \end{bmatrix}$,

(*a*) prove that the characteristic equation is

$$\lambda^2 - (a + d)\lambda + (ad - bc) = 0;$$

(*b*) prove that the sum of the eigenvalues (if they exist) is $(a + d)$;
(*c*) prove that the product of the eigenvalues (if they exist) is $\det(\mathbf{M})$;
(*d*) verify the Cayley–Hamilton theorem directly for 2×2 matrices.

3 Find the angle between the eigenvectors of the following matrices:

(*a*) $\begin{bmatrix} 1 & 3 \\ 3 & 1 \end{bmatrix}$ (*b*) $\begin{bmatrix} 1 & 2 \\ 2 & -2 \end{bmatrix}$ (*c*) $\begin{bmatrix} 3 & 4 \\ 4 & -3 \end{bmatrix}$ (*d*) $\begin{bmatrix} 1 & -4 \\ -4 & 3 \end{bmatrix}$

What have all the matrices in common?

4 (*a*) Find the eigenvalues and eigenvectors of the matrix $\mathbf{M} = \begin{bmatrix} 2 & -1 \\ 1 & 4 \end{bmatrix}$.

(*b*) Why can you not express $\mathbf{M}$ in the form $\mathbf{U\Lambda U}^{-1}$?

5 (This question requires a knowledge of complex numbers.)

(*a*) Find the complex eigenvalues of $\mathbf{M} = \begin{bmatrix} 2 & 3 \\ -3 & 2 \end{bmatrix}$. Calculate the modulus and argument in each case.

(*b*) Sketch the effect of the transformation represented by $\mathbf{M}$ on the unit square. Hence express the above transformation as a combination of two basic transformations.

Compare your answers to parts (*a*) and (*b*).

SUMMARY

(1) An *eigenvector* of $\mathbf{M}$ is a non-zero vector $\mathbf{x}$ such that $\mathbf{Mx} = \lambda\mathbf{x}$; λ is the corresponding *eigenvalue*.

(2) To find the eigenvalues, solve $\det(\mathbf{M} - \lambda\mathbf{I}) = 0$. This equation in λ is known as the *characteristic equation*. The eigenvectors are then found from $(\mathbf{M} - \lambda\mathbf{I})\mathbf{x} = \mathbf{0}$.

(3) If $\mathbf{M}$ has real, distinct eigenvalues and eigenvectors, then it can be expressed in the form

$$\mathbf{M} = \mathbf{U\Lambda U}^{-1},$$

where the columns of $\mathbf{U}$ are the eigenvectors of $\mathbf{M}$ and the matrix $\mathbf{\Lambda}$ is a diagonal matrix with entries the corresponding eigenvalues of $\mathbf{M}$.

(4) If $\mathbf{M} = \mathbf{U\Lambda U}^{-1}$, then $\mathbf{M}^n = \mathbf{U\Lambda}^n\mathbf{U}^{-1}$.

(5) The *Cayley–Hamilton theorem*: A square matrix satisfies its own characteristic equation.

Revision exercises 1–4

Revision exercise 1

A1 Find the image of the line $\mathbf{r} = \begin{bmatrix} 3 \\ 1 \end{bmatrix} + t\begin{bmatrix} -2 \\ 2 \end{bmatrix}$ under the linear transformation represented by the matrix $\begin{bmatrix} 1 & 2 \\ 0 & 1 \end{bmatrix}$.

A2 Under a certain linear transformation, the image of the point $(2, 3)$ is $(-7, 4)$ and the image of the point $(3, 5)$ is $(-1, 6)$. What is the matrix which represents this transformation?

A3 Express the vector $\begin{bmatrix} -6 \\ 1 \end{bmatrix}$ as a linear combination of the vectors $\begin{bmatrix} 1 \\ -3 \end{bmatrix}$ and $\begin{bmatrix} -1 \\ 2 \end{bmatrix}$.

A4 Prove that the transformation $\mathbf{S}: \begin{bmatrix} x \\ y \end{bmatrix} \mapsto \begin{bmatrix} 2x - y \\ x + 3y \end{bmatrix}$ is a linear transformation.

A5 Prove that the transformation $\mathbf{T}: \begin{bmatrix} x \\ y \end{bmatrix} \mapsto \begin{bmatrix} 2x + 7y \\ 3y^2 \end{bmatrix}$ is not a linear transformation.

B1 Under a linear transformation, the image of $(-1, 0)$ is $(5, -3)$ and the image of $(1, 1)$ is $(3, 2)$. Find
(*a*) the image of $(6, -2)$;
(*b*) the matrix $\mathbf{A}$ which represents this transformation;
(*c*) the image of the line $y = x + 1$.

B2 Find the image of the line $x + y = 1$ under the transformation represented by the matrix $\begin{bmatrix} -3 & 4 \\ -4 & -3 \end{bmatrix}$. Also find the image of the line $y = -2x$ under the same transformation. Find the intersection of the two original lines and verify that its image is the intersection of the two image lines.

B3 After the transformation represented by the matrix $\begin{bmatrix} 4 & 3 \\ 3 & 2 \end{bmatrix}$, the equation of a line is

$$\frac{x+1}{2} = \frac{y-2}{3}.$$

What was its equation before the transformation?

B4 Find the image of the line $2x + 3y = 6$ under the transformation represented by the matrix $\begin{bmatrix} 1 & -1 \\ 1 & 1 \end{bmatrix}$. What is the angle between the original line and its image?

B5 By considering points of the form $\left(p, \frac{1}{p}\right)$, find the images of the curve $y = \frac{1}{x}$ under the transformations represented by the following matrices:

(*a*) $\begin{bmatrix} 1 & 0 \\ 0 & -1 \end{bmatrix}$ (*b*) $\begin{bmatrix} 2 & 0 \\ 0 & \frac{1}{2} \end{bmatrix}$

(*c*) $\begin{bmatrix} 0 & -1 \\ 1 & 0 \end{bmatrix}$ (*d*) $\begin{bmatrix} 3 & 0 \\ 0 & 3 \end{bmatrix}$

Revision exercise 2

A1 Solve the equations
$$\left.\begin{aligned} 2x - 3y &= 1 \\ -5x + 7y &= -4 \end{aligned}\right\}$$

A2 Use elementary matrices to find the inverse of the matrix $\begin{bmatrix} 4 & 1 \\ -3 & -2 \end{bmatrix}$.

A3 Find the matrix which represents a rotation of 150° about (0, 0).

A4 *State* whether the following pairs of equations have a unique solution, no solution, or an infinite number of solutions:

(*a*) $\left.\begin{aligned} 3x - y &= 11 \\ x - 3y &= 8 \end{aligned}\right\}$ (*b*) $\left.\begin{aligned} 7x + 4y &= 3 \\ 21x + 12y &= 10 \end{aligned}\right\}$

(*c*) $\left.\begin{aligned} 17x - 19y &= 31 \\ 51x - 57y &= 93 \end{aligned}\right\}$ (*d*) $\left.\begin{aligned} 76x + 247y &= 189 \\ 92x + 299y &= 288 \end{aligned}\right\}$

A5 Draw the image of the unit square under the transformation represented by the matrix $\begin{bmatrix} 0.6 & 0.8 \\ 0.8 & -0.6 \end{bmatrix}$. Give a geometrical description of this transformation.

B1 (*a*) Draw the image of the grid formed by the lines $x = -1, 0, 1, 2$ and $y = -1, 0, 1, 2$ under the transformation represented by the matrix $\begin{bmatrix} 2 & -1 \\ 5 & 3 \end{bmatrix}$. Mark the point (2, 8) on your diagram and hence write down an approximate solution for $\begin{bmatrix} 2 & -1 \\ 5 & 3 \end{bmatrix}\begin{bmatrix} x \\ y \end{bmatrix} = \begin{bmatrix} 2 \\ 8 \end{bmatrix}$.

(*b*) Solve the equation by an exact method.

B2 Find $\mathbf{A}^{60}$, where $\mathbf{A} = \begin{bmatrix} \frac{1}{2} & -\frac{1}{2}\sqrt{3} \\ \frac{1}{2}\sqrt{3} & \frac{1}{2} \end{bmatrix}$.

B3 Solve the equation $\begin{bmatrix} 3 & 1 \\ 7 & 4 \end{bmatrix}\begin{bmatrix} x \\ y \end{bmatrix} = \begin{bmatrix} 4 \\ -3 \end{bmatrix}$ by premultiplying by the elementary matrices $\mathbf{E}_1 = \begin{bmatrix} \frac{1}{3} & 0 \\ 0 & 1 \end{bmatrix}$, $\mathbf{E}_2 = \begin{bmatrix} 1 & 0 \\ -7 & 1 \end{bmatrix}$, $\mathbf{E}_3 = \begin{bmatrix} 1 & 0 \\ 0 & \frac{3}{5} \end{bmatrix}$, $\mathbf{E}_4 = \begin{bmatrix} 1 & -\frac{1}{3} \\ 0 & 1 \end{bmatrix}$ in turn. To what row-operations do these matrices correspond?

Work out the matrix product $\mathbf{E}_4\mathbf{E}_3\mathbf{E}_2\mathbf{E}_1$. What does this product represent?

B4 Write the matrix $\mathbf{M} = \begin{bmatrix} -11 & 4 \\ -6 & 2 \end{bmatrix}$ as the product of elementary matrices, and hence describe the transformation represented by $\mathbf{M}$ as a sequence of basic transformations.

B5 If $\mathbf{P} = \begin{bmatrix} 0 & 1 \\ 1 & 0 \end{bmatrix}$ and $\mathbf{Q} = \begin{bmatrix} 1 & 0 \\ 0 & -1 \end{bmatrix}$, describe the transformations represented by the matrices **P**, **Q**, **PQ** and **QP**.

(*a*) If $\mathbf{R}^2 = \mathbf{PQ}$, find **R** (there are two possible answers).

(*b*) If $(\mathbf{QP})^n = \mathbf{I}$, the identity matrix, find the smallest positive integer value of n.

(*c*) If $\mathbf{SP} = \mathbf{PQ}$, find **S**.

Revision exercise 3

A1 Find the fixed points of the transformations represented by the matrices (*a*) $\begin{bmatrix} 0 & 1 \\ 1 & 0 \end{bmatrix}$, (*b*) $\begin{bmatrix} 0 & -1 \\ 1 & 0 \end{bmatrix}$.

A2 The triangle ABC has coordinates $A(2, 3)$, $B(3, 5)$, $C(-1, 6)$. $A'B'C'$ is the image of ABC under the transformation with matrix $\begin{bmatrix} 4 & -1 \\ -2 & 3 \end{bmatrix}$. Find the value of $\dfrac{\text{area of } ABC}{\text{area of } A'B'C'}$.

A3 If $\mathbf{M} = \begin{bmatrix} \frac{1}{4} & \frac{2}{3} \\ \frac{3}{4} & \frac{1}{3} \end{bmatrix}$, find a non-zero vector **x** such that $\mathbf{Mx} = \mathbf{x}$.

A4 Find a matrix similar to $\begin{bmatrix} 3 & -1 \\ 4 & 2 \end{bmatrix}$.

A5 Find the matrix which represents a one-way stretch with invariant line $y = -x$, parallel to $y = x$, of factor 3.

B1 Find the invariant points of the transformation represented by the matrix $\begin{bmatrix} 5 & 4 \\ 2 & 3 \end{bmatrix}$ and hence describe it fully.

B2 If **M** is the matrix $\frac{1}{5}\begin{bmatrix} 3 & 4 \\ 4 & -3 \end{bmatrix}$,

(*a*) calculate $\mathbf{M}^2$;

(*b*) find the vectors $\mathbf{M}\begin{bmatrix} 2 \\ 1 \end{bmatrix}$ and $\mathbf{M}\begin{bmatrix} -1 \\ 2 \end{bmatrix}$;

(*c*) give a precise geometrical description of the linear transformation represented by the matrix **M**.

B3 Find **S**, the matrix representing a reflection in the line $y = 2x$, and **T**, the matrix representing a reflection in the line $2y = x$. Calculate **ST** and **TS** and give a geometrical description of the transformations represented by these matrices.

B4 Find (*a*) the coordinates of the reflection of the point $P(a, b)$ in the line $2y = 3x$;

(*b*) the coordinates (c, d) of Q, the foot of the perpendicular from P to the line $2y = 3x$.

Hence find the matrix representing a projection parallel to $3y + 2x = 0$ onto the line $2y = 3x$.

B5 The transformation represented by the matrix $\mathbf{M} = \begin{bmatrix} \frac{1}{2} & \frac{1}{2}\sqrt{3} \\ \frac{1}{2}\sqrt{3} & -\frac{1}{2} \end{bmatrix}$ is a reflection in the line $y = kx$. Find k.

The matrix **N** is $\begin{bmatrix} \cos 2\theta & \sin 2\theta \\ \sin 2\theta & -\cos 2\theta \end{bmatrix}$. For what values of θ is $\mathbf{MN} = \mathbf{NM}$?

Revision exercise 4

A1 Find the eigenvalues and eigenvectors of the matrix $\begin{bmatrix} 7 & 4 \\ -2 & 1 \end{bmatrix}$.

A2 Show that $\mathbf{M} = \begin{bmatrix} -3 & 4 \\ 2 & 4 \end{bmatrix}$ satisfies its own characteristic equation.

A3 Give a geometrical description of the transformation represented by the matrix $\begin{bmatrix} 4 & 2 \\ 6 & 5 \end{bmatrix}$.

A4 Express the matrix $\mathbf{M} = \begin{bmatrix} -2 & 3 \\ -2 & 5 \end{bmatrix}$ in the form $\mathbf{U\Lambda U}^{-1}$, where $\mathbf{\Lambda}$ is a diagonal matrix.

A5 Find the matrix for a two-way stretch in the oblique directions $y = 2x$ and $y = \frac{1}{2}x$, with stretch factors 2 and 3.

B1 Find $\mathbf{M}^3$, where $\mathbf{M} = \begin{bmatrix} 8 & 2 \\ -1 & 5 \end{bmatrix}$, by the two different methods:

(*a*) writing $\mathbf{M} = \mathbf{U\Lambda U}^{-1}$, with $\mathbf{\Lambda}$ a diagonal matrix;
(*b*) using the Cayley–Hamilton theorem.

B2 Find the eigenvalues of the matrix $\mathbf{A} = \begin{bmatrix} 1 & 1 \\ -2 & 4 \end{bmatrix}$, and show that the eigenvalues of $\mathbf{A}^2$ are the squares of the eigenvalues of $\mathbf{A}$. Find the eigenvectors of both $\mathbf{A}$ and $\mathbf{A}^2$.

B3 A linear transformation has matrix $\mathbf{M} = \begin{bmatrix} 3 & \sqrt{2} \\ \sqrt{2} & 2 \end{bmatrix}$. Find the equation of the image of the line $y = 3x$ under this transformation. For what values of m is the line $y = mx$ mapped onto itself?

B4 A linear transformation of the plane has eigenvectors $\begin{bmatrix} 2 \\ 1 \end{bmatrix}$ and $\begin{bmatrix} -1 \\ 3 \end{bmatrix}$, with corresponding eigenvalues 2 and 3.

(*a*) Write down the images of $\begin{bmatrix} 2 \\ 1 \end{bmatrix}$ and $\begin{bmatrix} -1 \\ 3 \end{bmatrix}$ under this transformation.

(*b*) Express $\begin{bmatrix} 1 \\ 0 \end{bmatrix}$ and $\begin{bmatrix} 0 \\ 1 \end{bmatrix}$ as linear combinations of $\begin{bmatrix} 2 \\ 1 \end{bmatrix}$ and $\begin{bmatrix} -1 \\ 3 \end{bmatrix}$ and deduce the images of $\begin{bmatrix} 1 \\ 0 \end{bmatrix}$ and $\begin{bmatrix} 0 \\ 1 \end{bmatrix}$.

(*c*) Hence write down the matrix representing this transformation.

B5 A matrix of the form $\begin{bmatrix} a & 1-b \\ 1-a & b \end{bmatrix}$ where all the elements are positive (so $0 < a < 1$ and $0 < b < 1$), is called a *stochastic matrix*. Show that such a matrix always has 1 as an eigenvalue, and find the other eigenvalue. Find also the corresponding eigenvectors.

5

Transformations in three dimensions

In Chapters 1–4 we met a number of ideas about transformations of two-dimensional space. Similar ideas apply in three dimensions and in the next three chapters we shall investigate transformations in three dimensions more fully.

5.1 IMAGE OF THE UNIT CUBE

In two dimensions we often began with the unit square. In three dimensions we begin with the unit cube (Fig. 1).

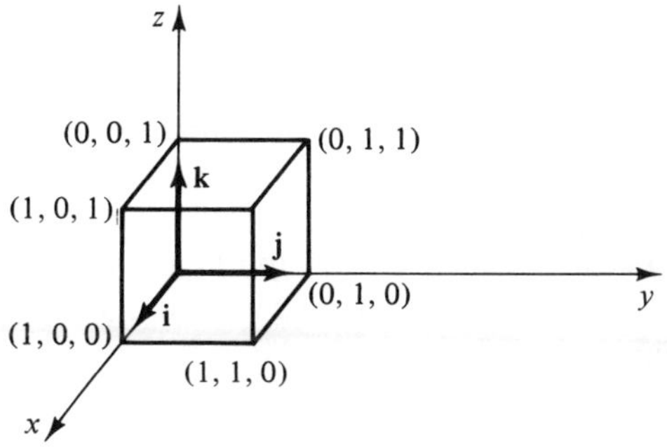

Figure 1

Example 1
Find the image of the unit cube under the transformation represented by the matrix $\begin{bmatrix} 3 & -2 & 1 \\ 1 & 4 & 1 \\ 2 & 2 & 3 \end{bmatrix}$.

Solution
The images of **i**, **j** and **k** are

$$\begin{bmatrix} 3 & -2 & 1 \\ 1 & 4 & 1 \\ 2 & 2 & 3 \end{bmatrix}\begin{bmatrix} 1 \\ 0 \\ 0 \end{bmatrix} = \begin{bmatrix} 3 \\ 1 \\ 2 \end{bmatrix}, \quad \begin{bmatrix} 3 & -2 & 1 \\ 1 & 4 & 1 \\ 2 & 2 & 3 \end{bmatrix}\begin{bmatrix} 0 \\ 1 \\ 0 \end{bmatrix} = \begin{bmatrix} -2 \\ 4 \\ 2 \end{bmatrix}$$

and $$\begin{bmatrix} 3 & -2 & 1 \\ 1 & 4 & 1 \\ 2 & 2 & 3 \end{bmatrix}\begin{bmatrix} 0 \\ 0 \\ 1 \end{bmatrix} = \begin{bmatrix} 1 \\ 1 \\ 3 \end{bmatrix}.$$

Note that the images of the unit vectors **i**, **j** and **k** are the columns of the matrix.

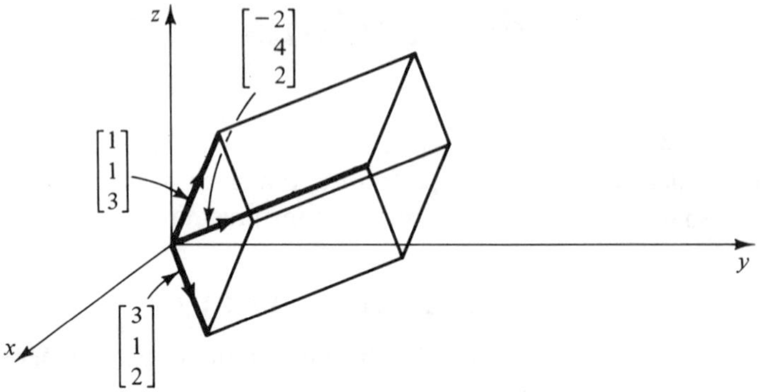

Figure 2

The image of the unit cube is shown in Fig. 2. The opposite faces of this solid are parallelograms and are parallel. It is called a *parallelepiped*. □

Q.1 In drawing Fig. 1 we have made some assumptions. Refer back to Chapter 1 and list any assumptions which you are making.

Conversely, if we know the images of **i**, **j** and **k**, and the transformation can be represented by a matrix, then we can write down the matrix of the transformation as shown in Example 2.

Example 2

Find the matrix **M** which represents the transformation in three dimensions in which the images of the vectors

$$\begin{bmatrix} 1 \\ 0 \\ 0 \end{bmatrix}, \begin{bmatrix} 0 \\ 1 \\ 0 \end{bmatrix} \text{ and } \begin{bmatrix} 0 \\ 0 \\ 1 \end{bmatrix} \text{ are } \begin{bmatrix} 1 \\ -2 \\ 3 \end{bmatrix}, \begin{bmatrix} 4 \\ 0 \\ -1 \end{bmatrix} \text{ and } \begin{bmatrix} 3 \\ 1 \\ 2 \end{bmatrix}, \text{ respectively.}$$

Solution

If $$\mathbf{M} = \begin{bmatrix} a & b & c \\ d & e & f \\ g & h & i \end{bmatrix}$$

then $$\mathbf{M}\begin{bmatrix} 1 \\ 0 \\ 0 \end{bmatrix} = \begin{bmatrix} a & b & c \\ d & e & f \\ g & h & i \end{bmatrix}\begin{bmatrix} 1 \\ 0 \\ 0 \end{bmatrix} = \begin{bmatrix} a \\ d \\ g \end{bmatrix} = \begin{bmatrix} 1 \\ -2 \\ 3 \end{bmatrix}.$$

Therefore $a = 1, \quad d = -2 \quad \text{and} \quad g = 3.$

Similarly
$$\begin{bmatrix} b \\ e \\ h \end{bmatrix} = \begin{bmatrix} 4 \\ 0 \\ -1 \end{bmatrix} \quad \text{and} \quad \begin{bmatrix} c \\ f \\ i \end{bmatrix} = \begin{bmatrix} 3 \\ 1 \\ 2 \end{bmatrix}.$$

Therefore
$$\mathbf{M} = \begin{bmatrix} 1 & 4 & 3 \\ -2 & 0 & 1 \\ 3 & -1 & 2 \end{bmatrix};$$

that is, the columns of **M** are the images of **i**, **j** and **k** respectively. □

5.2 LINEAR TRANSFORMATIONS

(a) Definition of a linear transformation

In the work in two dimensions we concentrated on the type of transformation known as a *linear transformation*, where the particular properties which had to hold were:

$$\mathbf{T}(k\mathbf{a}) = k\mathbf{T}(\mathbf{a}) \qquad (A)$$

and
$$\mathbf{T}(\mathbf{a} + \mathbf{b}) = \mathbf{T}(\mathbf{a}) + \mathbf{T}(\mathbf{b}) \qquad (B)$$

Exactly the same definition of a linear transformation can be taken in three dimensions, where **a** and **b** are any vectors in three-dimensional space and k is a real number.

Q.2 Under a linear transformation, is the image of the origin always the origin?

Q.3 Prove that a transformation **T** represented by a 3×3 matrix **M** is linear.

(*Hint:* if $\mathbf{M} = \begin{bmatrix} a & b & c \\ d & e & f \\ g & h & i \end{bmatrix}$, $\mathbf{a} = \begin{bmatrix} p \\ q \\ r \end{bmatrix}$, $\mathbf{b} = \begin{bmatrix} s \\ t \\ u \end{bmatrix}$ and k is a scalar, use matrix multiplication to show that

$$\mathbf{T}(k\mathbf{a}) = k\mathbf{T}(\mathbf{a})$$

and
$$\mathbf{T}(\mathbf{a} + \mathbf{b}) = \mathbf{T}(\mathbf{a}) + \mathbf{T}(\mathbf{b})$$

where
$$\mathbf{T}(\mathbf{a}) = \mathbf{M}\mathbf{a}.)$$

Sometimes our transformation is not given in matrix form but is given in the form

$$\mathbf{T}: \begin{bmatrix} x \\ y \\ z \end{bmatrix} \mapsto \begin{bmatrix} x \\ -y \\ 2x \end{bmatrix}.$$

Example 3

Prove that **T**, defined by the above mapping, is a linear transformation.

Solution

To prove this we have to go back to the definition of a linear transformation as given at the beginning of this section.

$$\text{Let } \mathbf{a} = \begin{bmatrix} p \\ q \\ r \end{bmatrix} \text{ and } \mathbf{b} = \begin{bmatrix} s \\ t \\ u \end{bmatrix}.$$

Therefore

$$\mathbf{a} + \mathbf{b} = \begin{bmatrix} p+s \\ q+t \\ r+u \end{bmatrix} \quad \text{and} \quad k\mathbf{a} = \begin{bmatrix} kp \\ kq \\ kr \end{bmatrix}$$

$$\Rightarrow \quad \mathbf{T}(\mathbf{a}+\mathbf{b}) = \mathbf{T}\begin{bmatrix} p+s \\ q+t \\ r+u \end{bmatrix} = \begin{bmatrix} p+s \\ -(q+t) \\ 2(p+s) \end{bmatrix}$$

$$= \begin{bmatrix} p \\ -q \\ 2p \end{bmatrix} + \begin{bmatrix} s \\ -t \\ 2s \end{bmatrix}$$

$$= \mathbf{T}(\mathbf{a}) + \mathbf{T}(\mathbf{b}),$$

so condition (*B*) of the definition is satisfied.

$$\mathbf{T}(k\mathbf{a}) = \mathbf{T}\begin{bmatrix} kp \\ kq \\ kr \end{bmatrix} = \begin{bmatrix} kp \\ -kq \\ 2kp \end{bmatrix}$$

$$= k\begin{bmatrix} p \\ -q \\ 2p \end{bmatrix}$$

$$= k\mathbf{T}(\mathbf{a}),$$

so condition (*A*) is also satisfied.

As **a**, **b** and *k* are arbitrary, we have shown that **T** is a linear transformation.

□

If we are trying to show that a transformation is *not* a linear transformation, often the best approach is to look for a 'counter-example', that is, a specific case which does not satisfy the definition.

Q.4 Show that the transformation $\mathbf{S}: \begin{bmatrix} x \\ y \\ z \end{bmatrix} \mapsto \begin{bmatrix} x \\ 12 \\ z+3 \end{bmatrix}$ is not a linear transformation.

(b) Vector equation of a line

In §1.2 we saw that the vector equation of the line through the points A and B whose position vectors are $\mathbf{a}$ and $\mathbf{b}$ is

$$\mathbf{r} = \mathbf{a} + t(\mathbf{b} - \mathbf{a}), \quad \text{where } t \text{ is a real number.}$$

Although we derived this equation for a line in a plane, the same derivation and result are true for a line in three-dimensional space.

Example 4
Find the vector equation of the line through the points A and B whose position vectors are $\mathbf{a} = \begin{bmatrix} 1 \\ 3 \\ -2 \end{bmatrix}$ and $\mathbf{b} = \begin{bmatrix} 4 \\ 0 \\ -1 \end{bmatrix}$.

Solution
See Fig. 3.

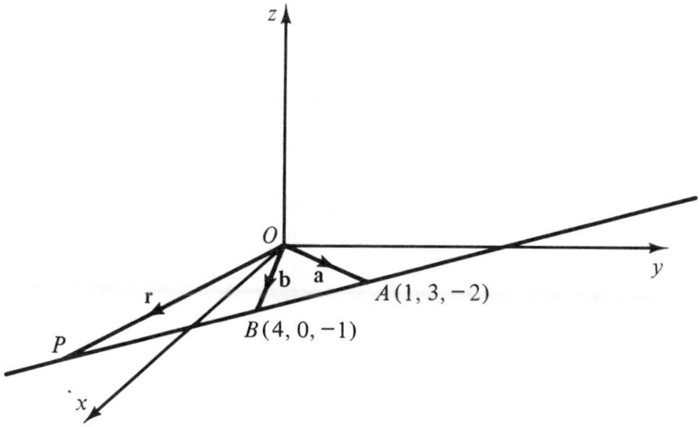

Figure 3

$$\mathbf{r} = \mathbf{a} + t(\mathbf{b} - \mathbf{a})$$

$$\Rightarrow \quad \mathbf{r} = \begin{bmatrix} 1 \\ 3 \\ -2 \end{bmatrix} + t\begin{bmatrix} 3 \\ -3 \\ 1 \end{bmatrix}, \quad \text{where } t \text{ is a real number.}$$ □

Example 5
Find the image of the line defined in Example 4 under the linear transformation represented by the matrix $\mathbf{M} = \begin{bmatrix} 1 & 4 & 3 \\ -2 & 0 & 1 \\ 3 & 1 & 5 \end{bmatrix}$.

Solution

$$\mathbf{T}\left(\begin{bmatrix} x \\ y \\ z \end{bmatrix}\right) = \mathbf{T}\left(\begin{bmatrix} 1 \\ 3 \\ -2 \end{bmatrix} + t\begin{bmatrix} 3 \\ -3 \\ 1 \end{bmatrix}\right) = \mathbf{T}\left(\begin{bmatrix} 1 \\ 3 \\ -2 \end{bmatrix}\right) + \mathbf{T}\left(t\begin{bmatrix} 3 \\ -3 \\ 1 \end{bmatrix}\right)$$

(using property *B*)

$$= \mathbf{T}\left(\begin{bmatrix} 1 \\ 3 \\ -2 \end{bmatrix}\right) + t\mathbf{T}\left(\begin{bmatrix} 3 \\ -3 \\ 1 \end{bmatrix}\right)$$

(using property *A*).

Now **T** is represented by the matrix $\begin{bmatrix} 1 & 4 & 3 \\ -2 & 0 & 1 \\ 3 & 1 & 5 \end{bmatrix}$,

so $$\mathbf{T}\left(\begin{bmatrix} x \\ y \\ z \end{bmatrix}\right) = \begin{bmatrix} 1 & 4 & 3 \\ -2 & 0 & 1 \\ 3 & 1 & 5 \end{bmatrix}\begin{bmatrix} 1 \\ 3 \\ -2 \end{bmatrix} + t\begin{bmatrix} 1 & 4 & 3 \\ -2 & 0 & 1 \\ 3 & 1 & 5 \end{bmatrix}\begin{bmatrix} 3 \\ -3 \\ 1 \end{bmatrix}$$

$$= \begin{bmatrix} 7 \\ -4 \\ -4 \end{bmatrix} + t\begin{bmatrix} -6 \\ -5 \\ 11 \end{bmatrix};$$

that is, the image has vector equation

$$\mathbf{r} = \begin{bmatrix} 7 \\ -4 \\ -4 \end{bmatrix} + t\begin{bmatrix} -6 \\ -5 \\ 11 \end{bmatrix}$$

which is the equation of the line through the point $(7, -4, -4)$ with direction $\begin{bmatrix} -6 \\ -5 \\ 11 \end{bmatrix}$.

This is a particular example of the result that 'in general, lines are mapped onto lines'. □

(c) Vector equation of a plane

The vectors $\mathbf{AB} = \mathbf{b} - \mathbf{a}$ and $\mathbf{AC} = \mathbf{c} - \mathbf{a}$ (Fig. 4, opposite).

If *P* is a point with a position vector **r** on the plane *ABC*, then

$$\mathbf{AP} = s\mathbf{AB} + t\mathbf{AC}, \quad \text{where } s \text{ and } t \text{ are real numbers.}$$

Now $$\mathbf{OP} = \mathbf{OA} + \mathbf{AP},$$

So $$\mathbf{r} = \mathbf{a} + s(\mathbf{b} - \mathbf{a}) + t(\mathbf{c} - \mathbf{a}).$$

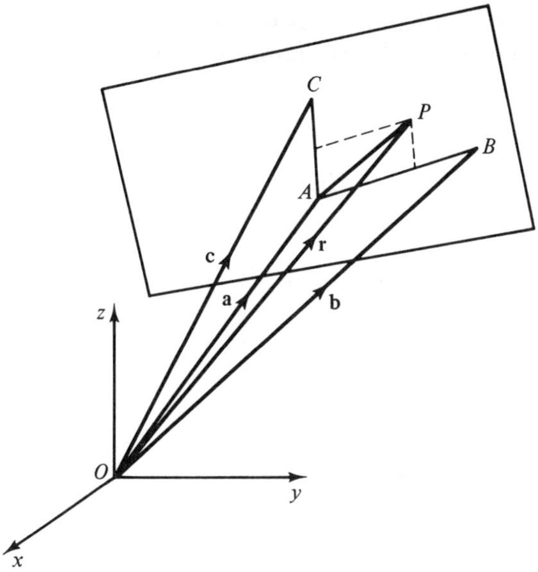

Figure 4

Example 6
A, B, C are points whose position vectors are

$$\mathbf{a} = \begin{bmatrix} 1 \\ 2 \\ -2 \end{bmatrix}, \quad \mathbf{b} = \begin{bmatrix} 3 \\ 2 \\ 4 \end{bmatrix}, \quad \mathbf{c} = \begin{bmatrix} 4 \\ 3 \\ -1 \end{bmatrix}.$$

Find the vector equation of the plane ABC.

Solution
Substituting the values of **a**, **b** and **c**, the vector equation of the plane is

$$\mathbf{r} = \begin{bmatrix} 1 \\ 2 \\ -2 \end{bmatrix} + s\begin{bmatrix} 2 \\ 6 \\ 6 \end{bmatrix} + t\begin{bmatrix} 3 \\ 1 \\ 1 \end{bmatrix}. \qquad \square$$

Q.5 Find the image of the plane ABC in Example 6 under the linear transformation represented by the matrix $\mathbf{M} = \begin{bmatrix} 1 & 4 & 3 \\ -2 & 0 & 1 \\ 3 & 1 & 5 \end{bmatrix}$.

In this case the image of the plane ABC is also a plane. It is true that 'in general, planes are mapped onto planes'. The exceptions would arise if $\mathbf{M}(\mathbf{b} - \mathbf{a})$ and $\mathbf{M}(\mathbf{c} - \mathbf{a})$ were in the same direction, or if one or both of $\mathbf{M}(\mathbf{b} - \mathbf{a})$ and $\mathbf{M}(\mathbf{c} - \mathbf{a})$ were equal to the zero vector.

Q.6 In the summary to Chapter 1 we listed six results which were a consequence of the definition of a linear transformation in two-dimensional space. Rewrite these six results to apply to linear transformations in three-dimensional space.

Exercise 5A

1 Find the matrix **M** which represents the transformation in three dimensions in which the images of the vectors

(*a*) $\begin{bmatrix}1\\0\\0\end{bmatrix}$, $\begin{bmatrix}0\\0\\1\end{bmatrix}$ and $\begin{bmatrix}0\\1\\0\end{bmatrix}$ are $\begin{bmatrix}2\\1\\4\end{bmatrix}$, $\begin{bmatrix}-1\\3\\2\end{bmatrix}$ and $\begin{bmatrix}4\\2\\0\end{bmatrix}$, respectively;

(*b*) $\begin{bmatrix}0\\2\\0\end{bmatrix}$, $\begin{bmatrix}1\\0\\0\end{bmatrix}$ and $\begin{bmatrix}0\\0\\3\end{bmatrix}$ are $\begin{bmatrix}0\\0\\1\end{bmatrix}$, $\begin{bmatrix}2\\0\\5\end{bmatrix}$ and $\begin{bmatrix}-2\\1\\6\end{bmatrix}$, respectively;

(*c*) $\begin{bmatrix}1\\0\\0\end{bmatrix}$, $\begin{bmatrix}0\\0\\1\end{bmatrix}$ and $\begin{bmatrix}0\\1\\0\end{bmatrix}$ are $\begin{bmatrix}3\\1\\0\end{bmatrix}$, $\begin{bmatrix}-1\\-1\\2\end{bmatrix}$ and $\begin{bmatrix}3\\1\\0\end{bmatrix}$, respectively.

2 What is the image of the line l given by $\mathbf{r} = \begin{bmatrix}2\\0\\0\end{bmatrix} + t\begin{bmatrix}1\\0\\0\end{bmatrix}$ under the transformation given by the matrix $\mathbf{M} = \begin{bmatrix}0 & 0 & 3\\0 & 1 & 2\\1 & -1 & 1\end{bmatrix}$?

Sketch l and its image l'. Are they skew lines?

3 Write down the vector equations of the following planes.

(*a*) the plane $y = 0$

(*b*) the plane $x = 0$

(*c*) the plane $x = y$

What are the images of these planes under the transformation represented by the matrix $\mathbf{M} = \begin{bmatrix}\frac{1}{\sqrt{2}} & -\frac{1}{\sqrt{2}} & 0\\ \frac{1}{\sqrt{2}} & \frac{1}{\sqrt{2}} & 0\\ 0 & 0 & 1\end{bmatrix}$?

Use your answers to help you describe the geometrical effect of **M**.

4 Find the image of the plane Π whose equation is

$$\mathbf{r} = \begin{bmatrix}1\\0\\0\end{bmatrix} + t\begin{bmatrix}1\\1\\1\end{bmatrix} + s\begin{bmatrix}-1\\-1\\2\end{bmatrix}$$

under the transformation represented by the matrix $\begin{bmatrix}0 & 0 & 1\\1 & 0 & 0\\0 & 1 & 0\end{bmatrix}$.

5 Determine which of the following mappings are linear. If they are linear, prove it; if not, give a counter-example.

(*a*) $\begin{bmatrix} x \\ y \\ z \end{bmatrix} \mapsto \begin{bmatrix} y \\ x \\ 2z \end{bmatrix}$ (*b*) $\begin{bmatrix} x \\ y \\ z \end{bmatrix} \mapsto \begin{bmatrix} 2z \\ y \\ x+z \end{bmatrix}$

(*c*) $\begin{bmatrix} x \\ y \\ z \end{bmatrix} \mapsto \begin{bmatrix} x \\ 2x^2 \\ 3z \end{bmatrix}$ (*d*) $\begin{bmatrix} x \\ y \\ z \end{bmatrix} \mapsto \begin{bmatrix} x-2 \\ y-2 \\ z+x \end{bmatrix}$

6 If $\mathbf{M} = \begin{bmatrix} 0 & 2 & 1 \\ -1 & 1 & 0 \\ 0 & 1 & 1 \end{bmatrix}$, find the image under **M** of

(*a*) the point p whose position vector is $\begin{bmatrix} 1 \\ 1 \\ 1 \end{bmatrix}$;

(*b*) the line l_1 whose equation is $\mathbf{r} = \begin{bmatrix} -1 \\ 0 \\ 0 \end{bmatrix} + t \begin{bmatrix} -1 \\ 0 \\ -1 \end{bmatrix}$;

(*c*) the line l_2 whose equation is $\mathbf{r} = \begin{bmatrix} -1 \\ 0 \\ 0 \end{bmatrix} + s \begin{bmatrix} 2 \\ 1 \\ 2 \end{bmatrix}$.

Do l_1 and l_2 define a plane? If they do, can you write down without further calculation the equation of the image plane?

5.3 SOME SIMPLE TRANSFORMATIONS

In the summary to Chapter 2 we listed the basic plane transformations. We will not attempt so comprehensive a list for 3 × 3 matrices, but using our knowledge of 2 × 2 matrices we can often write down the transformation represented by a matrix.

There are four basic types which we shall consider:

(a) Reflection in a plane

$\begin{bmatrix} 0 & 1 & 0 \\ 1 & 0 & 0 \\ 0 & 0 & 1 \end{bmatrix}$ represents a reflection in the $y = x$ plane (Fig. 5, overleaf).

Q.7 By finding the image of the unit cube, show that the transformation represented by $\begin{bmatrix} 1 & 0 & 0 \\ 0 & -1 & 0 \\ 0 & 0 & 1 \end{bmatrix}$ is a reflection in the plane $y = 0$.

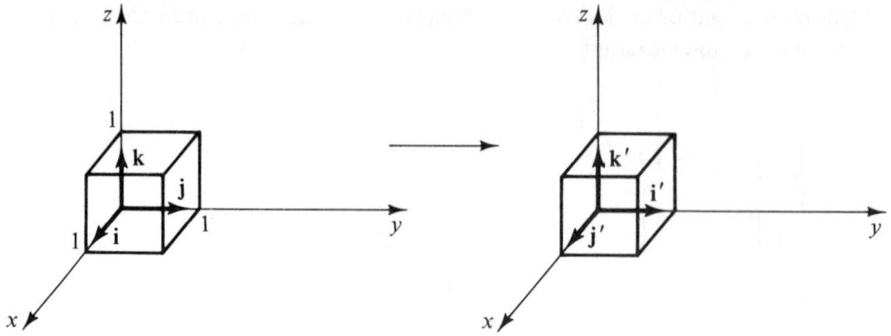

Figure 5

(b) Stretches along the axes

$$\begin{bmatrix} 2 & 0 & 0 \\ 0 & 3 & 0 \\ 0 & 0 & 4 \end{bmatrix}$$ represents a three-way stretch with factors 2, 3, 4 (Fig. 6).

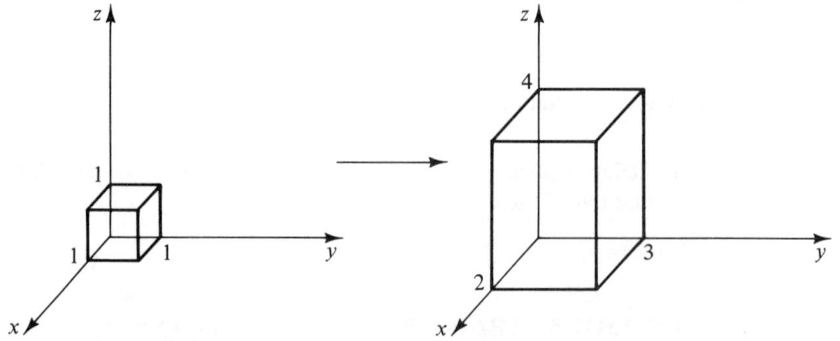

Figure 6

Note: if the factors are of the same value, we have an enlargement.

(c) Rotation about an axis

$$\begin{bmatrix} \cos\alpha & -\sin\alpha & 0 \\ \sin\alpha & \cos\alpha & 0 \\ 0 & 0 & 1 \end{bmatrix}$$ represents a rotation through an angle α about the z-axis (see Exercise 5A, question 3).

By 'a rotation' we mean a rotation of space about a directed axis, known as the axis of rotation. If l is the axis of rotation through the origin, the angle of rotation is positive if it is in the direction shown in Fig. 7.

Figure 7

So for a rotation about the z-axis, points on the positive x-axis will move in the direction of the positive y-axis (Fig. 8), and for a rotation about the y-axis, points on the positive x-axis will move in the direction of the negative z-axis (Fig. 9).

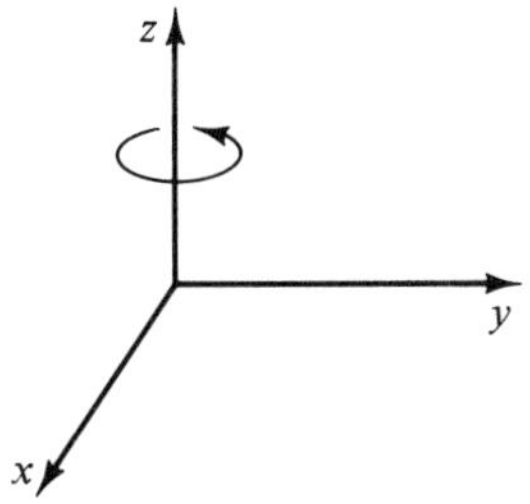

Figure 8

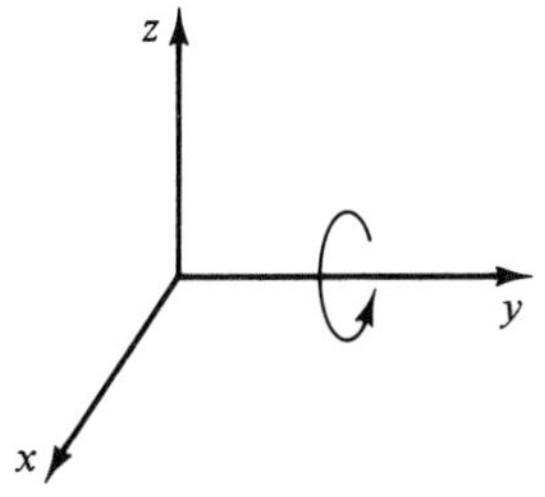

Figure 9

If l' is the same axis of rotation as l, but with its direction reversed, then a rotation of θ about l is equivalent to a rotation of $(2\pi - \theta)$ about l'.

(d) Shear with a plane invariant

$\begin{bmatrix} 1 & 0 & 1 \\ 0 & 1 & 0 \\ 0 & 0 & 1 \end{bmatrix}$ represents a shear in the direction of the x-axis with the plane $z = 0$ invariant (Fig. 10).

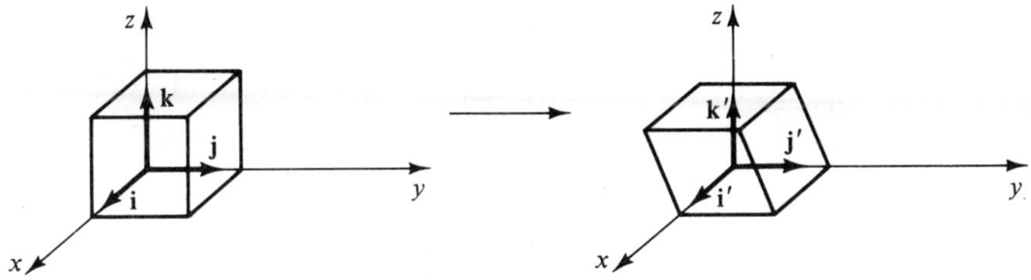

Figure 10

The ideas of the next section are also useful in identifying transformations represented by matrices.

5.4 FIXED POINTS OF A LINEAR TRANSFORMATION

In the transformations we were considering in § 5.3, points sometimes remained unchanged under the transformation. For example in (*a*) and (*d*), there was a plane of points which stayed the same, while in (*c*) the axis of rotation was unchanged. Such points are called *invariant points* (see Chapter 3).

To find invariant points we solve the equation

$$\mathbf{Mx} = \mathbf{x}.$$

For (*a*):
$$\begin{bmatrix} 0 & 1 & 0 \\ 1 & 0 & 0 \\ 0 & 0 & 1 \end{bmatrix}\begin{bmatrix} x \\ y \\ z \end{bmatrix} = \begin{bmatrix} x \\ y \\ z \end{bmatrix}$$

so
$$\begin{bmatrix} y \\ x \\ z \end{bmatrix} = \begin{bmatrix} x \\ y \\ z \end{bmatrix};$$

that is, the plane $x = y$ is invariant.

For (*c*):
$$\begin{bmatrix} \cos\alpha & -\sin\alpha & 0 \\ \sin\alpha & \cos\alpha & 0 \\ 0 & 0 & 1 \end{bmatrix}\begin{bmatrix} x \\ y \\ z \end{bmatrix} = \begin{bmatrix} x \\ y \\ z \end{bmatrix}$$

so
$$\begin{bmatrix} (\cos\alpha)x - (\sin\alpha)y \\ (\sin\alpha)x + (\cos\alpha)y \\ z \end{bmatrix} = \begin{bmatrix} x \\ y \\ z \end{bmatrix};$$

that is,
$$\left.\begin{aligned} (1 - \cos\alpha)x + (\sin\alpha)y &= 0 \\ (\sin\alpha)x - (1 - \cos\alpha)y &= 0 \\ z &= z \end{aligned}\right\}$$

Solving the first two equations gives $x = 0$, $y = 0$, provided α is not a multiple of 2π (in which case, the matrix is the identity matrix). So the line $\mathbf{r} = \begin{bmatrix} 0 \\ 0 \\ z \end{bmatrix}$ (that is, the z-axis) is invariant.

For (*d*):
$$\begin{bmatrix} 1 & 0 & 1 \\ 0 & 1 & 0 \\ 0 & 0 & 1 \end{bmatrix}\begin{bmatrix} x \\ y \\ z \end{bmatrix} = \begin{bmatrix} x \\ y \\ z \end{bmatrix}$$

so
$$\begin{bmatrix} x + z \\ y \\ z \end{bmatrix} = \begin{bmatrix} x \\ y \\ z \end{bmatrix};$$

that is, the plane $z = 0$ is invariant.

Example 7
Which points are invariant under the linear transformations represented by the matrices

$$(a)\ \begin{bmatrix} \frac{5}{4} & 0 & \frac{1}{4}\sqrt{3} \\ 0 & 3 & 0 \\ \frac{1}{4}\sqrt{3} & 0 & \frac{7}{4} \end{bmatrix} \qquad (b)\ \begin{bmatrix} 4 & 2 & -1 \\ 6 & 5 & -2 \\ -3 & -2 & 2 \end{bmatrix}?$$

Solution

(*a*) If $\begin{bmatrix} x \\ y \\ z \end{bmatrix}$ remains unchanged, then

$$\begin{bmatrix} \frac{5}{4} & 0 & \frac{1}{4}\sqrt{3} \\ 0 & 3 & 0 \\ \frac{1}{4}\sqrt{3} & 0 & \frac{7}{4} \end{bmatrix} \begin{bmatrix} x \\ y \\ z \end{bmatrix} = \begin{bmatrix} x \\ y \\ z \end{bmatrix}$$

that is,

$$\left.\begin{aligned} \frac{5x}{4} + \frac{\sqrt{3}z}{4} &= x \\ 3y &= y \\ \frac{\sqrt{3}x}{4} + \frac{7z}{4} &= z \end{aligned}\right\}$$

From the second equation, we see that $y = 0$, and the first and third equations reduce to $x = -\sqrt{3}z$.

So points whose position vectors are

$$\begin{bmatrix} -\sqrt{3}t \\ 0 \\ t \end{bmatrix} \quad \text{(put } z = t\text{)},$$

where t is a real number, are invariant; that is, there is a line of fixed points.

(*b*) If $\begin{bmatrix} x \\ y \\ z \end{bmatrix}$ remains unchanged, then

$$\begin{bmatrix} 4 & 2 & -1 \\ 6 & 5 & -2 \\ -3 & -2 & 2 \end{bmatrix} \begin{bmatrix} x \\ y \\ z \end{bmatrix} = \begin{bmatrix} x \\ y \\ z \end{bmatrix};$$

that is,

$$\left.\begin{aligned} 4x + 2y - z &= x \\ 6x + 5y - 2z &= y \\ -3x - 2y + 2z &= z \end{aligned}\right\}$$

which simplifies to

$$\left.\begin{aligned} 3x + 2y - z &= 0 \\ 6x + 4y - 2z &= 0 \\ -3x - 2y + z &= 0 \end{aligned}\right\}$$

These three equations are all multiples of the equation

$$3x + 2y - z = 0$$

which is the equation of a plane which is invariant under the transformation represented by the matrix $\begin{bmatrix} 4 & 2 & -1 \\ 6 & 5 & -2 \\ -3 & -2 & 2 \end{bmatrix}$. □

In three dimensions the following kinds of invariance can arise:

(1) a fixed line through the origin (e.g. the transformation could be a rotation);

(2) a fixed plane through the origin (e.g. the transformation could be a reflection);

(3) the whole space is fixed and we have the identity transformation.

In Example 7 we have given one example for each of (1) and (2). What other possible transformations can you think of?

Exercise 5B

1 By considering the effect on the unit cube, or more particularly on the unit vectors **i**, **j** and **k**, find the matrices which describe the following transformations:

(*a*) reflection in the plane $z = 0$

(*b*) rotation about the y-axis of 90°

(*c*) a shear in which the plane $y = 0$ is invariant and the point (2, 3, 0) goes to (6, 3, 0)

(*d*) a shear in which the plane $x = 0$ is invariant and the point with position vector $\begin{bmatrix} -1 \\ 2 \\ 6 \end{bmatrix}$ goes to the point with vector $\begin{bmatrix} -1 \\ 5 \\ 7 \end{bmatrix}$

(*e*) a reflection in the plane $y = z$

(*f*) a 180° rotation about the line $x = y = 0$; that is, the z-axis

2 What transformations are represented by the following matrices?

(*a*) $\begin{bmatrix} 2 & 0 & 0 \\ 0 & -2 & 0 \\ 0 & 0 & 3 \end{bmatrix}$ (*b*) $\begin{bmatrix} 4 & 0 & 0 \\ 0 & 4 & 0 \\ 0 & 0 & 4 \end{bmatrix}$ (*c*) $\begin{bmatrix} 1 & 0 & 0 \\ 0 & 0 & -1 \\ 0 & 1 & 0 \end{bmatrix}$

(*d*) $\begin{bmatrix} 1 & 0 & 0 \\ 0 & 1 & 0 \\ 0 & 3 & 1 \end{bmatrix}$ (*e*) $\begin{bmatrix} 0.6 & 0.8 & 0 \\ -0.8 & 0.6 & 0 \\ 0 & 0 & 1 \end{bmatrix}$ (*f*) $\begin{bmatrix} 1 & 0 & 0 \\ -2 & 1 & 0 \\ 0 & 0 & 1 \end{bmatrix}$

(*g*) $\begin{bmatrix} 1 & 0 & 0 \\ 0 & 1 & 0 \\ 0 & 0 & -1 \end{bmatrix}$ (*h*) $\begin{bmatrix} -1 & 0 & 0 \\ 0 & 1 & 0 \\ 0 & 0 & -1 \end{bmatrix}$ (*i*) $\begin{bmatrix} \frac{1}{\sqrt{2}} & 0 & \frac{1}{\sqrt{2}} \\ 0 & 1 & 0 \\ -\frac{1}{\sqrt{2}} & 0 & \frac{1}{\sqrt{2}} \end{bmatrix}$

3 $\mathbf{M} = \begin{bmatrix} 1 & 0 & 0 \\ 0 & -1 & 0 \\ 0 & 0 & 1 \end{bmatrix}$, $\mathbf{N} = \begin{bmatrix} 0 & 1 & 0 \\ -1 & 0 & 0 \\ 0 & 0 & 1 \end{bmatrix}$. Calculate **MN** and **NM**. Describe geometrically the transformations represented by **M**, **N**, **MN** and **NM**.

4 Find the fixed points of the following linear transformations:

(a) $\begin{bmatrix} 2 & 0 & 2 \\ 6 & 0 & 5 \\ -6 & 1 & -4 \end{bmatrix}$ (b) $\begin{bmatrix} -1 & -8 & -6 \\ 1 & 5 & 4 \\ -1 & -4 & -4 \end{bmatrix}$

(c) $\begin{bmatrix} \frac{1}{3} & -\frac{2}{3} & -\frac{2}{3} \\ -\frac{2}{3} & \frac{1}{3} & -\frac{2}{3} \\ -\frac{2}{3} & -\frac{2}{3} & \frac{1}{3} \end{bmatrix}$ (d) $\begin{bmatrix} \frac{1}{3} & \frac{2}{3} & -\frac{2}{3} \\ \frac{2}{3} & \frac{1}{3} & \frac{2}{3} \\ -\frac{2}{3} & \frac{2}{3} & \frac{1}{3} \end{bmatrix}$

The aim of this chapter has been to extend to three dimensions ideas with which you are already familiar in two dimensions. It is not so easy to 'spot' the answer with transformations in three dimensions, so it is important to develop a systematic approach to identifying a transformation.

Miscellaneous exercise 5

1 A transformation is defined by

$$\begin{bmatrix} x' \\ y' \\ z' \end{bmatrix} = \begin{bmatrix} -2 & 1 & 4 \\ 1 & 0 & -2 \\ 3 & 4 & -6 \end{bmatrix} \begin{bmatrix} x \\ y \\ z \end{bmatrix}.$$

Show that the set of planes perpendicular to the y-axis onto a set of parallel lines. What is the direction of these lines? Which of these planes is mapped onto a line through the origin? [SMP]

2 Show that under the transformation represented by the matrix $\begin{bmatrix} \frac{2}{3} & \frac{1}{3} & -\frac{1}{3} \\ \frac{1}{3} & \frac{2}{3} & \frac{1}{3} \\ -\frac{1}{3} & \frac{1}{3} & \frac{2}{3} \end{bmatrix}$ the whole space is mapped onto the plane $x - y + z = 0$.

Find the image under the transformation of

(a) the line $x = -y = z$

(b) the plane $x = 0$

(c) the plane $x = y$

Give a geometrical description of the transformation.

3 The matrix of a transformation is $\begin{bmatrix} 1 & -2 & -1 \\ 3 & 1 & 5 \\ -1 & -5 & -7 \end{bmatrix}$.

(a) Show that under this transformation the whole space is mapped onto the plane $2x - y - z = 0$.

(b) Find the image of the line $\mathbf{r} = \begin{bmatrix} 3 \\ 1 \\ 2 \end{bmatrix} + \lambda \begin{bmatrix} 9 \\ 8 \\ -7 \end{bmatrix}$.

(c) Find the set of points which is mapped onto the origin.

4 Write down the matrix $\mathbf{R}$ which represents a rotation about the z-axis of $\theta°$, and the matrix $\mathbf{S}$ which represents a reflection in the plane $y = 0$.

(a) What is $\mathbf{R}^{-1}$?

(*b*) Calculate $\mathbf{RSR}^{-1}$ and describe geometrically the transformation which it represents.

5 A matrix **M** is said to be transposed into the matrix $\mathbf{M}^{\mathrm{T}}$ if the first row of **M** becomes the first column of $\mathbf{M}^{\mathrm{T}}$, the second row of **M** become the second column of $\mathbf{M}^{\mathrm{T}}$, and so on. Write down the transposes of the matrices

$$\mathbf{M} = \begin{bmatrix} x \\ y \\ z \end{bmatrix} \quad \text{and} \quad \mathbf{T} = \begin{bmatrix} 0 & b & 0 \\ 0 & 0 & c \\ a & 0 & 0 \end{bmatrix}.$$

Calculate the matrix products $\mathbf{M}^{\mathrm{T}}\mathbf{M}$ and $\mathbf{TM}$, and show also that $(\mathbf{TM})^{\mathrm{T}} = \mathbf{M}^{\mathrm{T}}\mathbf{T}^{\mathrm{T}}$.

If the elements of **M** are the Cartesian coordinates of a point *P*, what information is provided by the element of $\mathbf{M}^{\mathrm{T}}\mathbf{M}$? [SMP]

If the matrix **T** describes a transformation of the point *P* of three-dimensional space, interpret geometrically the equation $(\mathbf{TM})^{\mathrm{T}}(\mathbf{TM}) = \mathbf{M}^{\mathrm{T}}\mathbf{M}$, and find the appropriate values of a, b and c.

SUMMARY

(1) If **T** is a transformation, **a** and **b** are any vectors in three-dimensional space and k is a real number, then **T** is a *linear transformation* if

$$\mathbf{T}(k\mathbf{a}) = k\mathbf{T}(\mathbf{a})$$

and

$$\mathbf{T}(\mathbf{a} + \mathbf{b}) = \mathbf{T}(\mathbf{a}) + \mathbf{T}(\mathbf{b}).$$

A consequence of this definition is that, for a linear transformation,

$$\mathbf{T}(\lambda\mathbf{a} + \mu\mathbf{b}) = \lambda\mathbf{T}(\mathbf{a}) + \mu\mathbf{T}(\mathbf{b}).$$

(2) *Invariant points* are found by solving $\mathbf{M}\begin{bmatrix} x \\ y \\ z \end{bmatrix} = \begin{bmatrix} x \\ y \\ z \end{bmatrix}$.

6

Linear equations in three unknowns

6.1 ELIMINATION METHOD

For two equations in two unknowns we saw that the simplest solution was the straightforward elimination method. We now apply the same ideas to three equations in three unknowns.

Example 1

Solve the equations

$$\left.\begin{aligned} x - 2y - z &= 6 \\ 3x + y + 5z &= -4 \\ -4x + 2y - 3z &= 7 \end{aligned}\right\} \qquad \begin{aligned} &(A) \\ &(B) \\ &(C) \end{aligned}$$

Solution

We begin by eliminating x between equations (A) and (B), and then between (A) and (C).

$(B) - 3 \times (A)$: $\quad 7y + 8z = -22 \qquad (D)$

$(C) + 4 \times (A)$: $\quad -6y - 7z = 31 \qquad (E)$

The problem now reduces to two equations in two unknowns:

$(D) + (E)$: $\quad y + z = 9 \qquad (F)$

$(D) - 7 \times (F)$: $\quad z = -85$

Therefore, from (F): $\quad y = 94,$

and substituting in (A): $\quad x = 109.$

So $\quad x = 109, \quad y = 94, \quad z = -85.$ □

Example 2

Solve the equations

$$\left.\begin{aligned} x - 2y - z &= 6 \\ 3x + y + 5z &= -4 \\ -x - 5y - 7z &= 16 \end{aligned}\right\} \qquad \begin{aligned} &(A) \\ &(B) \\ &(C) \end{aligned}$$

Solution

$(B) - 3 \times (A)$: $\quad 7y + 8z = -22 \qquad (D)$

$(C) + (A)$: $\quad -7y - 8z = 22 \qquad (E)$

Equations (D) and (E) are the same equation, so we have an infinite number of solutions.

Let $z = \lambda$ (an arbitrary value),

$$\Rightarrow \quad y = -\tfrac{22}{7} - \tfrac{8}{7}\lambda$$

and substituting in (A):

$$x = 6 + 2(-\tfrac{22}{7} - \tfrac{8}{7}\lambda) + \lambda$$
$$= -\tfrac{2}{7} - \tfrac{9}{7}\lambda.$$

So $$x = -\tfrac{2}{7} - \tfrac{9}{7}\lambda, \quad y = -\tfrac{22}{7} - \tfrac{8}{7}\lambda, \quad z = \lambda.$$ □

Example 3
Solve the equations

$$\left.\begin{aligned} x - 2y - z &= 4 \quad &(A)\\ 3x + y + 5z &= -4 \quad &(B)\\ -x - 5y - 7z &= 10 \quad &(C)\end{aligned}\right\}$$

Solution

$3 \times (A) - (B)$: $$-7y - 8z = 22 \qquad (D)$$

$(C) + (A)$: $$-7y - 8z = 16 \qquad (E)$$

These equations are inconsistent, since $-7y - 8z$ cannot equal both 22 and 16, so the solution set is empty. □

6.2 GEOMETRICAL INTERPRETATION

In two-dimensional space an equation of the form $ax + by = r$ represents a straight line. The corresponding result for three-dimensional space is that an equation of the form $ax + by + cz = r$ represents a plane. The vector $\begin{bmatrix} a \\ b \\ c \end{bmatrix}$ is perpendicular to the plane and therefore gives the direction of the plane.

So the solution of the three linear equations

$$ax + by + cz = r$$
$$dx + ey + fz = s$$
$$gx + hy + iz = t$$

can be thought of as the intersection of the three planes which they represent.

For three *distinct* planes there are five cases to consider:

(1) *The three planes meet in a unique point* (Fig. 1).

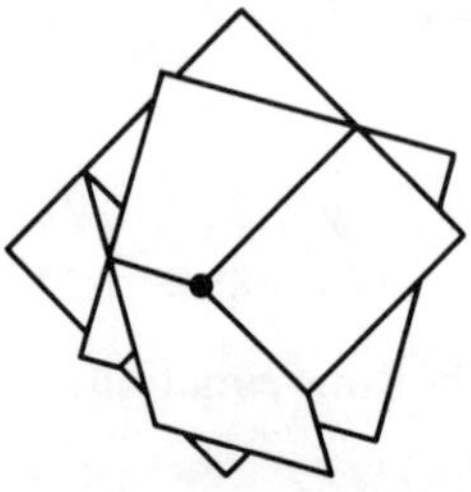

Figure 1

(2) *The three planes meet in a line* (that is, they form a sheaf) (Fig. 2).

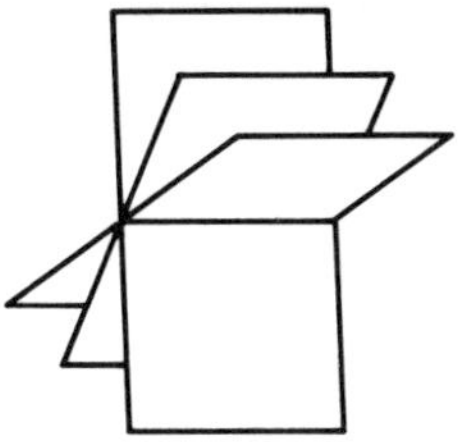

Figure 2

(3) *The three planes form a prism* (Fig. 3).

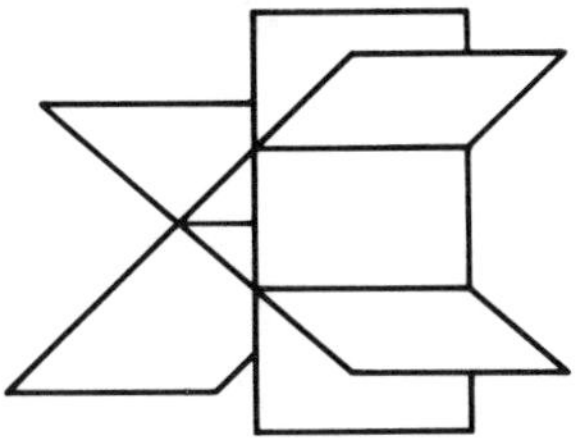

Figure 3

(4) *All three planes are parallel* (Fig. 4).

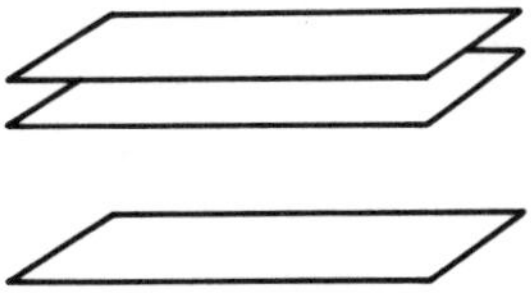

Figure 4

(5) *Two of the planes are parallel* (Fig. 5).

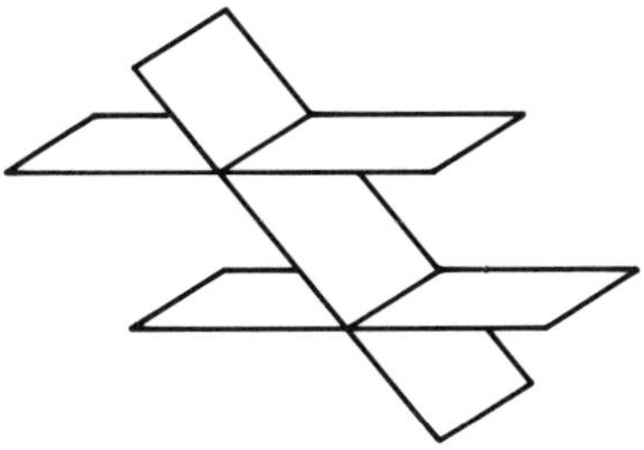

Figure 5

Q.1 What happens if the planes are not all distinct?

In summary, we see that there are four possible results for the intersection of three planes:
(1) The planes intersect in a unique point.
(2) The planes have no common point; that is, the solution set is empty.
(3) The planes intersect in a line.
(4) The planes intersect in a plane.

We can now give a geometrical interpretation of the solutions of the three examples in §6.1:

In Example 1, the three planes meet in the point $(109, 94, -85)$ – case (1).

In Example 2, the three planes meet in the line

$$\begin{bmatrix} x \\ y \\ z \end{bmatrix} = \begin{bmatrix} -\frac{2}{7} \\ -\frac{22}{7} \\ 0 \end{bmatrix} + \lambda \begin{bmatrix} -\frac{9}{7} \\ -\frac{8}{7} \\ 1 \end{bmatrix} \quad \text{– case (2).}$$

In Example 3, the three planes form a prism – case (3).

Exercise 6A

In each of the following questions find the solution set and explain its geometrical significance:

1 $\left.\begin{aligned} x + 2y - z &= 8 \\ 3x - y + 2z &= -5 \\ 4x + 2y + 3z &= -1 \end{aligned}\right\}$

2 $\left.\begin{aligned} 3x - 2y + 4z &= 24 \\ 2x + y - 3z &= -9 \\ 9x + y - 5z &= -3 \end{aligned}\right\}$

3 $\left.\begin{aligned} 2x - 5y + 3z &= 7 \\ x + 4y - 2z &= 7 \\ x - 22y + 12z &= 9 \end{aligned}\right\}$

4 $\left.\begin{aligned} 3x - y + 2z &= 5 \\ x + 2y - 3z &= 0 \\ 6x - 2y + 4z &= 10 \end{aligned}\right\}$

5 $\left.\begin{aligned} 2x - 4y + 4z &= 7 \\ x + 3y + 2z &= 5 \\ -3x + 6y - 6z &= 5 \end{aligned}\right\}$

6 $\left.\begin{aligned} x - y + 2z &= 3 \\ -x + 2y - 3z &= 4 \\ 2x - 3y + 5z &= -1 \end{aligned}\right\}$

7 $\left.\begin{aligned} 3x - y + 2z &= 4 \\ x + y + 5z &= 7 \\ 9x + y + 19z &= 13 \end{aligned}\right\}$

8 $\left.\begin{aligned} -x - y + z &= 3 \\ 2x + y - 3z &= -12 \\ x + 3y + z &= 9 \end{aligned}\right\}$

9 $\left.\begin{aligned} 3x - 2y + z &= -15 \\ 5x + 4y - z &= -1 \\ x + y + z &= 3 \end{aligned}\right\}$

10 $\left.\begin{aligned} 0.6x - 1.5y + 2.1z &= 0.9 \\ 2x - 5y + 7z &= 3 \\ x - 2.5y + 3.5z &= 1.5 \end{aligned}\right\}$

6.3 ELEMENTARY MATRICES

As in the two-dimensional case we can modify the elimination method so that the elimination is done systematically. To help show what is happening we write the equations in matrix form as well.

Example 4

Solve the equations

$$\left.\begin{aligned} x - 2y - z &= 6 \\ 3x + y + 5z &= -4 \\ -4x + 2y - 3z &= 7 \end{aligned}\right\} \qquad \begin{aligned} &R_1 \\ &R_2 \\ &R_3 \end{aligned}$$

(*Note:* R_i stands for the ith row.)

Solution

In matrix form

Stage 1

$$\begin{array}{ll} R_1 & x-2y-\ z=\ \ 6 \\ R_2 & 3x+\ y+5z=-4 \\ R_3 & -4x+2y-3z=\ \ 7 \end{array} \qquad \begin{bmatrix} 1 & -2 & -1 \\ 3 & 1 & 5 \\ -4 & 2 & -3 \end{bmatrix}\begin{bmatrix} x \\ y \\ z \end{bmatrix}=\begin{bmatrix} 6 \\ -4 \\ 7 \end{bmatrix}$$

Stage 2

$$\begin{array}{ll} R_1=R_1 & x-2y-\ z=\ \ 6 \\ R_2=R_2-3R_1 & 7y+8z=-22 \\ R_3=R_3 & -4x+2y-3z=\ \ 7 \end{array} \qquad \begin{bmatrix} 1 & -2 & -1 \\ 0 & 7 & 8 \\ -4 & 2 & -3 \end{bmatrix}\begin{bmatrix} x \\ y \\ z \end{bmatrix}=\begin{bmatrix} 6 \\ -22 \\ 7 \end{bmatrix}$$

Stage 3

$$\begin{array}{ll} R_1=R_1 & x-2y-\ z=\ \ 6 \\ R_2=R_2 & 7y+8z=-22 \\ R_3=R_3+4R_1 & -6y-7z=\ \ 31 \end{array} \qquad \begin{bmatrix} 1 & -2 & -1 \\ 0 & 7 & 8 \\ 0 & -6 & -7 \end{bmatrix}\begin{bmatrix} x \\ y \\ z \end{bmatrix}=\begin{bmatrix} 6 \\ -22 \\ 31 \end{bmatrix}$$

Stage 4

$$\begin{array}{ll} R_1=R_1 & x-2y-\ z=\ 6 \\ R_2=R_2+R_3 & y+\ z=\ 9 \\ R_3=R_3 & -6y-7z=31 \end{array} \qquad \begin{bmatrix} 1 & -2 & -1 \\ 0 & 1 & 1 \\ 0 & -6 & -7 \end{bmatrix}\begin{bmatrix} x \\ y \\ z \end{bmatrix}=\begin{bmatrix} 6 \\ 9 \\ 31 \end{bmatrix}$$

Stage 5

$$\begin{array}{ll} R_1=R_1 & x-2y-z=\ 6 \\ R_2=R_2 & y+z=\ 9 \\ R_3=R_3+6R_2 & -z=85 \end{array} \qquad \begin{bmatrix} 1 & -2 & -1 \\ 0 & 1 & 1 \\ 0 & 0 & -1 \end{bmatrix}\begin{bmatrix} x \\ y \\ z \end{bmatrix}=\begin{bmatrix} 6 \\ 9 \\ 85 \end{bmatrix}$$

Stage 6

$$\begin{array}{ll} R_1=R_1 & x-2y-z=\ 6 \\ R_2=R_2+R_3 & y\ \ =94 \\ R_3=R_3 & -z=85 \end{array} \qquad \begin{bmatrix} 1 & -2 & -1 \\ 0 & 1 & 0 \\ 0 & 0 & -1 \end{bmatrix}\begin{bmatrix} x \\ y \\ z \end{bmatrix}=\begin{bmatrix} 6 \\ 94 \\ 85 \end{bmatrix}$$

Stage 7

$$\begin{array}{ll} R_1=R_1-R_2 & x-2y\ \ =-79 \\ R_2=R_2 & y\ \ =\ \ 94 \\ R_3=R_3 & -z=\ \ 85 \end{array} \qquad \begin{bmatrix} 1 & -2 & 0 \\ 0 & 1 & 0 \\ 0 & 0 & -1 \end{bmatrix}\begin{bmatrix} x \\ y \\ z \end{bmatrix}=\begin{bmatrix} -79 \\ 94 \\ 85 \end{bmatrix}$$

Stage 8

$$\begin{array}{ll} R_1=R_1+2R_2 & x\ \ =109 \\ R_2=R_2 & y\ \ =\ 94 \\ R_3=R_3 & -z=\ 85 \end{array} \qquad \begin{bmatrix} 1 & 0 & 0 \\ 0 & 1 & 0 \\ 0 & 0 & -1 \end{bmatrix}\begin{bmatrix} x \\ y \\ z \end{bmatrix}=\begin{bmatrix} 109 \\ 94 \\ 85 \end{bmatrix}$$

Stage 9

$$\begin{array}{ll} R_1=R_1 & x\ \ =\ 109 \\ R_2=R_2 & y\ \ =\ \ 94 \\ R_3=-R_3 & z=-85 \end{array} \qquad \begin{bmatrix} 1 & 0 & 0 \\ 0 & 1 & 0 \\ 0 & 0 & 1 \end{bmatrix}\begin{bmatrix} x \\ y \\ z \end{bmatrix}=\begin{bmatrix} 109 \\ 94 \\ -85 \end{bmatrix}$$

Using this method we try to get a '0' in positions (2, 1) [position (2, 1) means second row and first column], (3, 1), (3,2), (2,3), (1,3) and (1,2) of the matrix, in that order, though sometimes it is possible to spot a quicker way of reducing the matrix to the identity. One of the main strengths of the systematic reduction is that it lends itself to computer solution. □

Q.2 Describe the effect of premultiplying the matrix $\mathbf{A}=\begin{bmatrix} a & b & c \\ d & e & f \\ g & h & i \end{bmatrix}$ by the following matrices:

$$(a)\ \begin{bmatrix} 6 & 0 & 0 \\ 0 & 1 & 0 \\ 0 & 0 & 1 \end{bmatrix} \qquad (b)\ \begin{bmatrix} 1 & 0 & 0 \\ -3 & 1 & 0 \\ 0 & 0 & 1 \end{bmatrix}$$

$$(c)\ \begin{bmatrix} 1 & 0 & 0 \\ 0 & 1 & 2 \\ 0 & 0 & 1 \end{bmatrix} \qquad (d)\ \begin{bmatrix} 1 & 0 & 0 \\ 0 & 0 & 1 \\ 0 & 1 & 0 \end{bmatrix}$$

Each of the matrices in Q.2 is an example of an *elementary matrix.*

For 3×3 matrices there are three types of elementary matrix:

(1) $\begin{bmatrix} k & 0 & 0 \\ 0 & 1 & 0 \\ 0 & 0 & 1 \end{bmatrix}, \begin{bmatrix} 1 & 0 & 0 \\ 0 & l & 0 \\ 0 & 0 & 1 \end{bmatrix}, \begin{bmatrix} 1 & 0 & 0 \\ 0 & 1 & 0 \\ 0 & 0 & m \end{bmatrix}$, which multiply one of the rows by a non-zero constant.

Geometrically, these matrices represent one-way stretches.

(2) $\begin{bmatrix} 1 & 0 & 0 \\ a & 1 & 0 \\ 0 & 0 & 1 \end{bmatrix}, \begin{bmatrix} 1 & 0 & 0 \\ 0 & 1 & 0 \\ b & 0 & 1 \end{bmatrix}, \begin{bmatrix} 1 & 0 & 0 \\ 0 & 1 & 0 \\ 0 & c & 1 \end{bmatrix}, \begin{bmatrix} 1 & 0 & 0 \\ 0 & 1 & d \\ 0 & 0 & 1 \end{bmatrix}, \begin{bmatrix} 1 & 0 & e \\ 0 & 1 & 0 \\ 0 & 0 & 1 \end{bmatrix},$
$\begin{bmatrix} 1 & f & 0 \\ 0 & 1 & 0 \\ 0 & 0 & 1 \end{bmatrix}$, which add a multiple of one row to another.

Geometrically, each of these matrices represents a shear.

(3) $\begin{bmatrix} 1 & 0 & 0 \\ 0 & 0 & 1 \\ 0 & 1 & 0 \end{bmatrix}, \begin{bmatrix} 0 & 1 & 0 \\ 1 & 0 & 0 \\ 0 & 0 & 1 \end{bmatrix}, \begin{bmatrix} 0 & 0 & 1 \\ 0 & 1 & 0 \\ 1 & 0 & 0 \end{bmatrix}$, which interchange two rows.

Geometrically, these matrices represent reflection in the planes $y = z$, $x = y$ and $x = z$, respectively.

Each of these elementary matrices can be obtained by applying the required operation to the identity matrix.

We now refer back to Example 4 and write down the elementary matrices which describe the transition from one stage to the next.

Q.3 Verify that the elementary matrices which would be used in Example 4 for stage 1 to stage 2, 2 to 3, 3 to 4, 4 to 5, 5 to 6, 6 to 7, 7 to 8 and 8 to 9 are respectively:

$$\mathbf{E}_1 = \begin{bmatrix} 1 & 0 & 0 \\ -3 & 1 & 0 \\ 0 & 0 & 1 \end{bmatrix} \qquad \mathbf{E}_2 = \begin{bmatrix} 1 & 0 & 0 \\ 0 & 1 & 0 \\ 4 & 0 & 1 \end{bmatrix} \qquad \mathbf{E}_3 = \begin{bmatrix} 1 & 0 & 0 \\ 0 & 1 & 1 \\ 0 & 0 & 1 \end{bmatrix}$$

$$\mathbf{E}_4 = \begin{bmatrix} 1 & 0 & 0 \\ 0 & 1 & 0 \\ 0 & 6 & 1 \end{bmatrix} \qquad \mathbf{E}_5 = \begin{bmatrix} 1 & 0 & 0 \\ 0 & 1 & 1 \\ 0 & 0 & 1 \end{bmatrix} \qquad \mathbf{E}_6 = \begin{bmatrix} 1 & 0 & -1 \\ 0 & 1 & 0 \\ 0 & 0 & 1 \end{bmatrix}$$

$$\mathbf{E}_7 = \begin{bmatrix} 1 & 2 & 0 \\ 0 & 1 & 0 \\ 0 & 0 & 1 \end{bmatrix} \qquad \mathbf{E}_8 = \begin{bmatrix} 1 & 0 & 0 \\ 0 & 1 & 0 \\ 0 & 0 & -1 \end{bmatrix}$$

Q.4 Evaluate $\mathbf{E}_8\mathbf{E}_7\mathbf{E}_6\mathbf{E}_5\mathbf{E}_4\mathbf{E}_3\mathbf{E}_2\mathbf{E}_1$ and verify that your answer is the inverse of the matrix $\begin{bmatrix} 1 & -2 & -1 \\ 3 & 1 & 5 \\ -4 & 2 & -3 \end{bmatrix}$.

Exercise 6B

1 Use the method of Example 4 to solve the equations

$$\left.\begin{aligned} x - y + 3z &= 8 \\ 2x - 3y + z &= -1 \\ 3x + 2y - 3z &= -2 \end{aligned}\right\}$$

Write down the elementary matrix which is used at each stage and hence find the inverse of the matrix $\begin{bmatrix} 1 & -1 & 3 \\ 2 & -3 & 1 \\ 3 & 2 & -3 \end{bmatrix}$.

2 Repeat question 1 for the equations

$$\left.\begin{aligned} 2x - y + 4z &= 7 \\ x + 2y + z &= 1 \\ -3x + 4y + 5z &= 2 \end{aligned}\right\}$$

and the matrix $\begin{bmatrix} 2 & -1 & 4 \\ 1 & 2 & 1 \\ -3 & 4 & 5 \end{bmatrix}$.

3 Find the inverses of the following matrices:

(*a*) $\begin{bmatrix} 4 & 0 & 4 \\ -2 & 1 & -2 \\ 0 & -3 & 1 \end{bmatrix}$ (*b*) $\begin{bmatrix} -5 & -12 & 25 \\ 3 & 7 & -15 \\ 2 & 4 & -9 \end{bmatrix}$ (*c*) $\begin{bmatrix} 3 & -2 & -8 \\ -1 & 1 & 4 \\ -5 & 5 & 22 \end{bmatrix}$

6.4 DETERMINANT OF A 3 × 3 MATRIX

With transformations in two dimensions we saw that the image of the unit square is a parallelogram and that the determinant measures the area scale factor of the transformation. A negative determinant indicates that an opposite transformation has taken place. For transformations in three dimensions we know that the image of the unit cube is a parallelepiped, so we could define the determinant of a 3×3 matrix to be the volume scale factor. We would expect a negative value if the transformation turns the cube 'inside out'.

The images of the unit vectors **i**, **j** and **k** are the columns of the matrix, so if

$$\mathbf{M} = \begin{bmatrix} a_1 & b_1 & c_1 \\ a_2 & b_2 & c_2 \\ a_3 & b_3 & c_3 \end{bmatrix}$$

we get a parallelepiped (Fig. 6). Its volume will be the same as that of any parallelepiped obtained from it by shearing. Elementary matrices of type 2 ($\begin{bmatrix} 1 & 0 & 0 \\ a & 1 & 0 \\ 0 & 0 & 1 \end{bmatrix}$ and so on) represent shears. Premultiplying **M** by a matrix of this form is equivalent to a row-operation on **M**.

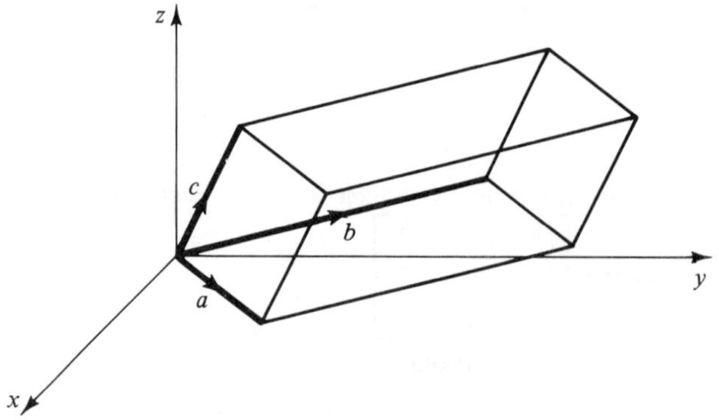

Figure 6

If R_i stands for the ith row, and we start with $\begin{bmatrix} a_1 & b_1 & c_1 \\ a_2 & b_2 & c_2 \\ a_3 & b_3 & c_3 \end{bmatrix}$,

$$\begin{aligned} R_2 &= R_2 - \frac{a_2}{a_1} R_1: \\ R_3 &= R_3 - \frac{a_3}{a_1} R_1: \end{aligned} \qquad \begin{bmatrix} a_1 & b_1 & c_1 \\ 0 & b_2' & c_2' \\ 0 & b_3' & c_3' \end{bmatrix},$$

where
$$b_2' = b_2 - \frac{a_2}{a_1} b_1, \qquad c_2' = c_2 - \frac{a_2}{a_1} c_1,$$
$$b_3' = b_3 - \frac{a_3}{a_1} b_1, \qquad c_3' = c_3 - \frac{a_3}{a_1} c_1$$

and we assume that $a_1 \neq 0$.

$$R_3 = R_3 - \frac{b_3'}{b_2'} R_2: \qquad \begin{bmatrix} a_1 & b_1 & c_1 \\ 0 & b_2' & c_2' \\ 0 & 0 & c_3'' \end{bmatrix}$$

where $c_3'' = c_3' - \dfrac{b_3'}{b_2'} c_2'$ and we assume that $b_2' \neq 0$.

Thus the parallelepiped with sides $\begin{bmatrix} a_1 \\ 0 \\ 0 \end{bmatrix}$, $\begin{bmatrix} b_1 \\ b_2' \\ 0 \end{bmatrix}$ and $\begin{bmatrix} c_1 \\ c_2' \\ c_3'' \end{bmatrix}$ has the same volume as the original parallelepiped (Fig. 7).

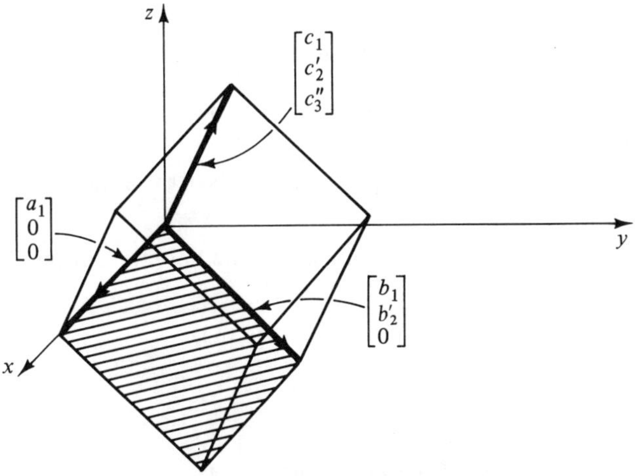

Figure 7

The shaded face lies in the plane $z = 0$ and has area $|a_1 \times b_2'|$ and hence the volume of the parallelepiped is $|a_1 \times b_2' \times c_3''|$.

Now

$$\begin{aligned}
a_1 \times b_2' \times c_3'' &= a_1 b_2'\left(c_3' - \frac{b_3'}{b_2'} c_2'\right) \\
&= a_1(b_2'c_3' - b_3'c_2') \\
&= a_1\left[\left(b_2 - \frac{a_2 b_1}{a_1}\right)\left(c_3 - \frac{a_3 c_1}{a_1}\right) - \left(b_3 - \frac{a_3 b_1}{a_1}\right)\left(c_2 - \frac{a_2 c_1}{a_1}\right)\right] \\
&= \frac{1}{a_1}[(a_1 b_2 - a_2 b_1)(a_1 c_3 - a_3 c_1) - (a_1 b_3 - a_3 b_1)(a_1 c_2 - a_2 c_1)] \\
&= \frac{1}{a_1}[a_1^2 b_2 c_3 - a_1 a_2 b_2 c_1 - a_1 a_2 b_1 c_3 + a_2 a_3 b_1 c_1 \\
&\qquad - a_1^2 b_3 c_2 + a_1 a_2 b_3 c_1 + a_1 a_3 b_1 c_2 - a_2 a_3 b_1 c_1] \\
&= a_1 b_2 c_3 - a_3 b_2 c_1 - a_2 b_1 c_3 - a_1 b_3 c_2 + a_2 b_3 c_1 + a_3 b_1 c_2 \\
&= a_1(b_2 c_3 - b_3 c_2) - a_2(b_1 c_3 - b_3 c_1) + a_3(b_1 c_2 - b_2 c_1).
\end{aligned}$$

Definition

If $\mathbf{M} = \begin{bmatrix} a_1 & b_1 & c_1 \\ a_2 & b_2 & c_2 \\ a_3 & b_3 & c_3 \end{bmatrix}$, the determinant of the 3×3 matrix $\mathbf{M}$ is given by

$$\det(\mathbf{M}) = a_1(b_2c_3 - b_3c_2) - a_2(b_1c_3 - b_3c_1) + a_3(b_1c_2 - b_2c_1).$$

Note: $\begin{vmatrix} a_1 & b_1 & c_1 \\ a_2 & b_2 & c_2 \\ a_3 & b_3 & c_3 \end{vmatrix}$ is an alternative notation often used for the determinant of the matrix $\mathbf{M}$.

In the derivation of $\det(\mathbf{M})$ we excluded the cases when (1) $a_1 = 0$ and (2) $b_2{}' = 0$.

(1) If $a_1 = 0$, simply change b_2 or c_2 to zero (if possible) instead of a_2, and proceed as before.

(2) If $b_2{}' = 0$ (that is, $a_1b_2 - b_2a_1 = 0$), the sides of the parallelepiped at stage 2 are $\begin{bmatrix} a_1 \\ 0 \\ 0 \end{bmatrix}$, $\begin{bmatrix} b_1 \\ 0 \\ 0 \end{bmatrix}$ and $\begin{bmatrix} c_1 \\ c_2 \\ c_3 \end{bmatrix}$, from which the volume can be calculated.

In both cases we get the same result for $\det(\mathbf{M})$.

Example 5

Evaluate the determinant of the matrix $\mathbf{M} = \begin{bmatrix} 2 & 7 & -3 \\ 4 & 0 & 1 \\ 6 & -1 & 2 \end{bmatrix}$.

Solution

$$\begin{aligned} \det(\mathbf{M}) &= 2(0 \times 2 - (-1) \times 1) - 4(7 \times 2 - (-1) \times (-3)) + 6(7 \times 1 - 0 \times (-3)) \\ &= 2 - 44 + 42 \\ &= 0. \end{aligned}$$

□

Exercise 6C

1 Find the determinants of the following matrices:

(*a*) $\begin{bmatrix} 0 & -1 & 2 \\ 1 & 3 & 0 \\ -1 & 2 & 1 \end{bmatrix}$ (*b*) $\begin{bmatrix} 2 & -1 & 2 \\ 1 & 1 & 3 \\ -4 & 0 & 2 \end{bmatrix}$

2 Evaluate the determinants of the following matrices:

(*a*)(i) $\begin{bmatrix} 1 & 1 & -3 \\ 5 & -2 & 0 \\ -2 & 1 & 4 \end{bmatrix}$ (ii) $\begin{bmatrix} 1 & 5 & -2 \\ 1 & -2 & 1 \\ -3 & 0 & 4 \end{bmatrix}$

(b)(i) $\begin{bmatrix} 0 & 7 & -2 \\ 1 & 2 & 0 \\ 3 & -1 & -1 \end{bmatrix}$ (ii) $\begin{bmatrix} 0 & 1 & 3 \\ 7 & 2 & -1 \\ -2 & 0 & -1 \end{bmatrix}$

(c)(i) $\begin{bmatrix} 1 & -2 & 3 \\ 4 & -5 & -2 \\ 1 & -3 & 7 \end{bmatrix}$ (ii) $\begin{bmatrix} 1 & 4 & 1 \\ -2 & -5 & -3 \\ 3 & -2 & 7 \end{bmatrix}$

Comment on your results.

3 Evaluate the determinants of the following matrices:

(a)(i) $\begin{bmatrix} 1 & 2 & -1 \\ 7 & 0 & 3 \\ -1 & 2 & 4 \end{bmatrix}$ (ii) $\begin{bmatrix} 7 & 0 & 3 \\ 1 & 2 & -1 \\ -1 & 2 & 4 \end{bmatrix}$

(b)(i) $\begin{bmatrix} 0 & 3 & -1 \\ 1 & 0 & -2 \\ 0 & 4 & 2 \end{bmatrix}$ (ii) $\begin{bmatrix} 0 & 4 & 2 \\ 1 & 0 & -2 \\ 0 & 3 & -1 \end{bmatrix}$

(c)(i) $\begin{bmatrix} 1 & 1 & 2 \\ -3 & 1 & 0 \\ 0 & 0 & 2 \end{bmatrix}$ (ii) $\begin{bmatrix} 0 & 0 & 2 \\ -3 & 1 & 0 \\ 1 & 1 & 2 \end{bmatrix}$

Comment on your results.

4 Evaluate the determinants of the following matrices:

(a) $\begin{bmatrix} 3 & -2 & 5 \\ 4 & 7 & 6 \\ 3 & -2 & 5 \end{bmatrix}$ (b) $\begin{bmatrix} 1 & -2 & 3 \\ 0 & 4 & 2 \\ 1 & -2 & 3 \end{bmatrix}$ (c) $\begin{bmatrix} -1 & 6 & 1 \\ -1 & 6 & 1 \\ 3 & -2 & 0 \end{bmatrix}$

(d) $\begin{bmatrix} 2 & 4 & 0 \\ 1 & 2 & 0 \\ -2 & 3 & 1 \end{bmatrix}$ (e) $\begin{bmatrix} 1 & 3 & 1 \\ 1 & -1 & 1 \\ 2 & 4 & 2 \end{bmatrix}$ (f) $\begin{bmatrix} 3 & 9 & 1 \\ -1 & -3 & 2 \\ 2 & 6 & 4 \end{bmatrix}$

Comment on your results.

5 If $\mathbf{A} = \begin{bmatrix} 1 & -1 & 0 \\ 7 & 0 & -3 \\ 1 & 0 & 2 \end{bmatrix}$ and $\mathbf{B} = \begin{bmatrix} -1 & 0 & 0 \\ 3 & 1 & 2 \\ -1 & 0 & 3 \end{bmatrix}$, calculate the matrix product **AB** and sum $(\mathbf{A} + \mathbf{B})$.

Find det(**A**), det(**B**), det(**AB**) and det($\mathbf{A} + \mathbf{B}$). What do you notice?

6 Find the matrix of the transformation which transforms $A(1,0,0)$, $B(0,1,0)$ and $C(0,0,1)$ to $A'(3,-1,2)$, $B'(-1,2,0)$ and $C'(1,1,2)$. Hence find the volume of the parallelepiped defined by the vectors **OA**$'$, **OB**$'$ and **OC**$'$.

7 A parallelepiped (Fig. 8) has vertices $A(1,1,1)$, $B(-2,1,3)$, $C(-2,2,6)$, $D(1,2,4)$, $E(2,3,0)$, $F(-1,3,2)$, $G(-1,4,5)$ and $H(2,4,3)$. Find its volume.

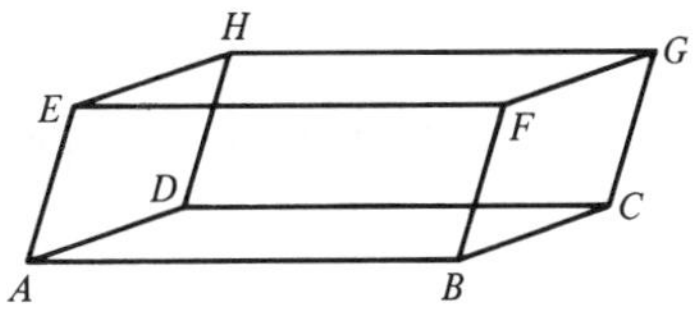

Figure 8

8 For each of the following transformations **T** in three-dimensional space:
(i) *write down* the volume scale factor;
(ii) find the matrix for **T** and the value of the determinant for this matrix.
(*a*) **T** is a shear with the xy-plane invariant in which $(0, 0, 1) \to (-2, 1, 1)$.
(*b*) **T** is a rotation through 60° about the y-axis.
(*c*) **T** is a reflection in the plane $y = 0$.
(*d*) **T** is a two-way stretch, factor 2 parallel to the x-axis and factor 5 parallel to the z-axis.
(*e*) **T** is a projection onto the yz-plane parallel to the x-axis.
(*f*) **T** is an enlargement centre O, scale factor 3.
(*g*) **T** is an enlargement centre O, scale factor -1.
(*h*) **T** is a reflection in the plane $x = z$.
Explain the significance of the minus signs in your answers to parts (*c*), (*g*) and (*h*).

6.5 SOME PROPERTIES OF DETERMINANTS

In this section we switch from the main theme of this chapter to investigate some of the properties of determinants. You will probably have guessed some of these properties from your answers to Exercise 6C. The section ends with an alternative method for finding the inverse of a matrix.

Result 1
The determinant of a matrix is unaltered if rows and columns are interchanged (see Exercise 6C, question 2).

Q.5 If $\mathbf{M} = \begin{bmatrix} a_1 & b_1 & c_1 \\ a_2 & b_2 & c_2 \\ a_3 & b_3 & c_3 \end{bmatrix}$ and $\mathbf{M}^T = \begin{bmatrix} a_1 & a_2 & a_3 \\ b_1 & b_2 & b_3 \\ c_1 & c_2 & c_3 \end{bmatrix}$, show, by direct expansion, that

$$\det(\mathbf{M}^T) = \det(\mathbf{M}).$$

Result 2

$$\det(\mathbf{AB}) = \det(\mathbf{A}) \times \det(\mathbf{B})$$

As the determinant of a matrix has been defined to be the volume scale factor of the transformation represented by the matrix, by considering successive transformations represented by the matrices **B** then **A**, it follows immediately that

$$\det(\mathbf{AB}) = \det(\mathbf{A}) \times \det(\mathbf{B})$$

Result 3
If a row of a matrix is multiplied by a number k, the determinant of the matrix is multiplied by k.

Multiplying a row by k is equivalent to premultiplying a matrix by an elementary matrix of type 1 ($\begin{bmatrix} k & 0 & 0 \\ 0 & 1 & 0 \\ 0 & 0 & 1 \end{bmatrix}$, and so on).

If $$\mathbf{E}_1 = \begin{bmatrix} k & 0 & 0 \\ 0 & 1 & 0 \\ 0 & 0 & 1 \end{bmatrix}, \quad \det(\mathbf{E}_1) = k,$$

so $$\det(\mathbf{E}_1\mathbf{M}) = \det(\mathbf{E}_1) \times \det(\mathbf{M}) \quad \text{(from Result 2)}$$
$$= k \det(\mathbf{M}).$$

For example,

$$\det\left(\begin{bmatrix} 6 & 9 & 12 \\ 5 & 15 & -5 \\ 1 & 0 & -3 \end{bmatrix}\right) = 3\det\left(\begin{bmatrix} 2 & 3 & 4 \\ 5 & 15 & -5 \\ 1 & 0 & -3 \end{bmatrix}\right) = 5 \times 3\det\left(\begin{bmatrix} 2 & 3 & 4 \\ 1 & 3 & -1 \\ 1 & 0 & -3 \end{bmatrix}\right)$$

Result 4
If to any row of a matrix is added a multiple of another row, the determinant of the matrix is unaltered.

This is equivalent to premultiplying a matrix by an elementary matrix of type 2 ($\begin{bmatrix} 1 & 0 & 0 \\ a & 1 & 0 \\ 0 & 0 & 1 \end{bmatrix}$, and so on).

If $$\mathbf{E}_2 = \begin{bmatrix} 1 & 0 & 0 \\ a & 1 & 0 \\ 0 & 0 & 1 \end{bmatrix}, \quad \det(\mathbf{E}_2) = 1,$$

so $$\det(\mathbf{E}_2\mathbf{M}) = \det(\mathbf{E}_2) \times \det(\mathbf{M}) \quad \text{(from Result 2)}$$
$$= \det(\mathbf{M}).$$

For example,

$$\det\left(\begin{bmatrix} 6 & -3 & 19 \\ 12 & -5 & 36 \\ 17 & -10 & 59 \end{bmatrix}\right) = \left(\begin{bmatrix} 6 & -3 & 19 \\ 0 & 1 & -2 \\ 17 & -10 & 59 \end{bmatrix}\right) \quad \text{(Why?)}$$
$$= \det\left(\begin{bmatrix} 6 & -3 & 19 \\ 0 & 1 & -2 \\ -1 & -1 & 2 \end{bmatrix}\right),$$

which has smaller numbers in the expansion.

Result 5
If two rows of a matrix are interchanged, the determinant of the matrix changes sign (see Exercise 6C, question 3).

This is equivalent to premultiplying by an elementary matrix of type 3 ($\begin{bmatrix} 0 & 1 & 0 \\ 1 & 0 & 0 \\ 0 & 0 & 1 \end{bmatrix}$, and so on).

If
$$\mathbf{E}_3 = \begin{bmatrix} 0 & 1 & 0 \\ 1 & 0 & 0 \\ 0 & 0 & 1 \end{bmatrix}, \quad \det(\mathbf{E}_3) = -1,$$

so
$$\begin{aligned} \det(\mathbf{E}_3\mathbf{M}) &= \det(\mathbf{E}_3) \times \det(\mathbf{M}) \quad \text{(from Result 2)} \\ &= -\det(\mathbf{M}). \end{aligned}$$

Result 6
If two rows of a matrix are the same, its determinant is zero.

This is a consequence of Result 5. Interchanging the two identical rows:

$$\begin{aligned} & \det(\mathbf{M}) = -\det(\mathbf{M}) \\ \Rightarrow\ & \det(\mathbf{M}) = 0. \end{aligned}$$

Q.6 If $\mathbf{A} = \begin{bmatrix} a_1 & b_1 & c_1 \\ a_2 & b_2 & c_2 \\ a_3 & b_3 & c_3 \end{bmatrix}$, prove that

$$\det(\mathbf{A}) = a_1 \times \det\left(\begin{bmatrix} b_2 & c_2 \\ b_3 & c_3 \end{bmatrix}\right) - a_2 \det\left(\begin{bmatrix} b_1 & c_1 \\ b_3 & c_3 \end{bmatrix}\right) + a_3 \det\left(\begin{bmatrix} b_1 & c_1 \\ b_2 & c_2 \end{bmatrix}\right).$$

Note how this last expression is written down. It is

$a_1 \times$ (the determinant of the 2×2 matrix left when the first row and first column are deleted: $\begin{bmatrix} \cancel{a_1} & \cancel{b_1} & \cancel{c_1} \\ \cancel{a_2} & b_2 & c_2 \\ \cancel{a_3} & b_3 & c_3 \end{bmatrix}$)

$-a_2 \times$ (the determinant of the 2×2 matrix left when the second row and first column are deleted: $\begin{bmatrix} \cancel{a_1} & b_1 & c_1 \\ \cancel{a_2} & \cancel{b_2} & \cancel{c_2} \\ \cancel{a_3} & b_3 & c_3 \end{bmatrix}$)

$+a_3 \times$ (the determinant of the 2×2 matrix left when the third row and first column are deleted: $\begin{bmatrix} \cancel{a_1} & b_1 & c_1 \\ \cancel{a_2} & b_2 & c_2 \\ \cancel{a_3} & \cancel{b_3} & \cancel{c_3} \end{bmatrix}$)

Cofactors

In the expansion of $\det(\mathbf{A})$ in Q.7,

$$\det\left(\begin{bmatrix} b_2 & c_2 \\ b_3 & c_3 \end{bmatrix}\right), \quad -\det\left(\begin{bmatrix} b_1 & c_1 \\ b_3 & c_3 \end{bmatrix}\right) \quad \text{and} \quad \det\left(\begin{bmatrix} b_1 & c_1 \\ c_2 & c_2 \end{bmatrix}\right)$$

are called the *cofactors* of a_1, a_2 and a_3, and are written as A_1, A_2 and A_3. Hence we can write

$$\det(\mathbf{M}) = a_1A_1 + a_2A_2 + a_3A_3.$$

We can define the cofactors of the other elements as follows: to find the cofactor X_{ij} of the element x_{ij} which is in the ith row and jth column, calculate the determinant of the remaining elements when the ith row and jth column are removed, and then multiply by $(-1)^{i+j}$. For example,

$$C_2 = (-1)^{2+3}\det\left(\begin{bmatrix} a_1 & b_1 \\ a_3 & b_3 \end{bmatrix}\right) \quad \text{(since } c_2 \text{ is in the second row and third column)}$$

$$= (-1)(a_1b_3 - a_3b_1).$$

Q.7 If $\mathbf{M} = \begin{bmatrix} a_1 & b_1 & c_1 \\ a_2 & b_2 & c_2 \\ a_3 & b_3 & c_3 \end{bmatrix}$, prove that

(*a*) $\det(\mathbf{M}) = a_2A_2 + b_2B_2 + c_2C_2$
(*b*) $\det(\mathbf{M}) = b_1B_1 + b_2B_2 + b_3B_3$
(*c*) $a_3A_1 + b_3B_1 + c_3C_1 = 0$

Using symmetry, write down other similar results.

Q.8 Using your results from Q.7, simplify

$$\begin{bmatrix} a_1 & b_1 & c_1 \\ a_2 & b_2 & c_2 \\ a_3 & b_3 & c_3 \end{bmatrix}\begin{bmatrix} A_1 & A_2 & A_3 \\ B_1 & B_2 & B_3 \\ C_1 & C_2 & C_3 \end{bmatrix}$$

An important consequence of the result of Q.8 is that the inverse of

$$\begin{bmatrix} a_1 & b_1 & c_1 \\ a_2 & b_2 & c_2 \\ a_3 & b_3 & c_3 \end{bmatrix} \quad \text{is} \quad \frac{1}{\det(\mathbf{M})}\begin{bmatrix} A_1 & A_2 & A_3 \\ B_1 & B_2 & B_3 \\ C_1 & C_2 & C_3 \end{bmatrix}$$

provided $\det(\mathbf{M}) \neq 0$. If $\det(\mathbf{M}) = 0$, there is no inverse.

Example 6

Find the inverse of the matrix $\mathbf{M} = \begin{bmatrix} 1 & -4 & 2 \\ 2 & 1 & 4 \\ 4 & 3 & -2 \end{bmatrix}$.

Solution

Using the same notation as earlier we calculate the cofactors:

$$\begin{aligned} A_1 &= -14, & A_2 &= -2, & A_3 &= -18 \\ B_1 &= 20, & B_2 &= -10, & B_3 &= 0 \\ C_1 &= 2, & C_2 &= -19, & C_3 &= 9 \end{aligned}$$

Now
$$\det(\mathbf{M}) = a_1A_1 + a_2A_2 + a_3A_3$$
$$= 1 \times (-14) + 2 \times (-2) + 4 \times (-18)$$
$$= -90$$
$$\Rightarrow \quad \mathbf{M}^{-1} = \frac{1}{-90}\begin{bmatrix} -14 & -2 & -18 \\ 20 & -10 & 0 \\ 2 & -19 & 9 \end{bmatrix}. \quad \square$$

Exercise 6D

1 Use the properties of determinants outlined above to help you evaluate the determinants of the following matrices:

(*a*) $\begin{bmatrix} 1 & 1 & 1 \\ 2 & 2 & 2 \\ 3 & 3 & 3 \end{bmatrix}$ (*b*) $\begin{bmatrix} 3 & 1 & -2 \\ 297 & 100 & -201 \\ 6 & 0 & 5 \end{bmatrix}$ (*c*) $\begin{bmatrix} 101 & 19 & 1 \\ 102 & 20 & 2 \\ 103 & 20 & 3 \end{bmatrix}$

(*d*) $\begin{bmatrix} 13 & 14 & 15 \\ 6 & 7 & 8 \\ 1 & 2 & 3 \end{bmatrix}$ (*e*) $\begin{bmatrix} 8 & 20 & 12 \\ 9 & 24 & 15 \\ 10 & 27 & 17 \end{bmatrix}$ (*f*) $\begin{bmatrix} 29 & 38 & 40 \\ 19 & 26 & 28 \\ 24 & 32 & 34 \end{bmatrix}$

2 Using the cofactor method, find the inverses of the following matrices. Check your answers by multiplying the original matrix and its inverse together.

(*a*) $\begin{bmatrix} 1 & 0 & -1 \\ 2 & 3 & 1 \\ 0 & -1 & 2 \end{bmatrix}$ (*b*) $\begin{bmatrix} -2 & 3 & 1 \\ 4 & 1 & -1 \\ 5 & 0 & -2 \end{bmatrix}$

(*c*) $\begin{bmatrix} 0 & 5 & -6 \\ 7 & -3 & 0 \\ 4 & 0 & -2 \end{bmatrix}$ (*d*) $\begin{bmatrix} -3 & 1 & 7 \\ 2 & 0 & -5 \\ 4 & 3 & 1 \end{bmatrix}$

6.6 MATRIX METHOD

The equations
$$\left.\begin{aligned} ax + by + cz &= r \\ dx + ey + fz &= s \\ gx + hy + iz &= t \end{aligned}\right\}$$
can be written in the form $\mathbf{Ax} = \mathbf{r}$, where
$$\mathbf{A} = \begin{bmatrix} a & b & c \\ d & e & f \\ g & h & i \end{bmatrix}, \quad \mathbf{x} = \begin{bmatrix} x \\ y \\ z \end{bmatrix} \quad \text{and} \quad \mathbf{r} = \begin{bmatrix} r \\ s \\ t \end{bmatrix}.$$

If the inverse of the matrix $\mathbf{A}$ exists, premultiplying $\mathbf{Ax} = \mathbf{r}$ by $\mathbf{A}^{-1}$ gives
$$\mathbf{A}^{-1}(\mathbf{Ax}) = \mathbf{A}^{-1}\mathbf{r}$$
$$\Rightarrow \quad \mathbf{Ix} = \mathbf{A}^{-1}\mathbf{r}$$
$$\Rightarrow \quad \mathbf{x} = \mathbf{A}^{-1}\mathbf{r};$$
that is, we get a unique solution for $\mathbf{x}$.

Q.9 Verify that $\begin{bmatrix} 13 & 8 & 9 \\ 11 & 7 & 8 \\ -10 & -6 & -7 \end{bmatrix}$ is the inverse of the matrix $\begin{bmatrix} 1 & -2 & -1 \\ 3 & 1 & 5 \\ -4 & 2 & -3 \end{bmatrix}$ and hence solve the equations

$$\left.\begin{aligned} x - 2y - z &= 6 \\ 3x + y + 5z &= -4 \\ -4x + 2y - 3z &= 7 \end{aligned}\right\}$$

We can show that a matrix **A** has an inverse if and only if

$$\det(\mathbf{A}) \neq 0.$$

If $\mathbf{A}^{-1}$ exists, then $\det(\mathbf{A}) \neq 0$, since if $\det(\mathbf{A}) = 0$, then whatever **B** is,

$$\begin{aligned} \det(\mathbf{AB}) &= \det(\mathbf{A}) \times \det(\mathbf{B}) \\ &= 0. \end{aligned}$$

As $\det(\mathbf{I}) = 1$, it follows that no **B** exists such that $\mathbf{AB} = \mathbf{I}$; that is, **A** does not have an inverse.

Conversely, if $\det(\mathbf{A}) \neq 0$, we can form the matrix

$$\frac{1}{\det(\mathbf{A})}\begin{bmatrix} A_1 & A_2 & A_3 \\ B_1 & B_2 & B_3 \\ C_1 & C_2 & C_3 \end{bmatrix}$$

which is the inverse of **A**. ($A_1, A_2, A_3, B_1, B_2, B_3, C_1, C_2, C_3$ are cofactors.)

We saw earlier that when $\mathbf{A}^{-1}$ exists, the equation $\mathbf{Ax} = \mathbf{r}$ has a unique solution. If $\det(\mathbf{A}) = 0$ (that is, **A** does not have an inverse), the equation $\mathbf{Ax} = \mathbf{r}$ has either an infinite set of solutions or the empty solution set (see Examples 2 and 3). That is:

$\det(\mathbf{A}) \neq 0 \quad \Leftrightarrow \quad$ there is a unique solution.

$\det(\mathbf{A}) = 0 \quad \Leftrightarrow \quad$ there is either an infinite set of solutions or the empty solution set.

Equations of the form $\mathbf{Ax} = \mathbf{0}$

Equations of this form are known as *homogeneous linear equations.* $\mathbf{x} = \mathbf{0}$ is always a solution of such equations.

If $\det(\mathbf{A}) \neq 0$, then it is the only solution, as the solution is unique.

If $\det(\mathbf{A}) = 0$, then there is an infinite set of solutions as it is not the empty solution set.

Example 7
Solve the equations

$$\left.\begin{aligned} x + y + z &= 0 \\ 2x + 3y - 4z &= 0 \\ 5x + 7y - 7z &= 0 \end{aligned}\right\}$$

Solution

If $\mathbf{A} = \begin{bmatrix} 1 & 1 & 1 \\ 2 & 3 & -4 \\ 5 & 7 & -7 \end{bmatrix}$, $\det(\mathbf{A}) = 0$, so there is an infinite solution set.

Reducing

$$\begin{bmatrix} 1 & 1 & 1 \\ 2 & 3 & -4 \\ 5 & 7 & -7 \end{bmatrix}\begin{bmatrix} x \\ y \\ z \end{bmatrix} = \begin{bmatrix} 0 \\ 0 \\ 0 \end{bmatrix}$$

using row operations we get

$$\begin{bmatrix} 1 & 1 & 1 \\ 0 & 1 & -6 \\ 0 & 0 & 0 \end{bmatrix}\begin{bmatrix} x \\ y \\ z \end{bmatrix} = \begin{bmatrix} 0 \\ 0 \\ 0 \end{bmatrix};$$

that is,

$$\begin{aligned} x + y + z &= 0 \\ y - 6z &= 0 \\ 0z &= 0 \end{aligned}$$

The last of these equations is satisfied by any value of z. Putting $z = \lambda$, we get $y = 6\lambda$ and $x = -7\lambda$, so the solution set is

$$\{(-7\lambda, 6\lambda, \lambda) : \lambda \in \mathbb{R}\}.$$

□

Exercise 6E

1 Using your answers to question 2 of Exercise 6D, find the solutions of

(*a*) $\left.\begin{aligned} x - z &= 3 \\ 2x + 3y + z &= -2 \\ -y + 2z &= 1 \end{aligned}\right\}$ (*b*) $\left.\begin{aligned} -2x + 3y + z &= -5 \\ 4x + y - z &= 4 \\ 5x - 2z &= 3 \end{aligned}\right\}$

(*c*) $\left.\begin{aligned} 10y - 12z &= -7 \\ 7x - 3y &= 2 \\ 4x - 2z &= 0 \end{aligned}\right\}$ (*d*) $\left.\begin{aligned} 3x - y - 7z &= -2 \\ 2x - 5z &= -1 \\ 4x + 3y - z &= 12 \end{aligned}\right\}$

2 For each of the following sets of homogeneous linear equations:
(i) find the value of the determinant of the associated matrix;
(ii) find the complete set of solutions.

(*a*) $\left.\begin{aligned} 3x - y + 7z &= 0 \\ x + 3y - 4z &= 0 \\ 7x + y + 10z &= 0 \end{aligned}\right\}$ (*b*) $\left.\begin{aligned} 2x + 5y - 11z &= 0 \\ x - 3y + z &= 0 \\ 5x - y + 2z &= 0 \end{aligned}\right\}$

$$(c)\quad \left.\begin{aligned} 2.4x - 0.6y + 2.3z &= 0 \\ 1.4x + 2.8y - 5.4z &= 0 \\ 3.4x - 4y + 10z &= 0 \end{aligned}\right\} \qquad (d)\quad \left.\begin{aligned} 3.2x - 2.5y + 3.4z &= 0 \\ 16x - 12.5y + 17z &= 0 \\ 19.2x - 15y + 20.4z &= 0 \end{aligned}\right\}$$

6.7 LINEAR EQUATIONS AND TRANSFORMATIONS

The equations

$$\left.\begin{aligned} x - 2y - z &= 6 \\ 3x + y + 5z &= -4 \\ -4x + 2y - 3z &= 7 \end{aligned}\right\}$$

can be written in the form

$$\begin{bmatrix} 1 & -2 & -1 \\ 3 & 1 & 5 \\ -4 & 2 & -3 \end{bmatrix}\begin{bmatrix} x \\ y \\ z \end{bmatrix} = \begin{bmatrix} 6 \\ -4 \\ 7 \end{bmatrix}.$$

But we know that the matrix $\begin{bmatrix} 1 & -2 & -1 \\ 3 & 1 & 5 \\ -4 & 2 & -3 \end{bmatrix}$ can be thought of as the matrix of a transformation of one three-dimensional space (with x-, y-, z-axes) into another three-dimensional space (with X-, Y-, Z-axes). The problem reduces to asking which point or points in the space on the left in Fig. 9 map onto the point $(6, -4, 7)$ in the space on the right.

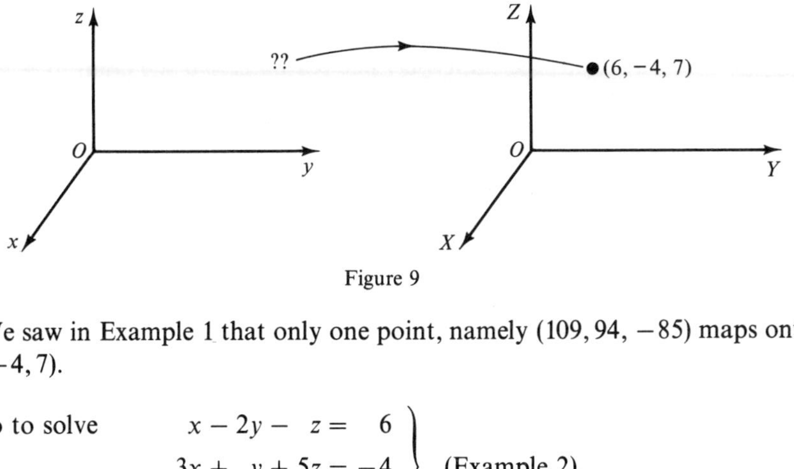

Figure 9

We saw in Example 1 that only one point, namely $(109, 94, -85)$ maps onto $(6, -4, 7)$.

So to solve

$$\left.\begin{aligned} x - 2y - z &= 6 \\ 3x + y + 5z &= -4 \\ -x - 5y - 7z &= 16 \end{aligned}\right\} \quad \text{(Example 2),}$$

we are really asking which point or points map onto the point $(6, -4, 16)$ under the transformation represented by the matrix $\begin{bmatrix} 1 & -2 & -1 \\ 3 & 1 & 5 \\ -1 & -5 & -7 \end{bmatrix}$.

In this case we find that all the image points lie on the plane $2X - Y - Z = 0$ and that each point on the plane is the image of more than one point from the three-dimensional space on the left (Fig. 10).

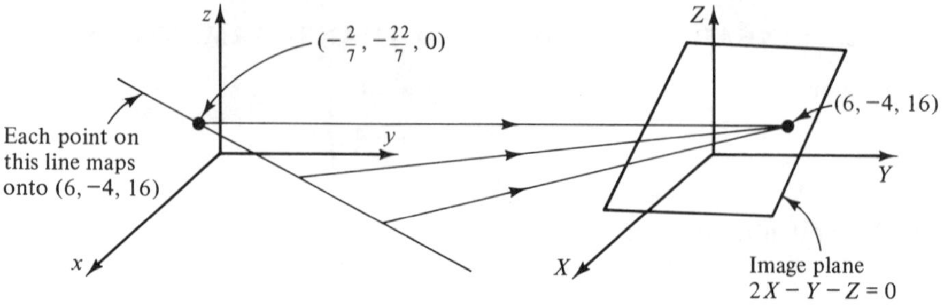

Figure 10

We found that the solution of Example 2 was the line

$$\mathbf{r} = \begin{bmatrix} -\frac{2}{7} \\ -\frac{22}{7} \\ 0 \end{bmatrix} + \lambda \begin{bmatrix} -\frac{9}{7} \\ -\frac{8}{7} \\ 1 \end{bmatrix}.$$

In Example 3, the equations were

$$\left.\begin{aligned} x - 2y - z &= 4 \\ 3x + y + 5z &= -4 \\ -x - 5y - 7z &= 10 \end{aligned}\right\}$$

and the solution set was the empty set. The reason is that the point (6, −4, 10) does *not* lie on the image plane $2X - Y - Z = 0$.

The ideas in this section will be new to you and are meant to be no more than an introduction. This approach will be developed more fully in Chapter 13.

The most important new idea in this chapter has been that of the determinant of a 3×3 matrix. While determinants are used in the solution of linear equations, they are very useful in other areas of mathematics.

Miscellaneous exercise 6

1 (*a*) Show that the word 'column' can be substituted for the word 'row' in Results 2–5 of §6.5 without altering the validity of the statements.

(*b*) Use *column* operations to simplify and then evaluate the determinants of the following matrices:

(i) $\begin{bmatrix} 3 & 5 & 2 \\ 6 & 10 & 3 \\ 9 & 15 & 1 \end{bmatrix}$ (ii) $\begin{bmatrix} 4 & 3 & 3 \\ 13 & 13 & 12 \\ 25 & 25 & 24 \end{bmatrix}$ (iii) $\begin{bmatrix} 3 & -2 & 1 \\ 5 & 4 & 9 \\ 9 & 13 & 22 \end{bmatrix}$

2 (*a*) By subtracting the first column from the second and third columns and then extracting common factors, show that

$$\det\left(\begin{bmatrix} 1 & 1 & 1 \\ a & b & c \\ a^2 & b^2 & c^2 \end{bmatrix}\right) = (b-a)(c-a)\det\left(\begin{bmatrix} 1 & 0 & 0 \\ a & 1 & 1 \\ a^2 & b+a & c+a \end{bmatrix}\right)$$

Complete the factorisation by subtracting the new second column from the third column, extracting a common factor and evaluating the resulting determinant.

(*b*) Factorise the determinants of the following matrices:

(i) $\begin{bmatrix} r & r^2 & r^3 \\ s & s^2 & s^3 \\ t & t^2 & t^3 \end{bmatrix}$ (ii) $\begin{bmatrix} x & y & z \\ 1 & 1 & 1 \\ x^3 & y^3 & z^3 \end{bmatrix}$ (iii) $\begin{bmatrix} 1 & l^2 & mn \\ 1 & m^2 & nl \\ 1 & n^2 & lm \end{bmatrix}$

(iv) $\begin{bmatrix} a-b & a^2-b^2 & 1 \\ b-c & b^2-c^2 & -1 \\ c-a & c^2-a^2 & 1 \end{bmatrix}$

3 For matrices **A** and **B**, show that

(*a*) $\det(\mathbf{AB}) = \det(\mathbf{BA})$

(*b*) in general, $\det(\mathbf{A}+\mathbf{B}) \neq \det(\mathbf{A}) + \det(\mathbf{B})$

(*c*) in general, $\det(k\mathbf{A}) \neq k\det(\mathbf{A})$

4 Solve the following equations:

(*a*) $\det\left(\begin{bmatrix} 2 & 2 & x \\ 3 & 3 & 3 \\ 5 & x & 5 \end{bmatrix}\right) = 0$ (*b*) $\det\left(\begin{bmatrix} (4-x) & 2 & 7 \\ 0 & (3-x) & 1 \\ 0 & 0 & (2+x) \end{bmatrix}\right) = 0$

(*c*) $\det\left(\begin{bmatrix} (2-x) & -1 & 6 \\ 3 & (-3-x) & 27 \\ 1 & -1 & (7-x) \end{bmatrix}\right) = 0$

5 For what value(s) of λ do the following sets of equations not have a unique solution? For this (these) value(s) of λ find the full solution set(s) in each case.

(*a*) $\left.\begin{aligned} 2x - 3y + 5z &= 4 \\ x + 2y - z &= 3 \\ x - y + \lambda z &= 4 \end{aligned}\right\}$ (*b*) $\left.\begin{aligned} x - 3y - 2z &= 0 \\ 2x + y - 5z &= 0 \\ x + \lambda y - 16z &= 0 \end{aligned}\right\}$

SUMMARY

(1) There are four possible results for the intersection of three planes:

(*a*) The planes intersect in a unique point.

(*b*) The planes have no common point, i.e. the solution set is empty – the planes form a prism or at least two are parallel.

(*c*) The planes intersect in a line – the planes form a sheaf.

(*d*) The planes intersect in a plane – the three planes then coincide.

(2) For 3×3 matrices there are three types of *elementary matrix*:

(*a*) $\begin{bmatrix} k & 0 & 0 \\ 0 & 1 & 0 \\ 0 & 0 & 1 \end{bmatrix}$, $\begin{bmatrix} 1 & 0 & 0 \\ 0 & l & 0 \\ 0 & 0 & 1 \end{bmatrix}$, $\begin{bmatrix} 1 & 0 & 0 \\ 0 & 1 & 0 \\ 0 & 0 & m \end{bmatrix}$, which multiply one of the rows by a constant;

(*b*) $\begin{bmatrix} 1 & 0 & 0 \\ a & 1 & 0 \\ 0 & 0 & 1 \end{bmatrix}$, $\begin{bmatrix} 1 & 0 & 0 \\ 0 & 1 & 0 \\ b & 0 & 1 \end{bmatrix}$, $\begin{bmatrix} 1 & 0 & 0 \\ 0 & 1 & 0 \\ 0 & c & 1 \end{bmatrix}$, $\begin{bmatrix} 1 & 0 & 0 \\ 0 & 1 & d \\ 0 & 0 & 1 \end{bmatrix}$,

$\begin{bmatrix} 1 & 0 & e \\ 0 & 1 & 0 \\ 0 & 0 & 1 \end{bmatrix}$, $\begin{bmatrix} 1 & f & 0 \\ 0 & 1 & 0 \\ 0 & 0 & 1 \end{bmatrix}$, which add a multiple of one row to another;

(*c*) $\begin{bmatrix} 1 & 0 & 0 \\ 0 & 0 & 1 \\ 0 & 1 & 0 \end{bmatrix}$, $\begin{bmatrix} 0 & 1 & 0 \\ 1 & 0 & 0 \\ 0 & 0 & 1 \end{bmatrix}$, $\begin{bmatrix} 0 & 0 & 1 \\ 0 & 1 & 0 \\ 1 & 0 & 0 \end{bmatrix}$, which interchange two rows.

(3) If $\mathbf{M} = \begin{bmatrix} a_1 & b_1 & c_1 \\ a_2 & b_2 & c_2 \\ a_3 & b_3 & c_3 \end{bmatrix}$, the *determinant* of the 3×3 matrix $\mathbf{M}$ is

$$\det(\mathbf{M}) = a_1(b_2c_3 - b_3c_2) - a_2(b_1c_3 - b_3c_1) + a_3(b_1c_2 - b_2c_1).$$

(4) Some properties of determinants:
(*a*) The determinant of a matrix is unaltered if rows and columns are interchanged.
(*b*) $\det(\mathbf{AB}) = \det(\mathbf{A}) \times \det(\mathbf{B})$
(*c*) If a row of a matrix is multiplied by a number k, the determinant of the matrix is multiplied by k.
(*d*) If to any row of a matrix is added a multiple of another row, the determinant of the matrix is unaltered.
(*e*) If two rows of a matrix are interchanged, the determinant of the matrix changes sign.
(*f*) If two rows of a matrix are the same, its determinant is zero.

(5) The *inverse* of $\mathbf{M} = \begin{bmatrix} a_1 & b_1 & c_1 \\ a_2 & b_2 & c_2 \\ a_3 & b_3 & c_3 \end{bmatrix}$ is $\dfrac{1}{\det(\mathbf{M})}\begin{bmatrix} A_1 & A_2 & A_3 \\ B_1 & B_2 & B_3 \\ C_1 & C_2 & C_3 \end{bmatrix}$, where $A_1, A_2, A_3, B_1, B_2, B_3, C_1, C_2, C_3$ are the cofactors of a_1, a_2, etc., provided $\det(\mathbf{M}) \neq 0$.

(6) The *cofactor* X_{ij} of the element x_{ij} is the determinant of the matrix of remaining elements when the ith row and the jth column are removed and then multiplied by $(-1)^{i+j}$.

(7) If $\mathbf{Ax} = \mathbf{r}$, then
(*a*) $\det(\mathbf{A}) \neq 0 \Leftrightarrow$ there is a unique solution.
(*b*) $\det(\mathbf{A}) = 0 \Leftrightarrow$ there is either an infinite set of solutions or the empty solution set.

(8) Equations of the form $\begin{bmatrix} a_1 & b_1 & c_1 \\ a_2 & b_2 & c_2 \\ a_3 & b_3 & c_3 \end{bmatrix}\begin{bmatrix} x \\ y \\ z \end{bmatrix} = \begin{bmatrix} 0 \\ 0 \\ 0 \end{bmatrix}$ (that is, $\mathbf{Ax} = \mathbf{0}$) are known as a *homogeneous set of equations*.

7

Eigenvalues and eigenvectors for 3×3 matrices

7.1 THE FIXED DIRECTIONS OF A LINEAR MAPPING

We saw in Chapter 4 that a knowledge of the invariant vectors under a transformation helped us to describe a transformation in two dimensions. We now investigate this problem for a transformation in three dimensions.

Example 1

What are the invariant vectors (if any) of the transformation represented by the matrix $\mathbf{M} = \begin{bmatrix} 2 & -1 & 6 \\ 3 & -3 & 27 \\ 1 & -1 & 7 \end{bmatrix}$?

Solution

If the direction of the vector $\begin{bmatrix} x \\ y \\ z \end{bmatrix}$ is unchanged, we can express this by the equation

$$\mathbf{Mx} = \lambda\mathbf{x} \quad \text{for some number } \lambda.$$

Therefore $\quad \mathbf{Mx} = \lambda\mathbf{Ix}$, where $\mathbf{I}$ is the 3×3 identity matrix

$$\Rightarrow \quad \mathbf{Mx} - \lambda\mathbf{Ix} = \mathbf{0}$$

$$\Rightarrow \quad (\mathbf{M} - \lambda\mathbf{I})\mathbf{x} = \mathbf{0};$$

that is,
$$\begin{bmatrix} 2-\lambda & -1 & 6 \\ 3 & -3-\lambda & 27 \\ 1 & -1 & 7-\lambda \end{bmatrix}\begin{bmatrix} x \\ y \\ z \end{bmatrix} = \begin{bmatrix} 0 \\ 0 \\ 0 \end{bmatrix}.$$

This is a homogeneous set of equations, and we saw in §6.6 that for such equations to have non-trivial solutions (that is, solutions other than $\begin{bmatrix} 0 \\ 0 \\ 0 \end{bmatrix}$),

$$\det(\mathbf{M} - \lambda\mathbf{I}) = 0,$$

so $$\det\left(\begin{bmatrix} 2-\lambda & -1 & 6 \\ 3 & -3-\lambda & 27 \\ 1 & -1 & 7-\lambda \end{bmatrix}\right) = 0$$

$$\Rightarrow \quad (2-\lambda)[(-3-\lambda)-(-27)] - 3[(-1)(7-\lambda)-(-6)] + 1[-27-(-3-\lambda)6] = 0$$

$$\Rightarrow \quad (2-\lambda)(\lambda^2 - 4\lambda + 6) - 3(-1+\lambda) + 1(-9+6\lambda) = 0$$

$$\Rightarrow \quad 2\lambda^2 - 8\lambda + 12 - \lambda^3 + 4\lambda^2 - 6\lambda + 3 - 3\lambda - 9 + 6\lambda = 0$$

$$\Rightarrow \quad -\lambda^3 + 6\lambda^2 - 11\lambda + 6 = 0$$

$$\Rightarrow \quad \lambda^3 - 6\lambda^2 + 11\lambda - 6 = 0,$$

$$\Rightarrow \quad (\lambda - 1)(\lambda - 2)(\lambda - 3) = 0$$

$$\Rightarrow \quad \lambda = 1, \quad 2 \quad \text{or} \quad 3.$$

These values of λ are the *eigenvalues* of the matrix $\mathbf{M}$, and the cubic equation arising from $\det(\mathbf{M} - \lambda\mathbf{I}) = 0$ is known as the *characteristic equation.*

To find the *eigenvectors* (that is, those non-zero vectors $\mathbf{x}$ which satisfy $\mathbf{Mx} = \lambda\mathbf{x}$), we substitute for λ into the equation $(\mathbf{M} - \lambda\mathbf{I})\mathbf{x} = \mathbf{0}$.

$\lambda = 1$ $$\begin{bmatrix} 1 & -1 & 6 \\ 3 & -4 & 27 \\ 1 & -1 & 6 \end{bmatrix}\begin{bmatrix} x \\ y \\ z \end{bmatrix} = \begin{bmatrix} 0 \\ 0 \\ 0 \end{bmatrix}$$

so
$$\left.\begin{aligned} x - y - 6z &= 0 \\ 3x - 4y + 27z &= 0 \\ x - y + 6z &= 0 \end{aligned}\right\} \quad \begin{matrix} (A) \\ (B) \\ (C) \end{matrix}$$

Eliminate x between equations (A) and (B) by finding $(B) - 3 \times (A)$:

$$-y + 9z = 0$$

$$\Rightarrow \quad y = 9z.$$

If $z = k$, $y = 9k$, and substituting in equation (A) we get $x = 3k$, so for $\lambda = 1$ an eigenvector is $\begin{bmatrix} 3 \\ 9 \\ 1 \end{bmatrix}$ (or any non-zero multiple of it).

$\lambda = 2$ $$\begin{bmatrix} 0 & -1 & 6 \\ 3 & -5 & 27 \\ 1 & -1 & 5 \end{bmatrix}\begin{bmatrix} x \\ y \\ z \end{bmatrix} = \begin{bmatrix} 0 \\ 0 \\ 0 \end{bmatrix}$$

so
$$\left.\begin{aligned} -y + 6z &= 0 \\ 3x - 5y + 27z &= 0 \\ x - y + 5z &= 0 \end{aligned}\right\} \quad \begin{matrix} (D) \\ (E) \\ (F) \end{matrix}$$

From equation (D), $y = 6z$. If $z = k'$, $y = 6k'$, and substituting in equation (F) we get $x = k'$, so for $\lambda = 2$ an eigenvector is $\begin{bmatrix} 1 \\ 6 \\ 1 \end{bmatrix}$ (or any non-zero multiple of it).

$\lambda = 3$

$$\begin{bmatrix} -1 & -1 & 6 \\ 3 & -6 & 27 \\ 1 & -1 & 4 \end{bmatrix}\begin{bmatrix} x \\ y \\ z \end{bmatrix} = \begin{bmatrix} 0 \\ 0 \\ 0 \end{bmatrix}$$

so

$$\left.\begin{aligned} -x - y + 6z &= 0 \\ 3x - 6y + 27z &= 0 \\ x - y + 4z &= 0 \end{aligned}\right\} \quad \begin{matrix} (G) \\ (H) \\ (I) \end{matrix}$$

Adding equations (G) and (I): $\quad -2y + 10z = 0$

$$\Rightarrow \quad y = 5z.$$

If $z = k''$, $y = 5k''$, and substituting in equation (I) we get $x = k''$, so for $\lambda = 3$ an eigenvector is $\begin{bmatrix} 1 \\ 5 \\ 1 \end{bmatrix}$ (or any non-zero multiple of it). □

For a 3 × 3 matrix, the characteristic equation is a cubic equation which has up to three different real solutions. Example 2 shows what happens when the eigenvalues are not all distinct.

Example 2
Find the *repeated eigenvalue* and corresponding *eigenvectors* of the following matrices:

$$(a)\begin{bmatrix} 2 & 2 & 1 \\ 2 & 5 & 2 \\ 3 & 6 & 4 \end{bmatrix} \qquad (b)\begin{bmatrix} 3 & 1 & 0 \\ -1 & 1 & 0 \\ 0 & 0 & -5 \end{bmatrix} \qquad (c)\begin{bmatrix} 3 & 0 & 0 \\ 0 & 3 & 0 \\ 0 & 0 & 3 \end{bmatrix}$$

Solution
(a) The characteristic equation simplifies to

$$(\lambda - 1)^2(\lambda - 9) = 0$$

so the eigenvalues are 1, 1 and 9.

When $\lambda = 1$,

$$\begin{bmatrix} 1 & 2 & 1 \\ 2 & 4 & 2 \\ 3 & 6 & 3 \end{bmatrix}\begin{bmatrix} x \\ y \\ z \end{bmatrix} = \begin{bmatrix} 0 \\ 0 \\ 0 \end{bmatrix},$$

so

$$\left.\begin{aligned} x + 2y + z &= 0 \\ 2x + 4y + 2z &= 0 \\ 3x + 6y + 3z &= 0 \end{aligned}\right\};$$

that is, any vector in the plane $x + 2y + z = 0$ is an eigenvector. Examples of vectors in this plane are

$$\begin{bmatrix} 1 \\ 0 \\ -1 \end{bmatrix}, \quad \begin{bmatrix} 0 \\ 1 \\ -2 \end{bmatrix} \quad \text{and} \quad \begin{bmatrix} 4 \\ -3 \\ 2 \end{bmatrix}.$$

In fact, any linear combination of vectors in different directions in this plane is an eigenvector. For example,

$$s\begin{bmatrix} 1 \\ 0 \\ -1 \end{bmatrix} + t\begin{bmatrix} 0 \\ 1 \\ -2 \end{bmatrix}: \quad s, t \in \mathbb{R}, \text{ and } s \text{ and } t \text{ not both zero}$$

is an eigenvector.

(*b*) The characteristic equation simplifies to

$$(\lambda - 2)^2(\lambda + 5) = 0$$

so the eigenvalues are 2, 2 and -5.

When $\lambda = 2$,
$$\begin{bmatrix} 1 & 1 & 0 \\ -1 & -1 & 0 \\ 0 & 0 & -7 \end{bmatrix}\begin{bmatrix} x \\ y \\ z \end{bmatrix} = \begin{bmatrix} 0 \\ 0 \\ 0 \end{bmatrix},$$

so
$$\left.\begin{aligned} x + y \quad &= 0 \\ -x - y \quad &= 0 \\ -7z &= 0 \end{aligned}\right\}$$

An eigenvector is therefore $\begin{bmatrix} 1 \\ -1 \\ 0 \end{bmatrix}$ (or any non-zero multiple of it).

Notice that in this case we can obtain only two 'distinct' eigenvectors for this matrix.

(*c*) The characteristic equation is

$$(3 - \lambda)^3 = 0,$$

so the eigenvalues are 3, 3 and 3.

In this case a vector

$$\begin{bmatrix} p \\ q \\ r \end{bmatrix}: \quad p, q, r \in \mathbb{R} \text{ and not all zero}$$

is an eigenvector. □

Exercise 7A

1 Show that $\begin{bmatrix} -2 \\ -5 \\ 3 \end{bmatrix}$ and $\begin{bmatrix} 6 \\ 5 \\ 11 \end{bmatrix}$ are eigenvectors of the matrix $\mathbf{M} = \begin{bmatrix} 1 & 2 & 4 \\ 2 & 1 & 3 \\ 3 & 3 & 7 \end{bmatrix}$ and find the corresponding eigenvalues. Find also the third eigenvalue and a corresponding eigenvector.

2 Find the characteristic equation, the real eigenvalues and the corresponding eigenvectors of each of the following matrices. (You will need to use your answers to parts (*a*)–(*c*) later, in Exercise 7B.)

(*a*) $\begin{bmatrix} 1 & 0 & 1 \\ 0 & 1 & 0 \\ 1 & 0 & 1 \end{bmatrix}$ (*b*) $\begin{bmatrix} 3 & 2 & 2 \\ 1 & 4 & 1 \\ -2 & -4 & -1 \end{bmatrix}$ (*c*) $\begin{bmatrix} -2 & 2 & 2 \\ 2 & 1 & 2 \\ -3 & -6 & -7 \end{bmatrix}$

(*d*) $\begin{bmatrix} 4 & 9 & 0 \\ 0 & -2 & 6 \\ 0 & 0 & 7 \end{bmatrix}$ (*e*) $\begin{bmatrix} 1 & 2 & 0 \\ 0 & -1 & 3 \\ 2 & 0 & -2 \end{bmatrix}$ (*f*) $\begin{bmatrix} 0 & \frac{1}{2} & 0 \\ 0 & \frac{1}{4} & 1 \\ 1 & \frac{1}{4} & 0 \end{bmatrix}$

3 The following matrices have a repeated eigenvalue. Find the eigenvalues and corresponding eigenvectors.

(*a*) $\begin{bmatrix} 2 & -1 & 1 \\ -1 & 2 & -1 \\ 1 & -1 & 2 \end{bmatrix}$ (*b*) $\begin{bmatrix} 1 & 2 & 1 \\ 0 & -2 & -4 \\ 0 & 3 & 5 \end{bmatrix}$

4 Find the angles between the eigenvectors of the matrix $\begin{bmatrix} 2 & 0 & 3 \\ 0 & 2 & 4 \\ 3 & 4 & 2 \end{bmatrix}$.

7.2 APPLICATIONS OF EIGENVALUES AND EIGENVECTORS

(a) Describing a transformation

Example 3

Describe the transformation represented by the matrix

$$\mathbf{M} = \begin{bmatrix} 2 & -1 & 6 \\ 3 & -3 & 27 \\ 1 & -1 & 7 \end{bmatrix}.$$

Solution

This is the same matrix as in Example 1, where we found the eigenvalues and eigenvectors to be:

Eigenvalue	*Eigenvector*
1	$\begin{bmatrix} 3 \\ 9 \\ 1 \end{bmatrix}$

Eigenvalues	*Eigenvectors*
2	$\begin{bmatrix}1\\6\\1\end{bmatrix}$
3	$\begin{bmatrix}1\\5\\1\end{bmatrix}$

(or any non-zero multiples of these vectors).

This means that, under the transformation represented by this matrix, points on the line $\mathbf{r} = k\begin{bmatrix}3\\9\\1\end{bmatrix}$ stay put, points on the line $\mathbf{r} = k'\begin{bmatrix}1\\6\\1\end{bmatrix}$ stay on the same line but are twice as far away from the origin, and points on the line $\mathbf{r} = k''\begin{bmatrix}1\\5\\1\end{bmatrix}$ stay on the same line but are three times as far away the origin. So we can describe the transformation represented by the matrix **M** as a three-way stretch in the oblique directions $\begin{bmatrix}3\\9\\1\end{bmatrix}, \begin{bmatrix}1\\6\\1\end{bmatrix}, \begin{bmatrix}1\\5\\1\end{bmatrix}$, with factors 1, 2 and 3 respectively. □

(b) Expression of M in the form $\mathbf{U\Lambda U}^{-1}$

An analogous result to that established in Chapter 4 for 2 × 2 matrices holds for 3 × 3 matrices, and you might like to see if you can produce a general proof similar to that on pp. 50–51 for the matrix **M** which has three real eigenvalues and three 'distinct' eigenvectors.

Q.1 In Example 1, $\mathbf{M} = \begin{bmatrix}2 & -1 & 6\\3 & -3 & 27\\1 & -1 & 7\end{bmatrix}$. **U** is now defined as the matrix which has the eigenvectors as its columns, that is, $\mathbf{U} = \begin{bmatrix}3 & 1 & 1\\9 & 6 & 5\\1 & 1 & 1\end{bmatrix}$, and $\mathbf{\Lambda}$ is the matrix with corresponding eigenvalues on the diagonal; that is $\mathbf{\Lambda} = \begin{bmatrix}1 & 0 & 0\\0 & 2 & 0\\0 & 0 & 3\end{bmatrix}$.

(*a*) Verify that $\mathbf{U}^{-1} = \begin{bmatrix} \frac{1}{2} & 0 & -\frac{1}{2} \\ -2 & 1 & -3 \\ \frac{3}{2} & -1 & \frac{9}{2} \end{bmatrix}$.

(*b*) Evaluate $\mathbf{U\Lambda U}^{-1}$ and check that it is equal to $\mathbf{M}$.

(c) To find powers of M

If $\qquad \mathbf{M} = \mathbf{U\Lambda U}^{-1}$,

then $\qquad \mathbf{M}^2 = (\mathbf{U\Lambda U}^{-1})(\mathbf{U\Lambda U}^{-1}) = \mathbf{U\Lambda}^2\mathbf{U}^{-1}$,

and $\qquad \mathbf{M}^3 = (\mathbf{U\Lambda}^2\mathbf{U}^{-1})(\mathbf{U\Lambda U}^{-1}) = \mathbf{U\Lambda}^3\mathbf{U}^{-1}$,

and so on, giving $\quad \mathbf{M}^n = \mathbf{U\Lambda}^n\mathbf{U}^{-1}$.

Q.2 Use this result to evaluate $\begin{bmatrix} 2 & -1 & 6 \\ 3 & -3 & 27 \\ 1 & -1 & 7 \end{bmatrix}^4$.

(d) The Cayley–Hamilton theorem

A square matrix satisfies its own characteristic equation.

The proof of this is similar to the proof for the 2 × 2 matrix when the matrix $\mathbf{M}$ can be expressed in the form $\mathbf{U\Lambda U}^{-1}$. See §4.4(b).

In Example 1 the characteristic equation is

$$\lambda^3 - 6\lambda^2 + 11\lambda - 6 = 0.$$

Q.3 Verify that $\qquad \mathbf{M}^3 - 6\mathbf{M}^2 + 11\mathbf{M} - 6\mathbf{I} = \mathbf{0} \qquad (A)$

for the matrix $\mathbf{M} = \begin{bmatrix} 2 & -1 & 6 \\ 3 & -3 & 27 \\ 1 & -1 & 7 \end{bmatrix}$.

We can now use this result to calculate the inverse $\mathbf{M}^{-1}$ of the matrix $\mathbf{M}$. Multiply the equation $\mathbf{M}^3 - 6\mathbf{M}^2 + 11\mathbf{M} - 6\mathbf{I} = \mathbf{0}$ by $\mathbf{M}^{-1}$ to give

$$\mathbf{M}^2 - 6\mathbf{M} + 11\mathbf{I} - 6\mathbf{M}^{-1} = \mathbf{0}$$

$$\Rightarrow \qquad \mathbf{M}^{-1} = \tfrac{1}{6}(\mathbf{M}^2 - 6\mathbf{M} + 11\mathbf{I}).$$

Q.4 Calculate the inverse of the matrix $\mathbf{M} = \begin{bmatrix} 2 & -1 & 6 \\ 3 & -3 & 27 \\ 1 & -1 & 7 \end{bmatrix}$ by this method, and check your result.

Exercise 7B

1 For each of the following matrices **M**:
(i) write **M** in the form $\mathbf{U\Lambda U^{-1}}$, where $\mathbf{\Lambda}$ is a diagonal matrix;
(ii) give a geometrical description of the transformation represented by **M**;
(iii) calculate $\mathbf{M}^5$;
(iv) use the Cayley–Hamilton theorem to calculate $\mathbf{M}^{-1}$.

(*a*) $\begin{bmatrix} 1 & 0 & 1 \\ 0 & 1 & 0 \\ 1 & 0 & 1 \end{bmatrix}$ (*b*) $\begin{bmatrix} 3 & 2 & 2 \\ 1 & 4 & 1 \\ -2 & -4 & -1 \end{bmatrix}$ (*c*) $\begin{bmatrix} -2 & 2 & 2 \\ 2 & 1 & 2 \\ -3 & -6 & -7 \end{bmatrix}$

2 (*a*) The matrix $\mathbf{M} = \begin{bmatrix} 2 & -1 & 1 \\ -1 & 2 & -1 \\ 1 & -1 & 2 \end{bmatrix}$ has a repeated eigenvalue (see Exercise 7A, question 3(*a*)). Verify that **M** can be written in the form $\mathbf{U\Lambda U^{-1}}$.

(*b*) Why can the matrix $\mathbf{M} = \begin{bmatrix} 1 & 2 & 1 \\ 0 & -2 & -4 \\ 0 & 3 & 5 \end{bmatrix}$ (see Exercise 7A, question 3(*b*)) not be expressed in the form $\mathbf{U\Lambda U^{-1}}$?

3 A matrix **M** has eigenvalues -2, 3 and 0, and corresponding eigenvectors $\begin{bmatrix} 1 \\ 3 \\ 3 \end{bmatrix}$, $\begin{bmatrix} 1 \\ 1 \\ 4 \end{bmatrix}$ and $\begin{bmatrix} 1 \\ 1 \\ 1 \end{bmatrix}$. Find **M**.

4 Express $\mathbf{M} = \begin{bmatrix} 1 & 1 & 1 \\ -2 & -2 & 1 \\ 2 & 2 & -1 \end{bmatrix}$ in the form $\mathbf{U\Lambda U^{-1}}$ and hence calculate $\mathbf{M}^n$.

5 If $\mathbf{P} = \begin{bmatrix} \frac{1}{2} & \frac{1}{4} & 0 \\ \frac{1}{2} & \frac{1}{2} & \frac{1}{2} \\ 0 & \frac{1}{4} & \frac{1}{2} \end{bmatrix}$, find the limit of $\mathbf{P}^n$ as $n \to \infty$.

6 Give a direct proof of the Cayley–Hamilton theorem for matrices of the form $\begin{bmatrix} a & b & c \\ 0 & d & e \\ 0 & 0 & f \end{bmatrix}$.

In this chapter we have seen how to find the eigenvalues and eigenvectors of a 3 × 3 matrix, such that lines in the directions of the eigenvectors are invariant under the transformation represented by the matrix.

Miscellaneous exercise 7

1 Express $\mathbf{P} = \begin{bmatrix} \frac{1}{2} & 1 & 0 \\ \frac{1}{2} & 0 & 0 \\ 0 & 0 & 1 \end{bmatrix}$ in the form $\mathbf{U\Lambda U}^{-1}$ and hence find the limit of $\mathbf{P}^n$ as $n \to \infty$.
Does it matter which two eigenvectors in the plane $x - 2y = 0$ are chosen?

2 If $\mathbf{D} = \begin{bmatrix} 3 & 0 & 0 \\ 0 & 1 & 0 \\ 0 & 0 & -1 \end{bmatrix}$ and $\mathbf{P} = \begin{bmatrix} 1 & 2 & 3 \\ 0 & -1 & 4 \\ 0 & 0 & 1 \end{bmatrix}$, compare the characteristic equations of $\mathbf{D}$ and $\mathbf{P}^{-1}\mathbf{DP}$. Explain your findings.

3 $\mathbf{A}$ and $\mathbf{B}$ are similar matrices if there is a non-singular matrix $\mathbf{P}$ for which $\mathbf{B} = \mathbf{P}^{-1}\mathbf{AP}$. Prove that similar matrices have the same characteristic equation.

4 Find two matrices, each of which has the characteristic equation

$$\lambda^3 - 2\lambda^2 - 5\lambda + 6 = 0.$$

5 Justify, if possible, the use of $\mathbf{M}^i = \mathbf{U\Lambda}^i\mathbf{U}^{-1}$ for rational i. Find $\begin{bmatrix} 1 & 0 & 1 \\ 0 & 1 & 0 \\ 1 & 0 & 1 \end{bmatrix}^{1/2}$.

6 The matrix $\mathbf{M} = \begin{bmatrix} a & b & c \\ d & e & f \\ g & h & i \end{bmatrix}$ has eigenvalues $\lambda_1, \lambda_2, \lambda_3$. Prove that

(*a*) $\lambda_1 + \lambda_2 + \lambda_3 = a + e + i$

(*b*) $\lambda_1\lambda_2\lambda_3 = \det(\mathbf{M})$.

SUMMARY

(1) An *eigenvector* of $\mathbf{M}$ is a non-zero vector $\begin{bmatrix} p \\ q \\ r \end{bmatrix}$ such that $\mathbf{M}\begin{bmatrix} p \\ q \\ r \end{bmatrix} = \lambda \begin{bmatrix} p \\ q \\ r \end{bmatrix}$; λ is the corresponding *eigenvalue*.

(2) To find the eigenvalues, solve $\det(\mathbf{M} - \lambda\mathbf{I}) = 0$. This equation in λ is known as the *characteristic equation*.

(3) If $\mathbf{M}$ has real eigenvalues and three 'distinct' eigenvectors, then it can be expressed in the form

$$\mathbf{M} = \mathbf{U\Lambda U}^{-1},$$

where the columns of $\mathbf{U}$ are the eigenvectors of $\mathbf{M}$ and the matrix $\mathbf{\Lambda}$ is a diagonal matrix with entries the corresponding eigenvalues of $\mathbf{M}$.

(4) If $\mathbf{M} = \mathbf{U\Lambda U}^{-1}$, then $\mathbf{M}^n = \mathbf{U\Lambda}^n\mathbf{U}^{-1}$.

(5) *The Cayley–Hamilton theorem:* A square matrix satisfies its own characteristic equation.

8

Matrices

We have already identified several different types of matrices, for example, diagonal matrices, elementary matrices and non-singular matrices, and seen some of their properties. The main aim of this chapter is to look more closely at two further particular types of matrices and investigate some of their properties. The miscellaneous exercise encourages you to explore for yourself some further results connected with matrices, as well as extending the ideas of this chapter to matrices with complex elements.

8.1 THE TRANSPOSE OF A MATRIX

Definition

The *transpose* of a matrix $\mathbf{M}$, written as $\mathbf{M}^{\mathrm{T}}$, is the matrix obtained by writing the rows of $\mathbf{M}$, in order, as columns.

For example, if $\mathbf{M} = \begin{bmatrix} 1 & 2 & 0 \\ -4 & 3 & 6 \end{bmatrix}$, then $\mathbf{M}^{\mathrm{T}} = \begin{bmatrix} 1 & -4 \\ 2 & 3 \\ 0 & 6 \end{bmatrix}$.

($\mathbf{M}'$, $\mathbf{M}^*$ and $\tilde{\mathbf{M}}$ are other notations which are sometimes used for the transpose of a matrix. Note that we shall use $\mathbf{M}^*$ for the complex conjugate of $\mathbf{M}$ later in this chapter.)

Q.1 Evaluate

(*a*) $\mathbf{A} + \mathbf{B}$ (*b*) $\mathbf{A}^{\mathrm{T}}$ (*c*) $\mathbf{B}^{\mathrm{T}}$ (*d*) $(\mathbf{A} + \mathbf{B})^{\mathrm{T}}$
(*e*) $\mathbf{AB}$ (*f*) $\mathbf{BA}$ (*g*) $(\mathbf{AB})^{\mathrm{T}}$ (*h*) $(\mathbf{BA})^{\mathrm{T}}$
(*i*) $\mathbf{A}^{\mathrm{T}}\mathbf{B}^{\mathrm{T}}$ (*j*) $\mathbf{B}^{\mathrm{T}}\mathbf{A}^{\mathrm{T}}$ (*k*) $\mathbf{A}^{\mathrm{T}} + \mathbf{B}^{\mathrm{T}}$

for (i) $\mathbf{A} = \begin{bmatrix} 2 & 3 \\ -4 & 1 \end{bmatrix}$, $\mathbf{B} = \begin{bmatrix} 1 & 0 \\ -3 & 6 \end{bmatrix}$,

and (ii) $\mathbf{A} = \begin{bmatrix} 1 & 2 & -5 \\ 3 & 0 & 4 \\ -1 & -3 & 2 \end{bmatrix}$, $\mathbf{B} = \begin{bmatrix} 6 & -5 & 1 \\ 4 & -3 & 7 \\ -1 & 2 & 0 \end{bmatrix}$.

You will notice from your answers to Q.1 that the transpose of a matrix appears to have the following properties.

Result 1

$$(\mathbf{A} + \mathbf{B})^{\mathrm{T}} = \mathbf{A}^{\mathrm{T}} + \mathbf{B}^{\mathrm{T}}$$

Result 2

$$(\mathbf{AB})^{\mathrm{T}} = \mathbf{B}^{\mathrm{T}}\mathbf{A}^{\mathrm{T}}$$

Q.2 If $\mathbf{A}$ is an arbitrary matrix, under what conditions are $\mathbf{A}^{\mathrm{T}}\mathbf{A}$ and $\mathbf{AA}^{\mathrm{T}}$ defined?

Q.3 If $\mathbf{A}$ is a 2×2 matrix, prove that $\det(\mathbf{A}) = \det(\mathbf{A}^{\mathrm{T}})$. Is this result also true if $\mathbf{A}$ is a 3×3 matrix?

Q.4 If $\mathbf{A} = \begin{bmatrix} a_{11} & a_{12} \\ a_{21} & a_{22} \end{bmatrix}$ and $\mathbf{B} = \begin{bmatrix} b_{11} & b_{12} \\ b_{21} & b_{22} \end{bmatrix}$, prove that $(\mathbf{AB})^{\mathrm{T}} = \mathbf{B}^{\mathrm{T}}\mathbf{A}^{\mathrm{T}}$.

Result 2, which you have proved for 2×2 matrices in Q.4, is true for matrices of any size.

Example 1
Prove Result 2 for 3×3 matrices.

Solution

If $$\mathbf{A} = \begin{bmatrix} a_{11} & a_{12} & a_{13} \\ a_{21} & a_{22} & a_{23} \\ a_{31} & a_{32} & a_{33} \end{bmatrix} \quad \text{and} \quad \mathbf{B} = \begin{bmatrix} b_{11} & b_{12} & b_{13} \\ b_{21} & b_{22} & b_{33} \\ b_{31} & b_{32} & b_{33} \end{bmatrix},$$

then the *ij*-element (i.e. the element in the ith row and jth column) of $(\mathbf{AB})^{\mathrm{T}}$, which is the *ji*-element of $\mathbf{AB}$, is

$$a_{j1}b_{1i} + a_{j2}b_{2i} + a_{j3}b_{3i}.$$

Now $$\mathbf{B}^{\mathrm{T}} = \begin{bmatrix} b_{11} & b_{21} & b_{31} \\ b_{12} & b_{22} & b_{32} \\ b_{13} & b_{23} & b_{33} \end{bmatrix} \quad \text{and} \quad \mathbf{A}^{\mathrm{T}} = \begin{bmatrix} a_{11} & a_{21} & a_{31} \\ a_{12} & a_{22} & a_{32} \\ a_{13} & a_{23} & a_{33} \end{bmatrix},$$

so the *ij*-element of $\mathbf{B}^{\mathrm{T}}\mathbf{A}^{\mathrm{T}}$ is

$$b_{1i}a_{j1} + b_{2i}a_{j2} + b_{3i}a_{j3}.$$

This is the same as the *ij*-element of $(\mathbf{AB})^{\mathrm{T}}$ above, so $(\mathbf{AB})^{\mathrm{T}} = \mathbf{B}^{\mathrm{T}}\mathbf{A}^{\mathrm{T}}$. □

Q.5 If $\mathbf{x}$ and $\mathbf{y}$ are column vectors, how is $\mathbf{x}^{\mathrm{T}}\mathbf{y}$ related to the scalar product $\mathbf{x} \cdot \mathbf{y}$?

8.2 ORTHOGONAL MATRICES

In this section we look more closely at those linear transformations which preserve distance. Such transformations are known as *isometries*. As the origin is an invariant point of a linear transformation, we shall therefore be considering isometries with a fixed point.

Q.6 Which of the transformations represented by the following matrices are isometries?

(a) $\begin{bmatrix} 1 & -4 \\ 0 & 1 \end{bmatrix}$ (b) $\begin{bmatrix} \frac{3}{5} & -\frac{4}{5} \\ \frac{4}{5} & \frac{3}{5} \end{bmatrix}$

(c) $\begin{bmatrix} 0 & -1 \\ -1 & 0 \end{bmatrix}$ (d) $\begin{bmatrix} 1 & -1 \\ 1 & 1 \end{bmatrix}$

(e) $\begin{bmatrix} 1 & 0 & 0 \\ 0 & 1 & 0 \\ 0 & 2 & 1 \end{bmatrix}$ (f) $\begin{bmatrix} 1 & 0 & 0 \\ 0 & 0.6 & 0.8 \\ 0 & -0.8 & 0.6 \end{bmatrix}$

Q.7 For each of the matrices **M** in Q.6, calculate $\mathbf{M}^T\mathbf{M}$.

Q.8 What do you notice about the results of Q.6 and Q.7?

Let us consider the images of $\begin{bmatrix} 1 \\ 0 \end{bmatrix}$ and $\begin{bmatrix} 0 \\ 1 \end{bmatrix}$ under the transformation represented by the matrix $\mathbf{M} = \begin{bmatrix} a & b \\ c & d \end{bmatrix}$.

$$\mathbf{M}\begin{bmatrix} 1 \\ 0 \end{bmatrix} = \begin{bmatrix} a \\ c \end{bmatrix} \quad \text{and} \quad \mathbf{M}\begin{bmatrix} 0 \\ 1 \end{bmatrix} = \begin{bmatrix} b \\ d \end{bmatrix}.$$

If the transformation is an isometry, the lengths of the vectors $\begin{bmatrix} a \\ b \end{bmatrix}$ and $\begin{bmatrix} b \\ d \end{bmatrix}$ will both be 1 and the angle between them will be 90°. (*Why?*)

So we get
$$a^2 + c^2 = 1,$$
$$b^2 + d^2 = 1$$

and
$$\begin{bmatrix} a \\ c \end{bmatrix} \cdot \begin{bmatrix} b \\ d \end{bmatrix} = ab + cd = 0.$$

Therefore
$$\mathbf{M}^T\mathbf{M} = \begin{bmatrix} a & c \\ b & d \end{bmatrix}\begin{bmatrix} a & b \\ c & d \end{bmatrix} = \begin{bmatrix} a^2 + c^2 & ab + cd \\ ab + cd & b^2 + d^2 \end{bmatrix}$$
$$= \begin{bmatrix} 1 & 0 \\ 0 & 1 \end{bmatrix}.$$

So
$$\mathbf{M}^T\mathbf{M} = \mathbf{I}.$$

Definition
A square matrix **M** is said to be *orthogonal* if $\mathbf{M}^T\mathbf{M} = \mathbf{I}$.

Result 3
The separate columns of an orthogonal matrix form unit vectors and are mutually orthogonal (i.e. perpendicular).

We can prove Result 3 for the two-dimensional case as follows:
If the columns of **M** are $\mathbf{x}_1$ and $\mathbf{x}_2$, then the rows of $\mathbf{M}^T$ are $\mathbf{x}_1{}^T$ and $\mathbf{x}_2{}^T$.

Therefore
$$\mathbf{M}^T\mathbf{M} = \begin{bmatrix} \mathbf{x}_1{}^T\mathbf{x}_1 & \mathbf{x}_1{}^T\mathbf{x}_2 \\ \mathbf{x}_2{}^T\mathbf{x}_1 & \mathbf{x}_2{}^T\mathbf{x}_2 \end{bmatrix} = \begin{bmatrix} 1 & 0 \\ 0 & 1 \end{bmatrix}$$

(as we are given that **M** is an orthogonal matrix)

$$\Rightarrow \quad \mathbf{x}_1{}^T\mathbf{x}_1 = \mathbf{x}_2{}^T\mathbf{x}_2 = 1;$$

that is,
$$\mathbf{x}_1 \cdot \mathbf{x}_1 = \mathbf{x}_2 \cdot \mathbf{x}_2 = 1 \quad \text{(see Q.5)}$$

so $\mathbf{x}_1$ and $\mathbf{x}_2$ are unit vectors.

And
$$\mathbf{x}_1{}^T\mathbf{x}_2 = \mathbf{x}_1 \cdot \mathbf{x}_2 = 0 \quad \text{(see Q.5).}$$

That is, $\mathbf{x}_1$ and $\mathbf{x}_2$ are perpendicular vectors.

From geometrical considerations, we know that in the two-dimensional case an isometry is either a rotation or a reflection, so the matrix **M** is of the form

$$\begin{bmatrix} \cos\theta & -\sin\theta \\ \sin\theta & \cos\theta \end{bmatrix} \quad \text{or} \quad \begin{bmatrix} \cos\theta & \sin\theta \\ \sin\theta & -\cos\theta \end{bmatrix}.$$

Q.9 Check Result 3 for the two matrices above.

Q.10 Using the method outlined above, prove Result 3 for the three-dimensional case.

We showed earlier that if an isometry is represented by a matrix **M**, then **M** is an orthogonal matrix (that is, $\mathbf{M}^T\mathbf{M} = \mathbf{I}$). We now prove the converse of this result.

Result 4
If **M** is an orthogonal matrix, then the transformation represented by **M** is an isometry.

If the points P and Q, with position vectors **p** and **q**, are mapped onto the points P' and Q', with position vectors $\mathbf{p}'$ and $\mathbf{q}'$, under the linear transformation represented by the orthogonal matrix **M**,

then
$$\mathbf{p}' = \mathbf{M}\mathbf{p}$$

and
$$\mathbf{q}' = \mathbf{M}\mathbf{q}.$$

Also
$$\mathbf{M}^T\mathbf{M} = \mathbf{I}, \quad \text{as } \mathbf{M} \text{ is an orthogonal matrix.}$$

The vector
$$\mathbf{PQ} = \mathbf{q} - \mathbf{p}$$

and the vector
$$\mathbf{P'Q'} = \mathbf{q}' - \mathbf{p}'$$

so
$$\begin{aligned}(\mathrm{P'Q'})^2 &= (\mathbf{q}' - \mathbf{p}')^T(\mathbf{q}' - \mathbf{p}') \quad \text{(see Q.5)} \\ &= (\mathbf{Mq} - \mathbf{Mp})^T(\mathbf{Mq} - \mathbf{Mp}) \\ &= [\mathbf{M}(\mathbf{q} - \mathbf{p})]^T[\mathbf{M}(\mathbf{q} - \mathbf{p})]\end{aligned}$$

$$\begin{aligned} &= [(\mathbf{q}-\mathbf{p})^T\mathbf{M}^T][\mathbf{M}(\mathbf{q}-\mathbf{p})] && \text{(from Result 2)} \\ &= (\mathbf{q}-\mathbf{p})^T(\mathbf{M}^T\mathbf{M})(\mathbf{q}-\mathbf{p}) \\ &= (\mathbf{q}-\mathbf{p})^T\mathbf{I}(\mathbf{q}-\mathbf{p}) && (\mathbf{M} \text{ is orthogonal}) \\ &= (\mathbf{q}-\mathbf{p})^T(\mathbf{q}-\mathbf{p}) \\ &= (PQ)^2; \end{aligned}$$

that is, distance is preserved.

As this is true for every pair of points P and Q, the transformation represented by **M** is an isometry.

Other properties of orthogonal matrices

Result 5(a)
If **M** is an orthogonal matrix, then $\det(\mathbf{M}) = \pm 1$.

$$\begin{aligned} &\mathbf{M}^T\mathbf{M} = \mathbf{I} \\ \Rightarrow\quad &\det(\mathbf{M}^T\mathbf{M}) = \det(\mathbf{M}^T) \times \det(\mathbf{M}) = \det(\mathbf{I}). \\ \Rightarrow\quad &(\det(\mathbf{M}))^2 = 1, \qquad \text{since } \det(\mathbf{M}^T) = \det(\mathbf{M}), \text{ see Q.3} \\ \Rightarrow\quad &\det(\mathbf{M}) = \pm 1. \end{aligned}$$

$\det(\mathbf{M}) = 1$ will correspond to a *direct* isometry, and $\det(\mathbf{M}) = -1$ will correspond to an *opposite* isometry.

Result 5(b)
For an orthogonal matrix **M**, $\mathbf{M}^{-1}$ exists and is equal to $\mathbf{M}^T$.

Q.11 Check this result for the two cases which arise with 2×2 matrices; that is

$$\mathbf{M} = \begin{bmatrix} \cos\theta & -\sin\theta \\ \sin\theta & \cos\theta \end{bmatrix} \quad\text{and}\quad \mathbf{M} = \begin{bmatrix} \cos\theta & \sin\theta \\ \sin\theta & -\cos\theta \end{bmatrix}.$$

In general, $\mathbf{M}^{-1}$ exists, as $\det(\mathbf{M}) \neq 0$ (see Result 5(*a*)).

As
$$\begin{aligned} &\mathbf{M}^T\mathbf{M} = \mathbf{I}, \\ &(\mathbf{M}^T\mathbf{M})\mathbf{M}^{-1} = \mathbf{I}\mathbf{M}^{-1} && (\text{postmultiplying by } \mathbf{M}^{-1}) \\ \Rightarrow\quad &\mathbf{M}^T(\mathbf{M}\mathbf{M}^{-1}) = \mathbf{M}^{-1} && (\text{associativity}) \\ \Rightarrow\quad &\mathbf{M}^T\mathbf{I} = \mathbf{M}^{-1} \\ \Rightarrow\quad &\mathbf{M}^T = \mathbf{M}^{-1}. \end{aligned}$$

Result 5(c)
The real eigenvalues of **M** are ± 1.

If **M** has a real eigenvalue λ and corresponding eigenvector **x**, then $\mathbf{Mx} = \lambda\mathbf{x}$. As

M is an isometry, the length of the vector **x** is not changed under the transformation, so $\lambda = \pm 1$.

We can now examine the various cases corresponding to the different possible roots of the characteristic equation of **M**.

If **M** is a 2×2 matrix there are four possible cases for λ_1 and λ_2, the eigenvalues of **M**:

(1) $\lambda_1 = +1, \lambda_2 = +1$
(2) $\lambda_1 = +1, \lambda_2 = -1$
(3) $\lambda_1 = -1, \lambda_2 = -1$
(4) no real eigenvalues.

Q.12 Verify that if

(*a*) $\lambda_1 = \lambda_2 = 1$, the transformation is the identity;

(*b*) $\lambda_1 = 1, \lambda_2 = -1$, the transformation is a reflection, the mirror line having normal $\mathbf{x}_2$ (the eigenvector corresponding to λ_2);

(*c*) $\lambda_1 = \lambda_2 = -1$, the transformation is a half-turn;

(*d*) there are no real eigenvalues, the transformation is a rotation, and the angle of rotation can be found by considering the image of $(1, 0)$.

Example 2

Identify the transformation represented by the matrix $\mathbf{M} = \begin{bmatrix} \frac{1}{3} & \frac{2}{3} & \frac{2}{3} \\ -\frac{2}{3} & \frac{2}{3} & -\frac{1}{3} \\ -\frac{2}{3} & -\frac{1}{3} & \frac{2}{3} \end{bmatrix}$.

Solution

It is an isometry, since $\mathbf{M}^T\mathbf{M} = \mathbf{I}$. To find the eigenvalues, we solve

$$\det(\mathbf{M} - \lambda\mathbf{I}) = \det\left(\begin{bmatrix} (\frac{1}{3} - \lambda) & \frac{2}{3} & \frac{2}{3} \\ -\frac{2}{3} & (\frac{2}{3} - \lambda) & -\frac{1}{3} \\ -\frac{2}{3} & -\frac{1}{3} & (\frac{2}{3} - \lambda) \end{bmatrix}\right) = 0.$$

After simplification, we get $(1 - \lambda)[(\frac{1}{3} - \lambda)^2 + \frac{8}{9}] = 0$, so $\lambda = 1$ is the only real eigenvalue.

As there is only one fixed direction, the transformation is a rotation with axis of rotation the corresponding eigenvector **x**.

$$\text{When } \lambda = 1, \quad \begin{bmatrix} -\frac{2}{3} & \frac{2}{3} & \frac{2}{3} \\ -\frac{2}{3} & -\frac{1}{3} & -\frac{1}{3} \\ -\frac{2}{3} & -\frac{1}{3} & -\frac{1}{3} \end{bmatrix} \begin{bmatrix} x \\ y \\ z \end{bmatrix} = \begin{bmatrix} 0 \\ 0 \\ 0 \end{bmatrix},$$

so an eigenvector is

$$\mathbf{x} = \begin{bmatrix} 0 \\ 1 \\ -1 \end{bmatrix}.$$

To find the angle of rotation, we choose a direction perpendicular to $\mathbf{x}$, for example $\begin{bmatrix}1\\0\\0\end{bmatrix}$, and find the angle through which this vector is rotated by $\mathbf{M}$:

$$\mathbf{M}\begin{bmatrix}1\\0\\0\end{bmatrix}=\begin{bmatrix}\frac{1}{3}\\-\frac{2}{3}\\-\frac{2}{3}\end{bmatrix},$$

and the angle between $\begin{bmatrix}1\\0\\0\end{bmatrix}$ and $\begin{bmatrix}\frac{1}{3}\\-\frac{2}{3}\\-\frac{2}{3}\end{bmatrix}$ is $\cos^{-1}\frac{1}{3}\approx 70.5°$. Thus, $\mathbf{M}$ represents a rotation of 70.5° about the line with direction $\begin{bmatrix}0\\1\\-1\end{bmatrix}$. □

We can summarise the six cases which can arise for a 3×3 matrix $\mathbf{M}$ with eigenvalues λ_1, λ_2, λ_3 and corresponding eigenvectors $\mathbf{x}_1$, $\mathbf{x}_2$, $\mathbf{x}_3$:

(1) $\lambda_1=\lambda_2=\lambda_3=1$; this is the identity transformation.

(2) $\lambda_1=1$, the only real eigenvalue; this is a rotation with axis $\mathbf{x}_1$.

(3) $\lambda_1=1$, $\lambda_2=\lambda_3=-1$; this is a special case of (2) – a half-turn.

(4) $\lambda_1=\lambda_2=1$, $\lambda_3=-1$; this is a reflection in the plane with normal $\mathbf{x}_3$.

(5) $\lambda_1=-1$, the only real eigenvalue; we call this transformation a rotary reflection, as it is a reflection in the plane with normal $\mathbf{x}_1$, followed by a rotation about this direction.

(6) $\lambda_1=\lambda_2=\lambda_3=-1$; this is a special case of (5) with a half-turn – it is called a central inversion and can also be obtained by enlarging (-1) times.

Exercise 8A

1 Show that the following matrices are orthogonal, and describe as completely as possible the isometries which they represent:

(*a*) $\begin{bmatrix}\frac{7}{25} & -\frac{24}{25}\\ -\frac{24}{25} & -\frac{7}{25}\end{bmatrix}$ (*b*) $\begin{bmatrix}\frac{5}{13} & -\frac{12}{13}\\ \frac{12}{13} & \frac{5}{13}\end{bmatrix}$

(*c*) $\begin{bmatrix}\frac{1}{\sqrt{2}} & 0 & \frac{1}{\sqrt{2}}\\ \frac{1}{\sqrt{2}} & 0 & -\frac{1}{\sqrt{2}}\\ 0 & 1 & 0\end{bmatrix}$ (*d*) $\begin{bmatrix}\frac{1}{\sqrt{2}} & 0 & \frac{1}{\sqrt{2}}\\ \frac{1}{\sqrt{2}} & 0 & -\frac{1}{\sqrt{2}}\\ 0 & -1 & 0\end{bmatrix}$

(*e*) $\begin{bmatrix}\frac{1}{3} & -\frac{2}{3} & -\frac{2}{3}\\ -\frac{2}{3} & \frac{1}{3} & -\frac{2}{3}\\ -\frac{2}{3} & -\frac{2}{3} & \frac{1}{3}\end{bmatrix}$ (*f*) $\begin{bmatrix}-\frac{7}{9} & \frac{4}{9} & \frac{4}{9}\\ \frac{4}{9} & -\frac{1}{9} & \frac{8}{9}\\ \frac{4}{9} & \frac{8}{9} & -\frac{1}{9}\end{bmatrix}$

2 Find an orthogonal matrix whose first row is a multiple of $[1 \quad 1 \quad 1]$.

3 Show that if **A** and **B** are orthogonal matrices, then **AB** and $\mathbf{A}^{-1}$ are also orthogonal.

4 Prove that if an orthogonal matrix is triangular (either upper or lower), then it is also diagonal.

5 Show that $\begin{bmatrix} \cos\phi & \sin\phi\sin\theta & \sin\phi\cos\theta \\ -\sin\phi & \cos\phi\sin\theta & \cos\phi\cos\theta \\ 0 & \cos\theta & -\sin\theta \end{bmatrix}$ is an orthogonal matrix.

8.3 SYMMETRIC MATRICES

Definition
M is a *symmetric matrix* if $\mathbf{M}^{\mathrm{T}} = \mathbf{M}$.

Q.13 Show that the matrix $\mathbf{M} = \begin{bmatrix} 2 & -2 & 0 \\ -2 & 1 & 2 \\ 0 & 2 & 0 \end{bmatrix}$ has three real eigenvalues and that the matrix which has the eigenvectors of unit length as its columns is an orthogonal matrix **U**. Also calculate $\mathbf{U}^{-1}\mathbf{MU}$.

The results of Q.13 are in fact true for any symmetric matrix **M** with real entries, namely:

(1) The eigenvalues are all real.

(2) The matrix **M** can always be diagonalised, that is, there exists a matrix **U** such that $\mathbf{U}^{-1}\mathbf{MU}$ is a diagonal matrix; furthermore, **U** is an orthogonal matrix.

(a) The eigenvalues of a symmetric matrix M with real entries are all real

Q.14 What is the characteristic equation for the symmetric matrix $\mathbf{M} = \begin{bmatrix} a & h \\ h & b \end{bmatrix}$ (with a, b, h all real numbers)?

Prove that the eigenvalues are both real and unequal unless $a = b$ and $h = 0$.

The corresponding proof for a 3×3 symmetric matrix with real entries uses the ideas of complex numbers.

We are given that $\mathbf{M}^{\mathrm{T}} = \mathbf{M}$ (symmetric)

and $\mathbf{M}^* = \mathbf{M}$, where $\mathbf{M}^*$ is the complex conjugate of **M**.

If λ is any eigenvalue of **M**, and **x** is the corresponding eigenvector,

$$\mathbf{Mx} = \lambda\mathbf{x}$$

$$\Rightarrow \quad \mathbf{x}^{\mathrm{T}}\mathbf{M} = \lambda\mathbf{x}^{\mathrm{T}} \qquad \text{(taking the transpose)}$$

$$\Rightarrow \quad (\mathbf{x}^*)^{\mathrm{T}}\mathbf{M} = \lambda^*(\mathbf{x}^*)^{\mathrm{T}} \qquad \text{(taking the complex conjugate)}$$

$$\Rightarrow \quad (\mathbf{x}^*)^{\mathrm{T}}\mathbf{Mx} = \lambda^*(\mathbf{x}^*)^{\mathrm{T}}\mathbf{x}$$

$$\Rightarrow \quad \lambda(\mathbf{x}^*)^{\mathrm{T}}\mathbf{x} = \lambda^*(\mathbf{x}^*)^{\mathrm{T}}\mathbf{x} \qquad \text{(using } \mathbf{Mx} = \lambda\mathbf{x}\text{)}$$

Since $(\mathbf{x}^*)^{\mathrm{T}}\mathbf{x} \neq 0,$ *(Why?)*

$$\lambda = \lambda^*;$$

that is, the eigenvalues of **M** are all real.

Note: The eigenvalues are not necessarily distinct for 3 × 3 matrices.

(b) $\mathbf{U}^{-1}\mathbf{MU}$ is a diagonal matrix with U an orthogonal matrix

We saw in Chapters 4 and 7 that if all the eigenvalues of a matrix **M** are real and there is a full set of 'distinct' associated eigenvectors, then **M** can be expressed in the form $\mathbf{M} = \mathbf{U\Lambda U}^{-1}$;

that is, $\mathbf{U}^{-1}\mathbf{MU} = \mathbf{\Lambda}$ (a diagonal matrix).

If **M** is a symmetric matrix we want to show that an orthogonal matrix **U** can always be formed. In constructing **U** we choose the eigenvectors of **M** which are of unit length.

We first show that distinct eigenvalues of **M** have mutually orthogonal eigenvectors.

$$\mathbf{Mx}_1 = \lambda_1\mathbf{x}_1 \quad \text{and} \quad \mathbf{Mx}_2 = \lambda_2\mathbf{x}_2 \quad (\lambda_1 \neq \lambda_2)$$

$$\Rightarrow \quad \lambda_1\mathbf{x}_1{}^{\mathrm{T}}\mathbf{x}_2 = (\mathbf{Mx}_1)^{\mathrm{T}}\mathbf{x}_2 = (\mathbf{x}_1{}^{\mathrm{T}}\mathbf{M}^{\mathrm{T}})\mathbf{x}_2$$

$$= \mathbf{x}_1{}^{\mathrm{T}}\mathbf{Mx}_2 \qquad (\text{as } \mathbf{M}^{\mathrm{T}} = \mathbf{M})$$

$$= \lambda_2\mathbf{x}_1{}^{\mathrm{T}}\mathbf{x}_2$$

$$\Rightarrow \quad (\lambda_1 - \lambda_2)\mathbf{x}_1{}^{\mathrm{T}}\mathbf{x}_2 = 0$$

$$\Rightarrow \quad \mathbf{x}_1{}^{\mathrm{T}}\mathbf{x}_2 = 0 \qquad (\text{as } \lambda_1 \neq \lambda_2)$$

That is, $\mathbf{x}_1 \cdot \mathbf{x}_2 = 0,$

so $\mathbf{x}_1$ and $\mathbf{x}_2$ are mutually orthogonal.

If **M** is a 2 × 2 symmetric matrix which is not diagonal, we know that the eigenvalues are real and distinct (see Q.14), so the eigenvectors are mutually orthogonal; therefore **U** is an orthogonal matrix.

If **M** is a 3 × 3 matrix with distinct eigenvalues, then apply the last result of the eigenvectors taken in pairs. How do we deal with the case where there is a repeated eigenvalue, say $\lambda_2 = \lambda_3$? If $\mathbf{x}_1$ and $\mathbf{x}_2$ are the two eigenvectors corresponding to λ_1 and λ_2, we know that $\mathbf{x}_2$ and $\mathbf{x}_3$ are orthogonal. We now choose a vector $\mathbf{x}_3$ such that

$$\mathbf{x}_3 \cdot \mathbf{x}_1 = 0 \quad \text{and} \quad \mathbf{x}_3 \cdot \mathbf{x}_2 = 0;$$

that is, $\mathbf{x}_3{}^{\mathrm{T}}\mathbf{x}_1 = 0$ and $\mathbf{x}_3{}^{\mathrm{T}}\mathbf{x}_2 = 0.$ *(A)*

Since $\mathbf{x}_1$ and $\mathbf{x}_2$ are eigenvectors of **M**, from *(A)* we get

$$\mathbf{x}_3{}^{\mathrm{T}}\mathbf{Mx}_1 = \mathbf{x}_3{}^{\mathrm{T}}\mathbf{Mx}_2 = 0. \qquad (B)$$

When we take the transpose of (B) and remember that $\mathbf{M}$ is a symmetric matrix, we get

$$\mathbf{x}_1{}^{\mathrm{T}}\mathbf{M}\mathbf{x}_3 = \mathbf{x}_2{}^{\mathrm{T}}\mathbf{M}\mathbf{x}_3 = 0;$$

that is, $\mathbf{M}\mathbf{x}_3$ is a vector orthogonal to $\mathbf{x}_1$ and $\mathbf{x}_2$, and is therefore a multiple of $\mathbf{x}_3$. Hence $\mathbf{x}_3$ is the third eigenvector of $\mathbf{M}$, and the three eigenvectors are mutually orthogonal.

Exercise 8B

1 If $\mathbf{A}$ is a 3×3 matrix, show that $\mathbf{A}^{\mathrm{T}}\mathbf{A}$ and $\mathbf{A} + \mathbf{A}^{\mathrm{T}}$ are both symmetric matrices.

2 Find an orthogonal matrix $\mathbf{U}$ such that $\mathbf{U}^{-1}\mathbf{M}\mathbf{U}$ is a diagonal matrix for each of the following matrices $\mathbf{M}$:

(a) $\begin{bmatrix} 17 & 6 \\ 6 & 8 \end{bmatrix}$ (b) $\begin{bmatrix} 6 & -2 \\ -2 & 9 \end{bmatrix}$ (c) $\begin{bmatrix} -\frac{1}{4} & \frac{5}{4} \\ \frac{5}{4} & -\frac{1}{4} \end{bmatrix}$

(d) $\begin{bmatrix} 1 & 0 & 1 \\ 0 & 1 & 0 \\ 1 & 0 & 1 \end{bmatrix}$ (e) $\begin{bmatrix} 0 & 0 & 3 \\ 0 & 0 & 4 \\ 3 & 4 & 0 \end{bmatrix}$ (f) $\begin{bmatrix} 2 & 0 & 36 \\ 0 & 50 & 0 \\ 36 & 0 & 23 \end{bmatrix}$

3 Show that if $\mathbf{U}$ is an orthogonal matrix and $\mathbf{M}$ is a symmetric matrix, then $\mathbf{U}^{-1}\mathbf{M}\mathbf{U}$ is always a symmetric matrix.

4 A square matrix $\mathbf{A}$ is called skew-symmetric if $\mathbf{A}^{\mathrm{T}} = -\mathbf{A}$. Prove that every square matrix can be written as the sum of a symmetric matrix and a skew-symmetric matrix.

In this chapter we have arrived at some particularly important results about symmetric and orthogonal matrices; namely, that if $\mathbf{M}$ is a symmetric matrix with real entries, then all its eigenvalues are real and there is an orthogonal matrix $\mathbf{U}$ such that $\mathbf{U}^{-1}\mathbf{M}\mathbf{U}$ is a diagonal matrix, the diagonal entries being the eigenvalues. We shall see the importance of these results in Chapters 9 and 11 when we discuss quadratic forms and change of basis.

Miscellaneous exercise 8

Questions 9–12 in this exercise require a knowledge of complex numbers.

1 Find two matrices $\mathbf{B}$ and $\mathbf{C}$ (where $\mathbf{B}$ is not a multiple of $\mathbf{C}$) which commute with $\mathbf{A} = \begin{bmatrix} 1 & 2 \\ -3 & 4 \end{bmatrix}$. What is the general form of a matrix which commutes with $\mathbf{A}$?

2 What can we say about a, b, c and d (all real numbers) if

$$\begin{bmatrix} a & b \\ c & d \end{bmatrix}^2 = \begin{bmatrix} a^2 & b^2 \\ c^2 & d^2 \end{bmatrix}?$$

3 If $\mathbf{A} = \begin{bmatrix} 0 & 1 \\ 1 & 2 \end{bmatrix}$, calculate $\mathbf{A}^2$, $\mathbf{A}^3$, $\mathbf{A}^4$ and $\mathbf{A}^5$. Write down a simple relation between $\mathbf{A}^{n+1}$, $\mathbf{A}^n$ and $\mathbf{A}^{n-1}$.

4 If $\mathbf{A}$ is a 2×2 matrix such that $\mathbf{A}^2 = \mathbf{I}$, what can you say about $\mathbf{A}$?

5 Show that the most general form of the matrix $\mathbf{U}$ such that $\mathbf{U}^{-1}\mathbf{MU} = \mathbf{D}$ is of the form $\begin{bmatrix} \lambda & \mu \\ \lambda & -\mu \end{bmatrix}$ where

$$\mathbf{M} = \begin{bmatrix} 3 & -2 \\ -2 & 3 \end{bmatrix} \quad \text{and} \quad \mathbf{D} = \begin{bmatrix} 1 & 0 \\ 0 & 5 \end{bmatrix}.$$

(*Hint:* write $\mathbf{U}^{-1}\mathbf{MU} = \mathbf{D}$ in the form $\mathbf{MU} = \mathbf{UD}$.)

6 Find the most general form for the matrix $\mathbf{U}$ such that $\mathbf{U}^{-1}\mathbf{MU} = \mathbf{D}$ where

$$\mathbf{M} = \begin{bmatrix} 2 & 0 & 0 \\ 0 & 0 & -3 \\ 0 & -3 & 0 \end{bmatrix} \quad \text{and} \quad \mathbf{D} = \begin{bmatrix} 2 & 0 & 0 \\ 0 & 3 & 0 \\ 0 & 0 & -3 \end{bmatrix}.$$

7 We say that $\mathbf{A}$ is *idempotent* if $\mathbf{A}^2 = \mathbf{A}$.

(*a*) If $\mathbf{A} = \begin{bmatrix} a & b \\ c & d \end{bmatrix}$, where a, b, c and d are real numbers, show that (i) if $a + d = 0$, then $b = c = 0$; (ii) if $a + d \neq 0$, $b \neq 0$ and $c = 0$, then either $\mathbf{A} = \begin{bmatrix} 1 & b \\ 0 & 0 \end{bmatrix}$ or $\mathbf{A} = \begin{bmatrix} 0 & b \\ 0 & 1 \end{bmatrix}$; (iii) if $a + d \neq 0$, then $bc \leqslant \frac{1}{4}$. (*Hint:* find a quadratic equation with roots a, d.) Interpret your results geometrically.

(*b*) What are the possible values for an eigenvalue of an idempotent matrix?

8 A square matrix $\mathbf{A}$ is *nilpotent* if $\mathbf{A}^n = \mathbf{0}$ for some integer $n > 1$.

(*a*) Show that $\mathbf{A} = \begin{bmatrix} -1 & -5 & 2 \\ -1 & -2 & 1 \\ -3 & -6 & 3 \end{bmatrix}$ is nilpotent.

(*b*) Find a 2×2 nilpotent matrix in which none of the elements in the matrix is zero.

(*c*) What are the possible eigenvalues of a nilpotent matrix?

9 If $\mathbf{AB} = -\mathbf{BA}$, the matrices $\mathbf{A}$ and $\mathbf{B}$ are said to be *anti-commutative* and the matrix $(\mathbf{AB} - \mathbf{BA})$ is known as the *commutator* of $\mathbf{A}$ and $\mathbf{B}$.

If $\mathbf{P} = \begin{bmatrix} 0 & 1 \\ 1 & 0 \end{bmatrix}$, $\mathbf{Q} = \begin{bmatrix} 1 & 0 \\ 0 & -1 \end{bmatrix}$ and $\mathbf{R} = \begin{bmatrix} 0 & -j \\ j & 0 \end{bmatrix}$ (where $j = \sqrt{-1}$), show that $\mathbf{P}$ and $\mathbf{Q}$, $\mathbf{Q}$ and $\mathbf{R}$, $\mathbf{P}$ and $\mathbf{R}$ are anti-commutative pairs. Calculate the commutator in each case and comment on your results. (These matrices are the Pauli spin matrices used in work on electron spin in quantum theory.)

10 A matrix $\mathbf{H}$ (in which the elements are complex numbers) is said to *Hermitian* if it is equal to its complex conjugate transposed, that is $(\mathbf{H}^*)^{\mathrm{T}} = \mathbf{H}$. (If the elements of $\mathbf{H}$ are real, then $\mathbf{H}$ is symmetric.)

A matrix $\mathbf{U}$ is said to be *unitary* if $(\mathbf{U}^*)^{\mathrm{T}}\mathbf{U} = \mathbf{I}$. (If the elements of $\mathbf{U}$ are real, then $\mathbf{U}$ is orthogonal.)

Prove the following results, which are analogous to the results obtained for real symmetric and orthogonal matrices.

(*a*) $(\mathbf{x}^*)^{\mathrm{T}}\mathbf{x}$ is real and positive, unless $\mathbf{x} = \mathbf{0}$.

(*b*) The eigenvalues of $\mathbf{H}$ are all real.

(*c*) If λ_1 and λ_2 are two distinct eigenvalues of $\mathbf{H}$, and $\mathbf{x}_1$ and $\mathbf{x}_2$ their corresponding eigenvectors, then $(\mathbf{x}_1{}^*)^{\mathrm{T}}\mathbf{x}_2 = 0 = (\mathbf{x}_2{}^*)^{\mathrm{T}}\mathbf{x}_1$.

(*d*) If all the eigenvectors of **H** are distinct, then we can find a unitary matrix **U** such that $\mathbf{U}^{-1}\mathbf{HU} = \mathbf{\Lambda}$, a diagonal matrix with its diagonal entries the eigenvalues of **H**.

(*e*) The product of any number of unitary matrices is unitary. (This implies a similar result for orthogonal matrices.)

(*f*) The product of Hermitian (and of symmetric) matrices is not in general Hermitian (or symmetric).

11 Prove that $\begin{bmatrix} \dfrac{1}{\sqrt{3}} & \dfrac{1+j}{\sqrt{3}} \\ \dfrac{1-j}{\sqrt{3}} & \dfrac{-1}{\sqrt{3}} \end{bmatrix}$ is unitary.

12 Find the eigenvalues of $\mathbf{H} = \begin{bmatrix} 2 & j\sqrt{5} \\ -j\sqrt{5} & -4 \end{bmatrix}$, and the corresponding eigenvectors.

Find the unitary matrix **U**, such that $\mathbf{U}^{-1}\mathbf{HU}$ is a diagonal matrix.

SUMMARY

Definitions

(1) The *transpose* of a matrix **M**, written as $\mathbf{M}^{\mathrm{T}}$, is the matrix obtained by writing the rows of **M**, in order, as columns.

(2) Transformations which preserve distance are known as *isometries*.

(3) A square matrix **M** is said to be *orthogonal* if $\mathbf{M}^{\mathrm{T}}\mathbf{M} = \mathbf{I}$.

(4) **M** is a *symmetric* matrix if $\mathbf{M}^{\mathrm{T}} = \mathbf{M}$.

Results

(1) $(\mathbf{A} + \mathbf{B})^{\mathrm{T}} = \mathbf{A}^{\mathrm{T}} + \mathbf{B}^{\mathrm{T}}$

(2) $(\mathbf{AB})^{\mathrm{T}} = \mathbf{B}^{\mathrm{T}}\mathbf{A}^{\mathrm{T}}$

(3) The separate columns of an orthogonal matrix form unit vectors and are mutually orthogonal.

(4) If **M** is an orthogonal matrix, then the transformation represented by **M** is an isometry.

(5) If **M** is an orthogonal matrix, then (*a*) $\det(\mathbf{M}) = \pm 1$, (*b*) $\mathbf{M}^{-1} = \mathbf{M}^{\mathrm{T}}$, and (*c*) the real eigenvalues of **M** are ± 1.

(6) If **M** is a symmetric matrix, then (*a*) the eigenvalues are all real, and (*b*) there exists an orthogonal matrix **U** such that $\mathbf{U}^{-1}\mathbf{MU}$ is a diagonal matrix.

9

Quadratic forms in two and three dimensions

Equations of the second degree, that is, equations of the form

$$ax^2 + 2hxy + by^2 + 2gx + 2fy + c = 0$$

are known as *conics*. They arise (and hence the name) if we take a section through a 'double cone' as is shown in the next section.

We shall see how we can reduce the equation of a conic to a simpler form by means of the simple transformations of translation and rotation.

Translation
By choosing the appropriate translation (further details are given in question 1 of the miscellaneous exercise), we can reduce the equation to the form

$$ax^2 + 2hxy + by^2 + k = 0$$

(that is, with no terms in x and y).

Rotation
The equation can be further reduced to the form

$$a'x^2 + b'y^2 + k' = 0$$

(that is, with no term in xy) by rotating the conic.

In this chapter, we shall not develop any of the properties of conics, but if you are interested in finding out more about conics, there are a number of suitable books available. Some of the basic results on conics are given on p. 17 of *Formulae in Advanced Mathematics with Statistical Tables* (Cambridge University Press, 1984).

9.1 SECTIONS OF A CONE

If we take a section through a 'double cone' (and not through the vertex), we get three different types of 'curves' (Fig. 1).

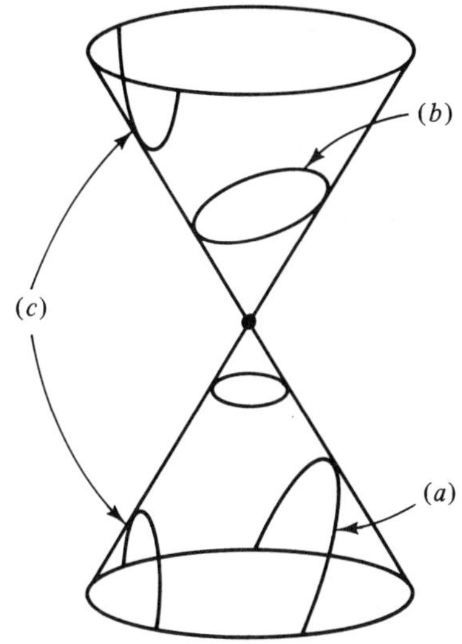

Figure 1

These curves and the standard form of their equations are:

(*a*) *The parabola:* the section is parallel to a generator of the cone (Fig. 2).

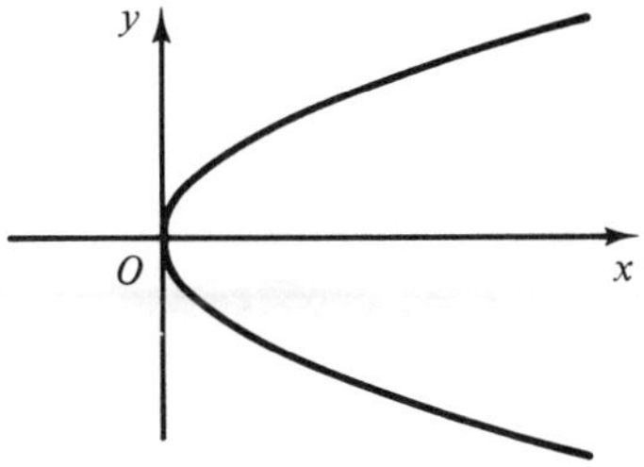

$$y^2 = 4ax$$

Figure 2

(*b*) *The ellipse:* the section cuts either the top or the bottom part of the cone, but not both, and is not parallel to a generator (Fig. 3).

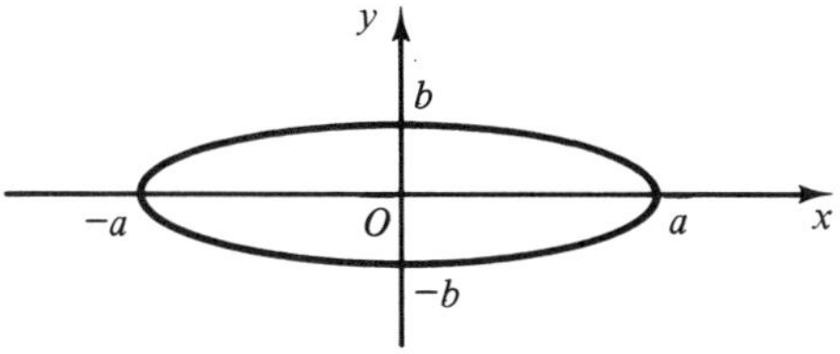

$$\frac{x^2}{a^2} + \frac{y^2}{b^2} = 1$$

Figure 3

(c) *The hyperbola:* the section cuts both parts of the cone (Fig. 4).

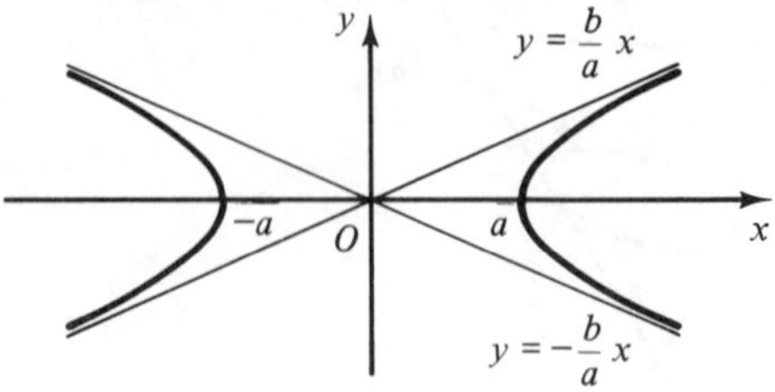

$$\frac{x^2}{a^2} - \frac{y^2}{b^2} = 1$$

Figure 4

If the section goes through the vertex of the cone, we get either a pair of straight lines or a point (Fig. 5)

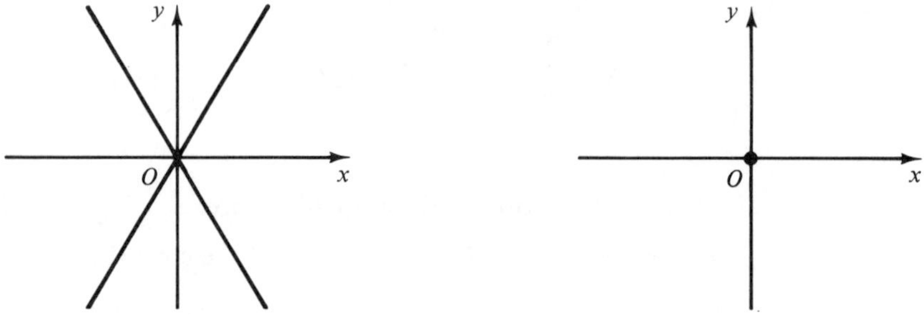

$$\frac{x^2}{a^2} - \frac{y^2}{b^2} = 0 \qquad x^2 + y^2 = 0$$

Figure 5

Exercise 9A

Identify the following conics and sketch their graphs:

1 $4x^2 + 9y^2 = 36$

2 $y^2 = 8x$

3 $x^2 - 2y^2 = 1$

4 $3x^2 + 4y^2 = 48$

5 $4x^2 - 3y^2 = 48$

6 $x^2 = 25 - y^2$

9.2 TRANSFORMATIONS OF CONICS

Example 1
Find the equation of the image of the hyperbola

$$2x^2 - 3y^2 = 1$$

under the transformation represented by the matrix $\begin{bmatrix} 1 & -1 \\ 1 & 1 \end{bmatrix}$.

Solution
There are two possible approaches:

Method 1

If (a, b) is a general point on the conic, we can find the image point (a', b') under the transformation, using

$$\begin{bmatrix} a' \\ b' \end{bmatrix} = \begin{bmatrix} 1 & -1 \\ 1 & 1 \end{bmatrix} \begin{bmatrix} a \\ b \end{bmatrix}.$$

$$\begin{bmatrix} a \\ b \end{bmatrix} = \begin{bmatrix} 1 & -1 \\ 1 & 1 \end{bmatrix}^{-1} \begin{bmatrix} a' \\ b' \end{bmatrix} = \begin{bmatrix} \frac{1}{2} & \frac{1}{2} \\ -\frac{1}{2} & \frac{1}{2} \end{bmatrix} \begin{bmatrix} a' \\ b' \end{bmatrix}$$

so $$a = \tfrac{1}{2}a' + \tfrac{1}{2}b'$$

and $$b = -\tfrac{1}{2}a' + \tfrac{1}{2}b'.$$

But (a, b) lies on the hyperbola $2x^2 - 3y^2 = 1$,

so $$2(\tfrac{1}{2}a' + \tfrac{1}{2}b')^2 - 3(-\tfrac{1}{2}a' + \tfrac{1}{2}b')^2 = 1$$

$$\Rightarrow \quad 2(\tfrac{1}{4}a'^2 + \tfrac{1}{2}a'b' + \tfrac{1}{4}b'^2) - 3(\tfrac{1}{4}a'^2 - \tfrac{1}{2}a'b' + \tfrac{1}{4}b'^2) = 1$$

$$\Rightarrow \quad -\tfrac{1}{4}a'^2 + \tfrac{5}{2}a'b' - \tfrac{1}{4}b'^2 = 1.$$

The equation of the image relative to the original xy-axes is therefore

$$-\tfrac{1}{4}x^2 + \tfrac{5}{2}xy - \tfrac{1}{4}y^2 = 1.$$

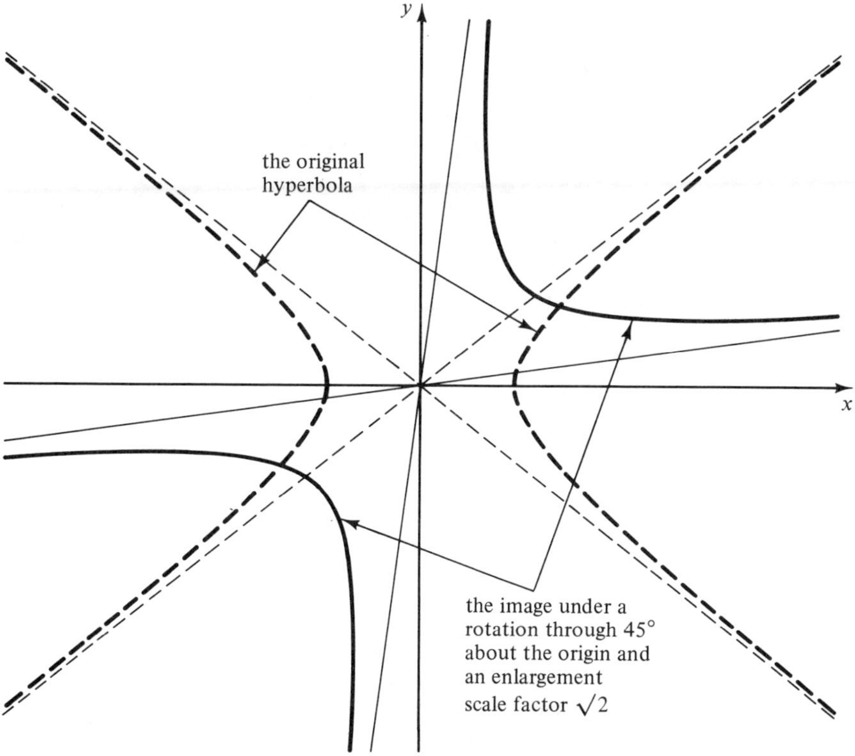

Figure 6

Method 2

This method is based on the fact that $2x^2 - 3y^2 = 1$ can be written in the form $\mathbf{x}^T\begin{bmatrix} 2 & 0 \\ 0 & -3 \end{bmatrix}\mathbf{x} = [1]$, where $\mathbf{x} = \begin{bmatrix} x \\ y \end{bmatrix}$.

Q.1 Check that $2x^2 - 3y^2 = 1$ can be written in the form

$$\mathbf{x}^T\begin{bmatrix} 2 & 0 \\ 0 & -3 \end{bmatrix}\mathbf{x} = [1], \quad \text{where } \mathbf{x} = \begin{bmatrix} x \\ y \end{bmatrix}.$$

If (x, y) is a general point on the conic and (x', y') its image under the transformation represented by $\mathbf{M} = \begin{bmatrix} 1 & -1 \\ 1 & 1 \end{bmatrix}$,

then $$\begin{bmatrix} x' \\ y' \end{bmatrix} = \mathbf{M}\begin{bmatrix} x \\ y \end{bmatrix};$$

that is, $$\mathbf{x}' = \mathbf{M}\mathbf{x}, \quad \text{where } \mathbf{x}' = \begin{bmatrix} x' \\ y' \end{bmatrix},$$

so $$\mathbf{x} = \mathbf{M}^{-1}\mathbf{x}'.$$

$$\mathbf{x}^T\begin{bmatrix} 2 & 0 \\ 0 & -3 \end{bmatrix}\mathbf{x} = [1] \quad \text{becomes} \quad (\mathbf{M}^{-1}\mathbf{x}')^T\begin{bmatrix} 2 & 0 \\ 0 & -3 \end{bmatrix}(\mathbf{M}^{-1}\mathbf{x}') = [1]$$

$$\Rightarrow \quad (\mathbf{x}')^T(\mathbf{M}^{-1})^T\begin{bmatrix} 2 & 0 \\ 0 & -3 \end{bmatrix}\mathbf{M}^{-1}\mathbf{x}' = [1].$$

Now $\mathbf{M} = \begin{bmatrix} 1 & -1 \\ 1 & 1 \end{bmatrix}$, so $\mathbf{M}^{-1} = \begin{bmatrix} \frac{1}{2} & \frac{1}{2} \\ -\frac{1}{2} & \frac{1}{2} \end{bmatrix}$ and $(\mathbf{M}^{-1})^T = \begin{bmatrix} \frac{1}{2} & -\frac{1}{2} \\ \frac{1}{2} & \frac{1}{2} \end{bmatrix}$.

Substituting for $(\mathbf{M}^{-1})^T$ in the equation we get

$$(\mathbf{x}')^T\left(\begin{bmatrix} \frac{1}{2} & -\frac{1}{2} \\ \frac{1}{2} & \frac{1}{2} \end{bmatrix}\begin{bmatrix} 2 & 0 \\ 0 & -3 \end{bmatrix}\begin{bmatrix} \frac{1}{2} & \frac{1}{2} \\ -\frac{1}{2} & \frac{1}{2} \end{bmatrix}\right)\mathbf{x}' = [1],$$

which simplifies to $$(\mathbf{x}')^T\begin{bmatrix} -\frac{1}{4} & \frac{5}{4} \\ \frac{5}{4} & -\frac{1}{4} \end{bmatrix}\mathbf{x}' = [1]$$

or $$-\tfrac{1}{4}x'^2 + \tfrac{5}{2}x'y' - \tfrac{1}{4}y'^2 = 1.$$

So the equation of the image is, as before,

$$-\tfrac{1}{4}x^2 + \tfrac{5}{2}xy - \tfrac{1}{4}y^2 = 1.$$ □

In practice, we usually want to do the reverse of Example 1, that is, to reduce a more complicated equation (such as $-\frac{1}{4}x^2 + \frac{5}{2}xy - \frac{1}{4}y^2 = 1$) to a more convenient form (such as $2x^2 - 3y^2 = 1$). This is the theme of the next section, where we use the ideas introduced in Method 2.

Exercise 9B

Find the equation of the image of each of the following conics under the transformations represented by the given matrices:

	Conic	Matrix
1	$2x^2 + 3y^2 = 1$	$\begin{bmatrix} 1 & 0 \\ 0 & 4 \end{bmatrix}$
2	$x^2 - y^2 = 4$	$\begin{bmatrix} \frac{1}{\sqrt{2}} & -\frac{1}{\sqrt{2}} \\ \frac{1}{\sqrt{2}} & \frac{1}{\sqrt{2}} \end{bmatrix}$
3	$x^2 + y^2 = 9$	$\begin{bmatrix} -1 & 0 \\ 0 & 4 \end{bmatrix}$
4	$\frac{x^2}{4} + \frac{y^2}{9} = 1$	$\begin{bmatrix} 2 & 0 \\ 0 & 3 \end{bmatrix}$
5	$5x^2 - y^2 = 1$	$\begin{bmatrix} 2 & -1 \\ 1 & 2 \end{bmatrix}$
6	$x^2 + y^2 = 1$	$\begin{bmatrix} \frac{3}{5} & -\frac{4}{5} \\ \frac{4}{5} & \frac{3}{5} \end{bmatrix}$

9.3 QUADRATIC FORMS IN TWO DIMENSIONS

Equations of the form $ax^2 + 2hxy + by^2 = 1$ (where a, b, h are real numbers) are known as quadratic forms in two dimensions. We have seen that equations of this form are equations of conics.

In a similar way to that of Method 2 in Example 1, the equation $ax^2 + 2hxy + by^2 = 1$ can be written in matrix form as

$$\begin{bmatrix} x & y \end{bmatrix}\begin{bmatrix} a & h \\ h & b \end{bmatrix}\begin{bmatrix} x \\ y \end{bmatrix} = [1];$$

that is, $\mathbf{x}^{\mathrm{T}}\mathbf{M}\mathbf{x} = [1]$, where $\mathbf{x} = \begin{bmatrix} x \\ y \end{bmatrix}$ and $\mathbf{M} = \begin{bmatrix} a & h \\ h & b \end{bmatrix}$.

(We shall see later why we choose $\mathbf{M}$ to be a symmetric matrix.)

We would like to be able to find an orthogonal transformation (which is an isometry and therefore does not change the shape of the curve) so that the equation of the conic can be expressed in standard form.

Let $\mathbf{U}$ be the matrix of an orthogonal transformation such that

$$\begin{bmatrix} x' \\ y' \end{bmatrix} = \mathbf{U}^{-1}\begin{bmatrix} x \\ y \end{bmatrix}.$$

That is, $\mathbf{x}' = \mathbf{U}^{-1}\mathbf{x}$ or $\mathbf{x} = \mathbf{U}\mathbf{x}'$.

At first sight this may appear to be the wrong way round, but it is consistent with the approach of §3.2, and furthermore leads to an expression which can be simplified as we now see.

The equation of the conic is

$$\begin{aligned} & \mathbf{x}^{\mathrm{T}}\mathbf{M}\mathbf{x} = [1] \\ \Rightarrow\quad & (\mathbf{U}\mathbf{x}')^{\mathrm{T}}\mathbf{M}(\mathbf{U}\mathbf{x}') = [1] \\ \Rightarrow\quad & (\mathbf{x}')^{\mathrm{T}}\mathbf{U}^{\mathrm{T}}\mathbf{M}\mathbf{U}\mathbf{x}' = [1] \\ \Rightarrow\quad & (\mathbf{x}')^{\mathrm{T}}(\mathbf{U}^{-1}\mathbf{M}\mathbf{U})\mathbf{x}' = [1], \quad \text{as } \mathbf{U}^{\mathrm{T}} = \mathbf{U}^{-1} \text{ for an orthogonal matrix.} \end{aligned}$$

In § 8.3 we saw that if $\mathbf{M}$ is a symmetric matrix (hence the reason why we wrote $\mathbf{M} = \begin{bmatrix} a & h \\ h & b \end{bmatrix}$), then we can find an orthogonal matrix $\mathbf{U}$ such that $\mathbf{U}^{-1}\mathbf{M}\mathbf{U}$ is a diagonal matrix, say $\begin{bmatrix} a' & 0 \\ 0 & b' \end{bmatrix}$.

So the new form of the conic is

$$(\mathbf{x}')^{\mathrm{T}}\begin{bmatrix} a' & 0 \\ 0 & b' \end{bmatrix}\mathbf{x}' = [1];$$

that is,

$$a'x'^2 + b'y'^2 = 1.$$

So, relative to the xy-axes, the new equation is

$$a'x^2 + b'y^2 = 1.$$

As the transformation is an isometry, we have not changed the nature of the conic, only its position; so we can identify the conic from the values of a' and b'. The following cases arise:

(1) If a' and b' are both positive, the conic is an ellipse.

(2) If a' and b' differ in sign, the conic is a hyperbola.

(3) If a' and b' are both non-positive, no locus exists.

(4) If one of a' or b' is zero and the other is positive, there is a pair of straight lines.

Example 2

Identify the conic $17x^2 + 12xy + 8y^2 = 1$.

Solution

The matrix $\mathbf{M} = \begin{bmatrix} 17 & 6 \\ 6 & 8 \end{bmatrix}$ has eigenvalues $\lambda = 5$ and 20 and the corresponding *unit* eigenvectors are $\begin{bmatrix} \frac{1}{\sqrt{5}} \\ -\frac{2}{\sqrt{5}} \end{bmatrix}$ and $\begin{bmatrix} \frac{2}{\sqrt{5}} \\ \frac{1}{\sqrt{5}} \end{bmatrix}$, so $\mathbf{U} = \begin{bmatrix} \frac{1}{\sqrt{5}} & \frac{2}{\sqrt{5}} \\ -\frac{2}{\sqrt{5}} & \frac{1}{\sqrt{5}} \end{bmatrix}$.

The new form of the conic is therefore $5x^2 + 20y^2 = 1$, which is an ellipse (Fig. 7).

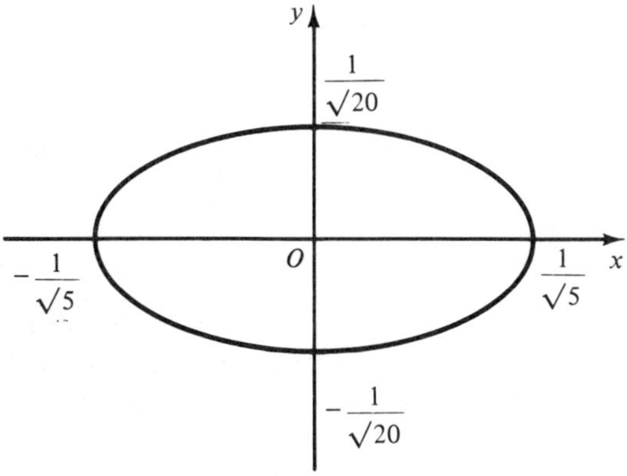

Figure 7

Now $\mathbf{x} = \mathbf{U}\mathbf{x}'$, so the original conic is obtained by applying the transformation represented by $\mathbf{U}$ to the image conic.

$\mathbf{U}$ represents a rotation through $-\cos^{-1}\left(\frac{1}{\sqrt{5}}\right) = -63.4°$, so the original conic is therefore as in Fig. 8.

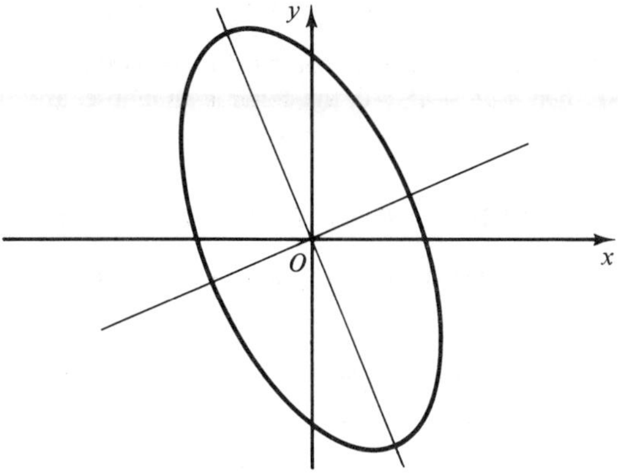

Figure 8

Note that the axes of the ellipse are in the directions of the eigenvectors of $\mathbf{M}$, that is $\begin{bmatrix} \frac{1}{\sqrt{5}} \\ -\frac{2}{\sqrt{5}} \end{bmatrix}$ and $\begin{bmatrix} \frac{2}{\sqrt{5}} \\ \frac{1}{\sqrt{5}} \end{bmatrix}$ referred to the original xy-axes, so their equations are $y = -2x$ and $y = \frac{1}{2}x$. □

Q.2 If we had chosen eigenvectors $\begin{bmatrix} -\frac{1}{\sqrt{5}} \\ \frac{2}{\sqrt{5}} \end{bmatrix}$ and $\begin{bmatrix} \frac{2}{\sqrt{5}} \\ \frac{1}{\sqrt{5}} \end{bmatrix}$, or $\begin{bmatrix} -\frac{1}{\sqrt{5}} \\ \frac{2}{\sqrt{5}} \end{bmatrix}$ and $\begin{bmatrix} -\frac{2}{\sqrt{5}} \\ -\frac{1}{\sqrt{5}} \end{bmatrix}$, or $\begin{bmatrix} \frac{1}{\sqrt{5}} \\ -\frac{2}{\sqrt{5}} \end{bmatrix}$ and $\begin{bmatrix} -\frac{2}{\sqrt{5}} \\ -\frac{1}{\sqrt{5}} \end{bmatrix}$, what difference would it have made to our answer?

We have rotated the conic so that its axes coincide with the xy-axes. An alternative approach would have been to choose new axes which coincide with the axes of the conic. This 'change of basis' is the subject of Chapter 11.

Exercise 9C

In questions 1–8, identify the conics and write them in the form $a'x^2 + b'y^2 = 1$. Find the equations of the axes of the conics.

1 $36x^2 - 24xy + 29y^2 = 1$ **2** $x^2 + 36xy - 14y^2 = 1$

3 $4x^2 + 2xy + 4y^2 = 1$ **4** $2x^2 - 4xy - y^2 = 1$

5 $xy = 8$ **6** $4x^2 - xy + 4y^2 = 10$

7 $5x^2 + 12xy - 4y^2 = 10$ **8** $4x^2 - 4xy + y^2 = 125$

9 By comparing the characteristic equations of $\begin{bmatrix} a & h \\ h & b \end{bmatrix}$ and $\begin{bmatrix} a' & 0 \\ 0 & b' \end{bmatrix}$, show that '$a + b$' and '$ab - h^2$' are invariant under the orthogonal transformation. Hence show that when $a + b > 0$, then if $ab - h^2 > 0$, the conic is an ellipse, and if $ab - h^2 < 0$, the conic is a hyperbola.

9.4 QUADRATIC FORMS IN THREE DIMENSIONS

In three dimensions the situation is very similar. The general form of a *central quadric* is

$$ax^2 + by^2 + cz^2 + 2fyz + 2gzx + 2hxy = 1 \quad \text{(where } a, b, c, f, g, h \text{ are real)},$$

which may be written in matrix form as

$$[x \quad y \quad z]\begin{bmatrix} a & h & g \\ h & b & f \\ g & f & c \end{bmatrix}\begin{bmatrix} x \\ y \\ z \end{bmatrix} = [1];$$

that is, $\mathbf{x}^{\mathrm{T}}\mathbf{M}\mathbf{x} = 1$, where $\mathbf{x} = \begin{bmatrix} x \\ y \\ z \end{bmatrix}$ and $\mathbf{M} = \begin{bmatrix} a & h & g \\ h & b & f \\ g & f & c \end{bmatrix}$.

It represents a surface in three dimensions.

Q.3 Write $3x^2 - 4y^2 + 2z^2 + 3yz - 6zx + 5xy = 1$ in the form

$$\mathbf{x}^{\mathrm{T}}\mathbf{M}\mathbf{x} = [1].$$

As in the two-dimensional case, we can choose an orthogonal matrix **U** so that the quadric can be expressed in the simpler form

$$a'x^2 + b'y^2 + c'z^2 = 1$$

where a', b' and c' are the eigenvalues of **M**. There are three main types of quadric surface, depending on the values of a', b' and c':

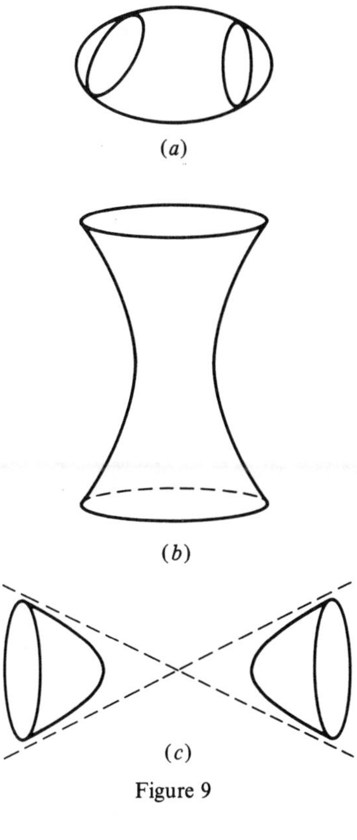

Figure 9

(1) If a', b', c' are all positive, the quadric surface is an *ellipsoid*, a surface in which every cross-section is an ellipse, rather like a rugby ball (Fig. 9(*a*)).

(2) If two of a', b', c' are positive and one negative, the quadric surface is a *hyperboloid of one sheet*, a surface like a waisted flower vase (Fig. 9(*b*)).

(3) If one of a', b', c' is positive and the other two negative, the quadric surface is a *hyperboloid of two sheets* (Fig. 9(c)).

Q.4 What happens if some of a', b', c' are zero?

Example 3

Identify the quadric surface

$$-2x^2 - 2y^2 + z^2 + 4yz + 4zx + 2xy = 1$$

and write it in the form $a'x^2 + b'y^2 + c'z^2 = 1$.

Solution

$\mathbf{M} = \begin{bmatrix} -2 & 1 & 2 \\ 1 & -2 & 2 \\ 2 & 2 & 1 \end{bmatrix}$, and this matrix has eigenvalues 3, -3, -3.

When $\lambda = 3$, the unit eigenvector is $\begin{bmatrix} \frac{1}{\sqrt{6}} \\ \frac{1}{\sqrt{6}} \\ \frac{2}{\sqrt{6}} \end{bmatrix}$.

When $\lambda = -3$, we get the equation of the plane $x + y + 2z = 0$, so we choose as eigenvectors any two vectors in the plane which are mutually perpendicular, for example,

$$\begin{bmatrix} \frac{2}{\sqrt{5}} \\ 0 \\ -\frac{1}{\sqrt{5}} \end{bmatrix} \quad \text{and} \quad \begin{bmatrix} \frac{1}{\sqrt{30}} \\ -\frac{5}{\sqrt{30}} \\ \frac{2}{\sqrt{30}} \end{bmatrix}.$$

These three eigenvectors give the principal axes of the quadric surface and the matrix $\mathbf{U}$ is

$$\begin{bmatrix} \frac{1}{\sqrt{6}} & \frac{2}{\sqrt{5}} & \frac{1}{\sqrt{30}} \\ \frac{1}{\sqrt{6}} & 0 & -\frac{5}{\sqrt{30}} \\ \frac{2}{\sqrt{6}} & -\frac{1}{\sqrt{5}} & \frac{2}{\sqrt{30}} \end{bmatrix}.$$

The new form of the equation is $3x^2 - 3y^2 - 3z^2 = 1$, so we have a hyperboloid of two sheets.

It should be noted that a consequence of two of the eigenvalues being equal is that the surface is a surface of revolution with its axis of symmetry in the direction

$\begin{bmatrix} 1 \\ 1 \\ 2 \end{bmatrix}$ (that is, in the direction perpendicular to the plane $x + y + 2z = 0$), and this explains the freedom of choice we have in choosing two of the principal axes.

If all three eigenvalues were equal, the surface would either be a sphere or would not exist. □

Exercise 9D

Identify the following quadric surfaces and write them in the form $ax^2 + by^2 + cz^2 = 1$. What are the principal axes?

1 $2x^2 - 6yz = 1$

2 $2x^2 + 2y^2 + 2z^2 - 2yz - 2zx - 2xy = 1$

3 $4x^2 + 5y^2 + 6z^2 - 4xy + 4yz = 1$

4 $-2x^2 - y^2 - 4xy - 4zy = 1$

5 $2yz + 2zx + 2xy = 1$

6 $x^2 + y^2 - 2z^2 - 2xy - 4zx - 4yz = 4$

7 $6xy + 8zx = 1$

8 $4x^2 + y^2 + 4z^2 - 4yz - 8zx + 4xy = 9$

By simple isometric transformations we have seen how quadratic forms in two and three dimensions can be expressed as the sum or difference of squared terms, and hence how we can identify the conic or quadric surface. We shall consider this topic from a different point of view in Chapter 11, when instead of transforming the conic or quadric surface we choose new axes. This is known as 'change of basis'.

Miscellaneous exercise 9

1 The general equation of a conic is

$$ax^2 + 2hxy + by^2 + 2gx + 2fy + c = 0.$$

Unless $f = h = 0$ this conic is not centred on the origin. We stated earlier in this chapter that by choosing the appropriate translation the equation can be reduced to the form

$$ax^2 + 2hxy + by^2 + k = 0$$

which has centre the origin.

If the centre is (α, β), the translation required is $-\begin{bmatrix} \alpha \\ \beta \end{bmatrix} = -\boldsymbol{\alpha}$. The old and new position vectors of a point on the conic are therefore connected by

$$\mathbf{x}' = \mathbf{x} - \boldsymbol{\alpha};$$

that is, $$\mathbf{x} = \mathbf{x}' + \boldsymbol{\alpha} \quad \text{or} \quad \begin{bmatrix} x \\ y \end{bmatrix} = \begin{bmatrix} x' \\ y' \end{bmatrix} + \begin{bmatrix} \alpha \\ \beta \end{bmatrix}.$$

If we substitute for x and y in the equation of the conic, we can equate the coefficients of x' and y' to zero and solve for α and β.

Use this method to find the centres of the following conics:

(a) $8x^2 - 12xy + 17y^2 + 10x - 12y + 17 = 0$

(b) $x^2 + 4xy - 2y^2 + 6x - 7y - 13 = 0$

When will the equations in α and β have no solution?

2 Apply the method of question 1 to find the centre of the following quadric surfaces:

(a) $x^2 + yz - xz + 10x - 4y - 2z + 8 = 0$

(b) $-2x^2 - 2y^2 + z^2 + 4yz + 4zx + 2xy + 22x + 4y + 2z - 2 = 0$

3 What condition must $a + b$ and/or $ab - h^2$ satisfy for the conic

$$ax^2 + 2hxy + by^2 = 1$$

to be a pair of straight lines?

Is it possible for the pair of lines not to be parallel?

4 A quadratic form $\mathbf{x}^T\mathbf{M}\mathbf{x}$ is said to be *positive definite* if

$$\mathbf{x}^T\mathbf{M}\mathbf{x} > 0 \quad \text{for all } \mathbf{x} \neq \mathbf{0}.$$

Prove that a quadratic form is positive definite if and only if its eigenvalues are positive.

SUMMARY

(1) Equations of the second degree of the form

$$ax^2 + 2hxy + by^2 + 2gx + 2fy + c = 0$$

are known as *conics*.

(2)

Name of curve	Standard form of the equation
Parabola	$y = 4ax$
Ellipse	$\frac{x^2}{a^2} + \frac{y^2}{b^2} = 1$
Hyperbola	$\frac{x^2}{a^2} - \frac{y^2}{b^2} = 1$

(3) $ax^2 + 2hxy + by^2 = 1$ can be written in matrix form as

$$[x \quad y]\begin{bmatrix} a & h \\ h & b \end{bmatrix}\begin{bmatrix} x \\ y \end{bmatrix} = [1];$$

that is, $\mathbf{x}^T\mathbf{M}\mathbf{x} = [1]$, where $\mathbf{M}$ is the symmetric matrix $\begin{bmatrix} a & h \\ h & b \end{bmatrix}$.

Similarly, $ax^2 + by^2 + cz^2 + 2fyz + 2gzx + 2hxy = 1$ can be written in matrix form as

$$[x \quad y \quad z]\begin{bmatrix} a & h & g \\ h & b & f \\ g & f & c \end{bmatrix}\begin{bmatrix} x \\ y \\ z \end{bmatrix} = [1].$$

(4) When the quadratic form $ax^2 + 2hxy + by^2 = 1$ is reduced to the form

$$a'x^2 + b'y^2 = 1,$$

then if
(*a*) a' and b' are positive, the conic is an *ellipse*;
(*b*) a' and b' differ in sign, the conic is a *hyperbola*.
Similarly, for three dimensions, with $a'x^2 + b'y^2 + c'z^2 = 1$, if
(*a*) a', b', c' are all positive, the quadric surface is an *ellipsoid*;
(*b*) two of a', b', c' are positive and one is negative, the quadric surface is a *hyperboloid of one sheet*;
(*c*) one of a', b', c' is positive and two are negative, the quadric surface is a *hyperboloid of two sheets*.

Revision exercises 5–9

Revision exercise 5

A1 Find the image of the line through the points $(2,1,-5)$, $(-4,2,1)$ under the transformation represented by the matrix $\begin{bmatrix} 2 & 1 & 4 \\ 3 & 0 & -2 \\ 1 & 1 & 5 \end{bmatrix}$.

A2 Describe geometrically the transformations represented by the matrices

(*a*) $\begin{bmatrix} 1 & 0 & 0 \\ 0 & 1 & 0 \\ -3 & 0 & 1 \end{bmatrix}$ (*b*) $\begin{bmatrix} 0 & 1 & 0 \\ -1 & 0 & 0 \\ 0 & 0 & 1 \end{bmatrix}$.

A3 Find the matrix which represents a reflection in the plane $z = y$.

A4 For the following matrices $\mathbf{M}$, calculate $\mathbf{M}^2$, $\mathbf{M}^3$ and $\mathbf{M}^4$:

(*a*) $\begin{bmatrix} 1 & 0 & 0 \\ 0 & \frac{1}{\sqrt{2}} & \frac{1}{\sqrt{2}} \\ 0 & \frac{1}{\sqrt{2}} & -\frac{1}{\sqrt{2}} \end{bmatrix}$ (*b*) $\begin{bmatrix} 1 & 0 & 0 \\ 0 & \frac{1}{\sqrt{2}} & -\frac{1}{\sqrt{2}} \\ 0 & \frac{1}{\sqrt{2}} & \frac{1}{\sqrt{2}} \end{bmatrix}$

In each case give a geometrical explanation for your results.

A5 Prove that the transformation $\mathbf{T}$: $\begin{bmatrix} x \\ y \\ z \end{bmatrix} \mapsto \begin{bmatrix} x+2 \\ y^2 \\ z \end{bmatrix}$ is not a linear transformation.

B1 Describe the geometrical effect of the transformation represented by the matrix $\begin{bmatrix} 1 & 0 & 0 \\ 0 & 0 & 0 \\ 0 & 0 & 1 \end{bmatrix}$. Find the set of points which are transformed into the point $(3,0,-1)$.

B2 Find the equation of the invariant plane for the linear transformation represented by the matrix $\begin{bmatrix} \frac{13}{9} & -\frac{4}{9} & \frac{2}{9} \\ -\frac{4}{9} & \frac{13}{9} & -\frac{2}{9} \\ \frac{2}{9} & -\frac{2}{9} & \frac{10}{9} \end{bmatrix}$.

Investigate what happens to points on the normal to this plane containing the origin under the linear transformation, and so give a geometric description of the linear transformation.

B3 $\mathbf{S}$ is a reflection in the plane $y = 0$, $\mathbf{T}$ is a reflection in the plane $x = z$ and $\mathbf{U}$ is a rotation about the x-axis of 90°. Write down the matrix representing each of these transformations, and give a geometrical description of the transformations $\mathbf{ST}$ and $\mathbf{SU}$.

B4

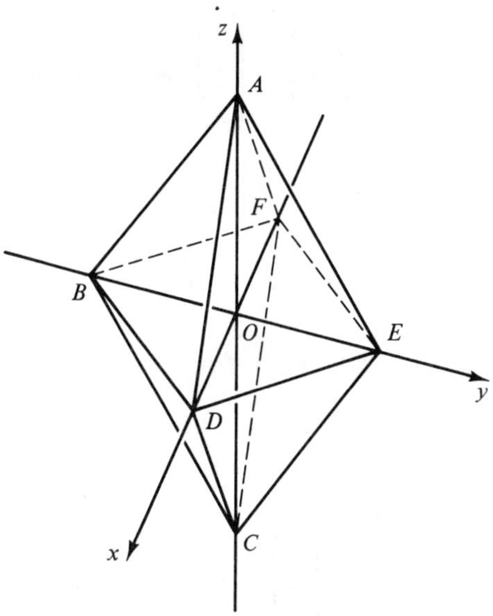

Figure 1

ABCDEF is a regular octahedron. By taking axes $Oxyz$ as shown, find the matrix representing the transformation in which B goes to E, C goes to F and D goes to A.

B5 Show that the linear transformation represented by the matrix $\begin{bmatrix} 2 & 1 & 0 \\ 1 & -3 & 2 \\ 7 & -7 & 6 \end{bmatrix}$ maps every point of three-dimensional space onto the plane $2x + 3y - z = 0$.

Which points are mapped onto the origin under this transformation?

Revision exercise 6

A1 Solve the equations

$$\left.\begin{aligned} x - y + 3z &= 12 \\ 2x + 4y - z &= -3 \\ -x + y + z &= 0 \end{aligned}\right\}$$

and interpret your result geometrically.

A2 Evaluate the determinants of the following matrices:

(*a*) $\begin{bmatrix} 2 & -1 & 3 \\ 4 & 1 & 6 \\ 2 & 0 & -5 \end{bmatrix}$ (*b*) $\begin{bmatrix} 10 & 6 & -7 \\ 11 & 8 & -5 \\ 9 & 5 & 12 \end{bmatrix}$

A3 Find the inverse of the matrix $\begin{bmatrix} -2 & 1 & 3 \\ 6 & 4 & 1 \\ -3 & 2 & 5 \end{bmatrix}$.

A4 If $\mathbf{M} = \begin{bmatrix} 1 & x & x^3 \\ 1 & a & a^3 \\ 1 & b & b^3 \end{bmatrix}$, where $a \neq b$, solve the equation $\det(\mathbf{M}) = 0$.

A5 Explain why $\begin{bmatrix} 1 & -1 & 1 \\ 3 & 1 & 7 \\ 1 & 1 & 3 \end{bmatrix}\begin{bmatrix} x \\ y \\ z \end{bmatrix} = \begin{bmatrix} 3 \\ 1 \\ 1 \end{bmatrix}$ has no solution.

B1 Find the solution set of the equations

$$\begin{bmatrix} 1 & 3 & a \\ 2 & -1 & -5 \\ 1 & 1 & 2 \end{bmatrix}\begin{bmatrix} x \\ y \\ z \end{bmatrix} = \begin{bmatrix} 4 \\ b \\ 1 \end{bmatrix}$$

in the following cases:

(*a*) $a = 9, b = -1$ (*b*) $a = 8, b = -1$ (*c*) $a = 8, b = -2\frac{1}{2}$

For what value of a does the equation

(*d*) $\begin{bmatrix} a & -5 & 2 \\ 3 & -1 & 1 \\ 1 & 2 & 1 \end{bmatrix}\begin{bmatrix} x \\ y \\ z \end{bmatrix} = \begin{bmatrix} 4 \\ 7 \\ 8 \end{bmatrix}$ not have a unique solution?

(*e*) $\begin{bmatrix} a & -10 & 4 \\ 3 & -1 & 1 \\ 1 & 2 & 1 \end{bmatrix}\begin{bmatrix} x \\ y \\ z \end{bmatrix} = \begin{bmatrix} 4 \\ 7 \\ 9 \end{bmatrix}$ not have a unique solution?

[SMP]

B2 (*a*) Prove that if the three vectors $\begin{bmatrix} a \\ b \\ c \end{bmatrix}, \begin{bmatrix} d \\ e \\ f \end{bmatrix}, \begin{bmatrix} g \\ h \\ i \end{bmatrix}$ lie in a plane through the origin, then

$$\det\left(\begin{bmatrix} a & d & g \\ b & e & h \\ c & f & i \end{bmatrix}\right) = 0.$$

(*b*) Find the matrix of the transformation which transforms $A(1, 0, 0)$, $B(0, 2, 0)$ and $C(0, 0, 3)$ to $A'(4, 1, -2)$, $B'(6, 3, 1)$ and $C'(-2, 1, 3)$. Hence find the volume of the parallelepiped defined by the vectors **OA**′, **OB**′, **OC**′.

B3 Let **A** stand for the matrix $\begin{bmatrix} 17 & -4 & 0 \\ 23 & 49 & 3 \\ 18 & 13 & 1 \end{bmatrix}$. Find two matrices $\mathbf{M}_1$, $\mathbf{M}_2$ such that

(*a*) each has only one non-zero entry off the leading diagonal;

(*b*) the product $\mathbf{M}_2\mathbf{M}_1\mathbf{A}$ has zeros above and to the right of the leading diagonal, so that its form is

$$\begin{bmatrix} * & 0 & 0 \\ * & * & 0 \\ * & * & * \end{bmatrix},$$

where the places indicated by the asterisks are occupied by numbers.

From your result deduce the value of the determinant of **A**. [SMP]

B4 Show that there are three values of k for which the equations

$$\left.\begin{aligned} kx + y + 2z &= 0 \\ x - ky &= 0 \\ 4x - 3y + kz &= 0 \end{aligned}\right\}$$

have a non-trivial solution, and find the solutions.

B5 The matrix $\mathbf{M} = \begin{bmatrix} 2 & 1 & -1 \\ -1 & \lambda & 2 \\ 1 & 1 & 0 \end{bmatrix}$. For what values of λ does $\mathbf{M}$ have an inverse?

In the case where $\lambda = 3$, find the inverse $\mathbf{M}^{-1}$ and hence, or otherwise, find the column vector $\mathbf{x}$ such that $\mathbf{Mx} = \begin{bmatrix} 2 \\ 1 \\ -1 \end{bmatrix}$. [MEI]

Revision exercise 7

A1 Show that $\begin{bmatrix} -3 \\ 0 \\ 0 \end{bmatrix}$, $\begin{bmatrix} 0 \\ 7 \\ 7 \end{bmatrix}$ and $\begin{bmatrix} 0 \\ 5 \\ -5 \end{bmatrix}$ are eigenvectors of the matrix $\begin{bmatrix} 2 & 0 & 0 \\ 0 & 0 & -3 \\ 0 & -3 & 0 \end{bmatrix}$ and find the corresponding eigenvalues.

A2 Find the eigenvalues and eigenvectors of the matrix $\begin{bmatrix} 2 & 1 & 3 \\ 0 & 3 & 1 \\ 4 & -4 & 0 \end{bmatrix}$.

A3 Give a geometrical description of the transformation represented by the matrix $\begin{bmatrix} 2 & 1 & 3 \\ 0 & 3 & 1 \\ 4 & -4 & 0 \end{bmatrix}$.

A4 Express the matrix $\begin{bmatrix} 2 & 1 & 3 \\ 0 & 3 & 1 \\ 4 & -4 & 0 \end{bmatrix}$ in the form $\mathbf{U\Lambda U}^{-1}$, where $\mathbf{\Lambda}$ is a diagonal matrix.

A5 Verify that the matrix $\begin{bmatrix} 0 & -2 & 1 \\ 0 & 1 & 3 \\ 0 & 0 & 2 \end{bmatrix}$ satisfies its own characteristic equation.

B1 A matrix $\mathbf{M}$ has eigenvalues 3, -3, 9 and corresponding eigenvectors $\begin{bmatrix} 1 \\ -2 \\ -2 \end{bmatrix}$, $\begin{bmatrix} -2 \\ 1 \\ -2 \end{bmatrix}$ and $\begin{bmatrix} -2 \\ -2 \\ 1 \end{bmatrix}$. Find $\mathbf{M}$.

B2 Find the eigenvalues and eigenvectors of the matrix $\mathbf{A} = \begin{bmatrix} 2 & -2 & 3 \\ 1 & 1 & 1 \\ 1 & 3 & -1 \end{bmatrix}$.

(*a*) Describe the effect of this linear transformation on points on the line $x = y = z$.

(*b*) Explain the nature of the transformation represented by the matrix $(\mathbf{A} - 3\mathbf{I})$, where $\mathbf{I}$ is the unit 3×3 matrix.

B3 If $\mathbf{P} = \begin{bmatrix} 0 & \frac{2}{3} & \frac{2}{3} \\ 1 & 0 & \frac{1}{3} \\ 0 & \frac{1}{3} & 0 \end{bmatrix}$, find the limit of $\mathbf{P}^n$ as $n \to \infty$. How is your result related to the eigenvectors of $\mathbf{P}$?

B4 What are the eigenvalues and eigenvectors of the matrix $\mathbf{M} = \begin{bmatrix} 0 & 1 & 1 \\ 1 & 0 & 1 \\ 1 & 1 & 0 \end{bmatrix}$? Hence find a non-singular matrix $\mathbf{P}$ such that $\mathbf{P}^{-1}\mathbf{M}\mathbf{P}$ is a diagonal matrix.

B5 Find a matrix $\mathbf{B}$ such that $\mathbf{B}^2 = \mathbf{A}$, where $\mathbf{A} = \begin{bmatrix} 1 & 0 & 6 \\ 0 & 9 & 5 \\ 0 & 0 & 4 \end{bmatrix}$.

Revision exercise 8

A1 Find an orthogonal matrix which has a multiple of $\begin{bmatrix} 2 \\ -1 \\ 3 \end{bmatrix}$ as its first column.

A2 If $\mathbf{A} = \begin{bmatrix} 7 & 2 \\ 2 & 4 \end{bmatrix}$, find a matrix $\mathbf{P}$ such that $\mathbf{P}^{\mathrm{T}}\mathbf{P} = \mathbf{I}$ and $\mathbf{P}^{-1}\mathbf{A}\mathbf{P}$ is diagonal.

A3 If $\mathbf{A}$ and $\mathbf{B}$ are symmetric matrices, are $\mathbf{A}^2$ and $\mathbf{AB}$ symmetric matrices?

A4 Show that the matrix $\begin{bmatrix} \frac{5}{13} & 0 & -\frac{12}{13} \\ 0 & 1 & 0 \\ \frac{12}{13} & 0 & \frac{5}{13} \end{bmatrix}$ is orthogonal, and describe the isometry which it represents.

A5 Prove that if the matrix $\mathbf{R}^{-1}\mathbf{X}\mathbf{R}$ is diagonal for some orthogonal matrix $\mathbf{R}$, then $\mathbf{X}$ is symmetric.

B1 Describe the transformation represented by the matrix $\begin{bmatrix} \frac{7}{9} & \frac{4}{9} & -\frac{4}{9} \\ \frac{4}{9} & \frac{1}{9} & \frac{8}{9} \\ -\frac{4}{9} & \frac{8}{9} & \frac{1}{9} \end{bmatrix}$.

B2 Find an orthogonal matrix $\mathbf{U}$ such that $\mathbf{U}^{-1}\mathbf{M}\mathbf{U}$ is a diagonal matrix for

$$\mathbf{M} = \begin{bmatrix} 6 & 2 & 4 \\ 2 & 9 & -2 \\ 4 & -2 & 6 \end{bmatrix}.$$

B3 (*a*) The matrix $\mathbf{A}$ is 3×3 and such that $\mathbf{A}^{-1} = \mathbf{A}^{\mathrm{T}}$ (that is, $\mathbf{A}$ is orthogonal), and

$$\begin{bmatrix} y_1 \\ y_2 \\ y_3 \end{bmatrix} = \mathbf{A} \begin{bmatrix} x_1 \\ x_2 \\ x_3 \end{bmatrix}.$$

Show that $y_1{}^2 + y_2{}^2 + y_3{}^2 = x_1{}^2 + x_2{}^2 + x_3{}^2$.

(*b*) The matrix $\begin{bmatrix} \frac{2}{3} & \frac{2}{3} & -\frac{1}{3} \\ a & b & 0 \\ c & d & e \end{bmatrix}$ is orthogonal (with b and e positive). Determine a, b, c, d, e. [SMP]

B4 (*a*) Show that a matrix and its transpose have the same eigenvalues. Are the eigenvectors the same?

(*b*) If λ is the eigenvalue of an orthogonal matrix, prove that $1/\lambda$ is also an eigenvalue. What is the corresponding eigenvector?

B5 The plane isometry $\mathbf{x} \mapsto \mathbf{Mx}$ is such that the matrix $\mathbf{M}$ has eigenvalues 1 and -1, with corresponding eigenvectors $\mathbf{u}$ and $\mathbf{v}$. It is given that for such an isometry

$$\mathbf{M}^{\mathrm{T}}\mathbf{M} = \mathbf{I}.$$

By considering $(\mathbf{Mu})^{\mathrm{T}}(\mathbf{Mv})$ in two different ways, show that $\mathbf{u}$ is perpendicular to $\mathbf{v}$.

Deduce the nature of the isometry by writing the position vector of the plane in the form $\alpha\mathbf{u} + \beta\mathbf{v}$.

Hence, or otherwise, find the image of the point (10, 10) under reflection in the line $y = 3x$. [SMP]

Revision exercise 9

A1 Sketch the graphs of the following conics:

(*a*) $16x^2 - 9y^2 = 1$ (*b*) $\dfrac{x^2}{25} + 4y^2 = 1$

A2 Find the equation of the image of the ellipse $2x^2 + 3y^2 = 1$ after a rotation of 45° about the origin.

A3 Write $3x^2 - 4y^2 + 2z^2 - 6xy + 4zy = 10$ in the form $\mathbf{x}^{\mathrm{T}}\mathbf{Mx} = [10]$, where $\mathbf{M}$ is a symmetric matrix.

A4 Identify the conic $\mathbf{x}^{\mathrm{T}}\begin{bmatrix} 0 & 2 \\ 2 & 0 \end{bmatrix}\mathbf{x} = [5]$ and sketch it.

A5 Find the lengths of the axes of the ellipse $5x^2 + 4xy + 2y^2 = 72$.

B1 Find the principal axis of the ellipsoid

$$3x^2 + 6y^2 + 2z^2 - 2xy - 2yz - 2zx = 1$$

associated with the integer eigenvalue of the corresponding matrix. [SMP]

B2 Find the eigenvalues of the matrix $\begin{bmatrix} 0 & 6 \\ 6 & 5 \end{bmatrix}$ and for each eigenvalue find a corresponding eigenvector. Use your result to sketch the curve given by the equation $12xy + 5y^2 = 36$.

B3 Find the equation of the ellipse which has axes of length 10 and 4, and with equations of the axes of symmetry $x + 3y = 0$ and $3x - y = 0$, respectively.

B4 Find the eigenvalues of the matrix $\mathbf{M} = \begin{bmatrix} 0 & 1 & -1 \\ 1 & 0 & 1 \\ -1 & 1 & 0 \end{bmatrix}$.

Construct an orthogonal matrix $\mathbf{P}$ such that $\mathbf{P}^{-1}\mathbf{MP}$ is a diagonal matrix.

Use the above results to express the equation of the surface

$$2xy + 2yz - 2zx = 1$$

in the form $ax'^2 + by'^2 + cz'^2 = 1$.

Show that this surface has an axis of rotational symmetry, and find the angles which this makes with the coordinate axes.

B5 Identify the following surfaces:

(*a*) $\mathbf{x}^{\mathrm{T}}\begin{bmatrix} 1 & 1 & 0 \\ 1 & 1 & 0 \\ 0 & 0 & -3 \end{bmatrix}\mathbf{x} = [0]$ (*b*) $\mathbf{x}^{\mathrm{T}}\begin{bmatrix} \frac{1}{2} & 1 & 0 \\ 1 & \frac{1}{2} & 0 \\ 0 & 0 & -\frac{7}{2} \end{bmatrix}\mathbf{x} = [1]$

(*c*) $\mathbf{x}^{\mathrm{T}}\begin{bmatrix} 6 & 1 & 0 \\ 1 & 6 & 0 \\ 0 & 0 & 6 \end{bmatrix}\mathbf{x} = [24]$

Examination questions 1: Chapters 1–9

1 Let
$$\mathbf{A} = \begin{bmatrix} 1 & 0 & 1 \\ 2 & 1 & 2 \\ 0 & -1 & 1 \end{bmatrix}.$$

Find elementary matrices $\mathbf{E}_1$, $\mathbf{E}_2$, $\mathbf{E}_3$ such that

(*a*) $\mathbf{E}_1\mathbf{A}$ has only one non-zero entry in the first column;

(*b*) $\mathbf{E}_2\mathbf{E}_1\mathbf{A}$ has only one non-zero entry in each of the first two columns;

(*c*) $\mathbf{E}_3\mathbf{E}_2\mathbf{E}_1\mathbf{A}$ is the identity matrix.

Use these results to find $\mathbf{A}^{-1}$. [SMP]

2 Linear transformations $\mathbf{L}_k$ of three-dimensional space into itself are given by the matrices
$$\mathbf{A}_k = \begin{bmatrix} 1 & 1 & 1 \\ 1 & k & 0 \\ 1 & 0 & 0 \end{bmatrix}.$$

(*a*) Find the image of the plane $x + y + z = 0$ under $\mathbf{L}_1$.

(*b*) Find the point which maps to $(1, 2, 3)$ under $\mathbf{L}_2$.

(*c*) Prove that $\mathbf{L}_0$ maps the whole space onto a plane, and give the equation of this plane. [O & C]

3 Identify the symmetry transformations represented by the matrices
$$\mathbf{P} = \begin{bmatrix} -1 & 0 \\ 0 & 1 \end{bmatrix} \quad \text{and} \quad \mathbf{Q} = \begin{bmatrix} -\frac{1}{2} & -\frac{1}{2}\sqrt{3} \\ \frac{1}{2}\sqrt{3} & -\frac{1}{2} \end{bmatrix}.$$

Describe geometrically the transformation given by the matrix $\mathbf{R}$ where
$$\mathbf{R} = \mathbf{Q}^{-1}\mathbf{P}\mathbf{Q}.$$

Verify your answer by evaluating the components of $\mathbf{R}$ and investigating the eigenvalues and eigenvectors of $\mathbf{R}$. [SMP]

4 Matrices $\mathbf{A}$, $\mathbf{D}$ are defined by
$$\mathbf{A} = \begin{bmatrix} 1 & -3 & -3 \\ -8 & 6 & -3 \\ 8 & -2 & 7 \end{bmatrix}, \quad \mathbf{D} = \begin{bmatrix} 1 & 0 & 0 \\ 0 & 4 & 0 \\ 0 & 0 & 9 \end{bmatrix}.$$

For each of the eigenvalues $1, 4, 9$ of $\mathbf{A}$ find a corresponding eigenvector. Write down a matrix $\mathbf{P}$ such that $\mathbf{P}^{-1}\mathbf{A}\mathbf{P} = \mathbf{D}$, and calculate $\mathbf{P}^{-1}$.

Write down a matrix $\mathbf{C}$ such that $\mathbf{C}^2 = \mathbf{D}$. Hence, or otherwise, find a matrix $\mathbf{B}$ such that $\mathbf{B}^2 = \mathbf{A}$. [SMP]

5 A linear transformation of the plane has eigenvectors $\begin{bmatrix}-1\\2\end{bmatrix}$ and $\begin{bmatrix}3\\1\end{bmatrix}$, with corresponding eigenvalues -1 and 2. Write down the images under the transformation of $\begin{bmatrix}-1\\2\end{bmatrix}$ and $\begin{bmatrix}3\\1\end{bmatrix}$, and deduce from these the images of $\begin{bmatrix}1\\0\end{bmatrix}$ and $\begin{bmatrix}0\\1\end{bmatrix}$. Hence write down the matrix of the transformation. [SMP]

6 Solve for x, y, z the equations

$$\left.\begin{aligned} x + 2y - z &= 4\\ 3x - 4y + 5z &= -2\\ 5x - 5y + 7z &= -1 \end{aligned}\right\}$$

Describe geometrically the intersection of the three planes given by these equations. [SMP]

7 The eigenvalues of the matrix

$$\mathbf{T} = \begin{bmatrix} a & b\\ c & d\end{bmatrix} \qquad (b > 0, \quad c \geqslant 0)$$

are equal. Prove that $a = d$ and $c = 0$.

If $\mathbf{T}$ maps the point $(-2, 1)$ into the point $(1, 2)$, prove that

$$\mathbf{T} = \begin{bmatrix} 2 & 5\\ 0 & 2\end{bmatrix},$$

and find the image of the line $y + 2x = 0$ under $\mathbf{T}$. [O]

8 $\mathbf{A}$ is the matrix $$\begin{bmatrix} 1 & 2 & -1\\ 2 & 1 & 0\\ 1 & 0 & 1\end{bmatrix}.$$

Find all the values of λ for which $\mathbf{Ax} = \lambda\mathbf{x}$ has a non-zero solution, by solving

$$\det(\mathbf{A} - \lambda\mathbf{I}) = 0$$

where $\mathbf{I}$ is the identity matrix and $\mathbf{x}$ is a 3×1 matrix.

For one such value of λ, find a non-zero vector $\mathbf{x}$ such that $\mathbf{Ax} = \lambda\mathbf{x}$.

Explain the geometrical significance of this result. [C]

9 Find the eigenvalues of the matrix $\begin{bmatrix} 3 & 2\\ 2 & 6\end{bmatrix}$ and for each eigenvalue find a corresponding eigenvector.

Use your results to sketch the plane curve given by the equation

$$3x^2 + 4xy + 6y^2 = 1.$$ [SMP]

10 Show that for $\alpha < 4$ the matrix $\begin{bmatrix} 1 & 2\\ 2 & \alpha\end{bmatrix}$ has non-zero eigenvalues of opposite sign.

What type of graph is represented by the equation

$$x^2 + 4xy + \alpha y^2 = 1$$

where $\alpha < 4$?

Find the principal axes of the curve

$$x^2 + 4xy + y^2 = 1.$$ [SMP]

11 Given that $f(\lambda) \equiv \det\left(\begin{bmatrix} \lambda & 0 & 2\lambda \\ 0 & \lambda & 1 \\ 1 & -1 & \lambda \end{bmatrix}\right)$, find f(2).

Find also the two values of λ, λ_1 and λ_2, for which **M** has no inverse, where

$$\mathbf{M} = \begin{bmatrix} \lambda & 0 & 2\lambda \\ 0 & \lambda & 1 \\ 1 & -1 & \lambda \end{bmatrix}.$$

If $\lambda \neq \lambda_1$ and $\lambda \neq \lambda_2$ find $\mathbf{M}^{-1}$ in terms of λ and write out **M** and $\mathbf{M}^{-1}$ if $\lambda = 2$. Check your result by evaluating $\mathbf{MM}^{-1}$ in this case. [L]

12 Solve completely the system of equations

$$\left.\begin{aligned} x + \ y + \ z &= 4 \\ kx - \ y + 3z &= 5 + k \\ 3x + 6y + kz &= 11 + k \end{aligned}\right\}$$

in the three cases $k = 1, 2, 3$.

Interpret each of your results geometrically. [O & C]

13 Show that the matrix of the linear transformation which reflects the xy-plane in the line $y = x \tan \theta$ is

$$\begin{bmatrix} \cos 2\theta & \sin 2\theta \\ \sin 2\theta & -\cos 2\theta \end{bmatrix}.$$

Find

(*a*) the coordinates of the reflection of the point $A(a, b)$ in the line $4y = 3x$;

(*b*) the coordinates (p, q) of B, the foot of the perpendicular from A to the line $4y = 3x$.

Given that **T** is the matrix of the transformation which maps every point A into its corresponding point B, find **T**. [T]

14 (*a*) A point P has coordinates (x, y) with respect to the cartesian axes Ox, Oy. Show that the transformation **R** with matrix **M**, where

$$\mathbf{M} = \frac{1}{\sqrt{2}}\begin{bmatrix} 1 & 1 \\ -1 & 1 \end{bmatrix},$$

rotates the line OP through $\pi/4$ in a clockwise direction. State the 2×2 matrix of the transformation **T** which reflects each point P in the line $x = 0$. Given that P has coordinates $(2, 1)$ show that the image of OP under the transformation **TR** is perpendicular to the image of OP under the transformation **RT**.

(*b*) Show that the transformation with matrix $\begin{bmatrix} 3 & 1 \\ 9 & 3 \end{bmatrix}$ transforms all points of the plane onto a straight line. Find the equation of this line. [L]

15 (*a*) If $\mathbf{X} = \begin{bmatrix} x \\ y \end{bmatrix}$, $\mathbf{X}_1 = \begin{bmatrix} x_1 \\ y_1 \end{bmatrix}$, $\mathbf{A} = \begin{bmatrix} -5 & 0 \\ 0 & 5 \end{bmatrix}$, find the image of the curve $y = x^2 + 2x + 1$ under the transformation $\mathbf{X}_1 = \mathbf{AX}$. Describe the effect of this transformation on the curve in geometrical terms.

(*b*) Given that

$$\left.\begin{aligned} x + \ y + \ z &= a \\ 2x - \ y + 2z &= b \\ 2x + 2y - \ z &= c \end{aligned}\right\}$$

find x, y, z in terms of a, b and c.

Hence, obtain the inverse of the matrix

$$\begin{bmatrix} 1 & 1 & 1 \\ 2 & -1 & 2 \\ 2 & 2 & -1 \end{bmatrix}.$$ [L]

16 Show that the conic

$$7x^2 - 6\sqrt{3}\,xy + 13y^2 = 64$$

is an ellipse; find the lengths of its axes and the inclination of the major axis to the x-axis. [SMP]

17 (*a*) For the two $n \times n$ non-singular matrices $\mathbf{A}$ and $\mathbf{B}$, prove that $(\mathbf{AB})^{-1} = \mathbf{B}^{-1}\mathbf{A}^{-1}$.

(*b*) Find the eigenvalues and corresponding eigenvectors for the matrix

$$\begin{bmatrix} 1 & 1 & -2 \\ -1 & 2 & 1 \\ 0 & 1 & -1 \end{bmatrix}.$$ [L]

18 (*a*) Show that, for all real values of p, q and r, the matrix

$$\begin{bmatrix} 1 & -q & p \\ q & 1 & -r \\ -p & r & 1 \end{bmatrix}$$

has an inverse.

(*b*) A mapping $(x, y) \mapsto (u, v)$ is given by

$$\begin{bmatrix} u \\ v \end{bmatrix} = \begin{bmatrix} 2 & 1 \\ -8 & -4 \end{bmatrix}\begin{bmatrix} x \\ y \end{bmatrix}.$$

Show briefly that this mapping is not one-to-one.

Find the locus, L, of all points which map to $(1, -4)$. Describe the locus of (u, v) as (x, y) is allowed to vary throughout the plane. Show that any given point, P, on this locus is the image of just one point on the y-axis and describe how the set of all points with image P is related to the locus L. [MEI]

19 A linear transformation is defined by the matrix $\mathbf{A} = \begin{bmatrix} 1 & 1 & 0 \\ 2 & 3 & 1 \\ -2 & 3 & 5 \end{bmatrix}$. Find a vector $\mathbf{v}$ such that $k\mathbf{v}$ is transformed into the zero vector for any scalar k.

Show that, for any vector $\mathbf{u}$, the vector $\mathbf{Au}$ lies in a certain plane, and give the equation of this plane.

Find the eigenvalues and eigenvectors of $\mathbf{A}$. [O]

20 Show that the eigenvalues of the matrix

$$\mathbf{P} = \begin{bmatrix} \frac{1}{4} & \frac{1}{2} \\ \frac{3}{4} & \frac{1}{2} \end{bmatrix}$$

are $-\frac{1}{4}$ and 1, and find corresponding eigenvectors. Deduce a matrix $\mathbf{A}$ such that

$$\mathbf{PA} = \mathbf{A\Lambda}, \quad \text{where} \quad \mathbf{\Lambda} = \begin{bmatrix} -\frac{1}{4} & 0 \\ 0 & 1 \end{bmatrix}.$$

Hence show that $$\mathbf{P}^n \to \begin{bmatrix} \frac{2}{5} & \frac{2}{5} \\ \frac{3}{5} & \frac{3}{5} \end{bmatrix} \quad \text{as } n \to \infty.$$ [SMP]

21 The matrix $\mathbf{M} = \begin{bmatrix} a & b \\ c & d \end{bmatrix}$, and $\mathbf{I} = \begin{bmatrix} 1 & 0 \\ 0 & 1 \end{bmatrix}$. Prove that, if $a + d \neq 0$, then

$$\mathbf{M} = \frac{1}{a+d}[\mathbf{M}^2 + (ad - bc)\mathbf{I}].$$

Prove also that, if $$\mathbf{M}^2 = \begin{bmatrix} p & q \\ r & s \end{bmatrix},$$

then $$p + s = (a+d)^2 - 2(ad - bc)$$

and $$ps - qr = (ad - bc)^2.$$

Hence, or otherwise, find four distinct matrices $\mathbf{M}$ such that

$$\mathbf{M}^2 = \begin{bmatrix} 2 & 1 \\ 2 & 3 \end{bmatrix}.$$

[C]

22 The matrix $\begin{bmatrix} k & 1 & 2 \\ 1 & 0 & 1 \\ 2 & 1 & \frac{5}{2} \end{bmatrix}$ is denoted by $\mathbf{A}_k$.

Evaluate the determinant of $\mathbf{A}_1$ and solve the equations

$$\left.\begin{aligned} x + \quad y + 2z &= \tfrac{3}{2} \\ x \qquad + \quad z &= 1 \\ 2x + \quad y + \tfrac{3}{2}z &= 2 \end{aligned}\right\}$$

Evaluate the determinant of $\mathbf{A}_{\frac{3}{2}}$. State what this value tells you about obtaining solutions of the equations

$$\begin{aligned} \tfrac{3}{2}x + \quad y + 2z &= \tfrac{3}{2} \\ x \qquad + \quad z &= 1, \\ 2x + \quad y + \tfrac{5}{2}z &= 2. \end{aligned}$$

Given that z has the value λ, where λ is an arbitrary constant, find, in terms of λ, corresponding values for x and y. [Cambridge Entrance]

23 Determine the eigenvalues of the matrix $\mathbf{A} = \begin{bmatrix} 5 & -3 \\ -3 & 5 \end{bmatrix}$ and hence find a matrix $\mathbf{P}$ such that $\mathbf{P}^T\mathbf{P} = \mathbf{I}$ and $\mathbf{P}^{-1}\mathbf{AP}$ is diagonal.

(*a*) If $\mathbf{A}$ is the matrix of a linear transformation $\mathbf{f}$, describe the geometrical effect of $\mathbf{f}$ in terms of a sequence of rotations and stretches parallel to the coordinate axes.

(*b*) If $\mathbf{r} = \begin{bmatrix} x \\ y \end{bmatrix}$, show that the conic $\mathbf{r}^T\mathbf{Ar} = 1$ is an ellipse. [O & C]

24 Find the values of λ for which the matrix $\mathbf{M}$, where $\mathbf{M} = \begin{bmatrix} 3-\lambda & -2 \\ -4 & 1-\lambda \end{bmatrix}$, is singular.

For each of these values of λ, describe the geometrical effect of the transformation

$\mathbf{T}: \begin{bmatrix} x \\ y \end{bmatrix} \mapsto \mathbf{M}\begin{bmatrix} x \\ y \end{bmatrix}$.

The matrix $\begin{bmatrix} 3 & -2 \\ -4 & 1 \end{bmatrix}$ is denoted by $\mathbf{A}$, and the transformation $\mathbf{S}$ maps $\begin{bmatrix} x \\ y \end{bmatrix}$ to $\mathbf{A}\begin{bmatrix} x \\ y \end{bmatrix}$. Find the equations of the two lines which are invariant under $\mathbf{S}$.

Describe the effect of **T** on each of these lines for each of the two values of λ found earlier. [C]

25 Find the inverse of the matrix $\begin{bmatrix} 1 & 1 & 1 \\ 1 & 2 & 3 \\ 3 & -2 & 2 \end{bmatrix}$ and hence solve the equations

$$\left.\begin{aligned} x + y + z &= 3 \\ x + 2y + 3z &= -5 \\ 3x - 2y + 2z &= 4 \end{aligned}\right\}$$

[SMP]

Projects 1–4

PROJECT 1 NUMERICAL SOLUTION OF EIGENVALUES USING THE POWER METHOD

If a 2×2 matrix $\mathbf{A}$ has distinct eigenvalues λ_1 and λ_2 with corresponding eigenvectors $\mathbf{e}_1$ and $\mathbf{e}_2$, then any vector $\mathbf{x}$ can be expressed as a linear combination of $\mathbf{e}_1$ and $\mathbf{e}_2$:

$$\mathbf{x} = a\mathbf{e}_1 + b\mathbf{e}_2$$

$$\Rightarrow \quad \mathbf{Ax} = \mathbf{A}(a\mathbf{e}_1 + b\mathbf{e}_2)$$

$$\Rightarrow \quad \mathbf{Ax} = a\mathbf{Ae}_1 + b\mathbf{Ae}_2$$

$$\Rightarrow \quad \mathbf{Ax} = a\lambda_1\mathbf{e}_1 + b\lambda_2\mathbf{e}_2, \text{ as } \mathbf{Ae}_1 = \lambda_1\mathbf{e}_1 \quad \text{and} \quad \mathbf{Ae}_2 = \lambda_2\mathbf{e}_2.$$

After repeated application we get

$$\mathbf{A}^n\mathbf{x} = a\lambda_1{}^n\mathbf{e}_1 + b\lambda_2{}^n\mathbf{e}_2$$
$$= \lambda_1{}^n\left[a\mathbf{e}_1 + b\left(\frac{\lambda_2}{\lambda_1}\right)^n\mathbf{e}_2\right].$$

Now if $|\lambda_1| > |\lambda_2|$, $\left(\frac{\lambda_2}{\lambda_1}\right)^n \to 0$, so the direction of $\mathbf{A}^n\mathbf{x}$ tends to the direction of $\mathbf{e}_1$. If we apply $\mathbf{A}$ often enough we should be able to find the eigenvector $\mathbf{e}_1$ and corresponding eigenvalue λ_1.

Note that this method gives the numerically largest eigenvalue, which in practice is often the only eigenvalue which is needed.

Example 1

Find the numerically largest eigenvalue and corresponding eigenvector of the matrix $\mathbf{A} = \begin{bmatrix} 4.2 & 3.5 \\ 3.5 & 2.7 \end{bmatrix}$.

Solution

If we start with $\mathbf{x}_1 = \begin{bmatrix} 1 \\ 1 \end{bmatrix}$,

$$\mathbf{x}_2 = \mathbf{Ax}_1 = \begin{bmatrix} 4.2 & 3.5 \\ 3.5 & 2.7 \end{bmatrix}\begin{bmatrix} 1 \\ 1 \end{bmatrix} = \begin{bmatrix} 7.7 \\ 6.2 \end{bmatrix}.$$

In order to be able to compare the directions of the vectors $\mathbf{x}_1, \mathbf{x}_2, \ldots$, we must have them in some standard form, for example as unit vectors or as vectors with the first component equal to 1.

If $\mathbf{x}_n = \mathbf{A}\mathbf{x}_{n-1}$, we get the following results:

n	$\mathbf{x}_n$	Vector $\mathbf{x}_n$ scaled so that its first component is 1
1	$\begin{bmatrix} 1 \\ 1 \end{bmatrix}$	$\begin{bmatrix} 1 \\ 1 \end{bmatrix}$
2	$\begin{bmatrix} 7.7 \\ 6.2 \end{bmatrix}$	$\begin{bmatrix} 1 \\ 0.805 \end{bmatrix}$
3	$\begin{bmatrix} 54.04 \\ 43.69 \end{bmatrix}$	$\begin{bmatrix} 1 \\ 0.808 \end{bmatrix}$
4	$\begin{bmatrix} 379.9 \\ 307.1 \end{bmatrix}$	$\begin{bmatrix} 1 \\ 0.808 \end{bmatrix}$

Therefore the eigenvector is $\begin{bmatrix} 1 \\ 0.808 \end{bmatrix}$. As $\mathbf{A}\begin{bmatrix} 1 \\ 0.808 \end{bmatrix} = \begin{bmatrix} 7.03 \\ 5.68 \end{bmatrix} = 7.03\begin{bmatrix} 1 \\ 0.808 \end{bmatrix}$, the corresponding eigenvalue is 7.03. □

Exercise

1 Use this method to find the numerically largest eigenvalue of the following matrices, correct to 3 s.f.:

(*a*) $\begin{bmatrix} 8.2 & 6.2 \\ 1.7 & -1.3 \end{bmatrix}$ (*b*) $\begin{bmatrix} 6.3 & 2.7 \\ 3.1 & 4.1 \end{bmatrix}$ (*c*) $\begin{bmatrix} 2.5 & -2.5 \\ 4.1 & 4.3 \end{bmatrix}$

2 Repeat question 1 for the following matrices:

(*a*) $\begin{bmatrix} 7 & 7 & 4 \\ 2 & 9 & 2 \\ 2 & 1 & 5 \end{bmatrix}$ (*b*) $\begin{bmatrix} 2 & 2 & 1 \\ 2 & 1 & 2 \\ 1 & 2 & 0 \end{bmatrix}$ (*c*) $\begin{bmatrix} 6 & 2 & 0 & 1 \\ 2 & 6 & 1 & 0 \\ 0 & 1 & 6 & 2 \\ 1 & 0 & 2 & 6 \end{bmatrix}$

PROJECT 2 THE SOLUTION OF LINEAR EQUATIONS USING ITERATION

The two methods introduced in this project are illustrated using as an example the linear equations

$$\left.\begin{aligned} 2x + y &= 5 \\ -x + 4y &= 2 \end{aligned}\right\}$$

These can be rearranged to give

$$\left.\begin{aligned} x &= \frac{5-y}{2} \\ y &= \frac{2+x}{4} \end{aligned}\right\}$$

The Jacobi method

This method uses the iterative formulae

$$x_{n+1} = \frac{5-y_n}{2}, \qquad y_{n+1} = \frac{2+x_n}{4}.$$

So, if we take suitable starting values, for example $x_1 = 0$, $y_1 = 0$, we get the following results:

n	x_n	y_n
1	0	0
2	2.5	0.5
3	2.25	1.125
4	1.937 5	1.062 5
5	1.968 75	0.984 375
6	2.007 81	0.992 188
7	2.003 91	1.001 95
8	1.999 02	1.000 98
9	1.999 51	0.999 756
10	2.000 12	0.999 878
11	2.000 06	1.000 03
12	1.999 98	1.000 02
13	1.999 99	0.999 996
14	2.000 00	0.999 998
15	2.000 00	1.000 00
16	2.000 00	1.000 00

So the solution is $x = 2.000\,00$, $y = 1.000\,00$, correct to 6 significant figures.

The Gauss–Seidel method

The method is very similar to the Jacobi method. The only difference is that the new value of x is used as soon as it is calculated, so we use

$$x_{n+1} = \frac{5-y_n}{2}, \qquad y_{n+1} = \frac{2+x_{n+1}}{4}.$$

Starting again with $x_1 = 0$, $y_1 = 0$, we get the following results:

n	x_n	y_n
1	0	0
2	2.5	1.125
3	1.937 5	0.984 375
4	2.007 81	1.001 95
5	1.999 02	0.999 756
6	2.000 12	1.000 03
7	1.999 98	0.999 996
8	2.000 00	1.000 00
9	2.000 00	1.000 00

Again this gives the solution $x = 2.000\,00$, $y = 1.000\,00$, correct to 6 significant figures.

These two methods do not always work for a set of linear equations, but the chances of success are greater if the coefficients on the leading diagonal are large relative to the other coefficients in each equation. Also, the Gauss–Seidel method is likely to converge more rapidly than the Jacobi method.

Exercise

1 Use both the Jacobi and Gauss–Seidel methods to solve the following sets of linear equations:

(*a*) $\left.\begin{aligned} 8x - 2y &= 7 \\ x + 13y &= -8 \end{aligned}\right\}$ (*b*) $\left.\begin{aligned} -4x + 2y &= 16.9 \\ 2x + 5y &= 9.7 \end{aligned}\right\}$

(*c*) $\left.\begin{aligned} 5x - y - 2z &= 2 \\ x + 7y - z &= -2 \\ 2x + 3y - 9z &= 12 \end{aligned}\right\}$ (*d*) $\left.\begin{aligned} 43x - 17y + 9z &= 83 \\ -12x + 32y - 13z &= 117 \\ 23x - 19y + 51z &= -43 \end{aligned}\right\}$

2 Illustrate graphically how these two iterations work by drawing the two lines and plotting the points (x_n, y_n) for the linear equations

$$\left.\begin{aligned} 2x + y &= 5 \\ -x + 4y &= 2 \end{aligned}\right\}$$

(For the Gauss–Seidel method, also plot (x_{n+1}, y_n).)

PROJECT 3 TRANSFORMATIONS OF THE FORM

$$\begin{bmatrix} x \\ y \end{bmatrix} \mapsto \begin{bmatrix} a & b \\ c & d \end{bmatrix}\begin{bmatrix} x \\ y \end{bmatrix} + \begin{bmatrix} e \\ f \end{bmatrix}$$

So far, we have been studying linear transformations and results connected with linear transformations. This project consists of a series of questions through which we investigate non-linear transformations of the form

$$\begin{bmatrix} x \\ y \end{bmatrix} \mapsto \begin{bmatrix} a & b \\ c & d \end{bmatrix}\begin{bmatrix} x \\ y \end{bmatrix} + \begin{bmatrix} e \\ f \end{bmatrix}.$$

Why is this not a linear transformation?

1 By first finding the invariant points, give a geometrical description of the following transformations:

(*a*) $\begin{bmatrix} x \\ y \end{bmatrix} \mapsto \begin{bmatrix} 0 & -1 \\ 1 & 0 \end{bmatrix}\begin{bmatrix} x \\ y \end{bmatrix} + \begin{bmatrix} 3 \\ -2 \end{bmatrix}$

(*b*) $\begin{bmatrix} x \\ y \end{bmatrix} \mapsto \begin{bmatrix} 0 & 1 \\ 1 & 0 \end{bmatrix}\begin{bmatrix} x \\ y \end{bmatrix} + \begin{bmatrix} -3 \\ 3 \end{bmatrix}$

(*c*) $\begin{bmatrix} x \\ y \end{bmatrix} \mapsto \begin{bmatrix} 7 & -4 \\ 9 & -5 \end{bmatrix}\begin{bmatrix} x \\ y \end{bmatrix} + \begin{bmatrix} 2 \\ 3 \end{bmatrix}$

2 Find the matrix representation of the following pairs of transformations and then describe each one as a single transformation:

(*a*) a reflection in $y = 0$, followed by the translation $\begin{bmatrix} 6 \\ 4 \end{bmatrix}$

(*b*) a reflection in $y = x$, followed by the translation $\begin{bmatrix} 3 \\ -1 \end{bmatrix}$

(*c*) a rotation of 90° about (0, 0), followed by the translation $\begin{bmatrix} -2 \\ 4 \end{bmatrix}$

What happens if the pairs of transformations are combined in the reverse order?

3 In order to find the matrix representation of a transformation, it may be necessary to think of the transformation as a sequence of simpler transformations, for example a rotation of 60° about the point $P(3, -4)$ can be achieved by translating P to the origin, performing the rotation and then translating back. Use this idea to find the matrix representations of (*a*) a rotation of 60° about the point $(3, -4)$, (*b*) a reflection in the line $x + y = 4$.

4 Find the single transformation equivalent to a rotation of 90° about the point (3, 5) followed by a reflection in the line $x + y = -2$.

5 Investigate the transformation represented by

$$\begin{bmatrix} x \\ y \end{bmatrix} \mapsto \begin{bmatrix} 2 & 3 \\ 6 & 9 \end{bmatrix}\begin{bmatrix} x \\ y \end{bmatrix} + \begin{bmatrix} 0 \\ 4 \end{bmatrix}.$$

6 Find the matrix representations of the following general transformations:

(*a*) a rotation through $\theta°$ about the point (p, q),

(*b*) a reflection in the line $y = (\tan\theta)x + c$.

7 For the transformation represented by

$$\begin{bmatrix} x \\ y \end{bmatrix} \mapsto \begin{bmatrix} 3 & 2 \\ 1 & -1 \end{bmatrix}\begin{bmatrix} x \\ y \end{bmatrix} + \begin{bmatrix} 1 \\ 3 \end{bmatrix},$$

investigate whether, under this transformation:

(*a*) lines are mapped onto lines;

(*b*) the intersection of two lines is mapped onto the intersection of the image lines;

(*c*) the distance between two points is invariant;

(*d*) the mid-point of a line segment is mapped onto the mid-point of the image line segment;

(*e*) non-collinear points are mapped onto non-collinear points;

(*f*) the angle between two lines is invariant;

(*g*) parallel lines are mapped onto parallel lines.

8 In general it is possible to find a transformation of this form in which three non-collinear points can be mapped onto any three non-collinear points. Find the matrix representation of the transformation in which the points $(2, -4)$, $(-1, 0)$, $(-2, 2)$ are mapped onto the points $(1, 1)$, $(1, 2)$, $(3, 1)$.

9 Show that a corollary of the result of question 8 is that any parallelogram can be mapped into a given square.

10 Transformations of the form

$$\begin{bmatrix} x \\ y \end{bmatrix} \mapsto \begin{bmatrix} a & b \\ c & d \end{bmatrix} \begin{bmatrix} x \\ y \end{bmatrix} + \begin{bmatrix} e \\ f \end{bmatrix}$$

are known as *affine transformations* and the associated geometry is known as *affine geometry*.

Under affine transformations, two of the most important invariant properties are

(1) Parallelism is preserved; and

(2) Ratios are preserved; that is, if P is the point on AB such that $\dfrac{AP}{PB} = \dfrac{\lambda}{\mu}$, then the image point P' is on the line $A'B'$ such that $\dfrac{A'P'}{P'B'} = \dfrac{\lambda}{\mu}$.

We are now able to prove a number of properties of triangles and parallelograms by looking at those properties of special triangles (for example, equilateral or isosceles triangles) and squares which will have remained invariant under an affine transformation.

Use these ideas to prove the following:

(*a*) The medians of a triangle are concurrent.

(*b*) The diagonals of a parallelogram bisect each other.

(*c*) The mid-points of the sides of a parallelogram form the vertices of another parallelogram.

PROJECT 4 EXTENSION TO *n*-DIMENSIONAL SPACE

So far, most of the ideas and results have been introduced using geometrical ideas, and we have restricted ourselves to work in two and three dimensions. We have used two different, but equivalent ways of representing a point: coordinates and position vectors. For example,

	Coordinates		Position vector
In two dimensions	(3, 4)	is equivalent to	$\begin{bmatrix} 3 \\ 4 \end{bmatrix}$
In three dimensions	(4, −2, 3)	is equivalent to	$\begin{bmatrix} 4 \\ -2 \\ 3 \end{bmatrix}$

How important is the link with geometry? You will probably have found it useful in helping you to 'picture' and to grasp the results, but many of these results can also be interpreted in other contexts. For example, the 2×1 vector may represent a probability. Alternatively, a set of linear equations may have arisen from a question about an electrical circuit, in which case the 2×1 or 3×1 vector may represent currents. As the results do not have to be tied to geometry, probability or electricity, we can look for some underlying structure which is common. All involve the use of column vectors, so we can think of the vectors $\begin{bmatrix} x \\ y \end{bmatrix}$ and $\begin{bmatrix} x \\ y \\ z \end{bmatrix}$ as abstract vectors.

What geometrical picture do you have of $\begin{bmatrix} x \\ y \\ z \\ t \end{bmatrix}$? This vector is difficult to visualise, but we can still consider it as the position vector of a 'point' in four-dimensional space. By analogy, for a point in n-dimensional space, we use an $n \times 1$ matrix (that is, a column vector). The usual laws for the addition, multiplication by a real number and multiplication of matrices apply.

This project consists of a series of questions extending the techniques and results which are independent of geometry to n-dimensional space. The methods of approach which you will need are similar to those developed for the two- and three-dimensional cases, though there may be more arithmetic and algebra involved.

(a) Linear transformations

1 Find the image of $\begin{bmatrix} 2 \\ -1 \\ 4 \\ 3 \end{bmatrix}$ under the transformation represented by the matrix $\begin{bmatrix} 4 & 2 & -3 & 1 \\ 6 & 0 & 1 & 4 \\ 2 & -4 & 3 & 0 \\ -5 & 1 & 4 & 3 \end{bmatrix}$.

2 T is a linear transformation and $\mathbf{T}\begin{bmatrix}1\\3\\0\\4\\2\end{bmatrix}=\begin{bmatrix}3\\1\\6\\4\\-3\end{bmatrix}$, $\mathbf{T}\begin{bmatrix}-2\\4\\1\\0\\6\end{bmatrix}=\begin{bmatrix}-1\\5\\4\\-2\\1\end{bmatrix}$.

Find, if possible:

(*a*) $\mathbf{T}\begin{bmatrix}0\\10\\1\\8\\10\end{bmatrix}$ (*b*) $\mathbf{T}\begin{bmatrix}5\\4\\-1\\10\\12\end{bmatrix}$

(b) Linear equations

3 Solve the following equations using systematic elimination, writing down the elementary matrix at each stage:

$$\left.\begin{aligned} x \qquad\qquad\quad - t &= 2\\ 2x + 3y + z \qquad &= 1\\ -5y + 4z \qquad &= -3\\ -z + 2t &= 4 \end{aligned}\right\}$$

4 If the elementary matrices you used in question 3 were $\mathbf{E}_1, \mathbf{E}_2, \ldots, \mathbf{E}_k$ in that order, evaluate $\mathbf{E}_k\mathbf{E}_{k-1}\ldots\mathbf{E}_2\mathbf{E}_1$ and verify that your answer is the inverse of the matrix $\begin{bmatrix}1 & 0 & 0 & -1\\ 2 & 3 & 1 & 0\\ 0 & -5 & 4 & 0\\ 0 & 0 & -1 & 2\end{bmatrix}$.

5 Solve the equations:

(*a*) $$\left.\begin{aligned} x + y - z + t &= 8\\ 2x \qquad + 3z \qquad &= -1\\ x - 5y + z - t &= 0\\ x + 2y \qquad + t &= 5 \end{aligned}\right\}$$

(*b*) $$\left.\begin{aligned} -5x - y + 4z + t &= 14\\ 2x - y + 3z - t &= 2\\ 3y - 7z + 7t &= 18\\ x + y - 2z + 3t &= 10 \end{aligned}\right\}$$

(c) Determinants

Definition

If $\mathbf{A}$ is the 4×4 matrix $\begin{bmatrix}a_1 & b_1 & c_1 & d_1\\ a_2 & b_2 & c_2 & d_2\\ a_3 & b_3 & c_3 & d_3\\ a_4 & b_4 & c_4 & d_4\end{bmatrix}$,

$$\det(\mathbf{A}) = a_1 \det\left(\begin{bmatrix} b_2 & c_2 & d_2 \\ b_3 & c_3 & d_3 \\ b_4 & c_4 & d_4 \end{bmatrix}\right) - a_2 \det\left(\begin{bmatrix} b_1 & c_1 & d_1 \\ b_3 & c_3 & d_3 \\ b_4 & c_4 & d_4 \end{bmatrix}\right)$$
$$+ a_3 \det\left(\begin{bmatrix} b_1 & c_1 & d_1 \\ b_2 & c_2 & d_2 \\ b_4 & c_4 & d_4 \end{bmatrix}\right) - a_4 \det\left(\begin{bmatrix} b_1 & c_1 & d_1 \\ b_2 & c_2 & d_2 \\ b_3 & c_3 & d_3 \end{bmatrix}\right)$$

In a similar way the determinant of a matrix of higher order can be defined.

6 Evaluate the determinants of the following matrices. You may find it helpful to use some of the properties of determinants listed in Chapter 6, which are true for determinants of any order.

(*a*) $\begin{bmatrix} 2 & -3 & 1 & 5 \\ 6 & 0 & 2 & -3 \\ 1 & -1 & 3 & 2 \\ 0 & 4 & -1 & 4 \end{bmatrix}$ (*b*) $\begin{bmatrix} 10 & 5 & -15 & -5 \\ 4 & 12 & 8 & -8 \\ 9 & 6 & 15 & -6 \\ 6 & 2 & -4 & 2 \end{bmatrix}$

(*c*) $\begin{bmatrix} 67 & 43 & 50 & 27 \\ 68 & 44 & 51 & 28 \\ 69 & 45 & 52 & 29 \\ 70 & 46 & 53 & 60 \end{bmatrix}$

(d) Eigenvalues and eigenvectors

7 Find the eigenvalues and eigenvectors of the matrix

$$\mathbf{A} = \begin{bmatrix} 6 & 1 & 1 & -1 \\ 1 & 3 & 1 & -1 \\ 1 & 1 & 3 & -1 \\ -1 & -1 & -1 & 6 \end{bmatrix}.$$

8 $\mathbf{P}$ is the matrix which has as its columns the unit eigenvectors of the matrix $\mathbf{A}$ in question 7.

(*a*) Find $\mathbf{P}^{\mathrm{T}}\mathbf{P}$.
(*b*) Hence write down $\mathbf{P}^{-1}$.
(*c*) Find $\mathbf{P}^{-1}\mathbf{A}\mathbf{P}$.
(*d*) Hence calculate $\mathbf{A}^5$.

9 Find an orthogonal transformation which reduces the quadratic form

$$6x^2 + 3y^2 + 3z^2 + 6t^2 + 2yz + 2zx + 2xy - 2xt - 2yt - 2zt$$

to the sum of squares.

10 Show that the following four-dimensional 'surface' is bounded, and find the smallest four-dimensional 'spherical' region within which the surface lies:

$$\tfrac{3}{2}x^2 + \tfrac{3}{2}y^2 + \tfrac{7}{2}z^2 + \tfrac{7}{2}t^2 - xy + zt = 1$$

10

Introduction to vector spaces

So far, most of the ideas and results have been introduced using geometrical ideas in two and three dimensions. In this chapter we look at several topics which are not connected with geometry, yet find that a number of the same results still hold.

10.1 SEQUENCES

The sequence defined by the relation

$$u_{n+2} = 3u_n - 2u_{n+1} \quad (n \geqslant 1) \tag{A}$$

with $u_1 = 1$ and $u_2 = 0$ has as its first six terms $1, 0, 3, -6, 21, -60$. What are the next two terms?

We introduce a notation for sequences and will refer to the above sequence as

$$\mathbf{p} = (1, 0, 3, -6, 21, -60, \ldots).$$

Another sequence which satisfies (A) and has starting values $u_1 = 0$, $u_2 = 1$ is

$$\mathbf{q} = (0, 1, -2, 7, -20, 61, \ldots).$$

We define the 'addition' of two sequences '$\mathbf{p} + \mathbf{q}$' as the sequence formed by adding corresponding terms of $\mathbf{p}$ and $\mathbf{q}$,

so $$\mathbf{p} + \mathbf{q} = (1, 1, 1, 1, 1, \ldots).$$

By inspection we see that $\mathbf{p} + \mathbf{q}$ also satisfies (A), with the starting values $u_1 = 1$ and $u_2 = 1$.

Q.1 Show that the sum of any two sequences which satisfy the relation (A) also satisfies relation (A).

If we call the set of all the sequences which satisfy the relation (A), S, we know therefore that $\mathbf{p} \in S$ and $\mathbf{q} \in S$. We have shown that $\mathbf{p} + \mathbf{q} \in S$ for these *particular* sequences $\mathbf{p}$ and $\mathbf{q}$. You have also shown in Q.1 that for *any* two sequences $\mathbf{s}_1, \mathbf{s}_2 \in S$, then $\mathbf{s}_1 + \mathbf{s}_2 \in S$. As the 'sum' of *any* two sequences in the set S is also in the set S, we say that S is *closed* with respect to 'addition' (as defined earlier).

If we multiply each term of the sequence $\mathbf{p}$ by 2 we define

$$2\mathbf{p} = (2, 0, 6, -12, 42, -120, \ldots).$$

We see that this sequence also belongs to S.

Q.2 How would you define the sequence $k\mathbf{p}$, where k is a real number? Show that $k\mathbf{p} \in S$.

The result of Q.2 leads us to say that S is *closed* under multiplication by a real number. Sometimes we say that S is closed under multiplication by a scalar, where the scalars are real numbers.

We are now able to define a *linear combination* of **p** and **q** (see also § 2.1) as

$$\lambda\mathbf{p} + \mu\mathbf{q}$$

for real numbers λ and μ. It is a consequence of the results of Q.1 and Q.2 that $\lambda\mathbf{p} + \mu\mathbf{q} \in S$.

Q.3 Express the sequence $\mathbf{r} = (3, -2, 13, -32, 103, \ldots)$ as a linear combination of **p** and **q**.

Q.4 (*a*) If the initial values are $u_1 = -6$ and $u_2 = 3$, write down the first four terms of this sequence **g**. Express **g** as a linear combination of **p** and **q**.

(*b*) If the initial values are $u_1 = a$ and $u_2 = b$, where a and b are real numbers, write down the first four terms of this sequence, **h**. Express **h** as a linear combination of **p** and **q**.

Would it have been possible in part (*b*) to express **h** in terms of just *one* of **p** or **q** for all choices of initial values a and b?

From Q.4 we have discovered that any elements of S can be written as a linear combination of **p** and **q**, and that both **p** and **q** are necessary. We call this set $\{\mathbf{p}, \mathbf{q}\}$, which can be used to generate all the elements in S, a *basis* for the set S. As there are two elements in the basis, we say that the set is of *dimension* 2.

Could there be three elements in the basis for the set S?

Q.5 If

$$\mathbf{p} = (1, 0, 3, -6, 21, -60, \ldots),$$

$$\mathbf{q} = (0, 1, -2, 7, -20, 61, \ldots)$$

and

$$\mathbf{r} = (3, -2, 13, -32, 103, -302, \ldots),$$

express

$$\mathbf{s} = (4, -1, 14, -31, 104, -301, \ldots)$$

as a linear combination of **p**, **q** and **r**. Is your answer unique?

The answer is not unique, for example,

$$\mathbf{s} = \mathbf{p} + \mathbf{q} + \mathbf{r}$$

or

$$\mathbf{s} = -2\mathbf{p} + 3\mathbf{q} + 2\mathbf{r}.$$

Subtracting, we get

$$\mathbf{0} = 3\mathbf{p} - 2\mathbf{q} - \mathbf{r},$$

where **0** stands for the zero sequence, that is, $\mathbf{0} = (0, 0, 0, \ldots)$.

That is, there is a linear combination of **p**, **q** and **r** which gives the zero sequence. When this happens we say that $\{\mathbf{p}, \mathbf{q}, \mathbf{r}\}$ are a *linearly dependent* set. In other words, in this case every time **r** appears we can replace it by $3\mathbf{p} - 2\mathbf{q}$, so **r** is unnecessary. A basis will contain the *minimum* number of elements necessary so that every element in the set can be expressed as a linear combination of the elements of the basis.

On the other hand, the set $\{\mathbf{p}, \mathbf{q}\}$ is a *linearly independent* set, as the only linear combination of **p** and **q**, $\lambda\mathbf{p} + \mu\mathbf{q}$, which gives the zero sequence is when $\lambda = \mu = 0$.

Q.6 Write down any two sequences **s** and **t** which belong to S (that is, they satisfy relation (A)), where $\mathbf{s} \neq k\mathbf{t}$, and express **r** (see Q.3) as a linear combination of **s** and **t**.

It is possible to express any sequence in S as a linear combination of **s** and **t** (show this), so **s** and **t** could equally well be used as a *basis* for S. Furthermore, $\{\mathbf{s}, \mathbf{t}\}$ is a linear independent set, as we were told that $\mathbf{s} \neq k\mathbf{t}$. So the basis for the set S is not unique. Given a basis, all the elements of the set can be uniquely expressed as a linear combination of the elements of that basis. For the set S, $\{\mathbf{p}, \mathbf{q}\}$ is a particularly simple set to use for a basis – why?

10.2 SYMMETRIC MATRICES

We met symmetric matrices in Chapter 8. Let S be the set of 2×2 symmetric matrices; that is,

$$S = \left\{\begin{bmatrix} a & h \\ h & b \end{bmatrix} : a, b, h \in \mathbb{R}\right\}$$

Q.7 If $\mathbf{A}, \mathbf{B} \in S$, are the following true?

(a) $\mathbf{A} + \mathbf{B} \in S$ (where the addition is matrix addition)

(b) $k\mathbf{A} \in S$ (where $k \in \mathbb{R}$)

(This question is really asking whether S is closed under (a) addition of matrices and (b) multiplication by real numbers.)

Q.8 $\mathbf{A}, \mathbf{B}, \mathbf{C}, \mathbf{D} \in S$, where

$$\mathbf{A} = \begin{bmatrix} 1 & 0 \\ 0 & 1 \end{bmatrix}, \quad \mathbf{B} = \begin{bmatrix} 0 & 1 \\ 1 & 0 \end{bmatrix}, \quad \mathbf{C} = \begin{bmatrix} 1 & 0 \\ 0 & -1 \end{bmatrix} \quad \text{and} \quad \mathbf{D} = \begin{bmatrix} -1 & 0 \\ 0 & 1 \end{bmatrix}.$$

(a) Is it possible to express the symmetric matrix $\mathbf{X} = \begin{bmatrix} 3 & 4 \\ 4 & 5 \end{bmatrix}$ as a linear combination of **A** and **B**?

(b) Express **X** as a linear combination of **A**, **B** and **C**.

(c) Express **X** as a linear combination of **A**, **B**, **C** and **D**. Is your answer unique?

(d) What is a basis for S, and what do you think the dimension should be?

(e) Find another basis for S.

Q.9 (*Harder*) Find a basis for the set of 3×3 symmetric matrices.

Q.10 Show that the set of 2×2 orthogonal matrices is (*a*) closed under matrix multiplication but (*b*) not closed under multiplication by real numbers.

10.3 DIFFERENTIAL EQUATIONS

Q.11 $y_1(x)$ and $y_2(x)$ are two solutions of the differential equation

$$\frac{d^2y}{dx^2} - 5\frac{dy}{dx} + 6y = 0.$$

Prove that $y_1(x) + y_2(x)$ and $ky_1(x)$ (where k is a real number) are also solutions.

So we are able to say that the set of solutions of this differential equation is closed under both addition and multiplication by real numbers.

It is shown in calculus books that the general form for the solution of this differential equation is

$$y(x) = Ae^{2x} + Be^{3x} \quad (A, B \in \mathbb{R}).$$

Q.12 Verify that $y(x) = Ae^{2x} + Be^{3x}$ satisfies

$$\frac{d^2y}{dx^2} - 5\frac{dy}{dx} + 6y = 0.$$

Choose a basis for the solution set of this differential equation. What is the dimension of this set?

So we can express any member of the infinite set of solutions of this differential equation simply as a linear combination of the basis elements.

Q.13 If $y_1(x)$ and $y_2(x)$ are two solutions of the differential equation

$$\frac{d^2y}{dx^2} - 5\frac{dy}{dx} + 6y = 30,$$

show that (*a*) $y_1(x) + y_2(x)$, and (*b*) $ky_1(x)$ (where $k \neq 1$) are *not* solutions. Where do the results of Q.11 break down?

This is an example of an infinite set of solutions which cannot be generated from two independent solutions, as the set is not closed under either addition or multiplication by real numbers. The important consequence is that there cannot be a basis for the solution set.

10.4 LINEAR EQUATIONS

Q.14 If (x_1, y_1, z_1) and (x_2, y_2, z_2) are solutions of the linear equations

$$\left.\begin{aligned} 3x + 4y - z &= 0 \\ 2x - y + 3z &= 0 \end{aligned}\right\},$$

are $(x_1 + x_2, y_1 + y_2, z_1 + z_2)$ and (kx_1, ky_1, kz_1) (where k is a real number) also solutions?

Q.15 Solve the equations in Q.14, and hence write down a basis for the solution set. What is the dimension of this solution set?

Because of the closure property proved in Q.14, any member of the solution set of these linear equations can be expressed as a linear combination of the basis elements. So if we consider all possible linear combinations of the basis elements we must have covered all the solutions of these linear equations.

Q.16 Why is it not possible to find a basis for the solution set of the linear equations

$$\left.\begin{aligned} 3x + 4y - z &= 7 \\ 2x + y + 3z &= 3 \end{aligned}\right\}?$$

10.5 GEOMETRICAL VECTORS

In Chapters 1–4 many of the concepts were introduced using geometrical ideas and we wrote vectors as **a**, **b**.

Q.17 Is the set of geometrical vectors in the plane closed under addition and multiplication by real numbers?

We referred in the early chapters to two-dimensional space. 'Two-dimensional' implies that the basis contains two vectors and that every vector in the space can be expressed as a linear combination of these two vectors. This is why the vectors **i** and **j** are referred to as the base vectors in Chapter 1; that is, the basis is the set $\{\mathbf{i}, \mathbf{j}\}$. Of course this is not the only possible basis. Any two linearly independent vectors will do.

Exercise 10A

1 Which of the following are closed under (i) addition, (ii) multiplication by real numbers? For those which are not, give a counter-example.

(*a*) all real solutions of $3x + 4y + 5z = 0$

(*b*) all real solutions of $3x + 4y + 5x \geqslant 0$

(*c*) all real solutions of $\left.\begin{aligned} 3x + 4y + 5z &= 12 \\ x + 2y + z &= 4 \end{aligned}\right\}$

(*d*) all real solutions of $\left.\begin{aligned} 3x + 4y + 5z &= 0 \\ x + 2y + z &= 0 \end{aligned}\right\}$

(*e*) all real solutions of $xy \geqslant 0$

(*f*) all polynomials in x of up to degree 3

(*g*) all quadratic polynomials in x

(*h*) all real solutions of the differential equation $\ddot{x} + 4x = 0$ (these are of the form $x = A\sin 2t + B\cos 2t$)

(*i*) matrices of the form $\begin{bmatrix} 0 & b \\ b & 0 \end{bmatrix}$ $(b \in \mathbb{R})$

2 For each of the examples in question 1 which are closed under both 'addition' and multiplication by real numbers, suggest a basis.

3 Solutions of

$$\left.\begin{aligned} 2w + x + 3y + z &= 0 \\ w - 2x + 5y - z &= 0 \end{aligned}\right\}$$

may be obtained by choosing w and x arbitrarily, and then solving for y and z. Find the solutions for which

(*a*) $w = 1, \quad x = 0$ (*b*) $w = 0, \quad x = 1$ (*c*) $w = 2, \quad x = 6.$

Call these **d**, **e**, **f**.

Write the vectors $\mathbf{a} = \begin{bmatrix} 2 \\ -2 \\ -1 \\ 1 \end{bmatrix}, \mathbf{b} = \begin{bmatrix} 1 \\ 3 \\ 0 \\ -5 \end{bmatrix}$ and $\mathbf{c} = \begin{bmatrix} 5 \\ -1 \\ -2 \\ -3 \end{bmatrix}$ in terms of **d**, **e**. Write each of the vectors **c**, **d**, **e**, **f** as a linear combination of **a**, **b**. Can any pair of **a**, **b**, **c**, **d**, **e**, **f** be chosen as a basis for the set of solution of the above equations?

10.6 VECTOR SPACES

Many of the examples both in the text and in Exercise 10A behave in the same way and are examples of a mathematical system which is called a *vector space*. Elements of a vector space are known as *vectors*. The two main rules we have been investigating are concerned with closure: namely, if $\mathbf{a}, \mathbf{b}, \in S$, then

(1) $$\mathbf{a} + \mathbf{b} \in S \quad \text{and}$$

(2) $$\lambda\mathbf{a} \in S \quad (\lambda \in \mathbb{R}).$$

There are a number of other rules which we have not examined but which are also true in these systems. A full definition will be given in Chapter 15.

Between several of the examples there is an even closer similarity. The sets in the examples in §§10.1, 10.2 and 10.5 all have dimension 2, so we can set up a one-to-one correspondence between the elements of the bases.

One possible correspondence is:

Sequences		*Differential equations*		*Geometrical vectors*
$\mathbf{p}$	$\Leftrightarrow$	e^{2x}	$\Leftrightarrow$	$\mathbf{i}$
$\mathbf{q}$	$\Leftrightarrow$	e^{3x}	$\Leftrightarrow$	$\mathbf{j}$

It is then also true that for $\lambda, \mu \in \mathbb{R}$,

$$\lambda\mathbf{p} + \mu\mathbf{q} \Leftrightarrow \lambda e^{2x} + \mu e^{3x} \Leftrightarrow \lambda\mathbf{i} + \mu\mathbf{j}.$$

We say that the vector spaces are *isomorphic* to each other. In fact all vector spaces of dimension 2 over the real numbers* are isomorphic to each other.

This chapter has provided an informal introduction to vector spaces and some of the terms we shall use in the next few chapters: closure, linear combination, linearly independent, basis and dimension. The most important result of this chapter is demonstrated by the examples of §§10.3 and 10.4, where we saw that if the solution set is closed under addition, and under multiplication by a real number, then the basis elements will generate the complete set of solutions.

The other theme of this chapter is that different mathematical 'objects' may in fact behave in the same way and that they have properties which are independent of the 'object' itself. This means that ideas which have been introduced using a geometrical approach (as in earlier chapters) may be applicable in other contexts, for example to polynomial equations or differential equations.

Miscellaneous exercise 10

1 In a magic square matrix, all rows and columns and diagonals have the same sum. The best known example is

$$\begin{bmatrix} 8 & 1 & 6 \\ 3 & 5 & 7 \\ 4 & 9 & 2 \end{bmatrix}.$$

The elements may be any rational numbers, although some books limit the discussion to sets of consecutive integers, as in the example given.

(*a*) Show that 3×3 magic squares are closed under addition and multiplication by rational numbers.

(*b*) Complete the following magic squares, if possible:

(i) $\begin{bmatrix} 1 & 2 & 3 \\ . & . & . \\ . & . & . \end{bmatrix}$ (ii) $\begin{bmatrix} 1 & . & 3 \\ . & 2 & . \\ . & . & . \end{bmatrix}$ (iii) $\begin{bmatrix} 1 & . & 3 \\ 2 & . & . \\ . & . & . \end{bmatrix}$

(iv) $\begin{bmatrix} 1 & . & . \\ . & . & 2 \\ . & 3 & . \end{bmatrix}$ (v) $\begin{bmatrix} 1 & . & . \\ . & 2 & . \\ . & . & 3 \end{bmatrix}$ (vi) $\begin{bmatrix} 1 & . & . \\ . & . & 2 \\ 1 & 2 & . \end{bmatrix}$

(*c*) What do you think is the dimension of the vector space of 3×3 magic square matrices? Choose a basis and express the magic square matrices found so far in terms of this basis.

(*d*) What is the dimension of the vector space of 2×2 magic square matrices?

2 Carry out an investigation into 4×4 magic square matrices.

* 'Over the real numbers' refers to the second property in which λ is a real number.

SUMMARY

Definitions

S is a set of elements and $\mathbf{u}$, $\mathbf{v}$, $\mathbf{w} \in S$.

(1) S is *closed under addition* if $\mathbf{u} + \mathbf{v} \in S$, for all $\mathbf{u}$, $\mathbf{v} \in S$.

(2) S is *closed under multiplication by real numbers* if $\lambda\mathbf{u} \in S$, for all $\lambda \in \mathbb{R}$.

(3) $\lambda\mathbf{u} + \mu\mathbf{v}$ is a *linear combination* of $\mathbf{u}$ and $\mathbf{v}$, where λ, $\mu \in \mathbb{R}$.

(4) The set $\{\mathbf{u}, \mathbf{v}\}$ is a *linearly independent* set if $\lambda\mathbf{u} + \mu\mathbf{v} = \mathbf{0}$ ($\lambda, \mu \in \mathbb{R}$) only when $\lambda = \mu = 0$.

(5) A linearly independent set $\{\mathbf{u}, \mathbf{v}, \mathbf{w}, \ldots\}$ is called a *basis* if every element in S can be expressed as a linear combination of that set $\{\mathbf{u}, \mathbf{v}, \mathbf{w}, \ldots\}$.

(6) The number of elements required to form a basis is called the *dimension* of the set.

11

Bases

Chapter 10 was an informal introduction to vector spaces and we referred to the elements of a vector space as vectors. This is a wider interpretation of the word 'vector' than was implied in the earlier part of this book, where we concentrated on geometric vectors. From now on, when we refer to a vector, we shall often have this wider interpretation in mind; our 'vectors' may be, for example, polynomials or matrices, or simply 'abstract' vectors, that is, objects which satisfy the definition of a vector space.

We begin by recalling some of the important definitions behind the idea of a basis before we investigate what happens when different bases are used.

11.1 BASIS

Definition 1

A vector $\mathbf{v}$ is said to be a *linear combination* of vectors $\mathbf{a}_1, \mathbf{a}_2, \ldots, \mathbf{a}_n$ if scalars $\lambda_1, \lambda_2, \ldots, \lambda_n$ (not all zero), can be found such that

$$\mathbf{v} = \lambda_1\mathbf{a}_1 + \lambda_2\mathbf{a}_2 + \ldots + \lambda_n\mathbf{a}_n.$$

Example 1

In the vector space V which consists of the set of 2×1 matrices with the components real numbers, that is,

$$V = \left\{\begin{bmatrix} p \\ q \end{bmatrix} : p, q \in \mathbb{R}\right\},$$

express the vector $\mathbf{v} = \begin{bmatrix} 4 \\ -3 \end{bmatrix}$ as a linear combination of

(*a*) $\mathbf{a}_1 = \begin{bmatrix} 2 \\ 1 \end{bmatrix}, \quad \mathbf{a}_2 = \begin{bmatrix} 1 \\ 3 \end{bmatrix}$ (*b*) $\mathbf{b}_1 = \begin{bmatrix} 4 \\ -2 \end{bmatrix}, \quad \mathbf{b}_2 = \begin{bmatrix} -2 \\ 1 \end{bmatrix}$

(*c*) $\mathbf{c}_1 = \begin{bmatrix} 1 \\ 0 \end{bmatrix}, \quad \mathbf{c}_2 = \begin{bmatrix} 0 \\ 1 \end{bmatrix}, \quad \mathbf{c}_3 = \begin{bmatrix} 3 \\ 2 \end{bmatrix}$

Solution

(*a*) If $\mathbf{v}$ is a linear combination of $\mathbf{a}_1$ and $\mathbf{a}_2$, then

$$\mathbf{v} = \lambda_1\mathbf{a}_1 + \lambda_2\mathbf{a}_2.$$

So

$$\begin{bmatrix} 4 \\ -3 \end{bmatrix} = \lambda_1\begin{bmatrix} 2 \\ 1 \end{bmatrix} + \lambda_2\begin{bmatrix} 1 \\ 3 \end{bmatrix};$$

that is,
$$\left.\begin{aligned} 4 &= 2\lambda_1 + \lambda_2 \\ -3 &= \lambda_1 + 3\lambda_2 \end{aligned}\right\} \quad \begin{matrix}(A)\\(B)\end{matrix}$$

$(A) - 2 \times (B)$: $\quad 10 = -5\lambda_2$

so $\quad \lambda_2 = -2$

and substituting in (B): $\quad \lambda_1 = 3.$

Hence $\quad \mathbf{v} = 3\mathbf{a}_1 - 2\mathbf{a}_2.$

(*b*) If $\mathbf{v} = \lambda_1\mathbf{b}_1 + \lambda_2\mathbf{b}_2$, we require

$$\begin{bmatrix} 4 \\ -3 \end{bmatrix} = \lambda_1\begin{bmatrix} 4 \\ -2 \end{bmatrix} + \lambda_2\begin{bmatrix} -2 \\ 1 \end{bmatrix};$$

that is,
$$\left.\begin{aligned} 4 &= 4\lambda_1 - 2\lambda_2 \\ -3 &= -2\lambda_1 + \lambda_2 \end{aligned}\right\} \quad \begin{matrix}(C)\\(D)\end{matrix}$$

Multiplying (D) by -2: $\quad 6 = 4\lambda_1 - 2\lambda_2. \quad (E)$

As $4\lambda_1 - 2\lambda_2$ cannot equal both 4 and 6 (from Equations (C) and (E)), there are no possible values of λ_1 and λ_2; so $\mathbf{v}$ cannot be expressed as a linear combination of $\mathbf{b}_1$ and $\mathbf{b}_2$.

(*c*) If $\mathbf{v} = \lambda_1\mathbf{c}_1 + \lambda_2\mathbf{c}_2 + \lambda_3\mathbf{c}_3$, we require

$$\begin{bmatrix} 4 \\ -3 \end{bmatrix} = \lambda_1\begin{bmatrix} 1 \\ 0 \end{bmatrix} + \lambda_2\begin{bmatrix} 0 \\ 1 \end{bmatrix} + \lambda_3\begin{bmatrix} 3 \\ 2 \end{bmatrix};$$

that is,
$$\left.\begin{aligned} 4 &= \lambda_1 \quad\quad + 3\lambda_3 \\ -3 &= \quad\quad \lambda_2 + 2\lambda_3 \end{aligned}\right\} \quad \begin{matrix}(F)\\(G)\end{matrix}$$

If $\quad \lambda_3 = 0$, then $\lambda_1 = 4$ and $\lambda_2 = -3$;

and if $\quad \lambda_3 = -1$, then $\lambda_1 = 7$ and $\lambda_2 = -1$.

So we see that there are not unique values for λ_1, λ_2 and λ_3. In fact, there is an infinite number of possible values for λ_1, λ_2, λ_3 (corresponding to a line of solutions if Equations (F) and (G) are considered as planes). □

Q.1 Express the vector $\mathbf{v} = \begin{bmatrix} p \\ q \end{bmatrix}$, where p and q are real numbers, as a linear combination of each of the three sets in Example 1.

You will notice from the answers to Example 1 and Q.1 that

(*a*) there is a unique expression for $\mathbf{v}$ as a linear combination of $\mathbf{a}_1$ and $\mathbf{a}_2$;

(*b*) $\mathbf{v}$ cannot always be expressed as a linear combination of $\mathbf{b}_1$ and $\mathbf{b}_2$;

(*c*) $\mathbf{v}$ can be written as a linear combination of $\mathbf{c}_1, \mathbf{c}_2$ and $\mathbf{c}_3$, but the answer is not unique.

The set $\{\mathbf{a}_1, \mathbf{a}_2\}$ in (*a*) and the set $\{\mathbf{c}_1, \mathbf{c}_2, \mathbf{c}_3\}$ in (*c*) are known as *spanning sets*, since any vector of the form $\begin{bmatrix} p \\ q \end{bmatrix}$ can be expressed as a linear combination of the vectors in the set.

However, in (*c*) we have more vectors in the spanning set than we need. Every time $\mathbf{c}_3$ appears, it can be replaced by $3\mathbf{c}_1 + 2\mathbf{c}_2$. If we have a connection between the vectors $\mathbf{c}_1, \mathbf{c}_2$ and $\mathbf{c}_3$, such as $3\mathbf{c}_1 + 2\mathbf{c}_2 - \mathbf{c}_3 = 0$, the set $\{\mathbf{c}_1, \mathbf{c}_2, \mathbf{c}_3\}$ is said to be *linearly dependent*.

Definition 2
A set of vectors $\{\mathbf{a}_1, \mathbf{a}_2, \ldots, \mathbf{a}_n\}$ is said to *span* a vector space V if every non-zero vector of V can be expressed as a linear combination of the set $\{\mathbf{a}_1, \mathbf{a}_2, \ldots, \mathbf{a}_n\}$.

Definition 3
A set of vectors $\{\mathbf{a}_1, \mathbf{a}_2, \ldots, \mathbf{a}_n\}$ is said to be *linearly dependent* if scalars $\lambda_1, \lambda_2, \ldots, \lambda_n$ (not all zero) can be found such that

$$\lambda_1\mathbf{a}_1 + \lambda_2\mathbf{a}_2 + \ldots + \lambda_n\mathbf{a}_n = \mathbf{0}.$$

Definition 4
If $\lambda_1\mathbf{a}_1 + \lambda_2\mathbf{a}_2 + \ldots + \lambda_n\mathbf{a}_n = \mathbf{0}$ only when $\lambda_1 = \lambda_2 = \ldots = \lambda_n = 0$, then the set of vectors $\{\mathbf{a}_1, \mathbf{a}_2, \ldots, \mathbf{a}_n\}$ is said to be *linearly independent*.

Example 2

Show that the vectors $\mathbf{a}_1 = \begin{bmatrix} 2 \\ 1 \end{bmatrix}$ and $\mathbf{a}_2 = \begin{bmatrix} 1 \\ 3 \end{bmatrix}$ are linearly independent. (These are the vectors in Example 1 (*a*).)

Solution

If $$\lambda_1\mathbf{a}_1 + \lambda_2\mathbf{a}_2 = \mathbf{0}$$

then $$\lambda_1\begin{bmatrix} 2 \\ 1 \end{bmatrix} + \lambda_2\begin{bmatrix} 1 \\ 3 \end{bmatrix} = \begin{bmatrix} 0 \\ 0 \end{bmatrix};$$

that is, $$\left.\begin{aligned} 2\lambda_1 + \lambda_2 &= 0 \\ \lambda_1 + 3\lambda_2 &= 0 \end{aligned}\right\} \qquad \begin{aligned} &(A) \\ &(B) \end{aligned}$$

$(A) - 2 \times (B)$: $$-5\lambda_2 = 0$$

so $$\lambda_2 = 0.$$

Substituting in (A): $$\lambda_1 = 0.$$

As no non-zero values of λ_1, λ_2 can be found, the set of vectors $\{\mathbf{a}_1, \mathbf{a}_2\}$ is *linearly independent*. □

However, for the vectors $\mathbf{b}_1 = \begin{bmatrix} 4 \\ -2 \end{bmatrix}$ and $\mathbf{b}_2 = \begin{bmatrix} -2 \\ 1 \end{bmatrix}$ of Example 1(*b*), $\mathbf{b}_1 + 2\mathbf{b}_2 = \mathbf{0}$, so the set of vectors $\{\mathbf{b}_1, \mathbf{b}_2\}$ is *linearly dependent*.

In Q.1 we saw that every vector of the form $\begin{bmatrix} p \\ q \end{bmatrix}$ can be uniquely expressed as a linear combination of $\mathbf{a}_1 = \begin{bmatrix} 2 \\ 1 \end{bmatrix}$ and $\mathbf{a}_2 = \begin{bmatrix} 1 \\ 3 \end{bmatrix}$ (the vectors in Example 1 (*a*)). We have also seen that this set of vectors $\{\mathbf{a}_1, \mathbf{a}_2\}$ is linearly independent and spans the vector space V. We say that the set $\{\mathbf{a}_1, \mathbf{a}_2\}$ is a *basis* for the vector space V.

Definition 5
A set of vectors which is linearly independent *and* spans a vector space is called a *basis* for the vector space.

The basis $\{\mathbf{a}_1, \mathbf{a}_2\}$ of Example 1 contains two elements, so we say that the vector space is of *dimension* 2.

Definition 6
The number of elements required to form a basis for a given vector space is called the *dimension* of that vector space.

Q.2 Prove that a necessary and sufficient condition for a vector to be uniquely expressible as a linear combination of $\mathbf{a}_1, \mathbf{a}_2, \ldots, \mathbf{a}_n$ is that the set $\{\mathbf{a}_1, \mathbf{a}_2, \ldots, \mathbf{a}_n\}$ is linearly independent.

So in a vector space V, each vector $\mathbf{v} \in V$ is *uniquely* expressed as a linear combination of the vectors in the basis.

This work on the basis of a vector space raises two questions:

(1) Does a basis always exist?

(2) If more than one basis exists, does each basis have the same number of elements?

We will return to these questions in Chapter 14.

Exercise 11A

1 Express the following vectors **a** as a linear combination of the vectors **b** and **c**:

(*a*) $\mathbf{a} = \begin{bmatrix} 1 \\ 4 \end{bmatrix}$ $\quad \mathbf{b} = \begin{bmatrix} -1 \\ 2 \end{bmatrix}$ $\quad \mathbf{c} = \begin{bmatrix} 2 \\ 2 \end{bmatrix}$

(*b*) $\mathbf{a} = \begin{bmatrix} 0 \\ 1 \end{bmatrix}$ $\quad \mathbf{b} = \begin{bmatrix} 2 \\ -3 \end{bmatrix}$ $\quad \mathbf{c} = \begin{bmatrix} 3 \\ -2 \end{bmatrix}$

(*c*) $\mathbf{a} = \begin{bmatrix} -1 \\ 5 \\ 1 \end{bmatrix}$ $\quad \mathbf{b} = \begin{bmatrix} 5 \\ 1 \\ 3 \end{bmatrix}$ $\quad \mathbf{c} = \begin{bmatrix} 3 \\ -2 \\ 1 \end{bmatrix}$

2 Which of the following sets of vectors are linearly independent?

(*a*) $\left\{ \begin{bmatrix} 1 \\ 1 \\ 0 \end{bmatrix}, \begin{bmatrix} -1 \\ 0 \\ 1 \end{bmatrix}, \begin{bmatrix} 5 \\ 3 \\ -2 \end{bmatrix} \right\}$ $\quad$ (*b*) $\left\{ \begin{bmatrix} 2 \\ 1 \\ 4 \end{bmatrix}, \begin{bmatrix} 1 \\ 0 \\ 1 \end{bmatrix}, \begin{bmatrix} 0 \\ 0 \\ 1 \end{bmatrix} \right\}$

(*c*) $\left\{ \begin{bmatrix} 2 \\ -1 \\ 1 \end{bmatrix}, \begin{bmatrix} 1 \\ 1 \\ 1 \end{bmatrix}, \begin{bmatrix} 0 \\ 1 \\ -1 \end{bmatrix} \right\}$ $\quad$ (*d*) $\left\{ \begin{bmatrix} 4 \\ -1 \\ 3 \end{bmatrix}, \begin{bmatrix} 0 \\ 0 \\ 0 \end{bmatrix}, \begin{bmatrix} 6 \\ 2 \\ -5 \end{bmatrix} \right\}$

(e) $\left\{\begin{bmatrix}2\\0\\-1\\3\end{bmatrix}, \begin{bmatrix}3\\2\\1\\2\end{bmatrix}, \begin{bmatrix}-1\\2\\3\\-4\end{bmatrix}\right\}$

3 Let L be the set of polynomials of degree 1 or less, that is

$$L = \{ax + b : a, b \in \mathbb{R}\}.$$

(*a*) Show that the polynomial $(2x - 1)$ can be expressed as a linear combination of $(x + 1)$ and $(x - 1)$.

(*b*) Are the polynomials $(2x + 3)$, $(x + 2)$, $(x - 5)$ linearly independent?

(*c*) Are $(2x + 3)$ and $(x + 2)$ linearly independent?

(*d*) Write $ax + b$ as a linear combination of $(2x + 3)$ and $(x + 2)$.

(*e*) Suggest a basis for L. What is the dimension of L?

4 S is the set of polynomials of degree 2, that is

$$S = \{px^2 + qx + r : p, q, r \in \mathbb{R}\}.$$

(*a*) Express $(3x^2 + 2x + 1)$ as a linear combination of the set $\{1, 2 + 3x, 1 + x^2\}$.

(*b*) Repeat part (*a*) for the general quadratic $(px^2 + qx + r)$.

(*c*) Show that the set $\{1, 2 + 3x, 1 + x^2\}$ is linearly independent.

5 Which of the following sets of vectors are linearly independent?

(*a*) $\left\{\begin{bmatrix}1 & 0\\0 & 1\end{bmatrix}, \begin{bmatrix}0 & 1\\1 & 0\end{bmatrix}, \begin{bmatrix}1 & -1\\-1 & 1\end{bmatrix}\right\}$

(*b*) $\left\{\begin{bmatrix}1 & 2\\0 & 3\end{bmatrix}, \begin{bmatrix}0 & 1\\3 & 2\end{bmatrix}, \begin{bmatrix}3 & 0\\2 & 1\end{bmatrix}\right\}$

6 Find a basis for the vector space spanned by each of the following sets of vectors:

(*a*) $\left\{\begin{bmatrix}2\\1\end{bmatrix}, \begin{bmatrix}3\\-1\end{bmatrix}, \begin{bmatrix}-4\\-2\end{bmatrix}, \begin{bmatrix}6\\1\end{bmatrix}\right\}$

(*b*) $\left\{\begin{bmatrix}3\\-1\\4\end{bmatrix}, \begin{bmatrix}2\\-2\\3\end{bmatrix}, \begin{bmatrix}-1\\3\\-2\end{bmatrix}\right\}$

(*c*) $\{1 + x,\ 2 - 3x,\ 4 + 6x\}$

(*d*) $\left\{\begin{bmatrix}4 & 2\\2 & -1\end{bmatrix}, \begin{bmatrix}1 & -3\\-3 & 5\end{bmatrix}, \begin{bmatrix}-2 & 4\\4 & -3\end{bmatrix}\right\}$

7 (*a*) $\{\mathbf{a}, \mathbf{b}, \mathbf{c}\}$ is a linearly independent set of vectors. Show that $\{\mathbf{a}, \mathbf{c}\}$ is also a linearly independent set.

(*b*) $\{\mathbf{a}, \mathbf{b}, \mathbf{c}\}$ is a linearly dependent set of vectors. Show that $\{\mathbf{a}, \mathbf{b}, \mathbf{c}, \mathbf{d}\}$ is also a linearly dependent set.

11.2 COORDINATES

In Chapter 1 we referred to equivalent ways of representing a point using either coordinates or a position vector, for example, if the point A has coordinates $(3, 4)$, the position vector of A is $\mathbf{a} = \begin{bmatrix}3\\4\end{bmatrix}$.

But in referring to the vector $\begin{bmatrix} 3 \\ 4 \end{bmatrix}$ we are assuming that a certain basis has been used. We mean $\mathbf{a} = 3\mathbf{i} + 4\mathbf{j}$, where $\{\mathbf{i}, \mathbf{j}\}$ is the familiar basis ($\mathbf{i}$ and $\mathbf{j}$ have the usual meaning).

If we had used the set $\{\mathbf{b}, \mathbf{c}\}$ as our basis, where $\mathbf{b} = \begin{bmatrix} 2 \\ 1 \end{bmatrix}$ and $\mathbf{c} = \begin{bmatrix} 1 \\ 3 \end{bmatrix}$, then $\mathbf{a} = 1\mathbf{b} + 1\mathbf{c}$, so the point A would have coordinates (1, 1) and position vector $\begin{bmatrix} 1 \\ 1 \end{bmatrix}$ (Fig. 1). (The word 'components' is sometimes used instead of coordinates.)

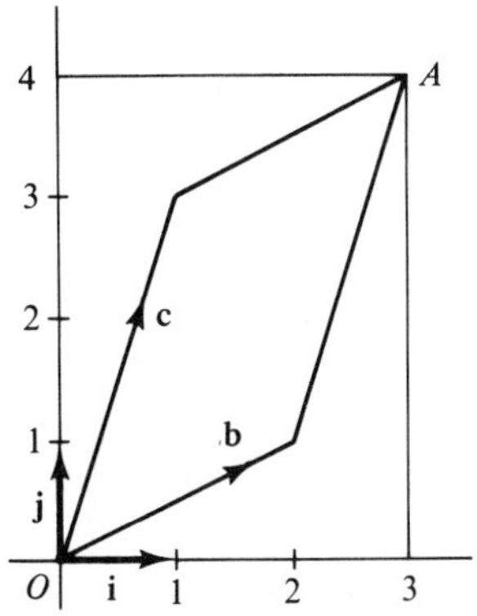

Figure 1

So the coordinates and the position vector of a point are dependent on the basis used.

Definition 7
If $\{\mathbf{a}_1, \mathbf{a}_2, \ldots, \mathbf{a}_n\}$ is a basis for the vector space V, and $\mathbf{v} = \lambda_1\mathbf{a}_1 + \lambda_2\mathbf{a}_2 + \ldots + \lambda_n\mathbf{a}_n$, then $(\lambda_1, \lambda_2, \ldots, \lambda_n)$ are called the coordinates or components of $\mathbf{v}$ with respect to the basis $\{\mathbf{a}_1, \mathbf{a}_2, \ldots, \mathbf{a}_n\}$.

Q.3 What are the coordinates of $\mathbf{p}$ and $\mathbf{q}$ relative to the basis $\{\mathbf{p}, \mathbf{q}\}$?

Example 3
Let M be the vector space of *symmetric* 2×2 matrices. Find the coordinates of the matrix $\mathbf{A} = \begin{bmatrix} 3 & 5 \\ 5 & 1 \end{bmatrix}$ relative to the basis

$$\left\{\begin{bmatrix} 2 & 1 \\ 1 & -1 \end{bmatrix}, \begin{bmatrix} 0 & -1 \\ -1 & 0 \end{bmatrix}, \begin{bmatrix} -1 & 0 \\ 0 & 3 \end{bmatrix}\right\}.$$

Solution

$$\mathbf{A} = \begin{bmatrix} 3 & 5 \\ 5 & 1 \end{bmatrix} = p\begin{bmatrix} 2 & 1 \\ 1 & -1 \end{bmatrix} + q\begin{bmatrix} 0 & -1 \\ -1 & 0 \end{bmatrix} + r\begin{bmatrix} -1 & 0 \\ 0 & 3 \end{bmatrix}$$

$$= \begin{bmatrix} 2p - r & p - q \\ p - q & -p + 3r \end{bmatrix};$$

that is,

$$\left.\begin{aligned} 2p - \quad r &= 3 \\ -p + 3r &= 1 \\ p - \quad q &= 5 \end{aligned}\right\}$$

which has solution $\quad p = 2, \quad q = -3, \quad r = 1.$

So the coordinates of **A** relative to this basis are $(2, -3, 1)$. □

Example 4

$A = \left\{\begin{bmatrix} 1 \\ 4 \end{bmatrix}, \begin{bmatrix} -3 \\ 2 \end{bmatrix}\right\}$. The coordinates of a point Q relative to the usual basis $\{\mathbf{i}, \mathbf{j}\}$ are $(3, 5)$. Find the coordinates of Q relative to the basis A.

Solution

If Q has coordinates (q_1, q_2) relative to basis A,

$$\begin{bmatrix} 3 \\ 5 \end{bmatrix} = q_1\begin{bmatrix} 1 \\ 4 \end{bmatrix} + q_2\begin{bmatrix} -3 \\ 2 \end{bmatrix}$$

$$= \begin{bmatrix} 1 & -3 \\ 4 & 2 \end{bmatrix}\begin{bmatrix} q_1 \\ q_2 \end{bmatrix}.$$

And so

$$\begin{bmatrix} q_1 \\ q_2 \end{bmatrix} = \begin{bmatrix} 1 & -3 \\ 4 & 2 \end{bmatrix}^{-1}\begin{bmatrix} 3 \\ 5 \end{bmatrix}$$

$$= \begin{bmatrix} \frac{1}{7} & \frac{3}{14} \\ -\frac{2}{7} & \frac{1}{14} \end{bmatrix}\begin{bmatrix} 3 \\ 5 \end{bmatrix}$$

$$= \begin{bmatrix} \frac{3}{2} \\ -\frac{1}{2} \end{bmatrix}.$$

The coordinates of Q relative to basis A are therefore $(\frac{3}{2}, -\frac{1}{2})$. □

More generally, we see that the coordinates (x_1, x_2) of a point R relative to $\{\mathbf{i}, \mathbf{j}\}$, and its coordinates (x_1', x_2') relative to basis A, are connected by

$$\begin{bmatrix} x_1 \\ x_2 \end{bmatrix} = \begin{bmatrix} 1 & -3 \\ 4 & 2 \end{bmatrix}\begin{bmatrix} x_1' \\ x_2' \end{bmatrix}$$

or

$$\mathbf{x} = \mathbf{P}\mathbf{x}'.$$

The columns of **P** give the coordinates of the elements of the basis A relative to $\{\mathbf{i}, \mathbf{j}\}$, and so **P** is the matrix of the transformation mapping $\{\mathbf{i}, \mathbf{j}\}$ to the basis A.

In general, if the coordinates of a point relative to basis $\{\boldsymbol{\alpha}_1, \boldsymbol{\alpha}_2\}$ are (x_1, x_2) and its coordinates relative to a new basis $\{\boldsymbol{\alpha}_1', \boldsymbol{\alpha}_2'\}$ are (x_1', x_2'), then

$$x_1\boldsymbol{\alpha}_1 + x_2\boldsymbol{\alpha}_2 = x_1'\boldsymbol{\alpha}_1' + x_2'\boldsymbol{\alpha}_2'.$$

Now $\boldsymbol{\alpha}_1'$ and $\boldsymbol{\alpha}_2'$ can be written as a linear combination of the basis $\{\boldsymbol{\alpha}_1, \boldsymbol{\alpha}_2\}$:

$$\boldsymbol{\alpha}_1' = a\boldsymbol{\alpha}_1 + b\boldsymbol{\alpha}_2$$

$$\boldsymbol{\alpha}_2' = c\boldsymbol{\alpha}_1 + d\boldsymbol{\alpha}_2.$$

Hence $$x_1\boldsymbol{\alpha}_1 + x_2\boldsymbol{\alpha}_2 = x_1'(a\boldsymbol{\alpha}_1 + b\boldsymbol{\alpha}_2) + x_2'(c\boldsymbol{\alpha}_1 + d\boldsymbol{\alpha}_2)$$
$$= (ax_1' + cx_2')\boldsymbol{\alpha}_1 + (bx_1' + dx_2')\boldsymbol{\alpha}_2$$

so $$\begin{bmatrix} x_1 \\ x_2 \end{bmatrix} = \begin{bmatrix} ax_1' + cx_2' \\ bx_1' + dx_2' \end{bmatrix} = \begin{bmatrix} a & c \\ b & d \end{bmatrix}\begin{bmatrix} x_1' \\ x_2' \end{bmatrix};$$

that is, $$\mathbf{x} = \mathbf{P}\mathbf{x}'.$$

Note that the columns of **P** give the coordinates of the new basis relative to the old basis.

Example 5

The coordinates of a point Q relative to the basis $A = \left\{\begin{bmatrix} 1 \\ 2 \end{bmatrix}, \begin{bmatrix} -2 \\ 1 \end{bmatrix}\right\}$ are $(3, -1)$.

Find its coordinates relative to the basis $B = \left\{\begin{bmatrix} 3 \\ 1 \end{bmatrix}, \begin{bmatrix} 1 \\ -1 \end{bmatrix}\right\}$.

Solution

We use the following notation:

Position vector	*Basis*
$\mathbf{x}$	$S = \{\mathbf{i}, \mathbf{j}\}$
$\mathbf{x}'$	A
$\mathbf{x}''$	B

Then $$\mathbf{x} = \begin{bmatrix} 1 & -2 \\ 2 & 1 \end{bmatrix}\mathbf{x}', \quad \text{changing basis from } S \text{ to } A,$$

and $$\mathbf{x} = \begin{bmatrix} 3 & 1 \\ 1 & -1 \end{bmatrix}\mathbf{x}'', \quad \text{changing basis from } S \text{ to } B.$$

Hence $$\mathbf{x}'' = \begin{bmatrix} 3 & 1 \\ 1 & -1 \end{bmatrix}^{-1}\mathbf{x} = \begin{bmatrix} \frac{1}{4} & \frac{1}{4} \\ \frac{1}{4} & -\frac{3}{4} \end{bmatrix}\mathbf{x}$$
$$= \begin{bmatrix} \frac{1}{4} & \frac{1}{4} \\ \frac{1}{4} & -\frac{3}{4} \end{bmatrix}\begin{bmatrix} 1 & -2 \\ 2 & 1 \end{bmatrix}\mathbf{x}'$$
$$= \begin{bmatrix} \frac{3}{4} & -\frac{1}{4} \\ -\frac{5}{4} & -\frac{5}{4} \end{bmatrix}\mathbf{x}'.$$

Since Q has coordinates $(3, -1)$ relative to the basis A, $\mathbf{x}' = \begin{bmatrix} 3 \\ -1 \end{bmatrix}$, and so

$$\mathbf{x}'' = \begin{bmatrix} \frac{3}{4} & -\frac{1}{4} \\ -\frac{5}{4} & -\frac{5}{4} \end{bmatrix}\begin{bmatrix} 3 \\ -1 \end{bmatrix} = \begin{bmatrix} \frac{5}{2} \\ -\frac{5}{2} \end{bmatrix}.$$

Q therefore has coordinates $(\frac{5}{2}, -\frac{5}{2})$ relative to the basis A. □

Exercise 11B

1 Find the coordinates of the following vectors $\mathbf{v}$ relative to the given basis:

(*a*) $\mathbf{v} = \begin{bmatrix} -2 \\ 13 \end{bmatrix}$, basis $= \left\{ \begin{bmatrix} 4 \\ -1 \end{bmatrix}, \begin{bmatrix} -2 \\ 3 \end{bmatrix} \right\}$

(*b*) $\mathbf{v} = \begin{bmatrix} 9 \\ 6 \\ -6 \end{bmatrix}$, basis $= \left\{ \begin{bmatrix} 2 \\ 1 \\ -3 \end{bmatrix}, \begin{bmatrix} 4 \\ -1 \\ 0 \end{bmatrix}, \begin{bmatrix} 3 \\ 0 \\ 2 \end{bmatrix} \right\}$

(*c*) $\mathbf{v} = \begin{bmatrix} 3 & -1 \\ 2 & -2 \end{bmatrix}$, basis $= \left\{ \begin{bmatrix} 1 & 1 \\ 0 & 0 \end{bmatrix}, \begin{bmatrix} 0 & 1 \\ 0 & 1 \end{bmatrix}, \begin{bmatrix} 0 & 0 \\ 1 & 1 \end{bmatrix} \right\}$

(*d*) $\mathbf{v} = 3t^2 + 5t + 6$, basis $= \{1, 1 + t, (1 + t)^2\}$

2 $A = \left\{ \begin{bmatrix} 1 \\ 2 \end{bmatrix}, \begin{bmatrix} -2 \\ 1 \end{bmatrix} \right\}$, $B = \left\{ \begin{bmatrix} 4 \\ 2 \end{bmatrix}, \begin{bmatrix} 3 \\ 1 \end{bmatrix} \right\}$.

A point Q has coordinates $(5, 4)$ relative to the basis $\{\mathbf{i}, \mathbf{j}\}$. Find the coordinates of Q, (*a*) relative to basis A, (*b*) relative to basis B.

3 The coordinates of the point P are given relative to basis A. Find the coordinates of P relative to basis B, where:

(*a*) P is the point $(2, 3)$, $A = \left\{ \begin{bmatrix} 3 \\ -1 \end{bmatrix}, \begin{bmatrix} 1 \\ 4 \end{bmatrix} \right\}$, $B = \left\{ \begin{bmatrix} 2 \\ 1 \end{bmatrix}, \begin{bmatrix} 3 \\ 2 \end{bmatrix} \right\}$

(*b*) P is the point $(1, 6)$, $A = \left\{ \begin{bmatrix} 1 \\ -2 \end{bmatrix}, \begin{bmatrix} 1 \\ 4 \end{bmatrix} \right\}$, $B = \left\{ \begin{bmatrix} 5 \\ -2 \end{bmatrix}, \begin{bmatrix} 3 \\ -1 \end{bmatrix} \right\}$

4 P has coordinates $(6, -4)$ when referred to basis $\left\{ \begin{bmatrix} 1 \\ -4 \end{bmatrix}, \begin{bmatrix} 2 \\ 2 \end{bmatrix} \right\}$. Find a new basis such that the coordinates of P become:

(*a*) $(1, 1)$ (*b*) $(1, 0)$ (*c*) $(0, 1)$

Are your answers unique?

5 P has coordinates $(1, 0)$ relative to basis $\{\mathbf{u}, \mathbf{v}\}$ and coordinates $(0, 1)$ relative to basis $\{\mathbf{u}', \mathbf{v}'\}$. If $\mathbf{u}$ and $\mathbf{v}$ are perpendicular, and $\mathbf{u}'$ and $\mathbf{v}'$ are perpendicular, what relationship is there between $\mathbf{u}$, $\mathbf{v}$, $\mathbf{u}'$ and $\mathbf{v}'$? What happens if they are not perpendicular?

11.3 CHANGE OF BASIS

Much of the work in this book is concerned with transformations, and we shall see in the next chapter that every linear transformation can be represented by a matrix. In this section we investigate what happens to the matrix of a transformation under a change of basis.

If, relative to the original basis, the transformation is represented by the matrix $\mathbf{M}$, the position vectors of a point $\mathbf{x}$ and its image $\mathbf{y}$ are related by $\mathbf{y} = \mathbf{Mx}$.

A new basis is chosen so that the position vectors of the point and its image are now $\mathbf{x}'$ and $\mathbf{y}'$.

So $$\mathbf{x} = \mathbf{Px}' \quad \text{and} \quad \mathbf{y} = \mathbf{Py}'.$$

Then $$\mathbf{y} = \mathbf{Mx}$$

becomes $$\mathbf{Py}' = \mathbf{M}(\mathbf{Px}');$$

that is, $$\mathbf{y}' = (\mathbf{P}^{-1}\mathbf{MP})\mathbf{x}'.$$

So the matrix which represents this transformation using the new basis is

$$\mathbf{P}^{-1}\mathbf{M}\mathbf{P} \quad \text{(note the order).}$$

We can represent this result diagrammatically as follows:

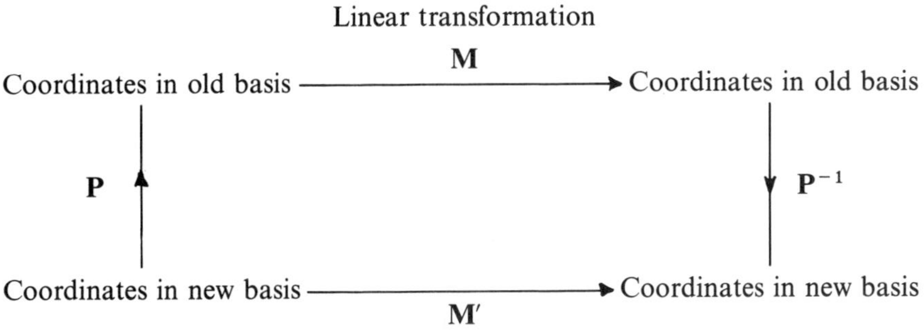

Going round this diagram each way we see that

$$\mathbf{M}' = \mathbf{P}^{-1}\mathbf{M}\mathbf{P}.$$

Definition 8
Matrices **M** and $\mathbf{P}^{-1}\mathbf{M}\mathbf{P}$ are said to be *similar matrices*, since they are different representations of the same linear transformation.

There are now two questions which we ask concerning linear transformations:

(1) Which properties of a linear transformation are independent of the choice of basis?

(2) Can we find a basis so that the matrix representing a linear transformation is as simple as possible?

For (1) there are two main results:

Result 1
Similar matrices have the same characteristic polynomial.

$$\begin{aligned}\det(\mathbf{P}^{-1}\mathbf{M}\mathbf{P} - \lambda\mathbf{I}) &= \det(\mathbf{P}^{-1}\mathbf{M}\mathbf{P} - \lambda\mathbf{P}^{-1}\mathbf{P})\\ &= \det[\mathbf{P}^{-1}(\mathbf{M} - \lambda\mathbf{I})\mathbf{P}]\\ &= \det(\mathbf{P}^{-1}) \times \det(\mathbf{M} - \lambda\mathbf{I}) \times \det(\mathbf{P})\\ &= \det(\mathbf{M} - \lambda\mathbf{I}), \quad (\text{as } \det(\mathbf{P}^{-1}) \times \det(\mathbf{P}) = 1).\end{aligned}$$

So the characteristic polynomial of a linear transformation is independent of the choice of basis. It follows that the eigenvalues are also invariant under the change of basis (but the eigenvectors are not – why?).

Result 2
Similar matrices have the same determinant.

$$\begin{aligned}\det(\mathbf{P}^{-1}\mathbf{M}\mathbf{P}) &= \det(\mathbf{P}^{-1}) \times \det(\mathbf{M}) \times \det(\mathbf{P})\\ &= \det(\mathbf{M}).\end{aligned}$$

So in two dimensions the area scale factor, and in three dimensions the volume scale factor, are independent of the choice of basis.

For (2) we saw in Chapter 4 that for 2×2 matrices $\mathbf{M}$ which had real distinct eigenvalues, we could write $\mathbf{M}$ in the form

$$\mathbf{M} = \mathbf{U}\mathbf{\Lambda}\mathbf{U}^{-1},$$

that is,

$$\mathbf{\Lambda} = \mathbf{U}^{-1}\mathbf{M}\mathbf{U}$$

where $\mathbf{\Lambda}$ is a diagonal matrix.

Q.4 How does this change of basis link up with the geometrical description in §4.3?

For larger square matrices with distinct real eigenvalues, a matrix $\mathbf{U}$ can always be found such that $\mathbf{U}^{-1}\mathbf{M}\mathbf{U}$ is a diagonal matrix.

11.4 TWO APPLICATIONS

(a) Quadratic forms in two dimensions

In Chapter 9 we saw that equations of the form $ax^2 + 2hxy + by^2 = 1$ represent conics. We simplified the form of the equation by rotating the conic so that its axes coincided with the x- and y-axes. We now have a fresh look at this problem by seeing what happens if we choose the axes of symmetry of the conic as the new basis vectors.

For example if the conic is the hyperbola in Fig. 2, we would choose the new basis vectors to be in the directions of the x'- and y'-axes.

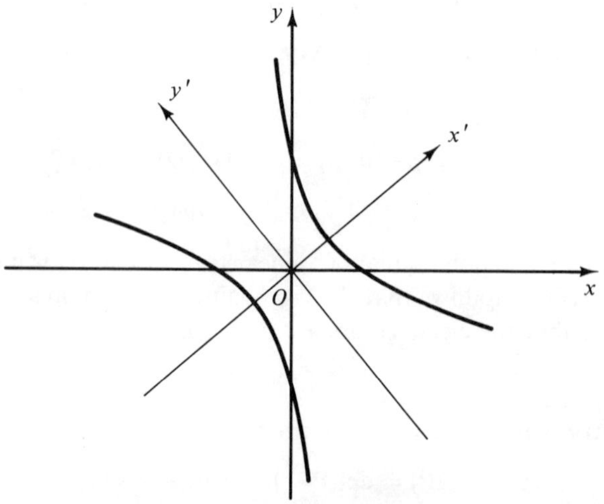

Figure 2

Example 6
Write the conic $17x^2 + 12xy + 8y^2 = 1$ in the form $a'x'^2 + b'y'^2 = 1$, and hence sketch it.

Solution
The equation $17x^2 + 12xy + 8y^2 = 1$ can be written in the form

$$[x \quad y]\begin{bmatrix} 17 & 6 \\ 6 & 8 \end{bmatrix}\begin{bmatrix} x \\ y \end{bmatrix} = [1] \quad (\text{see } §9.3),$$

that is,
$$\mathbf{x}^{\mathrm{T}}\mathbf{M}\mathbf{x} = [1] \qquad (A)$$

where $\mathbf{M}$ is the symmetric matrix $\begin{bmatrix} 17 & 6 \\ 6 & 8 \end{bmatrix}$.

This is the equation of the conic with respect to the usual basis, $\{\mathbf{i}, \mathbf{j}\}$.

If we have a new basis, the new position vector $\mathbf{x}'$ and the original position vector $\mathbf{x}$ are related by the equation

$$\mathbf{x} = \mathbf{P}\mathbf{x}'.$$

Equation (A) now becomes

$$(\mathbf{P}\mathbf{x}')^{\mathrm{T}}\mathbf{M}(\mathbf{P}\mathbf{x}') = [1]$$

so that
$$\mathbf{x}'^{\mathrm{T}}\mathbf{P}^{\mathrm{T}}\mathbf{M}\mathbf{P}\mathbf{x}' = [1]. \qquad (B)$$

We now recall two results from Chapter 8:

(1) If $\mathbf{M}$ is a *symmetric* matrix, we can find an *orthogonal* matrix $\mathbf{P}$ such that $\mathbf{P}^{-1}\mathbf{M}\mathbf{P}$ is a diagonal matrix.

(2) For an orthogonal matrix, $\mathbf{P}^{\mathrm{T}} = \mathbf{P}^{-1}$.

Combining these two results, equation (B) becomes

$$\mathbf{x}'^{\mathrm{T}}\mathbf{P}^{-1}\mathbf{M}\mathbf{P}\mathbf{x}' = [1]$$

$$\Rightarrow \qquad \mathbf{x}'^{\mathrm{T}}\mathbf{\Lambda}\mathbf{x} = [1];$$

that is,
$$a'x'^2 + b'y'^2 = 1, \quad \text{where } \mathbf{\Lambda} = \begin{bmatrix} a' & 0 \\ 0 & b' \end{bmatrix}.$$

For matrix $\mathbf{M} = \begin{bmatrix} 17 & 6 \\ 6 & 8 \end{bmatrix}$, to find the eigenvalues we solve $\det(\mathbf{M} - \lambda\mathbf{I}) = 0$:

$$(17 - \lambda)(8 - \lambda) - 36 = 0$$

$$\Rightarrow \qquad \lambda^2 - 25\lambda + 100 = 0$$

$$\Rightarrow \qquad (\lambda - 5)(\lambda - 20) = 0$$

$$\Rightarrow \qquad \lambda = 5 \quad \text{or} \quad 20.$$

If $\lambda = 5$, $\begin{bmatrix} 12 & 6 \\ 6 & 3 \end{bmatrix}\begin{bmatrix} x \\ y \end{bmatrix} = \begin{bmatrix} 0 \\ 0 \end{bmatrix}$, so the corresponding eigenvector is $k\begin{bmatrix} 1 \\ -2 \end{bmatrix}$, and if $\lambda = 20$, $\begin{bmatrix} -3 & 6 \\ 6 & -12 \end{bmatrix}\begin{bmatrix} x \\ y \end{bmatrix} = \begin{bmatrix} 0 \\ 0 \end{bmatrix}$, so the corresponding eigenvector is $k'\begin{bmatrix} 2 \\ 1 \end{bmatrix}$.

We therefore have

$$\Lambda = \begin{bmatrix} 5 & 0 \\ 0 & 20 \end{bmatrix} \quad \text{and} \quad \mathbf{P} = \begin{bmatrix} \frac{1}{\sqrt{5}} & \frac{2}{\sqrt{5}} \\ -\frac{2}{\sqrt{5}} & \frac{1}{\sqrt{5}} \end{bmatrix}$$

and the equation relative to the new axes is

$$5x'^2 + 20y'^2 = 1, \quad \text{which is an ellipse.}$$

The new basis is $\left\{ \begin{bmatrix} \frac{1}{\sqrt{5}} \\ -\frac{2}{\sqrt{5}} \end{bmatrix}, \begin{bmatrix} \frac{2}{\sqrt{5}} \\ \frac{1}{\sqrt{5}} \end{bmatrix} \right\}$, in which the basis vectors are the axes of the conic.

Since

$$\mathbf{P} = \begin{bmatrix} \frac{1}{\sqrt{5}} & \frac{2}{\sqrt{5}} \\ -\frac{2}{\sqrt{5}} & \frac{1}{\sqrt{5}} \end{bmatrix} = \begin{bmatrix} \cos\alpha & -\sin\alpha \\ \sin\alpha & \cos\alpha \end{bmatrix}, \quad \text{where } \alpha \approx -63.4°,$$

the new basis is obtained from the original basis by a rotation of $-63.4°$ (Fig. 3).

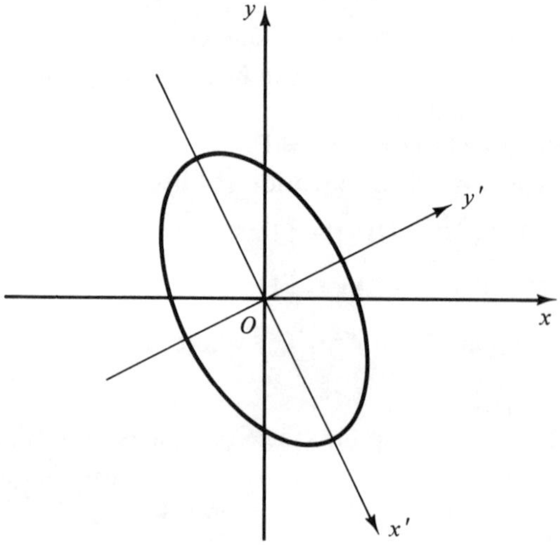

Figure 3

□

(b) Simultaneous differential equations

Example 7
Solve the simultaneous differential equations

$$\left.\begin{aligned} \dot{x} &= 2x + 3y \\ \dot{y} &= 2x + y \end{aligned}\right\}$$

where x and y are functions of t and dots denote differentiation with respect to t.

Solution
We write these equations in the form

$$\begin{bmatrix}\dot{x}\\ \dot{y}\end{bmatrix}=\begin{bmatrix}2 & 3\\ 2 & 1\end{bmatrix}\begin{bmatrix}x\\ y\end{bmatrix};$$

that is, $\dot{\mathbf{x}} = \mathbf{A}\mathbf{x}$, where $\mathbf{x} = \begin{bmatrix}x\\ y\end{bmatrix}$ and $\mathbf{A} = \begin{bmatrix}2 & 3\\ 2 & 1\end{bmatrix}$. (*A*)

If new variables $\begin{bmatrix}u\\ v\end{bmatrix}$ are connected to $\begin{bmatrix}x\\ y\end{bmatrix}$ by

$$\begin{bmatrix}x\\ y\end{bmatrix}=\mathbf{P}\begin{bmatrix}u\\ v\end{bmatrix}\quad \text{where } \mathbf{P} \text{ is a } 2\times 2 \text{ matrix},$$

equation (*A*) becomes

$$\mathbf{P}\dot{\mathbf{u}} = \mathbf{A}\mathbf{P}\mathbf{u};$$

that is,

$$\dot{\mathbf{u}} = \mathbf{P}^{-1}\mathbf{A}\mathbf{P}\mathbf{u}. \qquad (B)$$

If $\mathbf{A}$ has real distinct eigenvalues we can choose $\mathbf{P}$ so that $\mathbf{P}^{-1}\mathbf{A}\mathbf{P}$ is a diagonal matrix (see Chapter 4).

$$\begin{aligned} & \det(\mathbf{A}-\lambda\mathbf{I}) = 0\\ \Rightarrow\quad & (2-\lambda)(1-\lambda)-6=0\\ \Rightarrow\quad & \lambda^2-3\lambda-4=0\\ \Rightarrow\quad & (\lambda-4)(\lambda+1)=0\\ \Rightarrow\quad & \lambda = 4 \quad\text{or}\quad -1.\end{aligned}$$

For $\lambda = 4$,
$$\begin{bmatrix}-2 & 3\\ 2 & -3\end{bmatrix}\begin{bmatrix}x\\ y\end{bmatrix}=\begin{bmatrix}0\\ 0\end{bmatrix},\quad\text{so}\quad \begin{bmatrix}x\\ y\end{bmatrix}=k\begin{bmatrix}3\\ 2\end{bmatrix},$$

and for $\lambda = -1$,
$$\begin{bmatrix}3 & 3\\ 2 & 2\end{bmatrix}\begin{bmatrix}x\\ y\end{bmatrix}=\begin{bmatrix}0\\ 0\end{bmatrix},\quad\text{so}\quad \begin{bmatrix}x\\ y\end{bmatrix}=k'\begin{bmatrix}1\\ -1\end{bmatrix}.$$

So if $\mathbf{P} = \begin{bmatrix}3 & 1\\ 2 & -1\end{bmatrix}$, equation (*B*) becomes

$$\dot{\mathbf{u}} = \begin{bmatrix}4 & 0\\ 0 & -1\end{bmatrix}\mathbf{u};$$

that is,

$$\left.\begin{aligned}\dot{u} &= 4u\\ \dot{v} &= -v\end{aligned}\right\}$$

Solving these equations, we get

$$u = Ce^{4t}$$

$$v = De^{-t}$$

Hence
$$\begin{bmatrix} x \\ y \end{bmatrix} = \mathbf{P}\begin{bmatrix} u \\ v \end{bmatrix} = \begin{bmatrix} 3 & 1 \\ 2 & -1 \end{bmatrix}\begin{bmatrix} Ce^{4t} \\ De^{-t} \end{bmatrix};$$

that is, $x = 3Ce^{4t} + De^{-t}$ and $y = 2Ce^{4t} - De^{-t}$. □

Exercise 11C

1 A transformation is represented by the matrix **M** relative to the usual basis. Find the matrix which represents this transformation relative to a new basis A where:

(*a*) $\mathbf{M} = \begin{bmatrix} 2 & -1 \\ 4 & 3 \end{bmatrix}$, $A = \left\{\begin{bmatrix} 3 \\ 2 \end{bmatrix}, \begin{bmatrix} 2 \\ 1 \end{bmatrix}\right\}$

(*b*) $\mathbf{M} = \begin{bmatrix} 2 & 1 & 3 \\ 4 & -1 & 2 \\ 1 & 3 & 0 \end{bmatrix}$, $A = \left\{\begin{bmatrix} 1 \\ 1 \\ 1 \end{bmatrix}, \begin{bmatrix} 0 \\ 1 \\ 1 \end{bmatrix}, \begin{bmatrix} 0 \\ 0 \\ 1 \end{bmatrix}\right\}$

2 A point R has coordinates $(2, 3)$ referred to the usual basis. Find its coordinates with respect to the new basis $\left\{\begin{bmatrix} 1 \\ 1 \end{bmatrix}, \begin{bmatrix} -2 \\ 4 \end{bmatrix}\right\}$. A transformation **T** is a rotation of $+90°$ about the origin followed by an enlargement scale factor 2. Find the image of R with respect to the new basis.

(*a*) What is the matrix **M** representing **T** with respect to the $\{\mathbf{i}, \mathbf{j}\}$ basis?

(*b*) What is the matrix **M**′ representing **T** with respect to the new basis?

3 Repeat question 2 with the original coordinates of R being $(1, 5)$; the new basis $\left\{\begin{bmatrix} 0 \\ 1 \end{bmatrix}, \begin{bmatrix} 1 \\ 1 \end{bmatrix}\right\}$; and with **T** a shear with the y-axis invariant such that the image of $(2, 0)$ is $(2, 1)$, followed by a half-turn.

4 $\mathbf{M} = \begin{bmatrix} 1 & -4 \\ -3 & 2 \end{bmatrix}$. Find the eigenvalues λ_1, λ_2 and the eigenvectors $\mathbf{e}_1$, $\mathbf{e}_2$ of **M**.

P has coordinates $(4, 7)$ with respect to the basis $\{\mathbf{i}, \mathbf{j}\}$. Find the coordinates (a, b) of P with respect to $\{\mathbf{e}_1, \mathbf{e}_2\}$ as basis. Find the image P' of P under **M**.

Find the image of (a, b) under the matrix $\mathbf{M}' = \begin{bmatrix} \lambda_1 & 0 \\ 0 & \lambda_2 \end{bmatrix}$. Show that $\mathbf{M}'\begin{bmatrix} a \\ b \end{bmatrix}$ equals the vector $\mathbf{OP}'$ referred to $\{\mathbf{e}_1, \mathbf{e}_2\}$ as basis.

5 Write the following conics in the form $a'x'^2 + b'y'^2 = 1$, and hence sketch them:

(*a*) $5x^2 + 4xy + 2y^2 = 1$ (*b*) $x^2 + 4xy - 2y^2 = 1$

(*c*) $5x^2 - 24xy - 2y^2 = 1$ (*d*) $4x^2 + 24xy - 3y^2 = 1$

6 Solve the following simultaneous differential equations:

(*a*) $\left.\begin{aligned} \dot{x} &= 5x - 4y \\ \dot{y} &= -x + 2y \end{aligned}\right\}$ (*b*) $\left.\begin{aligned} \dot{x} &= 3x + 2y \\ \dot{y} &= 18x - 2y \end{aligned}\right\}$ (*c*) $\left.\begin{aligned} \dot{x} &= 9x + 3y \\ \dot{y} &= 12x + 4y \end{aligned}\right\}$

We began Chapter 1 by examining some of the assumptions we make when we answer questions on transformations. One further assumption we did not mention at that time concerns the coordinate system we are using. We assumed that we were using the usual xy-axes. In this chapter we have seen that both the coordinates of a point and the matrix representation of a transformation are dependent on the basis used.

Miscellaneous exercise 11

1 Let A, B be the arithmetical progressions given by

$$A = 4, 6, 8, 10, \ldots,$$
$$B = 3, 8, 13, 18, \ldots.$$

Show that C is an arithmetical progression where $C_n = 2A_n + 3B_n$ and A_n, B_n, C_n are the nth terms of the respective progressions.

Can *any* arithmetical progression be written as a linear combination of A and B? What can you say about the set of all arithmetical progressions?

2 A transformation is represented by the matrix $\begin{bmatrix} 3 & 2 \\ 1 & -1 \end{bmatrix}$ relative to the basis $\left\{\begin{bmatrix} 3 \\ 1 \end{bmatrix}, \begin{bmatrix} -2 \\ 3 \end{bmatrix}\right\}$. Find the matrix which represents this transformation relative to the basis $\left\{\begin{bmatrix} 4 \\ 5 \end{bmatrix}, \begin{bmatrix} 5 \\ 9 \end{bmatrix}\right\}$.

3 Write the conic $9x^2 + 12xy + 4y^2 = 1$ in the form $a'x'^2 + b'y'^2 = 1$, and hence sketch it.

4 Solve the simultaneous differential equations:

$$\left.\begin{aligned} 3\dot{x} + 2\dot{y} &= 2x - 8y \\ 4\dot{x} - \dot{y} &= 10x - 7y \end{aligned}\right\}$$

5 For a square matrix $\mathbf{A}$, the sum of the elements on the main diagonal is called the trace of $\mathbf{A}$, written $tr(\mathbf{A})$. $\mathbf{S}$ and $\mathbf{T}$ are square matrices. Show that

(*a*) $tr(\mathbf{ST}) = tr(\mathbf{TS})$,

(*b*) if $\mathbf{S}$ is similar to $\mathbf{T}$, then $tr(\mathbf{S}) = tr(\mathbf{T})$.

6 The points P, Q have coordinates $(3, 1)$ and $(-1, 3)$ respectively with respect to the basis $\{\mathbf{i}, \mathbf{j}\}$. If O is the origin, show that OQ and OP are perpendicular.

Find the coordinates of P, Q with respect to the basis $\{\mathbf{u}, \mathbf{v}\}$, where $\mathbf{u} = \begin{bmatrix} 2 \\ 5 \end{bmatrix}$ and $\mathbf{v} = \begin{bmatrix} -1 \\ 1 \end{bmatrix}$.

Are the vectors $\mathbf{u}$ and $\mathbf{v}$ perpendicular?

Are the vectors $\mathbf{i}$ and $\mathbf{j}$ perpendicular?

Are the vectors $\mathbf{OP}$ and $\mathbf{OQ}$ perpendicular irrespective of the basis used to describe them?

Does the scalar product $\mathbf{OP}.\mathbf{OQ} = 0$ regardless of the basis used?

7 (*a*) $\mathbf{u}$ and $\mathbf{v}$ are perpendicular unit vectors. $\mathbf{u}'$ and $\mathbf{v}'$ are a second pair of perpendicular unit vectors. The coordinates of P with respect to $\{\mathbf{u}, \mathbf{v}\}$ are (a, ka) and with respect to $\{\mathbf{u}', \mathbf{v}'\}$ are (ka, a).

If θ is the positive (anticlockwise) angle from $\mathbf{u}$ to $\mathbf{u}'$, show that

$$k = \pm\tan\left(45^\circ + \frac{\theta}{2}\right),$$

and explain the relationship between k, θ and the $\pm$ signs.

(*b*) If the angle between $\mathbf{u}$ and $\mathbf{v}$ is α and the angle between $\mathbf{u}'$ and $\mathbf{v}'$ is β, show that the representations (a, ka) and (ka, a) for P are impossible unless $\alpha = \beta$, and that in this case

$$k = \frac{\cos\theta - \cos\alpha}{1 - \cos(\alpha - \theta)}.$$

SUMMARY

Definitions

(1) A vector $\mathbf{v}$ is said to be a *linear combination* of vectors $\mathbf{a}_1, \mathbf{a}_2, \ldots, \mathbf{a}_n$ if scalars $\lambda_1, \lambda_2, \ldots, \lambda_n$ (not all zero) can be found such that $\mathbf{v} = \lambda_1 \mathbf{a}_1 + \lambda_2 \mathbf{a}_2 + \ldots + \lambda_n \mathbf{a}_n$.

(2) A set of vectors $\{\mathbf{a}_1, \mathbf{a}_2, \ldots, \mathbf{a}_n\}$ is said to *span* a vector space V if every non-zero vector of V can be expressed as a linear combination of the set $\{\mathbf{a}_1, \mathbf{a}_2, \ldots, \mathbf{a}_n\}$.

(3) A set of vectors $\{\mathbf{a}_1, \mathbf{a}_2, \ldots, \mathbf{a}_n\}$ is said to be *linearly dependent* if scalars $\lambda_1, \lambda_2, \ldots, \lambda_n$ (not all zero) can be found such that $\lambda_1 \mathbf{a}_1 + \lambda_2 \mathbf{a}_2 + \ldots + \lambda_n \mathbf{a}_n = \mathbf{0}$.

(4) If $\lambda_1 \mathbf{a}_1 + \lambda_2 \mathbf{a}_2 + \ldots + \lambda_n \mathbf{a}_n = \mathbf{0}$ only when $\lambda_1 = \lambda_2 = \ldots = \lambda_n = 0$, then the set of vectors $\{\mathbf{a}_1, \mathbf{a}_2, \ldots, \mathbf{a}_n\}$ is said to be *linearly independent*.

(5) A set of vectors which is linearly independent and spans a vector space is called a *basis* for this vector space.

(6) The number of elements required to form a basis for a given vector space is called the *dimension* of that vector space.

(7) If $\{\mathbf{a}_1, \mathbf{a}_2, \ldots, \mathbf{a}_n\}$ is a basis for the vector space V, and $\mathbf{v} = \lambda_1 \mathbf{a}_1 + \lambda_2 \mathbf{a}_2 + \ldots + \lambda_n \mathbf{a}_n$, then $(\lambda_1, \lambda_2, \ldots, \lambda_n)$ are called the *coordinates* or *components* of $\mathbf{v}$ with respect to the basis $\{\mathbf{a}_1, \mathbf{a}_2, \ldots, \mathbf{a}_n\}$.

(8) Matrices $\mathbf{M}$ and $\mathbf{P}^{-1}\mathbf{MP}$ are said to be *similar* matrices, since they are different representations of the same linear transformation.

Similar matrices have the same characteristic polynomial and the same determinant.

Change of basis

	Old basis	New basis
Position vector	$\mathbf{x}$	$\mathbf{x}' = \mathbf{P}^{-1}\mathbf{x}$ (as $\mathbf{x} = \mathbf{Px}'$)
Matrix representing a linear transformation	$\mathbf{M}$	$\mathbf{P}^{-1}\mathbf{MP}$

12

Linear transformations again

With the added knowledge of vector spaces, basis and dimension, we look again at linear transformations. In particular we shall show that every linear transformation can be represented by a matrix; we shall also introduce the dimension theorem.

12.1 LINEAR TRANSFORMATIONS

If you look back at the examples of linear transformations which we have met so far, you will recognise that both the domain and the codomain were the same vector space. However, in this chapter we shall see examples of linear transformations in which the domain and codomain are not the same set, though both sets will be vector spaces. The definition of a linear transformation is now written as:

Definition 1
If V and W are vector spaces and $\mathbf{T}$ is a mapping from V to W, then $\mathbf{T}$ is a *linear transformation* if it satisfies both of the following conditions:
(1) $\mathbf{T}(\mathbf{a} + \mathbf{b}) = \mathbf{T}(\mathbf{a}) + \mathbf{T}(\mathbf{b})$ for all $\mathbf{a}, \mathbf{b} \in V$;
(2) $\mathbf{T}(k\mathbf{a}) = k\mathbf{T}(\mathbf{a})$ for all $\mathbf{a} \in V$ and all real numbers k.

Example 1

$$V = \{px^2 + qx + r : p, q, r \in \mathbb{R}\}, \quad W = \{kx + l : k, l \in \mathbb{R}\}.$$

Show that the mapping $\mathbf{D}: ax^2 + bx + c \mapsto 2ax + b$ is a linear transformation.

Solution
Both sets V and W are vector spaces (they have bases $\{x^2, x, 1\}$ and $\{x, 1\}$ respectively). To prove linearity we have to check the two conditions of the definition.

(1) $$\mathbf{D}((a_1x^2 + b_1x + c_1) + (a_2x^2 + b_2x + c_2)) = 2(a_1 + a_2)x + (b_1 + b_2)$$

and $$\mathbf{D}(a_1x^2 + b_1x + c_1) + \mathbf{D}(a_2x^2 + b_2x + c_2) = (2a_1x + b_1) + (2a_2x + b_2).$$

(2) $$\mathbf{D}(k(ax^2 + bx + c)) = 2kax + kb$$

and $$k\mathbf{D}(ax^2 + bx + c) = k(2ax + b).$$

So both conditions are satisfied and $\mathbf{D}$ is a linear transformation. □

In Chapter 1 we saw that any transformation represented by a matrix is a linear transformation. We now show the converse, that is, 'any linear transformation can be represented by a matrix'.

To demonstrate the method, we look again at Example 1. Relative to the basis $\{x^2, x, 1\}$, the vector $(ax^2 + bx + c)$ has coordinates (a, b, c) and relative to the basis $\{x, 1\}$ the vector $(2ax + b)$ has coordinates $(2a, b)$. So $\mathbf{D}$ can be written as

$$\mathbf{D}: \begin{bmatrix} a \\ b \\ c \end{bmatrix} \mapsto \begin{bmatrix} 2a \\ b \end{bmatrix} = \begin{bmatrix} 2 & 0 & 0 \\ 0 & 1 & 0 \end{bmatrix} \begin{bmatrix} a \\ b \\ c \end{bmatrix}.$$

$\begin{bmatrix} 2 & 0 & 0 \\ 0 & 1 & 0 \end{bmatrix}$ is therefore the matrix which represents the transformation relative to the bases given. A similar process is always possible and so we have the following theorem:

Theorem 1
Every linear transformation can be represented by a matrix.

We give the proof of this theorem in the case when the domain V has dimension 3 and the codomain W has dimension 2. If a basis of V is $\{\mathbf{x}_1, \mathbf{x}_2, \mathbf{x}_3\}$ and a basis of W is $\{\mathbf{y}_1, \mathbf{y}_2\}$, then $\mathbf{T}(\mathbf{x}_1)$, $\mathbf{T}(\mathbf{x}_2)$ and $\mathbf{T}(\mathbf{x}_3)$ all belong to the image space (where $\mathbf{T}$ is the linear transformation), and therefore are linear combinations of $\mathbf{y}_1$ and $\mathbf{y}_2$,

so
$$\mathbf{T}(\mathbf{x}_1) = a\mathbf{y}_1 + b\mathbf{y}_2$$
$$\mathbf{T}(\mathbf{x}_2) = c\mathbf{y}_1 + d\mathbf{y}_2$$
$$\mathbf{T}(\mathbf{x}_3) = e\mathbf{y}_1 + f\mathbf{y}_2.$$

If $\mathbf{x} \in V$, $\mathbf{x}$ is a linear combination of $\mathbf{x}_1$, $\mathbf{x}_2$, $\mathbf{x}_3$,

so
$$\mathbf{x} = p\mathbf{x}_1 + q\mathbf{x}_2 + r\mathbf{x}_3.$$

Using the properties of a linear transformation:

$$\mathbf{T}(\mathbf{x}) = p(a\mathbf{y}_1 + b\mathbf{y}_2) + q(c\mathbf{y}_1 + d\mathbf{y}_2) + r(e\mathbf{y}_1 + f\mathbf{y}_2)$$
$$= (ap + cq + er)\mathbf{y}_1 + (bp + dq + fr)\mathbf{y}_2;$$

that is,
$$\mathbf{T}: \begin{bmatrix} p \\ q \\ r \end{bmatrix} \mapsto \begin{bmatrix} ap + cq + er \\ bp + dq + fr \end{bmatrix} = \begin{bmatrix} a & c & e \\ b & d & f \end{bmatrix} \begin{bmatrix} p \\ q \\ r \end{bmatrix}$$

so the matrix representing the transformation is $\begin{bmatrix} a & c & e \\ b & d & f \end{bmatrix}$.

Q.1 If V has dimension n and W has dimension m, what is the order of the matrix representing the transformation?

Exercise 12A

Determine which of the following mappings are linear. In the case of linear transformations, give a basis for each of the domain and codomain, and hence write down a matrix representing the linear transformation.

1 The domain is the set of polynomials of degree 2 or less in t, and the mapping is the operation of replacing t by $(t + 1)$.

2 The domain is the set of polynomials of degree 2 or less in t, and the mapping is definite integration over the interval $[0, x]$, that is,

$$at^2 + bt + c \mapsto \int_0^x (at^2 + bt + c)dt$$

3 The domain is the set of all 2×2 matrices and a matrix is mapped onto its determinant.

4 The domain is the set of all complex numbers and the mappings are defined as follows:

(*a*) $z \mapsto z + a$ (*b*) $z \mapsto bz$

(*c*) $z \mapsto z^*$ (*d*) $z \mapsto \dfrac{1}{z}$

(*e*) $z \mapsto |z|$ (*f*) $z \mapsto -2z^*$

5 The domain is the set of functions of the form $ax^2 + be^x + cxe^x + dx^2e^x$ and the mappings are

(*a*) $y \mapsto \dfrac{dy}{dx} - y$ (*b*) $y \mapsto \dfrac{d^2y}{dx^2} - 2\dfrac{dy}{dx} + y$

6 The domain is the set of 3×3 matrices and the 3×3 matrix is mapped onto its trace, that is:

$$\begin{bmatrix} a & b & c \\ d & e & f \\ g & h & i \end{bmatrix} \mapsto (a + e + i)$$

7 The domain is the set of polynomials of degree 2 or less. If $f(x)$ is in the domain, then

$$f(x) \mapsto \text{the polynomial } g(x),$$

where the graph of $y = g(x)$ is found by reflecting the graph of $y = f(x)$ in the line $x = 1$.

12.2 CANONICAL FORM

We saw in Chapter 1 that the matrix representing a linear transformation is not unique. In this section we see how, by systematically changing the basis of the *codomain* (but leaving the basis of the domain unaltered), the matrix can be reduced to a simpler form which is known as *canonical form.*

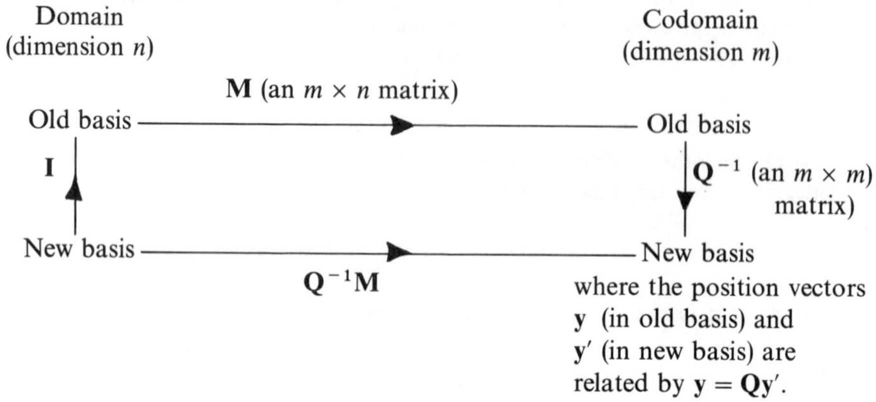

If we choose the matrix $\mathbf{Q}$ (and therefore also the matrix $\mathbf{Q}^{-1}$) to be an elementary matrix, then by repeated application, we can reduce the matrix representing the transformation to the form

$$\left[\begin{array}{cccccc|c} 1 & 0 & 0 & 0 & \dots & 0 & \\ 0 & 1 & 0 & 0 & \dots & 0 & \\ 0 & 0 & 1 & 0 & \dots & 0 & \mathbf{D} \\ \vdots & \vdots & \vdots & \vdots & & \vdots & \\ 0 & 0 & 0 & 0 & \dots & 1 & \\ \hline & & & \mathbf{0} & & & \mathbf{0} \end{array}\right]$$

where the top left-hand block is a $k \times k$ identity matrix $\mathbf{I}_k$, both bottom blocks (if they exist) contain zero everywhere and the top right-hand block (if it exists) is a $k \times (n-k)$ matrix of no particular type. This form is called *canonical form.*

Any $m \times n$ matrix can be reduced to canonical form by systematic multiplication by elementary matrices. The following example illustrates the general procedure.

Example 2

Reduce $\mathbf{M} = \begin{bmatrix} 1 & 2 & 1 \\ 2 & 5 & 3 \\ 5 & 14 & 9 \\ 7 & 18 & 11 \end{bmatrix}$ to canonical form.

Solution

	Matrix	*Elementary matrix*
	$\begin{bmatrix}1 & 2 & 1\\ 2 & 5 & 3\\ 5 & 14 & 9\\ 7 & 18 & 11\end{bmatrix}$	
Subtracting 7 × row 1 from row 4:	$\begin{bmatrix}1 & 2 & 1\\ 2 & 5 & 3\\ 5 & 14 & 9\\ 0 & 4 & 4\end{bmatrix}$	$\mathbf{E}_1 = \begin{bmatrix}1 & 0 & 0 & 0\\ 0 & 1 & 0 & 0\\ 0 & 0 & 1 & 0\\ -7 & 0 & 0 & 1\end{bmatrix}$
Subtracting 5 × row 1 from row 3:	$\begin{bmatrix}1 & 2 & 1\\ 2 & 5 & 3\\ 0 & 4 & 4\\ 0 & 4 & 4\end{bmatrix}$	$\mathbf{E}_2 = \begin{bmatrix}1 & 0 & 0 & 0\\ 0 & 1 & 0 & 0\\ -5 & 0 & 1 & 0\\ 0 & 0 & 0 & 1\end{bmatrix}$
Subtracting 2 × row 1 from row 2:	$\begin{bmatrix}1 & 2 & 1\\ 0 & 1 & 1\\ 0 & 4 & 4\\ 0 & 4 & 4\end{bmatrix}$	$\mathbf{E}_3 = \begin{bmatrix}1 & 0 & 0 & 0\\ -2 & 1 & 0 & 0\\ 0 & 0 & 1 & 0\\ 0 & 0 & 0 & 1\end{bmatrix}$
Subtracting 4 × row 2 from row 4:	$\begin{bmatrix}1 & 2 & 1\\ 0 & 1 & 1\\ 0 & 4 & 4\\ 0 & 0 & 0\end{bmatrix}$	$\mathbf{E}_4 = \begin{bmatrix}1 & 0 & 0 & 0\\ 0 & 1 & 0 & 0\\ 0 & 0 & 1 & 0\\ 0 & -4 & 0 & 1\end{bmatrix}$
Subtracting 4 × row 2 from row 3:	$\begin{bmatrix}1 & 2 & 1\\ 0 & 1 & 1\\ 0 & 0 & 0\\ 0 & 0 & 0\end{bmatrix}$	$\mathbf{E}_5 = \begin{bmatrix}1 & 0 & 0 & 0\\ 0 & 1 & 0 & 0\\ 0 & -4 & 1 & 0\\ 0 & 0 & 0 & 1\end{bmatrix}$
Subtracting 2 × row 2 from row 1:	$\begin{bmatrix}1 & 0 & -1\\ 0 & 1 & 1\\ 0 & 0 & 0\\ 0 & 0 & 0\end{bmatrix}$	$\mathbf{E}_6 = \begin{bmatrix}1 & -2 & 0 & 0\\ 0 & 1 & 0 & 0\\ 0 & 0 & 1 & 0\\ 0 & 0 & 0 & 1\end{bmatrix}$

This is now in canonical form, where

$$\mathbf{E}_6\mathbf{E}_5\mathbf{E}_4\mathbf{E}_3\mathbf{E}_2\mathbf{E}_1\mathbf{M} = \left[\begin{array}{cc|c} 1 & 0 & -1 \\ 0 & 1 & 1 \\ \hline 0 & 0 & 0 \\ 0 & 0 & 0 \end{array}\right].$$

With a little practice you will probably combine several of these steps; for example the first three steps can be combined by premultiplying by the matrix

$$\mathbf{E}_3\mathbf{E}_2\mathbf{E}_1 = \begin{bmatrix} 1 & 0 & 0 & 0 \\ -2 & 1 & 0 & 0 \\ -5 & 0 & 1 & 0 \\ -7 & 0 & 0 & 1 \end{bmatrix}.$$

Similarly, the fourth and fifth steps could be combined using the matrix $\begin{bmatrix} 1 & 0 & 0 & 0 \\ 0 & 1 & 0 & 0 \\ 0 & -4 & 1 & 0 \\ 0 & -4 & 0 & 1 \end{bmatrix}$. If in doubt, do not try to combine steps, as it is very easy to make mistakes. □

The process described is a general one. The only difficulty which can occur is that one of the elements on the diagonal may be zero, in which case it is necessary to interchange two rows by premultiplying by a suitable elementary matrix. If this is not sufficient (for example, if the first column contains nothing but zeros), it may be necessary to interchange two columns by postmultiplying by a suitable elementary matrix. This will not change the basis of the domain, only the order in which the vectors have been written down.

Exercise 12B

Reduce the following matrices to canonical forms:

1 $\begin{bmatrix} 4 & 0 & -3 \\ 1 & -1 & 4 \\ 2 & 2 & -11 \end{bmatrix}$

2 $\begin{bmatrix} 1 & 2 & 0 \\ 2 & 0 & 1 \\ 3 & 2 & 1 \\ 6 & 4 & 2 \\ 0 & -4 & 1 \\ 9 & 6 & 3 \end{bmatrix}$

3 $\begin{bmatrix} 2 & 0 & 3 & 1 \\ -1 & 5 & 6 & -3 \end{bmatrix}$

4 $\begin{bmatrix} 1 & 2 & 1 & -3 & 0 \\ 6 & 0 & 10 & 9 & 5 \\ 2 & 0 & 3 & 4 & 2 \end{bmatrix}$

5 $\begin{bmatrix} 1 & 4 & 3 & 0 \\ 2 & 1 & 0 & 1 \\ 3 & 0 & 1 & 1 \\ 0 & 5 & 2 & -1 \end{bmatrix}$

6 $\begin{bmatrix} 1 & 3 & 4 & 1 & 3 \\ 1 & 3 & 8 & 2 & 5 \\ 2 & 6 & -4 & 3 & 0 \\ 3 & 9 & 0 & 4 & 3 \end{bmatrix}$

12.3 IMAGE SPACE AND KERNEL

Example 3

Investigate the linear transformation **T** of $\mathbb{R}^3 \to \mathbb{R}^2$ in which $\mathbf{T}: \begin{bmatrix} x \\ y \\ z \end{bmatrix} \mapsto \begin{bmatrix} x \\ x \end{bmatrix}$.

Solution

(1) The matrix representing the transformation is the 2×3 matrix $\begin{bmatrix} 1 & 0 & 0 \\ 1 & 0 & 0 \end{bmatrix}$, as $\begin{bmatrix} x \\ x \end{bmatrix} = \begin{bmatrix} 1 & 0 & 0 \\ 1 & 0 & 0 \end{bmatrix} \begin{bmatrix} x \\ y \\ z \end{bmatrix}$.

(2) As the domain and codomain are different sets, we are not able to describe the transformation in geometric terms. We can illustrate it using a mapping diagram (Fig. 1). For example, the *image* of the point (3, 1, 4) in the domain is the point (3, 3) in the codomain.

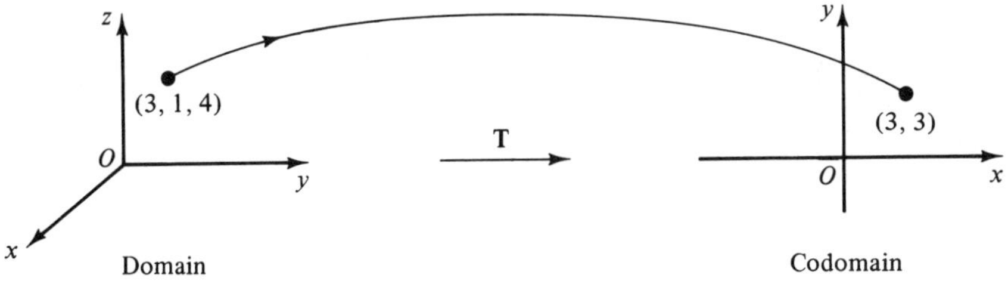

Figure 1

(3) The set of all the images is called the *image space* or *range* of the linear transformation **T**. In this example the image space is the line $y = x$ (in the codomain); that is, it is the line $\mathbf{r} = \lambda \begin{bmatrix} 1 \\ 1 \end{bmatrix}$ which goes through the origin. The image space is a one-dimensional vector space (a basis is $\left\{ \begin{bmatrix} 1 \\ 1 \end{bmatrix} \right\}$).

(4) As the domain is three-dimensional and the image space is one-dimensional, many points in the domain map onto a single point in the codomain: for example, all the points on the plane $x = 3$ in the domain map onto the point (3, 3) in the codomain. In particular, all points on the plane $x = 0$ in the domain map onto the origin in the codomain. The set of vectors in the domain which map onto the zero vector in the codomain has a special name – it is known as the *kernel* or the *null space* of the transformation. In this example the kernel is the set of vectors $\left\{ \begin{bmatrix} 0 \\ p \\ q \end{bmatrix} : p, q \in \mathbb{R} \right\}$. These form a two-dimensional vector space (a basis is $\begin{bmatrix} 0 \\ 1 \\ 0 \end{bmatrix}$ and $\begin{bmatrix} 0 \\ 0 \\ 1 \end{bmatrix}$). □

In Example 3 we introduced the terms image space or range, and kernel or null space.

Definition 2
The set of all the images under a linear transformation $\mathbf{T}$ is called *image space* or *range*. It is a subset of the codomain and need not be the same as the codomain.

$$\text{Image space} = \{\mathbf{T}(\mathbf{x}) : \mathbf{x} \in \text{domain}).$$

The dimension of the image space is called the *rank* of the linear transformation.

We saw in the last section that the matrix $\mathbf{M}$ representing a transformation can be expressed, when a suitable basis for the codomain is chosen, in canonical form; that is, in the form

$$\mathbf{M} = \left[\begin{array}{c|c} \mathbf{I}_k & \mathbf{D} \\ \hline \mathbf{0} & \mathbf{0} \end{array}\right].$$

If $\mathbf{x} = \begin{bmatrix} x_1 \\ x_2 \\ \vdots \\ x_n \end{bmatrix}$ is the domain, then $\mathbf{T}(\mathbf{x})$ is in the codomain. Now

$$\mathbf{T}(\mathbf{x}) = \mathbf{M}\mathbf{x} = \sum_{i=1}^{n} x_i \mathbf{M}_i$$

where $\mathbf{M}_i$ are the columns of $\mathbf{M}_i$; that is $\begin{bmatrix} 1 \\ 0 \\ \vdots \\ 0 \end{bmatrix}, \begin{bmatrix} 0 \\ 1 \\ \vdots \\ 0 \end{bmatrix}$, and so on.

Only k of these vectors are linearly independent, so the dimension of the image space is k. This is a particularly useful result, since once the transformation matrix has been reduced to canonical form the rank can be found from the size of the identity matrix in the top left-hand corner.

Definition 3
The set of vectors in the domain of $\mathbf{T}$ which map onto the zero vector in the codomain is known as the *kernel* or *null* space of the linear transformation.

$$\text{Kernel} = \{\mathbf{x} : \mathbf{T}(\mathbf{x}) = \mathbf{0}\}.$$

The dimension of the kernel is called the *nullity* of the linear transformation.

Notice that the kernel is a subset of the domain of $\mathbf{T}$ while the image space is a subset of the codomain.

Let us look again at Example 3. The domain is $\mathbb{R}^3$, the kernel is a two-dimensional vector space, while the image space is a one-dimensional vector space. The fact that

dimension of domain = dimension of kernel + dimension of image space

in this example is not an accident. It is an important result, known as the *dimension theorem*, which we shall prove in Chapter 14.

Theorem 2

For a linear transformation **T**,

dimension of image space + dimension of kernel = dimension of domain;

that is, rank + nullity = dimension of domain.

Example 4

Find the kernel and image space of the transformation **T** represented by the matrix $\mathbf{M} = \begin{bmatrix} 1 & 2 & 1 \\ 2 & 5 & 3 \\ 5 & 14 & 9 \\ 7 & 18 & 11 \end{bmatrix}$.

Solution

T is a linear mapping from $\mathbb{R}^3$ to $\mathbb{R}^4$. A basis for $\mathbb{R}^3$ is $\left\{ \begin{bmatrix} 1 \\ 0 \\ 0 \end{bmatrix}, \begin{bmatrix} 0 \\ 1 \\ 0 \end{bmatrix}, \begin{bmatrix} 0 \\ 0 \\ 1 \end{bmatrix} \right\}$ so the image space is spanned by

$$\left\{ \mathbf{M}\begin{bmatrix} 1 \\ 0 \\ 0 \end{bmatrix}, \mathbf{M}\begin{bmatrix} 0 \\ 1 \\ 0 \end{bmatrix}, \mathbf{M}\begin{bmatrix} 0 \\ 0 \\ 1 \end{bmatrix} \right\}; \quad \text{that is,} \left\{ \begin{bmatrix} 1 \\ 2 \\ 5 \\ 7 \end{bmatrix}, \begin{bmatrix} 2 \\ 5 \\ 14 \\ 18 \end{bmatrix}, \begin{bmatrix} 1 \\ 3 \\ 9 \\ 11 \end{bmatrix} \right\},$$

which are the columns of the matrix. If we call these vectors $\mathbf{c}_1, \mathbf{c}_2, \mathbf{c}_3$, we see that $\mathbf{c}_1 - \mathbf{c}_2 + \mathbf{c}_3 = \mathbf{0}$, (they are linearly dependent). However, any two of these vectors, for example $\begin{bmatrix} 1 \\ 2 \\ 5 \\ 7 \end{bmatrix}$ and $\begin{bmatrix} 1 \\ 3 \\ 9 \\ 11 \end{bmatrix}$, are linearly independent and so form a basis for the image space, which is therefore of dimension 2.

To find the kernel of the transformation we solve $\mathbf{T}(\mathbf{x}) = \mathbf{Mx} = \mathbf{0}$:

$$\begin{bmatrix} 1 & 2 & 1 \\ 2 & 5 & 3 \\ 5 & 14 & 9 \\ 7 & 18 & 11 \end{bmatrix} \begin{bmatrix} x \\ y \\ z \end{bmatrix} = \begin{bmatrix} 0 \\ 0 \\ 0 \\ 0 \end{bmatrix}$$

$$\left.\begin{aligned} x + 2y + z &= 0 \\ 2x + 5y + 3z &= 0 \\ 5x + 14y + 9z &= 0 \\ 7x + 18y + 11z &= 0 \end{aligned}\right\}$$

Subtracting appropriate multiples of the first equation from the others:

$$\left.\begin{aligned} x + 2y + z &= 0 \\ y + z &= 0 \\ 4y + 4z &= 0 \\ 4y + 4z &= 0 \end{aligned}\right\}$$

Subtracting 4 × second equation from third and fourth equations:

$$\left.\begin{aligned} x + 2y + z &= 0 \\ y + z &= 0 \\ 0 &= 0 \\ 0 &= 0 \end{aligned}\right\}$$

Subtracting 2 × second equation from the first equation:

$$\left.\begin{aligned} x - z &= 0 \\ y + z &= 0 \end{aligned}\right\}$$

If $x = \lambda$, then $z = \lambda$ and $y = -\lambda$, that is $\begin{bmatrix} x \\ y \\ z \end{bmatrix} = \lambda \begin{bmatrix} 1 \\ -1 \\ 1 \end{bmatrix}$; so the kernel is the one-dimensional vector space with basis $\left\{\begin{bmatrix} 1 \\ -1 \\ 1 \end{bmatrix}\right\}$. □

Q.2 How is this kernel related to the linear relation $\mathbf{c}_1 - \mathbf{c}_2 + \mathbf{c}_3 = \mathbf{0}$ which connects the columns of the matrix?

We can link this work with the ideas of the last section, where we saw that with a change of basis of the codomain (and $\mathbf{0}$ remains $\mathbf{0}$ under any change of basis – why?) but leaving the domain untouched, the matrix representing the transformation can be written in canonical form as

$$\left[\begin{array}{cc|c} 1 & 0 & -1 \\ 0 & 1 & 1 \\ \hline 0 & 0 & 0 \\ 0 & 0 & 0 \end{array}\right].$$

As the identity matrix in the top left-hand corner is of order 2, the dimension of the image space (the rank) is 2. We are therefore looking for two linearly independent vectors in the codomain which will be a basis for the image space, for example

$$\mathbf{M}\begin{bmatrix}1\\0\\0\end{bmatrix}=\begin{bmatrix}1\\2\\5\\7\end{bmatrix} \quad \text{and} \quad \mathbf{M}\begin{bmatrix}0\\1\\0\end{bmatrix}=\begin{bmatrix}2\\2\\14\\18\end{bmatrix}.$$

To find the kernel we solve

$$\begin{bmatrix}1&0&-1\\0&1&1\\0&0&0\\0&0&0\end{bmatrix}\begin{bmatrix}x\\y\\z\end{bmatrix}=\begin{bmatrix}0\\0\\0\\0\end{bmatrix}; \text{ that is, } \left.\begin{matrix}x-z=0\\y+z=0\end{matrix}\right\} \text{ as before.}$$

If $x=\lambda$, then $z=\lambda$ and $y=-\lambda$, that is, $\begin{bmatrix}x\\y\\z\end{bmatrix}=\lambda\begin{bmatrix}1\\-1\\1\end{bmatrix}$. So the kernel is the one-dimensional vector space with basis $\left\{\begin{bmatrix}1\\-1\\1\end{bmatrix}\right\}$.

Notice that: dimension of domain $=3$
dimension of image space $=2$
dimension of kernel $=1$,

which agrees with the dimension theorem.

Exercise 12C

1 Find the kernel and image space of the transformations represented by the following matrices. Verify Theorem 2 in each case.

(*a*) $\begin{bmatrix}1&3&5\\2&6&10\end{bmatrix}$ (*b*) $\begin{bmatrix}4&2&6\\1&3&4\\5&0&5\end{bmatrix}$ (*c*) $\begin{bmatrix}2&0\\-1&3\\4&-2\\7&7\end{bmatrix}$

(*d*) $\begin{bmatrix}-3&2\\4&9\\1&-2\end{bmatrix}$ (*e*) $\begin{bmatrix}2&4&4\\3&1&-1\\2&0&4\end{bmatrix}$ (*f*) $\begin{bmatrix}3&0&-1\\-2&-1&-1\\1&2&3\end{bmatrix}$

2 Find a 2×2 matrix $\mathbf{M}$ representing a linear transformation in which the image space is $\left\{\lambda\begin{bmatrix}1\\3\end{bmatrix}\right\}$ and the kernel is $\left\{\mu\begin{bmatrix}5\\4\end{bmatrix}\right\}$. What are the image space and kernel of the transformation represented by $\mathbf{M}^2$?

3 Find a matrix representing a linear transformation from $\mathbb{R}^3 \to \mathbb{R}^4$, in which a basis for the image space is $\left\{ \begin{bmatrix} 1 \\ 2 \\ -3 \\ 4 \end{bmatrix}, \begin{bmatrix} 0 \\ 2 \\ 1 \\ 5 \end{bmatrix} \right\}$.

4 Find a matrix representing a linear transformation from $\mathbb{R}^3 \to \mathbb{R}^2$, in which a basis for the kernel is $\left\{ \begin{bmatrix} 2 \\ 1 \\ 3 \end{bmatrix}, \begin{bmatrix} 1 \\ 0 \\ -1 \end{bmatrix} \right\}$.

5 $\mathbf{N} = \begin{bmatrix} 2 & 1 & -1 & 4 \\ 3 & 4 & 6 & 1 \\ -1 & 2 & 8 & -7 \end{bmatrix}$, $\mathbf{a} = \begin{bmatrix} 1 \\ 0 \\ 0 \\ 0 \end{bmatrix}$, $\mathbf{b} = \begin{bmatrix} 0 \\ 1 \\ 0 \\ 0 \end{bmatrix}$, $\mathbf{c} = \begin{bmatrix} 0 \\ 0 \\ 1 \\ 0 \end{bmatrix}$, $\mathbf{d} = \begin{bmatrix} 0 \\ 0 \\ 0 \\ 1 \end{bmatrix}$.

(*a*) Find two distinct linear relations connecting the columns of **N**.
(*b*) State two independent vectors of the kernel. Do they form a basis for the kernel?
(*c*) If the domain is spanned by **a**, **b**, **c**, **d**, state the dimension of the image space and give a basis for the image space.
(*d*) Find a linear relation connecting the rows of **N**, and deduce the cartesian equation of the plane that is the range. Show that this agrees with your answers to (*c*).

6 Find the kernel and image space of the transformation represented by $\mathbf{N}^{\mathrm{T}}$, the transpose of the matrix **N** in question 5.

There have been two main themes in this chapter. First, we have given the full definition of a linear transformation and shown how to prove the important result that every linear transformation can be represented by a matrix. So, in dealing with linear transformations it is perfectly general to use a matrix approach. Second, we have introduced the ideas of image space and kernel, applications of which we shall see in the next chapter.

Miscellaneous exercise 12

1 Find a 2×2 matrix **N** representing a linear transformation, in which the image space coincides with the kernel. What is $\mathbf{N}^2$?

2 $r(\mathbf{M})$ = rank of matrix **M**.
(*a*) If **A** and **B** are compatible for addition, prove that

$$r(\mathbf{A}+\mathbf{B}) \leqslant r(\mathbf{A}) + r(\mathbf{B}).$$

(*b*) If **C** and **D** are compatible for multiplication, what can you say about $r(\mathbf{CD})$?
(*c*) **A** is a 3×3 matrix and **B** is the same matrix with one extra column added. Can $r(\mathbf{B})$ be different from $r(\mathbf{A})$?

3 If $\mathbf{A}^{\mathrm{T}}$ is the transpose of **A**, then two products $\mathbf{A}^{\mathrm{T}}\mathbf{A}$ and $\mathbf{AA}^{\mathrm{T}}$ can be formed. If

(*a*) $\mathbf{A} = \begin{bmatrix} a & b \\ c & d \end{bmatrix}$ (*b*) $\mathbf{A} = \begin{bmatrix} a & b & c \\ d & e & f \end{bmatrix}$, investigate the products $\mathbf{AA}^T$ and $\mathbf{A}^T\mathbf{A}$ in each case and determine whether their ranks can be different from $r(\mathbf{A})$.

4 Some linear transformations can be regarded as 'projections', as can be illustrated by the following example. Figure 2 shows a two-dimensional representation of a cube in which we will assume that the 'projected' edges of the cube are of equal length. If we assume that the new axes are OX, OY as shown, then we have

$$\begin{bmatrix}1\\0\\0\end{bmatrix} \mapsto \begin{bmatrix}-\sqrt{3}\\-1\end{bmatrix}, \quad \begin{bmatrix}0\\1\\0\end{bmatrix} \mapsto \begin{bmatrix}\sqrt{3}\\-1\end{bmatrix} \quad \text{and} \quad \begin{bmatrix}0\\0\\1\end{bmatrix} \mapsto \begin{bmatrix}0\\2\end{bmatrix}$$

where the length of the projected sides is two units.

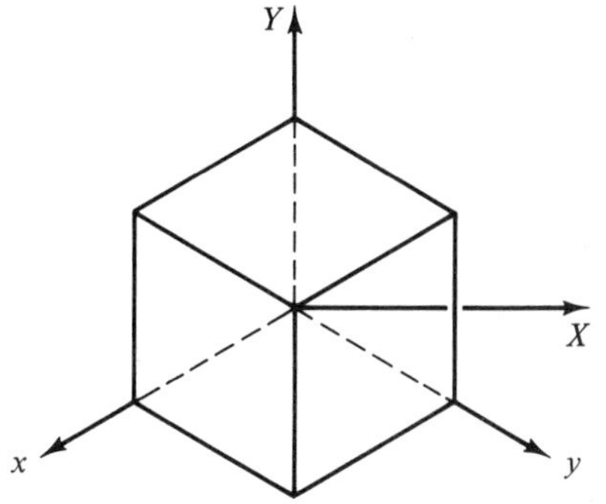

Figure 2

Find the matrix of the transformation and determine the kernel. Verify that the vertices of the cube are projected onto the vertices of a hexagon and the origin.

5 Another typical projection of a cube is shown in Figure 3. If the projected verticals and horizontals parallel to Ox are equal in length, select coordinates of V in the (X, Y) space and hence find the matrix of the transformation. Verify that the remaining vertices of the cube are projected onto the expected points and find the kernel of the transformation.

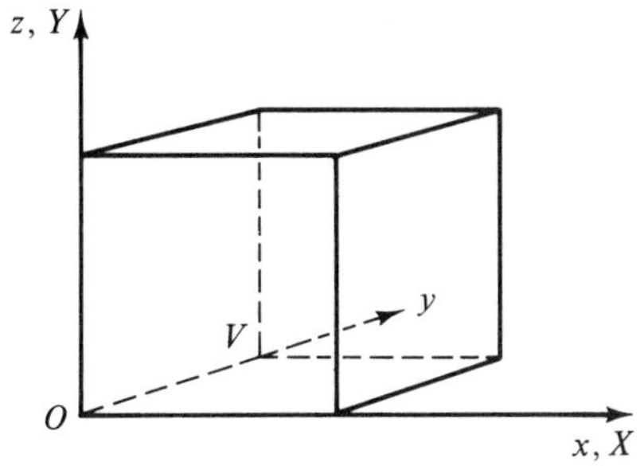

Figure 3

6 A cube in four-space has vertices at (a, b, c, d), where a, b, c, d take the values 0, 1 to give the 16 vertices. If the cube is projected by the matrix

$$\begin{bmatrix}2 & \sqrt{2} & 0 & -\sqrt{2}\\0 & \sqrt{2} & 2 & \sqrt{2}\end{bmatrix}$$

into two-dimensional space, find the coordinates of the transformed vertices and hence plot them and draw the projection of the cube in four-space.

What is the kernel of the transformation?

SUMMARY

Definitions

V and W are vector spaces and $\mathbf{T}$ is a mapping from V to W.

(1) $\mathbf{T}$ is a *linear transformation* if it satisfies
(*a*) $\mathbf{T}(\mathbf{a}+\mathbf{b}) = \mathbf{T}(\mathbf{a}) + \mathbf{T}(\mathbf{b})$ for all $\mathbf{a}, \mathbf{b} \in V$;
(*b*) $\mathbf{T}(k\mathbf{a}) = k\mathbf{T}(\mathbf{a})$ for all $\mathbf{a} \in V$ and all real numbers, k.

(2) *Image space* $= \{\mathbf{T}(\mathbf{x}) : \mathbf{x} \in \text{domain}\}$.

(3) The dimension of the image space is called the *rank* of $\mathbf{T}$.

(4) *Kernel* $= \{\mathbf{x} : \mathbf{T}(\mathbf{x}) = \mathbf{0}\}$. (The kernel is a subset of the domain.)

(5) The dimension of the kernel is called the *nullity of* $\mathbf{T}$.

(6) A matrix of the form $\left[\begin{array}{c|c} \mathbf{I}_k & \mathbf{D} \\ \hline \mathbf{0} & \mathbf{0} \end{array}\right]$ is said to be in *canonical form*.

Theorems

(1) Every linear transformation can be represented by a matrix.

(2) (The dimension theorem.) For a linear transformation, $\mathbf{T}$,

dimension of image space + dimension of kernel = dimension of domain;

that is, rank + nullity = dimension of domain.

13

Equations

In the last chapter we developed the ideas of rank, range and kernel. We now look at two applications of this work, seeing how the ideas can help us to solve systems of linear equations and differential equations and to understand the nature of the solutions.

13.1 LINEAR EQUATIONS

The set of equations

$$\left.\begin{aligned} a_{11}x_1 + a_{12}x_2 + \ldots + a_{1n}x_n &= d_1 \\ a_{21}x_1 + a_{22}x_2 + \ldots + a_{2n}x_n &= d_2 \\ \vdots \qquad \vdots \qquad\quad \vdots \quad &\quad\; \vdots \\ a_{m1}x_1 + a_{m2}x_2 + \ldots + a_{mn}x_n &= d_m \end{aligned}\right\}$$

is called a set of m linear equations in the n unknowns $x_1, x_2, \ldots, x_n$. The number of equations, m, need not necessarily be the same as the number of unknowns, n.

This set of equations can be written in matrix form as

$$\mathbf{Ax} = \mathbf{d}$$

where $\mathbf{A} = \begin{bmatrix} a_{11} & a_{12} & \ldots & a_{1n} \\ a_{21} & a_{22} & \ldots & a_{2n} \\ \vdots & \vdots & & \vdots \\ a_{m1} & a_{m2} & \ldots & a_{mn} \end{bmatrix}$, $\mathbf{x} = \begin{bmatrix} x_1 \\ x_2 \\ \vdots \\ x_n \end{bmatrix}$, $\mathbf{d} = \begin{bmatrix} d_1 \\ d_2 \\ \vdots \\ d_m \end{bmatrix}$.

Q.1 Check that $\begin{bmatrix} x \\ y \\ z \end{bmatrix} = \begin{bmatrix} 3 + \lambda \\ -2 + 2\lambda \\ \lambda \end{bmatrix}$

is a solution of the set of linear equations

$$\left.\begin{aligned} x + \;\; y - 3z &= \;\, 1 \\ 3x - 2y + \;\; z &= 13 \end{aligned}\right\}$$

If we put $\lambda = 5$ in Q.1 we get $\begin{bmatrix} x \\ y \\ z \end{bmatrix} = \begin{bmatrix} 8 \\ 8 \\ 5 \end{bmatrix}$

which is a *particular solution* of this set of linear equations. For different values of λ we get different particular solutions. Does the set of solutions

$$\left\{ \begin{bmatrix} x \\ y \\ z \end{bmatrix} = \begin{bmatrix} 3+\lambda \\ -2+2\lambda \\ \lambda \end{bmatrix};\quad \lambda \in \mathbb{R} \right\}$$

give us the complete set of solutions of these linear equations, or might we have missed some? We shall investigate this question in the next two sections.

13.2 HOMOGENEOUS LINEAR EQUATIONS

In the last section we expressed the set of linear equations in the form $\mathbf{Ax} = \mathbf{d}$.

If $\mathbf{d} = \mathbf{0}$ the set of equations is called a set of *homogeneous linear equations*.

We can interpret the equation $\mathbf{Ax} = \mathbf{0}$ using the ideas of Chapter 12 – if we have a linear transformation of $\mathbb{R}^n \to \mathbb{R}^m$ represented by the matrix $\mathbf{A}$, the set of solutions is therefore the kernel of this transformation; that is, those vectors $\mathbf{x} \in \mathbb{R}^n$ which are mapped onto $\mathbf{0} \in \mathbb{R}^m$.

We examine in more detail what could happen in the familiar case where we have three equations in three unknowns.

$$\left.\begin{aligned} a_1x + b_1y + c_1z &= 0 \\ a_2x + b_2y + c_2z &= 0 \\ a_3x + b_3y + c_3z &= 0 \end{aligned}\right\}$$

that is, $\mathbf{Ax} = \mathbf{0}$, where $\mathbf{A} = \begin{bmatrix} a_1 & b_1 & c_1 \\ a_2 & b_2 & c_2 \\ a_3 & b_3 & c_3 \end{bmatrix}$.

We are able to discover the nature of the solution set by looking at the rank of $\mathbf{A}$, which is the matrix of a transformation from $\mathbb{R}^3 \to \mathbb{R}^3$.

(1) $\text{Rank}(\mathbf{A}) = 3$: the dimension of the kernel $= 0$, so $\mathbf{x} = \mathbf{0}$ is the only solution.

(2) $\text{Rank}(\mathbf{A}) = 2$: the dimension of the kernel $= 1$, so the solution set is $\{\lambda\mathbf{p} : \lambda \in \mathbb{R}\}$, where $\mathbf{p}$ is a non-zero vector in the kernel.

(3) $\text{Rank}(\mathbf{A}) = 1$: the dimension of the kernel $= 2$, so the solution set is $\{\lambda\mathbf{p} + \mu\mathbf{q} : \lambda, \mu \in \mathbb{R}\}$, where $\mathbf{p}$ and $\mathbf{q}$ are two linearly independent vectors in the kernel. In other words, to find the complete solution set we need to find just two linearly independent solutions, and any other solution is a linear combination of these two.

(4) $\text{Rank}(\mathbf{A}) = 0$: the dimension of the kernel $= 3$, so all vectors in the domain are solutions.

In the general case where $\mathbf{A}$ is an $m \times n$ matrix, the kernel of the transformation represented by the matrix $\mathbf{A}$ gives us the complete solution of the set of homogeneous linear equations $\mathbf{Ax} = \mathbf{0}$. We can therefore be confident that we have not missed any.

Example 1
Find the solution of

$$\left.\begin{aligned} x + y + z + t &= 0 \\ 2x + 3y - z + 4t &= 0 \end{aligned}\right\}$$

Solution
This represents a mapping from $\mathbb{R}^4 \to \mathbb{R}^2$ and written in matrix form is

$$\begin{bmatrix} 1 & 1 & 1 & 1 \\ 2 & 3 & -1 & 4 \end{bmatrix} \begin{bmatrix} x \\ y \\ z \\ t \end{bmatrix} = \begin{bmatrix} 0 \\ 0 \end{bmatrix} \qquad (A)$$

so we are seeking the kernel of the linear transformation

$$\begin{bmatrix} x \\ y \\ z \\ t \end{bmatrix} \mapsto \begin{bmatrix} 1 & 1 & 1 & 1 \\ 2 & 3 & -1 & 4 \end{bmatrix} \begin{bmatrix} x \\ y \\ x \\ t \end{bmatrix}.$$

In the last chapter we saw that by changing the basis of the codomain, the matrix representing the transformation can be reduced to canonical form. This gives a valuable general method for finding the kernel, although it may not be the best method of tackling easy examples.

Subtracting $2 \times$ row 1 from row 2, equation (A) now becomes:

$$\begin{bmatrix} 1 & 1 & 1 & 1 \\ 0 & 1 & -3 & 2 \end{bmatrix} \begin{bmatrix} x \\ y \\ x \\ t \end{bmatrix} = \begin{bmatrix} 0 \\ 0 \end{bmatrix}.$$

Subtracting row 2 from row 1:

$$\left[\begin{array}{cc:cc} 1 & 0 & 4 & -1 \\ 0 & 1 & -3 & 2 \end{array}\right] \begin{bmatrix} x \\ y \\ z \\ t \end{bmatrix} = \begin{bmatrix} 0 \\ 0 \end{bmatrix} \qquad (B)$$

so the rank of this transformation is 2. As the dimension of the domain is 4, the dimension of the kernel is $(4 - 2) = 2$.

Multiplying out (B):

$$\left.\begin{aligned} x \quad + 4z - t &= 0 \\ y - 3z + 2t &= 0 \end{aligned}\right\}.$$

We are looking for two linearly independent solutions, as the dimension of the kernel is 2. Solving for x and y in terms of z and t we get

$$\begin{aligned} x &= -4z + t \\ y &= 3z - 2t, \end{aligned}$$

so
$$\begin{bmatrix} x \\ y \\ z \\ t \end{bmatrix} = z\begin{bmatrix} -4 \\ 3 \\ 1 \\ 0 \end{bmatrix} + t\begin{bmatrix} 1 \\ -2 \\ 0 \\ 1 \end{bmatrix}.$$

A basis for this kernel is therefore $\left\{\begin{bmatrix} -4 \\ 3 \\ 1 \\ 0 \end{bmatrix}, \begin{bmatrix} 1 \\ -2 \\ 0 \\ 1 \end{bmatrix}\right\}$.

Thus we have the complete solution set of the original equations, which is

$$\left\{\begin{bmatrix} x \\ y \\ z \\ t \end{bmatrix} = \lambda\begin{bmatrix} -4 \\ 3 \\ 1 \\ 0 \end{bmatrix} + \mu\begin{bmatrix} 1 \\ -2 \\ 0 \\ 1 \end{bmatrix} : \lambda, \mu \in \mathbb{R}\right\}.$$ □

Exercise 13A

1 Find the solutions of the following sets of linear equations:

(*a*) $\left.\begin{aligned} 2x + 3y - 4z &= 0 \\ x - 2y + 3z &= 0 \end{aligned}\right\}$

(*b*) $\left.\begin{aligned} 2x + 3y - z - 2t &= 0 \\ 3x - y + 2z + 3t &= 0 \\ x + 7y - 4z - 7t &= 0 \end{aligned}\right\}$

(*c*) $x + y - 2z + 3t = 0$

(*d*) $\left.\begin{aligned} x + 3y - z &= 0 \\ 3x - 12y + 12z &= 0 \\ 2x - y + 3z &= 0 \\ x + 11y + 9z &= 0 \end{aligned}\right\}$

2 For different values of p solve the equations

$$\left.\begin{aligned} x + 2y + 4z &= 0 \\ px - y - 2z &= 0 \end{aligned}\right\}$$

3 Show that $\mathbf{c}_1 = \begin{bmatrix} 3 \\ 1 \\ 1 \end{bmatrix}$, $\mathbf{c}_2 = \begin{bmatrix} 6 \\ 1 \\ 4 \end{bmatrix}$, $\mathbf{c}_3 = \begin{bmatrix} -4 \\ -1 \\ -2 \end{bmatrix}$ are a linearly dependent set of vectors. Hence write down the kernel of the transformation

$$\begin{bmatrix} x \\ y \\ z \end{bmatrix} \mapsto \begin{bmatrix} 3 & 6 & -4 \\ 1 & 1 & -1 \\ 1 & 4 & -2 \end{bmatrix}\begin{bmatrix} x \\ y \\ z \end{bmatrix}$$

and the solution of $\left.\begin{aligned} 3x + 6y - 4z &= 0 \\ x + y - z &= 0 \\ x + 4y - 2z &= 0 \end{aligned}\right\}$

4 For what solutions of λ do the following equations have a non-trivial solution?

$$\left.\begin{aligned} 2x + y + 3z &= 0 \\ (1+\lambda)x + \lambda y + (3+\lambda)z &= 0 \\ 2x + y + (1+\lambda)z &= 0 \end{aligned}\right\}$$

13.3 NON-HOMOGENEOUS LINEAR EQUATIONS

A set of linear equations can be written in matrix form as $\mathbf{Ax} = \mathbf{d}$. If $\mathbf{d} \neq \mathbf{0}$ then the set of equations is known as a *non-homogeneous set of linear equations.*

We begin by considering what happens when we have three equations in three unknowns:

$$\left.\begin{aligned} a_1x + b_1y + c_1z &= d_1 \\ a_2x + b_2y + c_2z &= d_2 \\ a_3x + b_3y + c_3z &= d_3 \end{aligned}\right\}$$

which is written in matrix form as $\mathbf{Ax} = \mathbf{d}$, where $\mathbf{d} = \begin{bmatrix} d_1 \\ d_2 \\ d_3 \end{bmatrix}$.

Thinking of this as a linear transformation of $\mathbb{R}^3 \to \mathbb{R}^3$ represented by the matrix $\mathbf{A}$, there will be solutions only if $\mathbf{d}$ belongs to the image space of the transformation. Consequently,

(1) if the rank of $\mathbf{A} = 3$, the dimension of the image space $= 3$, so $\mathbf{d}$ must belong to the image space under all circumstances;

(2) if the rank of $\mathbf{A} < 3$, the dimension of the image space <3, so $\mathbf{d}$ may or may not belong to the image space.

For example, with the equations

$$\left.\begin{aligned} x + y + z &= 1 \\ 2x + 2y + 2z &= 2 \\ 3x + 3y + 3z &= 4 \end{aligned}\right\}$$

that is,

$$\begin{bmatrix} 1 & 1 & 1 \\ 2 & 2 & 2 \\ 3 & 3 & 3 \end{bmatrix}\begin{bmatrix} x \\ y \\ z \end{bmatrix} = \begin{bmatrix} 1 \\ 2 \\ 4 \end{bmatrix}$$

or

$$\mathbf{Ax} = \mathbf{d},$$

the image space is the line $\mathbf{r} = \lambda\begin{bmatrix} 1 \\ 2 \\ 3 \end{bmatrix}$ (Fig. 1, overleaf).

Now $\mathbf{d} = \begin{bmatrix} 1 \\ 2 \\ 4 \end{bmatrix}$ does not lie in the image space, so there can be no vector $\mathbf{x}$ which satisfies $\mathbf{Ax} = \mathbf{d}$.

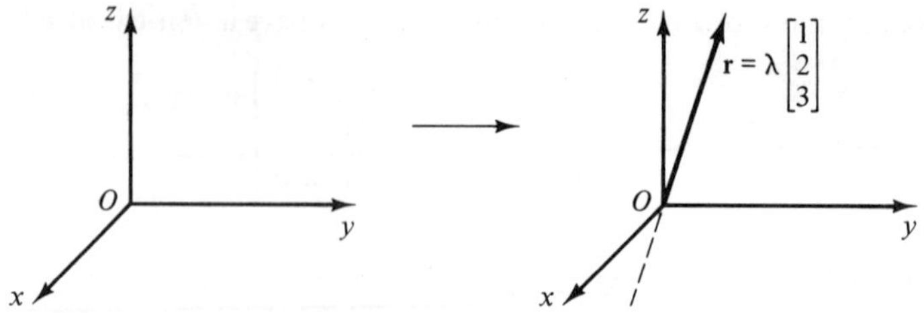

Figure 1

An alternative way of writing the original equations is

$$x \begin{bmatrix} a_1 \\ a_2 \\ a_3 \end{bmatrix} + y \begin{bmatrix} b_1 \\ b_2 \\ b_3 \end{bmatrix} + z \begin{bmatrix} c_1 \\ c_2 \\ c_3 \end{bmatrix} = \begin{bmatrix} d_1 \\ d_2 \\ d_3 \end{bmatrix}.$$

Hence, using the obvious notation,

$$x\mathbf{a} + y\mathbf{b} + z\mathbf{c} + (-1)\mathbf{d} = \mathbf{0}.$$

So, if solutions x, y, z exist, then $\mathbf{a}, \mathbf{b}, \mathbf{c}, \mathbf{d}$ are linearly dependent vectors. It follows that if we add $\mathbf{d}$ to the set of vectors $\{\mathbf{a}, \mathbf{b}, \mathbf{c}\}$, no further dimension is added to the space defined by $\{\mathbf{a}, \mathbf{b}, \mathbf{c}\}$. Consequently there will be a solution only if the rank of $\mathbf{A}$ is the same as the rank of $\begin{bmatrix} a_1 & b_1 & c_1 & d_1 \\ a_2 & b_2 & c_2 & d_2 \\ a_3 & b_3 & c_3 & d_3 \end{bmatrix}$ (which is written, as $\mathbf{A}|\mathbf{d}$); that is,

$$\operatorname{rank}(\mathbf{A}) = \operatorname{rank}(\mathbf{A}|\mathbf{d}).$$

These ideas can be extended to the general case where $\mathbf{A}$ is an $m \times n$ matrix, but before looking at any examples we prove an important theorem.

Theorem 1

The solution set of $\mathbf{Ax} = \mathbf{d}$ consists of all vectors $\mathbf{p} + \mathbf{k}$ where $\mathbf{p}$ is a particular solution and $\mathbf{k}$ is any member of the kernel of $\mathbf{A}$.

If $\mathbf{p}$ is a particular solution of $\mathbf{Ax} = \mathbf{d}$,

then $$\mathbf{Ap} = \mathbf{d}$$

so $$\mathbf{A}(\mathbf{x} - \mathbf{p}) = \mathbf{0}.$$

$(\mathbf{x} - \mathbf{p})$ therefore belongs to the kernel of the transformation represented by the matrix $\mathbf{A}$;

that is, $$\mathbf{x} - \mathbf{p} = \mathbf{k}, \quad \text{where } \mathbf{k} \in \text{kernel};$$

hence $$\mathbf{x} = \mathbf{p} + \mathbf{k}.$$

These solutions do not form a vector space, but a translated subspace, as illustrated in the next example.

Example 2
Find the solution of

$$\left.\begin{aligned} x + y - 3z &= 1 \\ 3x - 2y + z &= 13 \end{aligned}\right\}$$

Solution
Written in matrix form this is

$$\begin{bmatrix} 1 & 1 & -3 \\ 3 & -2 & 1 \end{bmatrix} \begin{bmatrix} x \\ y \\ z \end{bmatrix} = \begin{bmatrix} 1 \\ 13 \end{bmatrix}.$$

So we can think of the linear transformation from $\mathbb{R}^3 \to \mathbb{R}^2$ represented by the matrix $\begin{bmatrix} 1 & 1 & -3 \\ 3 & -2 & 1 \end{bmatrix}$.

We reduce this to canonical form, applying the same operations to the right-hand side.

$$\begin{bmatrix} 1 & 1 & -3 \\ 3 & -2 & 1 \end{bmatrix} \begin{bmatrix} x \\ y \\ z \end{bmatrix} = \begin{bmatrix} 1 \\ 13 \end{bmatrix}$$

Subtracting $3 \times$ row 1 from row 2:
$$\begin{bmatrix} 1 & 1 & -3 \\ 0 & -5 & 10 \end{bmatrix} \begin{bmatrix} x \\ y \\ z \end{bmatrix} = \begin{bmatrix} 1 \\ 10 \end{bmatrix}$$

Multiplying row 2 by $-\frac{1}{5}$:
$$\begin{bmatrix} 1 & 1 & -3 \\ 0 & 1 & -2 \end{bmatrix} \begin{bmatrix} x \\ y \\ z \end{bmatrix} = \begin{bmatrix} 1 \\ -2 \end{bmatrix}$$

Subtracting row 2 from row 1:
$$\left[\begin{array}{cc|c} 1 & 0 & -1 \\ 0 & 1 & -2 \end{array}\right] \begin{bmatrix} x \\ y \\ z \end{bmatrix} = \begin{bmatrix} 3 \\ -2 \end{bmatrix} \qquad (A)$$

This is now in canonical form. The rank of the matrix is 2, so the dimension of the image space is 2. Therefore the dimension of the kernel is $(3 - 2) = 1$.

Kernel
To find the kernel we have to solve

$$\begin{bmatrix} 1 & 0 & -1 \\ 0 & 1 & -2 \end{bmatrix} \begin{bmatrix} x \\ y \\ z \end{bmatrix} = \begin{bmatrix} 0 \\ 0 \end{bmatrix};$$

that is,
$$\left.\begin{aligned} x - z &= 0 \\ y - 2z &= 0 \end{aligned}\right\}$$

giving
$$x = z \quad \text{and} \quad y = 2z.$$

Hence $\begin{bmatrix} x \\ y \\ z \end{bmatrix} = z \begin{bmatrix} 1 \\ 2 \\ 1 \end{bmatrix}$, so a basis for the kernel is $\left\{ \begin{bmatrix} 1 \\ 2 \\ 1 \end{bmatrix} \right\}$.

Particular solution

In Equation (*A*), if $z = 0$, then $x = 3$ and $y = -2$, so $\begin{bmatrix} 3 \\ -2 \\ 0 \end{bmatrix}$ is a particular solution.

Applying Theorem 1, the complete solution set is

$$\left\{ \begin{bmatrix} x \\ y \\ z \end{bmatrix} = \begin{bmatrix} 3 \\ -2 \\ 0 \end{bmatrix} + \lambda \begin{bmatrix} 1 \\ 2 \\ 1 \end{bmatrix} : \lambda \in \mathbb{R} \right\}.$$

The solution set is the line through $(-3, 2, 0)$ with direction $\begin{bmatrix} 1 \\ 2 \\ 1 \end{bmatrix}$ (Fig. 2).

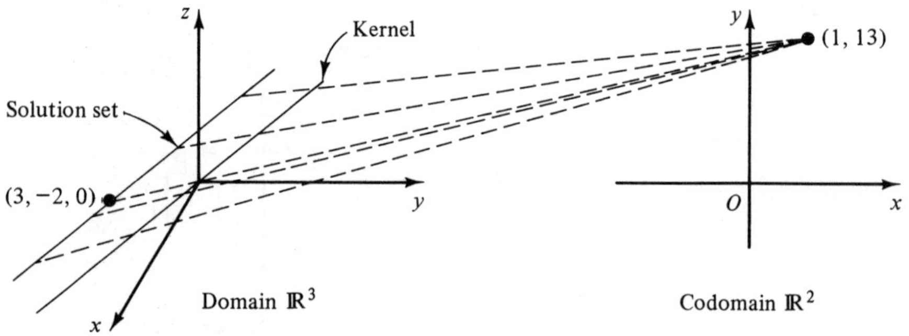

Figure 2

This is parallel to the kernel, which is the reason we refer to the solution set as a translated subspace. □

Example 3
Find the solution of

$$\left.\begin{aligned} x + y + 2z + 4t &= 3 \\ x \quad\;\; + z - 3t &= -1 \\ y + z + 7t &= 6 \end{aligned}\right\}$$

Solution
Written in matrix form this is

$$\begin{bmatrix} 1 & 1 & 2 & 4 \\ 1 & 0 & 1 & -3 \\ 0 & 1 & 1 & 7 \end{bmatrix} \begin{bmatrix} x \\ y \\ z \\ t \end{bmatrix} = \begin{bmatrix} 3 \\ -1 \\ 6 \end{bmatrix},$$

so we can think of the linear transformation from $\mathbb{R}^4 \to \mathbb{R}^3$ represented by the matrix $\begin{bmatrix} 1 & 1 & 2 & 4 \\ 1 & 0 & 1 & -3 \\ 0 & 1 & 1 & 7 \end{bmatrix}$.

We reduce this to canonical form:

$$\begin{bmatrix} 1 & 1 & 2 & 4 \\ 1 & 0 & 1 & -3 \\ 0 & 1 & 1 & 7 \end{bmatrix}\begin{bmatrix} x \\ y \\ z \\ t \end{bmatrix} = \begin{bmatrix} 3 \\ -1 \\ 6 \end{bmatrix}$$

Subtracting row 1 from row 2:

$$\begin{bmatrix} 1 & 1 & 2 & 4 \\ 0 & -1 & -1 & -7 \\ 0 & 1 & 1 & 7 \end{bmatrix}\begin{bmatrix} x \\ y \\ z \\ t \end{bmatrix} = \begin{bmatrix} 3 \\ -4 \\ 6 \end{bmatrix}$$

Adding row 2 to row 3:

$$\begin{bmatrix} 1 & 1 & 2 & 4 \\ 0 & -1 & -1 & -7 \\ 0 & 0 & 0 & 0 \end{bmatrix}\begin{bmatrix} x \\ y \\ z \\ t \end{bmatrix} = \begin{bmatrix} 3 \\ -4 \\ 2 \end{bmatrix}$$

With the transformation now represented by the matrix $\begin{bmatrix} 1 & 1 & 2 & 4 \\ 0 & -1 & -1 & -7 \\ 0 & 0 & 0 & 0 \end{bmatrix}$, any vector in the image space will be of the form $\begin{bmatrix} a \\ b \\ 0 \end{bmatrix}$.

Therefore $\begin{bmatrix} 3 \\ -4 \\ 2 \end{bmatrix}$ does not lie in the image space, so there are no values of x, y, z, t which satisfy the original equations.

We say that this set of equations is *inconsistent*. If a set of equations does have a solution we say that they are *consistent*. □

Exercise 13B

1 For what values of c, if any, do the following equations have a solution?

(*a*) $\left.\begin{aligned} 3x + y &= 8 \\ 2x - y &= 7 \\ 4x + 3y &= c \end{aligned}\right\}$ (*b*) $\left.\begin{aligned} 2x + y &- 10 \\ 3x - 2y &= 1 \\ 5x + 3y &= c \end{aligned}\right\}$ (*c*) $\left.\begin{aligned} 3x - 2y &= 9 \\ 5x - 8y &- 1 \\ cx + 3y &= 11 \end{aligned}\right\}$

2 Find values of a and b for which the equations

$$\left.\begin{aligned} 2x - y &= 5 \\ 6x - 3y &= a \\ x + y &= b \end{aligned}\right\}$$

have a solution.

3 Solve the following sets of equations (see Exercise 13A, question 1):

(*a*) $\left.\begin{aligned} 2x + 3y - 4z &= 4 \\ x - 2y + 3z &= 0 \end{aligned}\right\}$ (*b*) $\left.\begin{aligned} 2x + 3y - z - 2t &= -1 \\ 3x - y + 2z + 3t &= 12 \\ x + 7y - 4z - 7t &= -7 \end{aligned}\right\}$

(c) $x + y - 2z + 3t = 17$ (d) $\left.\begin{aligned} x + 3y - z &= 8 \\ 3x - 12y + 12z &= -24 \\ 2x - y + 3z &= 0 \\ x - 11y + 9z &= -24 \end{aligned}\right\}$

4 Find the kernel of the transformation

$$\begin{bmatrix} x \\ y \\ z \\ t \end{bmatrix} \mapsto \begin{bmatrix} 2 & 1 & 0 & -2 \\ 4 & 3 & 2 & 0 \end{bmatrix} \begin{bmatrix} x \\ y \\ z \\ t \end{bmatrix}$$

and solve the equations $\left.\begin{aligned} 2x + y - 2t &= 5 \\ 4x + 3y + 2z &= 9 \end{aligned}\right\}.$

5 Find the solutions for x, y, z, t of the equations

$$\left.\begin{aligned} 2x + 4y + 4z - t &= a \\ 3x - 3y + 3t &= b \\ x + 3y + 2z - t &= c \\ x - y + t &= d \end{aligned}\right\}$$

when (a) $a = 11$, $b = -5$, $c = 9$, $d = 1$
(b) $a = 3$, $b = -6$, $c = 8$, $d = -2$

13.4 LINEAR DIFFERENTIAL EQUATIONS

The same theory helps us to understand the nature of the solution of linear differential equations such as

$$\frac{d^2y}{dx^2} - 5\frac{dy}{dx} + 6y = 5\sin x - 15\cos x.$$

The techniques for solving such equations are given in books on calculus, where it is shown that the solution is made up of two parts – the particular integral and the complementary function. This is analogous to the solution of non-homogeneous linear equations, where the solution is made up of two parts – the particular solution and a member of the kernel.

If we write the left-hand side in the form

$$\left(\frac{d^2}{dx^2} - 5\frac{d}{dx} + 6\right)y$$

we can think of the *differential operator*, the expression within the brackets, as a mapping $\mathbf{T}$ from the set of suitable differential functions $y(x)$ to $z(x)$ where

$$z(x) = \frac{d^2y(x)}{dx^2} - 5\frac{dy(x)}{dx} + 6y(x).$$

For example,

$$y(x) \mapsto z(x)$$

$$e^{5x} \mapsto 6e^{5x}$$

$$2x^2 + 3x + 4 \mapsto 12x^2 - 2x + 13$$

$$\sin x \mapsto 5 \sin x - 5 \cos x$$

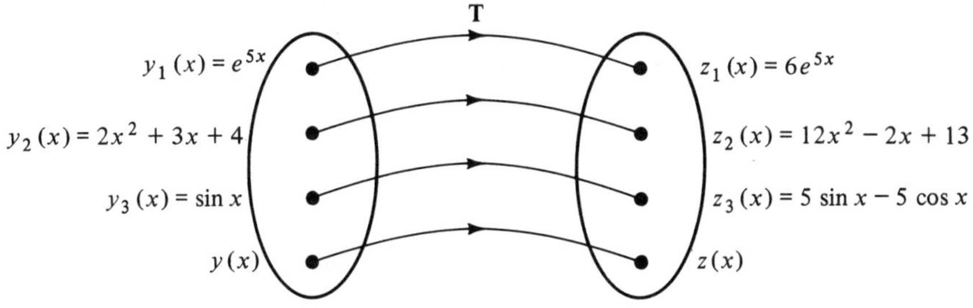

Figure 3

Solving the given differential equation is equivalent to finding those functions $y(x)$ which map onto $(5 \sin x - 15 \cos x)$.

We must first show that **T** is a linear transformation. Now

$$\mathbf{T}(y_1 + y_2) = \frac{d^2(y_1 + y_2)}{dx^2} - 5\frac{d(y_1 + y_2)}{dx} + 6(y_1 + y_2)$$

$$= \left(\frac{d^2y_1}{dx^2} - 5\frac{dy_1}{dx} + 6y_1\right) + \left(\frac{d^2y_2}{dx^2} - 5\frac{dy_2}{dx} + 6y^2\right)$$

$$= \mathbf{T}(y_1) + \mathbf{T}(y_2),$$

and

$$\mathbf{T}(ky_1) = \frac{d^2(ky_1)}{dx^2} - 5\frac{d(ky_1)}{dx} + 6(ky_1)$$

$$= k\left(\frac{d^2y_1}{dx^2} - 5\frac{dy_1}{dx} + 6y_1\right)$$

$$= k\mathbf{T}(y_1).$$

As **T** is a linear transformation, we are able to rewrite Theorem 1 to apply to linear differential equations:

Theorem 2

The solution set of $\mathbf{T}(y(x)) = f(x)$ consists of all functions $p(x) + k(x)$, where $p(x)$ is a particular solution and $k(x)$ is any member of the kernel of **T**.

Q.2 Prove Theorem 2.

For the differential equation at the beginning of this section, the complementary function (kernel) is

$$k(x) = Ae^{2x} + Be^{3x},$$

which is a two-dimensional vector space (the basis is $\{e^{2x}, e^{3x}\}$) and the particular solution is $p(x) = 2\sin x - \cos x$. So the complete solution is

$$y(x) = Ae^{2x} + Be^{3x} + 2\sin x - \cos x.$$

In general, the kernel of a linear differential equation of order n is an n-dimensional vector space.

Miscellaneous exercise 13

1 Prove algebraically that in all cases a pair of linear equations

$$\left.\begin{aligned} a_1x + b_1y + c_1z = 0 \\ a_2x + b_2y + c_2z = 0 \end{aligned}\right\}$$

where a_1, b_1, c_1 and a_2, b_2, c_2 are given real numbers, has a solution for (x, y, z) other than $(0, 0, 0)$.

Prove also that three linear equations

$$\left.\begin{aligned} a_1x + b_1y + c_1z = 0 \\ a_2x + b_2y + c_2z = 0 \\ a_2x + b_3y + c_3z = 0 \end{aligned}\right\}$$

have a solution other than $(x, y, z) = (0, 0, 0)$ if the three equations

$$\left.\begin{aligned} a_1X + a_2Y + a_3Z = 0 \\ b_1X + b_2Y + b_3Z = 0 \\ c_1X + c_2Y + c_3Z = 0 \end{aligned}\right\}$$

have a solution other than $(X, Y, Z) = (0, 0, 0)$. [Oxford Entrance]

2 Explain what is meant by the statement that the set Σ of functions of the form

$$a_1 + a_2x + a_3x^2 + a_4e^x + a_5xe^x + a_6x^2e^x$$

is a vector space (for the usual operations of addition and scalar multiplication). What is the dimension of Σ?

Prove that this set of functions is mapped into itself by the linear operator $\mathbf{L}$, defined by $\left(\frac{d}{dx} - 1\right)$ (so that $\mathbf{L}f(x)$ denotes $f'(x) - f(x)$). What is the null space for this mapping?

Express the mapping in matrix form: $\{a_i\} \mapsto \mathbf{M}\{a_i\}$ (where $\{a_i\}$ is a six-row column vector) and state the rank of the matrix $\mathbf{M}$.

Apply the results to obtain the general solution (assumed to lie within the space Σ) of the differential equation

$$\frac{dy}{dx} - y = 3x^2 + 2e^x.$$

Further, by applying the mapping $\mathbf{L}^2$ to Σ, obtain the general solution of

$$\frac{d^2y}{dx^2} - 2\frac{dy}{dx} + y = 3x^2 + 2e^x.$$

[Mathematical Association Diploma, 1966]

3 Show that the transformation **L**, of three-dimensional Euclidean space into itself, given by

$$\mathbf{L}(x, y, z) = (x - y + z, \quad 2x + y - 3z, \quad x + 2y - 4z),$$

is a linear transformation. Find the range space $R(\mathbf{L})$ and the null space, $N(\mathbf{L})$ of the transformation **L**. If **L** is expressed in the form

$$\mathbf{L}\colon \begin{bmatrix} x \\ y \\ z \end{bmatrix} \mapsto \mathbf{M} \begin{bmatrix} x \\ y \\ z \end{bmatrix},$$

where **M** is a 3×3 matrix, give the matrix **M**.

Hence, or otherwise, obtain the range spaces, $R(\mathbf{L}^2)$ and $R(\mathbf{L}^3)$, and the null spaces, $N(\mathbf{L}^2)$ and $N(\mathbf{L}^3)$ of the repeated transformations $\mathbf{L}^2$ and $\mathbf{L}^3$. Verify that

$$R(\mathbf{L}) \supseteq R(\mathbf{L}^2) \supseteq R(\mathbf{L}^3)$$

$$N(\mathbf{L}) \subseteq N(\mathbf{L}^2) \subseteq N(\mathbf{L}^3).$$

[Mathematical Association Diploma, 1968]

4 A *quaternion* is defined as $\quad x_0 + x_1 i + x_2 j + x_3 k,$

where $x_0, x_1, x_2, x_3 \in \mathbb{R}$ and i, j, k are such that

$$i^2 = j^2 = k^2 = -1$$

and

$$ij = -ji = k,$$

$$jk = -kj = i,$$

$$ki = -ik = j.$$

Multiplication is associative and distributive over addition.

Q is the set of quaternions and a mapping $\mathbf{T}\colon Q \to Q$ is defined by

$$\mathbf{T}(\mathbf{x}) = \mathbf{a} \times \mathbf{x},$$

where

$$\mathbf{a} = a_0 + a_1 i + a_2 j + a_3 k$$

and

$$\mathbf{x} = x_0 + x_1 i + x_2 j + x_3 k.$$

(*a*) Prove that this mapping is linear.

(*b*) Represent **T** by a 4×4 matrix.

(*c*) Write down the identity element under multiplication for quaternions. Hence find the right multiplicative inverse for the quaternion $1 + i + j + k$. Is this also the left inverse?

(*d*) Show that the right inverse of a non-zero quaternion is unique.

SUMMARY

The set of linear equations

$$\left.\begin{array}{l} a_{11}x_1 + a_{12}x_2 + \ldots + a_{1n}x_n = d_1 \\ a_{21}x_1 + a_{22}x_2 + \ldots + a_{2n}x_n = d_2 \\ \quad\vdots \qquad\quad \vdots \qquad\qquad\quad \vdots \qquad\quad \vdots \\ a_{m1}x_1 + a_{m2}x_2 + \ldots + a_{mn}x_n = d_m \end{array}\right\}$$

can be written in matrix form as $\mathbf{Ax} = \mathbf{d}$.

If $\mathbf{d} = \mathbf{0}$ we have a set of *homogeneous* linear equations.
If $\mathbf{d} \neq \mathbf{0}$ we have a set of *non-homogeneous* linear equations.

Theorem
The solution set of $\mathbf{Ax} = \mathbf{d}$ consists of all vectors $\mathbf{p} + \mathbf{k}$, where $\mathbf{p}$ is a particular solution and $\mathbf{k}$ is any member of the kernel of $\mathbf{A}$.

14

Vector spaces

We begin by reviewing the work so far. In Chapters 1–9 the study of linear transformations was introduced using geometrical ideas in two and three dimensions, and this was extended to n-dimensional vectors in Project 4. The next stage was to introduce non-geometrical examples which were seen to behave in a manner similar to the geometric vectors, and this led to an informal introduction to vector spaces, some results and applications.

In this chapter we look again at some of the ideas we have already met, but in a more general and abstract way, in which we try to pin down unambiguously the essential features and then define them rigorously. This has a number of advantages:

(1) Given any new situation we can test whether it behaves similarly.

(2) We can prove directly from the definitions some of the results which we have stated or hinted at previously.

(3) If a general result is proved, then it can be applied in particular situations.

14.1 VECTOR SPACES

In Chapter 10 we investigated the closure rules for a vector space, namely, that if $\mathbf{a}, \mathbf{b} \in S$, then

(1) $$\mathbf{a} + \mathbf{b} \in S, \text{ and}$$

(2) $$\lambda\mathbf{a} \in S \ (\lambda \in \mathbb{R}),$$

and we said that there are a number of other rules which are also true in these systems.

Q.1 What other common features can you identify?

You have probably listed many of the rules called axioms of a vector space, which we now define formally:

Definition 1

A *vector space, V, over the real numbers*, $\mathbb{R}$, is a set of elements $\mathbf{a}, \mathbf{b}, \mathbf{c}, \ldots,$ which are called vectors, together with the operations of vector addition and scalar multiplication, such that

(a) *Under addition*

(A1) Closure: $\mathbf{a} + \mathbf{b} \in V$ for all $\mathbf{a}, \mathbf{b} \in V$.

(A2) Identity: there is a vector $\mathbf{0} \in \mathbf{V}$ such that $\mathbf{a} + \mathbf{0} = \mathbf{0} + \mathbf{a} = \mathbf{a}$ for all $\mathbf{a} \in V$.

(A3) Associative: $\mathbf{a} + (\mathbf{b} + \mathbf{c}) = (\mathbf{a} + \mathbf{b}) + \mathbf{c}$ for all $\mathbf{a}, \mathbf{b}, \mathbf{c} \in V$.
(A4) Inverses: for each $\mathbf{a} \in V$, there exists a vector $(-\mathbf{a}) \in V$, such that

$$\mathbf{a} + (-\mathbf{a}) = (-\mathbf{a}) + \mathbf{a} = \mathbf{0}.$$

(A5) Commutative: $\mathbf{a} + \mathbf{b} = \mathbf{b} + \mathbf{a}$ for all $\mathbf{a}, \mathbf{b} \in V$.

(*b*) *Under scalar multiplication*
(M1) Closure: $\lambda\mathbf{a} \in V$ for all $\mathbf{a} \in V$ and $\lambda \in \mathbb{R}$.
(M2) Identity: $1\mathbf{a} = \mathbf{a}$ for all $\mathbf{a} \in V$.
(M3) Associative: $(\lambda\mu)\mathbf{a} = \lambda(\mu\mathbf{a})$ for all $\mathbf{a} \in V$ and $\lambda, \mu \in \mathbb{R}$.

(*c*) *Under addition and scalar multiplication*
(M4) Distributive: $\lambda(\mathbf{a} + \mathbf{b}) = \lambda\mathbf{a} + \lambda\mathbf{b}$ for all $\mathbf{a}, \mathbf{b} \in V$ and $\lambda \in \mathbb{R}$.
(M5) $(\lambda + \mu)\mathbf{a} = \lambda\mathbf{a} + \mu\mathbf{a}$ for all $\mathbf{a} \in V$ and $\lambda, \mu \in \mathbb{R}$.

This may seem to be a rather arbitrary selection of axioms, but in fact this set is found to be sufficient, and other properties can be proved to be consequences of them, as we shall see in the next sections.

A vector space may appear to be a complicated structure, as there are ten axioms, but in fact the first five axioms (A1–A5) simply state that the vectors form an Abelian group* under vector addition. If we are to verify that a set of elements forms a vector space, then all the axioms should be checked carefully. If the set of elements does *not* form a vector space, then it is necessary to find only one axiom which does not hold.

Another point to note with the axioms is that the '+' symbol has two different meanings. In one context it simply represents the law combining two vectors, while the other '+' is the operation of addition of real numbers. A similar comment also applies to multiplication. Sometimes the symbol '$\oplus$' is used for the vector addition to distinguish it from the scalar addition.

Exercise 14A

Which of the following sets form vector spaces over the real numbers? Assume the usual definitions of addition and scalar multiplication, except in questions 21 and 22 where alternative definitions are given. For those sets which are not vector spaces, list all the axioms which are not satisfied.

1 All polynomials of degree less than 3 with real coefficients

2 All polynomials of degree exactly 3 with real coefficients

3 All polynomials of degree less than 3 with rational coefficients

4 Complex numbers

5 All real solutions of $3x + 4y + 5z = 0$

6 All real solutions of $3x + 4y + 5z \geqslant 0$

7 All real solutions of $\left.\begin{aligned} 3x + 4y + 5z &= 12 \\ x + 2y + z &= 4 \end{aligned}\right\}$

* See Chapter 15.

8 All real solutions of $\left.\begin{aligned} 3x + 4y + 5z &= 0 \\ x + 2y + z &= 0 \end{aligned}\right\}$

9 All real solutions of $xy \geqslant 0$

10 All real solutions of $y = 3x - 1$

11 Matrices of the form $\begin{bmatrix} 0 & b \\ b & 0 \end{bmatrix}$, $b \in \mathbb{R}$

12 Singular 2×2 matrices with real entries

13 Real symmetric matrices

14 All real solutions of the differential equation $\ddot{x} + 4x = 0$

15 All real solutions of the differential equation $\ddot{x} + 5\dot{x} + 6x = 3e^t$

16 Even functions with domain $\mathbb{R}$

17 Rational numbers

18 The set of functions $f(x)$ for which $\int_0^1 f(x)dx = 1$

19 The set of functions $f(x)$ for which $f(0) = f(1)$

20 Real numbers

21 Positive real numbers with $x \oplus y = xy$ and $\lambda x = x^\lambda$

22 The set of ordered pairs of real numbers with $(x, y) \oplus (a, b) = (x + a, y + b)$ and $\lambda(x, y) = (0, \lambda y)$

14.2 CONSEQUENCES OF THE AXIOMS

One of the problems is that some results appear to be intuitively obvious, yet are not listed among the axioms. Provided that the set of axioms is sufficient, we should be able to prove these 'obvious' results directly from the axioms. This is sometimes compared to playing a game with a fixed set of rules (axioms). Examples 1 and 2 give some idea of the kinds of ways these proofs are developed and written out; you can try a couple for yourself in Q.2 and Q.3.

Example 1
Prove directly from the axioms that

$$0\mathbf{a} = \mathbf{0} \quad \text{for all } \mathbf{a} \in V.$$

Solution

$$\begin{aligned} \lambda\mathbf{a} &= (0 + \lambda)\mathbf{a} \quad &&(\text{since } 0 + \lambda = \lambda \text{ for real numbers}) \\ &= 0\mathbf{a} + \lambda\mathbf{a} \quad &&(\text{by axiom M5}). \end{aligned}$$

Adding $-(\lambda\mathbf{a})$ to both sides (it exists, by axiom A4):

$$\lambda\mathbf{a} + -(\lambda\mathbf{a}) = (0\mathbf{a} + \lambda\mathbf{a}) + -(\lambda\mathbf{a})$$

$$\lambda\mathbf{a} + -(\lambda\mathbf{a}) = 0\mathbf{a} + (\lambda\mathbf{a} + -(\lambda\mathbf{a})) \quad (\text{by axiom A3})$$

therefore $\quad \mathbf{0} = 0\mathbf{a} + \mathbf{0} \quad$ (by axiom A4),

so $\quad \mathbf{0} = 0\mathbf{a} \quad$ (by axiom A2). □

Example 2
Prove directly from the axioms that

$$\lambda\mathbf{0} = \mathbf{0} \quad \text{for all } \lambda \in \mathbb{R}.$$

Solution

$$\mathbf{0} = \mathbf{0} + \mathbf{0} \qquad \text{(by axiom A2, with } \mathbf{a} = \mathbf{0}\text{)}$$

$$\lambda\mathbf{0} = \lambda(\mathbf{0} + \mathbf{0}) \qquad \text{(premultiplying by } \lambda\text{)}$$

$$\lambda\mathbf{0} = \lambda\mathbf{0} + \lambda\mathbf{0} \qquad \text{(by axiom M4).}$$

Adding $-(\lambda\mathbf{0})$ to both sides (it exists, by axiom A4):

$$\lambda\mathbf{0} + -(\lambda\mathbf{0}) = (\lambda\mathbf{0} + \lambda\mathbf{0}) + -(\lambda\mathbf{0})$$

$$\lambda\mathbf{0} + -(\lambda\mathbf{0}) = \lambda\mathbf{0} + (\lambda\mathbf{0} + -(\lambda\mathbf{0})) \qquad \text{(by axiom A3)}$$

therefore $\mathbf{0} = \lambda\mathbf{0} + \mathbf{0}$ (by axiom A4)

so $\mathbf{0} = \lambda\mathbf{0}$ (by axiom A2). □

Q.2 Prove directly from the axioms that

$$(-\lambda)\mathbf{a} = \lambda(-\mathbf{a}) = -(\lambda\mathbf{a}) \quad \text{for all } \mathbf{a} \in V \text{ and } \lambda \in \mathbb{R}.$$

(*Hint:* start with $\mathbf{a} + (-\mathbf{a}) = \mathbf{0}$ or $\lambda + -\lambda = 0$.)

Q.3 Prove that, if $\lambda\mathbf{a} = \mathbf{0}$, then $\lambda = 0$ or $\mathbf{a} = \mathbf{0}$. (*Hint:* consider the two cases (*a*) $\lambda = 0$ and (*b*) $\lambda \neq 0$.)

14.3 FURTHER DEFINITIONS

Before we prove the basis theorem and the dimension theorem, which are two of the important results of this chapter, we recall some of the terms with which you are now familiar and define them rigorously for any vectors (that is, elements which belong to a vector space). This is necessary because we cannot rely on intuitive ideas in the proofs of these fundamental results.

Definition2
A vector $\mathbf{b}$ is said to be a *linear combination* of vectors $\mathbf{a}_1, \mathbf{a}_2, \ldots, \mathbf{a}_n$ if real numbers $\lambda_1, \lambda_2, \ldots, \lambda_n$ can be found such that

$$\mathbf{b} = \lambda_1\mathbf{a}_1 + \lambda_2\mathbf{a}_2 + \ldots + \lambda_n\mathbf{a}_n.$$

Definition 3
A set $\{\mathbf{a}_1, \mathbf{a}_2, \mathbf{a}_3, \ldots, \mathbf{a}_n\}$ of vectors is said to be *linearly dependent* if real numbers $\lambda_1, \lambda_2, \ldots, \lambda_n$ (not all zero) can be found such that

$$\lambda_1\mathbf{a}_1 + \lambda_2\mathbf{a}_2 + \ldots + \lambda_n\mathbf{a}_n = \mathbf{0}.$$

Definition 4
If $\lambda_1\mathbf{a}_1 + \lambda_2\mathbf{a}_2 + \ldots + \lambda_n\mathbf{a}_n = \mathbf{0}$ only when $\lambda_1 = \lambda_2 = \ldots = \lambda_n = 0$, then the set of vectors $\{\mathbf{a}_1, \mathbf{a}_2, \ldots, \mathbf{a}_n\}$ is said to be *linearly independent*.

Definition 5
A set of vectors $\{\mathbf{a}_1, \mathbf{a}_2, \ldots, \mathbf{a}_n\}$ is said to *span* a vector space V if every non-zero vector of V can be expressed as a linear combination of the set $\{\mathbf{a}_1, \mathbf{a}_2, \ldots, \mathbf{a}_n\}$.

Definition 6
A set of vectors which is linearly independent and spans a vector space is called a *basis* for the vector space.

Definition 7
The number of elements required to form a basis for a given vector space is called the *dimension* of the space.

We need to consider the particular case when the vector space consists of just one vector – the zero vector, $\mathbf{0}$. Geometrically, this vector would represent a single point (the origin), so the dimension of this particular vector space is taken as zero.

Definition 8
If $\{\mathbf{a}_1, \mathbf{a}_2, \ldots, \mathbf{a}_n\}$ is a basis for the vector space V, and $\mathbf{v} = \lambda_1\mathbf{a}_1 + \lambda_2\mathbf{a}_2 + \ldots + \lambda_n\mathbf{a}_n$, then $(\lambda_1, \lambda_2, \ldots, \lambda_n)$ are called the *coordinates* or *components* of $\mathbf{v}$ with respect to the basis $\{\mathbf{a}_1, \mathbf{a}_2, \ldots, \mathbf{a}_n\}$.

A new definition:

Definition 9
If U and V are both vector spaces and $U \subset V$, then we say that U is a *subspace* of V.

Q.4 If U is a non-empty subset of V, which axioms of Definition 1 form the minimum set that you must check to discover whether U is a subspace of V?

14.4 THE BASIS THEOREM

We have defined the dimension of a vector space as the number of elements required to form a basis. This definition is only meaningful if all the bases of a particular vector space have the same number of elements, that is, there is a unique answer. This theorem is known as the basis theorem.

The basis theorem
All bases of a vector space have the same number of elements.

The proof below assumes that the vector space has a finite dimension (for example, the vector space of all polynomials has infinite dimension), and is not the vector space $\{\mathbf{0}\}$.

Suppose that we have two different bases, $\{\mathbf{a}_1, \mathbf{a}_2, \ldots, \mathbf{a}_n\}$ and $\{\mathbf{b}_1, \mathbf{b}_2, \ldots, \mathbf{b}_m\}$. Both sets are therefore spanning sets and linearly independent, so none of the $\mathbf{a}_i$ or $\mathbf{b}_j$ can be the zero vector (otherwise they would not be linearly independent).

Suppose that $m > n$. We start with the basis which has the smaller number of elements, that is, $\{\mathbf{a}_1, \mathbf{a}_2, \mathbf{a}_3, \mathbf{a}_4, \ldots, \mathbf{a}_n\}$.

Step 1

$\{\mathbf{a}_1 + \mathbf{a}_2, \mathbf{a}_2, \mathbf{a}_3, \ldots, \mathbf{a}_n\}$ also forms a basis because

(1) it is a linearly independent set;

(Suppose $\qquad \lambda_1(\mathbf{a}_1 + \mathbf{a}_2) + \lambda_2\mathbf{a}_2 + \ldots + \lambda_n\mathbf{a}_n = \mathbf{0},$

then $\qquad \lambda_1\mathbf{a}_1 + (\lambda_1 + \lambda_2)\mathbf{a}_2 + \ldots + \lambda_n\mathbf{a}_n = \mathbf{0}.$

But $\{\mathbf{a}_1, \mathbf{a}_2, \ldots, \mathbf{a}_n\}$ is a linearly independent set, therefore $\lambda_1 = \lambda_1 + \lambda_2 = \lambda_3 = \ldots = \lambda_n = 0$; that is, $\lambda_i = 0$ for $i = 1, 2, 3, \ldots, n$.)

(2) it is a spanning set.

(As $\{\mathbf{a}_1, \mathbf{a}_2, \ldots, \mathbf{a}_n\}$ is a basis, any vector $\mathbf{x}$ can be expressed in the form

$$\begin{aligned}\mathbf{x} &= \alpha_1\mathbf{a}_1 + \alpha_2\mathbf{a}_2 + \ldots + \alpha_n\mathbf{a}_n \\ &= \alpha_1(\mathbf{a}_1 + \mathbf{a}_2) + (\alpha_1 - \alpha_2)\mathbf{a}_2 + \ldots + \alpha_n\mathbf{a}_n.)\end{aligned}$$

Step 2

Repeating this process, we can show that the set

$$\{\lambda_1\mathbf{a}_1 + \lambda_2\mathbf{a}_2 + \ldots + \lambda_n\mathbf{a}_n, \mathbf{a}_2, \mathbf{a}_3, \ldots, \mathbf{a}_n\},$$

where $\lambda_1 \neq 0$, is a basis.

Step 3

Since $\{\mathbf{a}_1, \mathbf{a}_2, \ldots, \mathbf{a}_n\}$ is a basis, we can write

$$\mathbf{b}_1 = \lambda_1\mathbf{a}_1 + \lambda_2\mathbf{a}_2 + \ldots + \lambda_n\mathbf{a}_n.$$

At least one of the λ_i must be non-zero. For convenience we assume that $\lambda_1 \neq 0$. So, by Step 2, $\{\mathbf{b}_1, \mathbf{a}_2, \mathbf{a}_3, \ldots, \mathbf{a}_n\}$ is a basis.

Step 4

We can now write $\mathbf{b}_2$ as a linear combination of this new basis, so

$$\mathbf{b}_2 = \mu_1\mathbf{b}_1 + \mu_2\mathbf{a}_2 + \mu_3\mathbf{a}_3 + \ldots + \mu_n\mathbf{a}_n.$$

At least one of the set $\{\mu_2, \mu_3, \ldots, \mu_n\}$ must be non-zero, for if μ_1 is the only non-zero coefficient, then $\{\mathbf{b}_1, \mathbf{b}_2\}$ is a linearly dependent set. For convenience we assume that $\mu_2 \neq 0$.

Step 5
As $\{\mathbf{a}_2, \mathbf{b}_1, \mathbf{a}_3, \ldots, \mathbf{a}_n\}$ is a basis and

$$\mathbf{b}_2 = \mu_2\mathbf{a}_2 + \mu_1\mathbf{b}_1 + \mu_3\mathbf{a}_3 + \ldots + \mu_n\mathbf{a}_n, \quad \text{where } \mu_2 \neq 0,$$

applying the results of Steps 1–3, we see that $\{\mathbf{b}_2, \mathbf{b}_1, \mathbf{a}_3, \ldots, \mathbf{a}_n\}$ is also a basis.

Step 6
Continuing this process, we find that $\{\mathbf{b}_1, \mathbf{b}_2, \ldots, \mathbf{b}_n\}$ is also a basis.

Step 7
But we are given that $\{\mathbf{b}_1, \mathbf{b}_2, \ldots, \mathbf{b}_m\}$ is a basis, so the proper subset $\{\mathbf{b}_1, \mathbf{b}_2, \ldots, \mathbf{b}_n\}$ cannot also be a basis. (*Why?*) Thus, our initial assumption that $m > n$ leads to a contradiction.

Similarly, it can be shown that $n > m$ also leads to a contradiction, so

$$m = n.$$

Conclusion
Any two bases of a finite dimensional vector space have the same number of elements.

Exercise 14B

1 Prove that a non-empty subset U of a vector space V over the real numbers $\mathbb{R}$ is a subspace if and only if $\lambda\mathbf{a} + \mu\mathbf{b} \in U$ for all λ, $\mu \in \mathbb{R}$ and $\mathbf{a}$, $\mathbf{b} \in U$.

2 For each of the following vector spaces V and subsets S, determine whether S is a subspace of V:

(*a*) $V = \left\{ \begin{bmatrix} p \\ q \\ r \end{bmatrix} : p, q, r \in \mathbb{R} \right\}, \quad S = \left\{ \begin{bmatrix} p \\ q \\ r \end{bmatrix} : p + q + r = 0 \right\}$

(*b*) $V = \left\{ \begin{bmatrix} p \\ q \\ r \end{bmatrix} : p, q, r \in \mathbb{R} \right\}, \quad S = \left\{ \begin{bmatrix} p \\ q \\ r \end{bmatrix} : pqr > 0 \right\}$

(*c*) $V = \left\{ \begin{bmatrix} p \\ q \end{bmatrix} : p, q \in \mathbb{R} \right\}, \quad S = \left\{ \begin{bmatrix} p \\ q \end{bmatrix} : p^2 + q^2 = 1 \right\}$

(*d*) $V = \left\{ \begin{bmatrix} p \\ q \\ r \\ s \end{bmatrix} : p, q, r, s \in \mathbb{R} \right\}, \quad S = \left\{ \begin{bmatrix} p \\ q \\ r \\ s \end{bmatrix} : \begin{matrix} p = 2s \\ p + s = q + r \end{matrix} \right\}$

(*e*) $V = \{\text{polynomials of degree} \leqslant 4\}$
$S = \{\text{polynomials of degree exactly } 3\}$

(*f*) $V = \{\text{real functions with domain } \mathbb{R}\}$
$S = \{\text{functions satisfying } f(x) = f(1 - x) \text{ for all } x\}$

3 Prove directly from the axioms that:
(*a*) If $\mathbf{a} + \mathbf{c} = \mathbf{b} + \mathbf{c}$, then $\mathbf{a} = \mathbf{b}$.
(*b*) If $\lambda\mathbf{a} = \lambda\mathbf{b}$, then $\lambda = 0$ or $\mathbf{a} = \mathbf{b}$.
(*c*) If $\lambda\mathbf{a} = \mu\mathbf{a}$, then $\lambda = \mu$ or $\mathbf{a} = \mathbf{0}$.
(*d*) If $\mathbf{a} + \mathbf{b} = \mathbf{a}$, then $\mathbf{b} = \mathbf{0}$.

4 Let $V = \left\{ \begin{bmatrix} a \\ b \\ -a \\ -b \end{bmatrix} : a, b \in \mathbb{R} \right\}$ be a subset of $\mathbb{R}^4$.
(*a*) Show that V is a subspace of $\mathbb{R}$.
(*b*) What is a basis for V?
(*c*) Extend this basis to give a basis for $\mathbb{R}^4$.

5 'If a set of vectors is linearly dependent, each vector can be expressed as a linear combination of the other vectors.' Provide an example showing that this statement is untrue and give a correct modified version of the statement.

6 $\{\mathbf{a}, \mathbf{b}, \mathbf{c}\}$ is a basis for V over $\mathbb{R}$. If $\lambda\mu\nu \neq 0$, prove that $\{\lambda\mathbf{a}, \mu\mathbf{b}, \nu\mathbf{c}\}$ is also a basis.

7 If $\{\mathbf{x}_1, \mathbf{x}_2, \mathbf{x}_3\}$ is a linearly independent set of vectors, prove that the set $\{\mathbf{x}_1, a\mathbf{x}_1 + \mathbf{x}_2, b\mathbf{x}_1 + c\mathbf{x}_2 + \mathbf{x}_3\}$ is also linearly independent.

8 The vectors $\mathbf{a}_1, \mathbf{a}_2, \mathbf{a}_3, \mathbf{a}_4$ form a basis for the vector space V over the real numbers $\mathbb{R}$. The vector $\mathbf{y} = x_1\mathbf{a}_1 + x_2\mathbf{a}_2 + x_3\mathbf{a}_3 + x_4\mathbf{a}_4$, where $x_1, x_2, x_3, x_4 \in \mathbb{R}$. State for each of the following subsets of V whether or not it constitutes a subspace, giving brief but sufficient reasons for your answer:
(*a*) all $\mathbf{y}$ with $x_1 = 0$
(*b*) all $\mathbf{y}$ with $2x_1 + x_2 = 3$
(*c*) all $\mathbf{y}$ with $x_1 \in \mathbb{Z}$.
When the subset is a subspace, give a basis for the subspace in terms of $\mathbf{a}_1, \mathbf{a}_2, \mathbf{a}_3, \mathbf{a}_4$.
[SMP]

14.5 LINEAR TRANSFORMATIONS

In Chapter 12 we gave the full definitions of a linear transformation, image space and kernel, and then introduced the dimension theorem. We did not attempt to prove it then for two reasons:
(1) We had not checked that the image space and kernel were both vector spaces, and therefore, we could not necessarily apply the term *dimension* to them.
(2) We had not proved the basis theorem.

We first prove that the image space and kernel are both subspaces. If $\mathbf{T}: V \to W$ is a linear transformation, where V and W are both vector spaces, then the image space is a subset of W and the kernel is a subset of V.

We can represent this diagrammatically as in Fig. 1 (opposite).

We saw in Q.4 that we have to check only axioms A1 and M1 to verify that a non-empty subset of a vector space is a subspace.

Theorem 1
If $\mathbf{T}: V \to W$ is a linear transformation, where V and W are both vector spaces, then the image space of $\mathbf{T}$ is a subspace of W.

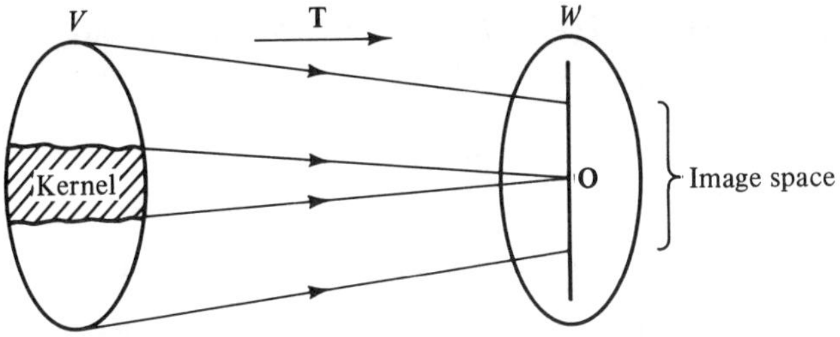

Figure 1

As $\mathbf{0} \in V$, $\mathbf{T}(\mathbf{0}) = \mathbf{0} \in W$, so the image space is a non-empty subset of W. We need therefore check only axioms A1 and M1:

(A1) If $\mathbf{p}, \mathbf{q} \in$ image space of $\mathbf{T}$,

$$\mathbf{p} = \mathbf{T}(\mathbf{a}) \quad \text{and} \quad \mathbf{q} = \mathbf{T}(\mathbf{b}) \quad \text{for some } \mathbf{a}, \mathbf{b} \in V.$$

Therefore
$$\begin{aligned} \mathbf{p} + \mathbf{q} &= \mathbf{T}(\mathbf{a}) + \mathbf{T}(\mathbf{b}) \\ &= \mathbf{T}(\mathbf{a} + \mathbf{b}) \qquad (\mathbf{T} \text{ is a linear transformation}), \end{aligned}$$

so $\mathbf{p} + \mathbf{q} \in$ image space of $\mathbf{T}$.
Hence, we have closure under addition.

(M1)
$$\begin{aligned} \lambda\mathbf{p} &= \lambda\mathbf{T}(\mathbf{a}) \\ &= \mathbf{T}(\lambda\mathbf{a}) \quad (\mathbf{T} \text{ is a linear transformation}) \end{aligned}$$

so $\lambda\mathbf{p} \in$ image space of $\mathbf{T}$.
Hence, we have closure under multiplication by a real number.

So the image space of **T** is a vector space. The dimension of the image space is called the *rank* of the linear transformation.

Theorem 2
If **T** is a linear transformation then the kernel of **T** is a vector space.

As $\mathbf{0} \in V$ and $\mathbf{T}(\mathbf{0}) = \mathbf{0}$, $\mathbf{0} \in$ kernel of **T**, so the kernel is a non-empty subset of V. As above, we need check only axioms A1 and M1:

(A1) If $\mathbf{x}, \mathbf{y} \in$ kernel of **T**, then $\mathbf{T}(\mathbf{x}) = \mathbf{T}(\mathbf{y}) = \mathbf{0}$, so

$$\begin{aligned} \mathbf{T}(\mathbf{x} + \mathbf{y}) &= \mathbf{T}(\mathbf{x}) + \mathbf{T}(\mathbf{y}) \quad (\mathbf{T} \text{ is a linear transformation}) \\ &= \mathbf{0} + \mathbf{0} \\ &= \mathbf{0}, \end{aligned}$$

so $\mathbf{x} + \mathbf{y} \in$ kernel of **T**.
Hence, we have closure under addition.

(M1) If $\mathbf{x} \in$ kernel of **T**, then $\mathbf{T}(\mathbf{x}) = \mathbf{0}$, so $$\begin{aligned} \mathbf{T}(\lambda\mathbf{x}) &= \lambda\mathbf{T}(\mathbf{x}) \quad (\mathbf{T} \text{ is a linear transformation}) \\ &= \lambda\mathbf{0} \\ &= \mathbf{0} \quad (\text{see Example 2}), \end{aligned}$$

so $\lambda\mathbf{x} \in$ kernel of $\mathbf{T}$.

Hence, we have closure under multiplication by a real number.

So the kernel of $\mathbf{T}$ is a vector space. The dimension of the kernel is called the *nullity* of the linear transformation.

If the image space $= \{\mathbf{0}\}$, the rank $= 0$, and if the kernel $= \{\mathbf{0}\}$, the nullity $= 0$.

We are now in a position to prove the important *dimension theorem*, a result which we used in Chapter 12 when we were finding the complete set of solutions of linear equations.

Theorem 3 (the dimension theorem)
If $\mathbf{T}$ is a linear transformation,

dimension of image space + dimension of kernel = dimension of domain;

that is, rank + nullity = dimension of domain.

Let the dimension of the domain be n and the dimension of the kernel be k.

Choose a basis $\{\mathbf{a}_1, \mathbf{a}_2, \ldots, \mathbf{a}_k\}$ of the kernel – it may be the empty set if the kernel of $\mathbf{T} = \{\mathbf{0}\}$.

Step 1
Now extend the basis of the kernel to give a basis for the domain.

If $\{\mathbf{a}_1, \mathbf{a}_2, \ldots, \mathbf{a}_k\}$ does not span the domain, then there is a vector $\mathbf{a}_{k+1}$ which does not belong to the kernel. Either $\{\mathbf{a}_1, \mathbf{a}_2, \ldots, \mathbf{a}_k, \mathbf{a}_{k+1}\}$ spans the domain, or there is another vector $\mathbf{a}_{k+2}$ which belongs to the domain and does not belong to the set of vectors $\{\mathbf{a}_1, \mathbf{a}_2, \ldots, \mathbf{a}_{k+1}\}$.

Continuing in this way, we can find a set of linearly independent vectors which span the domain. Let the basis of the domain be $\{\mathbf{a}_1, \ldots, \mathbf{a}_k, \mathbf{a}_{k+1}, \ldots, \mathbf{a}_n\}$.

Step 2
We now find a basis for the image space. As $\{\mathbf{a}_1, \mathbf{a}_2, \ldots, \mathbf{a}_n\}$ spans the domain, then $\{\mathbf{T}(\mathbf{a}_1), \mathbf{T}(\mathbf{a}_2), \ldots, \mathbf{T}(\mathbf{a}_n)\}$ spans the image space. Now $\mathbf{T}(\mathbf{a}_1) = \mathbf{T}(\mathbf{a}_2) = \ldots = \mathbf{T}(\mathbf{a}_k) = \mathbf{0}$.

Two cases arise:

(1) If $k = n$, the image space $= \{\mathbf{0}\}$, so we have:

$$\begin{aligned} \text{rank} &= 0 \\ \text{nullity} &= n \\ \text{dimension of domain} &= n, \end{aligned}$$

and the result follows.

(2) If $k < n$, $\{\mathbf{T}(\mathbf{a}_{k+1}), \mathbf{T}(\mathbf{a}_{k+2}), \ldots, \mathbf{T}(\mathbf{a}_n)\}$ spans the image space. Is this set linearly independent as well?

Let us assume that $\sum_{i=k+1}^{n} \lambda_i \mathbf{T}(\mathbf{a}_i) = \mathbf{0}$,

so $$\mathbf{T}\left[\sum_{i=k+1}^{n} \lambda_i \mathbf{a}_i\right] = \mathbf{0} \quad (\mathbf{T} \text{ is a linear transformation});$$

that is, $\sum_{i=k+1}^{n} \lambda_i \mathbf{a}_i$ belongs to the kernel.

So $$\sum_{i=k+1}^{n} \lambda_i \mathbf{a}_i = \sum_{j=1}^{k} \mu_j \mathbf{a}_j, \quad \text{as } \mathbf{a}_1, \ldots, \mathbf{a}_k \text{ is a basis of the kernel.}$$

Therefore $$\sum_{j=1}^{k} \mu_j \mathbf{a}_j - \sum_{i=k+1}^{n} \lambda_i \mathbf{a}_i = \mathbf{0}.$$

But $\{\mathbf{a}_1, \mathbf{a}_2, \ldots, \mathbf{a}_n\}$ is a basis of the domain, so it is a linearly independent set. The λs and μs must therefore all be zero, so the set $\{\mathbf{T}(\mathbf{a}_{k+1}), \ldots, \mathbf{T}(\mathbf{a}_n)\}$ is a linearly independent set. As we already know that this set spans the image space, it is a basis for the image space.

Conclusion

	Basis	Dimension
Domain	$\{\mathbf{a}_1, \ldots, \mathbf{a}_n\}$	n
Kernel	$\{\mathbf{a}_1, \ldots, \mathbf{a}_k\}$	k
Image space	$\{\mathbf{T}(\mathbf{a}_{k+1}), \ldots, \mathbf{T}(\mathbf{a}_n)\}$	$n-k$

Hence,

dimension of image space + dimension of kernel = dimension of domain;

that is, rank + nullity = dimension of domain.

Exercise 14C

1 Show that, if $\mathbf{T}$ is a linear transformation and $\{\mathbf{T}(\mathbf{x}_1), \mathbf{T}(\mathbf{x}_2), \ldots, \mathbf{T}(\mathbf{x}_n)\}$ is a set of linearly independent vectors, then $\{\mathbf{x}_1, \mathbf{x}_2, \ldots, \mathbf{x}_n\}$ is also a linearly independent set. Give an example to show that the converse is not necessarily true.

2 $\mathbf{T}: V \to V$ is a linear transformation. Prove that
(*a*) kernel of $\mathbf{T}^2 \supset$ kernel of $\mathbf{T}$;
(*b*) image space of $\mathbf{T}^2 \subset$ image space of $\mathbf{T}$.

3 $\mathbf{T}$ is a linear transformation from V to W, and U is a subspace of V. Prove that the image of U under $\mathbf{T}$ is a subspace of W.

4 V is a three-dimensional vector space and $\mathbf{T}: V \to V$ is a linear transformation of V. Prove that the vectors of the form $\{\mathbf{v} \in V: \mathbf{T}(\mathbf{v}) = \mathbf{0}\}$ and $\{\mathbf{T}(\mathbf{v}): \mathbf{v} \in V\}$ give subspaces of V. If $\nu(\mathbf{T})$, $\rho(\mathbf{T})$ respectively are the dimensions of these spaces, show that $\rho(\mathbf{T}) + \nu(\mathbf{T}) = 3$. (If you quote a general theorem you must prove it.) [MEI]

5 Given a linear transformation **T** from an n-dimensional vector space V to itself, the *rank* of **T** is defined to be the dimension of the range of **T** and the *nullity* of **T** is the dimension of the kernel of **T**. State a theorem connecting these two quantities with n.

Suppose **S** is another linear transformation from V to itself and that the composite transformation **ST** has nullity zero. Prove that the range of **T** is the whole of V.

[SMP]

6 Let V be a finite-dimensional vector space over the real numbers. Let $\boldsymbol{\theta}$ be a linear transformation of V into itself such that $\boldsymbol{\theta}^2$ is the identity; that is, $\boldsymbol{\theta}(\boldsymbol{\theta}(\mathbf{v})) = \mathbf{v}$ for all $\mathbf{v} \in V$. Let

$$W_1 = \{\mathbf{w} : \mathbf{w} \in V \text{ and } \boldsymbol{\theta}(\mathbf{w}) = \mathbf{w}\},$$

$$W_2 = \{\mathbf{w} : \mathbf{w} \in V \text{ and } \boldsymbol{\theta}(\mathbf{w}) = -\mathbf{w}\}.$$

Prove that W_1 and W_2 are vector subspaces of V.

By considering, for an arbitrary vector $\mathbf{v} \in V$, the vectors

$$\frac{\mathbf{v} + \boldsymbol{\theta}(\mathbf{v})}{2} \quad \text{and} \quad \frac{\mathbf{v} - \boldsymbol{\theta}(\mathbf{v})}{2}$$

(or otherwise), prove that $V = W_1 + W_2$, where $W_1 + W_2$ is the set of all vectors, $\mathbf{x}$, of the form $\mathbf{x} = \mathbf{w}_1 + \mathbf{w}_2$ with $\mathbf{w}_1 \in W_1$ and $\mathbf{w}_2 \in W_2$.

If V is Euclidean three-dimensional space, identify the spaces W_1 and W_2 corresponding to the linear mapping $\boldsymbol{\theta}$ with matrix

$$\begin{bmatrix} 1 & 0 & 0 \\ 0 & 1 & -1 \\ 0 & 0 & -1 \end{bmatrix}.$$

[SMP]

In this chapter we have rounded off work which was first introduced in Chapter 1. There the ideas were introduced using concrete examples, and gradually we have approached these ideas in a more abstract way. So in this chapter we have met the abstract definition of a vector space and been able to prove two important theorems – the basis theorem and the dimension theorem.

Miscellaneous exercise 14

1 A definition is given of A as the set of all ordered pairs of real numbers $(r, \theta) = \mathbf{a}$, where $\mathbf{a} + \mathbf{a}' = (rr', \theta + \theta')$ and $t\mathbf{a} = (r^t, t\theta)$.

Examine A to see whether it satisfies the axioms of a vector space over the real numbers.

Can a vector space be obtained by placing restrictions on r or θ or both?

[SMP]

2 If U and V are subspaces of a vector space W over the real numbers $\mathbb{R}$, show that $U \cap V$ (defined in the obvious way) is a vector space, but that $U \cup V$ may not be. What can you say about the dimension of $U \cap V$?

3 If U and V are subspaces of a vector space W over the real numbers $\mathbb{R}$, the sum of U and V, written $U + V$, consists of all the vectors $\mathbf{u} + \mathbf{v}$, where $\mathbf{u} \in U$ and $\mathbf{v} \in V$.

(*a*) Prove that $U + V$ is also a subspace of W and give a geometrical illustration.

(*b*) What can you say about the dimension of $U + V$? In what ways does it depend upon the dimension of $U \cap V$?

4 If M is the vector space of 3×3 matrices over the real numbers $\mathbb{R}$, and S and A are the subspaces of symmetric and antisymmetric matrices respectively, prove that $S \cap A = \varnothing$ and $M = S + A$.
(For symmetric matrices $\mathbf{M}^{\mathrm{T}} = \mathbf{M}$; for antisymmetric matrices $\mathbf{M}^{\mathrm{T}} = -\mathbf{M}$.)

5 W is the set of all real functions with domain $\mathbb{R}$. U is the subset of W for which $f(-x) = f(x)$ for all $x \in \mathbb{R}$, while V is the subset for which $f(-x) = -f(x)$ for all $x \in \mathbb{R}$.
(*a*) Show that U and V are both subspaces of W.
(*b*) What is $U \cap V$?
(*c*) Show that $U + V = W$.

6 V and W are vector spaces over the real numbers, and $\mathbf{S}, \mathbf{T}$ are linear transformations from V to W. New mappings, $(\mathbf{S} + \mathbf{T})$ and $(k\mathbf{S})$ (where $k \in \mathbb{R}$), are defined as follows:

if $\mathbf{v} \in V$, $$(\mathbf{S} + \mathbf{T})(\mathbf{v}) = \mathbf{S}(\mathbf{v}) + \mathbf{T}(\mathbf{v})$$

and $$(k\mathbf{S})(\mathbf{v}) = k(\mathbf{S}(\mathbf{v})).$$

(*a*) Show that $(\mathbf{S} + \mathbf{T})$ and $(k\mathbf{S})$ are both linear transformations.
(*b*) Show that the set of all linear transformations from V to W with the operations defined above forms a vector space.

SUMMARY

Definitions

(1) A *vector space, V, over the real numbers*, $\mathbb{R}$, is a set of elements $\mathbf{a}, \mathbf{b}, \mathbf{c}, \ldots$, which are called *vectors*, together with the operations of vector addition and scalar multiplication, such that

(*a*) *Under addition*

(A1) Closure: $\mathbf{a} + \mathbf{b} \in V$ for all $\mathbf{a}, \mathbf{b} \in V$.

(A2) Identity: there is a vector $\mathbf{0} \in V$ such that

$$\mathbf{a} + \mathbf{0} = \mathbf{0} + \mathbf{a} = \mathbf{a} \quad \text{for all } \mathbf{a}, \mathbf{b} \in V.$$

(A3) Associative: $\mathbf{a} + (\mathbf{b} + \mathbf{c}) = (\mathbf{a} + \mathbf{b}) + \mathbf{c}$ for all $\mathbf{a}, \mathbf{b}, \mathbf{c} \in V$.

(A4) Inverses: for each $\mathbf{a} \in V$, there exists a vector $(-\mathbf{a}) \in V$, such that

$$\mathbf{a} + (-\mathbf{a}) = (-\mathbf{a}) + \mathbf{a} = \mathbf{0}.$$

(A5) Commutative: $\mathbf{a} + \mathbf{b} = \mathbf{b} + \mathbf{a}$ for all $\mathbf{a}, \mathbf{b} \in V$.

(*b*) *Under scalar multiplication*

(M1) Closure: $\lambda\mathbf{a} \in V$ for all $\mathbf{a} \in V$ and $\lambda \in \mathbb{R}$.

(M2) Identity: $1\mathbf{a} = \mathbf{a}$ for all $\mathbf{a} \in V$.

(M3) Associative: $(\lambda\mu)\mathbf{a} = \lambda(\mu\mathbf{a})$ for all $\mathbf{a} \in V$ and $\lambda, \mu \in \mathbb{R}$.

(*c*) *Under addition and scalar multiplication*

(M4) Distributive: $\lambda(\mathbf{a} + \mathbf{b}) = \lambda\mathbf{a} + \lambda\mathbf{b}$ for all $\mathbf{a}, \mathbf{b} \in V$ and $\lambda \in \mathbb{R}$.

(M5) $(\lambda + \mu)\mathbf{a} = \lambda\mathbf{a} + \mu\mathbf{a}$ for all $\mathbf{a} \in V$ and $\lambda, \mu \in \mathbb{R}$.

(2) If U and V are both vector spaces and $U \subset V$, then we say that U is a subspace of V.

Theorems

(1) (*The basis theorem*) All bases of a vector space have the same number of elements.

(2) If **T** is a linear transformation, then the image space of **T** is a vector space.

(3) If **T** is a linear transformation, then the kernel of **T** is a vector space.

(4) (*The dimension theorem*) If **T** is a linear transformation,

dimension of image space + dimension of kernel = dimension of domain;

that is, rank + nullity = dimension of domain.

Revision exercises 11–14

Revision exercise 11

A1 Vectors $\mathbf{u} = \begin{bmatrix} 1 \\ -2 \end{bmatrix}$ and $\mathbf{v} = \begin{bmatrix} 1 \\ 4 \end{bmatrix}$ form a basis for a two-dimensional vector space.

Express the vectors $\begin{bmatrix} 5 \\ -2 \end{bmatrix}$ and $\begin{bmatrix} 3 \\ -1 \end{bmatrix}$ as linear combinations of $\mathbf{u}$ and $\mathbf{v}$.

A2 V is the vector space of all 2×2 matrices with real elements. Find a basis for this vector space.

A3 A point P has coordinates $(3, -1)$ relative to the basis $\{\mathbf{i}, \mathbf{j}\}$. Find the coordinates of P relative to the basis $\left\{\begin{bmatrix} 7 \\ 5 \end{bmatrix}, \begin{bmatrix} -3 \\ 4 \end{bmatrix}\right\}$.

A4 A transformation is represented by the matrix $\begin{bmatrix} 1 & 3 \\ 0 & 1 \end{bmatrix}$ relative to the usual basis.

What is the matrix which represents this transformation relative to the basis $\left\{\begin{bmatrix} 2 \\ 1 \end{bmatrix}, \begin{bmatrix} 1 \\ 2 \end{bmatrix}\right\}$?

A5 If $\{\mathbf{a}, \mathbf{b}, \mathbf{c}\}$ is a linearly independent set of vectors, prove that the set $\{\mathbf{a} + \mathbf{b}, \mathbf{a} - 2\mathbf{b}, 3\mathbf{a} + 2\mathbf{b} + \mathbf{c}\}$ is also a linearly independent set.

B1 Find p so that each of the following sets of vectors is linearly dependent:

(*a*) $\left\{\begin{bmatrix} p-1 \\ 1 \end{bmatrix}, \begin{bmatrix} 4 \\ p-1 \end{bmatrix}\right\}$ (*b*) $\left\{\begin{bmatrix} p-3 \\ -2 \\ 1 \end{bmatrix}, \begin{bmatrix} -2 \\ -2 \\ p \end{bmatrix}, \begin{bmatrix} -3 \\ p-4 \\ 3 \end{bmatrix}\right\}$

B2 Write the conic $3x^2 - 12xy - 2y^2 = 1$ in the form $a'x'^2 + b'y'^2 = 1$, and hence sketch the original conic.

B3 A point R has coordinates $(-1, -2)$ referred to the usual basis. Find its coordinates with respect to the new basis $\left\{\begin{bmatrix} -1 \\ -1 \end{bmatrix}, \begin{bmatrix} 1 \\ 2 \end{bmatrix}\right\}$. A transformation $\mathbf{T}$ is a half-turn about the origin followed by a reflection in the line $y = x$. Find the image of R with respect to this new basis.

(*a*) What is the matrix $\mathbf{M}$ representing $\mathbf{T}$ with respect to the $\{\mathbf{i}, \mathbf{j}\}$ basis?
(*b*) What is the matrix $\mathbf{M}'$ representing $\mathbf{T}$ with respect to the new basis?

B4 Solve the simultaneous differential equations:

$$\left.\begin{aligned} \dot{x} &= 7x + 4y \\ \dot{y} &= -2x + y \end{aligned}\right\}$$

B5 (*a*) Prove that if $\mathbf{S}$ and $\mathbf{T}$ are similar matrices then $\mathbf{S}^2$ and $\mathbf{T}^2$ are also similar.

(*b*) $\mathbf{A}$ and $\mathbf{B}$ are square matrices with the same eigenvalues. Show that they are similar matrices.

Revision exercise 12

A1 The domain is the set of polynomials of degree 2 or less in x, and the mapping is

$$a + bx + cx^2 \mapsto c + ax + bx^2, \quad \text{where } a, b, c \in \mathbb{R}.$$

Is the mapping linear?

A2 Give a basis for each of the domain and codomain and hence write down a matrix representing the linear transformation

$$\begin{bmatrix} x \\ y \\ z \\ t \end{bmatrix} \mapsto \begin{bmatrix} 3x + z \\ t - 4y \\ x + y + z \end{bmatrix}.$$

A3 Reduce the matrix $\begin{bmatrix} 4 & 9 & -2 & 4 \\ 2 & -1 & 0 & -2 \\ 1 & 5 & -1 & 3 \end{bmatrix}$ to canonical form.

A4 Find the kernel and image space of the transformation represented by the matrix $\begin{bmatrix} 5 & 7 & -3 \\ 2 & 1 & 3 \\ 1 & 2 & -2 \end{bmatrix}$.

A5 $\mathbf{M}$ is a 5×4 matrix with rank 3. What is the dimension of the kernel of the transformation represented by the matrix $\mathbf{M}$?

B1 V is the vector space of all 2×2 matrices (whose elements are real numbers). $\mathbf{T}$ is a linear transformation from V to V defined by

$$\mathbf{T}(\mathbf{X}) = \begin{bmatrix} 2 & -4 \\ -3 & 6 \end{bmatrix}\mathbf{X}, \quad \text{where } \mathbf{X} \in V.$$

Find the kernel and the image space of $\mathbf{T}$.

B2 A transformation $\mathbf{S}: \mathbb{R}^3 \to \mathbb{R}^2$ is represented by the matrix $\mathbf{M} = \begin{bmatrix} 3 & 0 & 4 \\ 2 & -1 & 3 \end{bmatrix}$. By considering the transformation represented by the matrix product $\mathbf{M}^T\mathbf{M}$, explain why $\det(\mathbf{M}^T\mathbf{M}) = 0$.

B3 F is the set of functions of the form $f(x) = (a + bx + cx^2)e^{-2x}$, where a, b, $c \in \mathbb{R}$. Show that the mapping $\mathbf{D}: F \to F$ defined by $\mathbf{D}(f(x)) = f'(x)$ is a linear transformation. Give a basis for the domain and the codomain, and hence write down a matrix representing this linear transformation. Find the kernel of $\mathbf{D}$.

B4 (*a*) Give an example of a 3×3 matrix $\mathbf{M}$ and vectors $\mathbf{p}$, $\mathbf{q}$, $\mathbf{r}$ for which $\mathbf{p}$, $\mathbf{q}$, $\mathbf{r}$ are linearly independent but $\mathbf{Mp}$, $\mathbf{Mq}$, $\mathbf{Mr}$ are linearly dependent.

(*b*) Show that if $\mathbf{T}$ is a linear transformation and $\mathbf{T}(\mathbf{x})$, $\mathbf{T}(\mathbf{y})$, $\mathbf{T}(\mathbf{z})$ are linearly independent, then so are $\mathbf{x}$, $\mathbf{y}$, $\mathbf{z}$.

B5 Show that the sequence of row operations

(*a*) adding $2 \times$ row 1 to row 2 and subtracting row 1 from row 3,

(*b*) multiplying row 2 by $\frac{1}{10}$,

(*c*) adding $4 \times$ row 2 to row 3, followed by the sequence of column operations,

(*d*) subtracting $7 \times$ column 1 from column 2, adding $4 \times$ column 1 to column 3, and subtracting $2 \times$ column 1 from column 4, (*e*) adding $\frac{1}{2}\times$ column 2 to column 3 and subtracting $\frac{1}{2}\times$ column 2 from column 4,

reduce the matrix $$\mathbf{A} = \begin{bmatrix} 1 & 7 & -4 & 2 \\ -2 & -4 & 3 & 1 \\ 1 & 3 & -2 & 0 \end{bmatrix},$$

to the canonical form $$\mathbf{C} = \begin{bmatrix} 1 & 0 & 0 & 0 \\ 0 & 1 & 0 & 0 \\ 0 & 0 & 0 & 0 \end{bmatrix}.$$

Hence find non-singular matrices **P**, **Q** such that

$$\mathbf{PAQ} = \mathbf{C}.$$

Show that the equation $$\mathbf{Ax} = \mathbf{y},$$

where **x**, **y** are column matrices of 4, 3 rows respectively, can be written in the form

$$\mathbf{Cx}' = \mathbf{y}'$$

and state (in terms of **P** and **Q**) the relations connecting **x** with **x**′ and **y** with **y**′.

Write down an expression for a general element of the kernel of the linear transformation represented by **C**. Deduce an expression for a general element of the kernel of the linear transformation represented by **A**. [SMP]

Revision exercise 13

A1 Find the dimension of the solution set of the following sets of homogeneous linear equations:

(*a*) $2x + 3y - z = 0$ (*b*) $\left.\begin{aligned} 3x - y + z &= 0 \\ x - y &= 0 \end{aligned}\right\}$

A2 For what values of a, b, c is $\left.\begin{aligned} 2x - 4y - z &= a \\ 3x - y + z &= b \\ 4x + 2y + 3z &= c \end{aligned}\right\}$

a consistent set of equations?

A3 Under the transformation $\mathbf{T}: \begin{bmatrix} x \\ y \\ z \\ t \end{bmatrix} \mapsto \begin{bmatrix} x-y \\ y-z \\ z-t \end{bmatrix}$, $\mathbf{T}(\mathbf{x}) = \begin{bmatrix} 3 \\ 1 \\ 2 \end{bmatrix}$. Find **x**.

A4 Find all the solutions of the equations $\mathbf{Ax} = \mathbf{b}$, where $\mathbf{A} = \begin{bmatrix} 1 & 0 & 3 \\ 0 & 1 & -2 \\ 0 & 0 & 0 \end{bmatrix}$ and **b** is

(*a*) $\begin{bmatrix} 0 \\ 0 \\ 0 \end{bmatrix}$ (*b*) $\begin{bmatrix} 4 \\ 3 \\ 1 \end{bmatrix}$ (*c*) $\begin{bmatrix} -2 \\ 4 \\ 0 \end{bmatrix}$.

A5 Calculate the ranks of the matrices

$$\begin{bmatrix} 4 & -3 & 1 & 1 \\ 2 & 1 & 3 & -3 \\ 1 & -2 & -1 & 2 \end{bmatrix} \quad \text{and} \quad \begin{bmatrix} 4 & -3 & 1 & 1 & -2 \\ 2 & 1 & 3 & -3 & -4 \\ 1 & -2 & -1 & 2 & 3 \end{bmatrix}.$$

Hence explain why

$$\left.\begin{aligned} 4x - 3y + z + t &= -2 \\ 2x + y + 3z - 3t &= -4 \\ x - 2y - z + 2t &= 3 \end{aligned}\right\}$$

is an inconsistent set of linear equations.

B1 If (x, y, z) satisfies

$$\left.\begin{aligned} 2x + 3y - 5z &= 39 \\ 4x - 6y + 2z &= -30 \end{aligned}\right\},$$

find the minimum value of $x^2 + y^2 + z^2$ and the corresponding values of (x, y, z). Suggest a geometrical problem for which this is a solution.

B2 If $\mathbf{c}_1 = \begin{bmatrix} 1 \\ 4 \end{bmatrix}, \mathbf{c}_2 = \begin{bmatrix} 2 \\ -1 \end{bmatrix}, \mathbf{c}_3 = \begin{bmatrix} 3 \\ 3 \end{bmatrix}, \mathbf{c}_4 = \begin{bmatrix} 4 \\ 7 \end{bmatrix}$, find linear relations between $\mathbf{c}_1, \mathbf{c}_2, \mathbf{c}_3$ and $\mathbf{c}_2, \mathbf{c}_3, \mathbf{c}_4$. Hence find the kernel of the transformation

$$\begin{bmatrix} x \\ y \\ z \\ t \end{bmatrix} \mapsto \begin{bmatrix} 1 & 2 & 3 & 4 \\ 4 & -1 & 3 & 7 \end{bmatrix} \begin{bmatrix} x \\ y \\ z \\ t \end{bmatrix}$$

and solve the equations

$$\left.\begin{aligned} x + 2y + 3z + 4t &= -1 \\ 4x - y + 3z + 7t &= 14 \end{aligned}\right\}$$

B3 P is the vector space of polynomials of degree 2 or less, with real coefficients. The mapping $\mathbf{T}: P \to P$ is defined by $\mathbf{T}(ax^2 + bx + c) = (a + c)x + (2b - c)$.

(*a*) Find the kernel of $\mathbf{T}$.

(*b*) Hence, or otherwise, find all the polynomials which are mapped by $\mathbf{T}$ onto $(2x - 3)$.

B4 N is the set of vectors in $\mathbb{R}^3$ and the mapping $\mathbf{T}: N \to N$ is defined by

$\mathbf{T}(\mathbf{v}) = \begin{bmatrix} 2 \\ 1 \\ -3 \end{bmatrix} \wedge \mathbf{v}$ (where $\wedge$ denotes the vector product).

(*a*) Prove that $\mathbf{T}$ is a linear transformation.

(*b*) Find a matrix representing this transformation.

(*c*) Find the kernel and image space.

(*d*) Solve the vector equations $\begin{bmatrix} 2 \\ 1 \\ -3 \end{bmatrix} \wedge \mathbf{v} = \mathbf{a}$ where

(i) $\mathbf{a} = \begin{bmatrix} 3 \\ -1 \\ 2 \end{bmatrix}$, (ii) $\mathbf{a} = \begin{bmatrix} 1 \\ 1 \\ 1 \end{bmatrix}$.

B5 Find necessary and sufficient conditions on the real numbers a and b for the equations

$$\left.\begin{aligned} 2x + y + 4z &= 2 \\ x - y + az &= 1 \\ x + 2y + bz &= 1 \\ 3x - 2y + z &= -1 \end{aligned}\right\}$$

to have a solution.

Find the solution when it exists. □

Revision exercise 14

A1 Give three examples of vector spaces, stating a basis in each case.

A2 V is a vector space. Prove directly from the vector space axioms that

$$0\mathbf{a} = \mathbf{0} \quad \text{for all } \mathbf{a} \in V.$$

(Start with $0 + 0 = 0$.)

A3 $\{\mathbf{x}_1, \mathbf{x}_2, \mathbf{x}_3\}$ is a basis of the vector space V over the real numbers $\mathbb{R}$. Prove that $\{\mathbf{x}_1 + \mathbf{x}_2, \mathbf{x}_2 + \mathbf{x}_3, \mathbf{x}_3 + \mathbf{x}_1\}$ is also a basis.

A4 V is the set of all real 2×2 matrices. Determine which (if any) of the following subsets are subspaces:

(*a*) the set of all symmetric 2×2 matrices

(*b*) the set of all non-singular 2×2 matrices

(*c*) the set of all 2×2 matrices of the form $\begin{bmatrix} 0 & a \\ b & 0 \end{bmatrix}$, where $a, b \in \mathbb{R}$.

A5 V is a vector space and $\mathbf{T}$ is a linear transformation from V to V. Prove that the kernel of $\mathbf{T}^2$ is a subset of the kernel of $\mathbf{T}$.

B1 Prove that the set of all real solutions of the equations $2x - 3y + 7z = 0$ forms a vector space over the real numbers.

B2 In $\mathbb{R}^4$, L is the subspace consisting of all vectors of the form $\begin{bmatrix} p \\ 2p \\ q \\ 2q \end{bmatrix}$, where $p, q \in \mathbb{R}$,

and M is the subspace consisting of all vectors of the form $\begin{bmatrix} a \\ 3b \\ c \\ a + b + c \end{bmatrix}$, where a, b, $c \in \mathbb{R}$. Describe the subspace $L \cap M$.

B3 Define the terms linear independence and basis of a vector space.

(*a*) Prove that the vectors $\mathbf{u} = (1, 2, 1)$, $\mathbf{v} = (1, 0, 1)$ and $\mathbf{w} = (-1, 2, -1)$ do not form a basis for three-dimensional space. Find a vector $\mathbf{k}$ such that $\{\mathbf{u}, \mathbf{v}, \mathbf{k}\}$ is a basis for this space.

In this space, show that the set of all vectors (x_1, x_2, x_3) such that $x_1 + x_2 + x_3 = 0$ forms a two-dimensional space contained in the three-dimensional space.

(*b*) Show that if **u** and **v** are vectors in a two-dimensional space such that real numbers a, b, c, d exist for which

$$a\mathbf{u} + b\mathbf{v} = (1, 0) \quad \text{and} \quad c\mathbf{u} + d\mathbf{v} = (0, 1),$$

then **u** and **v** must form a basis for the space. [MEI]

B4 You are given the following definitions relating to vector spaces:

(1) A set of vectors *spans* a space if every vector of the space can be expressed as a linear combination of elements of the set.

(2) A set of vectors which is linearly independent and spans a space is called a *basis*.

(3) The number of elements required to form a basis is called the *dimension* of the space.

From these definitions prove carefully that, if V_a and V_b are two different two-dimensional subspaces of a three-dimensional vector space V, then their common elements form a one-dimensonal subspace of V. [SMP]

B5 Fill in the essential words which are omitted from the following definition: 'A set $\{\mathbf{a}, \mathbf{b}, \mathbf{c}\}$ of vectors is *linearly dependent* if scalars $\alpha, \beta, \gamma, \ldots\ldots\ldots$, can be found such that $\alpha\mathbf{a} + \beta\mathbf{b} + \gamma\mathbf{c} = \mathbf{0}$.' Explain why these words are needed in the definition.

Two sets of linearly independent vectors, $\{\mathbf{a}, \mathbf{b}, \mathbf{c}\}$ and $\{\mathbf{r}, \mathbf{s}\}$, are given, and the intersection of the spaces spanned by them is a one-dimensional vector space. Prove that the set $\{\mathbf{a}, \mathbf{b}, \mathbf{c}, \mathbf{r}, \mathbf{s}\}$ is linearly dependent. Deduce that the dimension of the space spanned by $\{\mathbf{a}, \mathbf{b}, \mathbf{c}, \mathbf{r}, \mathbf{s}\}$ is less than or equal to 4. In your proof, careful attention should be given to the possibility that coefficients might be zero.

Prove that if the dimension of the space spanned by $\{\mathbf{a}, \mathbf{b}, \mathbf{c}, \mathbf{r}, \mathbf{s}\}$ were equal to 3, then the intersection of the spaces spanned by $\{\mathbf{a}, \mathbf{b}, \mathbf{c}\}$ and $\{\mathbf{r}, \mathbf{s}\}$ would have dimension 2 (contradicting the information at the beginning of the previous paragraph).

Hence prove that the space spanned by $\{\mathbf{a}, \mathbf{b}, \mathbf{c}, \mathbf{r}, \mathbf{s}\}$ has dimension 4. [SMP]

15

Groups 1

In Chapter 14 the axioms of a vector space were listed and there was the comment that 'the first five axioms simply state that the vectors form an Abelian group under vector addition'. The group is one of the most commonly occurring structures in mathematics, with examples arising in many different contexts. In this chapter, the formal definition of a group is given and we meet a variety of examples of groups.

15.1 SYMMETRY TRANSFORMATIONS

We are all familiar with the idea of symmetry, and recognise symmetry in geometrical shapes, graphs, wallpaper patterns, etc. A symmetry transformation is defined as a transformation which leaves the 'object' in the same position, so it looks the same, though individual points may move.

For example, with the letter 

, there are two symmetry transformations:

(1) reflection in the axis l, and
(2) the identity;

while for the letter O, there are an infinite number of symmetry transformations:

(1) reflection in any axis passing through the centre,
(2) rotation through any angle about the centre, and
(3) the identity.

Symmetries of a rectangle

The rectangle possesses four symmetry transformations:

Original position	Transformation	Final position
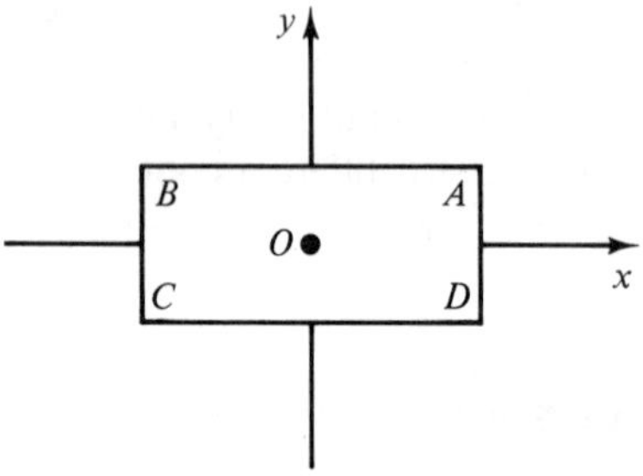	**I:** identity	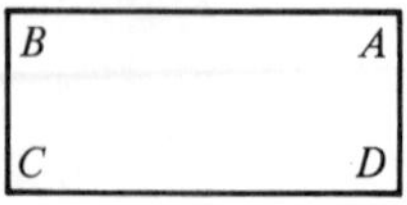
	X: reflection in the x-axis	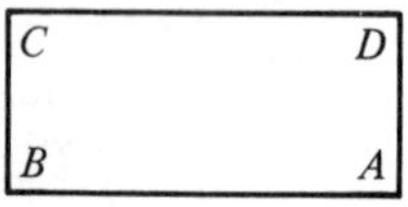
	Y: reflection in the y-axis	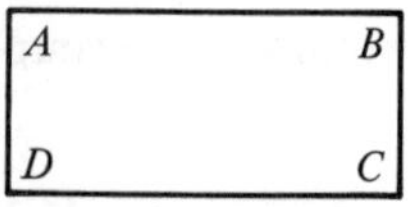
	H: 180° rotation about the centre, O	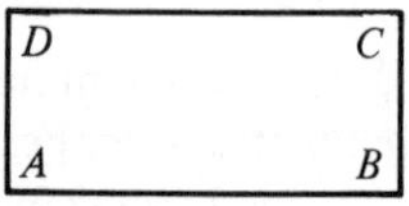

Since we are dealing with transformations, we can combine two transformations, written **X** $*$ **Y**, to form a new transformation. We take **X** $*$ **Y** to mean transformation **Y** followed by transformation **X**:

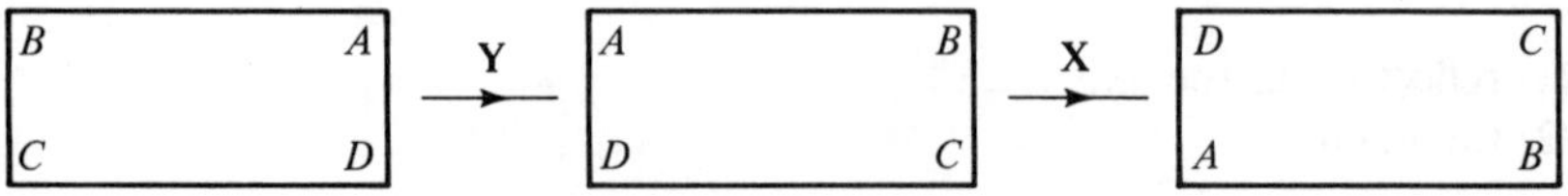

So **X** $*$ **Y** = **H**.

We have taken two transformations and combined them using the operation $*$, combination of transformations. The results are usually presented as a table:

$*$	**I**	**X**	**Y**	**H**
I				
X			**X** $*$ **Y** = **H**	
Y				
H				

Such a table is known as a *Cayley table.*

Q.1 Complete the Cayley table for the symmetries of the rectangle under the operation $*$, combination of transformations.

15.2 PERMUTATIONS

Permutations provide us with another way of describing symmetry transformations. For example, $ABCD$ is a rectangle and these vertices are at positions 1234. Then the half-turn symmetry transformation is

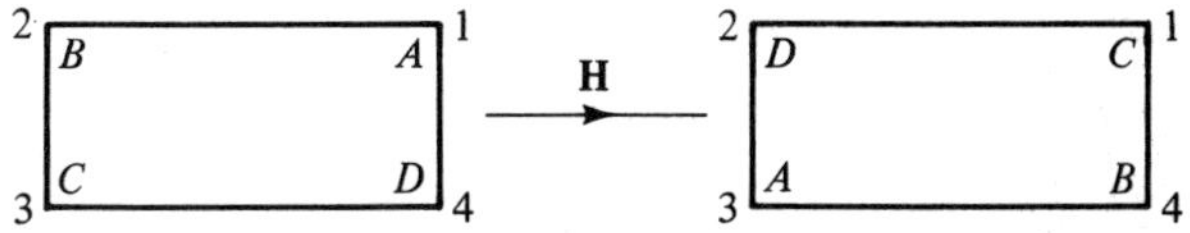

This can be specified by saying that the vertex in position 1 moves to position 3, the vertex in position 2 moves to position 4, and so on. This is written as $\pi_h = \begin{pmatrix} 1 & 2 & 3 & 4 \\ 3 & 4 & 1 & 2 \end{pmatrix}$. So the two reflections can be written as

$$\pi_x = \begin{pmatrix} 1 & 2 & 3 & 4 \\ 4 & 3 & 2 & 1 \end{pmatrix} \quad \text{and} \quad \pi_y = \begin{pmatrix} 1 & 2 & 3 & 4 \\ 2 & 1 & 4 & 3 \end{pmatrix},$$

and the identity as $$\pi_i = \begin{pmatrix} 1 & 2 & 3 & 4 \\ 1 & 2 & 3 & 4 \end{pmatrix}.$$

Rearrangements of elements among themselves are called *permutations*.

Given two permutations $\pi_x = \begin{pmatrix} 1 & 2 & 3 & 4 \\ 4 & 3 & 2 & 1 \end{pmatrix}$ and $\pi_y = \begin{pmatrix} 1 & 2 & 3 & 4 \\ 2 & 1 & 4 & 3 \end{pmatrix}$, we can combine them to obtain a third permutation. $\pi_x \circ \pi_y$ means permutation π_y followed by permutation π_x, so under π_y the vertex in position 1 goes to position 2, which under π_x goes to position 3; that is,

$$1 \overset{\pi_y}{\rightarrow} 2 \overset{\pi_x}{\rightarrow} 3.$$

Similarly, $$2 \overset{\pi_y}{\rightarrow} 1 \overset{\pi_x}{\rightarrow} 4$$

and $$3 \overset{\pi_y}{\rightarrow} 4 \overset{\pi_x}{\rightarrow} 1$$

and $$4 \overset{\pi_y}{\rightarrow} 3 \overset{\pi_x}{\rightarrow} 1.$$

Therefore $$\begin{pmatrix} 1 & 2 & 3 & 4 \\ 4 & 3 & 2 & 1 \end{pmatrix} \circ \begin{pmatrix} 1 & 2 & 3 & 4 \\ 2 & 1 & 4 & 3 \end{pmatrix} = \begin{pmatrix} 1 & 2 & 3 & 4 \\ 3 & 4 & 1 & 2 \end{pmatrix}$$

or $$\pi_x \circ \pi_y = \pi_h,$$

which confirms our earlier result.

15.3 SYMMETRIES OF AN EQUILATERAL TRIANGLE AND A SQUARE

(a) Equilateral triangle

Original position	Transformation	Final position	Permutation
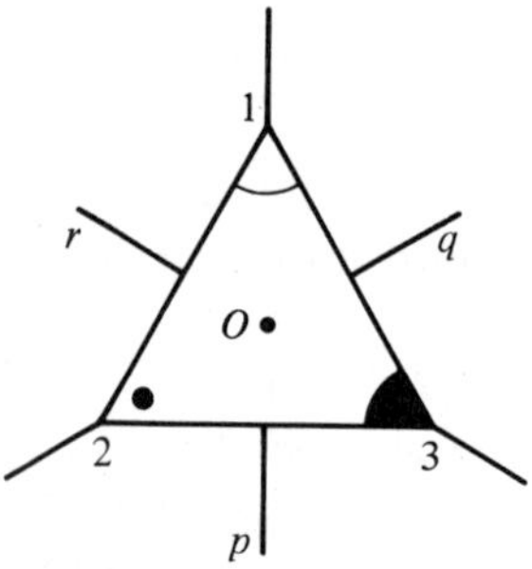	**I:** identity		$\begin{pmatrix}1 & 2 & 3\\1 & 2 & 3\end{pmatrix}$
	A: 120° rotation about O	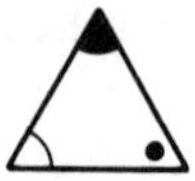	$\begin{pmatrix}1 & 2 & 3\\2 & 3 & 1\end{pmatrix}$
	B: 240° rotation about O	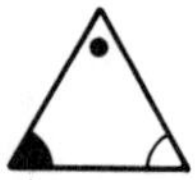	$\begin{pmatrix}1 & 2 & 3\\3 & 1 & 2\end{pmatrix}$
	P: reflection in p		$\begin{pmatrix}1 & 2 & 3\\1 & 3 & 2\end{pmatrix}$
	Q: reflection in q		$\begin{pmatrix}1 & 2 & 3\\3 & 2 & 1\end{pmatrix}$
	R: reflection in r		$\begin{pmatrix}1 & 2 & 3\\2 & 1 & 3\end{pmatrix}$

(b) Square

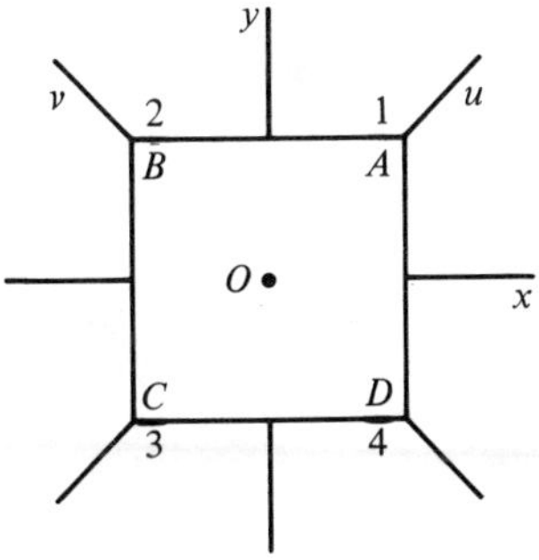

Original position	Transformation	Final position	Permutation
	I: identity	B A C D	$\begin{pmatrix}1 & 2 & 3 & 4\\1 & 2 & 3 & 4\end{pmatrix}$
	Q: 90° rotation about *O*	A D B C	$\begin{pmatrix}1 & 2 & 3 & 4\\2 & 3 & 4 & 1\end{pmatrix}$
	H: 180° rotation about *O*	D C A B	$\begin{pmatrix}1 & 2 & 3 & 4\\3 & 4 & 1 & 2\end{pmatrix}$
	T: 270° rotation about *O*	C B D A	$\begin{pmatrix}1 & 2 & 3 & 4\\4 & 1 & 2 & 3\end{pmatrix}$
	X: reflection in *x*	C D B A	$\begin{pmatrix}1 & 2 & 3 & 4\\4 & 3 & 2 & 1\end{pmatrix}$
	Y: reflection in *y*	A B D C	$\begin{pmatrix}1 & 2 & 3 & 4\\2 & 1 & 4 & 3\end{pmatrix}$
	U: reflection in *u*	D A C B	$\begin{pmatrix}1 & 2 & 3 & 4\\1 & 4 & 3 & 2\end{pmatrix}$
	V: reflection in *v*	B C A D	$\begin{pmatrix}1 & 2 & 3 & 4\\3 & 2 & 1 & 4\end{pmatrix}$

Q.2 Complete the following Cayley tables for the symmetries of (*a*) the equilateral triangle and (*b*) the square, under the operation of combination of transformations, $*$:

(*a*)

$*$	I	A	B	P	Q	R
I	I	A	B	P	Q	R
A	A					Q
B	B				R	
P	P	Q		I		
Q	Q		P		I	
R	R					I

(*b*)

$*$	I	Q	H	T	X	Y	U	V
I	I	Q	H	T	X	Y	U	V
Q	Q	H	T	I			Y	
H	H	T	I	Q		X		
T	T	I	Q	H	V			
X	X				I			
Y	Y	U				I		T
U	U						I	
V	V		U					I

Exercise 15A

1 Construct the Cayley tables for the symmetry transformations of the following figures:
   (*a*) an isosceles triangle
   (*b*) a rhombus
   (*c*) the letter H
   (*d*) a kite
   (*e*) the shape 
   (*f*) an ellipse

2 Describe some simple figures which have two, three, five symmetries (including the identity symmetry).

3 Describe the symmetries of the graphs of
   (*a*) $x^2 - 4y^2 = 1$
   (*b*) $y = \dfrac{1}{x}$
   (*c*) $|y| = \dfrac{1}{|x|}$
   (*d*) $x^2 + y^2 = 1$
   (*e*) $x^{2/3} + y^{2/3} = a^{2/3}$

4 Describe the symmetries of (*a*) a regular pentagon, (*b*) a regular hexagon.

5 Find the following composition of permutations of the set $\{1, 2, 3, 4\}$:
   (*a*) $\begin{pmatrix} 1 & 2 & 3 & 4 \\ 3 & 1 & 4 & 2 \end{pmatrix} \circ \begin{pmatrix} 1 & 2 & 3 & 4 \\ 1 & 4 & 2 & 3 \end{pmatrix}$

(b) $\begin{pmatrix} 1 & 2 & 3 & 4 \\ 2 & 1 & 3 & 4 \end{pmatrix} \circ \begin{pmatrix} 1 & 2 & 3 & 4 \\ 1 & 2 & 4 & 3 \end{pmatrix}$

(c) $\begin{pmatrix} 1 & 2 & 3 & 4 \\ 4 & 3 & 2 & 1 \end{pmatrix} \circ \begin{pmatrix} 1 & 2 & 3 & 4 \\ 3 & 2 & 1 & 4 \end{pmatrix}$

(d) $\begin{pmatrix} 1 & 2 & 3 & 4 \\ 2 & 4 & 1 & 3 \end{pmatrix} \circ \begin{pmatrix} 1 & 2 & 3 & 4 \\ 3 & 4 & 1 & 2 \end{pmatrix}$

6 If permutations $\pi_1 = \begin{pmatrix} 1 & 2 & 3 & 4 & 5 \\ 3 & 1 & 4 & 2 & 5 \end{pmatrix}$, $\pi_2 = \begin{pmatrix} 1 & 2 & 3 & 4 & 5 \\ 4 & 2 & 1 & 5 & 3 \end{pmatrix}$ and $\pi_3 = \begin{pmatrix} 1 & 2 & 3 & 4 & 5 \\ 5 & 2 & 3 & 1 & 4 \end{pmatrix}$, find

(a) $\pi_1 \circ \pi_2$ (b) $\pi_3 \circ (\pi_2 \circ \pi_1)$ (c) ${\pi_2}^3$ (d) $(\pi_3 \circ \pi_2)^2$

7 The permutation $\pi = \begin{pmatrix} 1 & 2 & 3 & 4 & 5 \\ 3 & 5 & 4 & 1 & 2 \end{pmatrix}$. If $\pi^n = \begin{pmatrix} 1 & 2 & 3 & 4 & 5 \\ 1 & 2 & 3 & 4 & 5 \end{pmatrix}$, find n.

8 The six permutations of the set $\{p, q, r\}$ are

$$\pi_1 = \begin{pmatrix} p & q & r \\ p & q & r \end{pmatrix}, \quad \pi_2 = \begin{pmatrix} p & q & r \\ q & r & p \end{pmatrix}, \quad \pi_3 = \begin{pmatrix} p & q & r \\ r & p & q \end{pmatrix},$$

$$\pi_4 = \begin{pmatrix} p & q & r \\ q & p & r \end{pmatrix}, \quad \pi_5 = \begin{pmatrix} p & q & r \\ r & q & p \end{pmatrix}, \quad \pi_6 = \begin{pmatrix} p & q & r \\ p & r & q \end{pmatrix}.$$

(a) Does $\pi_4 \circ \pi_2 = \pi_2 \circ \pi_4$?
(b) Does $\pi_3 \circ (\pi_5 \circ \pi_2) = (\pi_3 \circ \pi_5) \circ \pi_2$?
(c) Find π_i and π_j such that $\pi_6 \circ \pi_i = \pi_3$ and $\pi_j \circ \pi_2 = \pi_1$.

15.4 GROUPS OF SYMMETRIES

In the last two sections we completed the Cayley tables for the symmetries of the rectangle, equilateral triangle and square, under the operation composition of transformations, represented by $*$. The tables were:

Rectangle

*	I	X	Y	H
I	I	X	Y	H
X	X	I	H	Y
Y	Y	H	I	X
H	H	Y	X	I

Equilateral triangle

*	I	A	B	P	Q	R
I	I	A	B	P	Q	R
A	A	B	I	R	P	Q
B	B	I	A	Q	R	P
P	P	Q	R	I	A	B
Q	Q	R	P	B	I	A
R	R	P	Q	A	B	I

Square

*	I	Q	H	T	X	Y	U	V
I	I	Q	H	T	X	Y	U	V
Q	Q	H	T	I	U	V	Y	X
H	H	T	I	Q	Y	X	V	U
T	T	I	Q	H	V	U	X	Y
X	X	V	Y	U	I	H	T	Q
Y	Y	U	X	V	H	I	Q	T
U	U	X	V	Y	Q	T	I	H
V	V	Y	U	X	T	Q	H	I

A careful examination of these tables will show that they have a number of properties in common:

Closure: no new element is needed to complete the table – the answer when two symmetries are combined is always one of the symmetries under discussion.

Identity: there is a 'stay-put' symmetry – **I** in each case.

Inverse: for each symmetry there is another symmetry which will 'undo' it; that is, which will return it to the 'stay-put' symmetry.

Associative: this is not an easy property to spot but it is necessary so that a unique answer is arrived at when three or more symmetries are combined – remember that 'combination of transformations' is a *binary* operation, that is, *two* symmetries are combined; so with $\mathbf{L} * \mathbf{M} * \mathbf{N}$, either $(\mathbf{L} * \mathbf{M})$ or $(\mathbf{M} * \mathbf{N})$ would have to be done first.

So in order to have a group we must first have a *set of elements* and a *binary operation* defined on the elements of the set. The four rules of closure, associativity, existence of an identity and existence of inverses must also hold. The formal definition of a group is:

Definition 1

A *group* G is a set of elements and a binary operation $\circ$ such that

(1) *Closure:* $a \circ b \in G$ for all $a, b \in G$.

(2) *Associative:* $(a \circ b) \circ c = a \circ (b \circ c)$ for all $a, b, c \in G$.

(3) *Identity:* there is an identity element $e \in G$ such that

$$e \circ a = a \circ e = a \quad \text{for all } a \in G.$$

(4) *Inverse:* each element $a \in G$ has an inverse $a^{-1} \in G$ such that

$$a \circ a^{-1} = a^{-1} \circ a = e.$$

If, as well, (5) *Commutative:*

$$a \circ b = b \circ a \quad \text{for all } a,\ b \in G,$$

then the group is commutative and is called an *Abelian group*.*

(*Note:* '=' means 'is the same element as'.)

* Named after the Norwegian mathematician Niels Henrik Abel (1802–1829).

The symmetry group of the rectangle is commutative but the symmetry groups of the equilateral triangle and square are not commutative.

15.5 SOME PROPERTIES OF GROUPS

(a) Order of a group

Definition 2
A group G is said to be *finite* if G has a finite number of elements. The number of elements in a finite group is called the *order* of the group. A group with an infinite number of elements is called an *infinite group*.

Q.3 What is the order of the symmetry group of (*a*) the rectangle, (*b*) the equilateral triangle, (*c*) the square?

An example of an infinite group is the set of all two-dimensional vectors under the operation, addition of vectors.

(b) The Latin square property of a finite group

Each element appears once and only once in each row and column of a Cayley table.

Suppose that the p-row contains the element g twice; that is,

$\circ$	$\dots$	x	$\dots$	y
$\vdots$		$\vdots$		$\vdots$
p	$\dots$	g	$\dots$	g

where x and y are distinct elements.

So $\quad g = p \circ x = p \circ y$

therefore $\quad p^{-1} \circ (p \circ x) = p^{-1} \circ (p \circ y) \quad$ (premultiplying by p^{-1})

$\Rightarrow \quad (p^{-1} \circ p) \circ x = (p^{-1} \circ p) \circ y \quad$ (associativity)

$\Rightarrow \quad e \circ x = e \circ y \quad$ (inverses)

$\Rightarrow \quad x = y \quad$ (identity).

This contradicts the statement that x and y are distinct elements, so our original assumption that g appears twice is false; an element cannot appear more than once in any row. Because each row contains the same number of elements as there are in the group, *each* element will appear only *once* in each row. A similar argument is used to prove that each element will appear once and only once in each column.

However, the converse of this result is not true; that is, the Latin square property does not imply that we have a group. A counter-example is given in Q.4.

Q.4

$\circ$	e	a	b	c	d
e	e	a	b	c	d
a	a	e	c	d	b
b	b	d	e	a	c
c	c	b	d	e	a
d	d	c	a	b	e

Why is this Latin square not a group table?

(c) The equation $a \circ x = b$ has a unique solution in G

One important consequence of the group axioms is that in a group G, equations of the form $a \circ x = b$, where $a, b \in G$, have a unique solution. In proving this result all four axioms of a group are used – this gives us another reason for investigating sets and binary operations where these four properties hold.

If a solution to $a \circ x = b$ exists,

then $\quad a^{-1} \circ (a \circ x) = a^{-1} \circ b \quad$ (premultiplying by a^{-1})

$\Rightarrow \quad (a^{-1} \circ a) \circ x = a^{-1} \circ b \quad$ (associativity)

$\Rightarrow \quad e \circ x = a^{-1} \circ b \quad$ (inverses)

$\Rightarrow \quad x = a^{-1} \circ b \quad$ (identity).

Now $\quad a^{-1} \in G \;$ and $\; b \in G$,

so, by closure $\quad a^{-1} \circ b \in G$.

We need to check that $x = a^{-1} \circ b$ does satisfy the equation $a \circ x = b$. It does, since

$$a \circ (a^{-1} \circ b) = (a \circ a^{-1}) \circ b = e \circ b = b.$$

Thus, $a \circ x = b$ has the unique solution $x = a^{-1} \circ b$.

(d) The cancellation laws

If $\quad a \circ x = a \circ y$

then $\quad a^{-1} \circ (a \circ x) = a^{-1} \circ (a \circ y) \quad$ (premultiplying by a^{-1})

$\Rightarrow \quad (a^{-1} \circ a) \circ x = (a^{-1} \circ a) \circ y \quad$ (associativity)

$\Rightarrow \quad e \circ x = e \circ y \quad$ (inverses)

$\Rightarrow \quad x = y \quad$ (identity);

that is, $\quad a \circ x = a \circ y \;\Rightarrow\; x = y$

and we say that we have 'cancelled a on the left'.

This proof is similar to the proof of the Latin square property. It is essentially the same result, the main difference being that for the Latin square property, the group G has to be of finite order, while the cancellation laws apply to both finite and infinite groups.

Q.5 Prove the right cancellation law:

$$x \circ a = y \circ a \quad \Rightarrow \quad x = y.$$

(e) (i) The identity element is unique

Suppose that both e and f are identity elements,

then $\quad e \circ f = f \quad$ (e is an identity)

and $\quad e \circ f = e \quad$ (f is an identity);

that is, $\quad e = f,$

and the result follows.

(ii) The inverse of an element is unique

Suppose that b and c are both inverses of a.

Now $\quad (b \circ a) \circ c = b \circ (a \circ c) \quad$ (associativity),

so $\quad e \circ c = b \circ e \quad$ (inverses);

that is, $\quad c = b \quad$ (identity).

Thus a^{-1} is unique.

(f) Subgroups

Definition 3
If H is a subset of a group which itself forms a group under the same operation, then H is a *subgroup* of the group G.

Example 1
Show that $H = \{\mathbf{I}, \mathbf{X}\}$ is a subgroup of the group of symmetries of the rectangle.

Solution
The Cayley table is:

*	**I**	**X**
I	**I**	**X**
X	**X**	**I**

We need to check the axioms of a group:

(1) *Closure:* Only **I** and **X** appear in the Cayley table, so we have closure.

(2) *Associative:* Since associativity holds for the group G, and H is a subset of G, it must also hold for the subset.

(3) *Identity:* **I** is the identity element.
(4) *Inverse:* Each element in H has an inverse:

Element	*Inverse*
I	**I**
X	**X**

□

This example shows that in order to check that H is a subgroup of G (both under the operation $*$), we need only check the closure, identity and inverse axioms.

Q.6 List the subgroups of the symmetries of (*a*) the rectangle, (*b*) the equilateral triangle, and (*c*) the square. (*Note:* apart from $\{\mathbf{I}\}$ and G itself (which are always subgroups of a group G), the symmetry group of the rectangle has three proper subgroups, the equilateral triangle has four proper subgroups and the square has eight proper subgroups.)

Q.7 What do you notice about the orders of the subgroups and the order of the group?

Your answer to Q.7 demonstrates the truth of *Lagrange's theorem*, which will be proved in the next chapter.

15.6 OTHER EXAMPLES OF GROUPS

So far our examples of groups have been restricted to symmetries and permutations. In this section we see a number of the different types of examples which arise in other branches of mathematics. Further examples of groups appear in Exercise 15B.

A note about associativity

In many cases it would be a long process to check associativity, but fortunately there are quite a few situations in which associativity can be recognised, and standard results quoted. These include:

(1) multiplication and addition in number systems such as the integers, rationals, reals, complex numbers and in modulo arithmetic;

(2) situations in which $a \circ b \circ c$ means 'c followed by b followed by a'; for example, composition of functions, composition by transformations, composition of permutations, adding and multiplication of matrices.

(a) Number systems

The following sets of numbers form Abelian groups:

(1) Under addition: $\mathbb{Z}$, the set of integers;
$\mathbb{Q}$, the set of rational numbers;
$\mathbb{R}$, the set of real numbers;
$\mathbb{C}$, the set of complex numbers.

(2) If the number 0 is excluded, $\mathbb{Q}$, $\mathbb{R}$ and $\mathbb{C}$ form Abelian groups under multiplication. (Why has 0 to be excluded?)

(3) Sets of numbers under modulo arithmetic; for example, the set $\{2, 4, 6, 8\}$ under multiplication modulo 10 (by 'multiplication modulo 10', we mean the remainder on division by 10 when the two numbers are multiplied together under ordinary multiplication). The Cayley table is:

$\times_{10}$	2	4	6	8
2	4	8	2	6
4	8	6	4	2
6	2	4	6	8
8	6	2	8	4

Notice that the identity element is 6.

(b) Functions

Example 2

$$i: x \mapsto x \qquad a: x \mapsto \frac{1}{x} \qquad b: x \mapsto -x \qquad c: x \mapsto -\frac{1}{x}$$

are four functions. Do they form a group under composition of functions?

Solution
We begin by completing the Cayley table:

$\circ$	i	a	b	c
i	i	a	b	c
a	a	i	c	b
b	b	c	i	a
c	c	b	a	i

for example, $$a \circ b(x) = a(-x) = -\frac{1}{x} \quad \Rightarrow \quad a \circ b = c.$$

(1) *Closure:* Seen from the Cayley table.
(2) *Associative:* $p \circ (q \circ r) = (p \circ q) \circ r$, as composition of functions is associative (both terms mean 'function r followed by function q followed by function p').
(3) *Identity:* i is the identity function.
(4) *Inverse:* Each function is its own inverse.

So we have a group. □

(c) Matrices

Example 3
Show that the set of matrices

$$\left\{\begin{bmatrix}1 & 0\\0 & 1\end{bmatrix}, \begin{bmatrix}0 & -1\\1 & 0\end{bmatrix}, \begin{bmatrix}-1 & 0\\0 & -1\end{bmatrix}, \begin{bmatrix}0 & 1\\-1 & 0\end{bmatrix}\right\}$$

under matrix multiplication forms a group.

Solution

The Cayley table is:

$\times$	$\begin{bmatrix} 1 & 0 \\ 0 & 1 \end{bmatrix}$	$\begin{bmatrix} 0 & -1 \\ 1 & 0 \end{bmatrix}$	$\begin{bmatrix} -1 & 0 \\ 0 & -1 \end{bmatrix}$	$\begin{bmatrix} 0 & 1 \\ -1 & 0 \end{bmatrix}$
$\begin{bmatrix} 1 & 0 \\ 0 & 1 \end{bmatrix}$	$\begin{bmatrix} 1 & 0 \\ 0 & 1 \end{bmatrix}$	$\begin{bmatrix} 0 & -1 \\ 1 & 0 \end{bmatrix}$	$\begin{bmatrix} -1 & 0 \\ 0 & -1 \end{bmatrix}$	$\begin{bmatrix} 0 & 1 \\ -1 & 0 \end{bmatrix}$
$\begin{bmatrix} 0 & -1 \\ 1 & 0 \end{bmatrix}$	$\begin{bmatrix} 0 & -1 \\ 1 & 0 \end{bmatrix}$	$\begin{bmatrix} -1 & 0 \\ 0 & -1 \end{bmatrix}$	$\begin{bmatrix} 0 & 1 \\ -1 & 0 \end{bmatrix}$	$\begin{bmatrix} 1 & 0 \\ 0 & 1 \end{bmatrix}$
$\begin{bmatrix} -1 & 0 \\ 0 & -1 \end{bmatrix}$	$\begin{bmatrix} -1 & 0 \\ 0 & -1 \end{bmatrix}$	$\begin{bmatrix} 0 & 1 \\ -1 & 0 \end{bmatrix}$	$\begin{bmatrix} 1 & 0 \\ 0 & 1 \end{bmatrix}$	$\begin{bmatrix} 0 & -1 \\ 1 & 0 \end{bmatrix}$
$\begin{bmatrix} 0 & 1 \\ -1 & 0 \end{bmatrix}$	$\begin{bmatrix} 0 & 1 \\ -1 & 0 \end{bmatrix}$	$\begin{bmatrix} 1 & 0 \\ 0 & 1 \end{bmatrix}$	$\begin{bmatrix} 0 & -1 \\ 1 & 0 \end{bmatrix}$	$\begin{bmatrix} -1 & 0 \\ 0 & -1 \end{bmatrix}$

(1) *Closure:* Seen from the Cayley table.

(2) *Associative:* Matrix multiplication is associative, so it will be true for this set of matrices.

(3) *Identity:* $\begin{bmatrix} 1 & 0 \\ 0 & 1 \end{bmatrix}$ is the identity matrix.

(4) *Inverse:*

Element	*Inverse*
$\begin{bmatrix} 1 & 0 \\ 0 & 1 \end{bmatrix}$	$\begin{bmatrix} 1 & 0 \\ 0 & 1 \end{bmatrix}$
$\begin{bmatrix} 0 & -1 \\ 1 & 0 \end{bmatrix}$	$\begin{bmatrix} 0 & 1 \\ -1 & 0 \end{bmatrix}$
$\begin{bmatrix} -1 & 0 \\ 0 & -1 \end{bmatrix}$	$\begin{bmatrix} -1 & 0 \\ 0 & -1 \end{bmatrix}$
$\begin{bmatrix} 0 & 1 \\ -1 & 0 \end{bmatrix}$	$\begin{bmatrix} 0 & -1 \\ 1 & 0 \end{bmatrix}$

So we have a group. □

Example 4

Show that the set of matrices of the form $\begin{bmatrix} x & -y \\ y & x \end{bmatrix}$, where $x^2 + y^2 \neq 0$ and $x, y \in \mathbb{R}$, forms a group under multiplication.

Solution

As $\det\left(\begin{bmatrix} x & -y \\ y & x \end{bmatrix}\right) = x^2 + y^2$, the condition $x^2 + y^2 \neq 0$ is equivalent to $\det\left(\begin{bmatrix} x & -y \\ y & x \end{bmatrix}\right) \neq 0$.

(1) *Closure:* $\begin{bmatrix} x & -y \\ y & x \end{bmatrix}\begin{bmatrix} a & -b \\ b & a \end{bmatrix} = \begin{bmatrix} (ax-by) & -(bx+ay) \\ (ay+bx) & (-by+ax) \end{bmatrix}$

(*a*) $(ax - by) \in \mathbb{R}$ and $(bx + ay) \in \mathbb{R}$, as $a, b, c, y \in \mathbb{R}$;

(*b*) the matrix is of the correct form, with the leading diagonal terms the same and the other diagonal terms of opposite sign;

(*c*) the determinant of the product is equal to the product of the determinants, which are both non-zero, therefore the '$x^2 + y^2 \neq 0$' condition is also satisfied.

(2) *Associative:* Matrix multiplication is associative, so it will be true for this set of matrices.

(3) *Identity:* $\begin{bmatrix} 1 & 0 \\ 0 & 1 \end{bmatrix}$ is the identity – it is of the correct form, with $x = 1$, $y = 0$ and the determinant not 0.

(4) *Inverse:* The inverse of $\begin{bmatrix} x & -y \\ y & x \end{bmatrix}$ is $\begin{bmatrix} \dfrac{x}{x^2+y^2} & \dfrac{y}{x^2+y^2} \\ -\dfrac{y}{x^2+y^2} & \dfrac{x}{x^2+y^2} \end{bmatrix}$. This is the correct form, with 'x' $= \dfrac{x}{x^2+y^2}$ and 'y' $= -\dfrac{y}{x^2+y^2}$ and the determinant $= \dfrac{1}{x^2+y^2} \neq 0$.

So we have a group. □

(d) Groups defined algebraically

Example 5

Show that the set $\mathbb{Z}$ forms a group under the operation $\circ$ defined by $a \circ b = a + b + 1$.

Solution

(1) *Closure:* For all $a, b \in \mathbb{Z}$, $a + b + 1$ is an integer.

(2) *Associative:*

$$(a \circ b) \circ c = (a + b + 1) \circ c = a + b + c + 2$$

$$a \circ (b \circ c) = a \circ (b + c + 1) = a + b + c + 2.$$

So $\quad (a \circ b) \circ c = a \circ (b \circ c)$ for all $a, b, c \in \mathbb{Z}$.

(3) *Identity:* -1 is the identity element,

as $\quad a \circ -1 = a - 1 + 1 = a$

and $\quad -1 \circ a = -1 + a + 1 = a.$

(4) *Inverse:* For each $a \in \mathbb{Z}$, $(-2-a)$ is the inverse of a,

as $$a \circ (-2-a) = a + (-2-a) + 1 = -1$$

and $$(-2-a) \circ a = (-2-a) + a + 1 = -1.$$

Thus $\mathbb{Z}$ forms a group under $\circ$. □

Exercise 15B

1 Determine whether the following sets are closed, associative, commutative under the given operations. In each case, does the set contain an identity element for the given operation? If it has an identity element, does every element have an inverse?

Set	Operation
(*a*) even integers	addition
(*b*) $\left\{\begin{bmatrix} a & b \\ c & d \end{bmatrix} : a, b, c, d \in \mathbb{Q}\right\}$	matrix multiplication
(*c*) positive integers	$a * b = \sqrt{(ab)}$
(*d*) integers	$a * b = 5^{a+b}$
(*e*) real numbers	$a * b = \dfrac{a+b}{2}$
(*f*) real numbers	$a * b = a + b + ab$
(*g*) $\{1, 2, 3, 4, 5\}$	multiplication modulo 6
(*h*) $\{(a, b): a, b \in \mathbb{Z} \text{ and } b \neq 0\}$	$(a, b) * (c, d) = (ac, bd)$
(*i*) $\{(a, b): a, b \in \mathbb{R} \text{ and } b \neq 0\}$	$(a, b) * (c, d) = (ad + bc, bd)$
(*j*) $\{a + b\sqrt{3}: a, b \in \mathbb{Q} \text{ and } a, b \text{ not both zero}\}$	multiplication

2 Show that the following sets are groups under the given operations:

(*a*) $\{2, 4, 8, 10, 14, 16\}$ under multiplication modulo 18

(*b*) $\{3, 6, 9, 12\}$ under multiplication modulo 15

(*c*) $\{2, 4, 6, 8, 10, 12\}$ under multiplication modulo 14

(*d*) $\{0, 1, 2, 3, 4, 5\}$ under addition modulo 6

(*e*) $\left\{\begin{bmatrix} 1 & 0 \\ 0 & 1 \end{bmatrix}, \begin{bmatrix} 1 & 0 \\ 0 & -1 \end{bmatrix}, \begin{bmatrix} -1 & 0 \\ 0 & -1 \end{bmatrix}, \begin{bmatrix} -1 & 0 \\ 0 & 1 \end{bmatrix}\right\}$ under matrix multiplication

(*f*) $\left\{\begin{bmatrix} 0 & 0 \\ 1 & 1 \end{bmatrix}, \begin{bmatrix} 0 & 0 \\ -1 & -1 \end{bmatrix}, \begin{bmatrix} 0 & 0 \\ j & j \end{bmatrix}, \begin{bmatrix} 0 & 0 \\ -j & -j \end{bmatrix}\right\}$ under matrix multiplication

(*g*) $\left\{\begin{bmatrix} 1 & 0 \\ 0 & 1 \end{bmatrix}, \begin{bmatrix} 0 & -1 \\ 1 & 0 \end{bmatrix}, \begin{bmatrix} -1 & 0 \\ 0 & -1 \end{bmatrix}, \begin{bmatrix} 0 & 1 \\ -1 & 0 \end{bmatrix}, \begin{bmatrix} 1 & 0 \\ 0 & -1 \end{bmatrix}, \begin{bmatrix} 0 & 1 \\ 1 & 0 \end{bmatrix}, \begin{bmatrix} -1 & 0 \\ 0 & 1 \end{bmatrix}, \begin{bmatrix} 0 & -1 \\ -1 & 0 \end{bmatrix}\right\}$ under matrix multiplication

(h) $\left\{\begin{bmatrix}1&0&0\\0&1&0\\0&0&1\end{bmatrix}, \begin{bmatrix}0&0&1\\1&0&0\\0&1&0\end{bmatrix}, \begin{bmatrix}0&1&0\\0&0&1\\1&0&0\end{bmatrix},\right.$
$\left.\begin{bmatrix}0&1&0\\1&0&0\\0&0&1\end{bmatrix}, \begin{bmatrix}1&0&0\\0&0&1\\0&1&0\end{bmatrix}, \begin{bmatrix}0&0&1\\0&1&0\\1&0&0\end{bmatrix}\right\}$ under matrix multiplication

(i) $\left\{f\colon x \to x,\ g\colon x \to 1 - \dfrac{1}{x},\ h\colon x \to \dfrac{1}{1-x}\right\}$ under composition of functions

(j) $\left\{p\colon x \to x,\quad q\colon x \to \dfrac{2}{2-x},\quad r\colon x \to \dfrac{x-2}{x-1},\quad s\colon x \to \dfrac{2(x-1)}{x}\right\}$ under composition of functions

(k) $\left\{s\colon x \to x,\quad t\colon x \to 1 - \dfrac{1}{2x},\quad u\colon x \to \dfrac{1-x}{1-2x},\quad v\colon x \to \dfrac{1}{2-2x}\right\}$ under composition of functions

(l) $\left\{i\colon x \to x,\ f\colon x \to 1-x,\ g\colon x \to \dfrac{1}{x},\ p\colon x \to \dfrac{x-1}{x},\ q\colon x \to \dfrac{1}{1-x},\ r\colon x \to \dfrac{x}{x-1}\right\}$ under composition of functions

3 List all the subgroups of the groups defined in question 2.

4 Produce as many different Latin squares as you can with
(a) two elements, a, b; (b) three elements, a, b, c.
How many of these represent groups?

5 For each of the Latin squares below, test whether it is a group table. If it is not a group, which axioms do not hold?

(a)

*	a	b	c	d
a	b	c	d	a
b	a	b	c	d
c	d	a	b	c
d	c	d	a	b

(b)

*	i	a	b	c	d
i	i	a	b	c	d
a	a	c	i	d	b
b	b	i	d	a	c
c	c	d	a	b	i
d	b	d	c	i	a

(c)

*	i	a	b	c	d
i	i	a	b	c	d
a	a	i	c	d	b
b	b	d	a	i	c
c	c	b	d	a	i
d	d	c	i	b	a

6 Show that the set of matrices of the form $\begin{bmatrix}\cos\theta & -\sin\theta\\ \sin\theta & \cos\theta\end{bmatrix}$, where $\theta \in \mathbb{R}$, forms a group under multiplication.

7 Show that the set of matrices $\left\{\begin{bmatrix}p & 0\\ q & r\end{bmatrix} : p, q, r \in \mathbb{Q} \text{ and } pr \neq 0\right\}$ forms a group under matrix multiplication.

8 Show that the set of real numbers, excluding -1, forms a group under the operation $\circ$ defined by $a \circ b = a + b + ab$.

9 In a group, an element and its inverse commute. What does this tell you about the positions of the identity element in a Cayley table? What can you say about the number of times the identity element appears on the leading diagonal in the Cayley table of a group of even order?

10 What is the smallest group of matrices under matrix multiplication which contains the matrix $\begin{bmatrix}2 & 7\\ -1 & -3\end{bmatrix}$?

This chapter has been the first of two chapters about groups. Its main aim has been to introduce you to the definition of a group and a variety of examples of groups.

Miscellaneous exercise 15

1 A cuboid has vertices at the eight points $(\pm 1, \pm 1, \pm 1)$. The eight symmetry transformations of the cuboid are:

I: identity

X: reflection in the plane $x = 0$

Y: reflection in the plane $y = 0$

Z: reflection in the plane $z = 0$

P: 180° rotation about the x-axis

Q: 180° rotation about the y-axis

R: 180° rotation about the z-axis

C: central inversion

A central inversion is the transformation represented by the matrix
$$\begin{bmatrix} -1 & 0 & 0 \\ 0 & -1 & 0 \\ 0 & 0 & -1 \end{bmatrix}.$$
Show that the symmetry transformations of the cuboid form an Abelian group.

2 In a group table, a rectangle is drawn which has the identity element e in one corner:

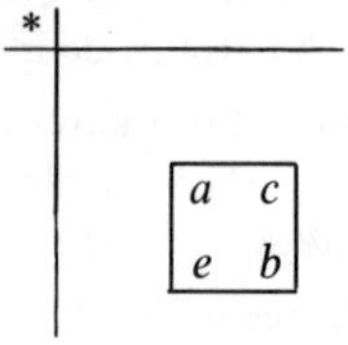

Prove that $c = a * b$.

3 In the definition of a group given in this chapter, we could have replaced axioms (3) and (4) by

(3) *Left identity*: there is an identity element $e \in G$ such that $e \circ a = a$ for all $a \in G$.

(4) *Left inverse*: each element $a \in G$ has an inverse $a^{-1} \in G$ such that $a^{-1} \circ a = e$.

Prove directly from these new axioms that e is also a right identity, and that a^{-1} is also a right inverse.

4 P and Q are subgroups of a group G. Prove that $P \cap Q$ is a subgroup of G. Is $P \cup Q$ a subgroup of G?

5 In a group G with identity e, every element $x \in G$ except the identity element satisfies $x^2 = e$. Prove that G is an Abelian group.

SUMMARY

Definitions

(1) A *group* G is a set of elements and a binary operation $\circ$ such that

(*a*) *Closure:* $a \circ b \in G$ for all $a, b \in G$.

(*b*) *Associative:* $(a \circ b) \circ c = a \circ (b \circ c)$ for all $a, b, c \in G$.

(*c*) *Identity:* there is an identity element $e \in G$ such that

$$e \circ a = a \circ e = a \quad \text{for all } a \in G.$$

(*d*) *Inverse:* each element $a \in G$ has an inverse $a^{-1} \in G$ such that

$$a \circ a^{-1} = a^{-1} \circ a = e.$$

If, as well, (*e*) *Commutative:*

$$a \circ b = b \circ a \quad \text{for all } a, b \in G,$$

then the group is commutative and is called an *Abelian group*.

(2) A group G is said to be *finite* if G has a finite number of elements. The number of elements in a finite group is called the *order* of the group. A group with an infinite number of elements is called an *infinite group*.

(3) If H is a subset of a group which itself forms a group under the same operation, then H is a *subgroup* of the group G.

16

Groups 2

We continue the theme of Chapter 15, in which the group structure was defined and a variety of examples of groups was given. This chapter is more abstract in approach. We are concerned with the classification of groups (we list all the abstract groups of order not exceeding 6) and results which are true for certain types of groups. These general results can then be applied to particular groups if we wish.

16.1 ISOMORPHISM

In the last chapter we met a number of examples of groups. Let us now look more closely at some of the groups of order 4.

(1) Symmetries of the rectangle under composition of transformations:

*	I	H	X	Y
I	I	H	X	Y
H	H	I	Y	X
X	X	Y	I	H
Y	Y	X	H	I

(2) $\{0, 1, 2, 3\}$ under + (mod 4):

$+_4$	0	1	2	3
0	0	1	2	3
1	1	2	3	0
2	2	3	0	1
3	3	0	1	2

(3) $\{2, 4, 6, 8\}$ under $\times$ (mod 10):

$\times_{10}$	2	4	6	8
2	4	8	2	6
4	8	6	4	2
6	2	4	6	8
8	6	2	8	4

(4) $i: x \to x$, $a: x \to \frac{1}{x}$, $b: x \to -x$, $c: x \to -\frac{1}{x}$ under composition of functions:

$\circ$	i	a	b	c
i	i	a	b	c
a	a	i	c	b
b	b	c	i	a
c	c	b	a	i

(5) Rotation of a square under composition of transformations:

*	**I**	**Q**	**H**	**T**
I	**I**	**Q**	**H**	**T**
Q	**Q**	**H**	**T**	**I**
H	**H**	**T**	**I**	**Q**
T	**T**	**I**	**Q**	**H**

An examination of these Cayley tables will show that tables (1) and (4) have the same pattern and tables (2) and (5) also have the same pattern. If in table (2) we replaced 0 by **I**, 1 by **Q**, 2 by **H** and 3 by **T**, we would end up with table (5). So, for example, $2 +_4 3 = 1$ would correspond to $\mathbf{H} * \mathbf{T} = \mathbf{Q}$.

We say that these two groups are *isomorphic* (in Greek, 'isos' means equal and 'morphe' means form or pattern).

There are four parts of the definition of 'isomorphic'. Referring to the example just given, we have

(*a*) two set: $\{0, 1, 2, 3\}$ and $\{\mathbf{I}, \mathbf{Q}, \mathbf{H}, \mathbf{T}\}$;

(*b*) two operations: $+_4$ and composition of functions (represented by $*$);

(*c*) a one-to-one correspondence between the elements:

$$0 \leftrightarrow \mathbf{I}$$

$$1 \leftrightarrow \mathbf{Q}$$

$$2 \leftrightarrow \mathbf{H}$$

$$3 \leftrightarrow \mathbf{T};$$

(*d*) if a binary operation is performed in one system, it is copied exactly in the other; for example, $1 +_4 2 = 3$ becomes $\mathbf{Q} * \mathbf{H} = \mathbf{T}$, which is correct.

Definition 1

Two groups $(G, *)$ and $(H, \circ)$ are *isomorphic* if there is a one-to-one mapping such that, if $a \leftrightarrow x$ and $b \leftrightarrow y$ (where $a, b \in G$ and $x, y \in H$), then

$$a * b \leftrightarrow x \circ y \quad \text{(Fig. 1).}$$

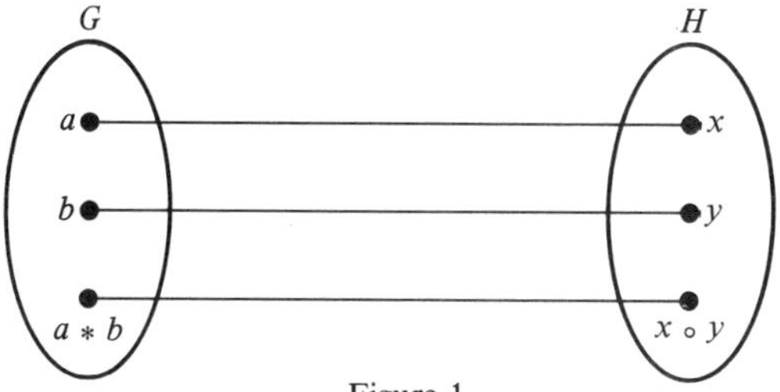

Figure 1

As the mapping is one-to-one, it follows that if two finite groups are isomorphic, then they have the same order. The definition of 'isomorphic' does not make any reference to the order of the groups, so it is also applicable to infinite groups.

Q.1 Show that the groups with tables (1) and (4) are isomorphic.

If we compare the groups in tables (2) and (3) it is not obvious that they have the same pattern. However, if we rewrite table (3) with the elements in a different order, we get:

$\times_{10}$	6	2	4	8
6	6	2	4	8
2	2	4	8	6
4	4	8	6	2
8	8	6	2	4

The correspondence is obvious:

$$0 \leftrightarrow 6$$

$$1 \leftrightarrow 2$$

$$2 \leftrightarrow 4$$

$$3 \leftrightarrow 8,$$

and we can then show that the groups with tables (2) and (3) are isomorphic.

Q.2 The correspondence is not necessarily unique. Show that the one-to-one mapping

$$0 \leftrightarrow 6$$

$$1 \leftrightarrow 8$$

$$2 \leftrightarrow 4$$

$$3 \leftrightarrow 2$$

could also have been used to show that the groups with tables (2) and (3) are isomorphic.

From this analysis of examples of groups of order 4, it looks as if there are only two essentially different types of groups, which have the forms

*	a	b	c	d
a	a	b	c	d
b	b	c	d	e
c	c	d	e	a
d	d	e	a	b

and

$\circ$	p	q	r	s
p	p	q	r	s
q	q	p	s	r
r	r	s	p	q
s	s	r	q	p

In §16.3 we shall show that there are no more different types of groups of order

4. Hence (1) and (4) are examples of one abstract group, and (2), (3) and (5) are examples of the other abstract group of order 4.

Q.3 If the two groups $(G, *)$ and $(H, \circ)$ are isomorphic, show that
(*a*) the identity element of G corresponds to the identity element of H;
(*b*) if $a \in G$ corresponds to $x \in H$, then $a^{-1} \in G$ will correspond to $x^{-1} \in H$;
that is, inverses in G correspond to inverses in H.

Exercise 16A

1 Determine which of the following groups of order 4 are isomorphic (see Exercise 15B, question 2):

(*a*) $\{3, 6, 9, 12\}$ under multiplication modulo 15

(*b*) $\left\{\begin{bmatrix}1 & 0\\0 & 1\end{bmatrix}, \begin{bmatrix}1 & 0\\0 & -1\end{bmatrix}, \begin{bmatrix}-1 & 0\\0 & -1\end{bmatrix}, \begin{bmatrix}-1 & 0\\0 & 1\end{bmatrix}\right\}$ under matrix multiplication

(*c*) $\left\{\begin{bmatrix}0 & 0\\1 & 1\end{bmatrix}, \begin{bmatrix}0 & 0\\-1 & -1\end{bmatrix}, \begin{bmatrix}0 & 0\\j & j\end{bmatrix}, \begin{bmatrix}0 & 0\\-j & -j\end{bmatrix}\right\}$ under matrix multiplication

(*d*) $\left\{p: x \to x,\ q: x \to \dfrac{2}{2-x},\ r: x \to \dfrac{x-2}{x-1},\ s: x \to \dfrac{2(x-1)}{x}\right\}$ under composition of functions

(*e*) $\left\{s: x \to x,\ t: x \to 1 - \dfrac{1}{2x},\ u: x \to \dfrac{1-x}{1-2x},\ v: x \to \dfrac{1}{2-2x}\right\}$ under composition of functions

2 Determine which of the following groups of order 6 are isomorphic (see Exercise 15B, question 2):

(*a*) $\{2, 4, 8, 10, 14, 16\}$ under multiplication modulo 18

(*b*) $\{2, 4, 6, 8, 10, 12\}$ under multiplication modulo 14

(*c*) $\left\{\begin{bmatrix}1 & 0 & 0\\0 & 1 & 0\\0 & 0 & 1\end{bmatrix}, \begin{bmatrix}0 & 0 & 1\\1 & 0 & 0\\0 & 1 & 0\end{bmatrix}, \begin{bmatrix}0 & 1 & 0\\0 & 0 & 1\\1 & 0 & 0\end{bmatrix},\right.$
$\left.\begin{bmatrix}0 & 1 & 0\\1 & 0 & 0\\0 & 0 & 1\end{bmatrix}, \begin{bmatrix}1 & 0 & 0\\0 & 0 & 1\\0 & 1 & 0\end{bmatrix}, \begin{bmatrix}0 & 0 & 1\\0 & 1 & 0\\1 & 0 & 0\end{bmatrix}\right\}$ under matrix multiplication

(*d*) $\left\{i: x \mapsto x,\ f: x \mapsto 1 - x,\ g: x \mapsto \dfrac{1}{x},\ p: x \mapsto \dfrac{x-1}{x},\ g: x \mapsto \dfrac{1}{1-x},\right.$
$\left. r: x \mapsto \dfrac{x}{x-1}\right\}$ under composition of functions

3 Give examples of geometric groups which are isomorphic to

(*a*) $\{1, 3, 7, 9\}$ under multiplication modulo 10

(*b*) $\left\{i: x \mapsto x,\ a: x \mapsto \dfrac{1}{x},\ b: x \mapsto -x,\ c: x \mapsto -\dfrac{1}{x}\right\}$ under composition of functions

(*c*) $\{1,\ -1,\ \tfrac{1}{2}(1 + j\sqrt{3}),\ \tfrac{1}{2}(1 - j\sqrt{3}),\ \tfrac{1}{2}(-1 + j\sqrt{3}),\ \tfrac{1}{2}(-1 - j\sqrt{3})\}$ under multiplication of complex numbers (*d*) $\left\{\begin{bmatrix}1 & 0\\0 & 1\end{bmatrix}, \begin{bmatrix}\omega & 0\\0 & \omega^2\end{bmatrix}, \begin{bmatrix}\omega^2 & 0\\0 & \omega\end{bmatrix}\right\}$, where $\omega^3 = 1$, under matrix multiplication

4 Prove that the groups $\left\{\begin{bmatrix}1 & 0\\m & 1\end{bmatrix} : m \in \mathbb{Z}\right\}$ under matrix multiplication and $\left\{\begin{bmatrix}n & 0\\0 & n\end{bmatrix} : n \in \mathbb{Z}\right\}$ under matrix addition, are isomorphic.

5 Show that the group of symmetries of a rhombus is isomorphic to the group of symmetries of a rectangle. How many different one-to-one correspondences are there?

6 Prove that the group of symmetries of an equilateral triangle is isomorphic to the permutation group of the set $\{a, b, c\}$.

7 Prove that all groups with just three elements are isomorphic.

8 Prove that an Abelian group cannot be isomorphic to a non-Abelian group.

16.2 FURTHER PROPERTIES OF GROUPS

Many of the definitions and results of this section will be illustrated using the symmetry group of the equilateral triangle G, which has the Cayley table:

*	I	A	B	P	Q	R
I	I	A	B	P	Q	R
A	A	B	I	R	P	Q
B	B	I	A	Q	R	P
P	P	Q	R	I	A	B
Q	Q	R	P	B	I	A
R	R	P	Q	A	B	I

(Transformations **I**, **A**, **B**, **P**, **Q**, **R** are defined in §15.1.)

(a) Generators

The elements $\{\mathbf{I}, \mathbf{A}, \mathbf{B}, \mathbf{P}, \mathbf{Q}, \mathbf{R}\}$ of the symmetries of the equilateral triangle can be expressed in terms of the elements **A** and **P** as

$$\{\mathbf{P}^2 \text{ (or } \mathbf{A}^3), \quad \mathbf{A}, \quad \mathbf{A}^2, \quad \mathbf{P}, \quad \mathbf{A}^2\mathbf{P}, \quad \mathbf{AP}\}.$$

We say that this group is *generated* by **A** and **P**.

Definition 2
A group G is *generated* by elements $a_1, a_2, \ldots, a_n, \ldots$ if every element of G can be expressed in terms of a combination of some or all of the a_i's.

Q.4 Show that the symmetry group of the square can be generated by two elements.

Q.5 How many elements are needed to generate the symmetry group of the rectangle?

(b) Cyclic groups

Definition 3
A group G which is generated by a single element is called a *cyclic group*.

The subgroup $\{\mathbf{I}, \mathbf{Q}, \mathbf{H}, \mathbf{T}\}$ of the symmetries of the square is a cyclic group, as it can be generated by the element $\mathbf{Q}$:

$$\mathbf{Q}^2 = \mathbf{H}, \quad \mathbf{Q}^3 = \mathbf{T} \quad \text{and} \quad \mathbf{Q}^4 = \mathbf{I}.$$

Q.6 Could the subgroup $\{\mathbf{I}, \mathbf{Q}, \mathbf{H}, \mathbf{T}\}$ above be generated by either $\mathbf{H}$ or $\mathbf{T}$?

(c) Period of an element

Definition 4
The *period* of an element g is the smallest positive integer k such that

$$g^k = e \quad \text{(the identity element).}$$

(Some books refer to the *order* of the element.)

For the symmetry group of the equilateral triangle, $\mathbf{A}^3 = \mathbf{I}$ and $\mathbf{P}^2 = \mathbf{I}$, so the period of $\mathbf{A}$ is 3 and the period of $\mathbf{P}$ is 2.

(d) Cosets

Definition 5
If H is a subgroup of a group G, with $H = \{h_1, h_2, h_3, \ldots, h_n\}$, the set $xH = \{x * h_1, x * h_2, \ldots, x * h_n\}$ is called the *left coset* of H by x.

$H = \{\mathbf{I}, \mathbf{P}\}$ is a subgroup of the symmetry group of the equilateral triangle, and there are six left cosets of H:

$$\mathbf{I}H = \{\mathbf{I}, \mathbf{P}\}$$

$$\mathbf{A}H = \{\mathbf{A}, \mathbf{R}\}$$

$$\mathbf{B}H = \{\mathbf{B}, \mathbf{Q}\}$$

$$\mathbf{P}H = \{\mathbf{P}, \mathbf{I}\}$$

$$\mathbf{Q}H = \{\mathbf{Q}, \mathbf{B}\}$$

$$\mathbf{R}H = \{\mathbf{P}, \mathbf{A}\}$$

We notice that

(1) xH and yH (for $x, y \in G$) are either the same or disjoint sets, and
(2) xH (for $x \in G$) has the same number of elements as H.

We can write $G = \mathbf{I}H \cup \mathbf{A}H \cup \mathbf{B}H$. These sets are disjoint and contain the same number of elements, so the order of the subgroup H is a factor of the order of the group G. This example illustrates the approach to the proof of Lagrange's theorem.

(e) Lagrange's theorem

If H is a subgroup of a finite group G, then the order of H is a factor of the order of G.

Let $H = \{e, a_1, a_2, \ldots, a_{h-1}\}$ be a subgroup of G.

The proof is made up of three steps:

(1) If $x \notin H$, then H and xH are disjoint sets.

Suppose $\quad a_i \in H \quad \text{and} \quad a_i \in xH;$

that is, $\quad a_i = xa_j \quad$ for some j,

therefore $\quad x = a_i a_j^{-1} \quad$ (postmultiplying by a_j^{-1}).

But both a_i and $a_j^{-1} \in H$, so by closure $a_i a_j^{-1} \in H$, thus contradicting the fact that $x \notin H$. So our assumption that there is an element a_i which belongs to both H and xH is incorrect, and the two sets H and xH must be disjoint.

(2) If y is now chosen (if it exists) which belongs to G but does not belong to H or xH, then xH and yH are disjoint sets.

Suppose they are *not* disjoint and that

$$xa_i = ya_j,$$

therefore

$$y = xa_i a_j^{-1}.$$

But $a_i a_j^{-1} \in H$, so $y \in xH$. This is a contradiction, since $y \notin xH$.

Now take z (if it exists) such that $z \in G$, $z \notin H$, $z \notin xH$, $z \notin yH$, and form zH. From above, it follows that zH is disjoint from H, xH and yH.

Repeat this process until every element of G (which is finite) is included in one of these sets. At this stage, the elements of G are partitioned into, say, p disjoint sets.

(3) All the sets contain exactly h different elements.

Suppose xH contained less than h elements, then for some i and j,

$$\begin{aligned} & xa_i = xa_j \\ \Rightarrow\quad & x^{-1}(xa_i) = x^{-1}(xa_j) \quad \text{(premultiplying by } x^{-1}) \\ \Rightarrow\quad & (x^{-1}x)a_i = (x^{-1}x)a_j \quad \text{(associativity)} \\ \Rightarrow\quad & ea_i = es_j \quad \text{(inverses)} \\ \Rightarrow\quad & a_i = a_j \quad \text{(identity).} \end{aligned}$$

This is a contradiction, since we know that the h elements of H are distinct.

Hence, the g elements of G can be partitioned into p sets, each of which contains h elements. This implies that $g = ph$, and we have proved Lagrange's theorem.

(f) The period of an element is a factor of the order of the group

If $a \in G$ and has period k (that is, $a^k = e$), then $\{e, a, a^2, \ldots, a^{k-1}\}$ is a cyclic subgroup with k elements, so by Lagrange's theorem, k is a factor of the order of the group.

(g) A group of prime order is cyclic

By Lagrange's theorem, a group of prime order cannot have any proper subgroups. If $a \in G$, where $a \neq e$, then the subgroup $\{e, a, a^2, \ldots, a^{k-1}\}$ is generated by the element a. As there are no proper subgroups, this must be the complete group G. So G is a cyclic group generated by the element a.

(h) Cayley's theorem

One of the reasons why permutation groups are important is:

> *Cayley's theorem*
> Any finite group of order n is isomorphic to a subgroup of the permutation group of n elements.

We saw earlier that each row of a Cayley table is a rearrangement of the elements of the group. So for each element $x \in G$ we can form the permutation based on the x-row of the table as its bottom line. So for the symmetry group of the equilateral triangle, we would form the permutations

$$\pi_i = \begin{pmatrix} \mathbf{I} & \mathbf{A} & \mathbf{B} & \mathbf{P} & \mathbf{Q} & \mathbf{R} \\ \mathbf{I} & \mathbf{A} & \mathbf{B} & \mathbf{P} & \mathbf{Q} & \mathbf{R} \end{pmatrix}, \quad \pi_a = \begin{pmatrix} \mathbf{I} & \mathbf{A} & \mathbf{B} & \mathbf{P} & \mathbf{Q} & \mathbf{R} \\ \mathbf{A} & \mathbf{B} & \mathbf{I} & \mathbf{R} & \mathbf{P} & \mathbf{Q} \end{pmatrix},$$

$$\pi_b = \begin{pmatrix} \mathbf{I} & \mathbf{A} & \mathbf{B} & \mathbf{P} & \mathbf{Q} & \mathbf{R} \\ \mathbf{B} & \mathbf{I} & \mathbf{A} & \mathbf{Q} & \mathbf{R} & \mathbf{P} \end{pmatrix}, \quad \pi_p = \begin{pmatrix} \mathbf{I} & \mathbf{A} & \mathbf{B} & \mathbf{P} & \mathbf{Q} & \mathbf{R} \\ \mathbf{P} & \mathbf{Q} & \mathbf{R} & \mathbf{I} & \mathbf{A} & \mathbf{B} \end{pmatrix},$$

$$\pi_q = \begin{pmatrix} \mathbf{I} & \mathbf{A} & \mathbf{B} & \mathbf{P} & \mathbf{Q} & \mathbf{R} \\ \mathbf{Q} & \mathbf{R} & \mathbf{P} & \mathbf{B} & \mathbf{I} & \mathbf{A} \end{pmatrix}, \quad \pi_r = \begin{pmatrix} \mathbf{I} & \mathbf{A} & \mathbf{B} & \mathbf{P} & \mathbf{Q} & \mathbf{R} \\ \mathbf{R} & \mathbf{P} & \mathbf{Q} & \mathbf{A} & \mathbf{B} & \mathbf{I} \end{pmatrix}.$$

In order to show that these permutations form a group which is isomorphic to the symmetry group of the equilateral triangle, we need to show that the composition of any two permutations corresponds to the composition of the corresponding transformations.

For example, if $\pi_b \leftrightarrow \mathbf{B}$ and $\pi_p \leftrightarrow \mathbf{P}$,

then we would want to show that $\pi_b \circ \pi_p \leftrightarrow \mathbf{B} * \mathbf{P}$.

Now

$$\pi_b = \begin{pmatrix} \mathbf{I} & \mathbf{A} & \mathbf{B} & \mathbf{P} & \mathbf{Q} & \mathbf{R} \\ \mathbf{B} & \mathbf{I} & \mathbf{A} & \mathbf{Q} & \mathbf{R} & \mathbf{P} \end{pmatrix} \quad \text{and} \quad \pi_p = \begin{pmatrix} \mathbf{I} & \mathbf{A} & \mathbf{B} & \mathbf{P} & \mathbf{Q} & \mathbf{R} \\ \mathbf{P} & \mathbf{Q} & \mathbf{R} & \mathbf{I} & \mathbf{A} & \mathbf{B} \end{pmatrix},$$

so
$$\pi_b \circ \pi_p = \begin{pmatrix} \mathbf{I} & \mathbf{A} & \mathbf{B} & \mathbf{P} & \mathbf{Q} & \mathbf{R} \\ \mathbf{Q} & \mathbf{R} & \mathbf{P} & \mathbf{B} & \mathbf{I} & \mathbf{A} \end{pmatrix} = \pi_q \quad \leftrightarrow \quad \mathbf{Q} = \mathbf{B} \circ \mathbf{P};$$

that is,
$$\pi_b \circ \pi_p \quad \leftrightarrow \quad \mathbf{B} \circ \mathbf{P}.$$

We can check all the other possible products in a similar way, thus illustrating the truth of this theorem.

In general, if the A-row of the Cayley table of a group of order n is

*	A_1	A_2	...	A_n
⋮	⋮	⋮		⋮
A	$A * A_1$	$A * A_2$	...	$A * A_n$
	⋮	⋮		⋮

then we can form the permutation $a = \begin{pmatrix} A_1 & A_2 & \dots & A_n \\ A * A_1 & A * A_2 & \dots & A * A_n \end{pmatrix}$.

If $\quad a_i = \begin{pmatrix} A_1 & A_2 & \dots & A_n \\ A_i * A_1 & A_i * A_2 & \dots & A_i * A_n \end{pmatrix} \quad \leftrightarrow \quad A_i$

and $\quad a_j = \begin{pmatrix} A_1 & A_2 & \dots & A_n \\ A_j * A_1 & A_j * A_2 & \dots & A_j * A_n \end{pmatrix} \quad \leftrightarrow \quad A_j$

then $a_i \circ a_j = \begin{pmatrix} A_1 & A_2 & \dots & A_n \\ (A_i * A_j) * A_1 & (A_i * A_j) * A_2 & \dots & (A_i * A_j) * A_n \end{pmatrix} \quad \leftrightarrow \quad A_i * A_j$.

Exercise 16B

1 The following is the Cayley table for a group with elements $\{e, a, b, c, p, q, r, s\}$:

*	e	a	b	c	p	q	r	s
e	e	a	b	c	p	q	r	s
a	a	e	s	r	q	p	c	b
b	b	q	e	s	r	a	p	c
c	c	r	q	e	s	b	a	p
p	p	s	r	q	e	c	b	a
q	q	b	c	p	a	r	s	e
r	r	c	p	a	b	s	e	q
s	s	p	a	b	c	e	q	r

(*a*) Find the subgroup generated by s.
(*b*) Find the subgroup generated by a.
(*c*) Find all the cyclic subgroups of this group.
(*d*) Find the subgroup generated by a and r.
(*e*) Find the subgroup generated by a and b.
(*f*) Find the left cosets of the subgroup $\{e, q, r, s\}$.
(*g*) Find the left cosets of the subgroup $\{e, a\}$.

2 Find the groups generated by the following matrices:

(*a*) $\begin{bmatrix} 4 & -7 \\ 3 & -5 \end{bmatrix}$ (*b*) $\begin{bmatrix} 3 & -1 \\ 7 & -2 \end{bmatrix}$ (c) $\begin{bmatrix} 5 & 13 \\ -2 & -5 \end{bmatrix}$

3 Find the group generated by the function $f: x \mapsto \dfrac{3x - 1}{7x - 2}$ ($x \in \mathbb{R}$ and $x \neq \frac{2}{7}$).

4 Find the group generated by the two functions:

$$f: x \mapsto \frac{3x-1}{7x-2} \ (x \in \mathbb{R}, x \neq \tfrac{2}{7}) \quad \text{and} \quad g: x \mapsto \frac{2x-1}{3x-2} \ (x \in \mathbb{R}, x \neq \tfrac{2}{3}).$$

5 How many different generators has a cyclic group of order (*a*) 4, (*b*) 5, (*c*) 6, (*d*) 20?

6 If P is a subgroup of Q, and Q is a subgroup of R, prove that P is a subgroup of R.

7 Prove that in a group, the inverse of $a * b$ is $b^{-1} * a^{-1}$.

8 Prove that every subgroup of a cyclic group is cyclic.

9 Prove that, if every element of a group is self-inverse, then the group is of order 2^n, where $n \in \mathbb{Z}$.

10 In a group with identity element e, every element $x \in G$ satisfies $x^2 = e$. Prove that G is an Abelian group.

11 Prove that in a group
(*a*) $ab = ca \Rightarrow ab^n = c^n a$ for all $n \in \mathbb{N}$;
(*b*) ab and ba have the same period.

12 a and b are elements of a group G. If $ab = ba$, prove that $ab^2 = b^2 a$. Is the converse of this result true?

13 a, b are elements of a group G. Prove that
(*a*) $(b^{-1}ab)^n = b^{-1}a^n b$ for all $n \in \mathbb{N}$;
(*b*) $b^{-1}ab$ has the same period as a.

14 The centre C of a group G is defined to be the set of all elements of the group which commute with every element of the group; that is, $c \in G$ if and only if $ac = ca$ for all $a \in G$. Show that C is a subgroup of G.

16.3 GROUPS OF ORDER NOT EXCEEDING 6

From the examples in §16.1 it appeared that there were only two essentially different types of groups of order 4. In this section we find all the abstract groups of order $\leqslant 6$.

When dealing with abstract groups, it is usual to omit the symbol for the group operation. So we write ab instead of $a * b$.

(a) Group of order 1

This is the trivial group with one element – the identity:

*	e
e	e

(b) Groups of order 2, 3 and 5

As the orders of these groups are prime, the groups will be cyclic. The Cayley tables are therefore:

$*$	e	a
e	e	a
a	a	e

$*$	e	a	a^2
e	e	a	a^2
a	a	a^2	e
a^2	a^2	e	a

$*$	e	a	a^2	a^3	a^4
e	e	a	a^2	a^3	a^4
a	a	a^2	a^3	a^4	e
a^2	a^2	a^3	a^4	e	a
a^3	a^3	a^4	e	a	a^2
a^4	a^4	e	a	a^2	a^3

(c) Groups of order 4

Apart from the identity, each element will have period 2 or 4. Two situations arise:

(1) If G contains an element a of period 4, the four elements are e, a, a^2, a^3; that is, the cyclic group of order 4.

(2) If there is no element of period 4, then all the other elements except the identity must have period 2. So if G contains the distinct elements e, a and b where $a^2 = b^2 = e$, the fourth element will be ab,

since if $ab = e = aa$, then $b = a$ (cancellation law),

if $ab = a$, then $b = e$

and if $ab = b$, then $a = e$,

none of which are possible.

So $G = \{e, a, b, ab\}$.

From closure considerations ba will equal one of these elements. Which one?

If $ba = e = aa$, then $b = a$, but a and b are distinct elements.

If $ba = a$, then $b = e$, but e and b are distinct elements.

If $ba = b$, then $a = e$, but e and a are distinct elements.

So $ba = ab$.

We can therefore complete the Cayley table:

$*$	e	a	b	ab
e	e	a	b	ab
a	a	e	ab	b
b	b	ab	e	a
ab	ab	b	a	e

This group is Abelian and is known as the Klein group. It is generated by the elements a and b where $a^2 = b^2 = e$ and $ab = ba$. The symmetry group of a rectangle is an example of a Klein group.

So there are only two different types of groups of order 4 – the cyclic group and the Klein group.

(d) Groups of order 6

(1) If G possesses an element a of period 6, then G is a cyclic group and has the elements $\{e, a, a^2, a^3, a^4, a^5\}$.

(2) If there is no element of period 6, then every other element, apart from the identity, will have period 2 or 3. There will be at least one element of period 2 and at least one element of period 3 since:

(*a*) If all the elements except the identity are of period 2, the set $\{e, a, b, ab\}$ would be a subgroup. This subgroup has order 4 and 4 is not a factor of 6.

(*b*) If all the elements except the identity are of period 3, then a^2 $(\neq e)$ is the inverse of the element a; that is, the distinct elements a and a^2 form an inverse pair. These inverse pairs plus the identity element would mean that G would have an odd number of elements.

Hence the group will be generated by the elements a and b where $a^2 = b^3 = e$ and the six elements are e, a, b, b^2, ab, ab^2.

We can check that these elements are all different; for example, if

$$
\begin{aligned}
& b = ab^2 & \\
& bb = (ab^2)b & \text{(postmultiplying by } b) \\
\Rightarrow\ & b^2 = a(b^2b) & \text{(associativity)} \\
\Rightarrow\ & b^2 = ae & (\text{since } b^3 = e) \\
\Rightarrow\ & b^2 = a & \text{(identity).}
\end{aligned}
$$

But $a^2 = e$ so $(b^2)^2 = b = e$, which contradicts our earlier assumption. Similar proofs can be written out for all other pairs.

From closure considerations, ba will equal one of these elements. Which one?

If $ba = e$, then $a = b^2$, which is not possible (see above).

If $ba = a$, then $b = e$, but e and b are distinct elements.

If $ba = b$, then $a = e$, but e and a are distinct elements.

If $ba = b^2$, then $a = b$, but a and b are distinct elements.

If $ba = ab$, then
$$
\begin{aligned}
(ba)^2 &= (ba)(ba) \\
&= b(ab)a \\
&= b(ba)a \\
&= b^2 \neq e
\end{aligned}
$$

and
$$\begin{aligned}(ba)^3 &= b^2(ba)\\ &= b^3a\\ &= a \neq e,\end{aligned}$$

so the element ba must have period 6, which contradicts our original assumption.

Hence $ba = ab^2$, the only element left.

Now
$$\begin{aligned}(ba)^2 = (ba)(ba) &= (ba)(ab^2)\\ &= beb^2\\ &= bb^2\\ &= e.\end{aligned}$$

So ba has period 2.

We can therefore complete the Cayley table:

$*$	e	a	b	b^2	ab	ab^2
e	e	a	b	b^2	ab	ab^2
a	a	e	ab	ab^2	b	b^2
b	b	ab^2	b^2	e	a	ab
b^2	b^2	ab	e	b	ab^2	a
ab	ab	b^2	ab^2	a	e	b
ab^2	ab^2	b	a	ab	b^2	e

This group is not Abelian, and is generated by the elements a and b where $a^2 = b^3 = e$ and $ba = ab^2$. The symmetry group of the equilateral triangle is an example of a non-Abelian group of order 6.

So there are only two different types of group of order 6, one of which is Abelian and the other non-Abelian.

16.4 GROUPS DEFINED USING GENERATORS

We saw in the last section that the non-Abelian group of order 6 could be generated using the elements a and b where $a^2 = b^3 = e$ and $ba = ab^2$. These defining relations and the axioms of a group are sufficient to enable you to simplify any expression and hence complete the Cayley table.

Example 1

For the group with $a^2 = b^3 = e$ and $ba = ab^2$, simplify $bab^{-1}ab^2$.

Solution

Note that brackets are unnecessary, since the operation is associative (one of the group axioms).

So
$$bab^{-1}ab^2 = ab^2b^{-1}ab^2 \quad (\text{since } ba = ab^2)$$
$$= abab^2 \quad (b^2b^{-1} = b)$$
$$= aab^2b^2 \quad (ba = ab^2)$$
$$= a^2b^3b$$
$$= b \quad (a^2 = b^3 = e). \qquad \square$$

For a general expression, we can use the relation $ba = a^2b$ to move the powers of a to the left and the powers of b to the right, so that any expression can be simplified to the form a^mb^n. As $a^2 = b^3 = e$, m can have the values 0 or 1, and n the values 0, 1, 2, so the distinct elements in this group are e, a, b, b^2, ab, ab^2.

Exercise 16C

1 Given the group with $r^3 = m^2 = e$ and $rm = mr^2$, prove that
(*a*) $(rm)^2 = e$ (*b*) $rmr = m$ (*c*) $r^2mrm = r$

2 Construct the Cayley tables for the groups defined by the relations:
(*a*) $a^3 = e$ (*b*) $a^2 = b^2 = (ab)^2 = e$
(*c*) $a^2 = b^4 = e$ and $ab = ba$ (*d*) $a^3 = b^2 = e$ and $ab = ba$
For each group give an example of a geometric group isomorphic to it.

3 Given that a, b, c are elements of a group and that $a^2 = b^2 = c^2 = e$ and also $ab = c$, show that $\{e, a, b, c\}$ is a subgroup.

4 Write down the elements of the group defined by the relations $a^2 = b^2 = c^2 = e$ and $(ab)^2 = (bc)^2 = (ca)^2 = e$. Complete the Cayley table.

5 Find the pair of generators and a set of defining relations for
(*a*) $\{1, 2, 4, 7, 8, 11, 13, 14\}$ under multiplication modulo 15
(*b*) $\{1, 2, 4, 5, 8, 10, 11, 13, 16, 17, 19, 20\}$ under multiplication modulo 21

16.5 GROUPS OF ISOMETRIES

An isometry of a plane is a one-to-one mapping of the plane onto itself which preserves distance and is called *direct* if it preserves the direction round the figure and *opposite* if the direction round the figure is reversed. An example is shown in Fig. 2.

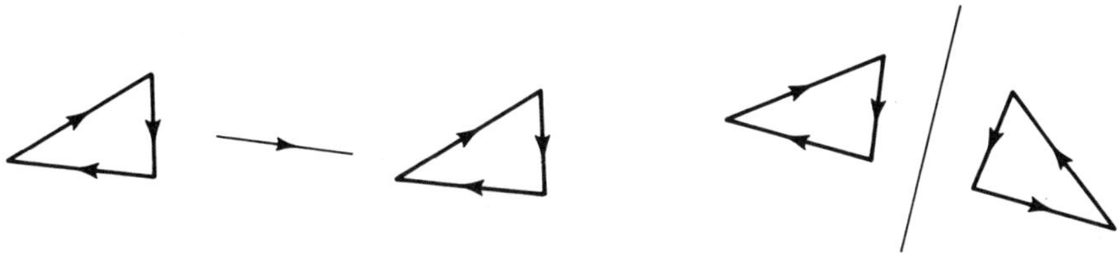

Translation – direct

Reflection – opposite

Figure 2

In the plane there are just four possible isometries: translation, rotation, reflection and glide-reflection. These isometries can be classified as follows:

	Direct	Opposite
With a fixed point	Rotation	Reflection
Without a fixed point	Translation	Glide-reflection

Theorem 1
The set of all isometries of the plane forms a group under composition of transformations.

A and B are two points of the plane and we denote the distance AB by $d(A, B)$. If $\mathbf{T}$ is an isometry then $d(\mathbf{T}(A), \mathbf{T}(B)) = d(A, B)$.

So for points A, B of the plane and isometries $\mathbf{S}$, $\mathbf{T}$ and $\mathbf{U}$:

(1) *Closure:*

$$\begin{aligned} d(\mathbf{T}(\mathbf{S}(A)), \mathbf{T}(\mathbf{S}(B))) &= d(\mathbf{S}(A), \mathbf{S}(B)) \quad \text{(as } \mathbf{T} \text{ is an isometry)} \\ &= d(A, B) \quad \text{(as } \mathbf{S} \text{ is an isometry),} \end{aligned}$$

so $\mathbf{TS}$ is an isometry.

(2) *Associative:* $\mathbf{U}(\mathbf{TS}) = (\mathbf{UT})\mathbf{S}$,

as both mean '$\mathbf{S}$ followed by $\mathbf{T}$ followed by $\mathbf{U}$'.

(3) *Identity:* The isometry $\mathbf{I}$, such that $\mathbf{I}(A) = A$ for all points of the plane.

(4) *Inverse:* As $\mathbf{T}$ is a one-to-one and onto mapping, an inverse $\mathbf{T}^{-1}$ exists; it is also an isometry since

$$\begin{aligned} d(A, B) &= d(\mathbf{T}(\mathbf{T}^{-1}(A)), \mathbf{T}(\mathbf{T}^{-1}(B))) \\ &= d(\mathbf{T}^{-1}(A), \mathbf{T}^{-1}(B)) \quad \text{(as } \mathbf{T} \text{ is an isometry).} \end{aligned}$$

So the set of all isometries of the plane forms a group under composition of transformations.

There are a number of important subgroups of the group of isometries of the plane, for example:

(*a*) the set of all direct isometries;
(*b*) the set of all rotations (including the identity) about a fixed point;
(*c*) the set of all translations of the plane (including the identity);
(*d*) the set of all isometries with a fixed point;
(*e*) the set of all isometries which map a given geometrical figure onto itself – this is known as the symmetry group of the figure. We have already met a number of examples of symmetry groups.

The definition of an isometry and the proof that the set of isometries forms a group can easily be extended for mappings of three-dimensional space onto itself.

A full classification of all three-dimensional isometries is fairly complicated, so we shall confine our attention to isometries with a fixed point. In §8.2 on orthogonal matrices we list the six possible cases which can arise from the different combinations of eigenvalues:

(1) the identity transformation;

(2) a rotation about an axis of rotation;

(3) a half-turn about an axis of rotation – this is a special case of (2);

(4) a reflection in a plane;

(5) a rotary reflection; that is, a reflection in a plane followed by a rotation with the normal to the plane being the axis of rotation;

(6) a central inversion – this is a special case of (5) with a half-turn; it can also be obtained by enlarging (-1) times with the fixed point the centre of enlargement.

Subgroups of the group of isometries include:

(*a*) the set of all direct isometries;

(*b*) the set of all rotations (including the identity) about a fixed axis of rotation;

(*c*) the set of all translations (including the identity);

(*d*) the set of all isometries with a fixed point;

(*e*) the set of all isometries which map a given geometrical solid onto itself – the symmetry group.

We end this chapter by looking briefly at one example of a symmetry group – the symmetry group of the regular tetrahedron (Fig. 3).

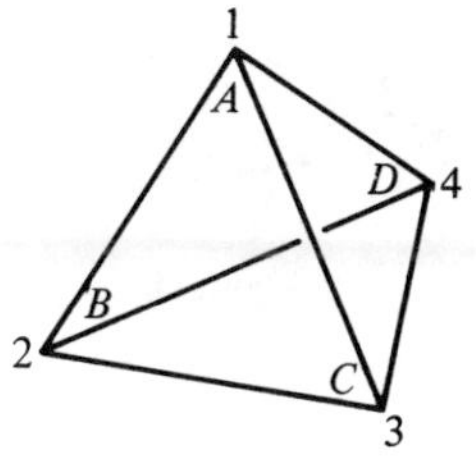

Figure 3

If the tetrahedron has vertices *ABCD* in positions 1234, then each symmetry transformation will effect a permutation of (1 2 3 4). There are therefore $4! = 24$ different symmetry transformations and they form a group which is isomorphic to the group of permutations of (1 2 3 4). Clearly, not all these transformations can be made by a physical movement of the regular tetrahedron; for example, try $\begin{pmatrix} 1 & 2 & 3 & 4 \\ 4 & 1 & 2 & 3 \end{pmatrix}$. By considering the axes of symmetry, we can identify the direct isometries which are:

(1) the identity transformation;

(2) three half-turns about a line joining a pair of mid-points of opposite sides;

(3) four rotations of $\frac{2\pi}{3}$ about each line through a vertex and the centre of the opposite face;

(4) four rotations of $\frac{4\pi}{3}$ about each line through a vertex and the centre of the opposite face.

These 12 direct isometries form a group which is known as the tetrahedron group. The other 12 isometries are all opposite isometries and are:

(5) six reflections in the planes of symmetry, each plane of reflection containing one edge and the mid-point of the opposite edge;

(6) six rotary reflections where the axis of rotation is the line joining the mid-points of opposite edges, and the plane of reflection is perpendicular to this line and passes through the mid-points of the other four edges of the tetrahedron.

Exercise 16D

1 Do all rotations of the plane form a group?

2 Prove that rotations and translations of a plane together form a group of transformations.

3 If $\mathbf{H}_A$, $\mathbf{H}_B$ and $\mathbf{H}_C$ are half-turns of the plane about the points A, B, C respectively, prove that $\mathbf{H}_A\mathbf{H}_B\mathbf{H}_C = \mathbf{H}_C\mathbf{H}_B\mathbf{H}_A$.

4 If **L**, **M**, **N** are reflections in lines l, m, n respectively, when does **LMN** = **NML**?

5 A group is generated by the isometries **L** and **H**, where **L** is a reflection in the line l and **H** is a half-turn about the point A, where A is not on l. Show that the group is infinite and contains reflections in an infinite set of lines.

6

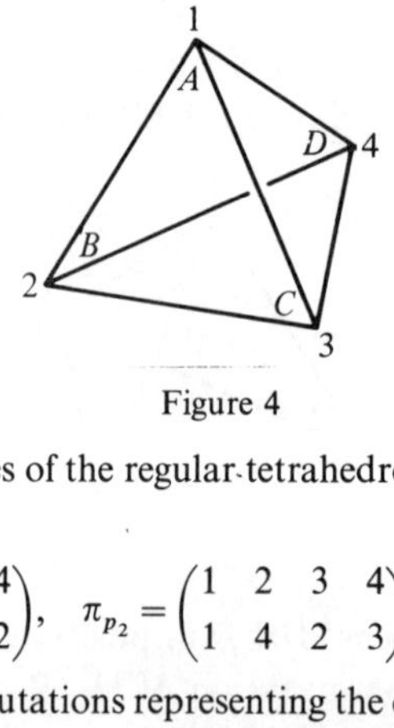

Figure 4

(*a*) Describe the symmetries of the regular tetrahedron (Fig. 4) which are represented by the permutations

$$\pi_{p_1} = \begin{pmatrix} 1 & 2 & 3 & 4 \\ 1 & 3 & 4 & 2 \end{pmatrix}, \quad \pi_{p_2} = \begin{pmatrix} 1 & 2 & 3 & 4 \\ 1 & 4 & 2 & 3 \end{pmatrix}, \quad \pi_x = \begin{pmatrix} 1 & 2 & 3 & 4 \\ 4 & 3 & 2 & 1 \end{pmatrix}.$$

(*b*) Write down the permutations representing the other nine direct isometries of the regular tetrahedron, and construct the Cayley table for the tetrahedral group. (Suggested notation for the other permutations: $\pi_i, \pi_{q_1}, \pi_{q_2}, \pi_{r_1}, \pi_{r_2}, \pi_{s_1}, \pi_{s_2}, \pi_y$ and π_z.)

(*c*) Find all the subgroups of the tetrahedron group.

In this chapter we have met a more abstract approach to the study of groups, and been able to identify, up to isomorphism, all the groups of order not exceeding six.

Miscellaneous exercise 16

1 If $(G, *)$ and $(H, \circ)$ are groups, we can form a new group which is called the *direct product* $G \times H$ of G and H, where the combination of two elements is defined by

$$(g_1, h_1)(g_2, h_2) = (g_1 * g_2, h_1 \circ h_2).$$

(*a*) Verify that $G \times H$ is a group.
(*b*) What is the order of $G \times H$?
(*c*) If both G and H are Abelian groups, prove that $G \times H$ is also an Abelian group.
(*d*) If G and H are cyclic groups, is $G \times H$ also a cyclic group?
(*e*) If P is a group of order 2, write out the Cayley table for $P \times P$. Name a group to which it is isomorphic. How many subgroups has the group $P \times P \times P$?

2 (*a*) Prove that the set $\{\pm 1, \pm i, \pm j, \pm k\}$, where $i^2 = j^2 = k^2 = -1$ and $ij = -ji = k$, $jk = -kj = i$, $ki = -ik = j$, forms a group under multiplication. This group is known as the *quaternion group*.
(*b*) Prove that this group is isomorphic to the set of matrices

$$\left\{\begin{bmatrix}1 & 0\\0 & 1\end{bmatrix}, \begin{bmatrix}-1 & 0\\0 & -1\end{bmatrix}, \begin{bmatrix}j & 0\\0 & -j\end{bmatrix}, \begin{bmatrix}-j & 0\\0 & j\end{bmatrix}, \begin{bmatrix}0 & 1\\-1 & 0\end{bmatrix}, \begin{bmatrix}0 & -1\\1 & 0\end{bmatrix}, \begin{bmatrix}0 & j\\j & 0\end{bmatrix}, \begin{bmatrix}0 & -j\\-j & 0\end{bmatrix}\right\},$$

where $j^2 = -1$, under multiplication of matrices.
(*c*) Prove that this group is also isomorphic to the group generated by the elements a and b where $a^4 = e$ (the identity element), and $a^2 = b^2$, $a^3b = ba$.

3 A permutation of the set $\{1, 2, 3, \ldots, n\}$ which interchanges just two elements and leaves all the others fixed is called a *transposition*; for example, $\begin{pmatrix}1 & 2 & 3 & 4 & 5\\1 & 4 & 3 & 2 & 5\end{pmatrix}$ is a transposition.

(*a*) Express the permutation $\begin{pmatrix}1 & 2 & 3\\3 & 1 & 2\end{pmatrix}$ as a product of transpositions. Is your answer unique?
(*b*) A permutation is called even or odd depending on whether it is the product of an even or odd number of transpositions; for example, $\begin{pmatrix}1 & 2 & 3\\3 & 1 & 2\end{pmatrix}$ is even, since it is the product of $\begin{pmatrix}1 & 2 & 3\\1 & 3 & 2\end{pmatrix}$ and $\begin{pmatrix}1 & 2 & 3\\3 & 2 & 1\end{pmatrix}$. List all the even permutations of $\{1, 2, 3\}$. Do they form a group?
(*c*) List all the odd permutations of $\{1, 2, 3, 4\}$. Do they form a group?
(*d*) Prove that there are an equal number of odd and even permutations of the set $\{1, 2, 3, \ldots, n\}$, for $n \geqslant 2$.

4 This question is about the rotational symmetries of a cube.
(*a*) Describe the axes of rotational symmetry of order (i) 4, (ii) 3, (iii) 2. How many such axes are there in each case?
(*b*) Each symmetry of the cube corresponds to a permutation of its diagonals. List the 23 permutations corresponding to the rotations in part (*a*).
(*c*) These 23 permutations and the identity permutation form a group. How many elements have period (i) 4, (ii) 3, (iii) 2?
(*d*) Is the group Abelian?
(*e*) Can you find subgroups of order (i), 6, (ii) 8, (iii) 12?

SUMMARY

Definitions

(1) Two groups $(G, *)$, and $(H, \circ)$ are *isomorphic* if there is a one-to-one mapping such that, if $a \leftrightarrow x$ and $b \leftrightarrow y$ (where $a, b \in G$ and $x, y \in H$), then $a * b \leftrightarrow x \circ y$.

(2) A group G is *generated* by elements $a_1, a_2, \ldots, a_n, \ldots$ if every element of G can be expressed in terms of a combination of some or all of the a_i's.

(3) A group G which is generated by a single element is called a *cyclic group*.

(4) The *period* of an element g is the smallest positive integer k such that $g^k = e$ (the identity element).

(5) If H is a subgroup of a group G, with $H = \{h_1, h_2, \ldots, h_n\}$, the set $xH = \{x * h_1, x * h_2, \ldots, x * h_n\}$ is called the *left coset* of H by x.

Theorems

(1) (*Lagrange's theorem*) If H is a subgroup of a finite group G, then the order of H is a factor of the order of G.

(2) (*Cayley's theorem*) Any finite group of order n is isomorphic to a subgroup of the permutation group of n elements.

(3) The set of all isometries of the plane forms a group under composition of transformations.

Other results

(1) The period of an element is a factor of the order of the group.

(2) A group of prime order is cyclic.

(3) Isometries of the plane:

	Direct	Opposite
With a fixed point	Rotation	Reflection
Without a fixed point	Translation	Glide-reflection

(4) Table of groups of order not exceeding 6

Order	Generators	Abelian	Some examples
1	e	Yes	The trivial group
2	a, where $a^2 = e$	Yes	$\left\{\begin{bmatrix}1 & 0\\ 0 & 1\end{bmatrix}, \begin{bmatrix}-1 & 0\\ 0 & -1\end{bmatrix}\right\}$, under multiplication $\{0, 1\}$, under addition modulo 2
3	a, where $a^3 = e$	Yes	$\{0, 1, 2\}$, under addition modulo 3 $\{1, \omega, \omega^2\}$, under multiplication, where $\omega^3 = 1$ Rotational subgroup of the symmetries of the equilateral triangle
4	a, where $a^4 = e$	Yes	$\{2, 4, 6, 8\}$, under multiplication modulo 10 Rotation subgroup of the symmetries of the square $\left\{x \to x, x \to \frac{1}{x}, x \to -x, x \to -\frac{1}{x}\right\}$ under composition of functions
	a, b where $a^2 = b^2 = e$ and $ab = ba$	Yes	Symmetries of a rectangle $\{1, 3, 5, 7\}$, under multiplication modulo 8 $\{1, -1, \mathrm{j}, -\mathrm{j}\}$, under multiplication
5	a, where $a^5 = e$	Yes	$\{0, 1, 2, 3, 4\}$, under addition modulo 5 Rotational symmetries of the pentagon
6	a, where $a^6 = e$	Yes	$\{1, 3, 5, 9, 11, 13\}$, under multiplication modulo 14 Rotational symmetries of the hexagon
	a, b where $a^2 = b^3 = e$ and $ba = ab^2$	No	Symmetries of the equilateral triangle $\left\{x \to x, x \to 1 - x, x \to \frac{1}{x}, x \to \frac{x-1}{x}, x \to \frac{1}{1-x}, x \to \frac{x}{x-1}\right\}$ under composition of functions

17

Rings and fields

In Chapter 15, we defined an algebraic structure in which we had a set and a single binary operation $\circ$. In this chapter we consider several algebraic structures in which we have a set and *two* binary operations.

17.1 FIELDS

In the step-by-step solution of the linear equation

$$5 + x = 3$$

we get

$$\begin{aligned} -5 + (5 + x) &= -5 + 3 \\ (-5 + 5) + x &= -5 + 3 \quad \text{(associativity)} \\ 0 + x &= -5 + 3 \quad \text{(inverses)} \\ x &= -5 + 3 \quad \text{(identity)} \end{aligned}$$

so

$$x = -2 \qquad \text{(closure);}$$

that is, each of the four axioms of a group are used in the solution.

What happens when we solve the equation $5 \times y + 3 = 7$, in which there are two operations, $\times$ and $+$?

$$\begin{aligned} (5 \times y + 3) + (-3) &= 7 + (-3) \\ 5 \times y + (3 + (-3)) &= 7 + (-3) \quad \text{(associativity under } +) \\ 5 \times y + 0 &= 7 + (-3) \quad \text{(inverses under } +) \\ 5 \times y &= 7 + (-3) \quad \text{(identity under } +) \\ 5 \times y &= 4 \qquad \text{(closure under } +) \\ 5^{-1} \times (5 \times y) &= 5^{-1} \times 4 \\ (5^{-1} \times 5) \times y &= 5^{-1} \times 4 \quad \text{(associativity under } \times) \\ 1 \times y &= 5^{-1} \times 4 \quad \text{(inverses under } \times) \\ y &= 5^{-1} \times 4 \quad \text{(identity under } \times) \\ y &= \tfrac{4}{5} \qquad \text{(closure under } \times). \end{aligned}$$

Here we used the group axioms under $+$ and the group axioms under $\times$: a sort of 'double-group'. There are two points to note:

(1) The element 0 (the identity under addition) does not have an inverse under

multiplication, so for the second group structure the set of numbers must be restricted.

(2) We have not used any rule in this example in which we combine the two operations of multiplication and addition. We say that multiplication is distributive over addition if

$$a \times (b + c) = (a \times b) + (a \times c)$$

and

$$(a + b) \times c = (a \times c) + (b \times c)$$

for all numbers a, b, c.

These results suggest the algebraic structure which is known as a *field*.

Definition 1

A field F is a non-empty set F on which two binary operations $\oplus$ and $\odot$ are defined, which satisfy the following conditions:

(1) F is an Abelian group under $\oplus$.

(2) F (excluding the identity element for $\oplus$) is an Abelian group under $\odot$.

(3) $\odot$ is distributive over $\oplus$.

We say that $(F, \oplus, \odot)$ is a field.

(*Notation:* In practice the symbols '+' and '.' are often used for the operations without implying that the operations are ordinary addition and multiplication. Under +, the identity is written as 0, and the inverse of a as $-a$. Under ., the identity is written as 1, and the inverse of a as a^{-1}.)

Important examples of fields are the following sets of numbers with the usual operations of addition and multiplication:

$\mathbb{R}$ – the real numbers,

$\mathbb{Q}$ – the rational numbers,

$\mathbb{C}$ – the complex numbers.

Example 1

Show that the set of matrices

$$M = \left\{\begin{bmatrix} x & -y \\ y & x \end{bmatrix} : x, y \in \mathbb{R}\right\}$$

forms a field under matrix addition and multiplication.

Solution

This is nearly the same set of matrices as in Example 4, Chapter 15. The only extra matrix is the zero matrix $\begin{bmatrix} 0 & 0 \\ 0 & 0 \end{bmatrix}$. In that example we showed that the set M, with the zero matrix excluded, is a group under matrix multiplication. We can check that it is commutative as well:

$$\begin{bmatrix} x & -y \\ y & x \end{bmatrix}\begin{bmatrix} a & -b \\ b & a \end{bmatrix} = \begin{bmatrix} (xa - yb) & -(xb + ya) \\ (ya + xb) & (-yb + xa) \end{bmatrix}$$

$$\begin{bmatrix} a & -b \\ b & a \end{bmatrix}\begin{bmatrix} x & -y \\ y & x \end{bmatrix} = \begin{bmatrix} (ax - by) & -(ay + bx) \\ (bx + ay) & (-by + ax) \end{bmatrix}$$

To show that M is an Abelian group under addition we have to check five axioms:

(1) *Closure:*

$$\begin{bmatrix} x & -y \\ y & x \end{bmatrix} + \begin{bmatrix} a & -b \\ b & a \end{bmatrix} = \begin{bmatrix} (x + a) & -(y + b) \\ (y + b) & (x + a) \end{bmatrix},$$

which is of the same form, and therefore belongs to M.

(2) *Associative:* This property holds for matrix addition in general.

(3) *Identity:* $\begin{bmatrix} 0 & 0 \\ 0 & 0 \end{bmatrix}$ is the identity and belongs to M.

(4) *Inverses:* The inverse of $\begin{bmatrix} x & -y \\ y & x \end{bmatrix}$ is $\begin{bmatrix} -x & y \\ -y & -x \end{bmatrix}$, which belongs to M, with 'x' $= -x$ and 'y' $= -y$.

(5) *Commutative:*

$$\begin{bmatrix} x & -y \\ y & x \end{bmatrix} + \begin{bmatrix} a & -b \\ b & a \end{bmatrix} = \begin{bmatrix} (x + a) & -(y + b) \\ (y + b) & (x + a) \end{bmatrix}$$

$$\begin{bmatrix} a & -b \\ b & a \end{bmatrix} + \begin{bmatrix} x & -y \\ y & x \end{bmatrix} = \begin{bmatrix} (a + x) & -(b + y) \\ (b + y) & (a + x) \end{bmatrix}$$

The distributive property holds, as it is true for matrices in general, so the set M is a field under the operations of matrix addition and multiplication. □

Result 1
In the field $(F, +, .)$, $a.0 = 0$ for all $a \in F$.

	$a = 0 + a$	(identity under $+$)
	$a.a = a.(0 + a)$	(premultiplying both sides by a)
	$a.a = a.0 + a.a$	(distributive law)
	$a.a + -(a.a) = (a.0 + a.a) + -(a.a)$	(adding inverse of $a.a$ to both sides)
	$a.a + -(a.a) = a.0 + (a.a + -(a.a))$	(associativity under $+$)
	$0 = a.0 + 0$	(inverses under $+$)
so	$0 = a.0$	(identity under $+$).

Result 2
If $a, b \in$ the field $(F, +, .)$ and $a.b = 0$, then either $a = 0$ or $b = 0$.

If $a = 0$, there is nothing further to prove.
If $a \neq 0$, then a has a multiplicative inverse.

$$\begin{aligned} a.b &= 0 \\ a^{-1}.(a.b) &= a^{-1}.0 \quad \text{(premultiplying both sides by } a^{-1}\text{)} \\ (a^{-1}.a).b &= a^{-1}.0 \quad \text{(associativity under .)} \\ 1.b &= a^{-1}.0 \quad \text{(inverses under .)} \\ b &= a^{-1}.0 \quad \text{(identity under .)} \\ b &= 0 \qquad\quad \text{(Result 1)} \end{aligned}$$

So either $\qquad a = 0 \quad \text{or} \quad b = 0.$

Q.1 Show that for a field F the *cancellation law* is true; that is, if $a \neq 0$, $a.b = a.c \Rightarrow b = c$.

This is a property which is also true for the integers, but they do not form a field. We shall be looking more carefully at the set of integers in §17.3.

17.2 AN ALTERNATIVE APPROACH

In Chapter 14 a careful examination of the many definitions and theorems about sets of vectors developed in earlier chapters led to the formal description of an abstract vector space. Throughout the work we have always assumed that we would wish to be able to multiply vectors by any real number; we have used the expression '... λ, $\mu \in \mathbb{R}$ ...' in our description of a vector space. Does $\mathbb{R}$ have some special properties that make it necessary or desirable that λ, μ should always belong to it and to no other set?

An example
A game involves moving a peg from one hole to another in a board in which the holes occupy positions which have *integer* (positive, negative or zero) coordinates with reference to a given hole O. The set of holes form what is often called a square lattice (Fig. 1).

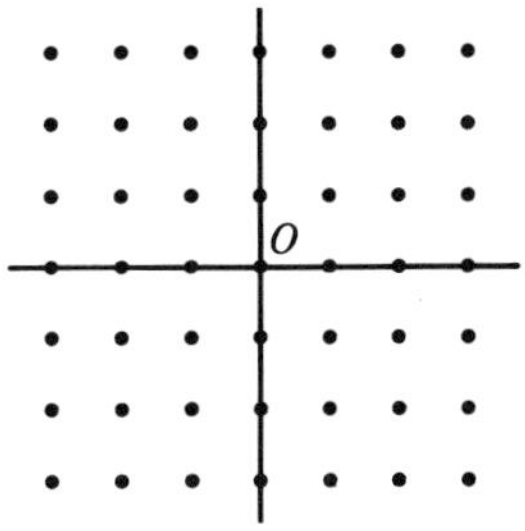

Figure 1

Assume that the board is arbitrarily large. Any possible move can be represented by a vector $\begin{bmatrix} a \\ b \end{bmatrix}$, where a, b must clearly be integers. Let the set of such vectors (moves) be the set V. Can V be a vector space? First we need to define multiplication by a scalar and immediately we see that $\lambda\begin{bmatrix} 1 \\ 2 \end{bmatrix}$, for example, is only possible if λ is an integer; $\frac{3}{4}\begin{bmatrix} 1 \\ 2 \end{bmatrix}$ is not a possible move (vector). If $\lambda = -3$, say, we can sensibly interpret $-3\begin{bmatrix} 1 \\ 2 \end{bmatrix}$ as the move $\begin{bmatrix} 1 \\ 2 \end{bmatrix}$ in reverse three times, and this is the same as $\begin{bmatrix} -3 \\ -6 \end{bmatrix}$. This suggests that we must try to define a vector space V over the integers. Does it satisfy the axioms?

If we check the list of requirements in Chapter 14 we find that they are all satisfied. The next step is to find a basis for V. The natural choice is $\mathbf{e}_1 = \begin{bmatrix} 1 \\ 0 \end{bmatrix}$ and $\mathbf{e}_2 = \begin{bmatrix} 0 \\ 1 \end{bmatrix}$; certainly any element of V can be expressed as a linear combination of $\mathbf{e}_1$ and $\mathbf{e}_2$:

$$\begin{bmatrix} a \\ b \end{bmatrix} = a\begin{bmatrix} 1 \\ 0 \end{bmatrix} + b\begin{bmatrix} 0 \\ 1 \end{bmatrix}.$$

But our work with bases tells us that we must be able to select *any* two independent vectors as a basis.

Suppose we choose $\begin{bmatrix} 2 \\ 0 \end{bmatrix}$ and $\begin{bmatrix} 0 \\ 1 \end{bmatrix}$; what are λ, μ such that

$$\begin{bmatrix} 1 \\ 1 \end{bmatrix} = \lambda\begin{bmatrix} 2 \\ 0 \end{bmatrix} + \mu\begin{bmatrix} 0 \\ 1 \end{bmatrix}?$$

$\lambda = \frac{1}{2}$ and $\mu = 1$. But λ cannot be $\frac{1}{2}$ since $\lambda \in \mathbb{Z}$. Hence $\begin{bmatrix} 2 \\ 0 \end{bmatrix}$ and $\begin{bmatrix} 0 \\ 1 \end{bmatrix}$ cannot form a basis, therefore V is not a vector space. In a vector space of dimension n we have stated and shown that any n linearly independent vectors will form a basis. To generalise the problem we can say that if we choose $\lambda\mathbf{e}_1$ instead of $\mathbf{e}_1$ as one of the base vectors, then we cannot express $\mathbf{e}_1$ as a linear combination of $\lambda\mathbf{e}_1$ and $\mathbf{e}_2$ unless we can find $\mu \in \mathbb{Z}$ such that $\mathbf{e}_1 = \mu(\lambda\mathbf{e}_1) \Rightarrow \mu\lambda = 1 \Rightarrow \mu = \dfrac{1}{\lambda}$. This will always be impossible unless $\lambda = 1$ or -1.

The set $\mathbb{Z}$ therefore seems to be unacceptable if V is to be a vector space.

Suppose we alter the game slightly, and say firstly that the board is of finite size with 'O' at the bottom left-hand corner so that the coordinates of the holes at the four corners are $(0, 0)$, $(n-1, 0)$, $(n-1, n-1)$ and $(0, n-1)$. Secondly if a particular move would take the peg 'off the board' then the move is completed by assuming that on reaching the end of any row or column the counting simply continues from the other end of the respective row or column; for example, a peg at $A(n-2, n-2)$ undergoing the 'move' $\begin{bmatrix} 0 \\ 3 \end{bmatrix}$ takes the peg from A to $B(n-2, 1)$ (Fig. 2).

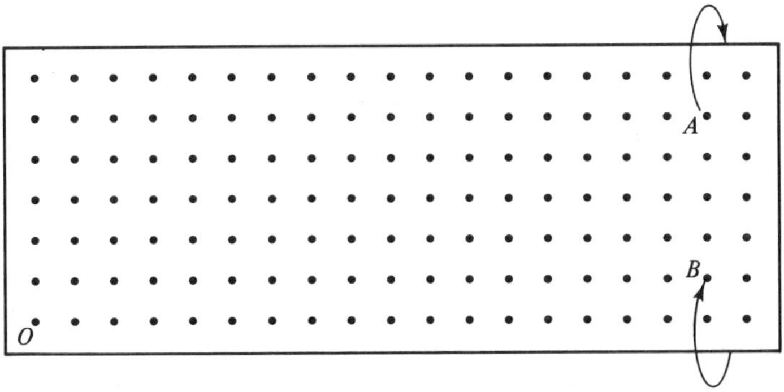

Figure 2

All our discussion so far about V remains unchanged except that

(1) The λ, μ now belong to a set of integers $<n$ and $>-n$.

(2) The arithmetic has altered: we now find that, for example, $(n-2)+7=5$. (You will recognise this as arithmetic modulo n.)

(3) The problem of finding μ such that $\mathbf{e}_1 = \mu(\lambda\mathbf{e}_1)$ may have a solution, for example, if $n = 9$ and $\lambda = 2$, then $\mu = 5$ because $\lambda\mu = 10 = 1$ (modulo 9); that is, the move $\begin{bmatrix} 1 \\ 0 \end{bmatrix}$ is the same as $\begin{bmatrix} 10 \\ 0 \end{bmatrix}$.

A reminder: $\mathbb{Z}_n$ means the set of integers $\{0, 1, 2, \ldots, (n-1)\}$.

Q.2 For the following values of n and λ, can you find $\mu \in \mathbb{Z}_n$ such that $\lambda\mu = 1$ (in $\mathbb{Z}_n$)?

(*a*) $n = 9, \quad \lambda = 4$
(*b*) $n = 9, \quad \lambda = 3$
(*c*) $n = 7, \quad \lambda = 6$
(*d*) $n = 7, \quad \lambda = 2$
(*e*) $n = 6, \quad \lambda = 4$
(*f*) $n = 6, \quad \lambda = 3$
(*g*) $n = 11$, $\lambda =$ any integer from 1 to 10 inclusive

These results suggest that in certain cases we can have all our requirements met so that V can be a vector space. These requirements will be met if the set to which λ, μ belong with the appropriate operations of 'add' and 'multiply' satisfies the axioms of a field.

The results of Q.2 together with the field axioms suggest that the set $\mathbb{Z}_n$ with the operations of addition and multiplication modulo n will be a field provided that n is a prime number. The next step is to prove this.

Example 2
Show that the set $F = \{0, 1, 2, 3, 4\}$ is a field under addition and multiplication modulo 5.

Solution
We draw up the Cayley tables under the two operations:

$\oplus_5$	0	1	2	3	4
0	0	1	2	3	4
1	1	2	3	4	0
2	2	3	4	0	1
3	3	4	0	1	2
4	4	0	1	2	3

$\otimes_5$	1	2	3	4
1	1	2	3	4
2	2	4	1	3
3	3	1	4	2
4	4	3	2	1

We can check that both these sets are Abelian groups. The distributive law holds as it is true for real numbers and we are just considering the remainder under division by 5.

Hence $\mathbb{Z}_5$, with addition and multiplication modulo 5, is a field. We may often speak of, and write, 'the field $\mathbb{Z}_5$'. □

Q.3 Check that $\mathbb{Z}_p$ is an Abelian group under addition modulo p.

To show that $\mathbb{Z}_p$ (with the zero element excluded) is an Abelian group under multiplication (modulo p) is more difficult. We can check that it is closed, commutative and associative, and 1 is the identity element. But what about inverses?

If we consider the ath column of the Cayley table it will contain the set of elements

$$S = \{1.a, 2.a, 3.a, \ldots, (p-1).a\}.$$

These are all distinct, since

if $\qquad r.a = s.a \quad \text{in } \mathbb{Z}_p$

then $\qquad r.a = sa + np \quad \text{in } \mathbb{Z};$

that is, $\qquad (r-s)a = np \quad \text{in } \mathbb{Z}.$

Now p is a divisor of np, but not of $(r-s)a$ unless $r - s = 0$.

Hence $S = \{1, 2, \ldots, (p-1)\}$, the elements having been listed above in some permuted order.

In particular there exists an element q for which $q.a = 1$ in $\mathbb{Z}_p$; this is the inverse of a.

So $\mathbb{Z}_p$, p prime, forms a field.

Exercise 17A

1 In each of the following equations find whether there is no solution, a unique solution or many solutions:

(*a*) $3x + 2 = 4$ in $\mathbb{Z}_5$ (*b*) $6x + 5 = 3$ in $\mathbb{Z}_9$
(*c*) $2x + 4 = 6$ in $\mathbb{Z}_8$ (*d*) $5x + 11 = 2$ in $\mathbb{Z}_{12}$
(*e*) $5(x + 1) = 3^{-1}(x + 4)$ in $\mathbb{Z}_{11}$ (*f*) $2^{-1}(x + 3) = 5$ in $\mathbb{Z}_9$

2 (*a*) Show that (i) $6^2 = 1$ in $\mathbb{Z}_7$,
(ii) $(n - 1)^2 = 1$ in $\mathbb{Z}_n$.

(*b*) What is a if $(n - 3)^2 = a$ in $\mathbb{Z}_n$? How many different values of x are there such that $x^2 = a$ in $\mathbb{Z}_{11}$ for some a?

3 Investigate the following equations:

(*a*) $x^2 = 1$ in $\mathbb{Z}_7$
(*b*) $(x + 1)(x + 2) = 3$ in $\mathbb{Z}_5$
(*c*) $2x^2 = 2$ in $\mathbb{Z}_6$

4 Find the image of $\begin{bmatrix} 1 \\ 4 \end{bmatrix}$ under

(*a*) matrix $\begin{bmatrix} 2 & -1 \\ 0 & 3 \end{bmatrix}$ in $\mathbb{Z}_5$ (*b*) matrix $\begin{bmatrix} 1 & 5 \\ 1 & 1 \end{bmatrix}$ in $\mathbb{Z}_6$

5 Show that the set of real numbers

$$S = \{a + b\sqrt{2}: a, b \in \mathbb{Q}\}$$

forms a field under matrix addition and multiplication.

6 Show that the set of matrices

$$M = \left\{\begin{bmatrix} x & 0 \\ 0 & y \end{bmatrix} : x, y \in \mathbb{Q}\right\}$$

forms a field under matrix addition and multiplication.

17.3 INTEGRAL DOMAINS AND RINGS

Why do the integers not form a field? We saw in the last section that only 1 and -1 had inverses under multiplication. A field requires the existence of inverses under multiplication for all elements. Yet for the integers the cancellation law (see Q.2) holds even though inverses do not exist. This leads us to the definition of a structure which is known as an *integral domain* as follows:

Definition 2
The set S with operations $+$ and $.$ is an *integral domain* if:
(1) S is an Abelian group under $+$.
(2) S is closed under $.$; $.$ is commutative and associative; a multiplicative identity (written as 1) exists and the cancellation law, that is if $a \neq 0$, $a . b = a . c \Rightarrow b = c$, holds.
(3) $.$ is distributive over $+$.

However, the cancellation law does not necessarily hold in all number systems. For example, in $\mathbb{Z}_{12}$, $6 \times 2 = 6 \times 4$, yet $2 \neq 4$. Even when the cancellation law holds, as with the even integers, there may not be a multiplicative identity. This leads us to the definition of a structure with fewer axioms, which is called a *ring*.

Definition 3
The set S with operations $+$ and $.$ is a *ring* if:
(1) S is an Abelian group under $+$.
(2) Under operation $.$, S is closed and associative.
(3) $.$ is distributive over $+$.

So all fields are integral domains, and all integral domains are rings.

We shall meet further examples of rings, integral domains and fields in Exercise 17B. In investigating which structure holds, it is often possible to quote the properties of other sets, for example the properties of real numbers. However, sometimes it is necessary to go through the tedious exercise of checking each axiom carefully, as we did in Example 1. In that example we had to quote a number of the properties of matrices under matrix addition and multiplication.

Exercise 17B

1 Complete the following table, giving an explanation for every negative answer. The operations are addition and multiplication in each case (multiplication meaning scalar product in the last part).

	Set	Commutative group under +	Group under . (if zero is excluded	Multiplication commutative	Distributive laws holds	$a.b = a.c$ and $a \neq 0 \Rightarrow b = c$
(*a*)	$\mathbb{Z}$					
(*b*)	$\mathbb{Z}_5$					
(*c*)	$\mathbb{Z}_6$					
(*d*)	$\{p + q\sqrt{3}: p, q \in \mathbb{Z}\}$					
(*e*)	$\mathbb{Q}$					
(*f*)	$\{p + q\sqrt{3}: p, q \in \mathbb{Q}\}$					
(*g*)	$\mathbb{R}$					
(*h*)	$\{p + qj: p, q \in \mathbb{R}\}$					
(*i*)	{polynomials with integer coefficients}					
(*j*)	{2 × 2 non-singular matrices with rational elements}					

Set	Commutative group under +	Group under . (if zero is excluded	Multiplication commutative	Distributive laws holds	$a.b = a.c$ and $a \neq 0$ $\Rightarrow b = c$
(*k*) {all 2×2 matrices with rational elements}					
(*l*) {two-dimensional vectors}					

2 Discuss which of the following sets (with the usual operations) are fields, integral domains, rings:

(*a*) {odd integers}
(*b*) {even integers}
(*c*) $\{a + b\sqrt{2}: a, b \in \mathbb{Z}\}$
(*d*) $\{a + b2^{1/4}: a, b \in \mathbb{Z}\}$
(*e*) $\{a + bj: a, b \in \mathbb{Z}\}$
(*f*) $\{a + bj: a, b \in \mathbb{Q}\}$
(*g*) $\{0, 2, 4, 6, 8, 10\}$ in $\mathbb{Z}_{12}$
(*h*) $\{1, 3, 5, 7, 9, 11\}$ in $\mathbb{Z}_{12}$
(*i*) {polynomials of even degree}
(*j*) $\left\{\begin{bmatrix} x & y \\ 0 & x \end{bmatrix}: x, y \in \mathbb{Q}\right\}$
(*k*) $\left\{\begin{bmatrix} a & 0 & 0 \\ 0 & b & 0 \\ 0 & 0 & c \end{bmatrix}: a, b, c \in \mathbb{Z}\right\}$
(*l*) $\left\{ \text{upper triangular matrices } \begin{bmatrix} a & b & c \\ 0 & d & e \\ 0 & 0 & f \end{bmatrix}: a, b, c, d, e, f \in \mathbb{Q}\right\}$
(*m*) $\{2 \times 2$ symmetrical matrices$\}$
(*n*) $\{3 \times 3$ orthogonal matrices$\}$

3 Operations $\otimes$ and $\oplus$ are defined on elements of $\mathbb{Q}$ as follows:

$$a \otimes b = a.b + a + b$$

$$a \oplus b = a + b + 1$$

(where + and . denote ordinary addition and multiplication).
Prove that $(\mathbb{Q}, \otimes, \odot)$ is a field.
What happens if the set $\mathbb{Q}$ is replaced by the set $\mathbb{Z}$?

4 Multiplication and addition for ordered pairs of real numbers are defined as follows:

$$(a, b) + (c, d) = (a + c, b + d)$$

$$(a, b).(c, d) = (ac - bd, ad + bc)$$

Prove that the set of ordered pairs of real numbers under these conditions forms a field.

17.4 DEDUCTION FROM THE AXIOMS

One of the central activities in all mathematics is that of proof. There are different types of proof, for example, proof by induction, proof by contradiction, proof by exhaustion. In the last few chapters we have been meeting another sort of proof, in which (i) we start from a set of axioms, and (ii) we use the rules of mathematical logic to deduce our results or theorems. We illustrate this method again in deriving some basic results for rings (which are also true for integral domains and fields – why?).

Example 3

If $(S, +, .)$ is a ring, prove that

(*a*) $0.a = a.0$ for all $a \in S$;

(*b*) $(-a).b = a.(-b) = -(a.b)$ for all $a, b \in S$;

(*c*) $(-a).(-b) = a.b$ for all $a, b \in S$.

Solution

(*a*) $a = 0 + a$ (identity under $+$)

$\Rightarrow$ $a.a = (0 + a).a$ (postmultiplying both sides by a)

$\Rightarrow$ $a.a = 0.a + a.a$ (distributive law)

$\Rightarrow$ $a.a + -(a.a) = (0.a + a.a) + -(a.a)$ (adding inverse of $a.a$ to both sides)

$\Rightarrow$ $a.a + -(a.a) = 0.a + (a.a + -(a.a))$ (associativity under $+$)

$\Rightarrow$ $0 = 0.a + 0$ (inverses under $+$)

$\Rightarrow$ $0 = 0.a$ (identity under $+$).

In §17.1 we proved that $a.0 = 0$ for all $a \in$ field F. The proof for a ring is identical.

(*b*) $a + -a = 0$ (inverses under $+$)

$\Rightarrow$ $(a + -a).b = 0.b$ (postmultiplying both sides by b)

$\Rightarrow$ $a.b + (-a).b = 0$ (distributive law and part (*a*))

$\Rightarrow$ $-(a.b) + (a.b + (-a).b) = -(a.b) + 0$ (adding inverse of $a.b$ to both sides)

$\Rightarrow$ $(-(a.b) + a.b) + (-a).b = -(a.b) + 0$ (associativity under $+$)

$\Rightarrow$ $0 + (-a).b = -(a.b) + 0$ (inverses under $+$)

$\Rightarrow$ $(-a).b = -(a.b)$ (identity under $+$).

Similarly, start with $a.(b + -b) = a.0$ to prove that $a.(-b) = -(a.b)$.

(c) $\quad (-a).(-b) = -((-a).b)$ (by part (b))

$\Rightarrow \quad (-a).(-b) = -(-(a.b))$ (by part (b))

$\Rightarrow \quad (-a).(-b) = a.b$ □

The set of real numbers $\mathbb{R}$ is a familiar example of a field and you will recognise in the results of Example 3 all the usual rules of signs in algebraic computations. Notice that these rules are thus seen to be a necessary consequence of the field structure of the real numbers.

Exercise 17C

In these questions, give reasons for each step in your proofs.

1 R is a ring and $a, b, c, d \in R$. Prove that
 (*a*) if $a + b = a$, then $b = 0$;
 (*b*) $(a + b).(c + d) = a.c + b.c + a.d + b.d$.

2 R is a ring with an identity element. Prove that the identity element is unique. (*Hint:* Assume that e and f are both elements and prove that $e = f$.)

3 You are given that $(R, +, .)$ is a ring. Assuming that for all $x \in R, x.0 = 0$, prove from the axioms that

$$x.(-y) = -(x.y),$$

where $-z$ means the additive inverse of z.
 The element $p \in R$ is such that

$$p.x = 0 \quad \Rightarrow \quad x = 0, \quad \text{where } x \in R.$$

Prove that $p.x = p.y \quad \Rightarrow \quad x = y$. [SMP]

4 A field contains a non-zero element x such that $x + x = 0$. Prove that $y + y = 0$ for every element y of the field. Give an example to show that this result need not hold in a ring. [SMP]

5 A ring $(R, +, .)$ is such that $a^2 = a$ for all $a \in R$. Prove that
 (*a*) $a + a = 0$ for all $a \in R$;
 (*b*) the ring is commutative.
(*Hint:* (*a*) expand $(a + a)^2$; (*b*) expand $(a + b)^2$.)

6 Prove that in an integral domain

$$a.b = 0 \quad \Rightarrow \quad a = 0 \quad \text{or} \quad b = 0.$$

(This is sometimes given as an alternative to the cancellation law in the set of axioms for an integral domain.)

7 Show that $x^2 = x$ implies $x = 0$ or $x = 1$ in an integral domain. Give a counter-example to show that the result is not necessarily true in a ring.

17.5 VECTORS SPACES OVER A FIELD

In Chapter 14 we defined a vector space in which the scalars belong to the set of real numbers. As the real numbers form a field we can extend this definition to a vector space over a field F, by saying that the scalars belong to the field F; that is,

$\lambda_1, \lambda_2 \in F$, rather than $\lambda_1, \lambda_2 \in \mathbb{R}$. Apart from this minor change, the definition remains the same.

17.6 FINITE GEOMETRY

We all have an intuitive idea of what we mean by a point and a straight line, by distance and shortest distance, and by the locus of a point that moves under certain constraints. The study of geometry in two dimensions has always meant the study of the properties of straight lines, triangles and so on; but what axioms have we been using? We can highlight the difficulties of this problem by trying to tackle a similar one; namely, what can we make of a geometry of a *finite* set of points only?

Normally we have an infinite set of points, whether we are thinking in one dimension (the set of points on a line), two dimensions (plane) or three dimensions; in addition, we can relate these points to the infinite set of real numbers by thinking of a coordinate system. The set $\mathbb{R}$ under addition and multiplication forms a field – will this be significant?

At the beginning of this chapter we looked at a 'game' played on a lattice. We found that if we restricted the number of points by having only integer values for coordinates and making the integer values equal to the remainder after division by a prime (that is, modulo p, p prime), then the set of numbers formed a field. Suppose we work with $p = 5$. Then the x- and y-coordinates can have the values of 0, 1, 2, 3, 4, and we have just 25 points (Fig. 3). What could we mean by the geometry of these points?

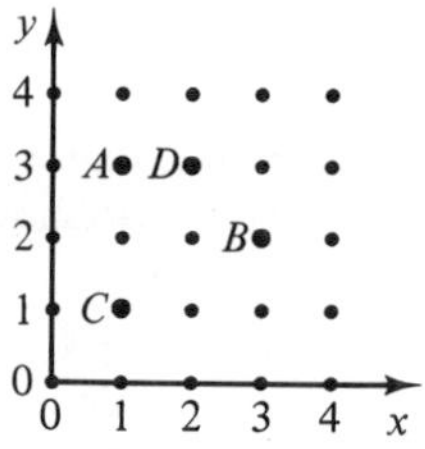

Figure 3

Q.4 What are the coordinates of A, B, C and D?

We have 25 points and a set of coordinates for each point. We now have a *line*. Our intuitive idea of a line breaks down because we have 'gaps' between the points. However, we have an algebraic definition of a line which we can use:

Definition 4
A *line* is the set of all those points whose coordinates (x, y) satisfy a linear equation with coefficients belonging to $\mathbb{Z}_5$, that is an equation $ax + by = c$, with a, b not both zero.

For example, $x + 2y = 1$ is such an equation. The point (2, 2) has coordinates satisfying the equation. Hence (2, 2) 'lies on' the 'line' $x + 2y = 1$.

Q.5 How many more points can you find on $x + 2y = 1$?

Two further definitions follow naturally:

Definition 5
Two lines are said to be *parallel* if they have no point in common.

Definition 6
The *intersection* of two lines is the set of points lying on both lines.

Clearly we are not confined to $\mathbb{Z}_5$ and can rewrite these definitions for $\mathbb{Z}_n$. The following examples will indicate how we can start to explore the properties of this new geometry.

Example 4
How many different lines are there in $\mathbb{Z}_3$?

Solution
In $\mathbb{Z}_3$ we can only have the integers 0, 1 and 2. A general line is $ax + by = c$, with $a, b, c \in \{0, 1, 2\}$. We cannot have $a = b = 0$, and we note that, for example $x + 2y = 1$ is the same as $2x + y = 2$, since the latter is just the former multiplied by 2.

The complete list is:

$$\begin{array}{rrr} x + y = 0, & x + y = 1, & x + y = 2, \\ x = 0, & x = 1, & x = 2, \\ y = 0, & y = 1, & y = 2, \\ x + 2y = 0, & x + 2y = 1, & x + 2y = 2, \end{array}$$

a total of 12 lines. □

Example 5
Using the list of equations above,

(*a*) find the equations of those lines containing the point $(2, 2)$;

(*b*) using a different symbol for each line, mark in a diagram all the points on each line.

Solution
(*a*) By inspection, $(2, 2)$ lies on

$$x = 2, \quad y = 2, \quad x + y = 1, \quad x + 2y = 0.$$

(*b*) Marking points on $x = 2$ with $\times$, $y = 2$ with ○, $x + y = 1$ with ●, $x + 2y = 0$ with □, we get Fig. 4:

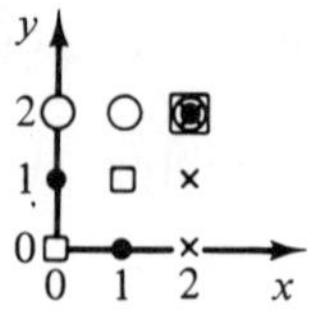

Figure 4

Example 6
Find the intersection of each of the following pairs of lines:

$$(a)\ \left.\begin{array}{r} x + \ y = 1 \\ 2x + 3y = 2 \end{array}\right\} \text{ in } \mathbb{Z}_5 \qquad (b)\ \left.\begin{array}{r} 4x + y = 3 \\ y = 5 \end{array}\right\} \text{ in } \mathbb{Z}_6$$

Solution
(*a*) First equation × 3: $3x + 3y = 3$

Second equation: $2x + 3y = 2$

Adding, we have $y = 0.$

Substituting in the first equation, $x = 1$, so the intersection is $(1, 0)$.
(*b*) Here we have $y = 5$ and hence

$$4x + 5 = 3$$

$$\Rightarrow \quad 4x = 4$$

$$\Rightarrow \quad x = 1 \quad \text{or} \quad 4,$$

and so there are *two* points of intersection, $(1, 5)$ and $(4, 5)$.
Notice that this has happened because $\mathbb{Z}_6$ is not a field. □

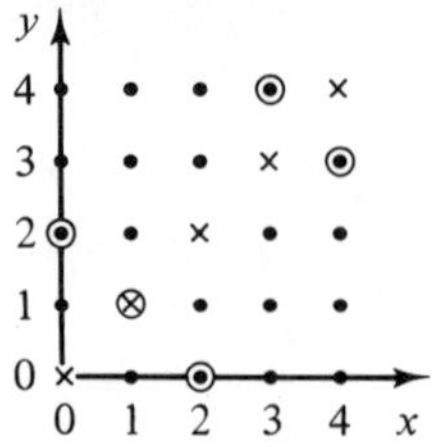

Figure 5

In $\mathbb{Z}_5$, Fig. 5 shows the line $x + 4y = 0$ (marked ×) and the line $x + y = 2$ (marked ○). Each has five points but cannot be called a 'straight' line.

Can we define distance in any way?

Whatever our definition is, we would want it to describe the 'shortest' distance between two points, and for consistency with the usual definition of distance it should satisfy the following axioms:

If $d(A, B)$ means the (shortest) distance between points A, B, then

(1) $d(A, B) \geqslant 0$
(2) $d(A, B) = 0$ if and only if $A = B$

(3) $d(A, B) = d(B, A)$
(4) $d(A, B) \leqslant d(A, C) + d(C, B)$

A definition of distance that satisfies axioms 1–4 is called a *metric*. If A, B are points whose coordinates are (x_1, y_1), (x_2, y_2) respectively, the following are examples of metrics:

(*a*) $d(A, B) = \sqrt{((x_1 - x_2)^2 + (y_1 - y_2)^2)}$: this is the definition we have always used in Euclidean geometry. It is the Euclidean metric.

(*b*) $d(A, B) = \max\{|x_1 - x_2|, |y_1 - y_2|\}$

(*c*) $d(A, B) = |x_1 - x_2| + |y_1 - y_2|$: this is often called the New York taxi-driver's metric – why?

Q.6 Check that axioms 1–4 are satisfied by these definitions.

However, if we try to find a metric for our finite geometry we run into trouble, as $\mathbb{Z}_p$ is not an ordered set and it is not meaningful to consider inequalities, which appear in axioms 1 and 4.

Exercise 17D

1 Find where each of the following pairs of lines meet:

(*a*) $\left.\begin{aligned} 2x + 3y &= 1 \\ x + y &= 2 \end{aligned}\right\}$ in $\mathbb{Z}_5$

(*b*) $\left.\begin{aligned} 2x + 3y &= 1 \\ x + 2y &= 4 \end{aligned}\right\}$ in $\mathbb{Z}_6$

(*c*) $\left.\begin{aligned} 3x + 4y &= 6 \\ 6x + 7y &= 8 \end{aligned}\right\}$ in $\mathbb{Z}_9$

2 List all the points on the lines $3x + y + 2 = 0, x + 2y = 0$ in $\mathbb{Z}_5$. Where do these lines intersect? Represent the lines on an appropriate diagram. Can you define the gradient of a line in this geometry?

3 In $\mathbb{Z}_5$, write down the other points on the line containing both $(2, 4)$ and $(3, 1)$ and the equation of this line. Is its representation unique?

4 Write down the equations of all the lines through the point $(1, 3)$ in $\mathbb{Z}_5$.

5 Do all lines in $\mathbb{Z}_5$ contain the same number of points? How many lines pass through each point?

A pair of points may be chosen in $\frac{1}{2}(25 \times 24) = 300$ ways. Deduce the number of distinct lines in this geometry.

6 In $\mathbb{Z}_5$, the line $2x + 3y + 4 = 0$ can be written $[2, 3, 4]$. Why is $[2, 3, 4] \equiv [1, 4, 2]$? In how many other ways can this line be written?

There are 125 ordered triads $[a, b, c]$ with $a, b, c \in \mathbb{Z}_5$. How many do not represent lines? Deduce the number of distinct lines.

7 In $\mathbb{Z}_6$ geometry, list all the points on the lines $x = 1$, $2x = 2$, $x + 3y + 2 = 0$, $4x + 2y + 1 = 0$. Comment on your answers.

8 In $\mathbb{Z}_p$ geometry (p prime), how many different points and lines are there?

So far when we have referred to a scalar we have meant the real numbers. By looking at some of the properties of these real numbers we have extended the definition of a scalar and arrived at an abstract algebraic structure which is called a field. The main aim of this chapter has been to give the formal definitions and examples of a field, an integral domain and a ring.

Miscellaneous exercise 17

1 Discuss whether $(a + b).(a + b) = a^2 + 2ab + b^2$ in $\mathbb{Z}_{12}$.

2 Multiplication and addition for ordered pairs of polynomials are defined as follows:

$$(f, g) + (h, k) = (fk + hg, gk)$$
$$(f, g).(h, k) = (fh, gk)$$

Two ordered pairs (p, q) and (r, s) are said to be equivalent if $ps = rq$. The second member of any ordered pair is not the zero polynomial.

Prove that under these conditions the distinct ordered pairs form a field.

3 If
$$a \otimes (b \oplus c) = (a \otimes b) \oplus (a \otimes c)$$
and
$$a \oplus (b \otimes c) = (a \oplus b) \otimes (a \oplus c)$$
for all $a, b, c \in S$, prove that neither $(S, \otimes, \oplus)$ nor $(S, \oplus, \otimes)$ is a field. (*Hint:* consider the elements corresponding to 0 and 1.)

4 On a suitable lattice (use graph paper), plot the points satisfying $y = x^2$ in $\mathbb{Z}_5$.

Also plot the points for $y = x^2$ in $\mathbb{Z}_7$ and $\mathbb{Z}_{11}$.

(*a*) How many members of the sets $\mathbb{Z}_5$, $\mathbb{Z}_7$, $\mathbb{Z}_{11}$ are perfect squares?

(*b*) How many perfect squares are there in $\mathbb{Z}_p$?

5 Is it possible to deduce $(a + b).c = a.c + b.c$ for all $a, b, c \in F$ from the other axioms for a field?

SUMMARY

Definitions

(1) A *field* $(F, +, .)$:

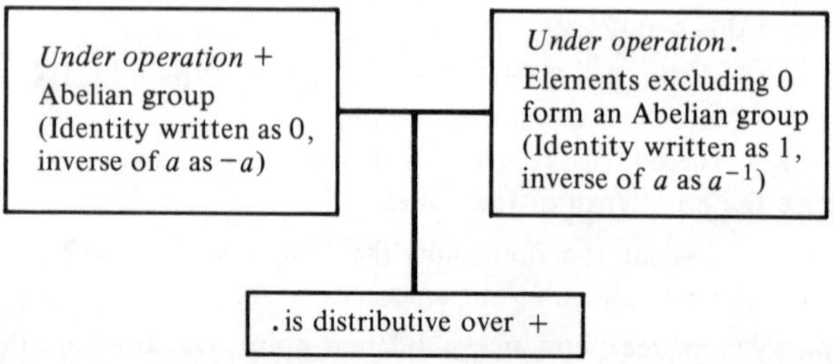
Under operation +
Abelian group
(Identity written as 0, inverse of a as $-a$)
Under operation .
Elements excluding 0 form an Abelian group
(Identity written as 1, inverse of a as a^{-1})
. is distributive over +

(2) A *ring* $(S, +, .)$:

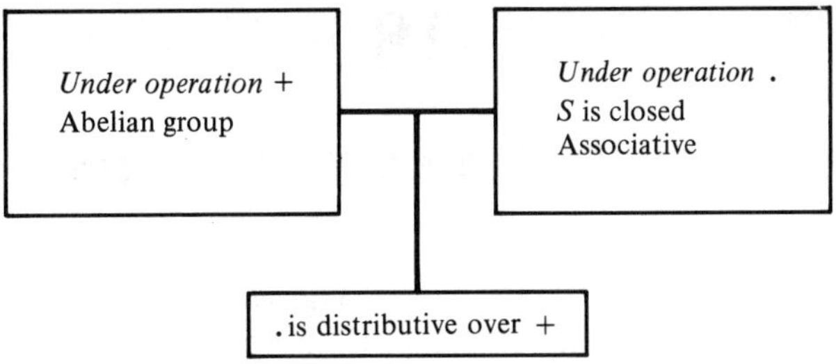

(3) An *integral domain* $(S, +, .)$:

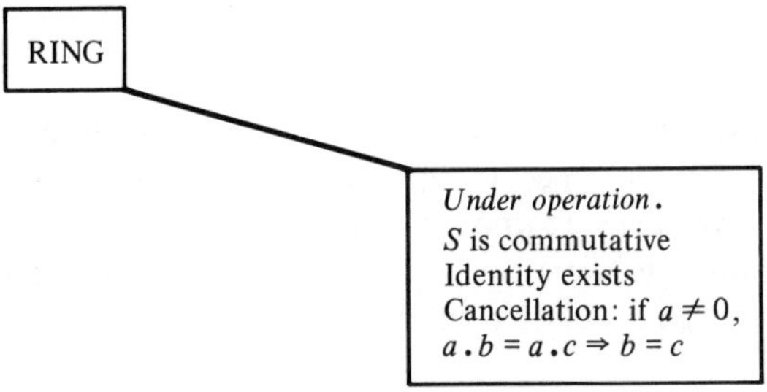

18

Equivalence relations

We find it useful to classify the member of mathematical systems according to certain properties. For example, isometries are classified as either direct or opposite, and groups according to isomorphism. In Chapter 3 we said that two 2×2 matrices are similar if there is a non-singular 2×2 matrix $\mathbf{P}$ such that

$$\mathbf{B} = \mathbf{P}^{-1}\mathbf{AP}.$$

In practice these two matrices are different representations of the same transformation but with respect to different bases. The relation 'is similar to' is an example of an *equivalence relation* defined on the set of all 2×2 matrices. An equivalence relation is an extension of the idea of equality, equality being measured according to a certain property.

18.1 EQUIVALENCE RELATIONS

Definition 1
If S is a set, then a (binary) *relation* R between the elements of S is defined if, for all $a, b \in S$, it is possible to decide whether
(1) a is related to b, written aRb, or
(2) a is *not* related to b, written $a \not{R} b$.

If $S = \{2, 4, 5, 12\}$ and the relation R is 'has a common factor with', then $2R4$ but $4 \not{R} 5$.

We can illustrate this relation by a diagram in which an arrow is drawn from a to b whenever aRb (Fig. 1).

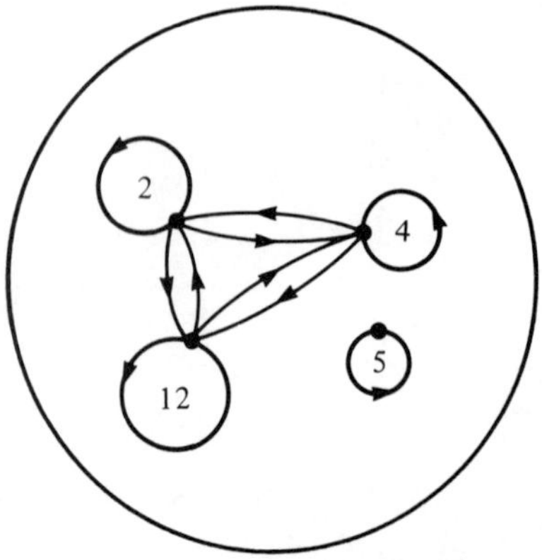

Figure 1

Q.1 For $S = \{2, 3, 4, 5, 6, 7\}$ sketch diagrams similar to Figure 1 for the following relations:

(*a*) a is a prime factor of b
(*b*) $a = b + 1$
(*c*) $|a - b|$ is even
(*d*) $|a - b|$ is odd
(*e*) $a > b$
(*f*) a and b are both even
(*g*) $a - b$ is divisible by 3

Q.2 For which relations in Q.1 is *every* element related to itself?

Q.3 For which relations in Q.1 is it true that *if* aRb, *then* bRa for all $a, b \in S$?

Q.4 For which relations in Q.1 is it true that *if* aRb *and* bRc, *then* aRc for all $a, b, c \in S$?

You will notice in Q.1, parts (*c*) and (*g*), that the diagram is broken up into clumps of elements, within which each element is related to itself and to all the other elements within that subset: the relation partitions the set S into disjoint subsets. This always happens when the relation has the three properties introduced in Q.2, Q.3 and Q.4. We now give formal definitions of these properties:

Definition 2
R is a relation defined on a set S.
(1) If, *for all* $a \in S$, then aRa, the relation is said to be *reflexive*.
(2) If, for all a, $b \in S$, *whenever* aRb then bRa, the relation is said to be *symmetric*.
(3) If, for all a, b, $c \in S$ (not necessarily all different), *whenever* aRb *and* bRc, then aRc, the relation is said to be *transitive*.

Definition 3
A relation which is reflexive, symmetric and transitive is called an *equivalence relation*.

Definition 4
The disjoint subsets formed by an equivalence relation are called *equivalence classes*. (*Notation:* $[x] = \{y \in S\colon yRx\}$ is called an equivalence class of x.)

Some comments on these definitions

(1) *Reflexive:* The key phrase here is 'for all', that is *each* element is related to itself; this is represented diagrammatically by

for each element $a \in S$.

If S is the set of positive integers and aRb if and only if a and b are both perfect squares, why is this relation not reflexive?

(2) *Symmetric:* The key word here is 'whenever'; this is represented diagrammatically by a  b, that is, *if* there is an arrow from a to b, *then* there will be an arrow from b to a.

If $S = \{2, 3, 4\}$ and aRb if and only if $a = b$, then the diagram is

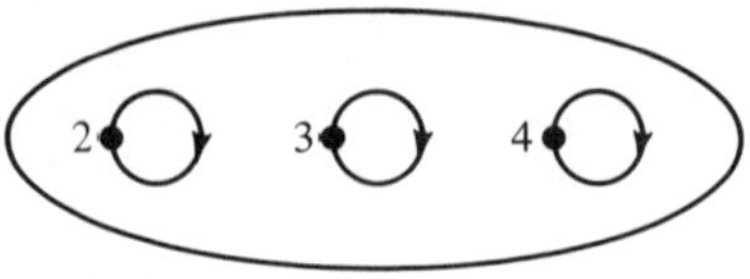

This relation is clearly reflexive, and because there are no arrows between distinct elements, it follows that the relation is symmetric as well. It never happens that there is an arrow from a to b without there being an arrow from b to a. In the definition we did not make any comment about a and b necessarily being different. What happens if they are the same?

(3) *Transitive:* Again the key word is 'whenever'; this is represented diagrammatically by

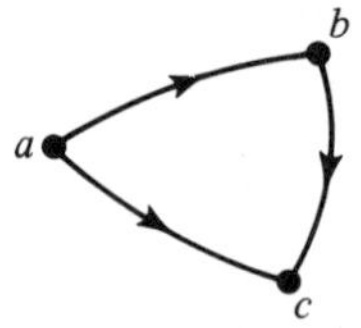

but note the comment in the definition that a, b and c do not necessarily have to be different.

If S is the set of boys and aRb if and only if a and b are brothers, then this relation is not transitive. As a counter-example choose a = John, b = James and c = John (a and c can be the same element).

Also note that the example given in (2) is transitive as well – no counter-example can be found.

(4) It is sometimes argued that a relation which is symmetric and transitive must also be reflexive. What is wrong with the following proof?

If $\quad xRy$ then yRx (symmetric property)

so $\quad xRx$ (transitive property);

that is, R is reflexive.

(5) The three properties, reflexive, symmetric and transitive, are all independent; that is, one cannot be deduced from the other two. In Exercise 18A you will find examples to demonstrate the eight possible combinations of true and false for these three properties.

(6) From observation, we have seen that an equivalence relation R on a set S partitions the set S into disjoint subsets called equivalence classes. The proof of this result is in two parts:

(*a*) to show that
$$S = \bigcup_{x \in S} [x];$$
that is, S is the union of all the equivalence classes;
(*b*) to show that

either
$$[x] \cap [y] = \varnothing \quad \text{or} \quad [x] = [y];$$
that is, the equivalence classes are either the same or disjoint.

Proof
(*a*) Since R is reflexive, $x \in [x]$ for every $x \in S$,

so
$$S = \bigcup_{x \in S} [x].$$

(*b*) If $\quad t \in [x] \cap [y], \quad$ then $\quad t \in [x] \quad$ and $\quad t \in [y];$

that is, $\quad tRx \quad$ and $\quad tRy.$

Let x_i be any element in $[x]$, so x_iRx.

But	xRt	(tRx and symmetric)
so	x_iRt	(transitive).
But	tRy	
so	x_iRy	(transitive);
that is,	$x_i \in [y]$.	

Since x_i was an arbitrary element in $[x]$, $[x]$ is a subset of $[y]$.
Similarly, it can be shown that $[y]$ is a subset of $[x]$, so if there is any element common to $[x]$ and $[y]$, then $[x] = [y]$.
Otherwise, $[x] \cap [y] = \varnothing$.

Example 1
S is the set of all 2×2 matrices, and the relation R is defined on S by '$\mathbf{A}R\mathbf{B}$ if and only if there exists a non-singular matrix $\mathbf{P} \in S$ such that
$$\mathbf{B} = \mathbf{P}^{-1}\mathbf{A}\mathbf{P} \quad (\mathbf{A}, \mathbf{B} \in S).\text{'}$$

Solution
Reflexive: For each $\mathbf{A} \in S$, $\mathbf{A} = \mathbf{I}^{-1}\mathbf{A}\mathbf{I}$, where $\mathbf{I} = \begin{bmatrix} 1 & 0 \\ 0 & 1 \end{bmatrix} \in S$ and is non-singular.

Symmetric: If $\mathbf{A}R\mathbf{B}$, then $\mathbf{B} = \mathbf{P}^{-1}\mathbf{A}\mathbf{P}$, where $\mathbf{P}$ is non-singular and $\mathbf{P} \in S$.

Therefore
$$\begin{aligned} \mathbf{A} &= \mathbf{P}\mathbf{B}\mathbf{P}^{-1} \\ &= (\mathbf{P}^{-1})^{-1}\mathbf{B}(\mathbf{P}^{-1}). \end{aligned}$$

Now, as $\mathbf{P}$ is non-singular, $\mathbf{P}^{-1}$ exists, is also non-singular and belongs to S.

So $$\mathbf{B}R\mathbf{A}.$$

Hence R is symmetric.

Transitive: If $$\mathbf{A}R\mathbf{B} \quad \text{and} \quad \mathbf{B}R\mathbf{C},$$

then $$\mathbf{B} = \mathbf{P}^{-1}\mathbf{A}\mathbf{P} \quad \text{and} \quad \mathbf{C} = \mathbf{Q}^{-1}\mathbf{B}\mathbf{Q},$$

with $\mathbf{P}, \mathbf{Q}$ both non-singular and $\mathbf{P}, \mathbf{Q} \in S$.

$$\begin{aligned} \mathbf{C} &= \mathbf{Q}^{-1}\mathbf{P}^{-1}\mathbf{A}\mathbf{P}\mathbf{Q} \\ &= (\mathbf{P}\mathbf{Q})^{-1}\mathbf{A}(\mathbf{P}\mathbf{Q}). \end{aligned}$$

Now, as $\mathbf{P}, \mathbf{Q}$ are non-singular, $\mathbf{PQ}$ is also non-singular and belongs to S.

So $$\mathbf{A}R\mathbf{C}.$$

Hence R is transitive.
So R is an equivalence relation on S. □

Example 2
Let S be the following set of matrices:

$$S = \left\{ \begin{bmatrix} a & -b \\ b & a \end{bmatrix} : a, b \in \mathbb{R}, \det\left(\begin{bmatrix} a & -b \\ b & a \end{bmatrix} \right) = 1 \right\}$$

A relation R is defined on the set of points in the plane by

$$(x_1, x_2)R(y_1, y_2)$$

if and only if $$\begin{bmatrix} x_1 \\ x_2 \end{bmatrix} = \mathbf{A} \begin{bmatrix} y_1 \\ y_2 \end{bmatrix} \quad \text{for some } \mathbf{A} \in S.$$

(*a*) Show that this relation is an equivalence relation.
(*b*) Describe the set of points in the equivalence class containing the point $(0, 2)$.

Solution

(*a*) *Reflexive*: Choosing $a = 1$, $b = 0$,

$$\mathbf{A} = \begin{bmatrix} 1 & 0 \\ 0 & 1 \end{bmatrix} \in S \quad \text{and} \quad \det(\mathbf{A}) = 1.$$

Then $$\begin{bmatrix} x_1 \\ x_2 \end{bmatrix} = \mathbf{A} \begin{bmatrix} x_1 \\ x_2 \end{bmatrix} \quad \text{for each} \begin{bmatrix} x_1 \\ x_2 \end{bmatrix};$$

that is, $$(x_1, x_2)R(x_1, x_2).$$

Symmetric: If $(x_1, x_2)R(y_1, y_2)$ then there exists $\mathbf{A} \in S$ such that

$$\begin{bmatrix} x_1 \\ x_2 \end{bmatrix} = \mathbf{A} \begin{bmatrix} y_1 \\ y_2 \end{bmatrix};$$

hence $$\begin{bmatrix} y_1 \\ y_2 \end{bmatrix} = \mathbf{A}^{-1}\begin{bmatrix} x_1 \\ x_2 \end{bmatrix}.$$

If $$\mathbf{A} = \begin{bmatrix} a & -b \\ b & a \end{bmatrix}, \text{ then } \mathbf{A}^{-1} = \begin{bmatrix} a & b \\ -b & a \end{bmatrix} = \begin{bmatrix} a & -(-b) \\ (-b) & a \end{bmatrix},$$

which is of the correct form, and

$$\det(\mathbf{A}^{-1}) = \frac{1}{\det(\mathbf{A})} = 1.$$

Therefore $$\mathbf{A}^{-1} \in S \quad \text{and so} \quad (y_1, y_2)R(x_1, x_2).$$

Transitive: If $(x_1, x_2)R(y_1, y_2)$ and $(y_1, y_2)R(z_1, z_2)$, then there exist $\mathbf{A}, \mathbf{B} \in S$ such that

$$\begin{bmatrix} x_1 \\ x_2 \end{bmatrix} = \mathbf{A}\begin{bmatrix} y_1 \\ y_2 \end{bmatrix} \quad \text{and} \quad \begin{bmatrix} y_1 \\ y_2 \end{bmatrix} = \mathbf{B}\begin{bmatrix} z_1 \\ z_2 \end{bmatrix};$$

hence $$\begin{bmatrix} x_1 \\ x_2 \end{bmatrix} = \mathbf{AB}\begin{bmatrix} z_1 \\ z_2 \end{bmatrix}.$$

If $$\mathbf{A} = \begin{bmatrix} a & -b \\ b & a \end{bmatrix} \quad \text{and} \quad \mathbf{B} = \begin{bmatrix} p & -q \\ q & p \end{bmatrix},$$

then $$\mathbf{AB} = \begin{bmatrix} (ap - bq) & -(aq + bp) \\ (aq + bp) & (ap - bq) \end{bmatrix},$$

which is of the correct form, and

$$\det(\mathbf{AB}) = \det(\mathbf{A}) \times \det(\mathbf{B}) = 1.$$

Therefore $$\mathbf{AB} \in S \quad \text{and so} \quad (x_1, x_2)R(z_1, z_2).$$

As the relation is reflexive, symmetric and transitive, it is an equivalence relation.

(*b*) The equivalence class $[(0, 2)] = \left\{(x, y): \begin{bmatrix} x \\ y \end{bmatrix} = \mathbf{A}\begin{bmatrix} 0 \\ 2 \end{bmatrix}, \mathbf{A} \in S\right\};$

that is, $$\begin{bmatrix} x \\ y \end{bmatrix} = \begin{bmatrix} a & -b \\ b & a \end{bmatrix}\begin{bmatrix} 0 \\ 2 \end{bmatrix}, \quad \text{where } a^2 + b^2 = 1$$
$$= \begin{bmatrix} -2b \\ 2a \end{bmatrix}.$$

So $$x = -2b, \quad y = 2a; \quad \text{that is, } b = -\frac{x}{2}, \quad a = \frac{y}{2}.$$

But $$a^2 + b^2 = 1.$$

Hence $$\left(\frac{y}{2}\right)^2 + \left(-\frac{x}{2}\right)^2 = 1;$$

that is, $$x^2 + y^2 = 4.$$

So $$[(0,2)] = \{(x, y): x^2 + y^2 = 4\},$$

which is the set of points on the circle centre (0, 0), radius 2. □

Exercise 18A

1 Complete the following table, indicating whether the relations on the given sets are reflexive, symmetric or transitive:

Set	Relation	Reflexive	Symmetric	Transitive
(*a*) {boys}	'is the brother of'	F	T	F
(*b*) {children}	'is the brother of'			
(*c*) {straight lines in the plane}	'is perpendicular to'			
(*d*) {straight lines in the plane}	'is parallel to or coincident with'			
(*e*) {triangles in the plane}	'is similar to'			
(*f*) {triangles in the plane}	'is congruent with'			
(*g*) $\mathbb{Z}$	xRy if and only if $xy > 0$			
(*h*) $\mathbb{Z}$	xRy if and only if $\lvert x - y\rvert$ is even			
(*i*) $\mathbb{Z}$	xRy if and only if $(x^2 - y^2)$ is an even integer			
(*j*) $\mathbb{Z}$	xRy if and only if $(x^2 - y^2)$ is an odd integer			
(*k*) $\mathbb{Z}$	xRy if and only if $(x - y)$ is divisible by 2 or 3			
(*l*) $\mathbb{Z}$	xRy if and only if $x < y$			
(*m*) $\mathbb{Z}^+$	xRy if and only if x is a factor of y			
(*n*) $\mathbb{Z}^+$	xRy if and only if $2x > y$			
(*o*) $\mathbb{Z}^+$	xRy if and only if $(x - y)$ is divisible by 5			
(*p*) $\mathbb{Z}^+$	xRy if and only if x has the same number of digits as y			
(*q*) $\mathbb{Z}^+$	xRy if and only if $\frac{x}{y}$ is an integer			

2 Describe the equivalence classes for each of the equivalence relations in question 1.

3 Invent other examples of sets and relations which are
(*a*) symmetric and transitive, but not reflexive
(*b*) reflexive and symmetric, but not transitive
(*c*) reflexive and transitive, but not symmetric
(*d*) reflexive, symmetric and transitive

4 (*a*) A relation R_1 is defined on the set

$$S_1 = \{(a, b): a, b \in \mathbb{Z} \text{ and } b \neq 0\}$$

by $(p, q)R_1(r, s)$ if and only if $ps = rq$.
Prove that this is an equivalence relation, and describe the equivalence classes.
(*b*) A relation R_2 is defined on the set

$$S_2 = \{(a, b): a, b \in \mathbb{Z}^+\}$$

by $(p, q)R_2(r, s)$ if and only if $p + s = q + r$.
Prove that this is an equivalence relation, and describe the equivalence classes.

5 S is the set of matrices $\left\{\begin{bmatrix} a & b \\ c & d \end{bmatrix}: a, b, c, d \in \mathbb{R}\right\}$.

(*a*) If $\mathbf{P} = \begin{bmatrix} 4 & -1 \\ -2 & 3 \end{bmatrix}$ and $\mathbf{Q} = \begin{bmatrix} 2 & 0 \\ 3 & -1 \end{bmatrix}$, find $\mathbf{A}$ and $\mathbf{B}$ such that $\mathbf{P} = \mathbf{AQ}$ and $\mathbf{Q} = \mathbf{BP}$, and verify that $\mathbf{A}^{-1} = \mathbf{B}$.
(*b*) A relation is now defined on the set S by '$\mathbf{P}$ is related to $\mathbf{Q}$ if and only if there exists a non-singular matrix $\mathbf{A}$, such that $\mathbf{P} = \mathbf{AQ}$'. Is this relation an equivalence relation?

6 A relation R is defined on the set of 2×1 matrices as follows: '$\begin{bmatrix} x_1 \\ x_2 \end{bmatrix} R \begin{bmatrix} y_1 \\ y_2 \end{bmatrix}$ if you can find a value of $\lambda \in \mathbb{R}$ which will make the statement $\begin{bmatrix} 1 & \lambda \\ 0 & 1 \end{bmatrix}\begin{bmatrix} x_1 \\ x_2 \end{bmatrix} = \begin{bmatrix} y_1 \\ y_2 \end{bmatrix}$ true.'
(*a*) Show that this relation is an equivalence relation.
(*b*) Find three 2×1 matrices each related to $\begin{bmatrix} 4 \\ 3 \end{bmatrix}$.
(*c*) Describe fully the equivalence class $\left[\begin{bmatrix} 4 \\ 3 \end{bmatrix}\right]$.

7 Let S be the following set of matrices:

$$S = \left\{\begin{bmatrix} 2 - a & 1 - a \\ a - 1 & a \end{bmatrix}: a \in \mathbb{R}\right\}.$$

A relation R is defined on the set of points in the plane by

$$(x_1, x_2)R(y_1, y_2)$$

if and only if $\begin{bmatrix} x_1 \\ x_2 \end{bmatrix} = \mathbf{A}\begin{bmatrix} y_1 \\ y_2 \end{bmatrix}$ for some $\mathbf{A} \in S$.
(*a*) Show that the relation is an equivalence relation.
(*b*) Describe the set of points in the equivalence class containing the point $(0, 2)$.

8 How many distinct equivalence relations can be defined on the set $\{x, y, z\}$?

18.2 CONGRUENCES

A familiar partitioning of the set of integers into equivalence classes arises from the relation R defined by 'xRy if and only if $(x - y)$ is divisible by an integer n; that is, $x - y = kn$ for some integer k'. This is an equivalence relation on the set of integers since it is reflexive, symmetric and transitive:

Reflexive: xRx for all $x \in \mathbb{Z}$, since $x - x = 0n$ and $0 \in \mathbb{Z}$.

Symmetric: If xRy, then $x - y = kn$, where $k \in \mathbb{Z}$,

so $$y - x = (-k)n;$$

that is, $$yRx \text{ as } -k \in \mathbb{Z}.$$

Transitive: If xRy and yRz, then

$$x - y = kn, \quad \text{where } k \in \mathbb{Z}$$

and $$y - z = ln, \quad \text{where } l \in \mathbb{Z}.$$

Adding: $$x - z = (k + l)n,$$

thus $$xRz \text{ as } (k + l) \in \mathbb{Z}.$$

For the case when $n = 5$, the equivalence classes are:

$$[0] = \{\ldots, -10, -5, 0, 5, 10, \ldots\} = \{5k : k \in \mathbb{Z}\}$$
$$[1] = \{\ldots, -9, -4, 1, 6, 11, \ldots] = \{5k + 1 : k \in \mathbb{Z}\}$$
$$[2] = \{\ldots, -8, -3, 2, 7, 12, \ldots\} = \{5k + 2 : k \in \mathbb{Z}\}$$
$$[3] = \{\ldots, -7, -2, 3, 8, 13, \ldots\} = \{5k + 3 : k \in \mathbb{Z}\}$$
$$[4] = \{\ldots, -6, -1, 4, 9, 14, \ldots\} = \{5k + 4 : k \in \mathbb{Z}\}$$

These equivalence classes are known as the congruence classes (or residue classes) modulo n (equal to 5 in this example), and we say that a is congruent to b modulo n (written $a \equiv b \pmod{n}$) if a and b belong to the same congruence class.

(a) Algebra of congruences

The congruence classes modulo 5 are [0], [1], [2], [3], [4].

Addition

Suppose we choose an element from [2] and an element from [4] and add them together:

$$2 + 4 = 6$$
$$-8 + 9 = 1$$
$$7 + -11 = -4$$
$$12 + 14 = 26$$

In each of these examples, the sum is an element of [1]. We can easily show that this is always true.

If $a \in [2]$ and $b \in [4]$, then a and b can be expressed in the forms

$$a = 5k + 2, \quad b = 5l + 4, \quad \text{where } k, l \in \mathbb{Z}$$

so

$$a + b = (5k + 2) + (5l + 4)$$
$$= 5(k + l + 1) + 1,$$

which belongs to [1] since $(k + l + 1) \in \mathbb{Z}$. This means that if we take one integer from [2] and another from [4] and add them together, the result is always an integer in [1]. This naturally gives rise to what we may regard as 'addition' of congruences, and we write $[2] + [4] = [1]$.

The complete table for addition of congruences is:

+	[0]	[1]	[2]	[3]	[4]
[0]	[0]	[1]	[2]	[3]	[4]
[1]	[1]	[2]	[3]	[4]	[0]
[2]	[2]	[3]	[4]	[0]	[1]
[3]	[3]	[4]	[0]	[1]	[2]
[4]	[4]	[0]	[1]	[2]	[3]

(*Note:* although we use the symbol '+' for addition, it does not have the same meaning as the '+' for addition of real numbers.)

Multiplication

As above, $a = 5k + 2 \quad \text{and} \quad b = 5l + 4$

so

$$ab = 25kl + 20k + 10l + 8$$
$$= 5(5kl + 4k + 2l + 1) + 3.$$

Hence $ab \in [3], \quad \text{since } (5kl + 4k + 2l + 1) \in \mathbb{Z},$

and we write $[2] \times [4] = [3]$.

The complete table for multiplication of congruences is:

×	[0]	[1]	[2]	[3]	[4]
[0]	[0]	[0]	[0]	[0]	[0]
[1]	[0]	[1]	[2]	[3]	[4]
[2]	[0]	[2]	[4]	[1]	[3]
[3]	[0]	[3]	[1]	[4]	[2]
[4]	[0]	[4]	[3]	[2]	[1]

You will notice that these tables are very similar to the tables for $\mathbb{Z}_5$ under $\oplus_5$ and $\otimes_5$ which we met in the last chapter. This set of congruences modulo 5 under + and × is *isomorphic* to $\mathbb{Z}_5$ under $\oplus_5$ and $\otimes_5$; that is, they have exactly the same structure. The same is true for the set of congruences modulo n and of $\mathbb{Z}_n$ under the appropriate operations. So it does not matter whether we think of

$0, 1, 2, \ldots, (n-1)$ as the ordinary integers under addition and multiplication modulo n, or interpret them as labels for the n disjoint congruence classes modulo n.

(b) Some results

If $\quad p \equiv q \pmod{n}$ and $r \equiv s \pmod{n}$,

then (1) $\quad p + r \equiv q + s \pmod{n}$

(2) $\quad p - r \equiv q - s \pmod{n}$

(3) $\quad pr \equiv qs \pmod{n}$.

Also (4) if $ax \equiv ay \pmod{n}$, then $x \equiv y \pmod{n}$ if a and n are coprime.

Proofs
By definition we have $\quad p - q = kn, \quad k \in \mathbb{Z}$

and $\quad r - s = ln, \quad l \in \mathbb{Z}$.

(1) $\quad (p + r) - (q + s) = (k + l)n;$

that is, $\quad (p + r) \equiv (q + s) \pmod{n}$.

(2) $\quad (p - r) - (q - s) = (k - l)n;$

that is, $\quad (p - r) \equiv (q - s) \pmod{n}$.

(3)
$$pr - qs = (q + kn)(s + ln) - qs$$
$$= (kln + ql + ks)n;$$

that is, $\quad pr \equiv qs \pmod{n}$.

(4) $\quad ax - ay = tn, \quad t \in \mathbb{Z}$.

So $\quad a(x - y) = tn$

$$(x - y) = \left(\frac{t}{a}\right)n = t_1 n, \quad \text{as } a \text{ and } n \text{ are coprime;}$$

that is, $\quad x \equiv y \pmod{n}$.

(c) Congruence equations

Example 3
Solve the congruence equation $x + 3 \equiv 1 \pmod{5}$.

Solution

$$x + 3 \equiv 1 \pmod{5}$$
$$x + 3 - 3 \equiv 1 - 3 \pmod{5} \quad \text{(by Result 2)}$$

$$\Rightarrow \qquad x \equiv -2 \pmod 5$$

$$\Rightarrow \qquad x \equiv 3 \pmod 5$$ □

Example 4

Solve the congruence equation $x^2 \equiv 3 \pmod 5$.

Solution

As each integer is congruent to one of the integers 0, 1, 2, 3, 4 we can check each of these five values to see whether it satisfies our equation:

x	0	1	2	3	4	(mod 5)
x^2	0	1	4	4	1	(mod 5)

It follows therefore that $x^2 \equiv 3 \pmod 5$ has no solution. □

Example 5

Solve the congruence equation $2x \equiv 4 \pmod 6$.

Solution

We apply the same method as in Example 4, and try the integers 0, 1, 2, 3, 4, 5 (it is modulo 6 this time):

x	0	1	2	3	4	5	(mod 6)
$2x$	0	2	4	0	2	4	(mod 6)

So the solutions are $x \equiv 2, 5 \pmod 6$.

Note that in this case Result 4 is not applicable, since 2 and 6 are not coprime. □

(d) Fermat's theorem

If p is prime and a and p have no common factor except 1, then $a^{p-1} \equiv (\text{mod } p)$.

If we consider the set of congruences modulo p,

$$\{[0], [1], \ldots, [p-1]\},$$

and the following set

$$\{[0a], [1a], [2a], \ldots, [(p-1)a]\}, \quad \text{where } a \not\equiv 0 \pmod p,$$

then both sets contain p distinct elements, since in the second set if $[ra] = [sa]$, then

$$ra \equiv sa \pmod p,$$

so

$$r \equiv s \pmod p \quad \text{(by Result 4);}$$

that is,

$$r = s \quad (\text{as } 1 \leqslant r \text{ and } s \leqslant p-1).$$

As there are only p distinct congruences modulo p, both sets must be the same.

Now
$$
\begin{aligned}
[0] &= [0a] \\
[1] &= [ra] \text{ for some } r; \quad \text{that is,} \quad 1 \equiv ra \pmod p, \\
[2] &= [sa] \text{ for some } s; \quad \text{that is,} \quad 2 \equiv sa \pmod p, \\
&\;\vdots \\
[p-1] &= [ta] \text{ for some } t; \quad \text{that is,} \quad (p-1) \equiv ta \pmod p.
\end{aligned}
$$

By multiplication of congruences (Result 3), it follows that

$$1 \times 2 \times \ldots \times (p-1) \equiv a \times (2a) \times \ldots \times ((p-1)a) \pmod p;$$

that is,
$$(p-1)! \equiv (p-1)!\, a^{p-1} \pmod p.$$

Now $(p-1)!$ and p have no common factor except 1, so (using Result 4)

$$1 \equiv a^{p-1} \pmod p.$$

Example 6
Prove that $5^{10} \equiv 1 \pmod{11}$.

Solution
This is a direct application of Fermat's theorem, with $a = 5$, $p = 11$, where p is prime and a and p have no common factor except 1. □

There is an alternative but very similar proof of Fermat's theorem using the fact that $\mathbb{Z}_p$ is a field.

Consider the set $S = \{1a, 2a, \ldots, (p-1)a\}$ in $\mathbb{Z}_p$. These are the entries in the ath column of the multiplication table for $\mathbb{Z}_p$, so

$$S = \{1, 2, \ldots, (p-1)\},$$

the elements being listed in some permuted order (using the Latin square property of a group). We take the product of the elements in both these sets to give

$$
\begin{aligned}
& (1a)(2a)\ldots((p-1)a) = 1 \times 2 \times \ldots \times (p-1) \\
\Rightarrow \quad & (p-1)!\, a^{p-1} = (p-1)! \\
\Rightarrow \quad & a^{p-1} = 1, \quad (\text{since } (p-1)! \neq 0.
\end{aligned}
$$

Because of the isomorphism referred to earlier, results for congruences have their parallel in $\mathbb{Z}_n$, and vice versa. So a problem may be set as:

(*a*) Solve the congruence equation $2x \equiv 3 \pmod 5$,

or

(*b*) Solve the equation $2x = 3$ in $\mathbb{Z}_5$.

In (*a*), the solution is $x \equiv 4 \pmod 5$, while in (*b*), the solution is $x = 4$.

Exercise 18B

1 Solve the following congruence equations:

(*a*) $x + 7 \equiv 5 \pmod 9$ (*b*) $2x + 3 \equiv 1 \pmod 7$ (*c*) $3x + 5 \equiv 2 \pmod{11}$

(*d*) $4x + 5 \equiv 3 \pmod 6$ (*e*) $3x \equiv 6 \pmod 9$ (*f*) $4x \equiv 3 \pmod 6$

(*g*) $3x^2 + 4x + 2 \equiv 0 \pmod 6$ (*h*) $3x^2 + 4x + 2 \equiv 0 \pmod 7$

(*i*) $x^3 \equiv 5 \pmod 7$ (*j*) $x^2 \equiv 6 \pmod{10}$

2 Solve the following congruence equations in modulo 7:

(*a*) $\left.\begin{aligned} 2x + 3y &\equiv 4 \\ x + 4y &\equiv 1 \end{aligned}\right\}$ (*b*) $\left.\begin{aligned} 3x + y &\equiv 4 \\ 5x + 4y &\equiv 2 \end{aligned}\right\}$ (*c*) $\left.\begin{aligned} 2x + 5y &\equiv 4 \\ 3x + 4y &\equiv 5 \end{aligned}\right\}$

3 (*a*) Find the remainder when 2^{80} is divided by 81.
(*b*) Prove that $7^{2n} + 3$ is divisible by 4 for integers $n \geqslant 0$.

4 Prove that if $p \equiv q \pmod n$, then $p^r \equiv q^r \pmod n$ for positive integral r.

5 Show that $\sum_{i=0}^{23} 3(5^i)$ is divisible by 7.

6 Give a counter-example to show that the converse of Fermat's theorem is not true; that is, if $a^{p-1} \equiv 1 \pmod p$, then p is not necessarily prime.

7 Any number N can be written in the form

$$N = a_0 + a_1 \times 10 + a_2 \times 10^2 + \ldots + a_n \times 10^n.$$

(*a*) Use congruences to prove that if a number N is divisible by 9, then the sum of its digits is also divisible by 9.

(*b*) Use congruences to prove that if a number N is divisible by 11, then the difference between the sum of the digits in the odd numbered places and the sum of the digits in the even numbered places is also divisible by 11.

8 Prove that the congruence equation $Ax \equiv B \pmod n$ has no solution if the highest common factor of A and n is not a factor of B.

Miscellaneous exercise 18

1 Let g and h be two elements of a group G. We say that g is *conjugate* to h in G if there exists an element $k \in G$ such that

$$kgk^{-1} = h.$$

(*a*) Prove that 'is conjugate to' is an equivalence relation on G.

(*b*) Prove that if g and h are two conjugate elements, then g and h have the same order.

(*c*) Prove that in an Abelian group each element is conjugate to itself alone.

(*d*) For the group of symmetries of the equilateral triangle, what are the equivalence classes under this relation?

(*e*) Repeat part (*d*) for the group of symmetries of the square.

(*f*) How do the results of parts (*d*) and (*e*) illustrate the geometric idea of conjugation as 'giving the same transformation in a different place'?

2 Verify that $(x-1)(x-2)(x-3)(x-4)(x-5)(x-6) \equiv x^6 - 1 \pmod 7$. Hence confirm that $6! \equiv -1 \pmod 7$. (This is a particular case of Wilson's theorem, which states that if p is prime, then $(p-1)! \equiv -1 \pmod p$.)

3 (*a*) R_1 and R_2 are two equivalence relations on the same set S. Is the relation 'R_1 and R_2' an equivalence relation? If so, describe the partitioning effected by this relation and those effected by R_1 and R_2 separately. Illustrate your answer with an example.
(*b*) Repeat part (*a*) for the relation 'R_1 or R_2'.

4 If
$$M = \left\{\begin{bmatrix} a & b \\ c & d \end{bmatrix} : a, b, c, d \in \mathbb{Z}_7\right\} \quad \text{and} \quad \mathbf{A} = \begin{bmatrix} 4 & 1 \\ 3 & 2 \end{bmatrix} \in M,$$
find matrices **P** and **D** in the set M with **D** of the form $\begin{bmatrix} u & 0 \\ 0 & v \end{bmatrix}$ such that $\mathbf{A} = \mathbf{PDP}^{-1}$.
Hence find $\mathbf{A}^{10}$.

5 (*a*) A woman, when asked how many eggs she had, replied: 'Taken in groups of 11, five remain over, and taken in groups of 23, three remain over.' What is the least number of eggs she could have?
(*b*) The same woman, on another occasion, replied: 'Taken in groups of 2, 3, 4, 5, 6 and 7, there remain 1, 2, 3, 4, 5 and no eggs, respectively.' What is the least number of eggs she could have?

6 Prove that congruence modulo $(-m)$ is equivalent to congruence modulo m.

SUMMARY

Definitions

(1) If S is a set, then a (binary) *relation* R between the elements of S is defined if, for all $a, b \in S$, it is possible to decide whether
(*a*) a is related to b, written aRb, or
(*b*) a is not related to b, written $a\not{R}b$.

(2) R is a relation defined on a set S. The relation is
(*a*) *reflexive* if aRa for all $a \in S$;
(*b*) *symmetric* if whenever aRb, then bRa for all $a, b \in S$;
(*c*) *transitive* if whenever aRb and bRc, then aRc for all $a, b, c \in S$ (not necessarily all different).

(3) A relation which is reflexive, symmetric and transitive is called an *equivalence relation*.

(4) The disjoint subsets formed by an equivalence relation are called *equivalence classes*: $[x] = \{y \in S : yRx\}$ is called an equivalence class of x.

(5) a is *congruent* to b modulo n (written $a \equiv b \pmod{n}$) if a and b belong to the same congruence class under the relation 'xRy if and only if $(x - y)$ is divisible by n'.

Results

(1) If $p \equiv q \pmod{n}$ and $r \equiv s \pmod{n}$,

then (*a*) $$p + r \equiv q + s \pmod{n}$$

(*b*) $$p - r \equiv q + s \pmod{n}$$

(*c*) $$pr \equiv qs \pmod{n}.$$

Also (*d*) if $ax \equiv ay \pmod{n}$, then $x \equiv y \pmod{n}$ if a and n are coprime.

(2) *Fermat's theorem*: If p is prime and a and p have no common factors except 1, then $a^{p-1} \equiv 1 \pmod{p}$.

19

Some applications

It is surprising how often the type of mathematics developed in this book is found to be useful by physicists, economists and many other users. The nineteenth-century physicist P. G. Tait, commenting about matrix theory, once said ‘Cayley is forging the weapons for future generations of physicists’. So in this chapter we outline briefly several illustrations to try to give some idea of the range of applications. It will not be possible to go into great detail, as considerable background knowledge of the area of application is needed, which is outside the scope of this book.

19.1 VIBRATIONS

The problem of finding the natural frequencies of an oscillating system is essentially an eigenvalue problem. Small distortions in structures such as suspension bridges or aircraft frames as well as vibrations within molecules are examples, but we will illustrate this application by looking at a simple mechanical system which consists of two equal masses joined by three similar springs of stiffness k, as in Fig. 1.

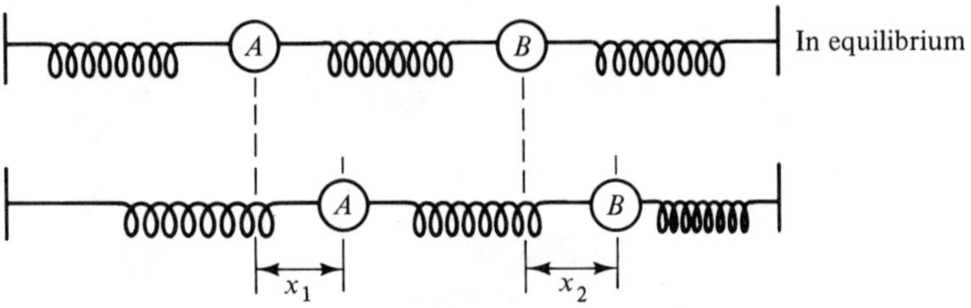

Figure 1

In equilibrium x_1 and x_2 denote the particles’ displacements from their equilibrium positions.

Applying Newton’s second law to particle A of mass m:

$$m\ddot{x}_1 = k(x_2 - x_1) - kx_1$$

and to particle B of mass m:

$$m\ddot{x}_2 = k(x_1 - x_2) - kx_2;$$

that is, $\quad m\ddot{x}_1 = k(x_2 - 2x_1)$

and $\quad m\ddot{x}_2 = k(x_1 - 2x_2).$

This can be written in matrix form as

$$\ddot{\mathbf{x}} = \frac{k}{m}\begin{bmatrix} -2 & 1 \\ 1 & -2 \end{bmatrix}\mathbf{x}, \quad \text{where } \mathbf{x} = \begin{bmatrix} x_1 \\ x_2 \end{bmatrix}.$$

That is, $\ddot{\mathbf{x}} = \mathbf{A}\mathbf{x}$, where $\mathbf{A}$ is the symmetric matrix $\begin{bmatrix} \frac{-2k}{m} & \frac{k}{m} \\ \frac{k}{m} & \frac{-2k}{m} \end{bmatrix}$.

If we change the variables to $\mathbf{y} = \begin{bmatrix} y_1 \\ y_2 \end{bmatrix}$, where $\mathbf{x} = \mathbf{B}\mathbf{y}$, then $\ddot{\mathbf{y}} = (\mathbf{B}^{-1}\mathbf{A}\mathbf{B})\mathbf{y}$.

Now, as $\mathbf{A}$ is a symmetric matrix, we can find $\mathbf{B}$ so that $\mathbf{B}^{-1}\mathbf{A}\mathbf{B}$ is a diagonal matrix (§8.3), with the eigenvalues of $\mathbf{A}$ on the diagonal.

$$\det\left(\begin{bmatrix} \left(\frac{-2k}{m} - \lambda\right) & \frac{k}{m} \\ \frac{k}{m} & \left(\frac{-2k}{m} - \lambda\right) \end{bmatrix}\right) = 0$$

$$\Rightarrow \qquad \left(\frac{-2k}{m} - \lambda\right)^2 - \left(\frac{k}{m}\right)^2 = 0$$

$$\Rightarrow \qquad \frac{-2k}{m} - \lambda = \pm\frac{k}{m},$$

so

$$\lambda = \frac{-k}{m} \quad \text{or} \quad \frac{-3k}{m}.$$

Hence

$$\ddot{\mathbf{y}} = \begin{bmatrix} \frac{-k}{m} & 0 \\ 0 & \frac{-3k}{m} \end{bmatrix}\mathbf{y};$$

that is,

$$\ddot{y}_1 = \frac{-k}{m}y_1, \quad \text{so } y_1(k) = R_1\cos\left(t\sqrt{\left(\frac{k}{m}\right)} + \varepsilon_1\right)$$

and

$$\ddot{y}_2 = \frac{-3k}{m}y_2, \quad \text{so } y_2(t) = R_2\cos\left(t\sqrt{\left(\frac{3k}{m}\right)} + \varepsilon_2\right),$$

and from $\mathbf{x} = \mathbf{B}\mathbf{y}$, where $\mathbf{B}$ is the matrix whose columns are the eigenvectors of $\mathbf{A}$, we can find x_1 and x_2 as linear combinations of

$$\cos\left(t\sqrt{\left(\frac{k}{m}\right)} + \varepsilon_1\right) \quad \text{and} \quad \cos\left(t\sqrt{\left(\frac{3k}{m}\right)} + \varepsilon_2\right).$$

The linear constants can be found using the initial conditions of the problems. $\sqrt{\left(\frac{k}{m}\right)}$ and $\sqrt{\left(\frac{3k}{m}\right)}$ are the *natural frequencies* of the system, and the two solutions $y_1(t)$ and $y_2(t)$ are referred to as the *normal modes of oscillation*.

19.2 MOMENT OF INERTIA

In rigid body mechanics, many of the equations for motion involve a quantity known as the moment of inertia. The moment of inertia about the axis OA is defined by:

$$\text{Moment of inertia about the axis } OA = \Sigma m_i(P_iN_i)^2,$$

summed over all the elements of the rigid body, where P_iN_i is perpendicular to OA (Fig. 2). The vector $\hat{\mathbf{a}} = \begin{bmatrix} a \\ b \\ c \end{bmatrix}$ is the unit vector in the direction OA, therefore $a^2 + b^2 + c^2 = 1$.

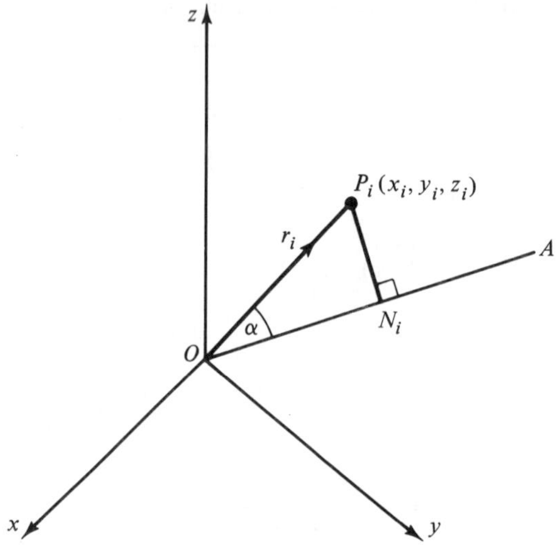

Figure 2

$$P_iN_i^2 = OP_i^2 - ON_i^2 = r_i^2 - (r_i \cos\alpha)^2.$$

But $r_i \cos\alpha$ is the projection of OP_i in the direction of vector $\hat{\boldsymbol{\alpha}}$

therefore $$r_i \cos\alpha = \mathbf{r}_i \cdot \hat{\mathbf{a}}$$
$$= ax_i + by_i + cz_i.$$

So, the moment of inertia about the axis OA

$$= \Sigma m_i(x_i^2 + y_i^2 + z_i^2 - (ax_i + by_i + cz_i)^2)$$
$$= \Sigma m_i((1 - a^2)x_i^2 + (1 - b^2)y_i^2 + (1 - c^2)z_i^2 - 2abx_iy_i - 2acx_iz_i - 2bcy_iz_i)$$
$$= \Sigma m_i((b^2 + c^2)x_i^2 + (a^2 + c^2)y_i^2 + (a^2 + b^2)z_i^2 - 2abx_iy_i - 2acx_iz_i - 2bcy_iz_i)$$
$$= (\Sigma m_i(y_i^2 + z_i^2))a^2 + (\Sigma m_i(x_i^2 + z_i^2))b^2 + (\Sigma m_i(x_i^2 + y_i^2))c^2$$
$$- 2(\Sigma m_ix_iy_i)ab - 2(\Sigma m_iy_iz_i)bc - 2(\Sigma m_ix_iz_i)ac$$
$$= Aa^2 + Bb^2 + Cc^2 - 2Hab - 2Fbc - 2Gac,$$

where $A = \Sigma m_i(y_i^2 + z_i^2)$, $B = \Sigma m_i(x_i^2 + z_i^2)$, $C = \Sigma m_i(x_i^2 + y_i^2)$,

$F = \Sigma m_i y_i z_i$, $G = \Sigma m_i x_i z_i$, $H = \Sigma m_i x_i y_i$.

The matrix $\mathbf{I} = \begin{bmatrix} A & -H & -G \\ -H & B & -F \\ -G & -F & C \end{bmatrix}$ is known as the *inertia matrix*. The inertia matrix is relative to the fixed axes $Oxyz$. As $\mathbf{I}$ is a symmetric matrix we can find a new set of axes $Ox'y'z'$ so that the inertia matrix $\mathbf{I}'$ is a diagonal matrix – this problem is very similar to reducing a quadric surface to a simple form by changing the axes. The new axes Ox', Oy' and Oz' are called the *principal axes* of the body. One important consequence is that if a body rotates about a principal axis then the angular momentum and angular velocity have the same direction.

19.3 DIMENSIONAL ANALYSIS

Many problems in dimensional analysis reduce to the solution of linear equations as illustrated by the following example.

It is believed that the drag due to the formation of waves on a body of length l moving in a liquid with speed v is related in some way to its length, the density of the liquid ρ, its speed, and the acceleration due to gravity.

If $$D = kl^x\rho^y v^z g^t,$$

then $$[MLT^{-2}] = [L]^x[ML^{-3}]^y[LT^{-1}]^z[LT^{-2}]^t.$$

From L: $$1 = x - 3y + z + t.$$

From M: $$1 = y.$$

From T: $$-2 = -z - 2t.$$

In matrix form this is

$$\begin{bmatrix} 1 & -3 & 1 & 1 \\ 0 & 1 & 0 & 0 \\ 0 & 0 & -1 & -2 \end{bmatrix}\begin{bmatrix} x \\ y \\ z \\ t \end{bmatrix} = \begin{bmatrix} 1 \\ 1 \\ -2 \end{bmatrix}.$$

On reduction to canonical form using row operations we get

$$\begin{bmatrix} 1 & 0 & 0 & -1 \\ 0 & 1 & 0 & 0 \\ 0 & 0 & 1 & 2 \end{bmatrix}\begin{bmatrix} x \\ y \\ z \\ t \end{bmatrix} = \begin{bmatrix} 2 \\ 1 \\ 2 \end{bmatrix}.$$

Using the ideas of Chapter 13, the general solution is composed of two parts, a particular solution and the kernel.

Particular solution

Putting $t=0$ we get $x=2$, $y=1$, $z=2$. So a particular solution is

$$\begin{bmatrix} x \\ y \\ z \\ t \end{bmatrix} = \begin{bmatrix} 2 \\ 1 \\ 2 \\ 0 \end{bmatrix}.$$

Kernel

This is of dimension 1, as the domain is of dimension 4 and the rank is 3.

We solve
$$\begin{bmatrix} 1 & 0 & 0 & -1 \\ 0 & 1 & 0 & 0 \\ 0 & 0 & 1 & 2 \end{bmatrix} \begin{bmatrix} x \\ y \\ z \\ t \end{bmatrix} = \begin{bmatrix} 0 \\ 0 \\ 0 \end{bmatrix},$$

so
$$\left.\begin{aligned} x - t &= 0 \\ y &= 0 \\ z + 2t &= 0 \end{aligned}\right\}.$$

Putting $t = \lambda$ gives the solution $\begin{bmatrix} x \\ y \\ z \\ t \end{bmatrix} = \lambda \begin{bmatrix} 1 \\ 0 \\ -2 \\ 1 \end{bmatrix}.$

Hence the complete solution is

$$\begin{bmatrix} x \\ y \\ z \\ t \end{bmatrix} = \begin{bmatrix} 2 \\ 1 \\ 2 \\ 0 \end{bmatrix} + \lambda \begin{bmatrix} 1 \\ 0 \\ -2 \\ 1 \end{bmatrix}$$

and
$$D = kl^{2+\lambda}\rho^1 v^{2-2\lambda} g^{\lambda};$$

that is,
$$D = kl^2\rho v^2 \left\{\frac{lg}{v^2}\right\}^{\lambda} \quad \text{for real } \lambda.$$

$\dfrac{v}{\surd(lg)}\left(\text{or sometimes } \dfrac{v^2}{lg}\right)$ is referred to as the *Froude number* in fluid dynamics. It is a dimensionless number used in problems involving fluids with free surfaces, for example, waves.

19.4 ELECTRICAL CIRCUITS

The solution of an electrical circuit can be reduced to solving a matrix equation. In practice this is often done using the matrix subroutines on a computer.

Notation (Fig. 3)

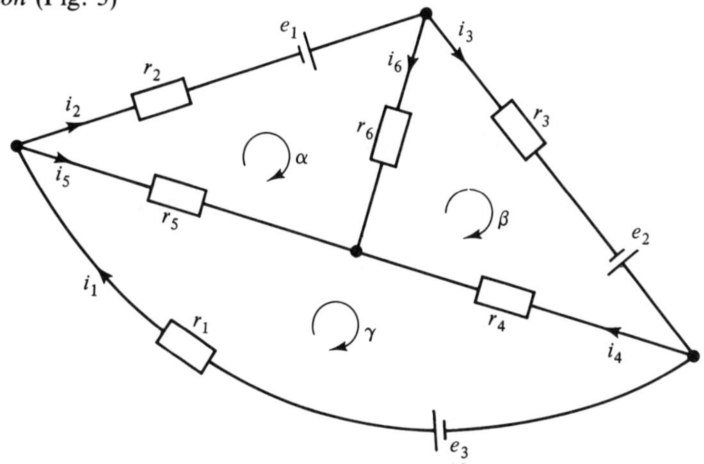

Figure 3

The loop current matrix $\mathbf{J} = \begin{bmatrix} \alpha \\ \beta \\ \gamma \end{bmatrix}$, the currents in the branches $\mathbf{i} = \begin{bmatrix} i_1 \\ i_2 \\ i_3 \\ i_4 \\ i_5 \\ i_6 \end{bmatrix}$,

$\mathbf{e} = \begin{bmatrix} e_1 \\ e_2 \\ e_3 \end{bmatrix}$ are the e.m.f.s in the loops, and $\mathbf{v} = \begin{bmatrix} v_1 \\ v_2 \\ v_3 \\ v_4 \\ v_5 \\ v_6 \end{bmatrix}$ where $v_1, v_2, v_3, v_4, v_5, v_6$ are the voltage drops in the branches with currents $i_1, i_2, i_3, i_4, i_5, i_6$.

From the definition of loop currents we get

$$
\begin{aligned}
i_1 &= \gamma \\
i_2 &= \alpha \\
i_3 &= \beta \\
i_4 &= \beta - \gamma \\
i_5 &= -\alpha + \gamma \\
i_6 &= \alpha - \beta
\end{aligned}
$$

that is, $\mathbf{i} = \mathbf{MJ}$, where $\mathbf{M} = \begin{bmatrix} 0 & 0 & 1 \\ 1 & 0 & 0 \\ 0 & 1 & 0 \\ 0 & 1 & -1 \\ -1 & 0 & 1 \\ 1 & -1 & 0 \end{bmatrix}$. (A)

Using this approach Kirchhoff's first law is taken care of: $i_1 = i_2 + i_5$ follows automatically.

Effectively using Kirchhoff's second law for each loop, we get

$$v_2 + v_6 - v_5 = e_1$$
$$v_3 + v_4 - v_6 = e_2$$
$$v_1 + v_5 - v_4 = e_3$$

and
$$\mathbf{e} = \begin{bmatrix} 0 & 1 & 0 & 0 & -1 & 1 \\ 0 & 0 & 1 & 1 & 0 & -1 \\ 1 & 0 & 0 & -1 & 1 & 0 \end{bmatrix} \mathbf{v};$$

that is, $\mathbf{e} = \mathbf{M}^{\mathrm{T}}\mathbf{v}$. (B)

Applying Ohm's law to each branch:

$$\mathbf{v} = \begin{bmatrix} r_1 & 0 & 0 & 0 & 0 & 0 \\ 0 & r_2 & 0 & 0 & 0 & 0 \\ 0 & 0 & r_3 & 0 & 0 & 0 \\ 0 & 0 & 0 & r_4 & 0 & 0 \\ 0 & 0 & 0 & 0 & r_5 & 0 \\ 0 & 0 & 0 & 0 & 0 & r_6 \end{bmatrix} \mathbf{e};$$

that is, $\mathbf{v} = \mathbf{Ri}$. (C)

Combining equations (A), (B) and (C):

$$\begin{aligned} \mathbf{e} &= \mathbf{M}^{\mathrm{T}}\mathbf{v} \\ &= \mathbf{M}^{\mathrm{T}}\mathbf{Ri} \\ &= (\mathbf{M}^{\mathrm{T}}\mathbf{RM})\mathbf{J} \end{aligned}$$

so
$$\mathbf{J} = (\mathbf{M}^{\mathrm{T}}\mathbf{RM})^{-1}\mathbf{e}.$$

Matrices **M**, **R** and **e** can be written down directly from the circuit, and then **J** can be calculated.

19.5 FOUR-TERMINAL NETWORKS

With a four-terminal network we can find a relation between the input $\begin{bmatrix} V_1 \\ I_1 \end{bmatrix}$ and the output $\begin{bmatrix} V_2 \\ I_2 \end{bmatrix}$ using the fact that all complicated networks are composed of combinations of the two basic networks shown in Fig. 4.

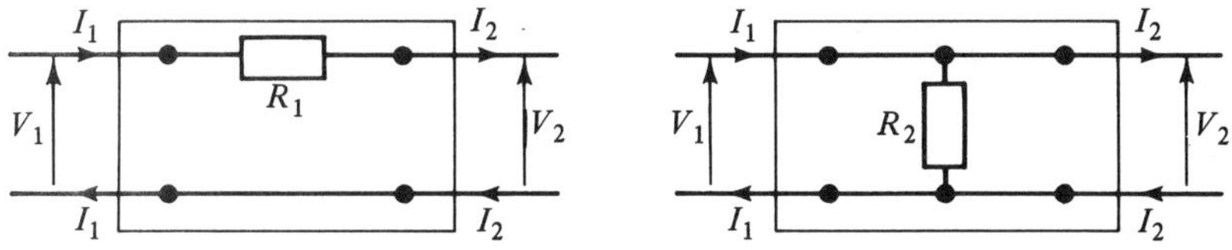

Figure 4

$$V_2 = V_1 - I_1R_1$$

and $\quad I_2 = I_1;$

$$V_2 = V_1$$

and $\quad I_2 = I_1 - \dfrac{V_1}{R_2};$

that is, $\begin{bmatrix} V_2 \\ I_2 \end{bmatrix} = \begin{bmatrix} 1 & -R_1 \\ 0 & 1 \end{bmatrix} \begin{bmatrix} V_1 \\ I_1 \end{bmatrix}.$ $\qquad$ that is, $\begin{bmatrix} V_2 \\ I_2 \end{bmatrix} = \begin{bmatrix} 1 & 0 \\ -1/R_2 & 1 \end{bmatrix} \begin{bmatrix} V_1 \\ I_1 \end{bmatrix}.$

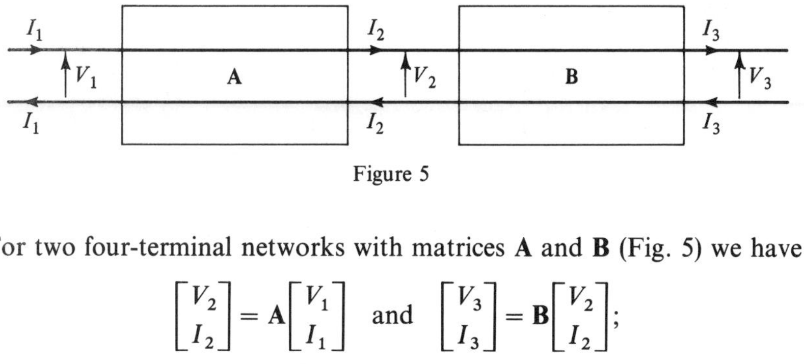

Figure 5

For two four-terminal networks with matrices **A** and **B** (Fig. 5) we have

$$\begin{bmatrix} V_2 \\ I_2 \end{bmatrix} = \mathbf{A}\begin{bmatrix} V_1 \\ I_1 \end{bmatrix} \quad \text{and} \quad \begin{bmatrix} V_3 \\ I_3 \end{bmatrix} = \mathbf{B}\begin{bmatrix} V_2 \\ I_2 \end{bmatrix};$$

therefore

$$\begin{bmatrix} V_3 \\ I_3 \end{bmatrix} = \mathbf{BA}\begin{bmatrix} V_1 \\ I_1 \end{bmatrix}.$$

The system is equivalent to a single four-terminal network with matrix **BA**. So, if n similar networks (each with matrix **A**) are connected together, it is equivalent to a single four-terminal network with matrix $\mathbf{A}^n$.

The basic matrices are of the same form for impedances, that is,

$$\begin{bmatrix} 1 & -z \\ 0 & 0 \end{bmatrix} \quad \text{and} \quad \begin{bmatrix} 1 & 0 \\ -\dfrac{1}{z} & 1 \end{bmatrix}.$$

19.6 MARKOV PROCESSES

The essential feature of a Markov process (named after the Russian mathematician A. A. Markov) is that the event we are considering is dependent only on the event immediately preceding it. For example, if we take the weather on a particular day to be either wet or fine and the probability of a wet day following a wet day to be $\frac{1}{2}$, whereas the probability of a wet day following a fine day is $\frac{1}{4}$, then this situation may be represented by the matrix:

$$\begin{array}{lll} & & \textit{first day} \\ & & \begin{array}{cc} W & F \end{array} \\ \mathbf{M} = \begin{array}{l} \textit{second} \\ \textit{day} \end{array} & \begin{array}{c} W \\ F \end{array} & \begin{bmatrix} \frac{1}{2} & \frac{1}{4} \\ \frac{1}{2} & \frac{3}{4} \end{bmatrix} \end{array}$$

(This is the same matrix as in Miscellaneous exercise 4, question 1.)

The relation between the weather one day and the weather on the next-but-one day is represented by $\mathbf{M}^2$ and the long-term prospect for the weather by $\mathbf{M}^n$ as $n \to \infty$.

M is an example of a *stochastic matrix* (all the entries are non-negative, and the sum of the entries in each column is 1). In general, a 2×2 stochastic matrix always has an eigenvalue of 1 and the modulus of the other eigenvalue is less than 1. So if we write **M** in the form

$$\mathbf{M} = \mathbf{P\Lambda P}^{-1}, \quad \text{where } \mathbf{\Lambda} = \begin{bmatrix} 1 & 0 \\ 0 & \lambda \end{bmatrix} \quad \text{with } |\lambda| < 1,$$

then

$$\begin{aligned} \mathbf{M}^n &= \mathbf{P\Lambda}^n\mathbf{P}^{-1} \\ &\to \mathbf{P}\begin{bmatrix} 1 & 0 \\ 0 & 0 \end{bmatrix}\mathbf{P}^{-1} \quad \text{as} \quad n \to \infty. \end{aligned}$$

That is, $\mathbf{M}^n$ reaches a limiting matrix. In this example,

$$\mathbf{M}^n \to \begin{bmatrix} \frac{1}{3} & \frac{1}{3} \\ \frac{2}{3} & \frac{2}{3} \end{bmatrix},$$

so in the long run we would expect a third of the days to be wet and two-thirds of the days to be fine.

This is one example of a probability problem but there are a large number of similar problems which arise in the physical, biological and social sciences: for example, diffusion theory and Brownian motion in the physical sciences, genetic theory in the biological sciences and population movement in the social sciences.

19.7 GENETIC THEORY

The theory of genetics was developed by G. Mendel and states that the inheritance of any given characteristic is governed by a pair of genes, each of which may be of two types which we will call G and g. There are three possible combinations:

(1) GG – known as homozygous dominant (D),
(2) Gg or gG – known as heterozygous (H), and
(3) gg – known as homozygous recessive (R).

In the mating of two animals, the offspring inherits one gene from each parent, and the basic assumption of genetic theory is that these genes are selected at random and independently of each other.

In a controlled experiment it is ensured that in the mating process one of the parents is heterozygous, but nothing is known about the other 'parent'. The probabilities of the different types of offspring are given in the following matrix:

$$\begin{array}{cc} & \textit{parent} \\ & \begin{array}{ccc} D & H & R \end{array} \\ \textit{offspring}\ \begin{array}{c} D \\ H \\ R \end{array} & \begin{bmatrix} \frac{1}{2} & \frac{1}{4} & 0 \\ \frac{1}{2} & \frac{1}{2} & \frac{1}{2} \\ 0 & \frac{1}{4} & \frac{1}{2} \end{bmatrix}. \end{array}$$

This is a stochastic matrix. Using matrix methods we can investigate the proportions of each type of offspring in each generation and what will happen eventually. In this example it will settle down to give a quarter D, half H and quarter R.

This is a simple example but it illustrates how matrices may be used in this sort of analysis. Similar techniques are applicable with more complex breeding situations.

19.8 THE JACOBIAN

$u = f(x, y)$, $v = g(x, y)$ is a transformation from the (x, y) coordinate system to the (u, v) coordinate system. For example,

$$r = \sqrt{(x^2 + y^2)}, \quad \theta = \tan^{-1}\left(\frac{y}{x}\right)$$

is the transformation from cartesian cordinates to polar coordinates.

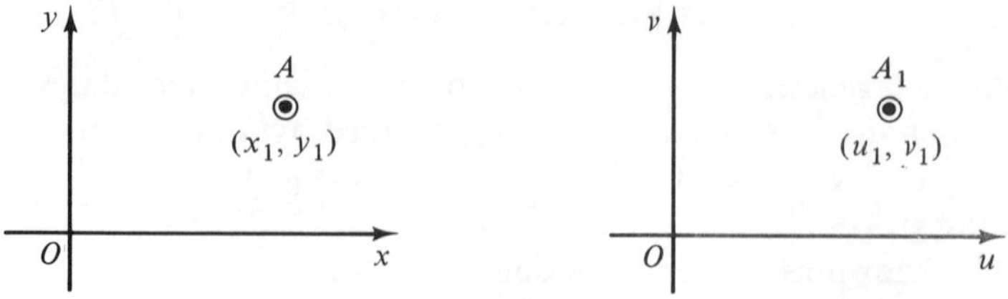

Figure 6

If a small area A round the point (x_1, y_1) is transformed into a small area A_1 round the point (u_1, v_1) (Fig. 6), then approximately

$$A_1 = \pm\det\left(\left[\frac{\partial(u_1, v_1)}{\partial(x_1, y_1)}\right]\right)A,$$

where $$\frac{\partial(u, v)}{\partial(x, y)} = \begin{bmatrix} \dfrac{\partial u}{\partial x} & \dfrac{\partial u}{\partial y} \\ \dfrac{\partial v}{\partial x} & \dfrac{\partial v}{\partial y} \end{bmatrix}$$ is known as the *Jacobian matrix.*

The determinant of the Jacobian matrix is an 'area' scale factor.

The formula for a change of variable in a double integral is therefore

$$\iint_{A_{xy}} f(x, y)\, dx\, dy = \iint_{A_{uv}} F(u, v)\left\{\det\left(\left[\frac{\partial(x, y)}{\partial(u, v)}\right]\right)\right\} du\, dv,$$

where the corresponding areas in the (x, y) and (u, v) coordinate systems are respectively A_{xy} and A_{uv}.

For three variables, the determinant of the Jacobian matrix is a 'volume' scale factor.

Using matrix theory the chain rule,

$$\frac{\partial(u, v)}{\partial(f, g)} \cdot \frac{\partial(f, g)}{\partial(x, y)} = \frac{\partial(u, v)}{\partial(x, y)},$$

can be proved. As a special case we get

$$\frac{\partial(u, v)}{\partial(x, y)} \cdot \frac{\partial(x, y)}{\partial(u, v)} = 1;$$

that is, $$\frac{\partial(x, y)}{\partial(u, v)} = \left(\frac{\partial(u, v)}{\partial(x, y)}\right)^{-1}.$$

19.9 LORENTZ TRANSFORMATIONS

The group of linear transformations known as the Lorentz transformations is important in relativity and quantum mechanics.

The basic question is: 'For what linear transformations is the expression

$$x^2 + y^2 + z^2 - c^2t^2, \quad \text{where } c \text{ is the speed of light,}$$

invariant for observers moving at constant velocity v relative to each other?'

So in the two coordinate systems, (x, y, z, t) and (x', y', z', t'), we must have

$$x^2 + y^2 + z^2 - c^2t^2 = x'^2 + y'^2 + z'^2 - c^2t'^2.$$

If we consider the case when y and z remain unchanged, so that x and y are the only variables in the transformation, we are therefore looking for linear transformations

$$x' = px + qt$$

and

$$t' = rx + st$$

such that

$$x'^2 - c^2t'^2 = x^2 - c^2t^2.$$

The solution of this is

$$x' = \frac{x - vt}{\sqrt{\left(1 - \frac{v^2}{c^2}\right)}}$$

$$t' = \frac{-\frac{v}{c^2}x + t}{\sqrt{\left(1 - \frac{v^2}{c^2}\right)}},$$

which can be written in matrix form as

$$\begin{bmatrix} x' \\ t' \end{bmatrix} = \begin{bmatrix} \dfrac{1}{\sqrt{\left(1 - \frac{v^2}{c^2}\right)}} & \dfrac{-v}{\sqrt{\left(1 - \frac{v^2}{c^2}\right)}} \\ \dfrac{-v}{c^2\sqrt{\left(1 - \frac{v^2}{c^2}\right)}} & \dfrac{1}{\sqrt{\left(1 - \frac{v^2}{c^2}\right)}} \end{bmatrix} \begin{bmatrix} x \\ t \end{bmatrix};$$

that is,

$$\begin{bmatrix} x' \\ t' \end{bmatrix} = \mathbf{L}(v) \begin{bmatrix} x \\ t \end{bmatrix}.$$

The set of matrices $\{\mathbf{L}(v)\colon |v| < c\}$ forms a group under matrix multiplication, called the Lorentz group.

We can show that

$$\mathbf{L}(-v) = [\mathbf{L}(v)]^{-1},$$

and if

$$\mathbf{L}(v_1)\mathbf{L}(v_2) = \mathbf{L}(v_3),$$

then

$$v_3 = \frac{v_1 + v_2}{1 + \frac{v_1 v_1}{c^2}},$$

which is the rule for adding velocities in the special theory of relativity.

In the case when v is small compared with c, then $\frac{v}{c} \approx 0$, and we get the usual expressions for motion in classical mechanics, that is,

$$x' = x - vt \quad \text{and} \quad t' = t.$$

19.10 FOURIER SERIES

This application rests on the ideas of vector spaces but needs three further extensions to our work:

(1) An inner product of two vectors $\mathbf{v}_1 . \mathbf{v}_2$ is defined so that the answer is a scalar.

(2) Our vector space is of infinite dimension.

(3) A basis $\{\mathbf{v}_1, \mathbf{v}_2, \ldots, \mathbf{v}_n\}$ is said to be orthonormal if

$$\mathbf{v}_i . \mathbf{v}_j = \begin{cases} 0 \text{ whenever } i \neq j \\ 1 \text{ whenever } i = j. \end{cases}$$

The simplest example of an orthonormal basis for $\mathbb{R}^2$ is $\left\{\begin{bmatrix}1\\0\end{bmatrix}, \begin{bmatrix}0\\1\end{bmatrix}\right\}$, with the inner product being the usual scalar product.

There is a method, known as the Gram–Schmidt orthogonalization method, which will convert any basis into an orthonormal set.

The Fourier series of a function $f(x)$ is an expansion into sines and cosines:

$$f(x) = a_0 + a_1 \cos x + b_1 \sin x + a_2 \cos 2x + b_2 \sin 2x + \ldots,$$

$$g . h = \int_0^{2\pi} g(x)h(x)\, dx.$$

Since $$\int_0^{2\pi} \sin mx \cos nx \, dx = 0$$

and, for $m \neq n$, $$\int_0^{2\pi} \sin mx \sin nx \, dx = \int_0^{2\pi} \cos mx \cos nx \, dx = 0,$$

the sines and cosines form an orthogonal set of vectors. The Fourier series gives the coordinates of the vector $f(x)$ with respect to the (infinite) basis

$$\{1, \cos x, \sin x, \cos 2x, \sin 2x, \ldots\}.$$

19.11 LINEAR PROGRAMMING

In many examples in economics the problem reduces to a set of linear inequalities rather than linear equations. A vector $\mathbf{x}_0$ has to be found which satisfies $\mathbf{Ax} \leqslant \mathbf{b}$ and which also maximises some other linear function, for example, $c_1x_1 + c_2x_2 + \ldots + c_nx_n$.

The usual method of solution of a problem like this is to use the *simplex method*, which was developed by Dantzig.

The essential idea in the solution is to find a 'corner' of the feasible set (Fig. 7).

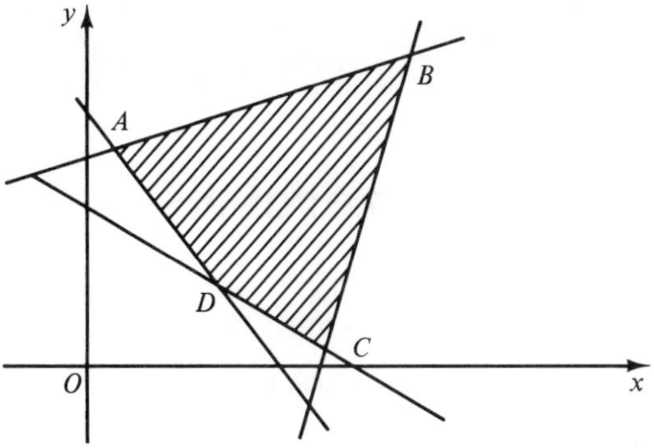

Figure 7

Starting at one of the 'corners', say A, move along one of the 'edges' through it, that is AB or AD here. Choose the 'edge' which increases the function to be maximised. This leads to a new corner with a bigger value of the function. Repeat this process until you reach a corner from which it is impossible to increase the value of the function by going along one of the edges. This then gives the optimal vector $\mathbf{x}_0$.

Revision exercises 15–18

Revision exercise 15

A1 Complete the table below to show which properties hold for the given sets and operations.

Set	Operation	Closed	Associative	Identity	Inverses
(*a*) {even integers}	addition				
(*b*) $\{a + b\sqrt{2} : a, b \in \mathbb{Q}$ and a, b not both zero$\}$	multiplication				
(*c*) {complex numbers with modulus 1}	addition				
(*d*) {complex numbers with modulus 1}	multiplication				

A2 Which of the following sets form groups under the given operations? Give your reasons.

(*a*) $\{1, 4, 7, 13\}$ under multiplication modulo 15

(*b*) {real 2×2 matrices} under matrix multiplication

(*c*) $\{3^k : k \in \mathbb{Z}\}$ under multiplication

A3 For permutations $\pi_1 = \begin{pmatrix} 1 & 2 & 3 & 4 \\ 3 & 1 & 4 & 2 \end{pmatrix}$ and $\pi_2 = \begin{pmatrix} 1 & 2 & 3 & 4 \\ 4 & 2 & 1 & 3 \end{pmatrix}$, find

(*a*) $\pi_1 \circ \pi_2$ (*b*) $\pi_2 \circ \pi_1$ (*c*) ${\pi_1}^3$

A4 Construct the Cayley tables for the symmetric transformations of

(*a*) the letter T

(*b*) the hyperbola $\dfrac{x^2}{a^2} - \dfrac{y^2}{b^2} = 1$

A5 Prove that the set of non-zero rational numbers forms a group under the operation $*$ defined by $a * b = 3ab$.

B1 A binary operation $*$ is defined on the set S of all ordered pairs (x, y), where $x, y \in \mathbb{R}$ (the set of real numbers) and where $y \neq 0$, by

$$(p, q) * (r, s) = (ps + r, qs).$$

(*a*) Is the operation $*$ commutative?

(*b*) State what you mean by an *identity element* of $(S, *)$. Verify that $(0, 1)$ is such an element.

(*c*) Show that S forms a group under $*$. [SMP]

B2 T is the set of all 2×2 real matrices $\begin{bmatrix} a & b \\ c & d \end{bmatrix}$ with $ad - bc = 1$. Prove that T is a group under matrix multiplication.

U is the set of 2×2 matrices:

$$U = \left\{\begin{bmatrix} p & -q \\ q & p \end{bmatrix} : p, q \text{ real but not both zero}\right\}.$$

Show that U is also a group under matrix multiplication. Establish whether either T or U is Abelian.

Four more sets of matrices are defined as follows:

$$V = \left\{\begin{bmatrix} p & 0 \\ 0 & p \end{bmatrix} : p \neq 0, p \text{ real}\right\}$$

$$W = \left\{\begin{bmatrix} 0 & -q \\ q & 0 \end{bmatrix} : q \neq 0, q \text{ real}\right\}$$

$$X = \left\{\begin{bmatrix} r & 0 \\ 0 & \frac{1}{r} \end{bmatrix} : r \neq 0, r \text{ real}\right\}$$

$$Y = \left\{\begin{bmatrix} p & -q \\ q & p \end{bmatrix} : p^2 + q^2 = 1;\ p, q \text{ real}\right\}$$

For each of V, W, X and Y, under matrix multiplication, state whether (*a*) it is a group, (*b*) it is a subgroup of T, (*c*) it is a subgroup of U. [SMP]

B3 List the eight subsets of the set $\{X, Y, Z\}$. Show that they form a group under the operation $*$ which is defined by $A * B = (A \cap B') \cup (A' \cap B)$. Identify all the subgroups of this group.

B4 $e: x \mapsto x, \quad f: x \mapsto 1 - x, \quad g: x \mapsto \dfrac{1}{x}$.

(*a*) Verify that $f^2 = g^2$. (*b*) Write down the function fg and show that $(fg)^2 = gf$. Hence (*c*) prove that $fgfgf = g$, and (*d*) express $(fg)^3$ in its simplest form.

Thus copy and complete the group table generated by f and g. Its elements are e, f, g, h, r, r^2, where $h = fgf$, $r = fg$, $r^2 = fgfg = (fg)^2$.

	e	f	g	h	r	r^2
e	e	f	g	h	r	r^2
f	f	e	r	r^2	g	h
g	g				h	f
h	h				f	g
r	r	h			r^2	e
r^2	r^2	g	h	f	e	r

List the elements of a subgroup of order 2 and those of a subgroup of order 3. Explain why there can be no subgroup of order 4. [SMP]

B5 Define (*a*) a binary operation on a set, (*b*) a closed binary operation on a set, (*c*) a group, (*d*) an Abelian group.

A set of matrices is defined by

$$M = \{\mathbf{I}, -\mathbf{I}, \mathbf{J}, -\mathbf{J}, \mathbf{K}, -\mathbf{K}, \mathbf{L}, -\mathbf{L}\},$$

where

$$\mathbf{I} = \begin{bmatrix} 1 & 0 \\ 0 & 1 \end{bmatrix}, \quad \mathbf{J} = \begin{bmatrix} j & 0 \\ 0 & -j \end{bmatrix}, \quad \mathbf{K} = \begin{bmatrix} 0 & 1 \\ -1 & 0 \end{bmatrix}, \quad \mathbf{L} = \begin{bmatrix} 0 & j \\ j & 0 \end{bmatrix} \quad \text{and} \quad j^2 = -1.$$

By constructing a matrix multiplication table for M, show that M forms a closed non-Abelian group with respect to matrix multiplication. [MEI]

Revision exercise 16

A1 The operations $\circ$ and $*$ are defined on the sets $P = \{p, q, r, s\}$ and $L = \{l, m, n, o\}$ by the following Cayley tables:

$\circ$	p	q	r	s
p	r	s	p	q
q	s	p	q	r
r	p	q	r	s
s	q	r	s	p

$*$	l	m	n	o
l	m	l	o	n
m	l	m	n	o
n	o	n	l	m
o	n	o	m	l

Show that $(P, \circ)$ and $(L, *)$ are isomorphic groups. State a geometric group to which they are each isomorphic.

A2 List the elements in the group generated by the matrices $\begin{bmatrix} 0 & 1 \\ -1 & 0 \end{bmatrix}$ and $\begin{bmatrix} -j & 0 \\ 0 & j \end{bmatrix}$ under matrix multiplication.

A3 Prove that 3 is a generator of a cyclic group of order 5 where the operation is multiplication modulo 11. What other elements generate this group?

A4 Show that the set of rotations about a fixed point forms a group under the operation of composition of transformations.

A5 a and b are elements of a group with identity element e. If $a^3 = b^2 = e$ and $ba = a^2b$,
(*a*) prove that $(ba)^2 = e$;
(*b*) find the simplest form of $(bab^{-1})^2$.

B1 Complete the table of products for a group consisting of the four elements e, a, b, c:

	e	a	b	c
e	e	a	b	c
a	a	b		
b	b			
c	c			

If the elements of the group are taken from the set of complex numbers and the group operation is the ordinary multiplication of complex numbers, find all possible selections of the numbers e, a, b, c.

Prove also that, to within isomorphism, there are only two groups of order 4. [SMP]

B2 The group G has identity e, and is generated by elements m and p such that $m^3 = p^2 = e$ and $m^2p = pm$, with e, m, p distinct. Show that G is of order 6.

Hence show that, if R and S denote the permutations $\begin{pmatrix} 1 & 2 & 3 & 4 & 5 \\ 1 & 5 & 2 & 4 & 3 \end{pmatrix}$ and $\begin{pmatrix} 1 & 2 & 3 & 4 & 5 \\ 4 & 2 & 5 & 1 & 3 \end{pmatrix}$ respectively, then R and S generate a group isomorphic to G.

[C]

B3 Let $G = (S, \circ)$ be a group and let k be any fixed element of the set S. Suppose that a new product $*$ is defined on the elements of S by

$$s_1 * s_2 = s_1 \circ k \circ s_2 \quad \text{for all } s_1, s_2 \in S.$$

Prove that $G^* = (S, *)$ is then also a group and determine its identity element and the inverse, under the operation $*$, of the general element s of S.

Prove that the mapping f from G to G^* defined by $f(s) = k^{-1} \circ s$ for all $s \in S$ (where k^{-1} is the inverse of k under the operation $\circ$) is an isomorphism and hence deduce that the groups G and G^* are isomorphic. [SMP]

B4 A group is defined by $a^4 = e$, $a^2 = b^2$, $ab = ba^3$. What is the order of this group? Write out the Cayley table and find the period of its elements.

B5 Let G be a group and let H be any non-empty subset of the elements of G. Prove that H is a *subgroup* of G if and only if

$$xy^{-1} \in H \quad \text{for all } x, y \in H.$$

The *centre* C of a group G is defined to be the set of all elements of G which commute with every element of G (that is, $c \in C$ if and only if $gc = cg$ for all $g \in G$). Prove that C is a subgroup of G.

Show that the set of matrices of the form

$$\begin{bmatrix} 1 & p & q \\ 0 & 1 & r \\ 0 & 0 & 1 \end{bmatrix},$$

where p, q, r are rational numbers, forms a group under matrix multiplication. Find the centre of this group. [SMP]

Revision exercise 17

A1 Show that the set $F = \{0, 2, 4, 6, 8\}$ forms a field under addition and multiplication modulo 10.

A2 Solve the following equations in $\mathbb{Z}_{11}$:

(*a*) $2x + 3 = 2$ (*b*) $(x + 3)(x + 4) = 5$ (*c*) $\begin{bmatrix} 4 & 3 \\ 2 & 1 \end{bmatrix}\begin{bmatrix} x \\ y \end{bmatrix} = \begin{bmatrix} 3 \\ 5 \end{bmatrix}$

A3 Does the set of non-singular 2×2 matrices form a field under matrix addition and multiplication?

A4 (*a*) List all the points on the lines $2x + 3y + 4 = 0$ and $x + y + 5 = 0$ in $\mathbb{Z}_7$. Where do these lines intersect?

(*b*) Find the equation of the line containing the points $(1, 4)$ and $(3, 2)$. Is your answer unique?

A5 Prove that in a field $a.b = a.c$ and $a \neq 0 \Rightarrow b = c$. Is this result true in an integral domain?

B1 A Gaussian integer is a complex number of the form $p + jq$, with p, q integers. Prove that the set of all Gaussian integers with the operations of addition and multiplication of complex numbers is a ring.

Is this ring also (*a*) an integral domain, (*b*) a field?

B2 The 'points' of a finite geometry are ordered pairs (x, y) where x and y are elements of $\mathbb{Z}_3$ (i.e. 0, 1 or 2). The 'lines' are sets of distinct points $\{A, B, C\}$ such that

$$A + B + C = (0, 0),$$

where $(x_1, y_1) + (x_2, y_2)$ denotes $(x_1 + x_2, y_1 + y_2)$, the addition being performed modulo 3.

(*a*) Write down all the lines through the point $(0, 0)$.

(*b*) Write down all the lines through the point $(1, 2)$.

(*c*) How many lines are there in all? How many of these lines do *not* meet a given line $\{A, B, C\}$?

(*d*) If $\{A, B, C\}$ is a line and (p, q) is any pair, prove that $\{A + (p, q), B + (p, q), C + (p, q)\}$ is also a line. Prove also that either these two lines are identical or else they have no point in common. [SMP]

B3 The set S consists of all ordered pairs of integers, that is

$$S = \{(m, n): m, n \in \mathbb{Z}\}.$$

The binary operations $\circ$ and $*$ on S are defined by

$$(m_1, n_1) \circ (m_2, n_2) = (m_1 - m_2, n_1 + n_2),$$

$$(m_1, n_1) * (m_2, n_2) = (m_1 m_2, 2n_1 n_2).$$

Determine which of the following statements are true and which are false, giving, in each case, a reason for your answer:

(*a*) The operation $\circ$ is associative.

(*b*) The set S forms a group under the operation $*$.

(*c*) The operation $*$ is distributive over the operation $\circ$.

Find an infinite subset of S which forms a group under $\circ$. Determine, giving reasons, whether or not this subset forms a ring under the operations $\circ$ and $*$. [C]

B4 $(R, +, .)$ is a ring with additive identity 0 and the additive inverse of a is denoted by $\bar{a}$. R contains a 'left identity element' l, i.e. an element such that

$$l.x = x \quad \text{for every } x \in R.$$

Prove that $$(a.l + \bar{a}).x = 0 \quad \text{for any } x, x \in R.$$

(You may use the standard result $\bar{a}.b = \overline{a.b}$ for any $a, b \in R$.)

Deduce that

$$a.l + \bar{a} + l$$

is also a left identity element. Further, show that if R has only *one* left identity element, then

$$a.l = a \quad \text{for any } a \in R.$$ [SMP]

B5 (*a*) Prove that if F_1 and F_2 are subfields of the same field F, then $F_1 \cap F_2$ is also a subfield.

(*b*) Prove that the only subfield of the field of rational numbers $\mathbb{Q}$ is $\mathbb{Q}$ itself.

Revision exercise 18

A1 Complete the following table, indicating whether the relations on the given sets are reflexive, symmetric or transitive.

Set	Relation	Reflexive	Symmetric	Transitive
(*a*) {triangles in the plane}	'have two vertices in common			
(*b*) $\mathbb{Z}^+$	xRy if and only if $xy = n^2$ for some integer n			
(*c*) $\mathbb{R}$	xRy if and only if $x^2 + x = y^2 + y$			
(*d*) $\mathbb{Z}$	xRy if and only if $x^2 \equiv y^2 \pmod 7$			

A2 Give examples of sets and relations which are
(*a*) reflexive but not symmetric or transitive
(*b*) symmetric but not reflexive or transitive
(*c*) transitive but not reflexive or symmetric

A3 The ordered pairs (a, b) and (c, d), where a, b, c, d are positive integers (greater than zero), are said to be in the relationship R if

$$ad - bc = 0.$$

Prove that R is an equivalence relation in the set of all such pairs.
With what type of number can each equivalence class be associated? [SMP]

A4 Solve the following congruence equations:
(*a*) $4x + 5 \equiv 2 \pmod 7$ (*b*) $6x \equiv 5 \pmod 9$
(*c*) $x^2 + 3x + 2 \equiv 0 \pmod 6$ (*d*) $x^2 + 3x + 3 \equiv 0 \pmod 6$

A5 For what positive integers m is it true that if $x^2 \equiv 0 \pmod m$, then $x \equiv 0 \pmod m$?

B1 Determine (giving reasons) which of the following properties define equivalence relations, and state the corresponding equivalence classes:
(*a*) parallelism among the set of straight lines
(*b*) possession of a factor in common among the set of positive integers
(*c*) equality of modulus among the set of complex numbers
(*d*) equality of radius among the set of circles [SMP]

B2 Prove that if m is an odd integer, then $m^2 \equiv 1 \pmod 8$. Hence show that it is not possible to express a positive integer of the form $8k + 7$ as the sum of three squares.

B3 If a and b are non-negative integers and p is a prime number, prove that

$$(a + b)^p \equiv a^p + b^p \pmod p.$$

Hence prove that $a^p \equiv a \pmod p$.

B4 Let S be the set of matrices

$$S = \left\{ \begin{bmatrix} (1 + b) & 2b \\ -\tfrac{1}{2}b & (1 - b) \end{bmatrix} : b \in \mathbb{R} \right\}.$$

A relation R is defined on the set of points in the plane by $(x_1, x_2)R(y_1, y_2)$ if and only if $\begin{bmatrix} x_1 \\ x_2 \end{bmatrix} = \mathbf{A}\begin{bmatrix} y_1 \\ y_2 \end{bmatrix}$ for some $\mathbf{A} \in S$.

(*a*) Show that this relation is an equivalence relation.

(*b*) Describe the set of points in the equivalence class containing the point $(0, 2)$.

B5 For each of the relations $R_1, R_2, \ldots, R_5$ defined below, state whether it is (i) reflexive, (ii) symmetric, (iii) transitive. For each relation which you consider to be an equivalence relation, give the equivalence classes.

(*a*) For $p, q \in \mathbb{N}$, $pR_1q \Leftrightarrow |p-q|$ is odd.

(*b*) For $p, q \in \mathbb{N}$, $pR_2q \Leftrightarrow p+q$ is even.

(*c*) For $p, q \in \mathbb{N}$, $pR_3q \Leftrightarrow p, q$ have a common divisor greater than unity.

(*d*) For $p, q \in \mathbb{Q}$, $pR_4q \Leftrightarrow p, q$ have the same denominator when in their lowest terms with positive denominators.

(*e*) For $p, q \in \{a, b, c, d, e, f\}$, $pR_5q \Leftrightarrow p * q = f$, where the operation $*$ is defined by the following table:

$*$	a	b	c	d	e	f
a	f	e	f	e	e	e
b	e	f	e	f	f	e
c	f	e	f	e	e	e
d	e	f	e	f	f	e
e	e	f	e	f	f	e
f	e	e	e	e	e	f

[C]

Examination questions 2: Chapters 10–19

1 Find the eigenvalues of the matrix **M**, where

$$\mathbf{M} = \begin{bmatrix} 3 & 4 \\ 4 & 3 \end{bmatrix}.$$

Find the corresponding eigenvectors and verify that they are orthogonal. Form an orthogonal matrix **P** such that $\mathbf{P}^{-1}\mathbf{MP}$ is a diagonal matrix, the entries being the eigenvalues. [SMP]

2 Find a basis for the kernel of the linear transformation **T**, where

$$\mathbf{T}: \begin{bmatrix} x \\ y \\ z \\ t \end{bmatrix} \mapsto \begin{bmatrix} 1 & 2 & 1 & 4 \\ 2 & 3 & 1 & 5 \\ 1 & 1 & 0 & 1 \end{bmatrix} \begin{bmatrix} x \\ y \\ z \\ t \end{bmatrix}.$$ [SMP]

3 Find the value of k for which the equations

$$\left.\begin{aligned} w + 2x - y - 3z &= 0 \\ w - x + 2y + 3z &= 0 \\ w + y + kz &= 0 \end{aligned}\right\}$$

have just two linearly independent solutions. Determine the solution set of the equations for this value of k. [SMP]

4 Find a linear relation connecting the rows of the matrix

$$\mathbf{M} = \begin{bmatrix} 1 & 2 & 0 & 3 \\ -2 & 1 & -5 & -1 \\ 0 & -1 & 1 & -1 \end{bmatrix}.$$

State the rank of **M**.

The linear transformation **T** is defined by

$$\mathbf{T}: \begin{bmatrix} x \\ y \\ z \\ t \end{bmatrix} \mapsto \mathbf{M} \begin{bmatrix} x \\ y \\ z \\ t \end{bmatrix}.$$

State the dimension of the kernel of **T**, and find a basis for the range of **T**. [SMP]

5 Is it true that $(x + 1)(x + 4) = x^2 + 5x + 4$

(*a*) in the ring $\mathbb{Z}_9$,

(*b*) in the field $\mathbb{Z}_{11}$?
Give reasons for your answers.
Hence, or otherwise, find all the solutions of

$$x^2 + 5x + 4 = 0$$

in $\mathbb{Z}_{11}$ and in $\mathbb{Z}_9$; indicate your method. [SMP]

6 The non-empty subset S of $\mathbb{Z}$ (with normal arithmetic) is such that

$$m \in S, n \in S \Rightarrow m - n \in S.$$

Show that
(*a*) $0 \in S$, and
(*b*) $m \in S \Rightarrow -m \in S$.
Hence prove that under addition S is an Abelian group. [SMP]

7 You are given that $(R, +, \times)$ is a ring.
By considering the identity $a + 0 = a$, or otherwise, prove directly from the axioms that, for all $a \in R$,

$$a \times 0 = 0 = 0 \times a.$$ [SMP]

8 Show that the set of points (x, y, z) which map to the point $(5, -4)$ under the transformation

$$\begin{bmatrix} x \\ y \\ z \end{bmatrix} \mapsto \begin{bmatrix} 1 & 3 & 5 \\ 2 & -1 & 3 \end{bmatrix} \begin{bmatrix} x \\ y \\ z \end{bmatrix}$$

is a line.
Express the line in the form $\mathbf{r} = \mathbf{a} + t\mathbf{u}$,

where the vectors **a** and **u** should be specified. [SMP]

9 V is a three-dimensional vector space and $\mathbf{T}: V \to V$ is a linear transformation of V. Prove that the vectors of the form

$$\{\mathbf{v} \in V: \mathbf{T}(\mathbf{v}) = \mathbf{0}\} \quad \text{and} \quad \{\mathbf{T}(\mathbf{v}): \mathbf{v} \in V\}$$

give subspaces of V. If $\nu(\mathbf{T})$, $\rho(\mathbf{T})$, respectively, are the dimensions of these spaces, show that

$$\rho(\mathbf{T}) + \nu(\mathbf{T}) = 3.$$

(If you quote a general theorem, you must prove it.)
If $\mathbf{T}^2 = \mathbf{0}$, the zero transformation, show that $\nu(\mathbf{T}) \geqslant 2$ and give a geometrical example for which $\nu(\mathbf{T}) = 2$. [MEI]

10 (*a*) Determine whether each of the following is an equivalence relation:
(i) '$\leqslant$' on the set $\mathbb{Z}$;
(ii) 'is similar to' for the set T of all triangles in a plane;
(iii) 'has the same number of vertices as' for the set P of all polygons in a plane.
(*b*) The set of residue classes of integers modulo 5, with the operations of addition and multiplication modulo 5 is denoted by $(\mathbb{Z}_5, +, .)$. Show, by forming appropriate tables or otherwise, that $(\mathbb{Z}_5, +, .)$ is a field. (You may assume that the distributive axiom is satisfied.)
Solve the equation $x^2 + 2x + 2 = 0$, in which unknown and constants are elements of $\mathbb{Z}_5$. [L]

11 (*a*) Let σ be a linear transformation from $\mathbb{R}^n$ to $\mathbb{R}^m$. Define the *range* of σ and the *null space* of σ. Prove that the range of σ is a subspace of $\mathbb{R}^m$ and that the null space of σ is a subspace of $\mathbb{R}^n$.

(*b*) Find the rank of the matrix **A** where

$$\mathbf{A} = \begin{bmatrix} 2 & -1 & 10 \\ -1 & 4 & -19 \\ 1 & 0 & 3 \\ 5 & 2 & 7 \end{bmatrix}.$$

Find also a basis for the subspace V of $\mathbb{R}^3$ which is defined by

$$V = \{\mathbf{X} \in \mathbb{R}^3 : \mathbf{AX} = \mathbf{0}\}.$$

[C]

12 X is the set $\{a + b\sqrt{2} : a \in \mathbb{Q}, b \in \mathbb{Q}\}$, where $\mathbb{Q}$ is the set of rational numbers. Prove that X, together with the usual operations of addition and multiplication, is a field.

Y is the set of numbers of the form $a + b\sqrt{2}$ where a and b can only take the values 0 and 1. Operations on Y are addition and multiplication, with the coefficients a and b being reduced modulo 2 where necessary. Prove that Y is not a field. [C]

13 (*a*) Show that the set of vectors

$$S = \left\{ \begin{bmatrix} 1 \\ 0 \\ 1 \end{bmatrix}, \begin{bmatrix} 0 \\ -1 \\ 0 \end{bmatrix}, \begin{bmatrix} 0 \\ 1 \\ 2 \end{bmatrix} \right\}$$

forms a basis for the linear (vector) space $\mathbb{R}^3$.

(*b*) L is a linear transformation from $\mathbb{R}^3$ to $\mathbb{R}^2$ defined by

$$L\begin{bmatrix} x \\ y \\ z \end{bmatrix} = \begin{bmatrix} 2x - y \\ x + z \\ 3x - 2y - z \end{bmatrix}.$$

(i) Find the null space of L, and state its dimension.

(ii) Show that
$$L\begin{bmatrix} 1 \\ 0 \\ 1 \end{bmatrix} = 2\begin{bmatrix} 1 \\ 0 \\ 1 \end{bmatrix} - 2\begin{bmatrix} 0 \\ -1 \\ 0 \end{bmatrix},$$

and express
$$L\begin{bmatrix} 0 \\ -1 \\ 0 \end{bmatrix} \text{ and } L\begin{bmatrix} 0 \\ 1 \\ 2 \end{bmatrix}$$

as linear combinations of the vectors of S. [C]

14 The set of all real 2×2 matrices forms a vector space V under addition and multiplication by real scalars. What is the dimension of this space? Find a basis for V.

For each of the following subsets determine whether it is a vector subspace of V:

(*a*) the set A of all 2×2 diagonal matrices;

(*b*) the set B of all symmetric 2×2 matrices;

(*c*) the set C of all singular 2×2 matrices.

In each case, either prove that it is a vector subspace and give a basis for it, or prove that it is not. [O & C]

15 S is the set of all 2×2 matrices. A relation ρ on S is defined as follows: 'given any $\mathbf{X}, \mathbf{Y} \in S$, then $\mathbf{X}\rho\mathbf{Y}$ if and only if a non-singular $\mathbf{M} \in S$ can be found such that

$\mathbf{X} = \mathbf{M}^{-1}\mathbf{Y}\mathbf{M}'$. Prove that ρ is an equivalence relation on S, and determine the equivalence class containing $\begin{bmatrix} 1 & 0 \\ 0 & 1 \end{bmatrix}$.

Determine whether or not the matrices $\begin{bmatrix} 0 & 0 \\ 1 & 1 \end{bmatrix}$ and $\begin{bmatrix} 1 & 1 \\ 1 & 1 \end{bmatrix}$ are in the same equivalence class. [C]

16 For a non-singular square matrix $\mathbf{M}$, show that $\mathbf{A}$ and $\mathbf{M}^{-1}\mathbf{A}\mathbf{M}$ have the same eigenvalues.

The transformation
$$\begin{bmatrix} x \\ y \end{bmatrix} = \mathbf{M}\begin{bmatrix} u \\ v \end{bmatrix}$$
is found to transform the differential equations
$$\left.\begin{aligned} \ddot{x} &= 4x - y \\ \ddot{y} &= 2x + y \end{aligned}\right\} \text{ to } \left\{\begin{aligned} \ddot{u} &= au \\ \ddot{v} &= bv. \end{aligned}\right.$$
Find a pair of possible values for the constants a and b. [SMP]

17 The operations $*$ and $\circ$ are defined over the set $S = \{0, 1, 2, 3\}$ as follows:
$$a * b = a + b + 1 \quad (\text{mod } 4),$$
$$a \circ b = a + b + ab \quad (\text{mod } 4).$$
Construct two tables, one for $*$ and one for $\circ$, on the set S.

Prove that $(S, *, \circ)$ is a commutative ring, and state whether or not it has a unity. State also, with a reason, whether or not $(S, *, \circ)$ is a field. [C]

18 The set P_2 consists of all polynomials in x, of degree less than or equal to 2, and having real coefficients i.e.
$$P_2 = \{ax^2 + bx + c : a, b, c \in \mathbb{R}\}.$$
Show that, with the usual operations of addition and of multiplication by a real number, P_2 is a linear (vector) space over $\mathbb{R}$, of dimension 3.

For each of the following subsets of P_2, determine whether or not it is a subspace, giving brief reasons for your answers. Give a basis for each subset which you consider to be a subspace.

(*a*) $\{f(x) \in P_2 : f(0) = 0\}$
(*b*) $\{f(x) \in P_2 : f(0) = 1\}$
(*c*) $\{f(x) \in P_2 : f(1) = 0\}$
(*d*) $\{f(x) \in P_2 : f(-x) = f(x) \quad \text{for all } x \in \mathbb{R}\}$ [C]

19 A group G of order 6 has identity e, and the other five elements are a, b, a^2, ab, a^2b.
(*a*) Given that $ab^2a = a^2$, prove that $b^2 = e$.
(*b*) Given in addition that $bab = a$, prove that $ab = ba$.
(*c*) Give the above conditions, explain why G is Abelian.
(*d*) Deduce from part (*c*) whether or not G is cyclic. [SMP]

20 (*a*) Given that $\mathbf{A}$ and $\mathbf{B}$, where
$$\mathbf{A} = \begin{bmatrix} 0 & 1 \\ 1 & 0 \end{bmatrix} \text{ and } \mathbf{B} = \begin{bmatrix} 0 & -1 \\ -1 & 0 \end{bmatrix},$$
are two elements of a group of order 4 under the operation of matrix multiplication, find the other two elements of the group. Denoting these two elements by $\mathbf{C}$ and $\mathbf{D}$, draw up a group operation table.

(*b*) The sets S and T are defined by

$$S = \{a + b\sqrt{3} : a, b \in \mathbb{Z}\},$$
$$T = \{a + b\sqrt{3} : a, b \in \mathbb{Q}\}.$$

For each of the above sets, determine whether or not, under the normal rules of addition and multiplication, it is (i) a ring, (ii) a field. Give reasons for your answers.

(The associative, commutative and distributive properties of addition and multiplication may be assumed.) [C]

21 Show that

(*a*) the set of symmetry transformations of the rhombus forms a group;

(*b*) the set of matrices $\{\mathbf{A}, \mathbf{B}, \mathbf{C}, \mathbf{D}\}$, where

$$\mathbf{A} = \begin{bmatrix} 1 & 0 \\ 0 & 1 \end{bmatrix}, \quad \mathbf{B} = \begin{bmatrix} 0 & 1 \\ -1 & 0 \end{bmatrix}, \quad \mathbf{C} = \begin{bmatrix} -1 & 0 \\ 0 & -1 \end{bmatrix}, \quad \mathbf{D} = \begin{bmatrix} 0 & -1 \\ 1 & 0 \end{bmatrix},$$

forms a group under matrix multiplication.

In each case state (i) the identity element, (ii) the inverse of each of the other elements.

State whether or not the groups are isomorphic and justify your answer.

(Associativity may be assumed in each case.) [L]

22 Give two examples of a vector space. In each example give a basis for the space.

Given that $\mathbf{r} = \begin{bmatrix} 1 \\ 2 \\ 3 \end{bmatrix}$ and $\mathbf{s} = \begin{bmatrix} 4 \\ 6 \\ 8 \end{bmatrix}$, write down

(*a*) a vector $\mathbf{u}$ such that $\mathbf{r}$, $\mathbf{s}$ and $\mathbf{u}$ are linearly dependent;

(*b*) a vector $\mathbf{v}$ such that $\mathbf{r}$, $\mathbf{s}$ and $\mathbf{v}$ are linearly independent.

The vectors $\mathbf{r}$ and $\mathbf{s}$ form a basis for the vector space V. Given that $\begin{bmatrix} 8 \\ 19 \\ z \end{bmatrix}$ is an element of this space, find the value of z.

The vector space V is transformed by the linear transformation represented by the matrix $\begin{bmatrix} 1 & 1 & 1 \\ 3 & 1 & 3 \\ 4 & 2 & 4 \end{bmatrix}$ into the vector space V'. Find a basis of the space V' and state its dimension. [L]

23 (*a*) A binary operation $\circ$ is defined on the set of real numbers by

$$a \circ b = 2a + 2b + ab + 2.$$

State whether the following statements are true or false, giving your reasons in each case:

(i) $\circ$ is commutative;
(ii) $\circ$ is associative;
(iii) there is an identity, e, such that $e \circ a = a \circ e = a$;
(iv) if $a \circ b = a \circ c$, then $b = c$.

(*b*) A binary operation $*$ is defined on the set of real numbers by

$$x * y = x + y - 2x^2y^2.$$

Discuss the associativity of $*$, and the existence of an identity and of inverses in the set. [MEI]

24

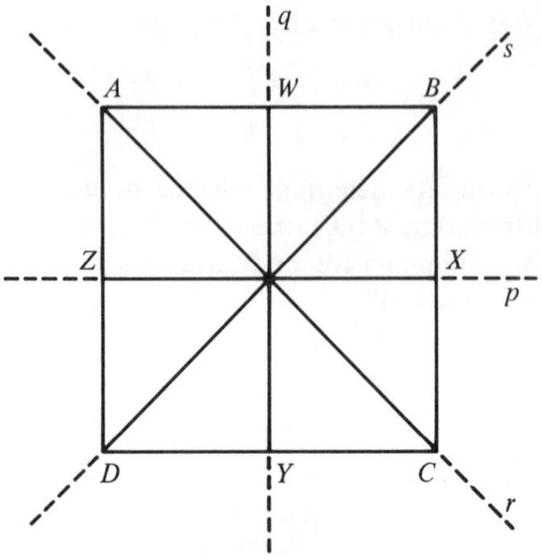

Figure 1

A group G consists of the eight transformations of the square $ABCD$ defined as follows. I, J, K and L are anticlockwise rotations about the centre through angles 0, $\frac{1}{2}\pi$, π and $\frac{3}{2}\pi$ respectively, and P, Q, R and S are reflections in the fixed lines p, q, r and s respectively. Find all the subgroups of G which contain exactly two elements. Show that any subgroup which contains both P and J must contain all eight elements, and find all the subgroups of G which contain exactly four elements. [O]

25 (*a*) Let V and W be subspaces of the linear (vector) space $\mathbb{R}^4$. The set of vectors of the form $\mathbf{v} + \mathbf{w}$, where $\mathbf{v} \in V$ and $\mathbf{w} \in W$ is denoted by $V + W$. Show that $V + W$ is a subspace of $\mathbb{R}^4$.

(*b*) S is the subspace of $\mathbb{R}^4$ spanned by the vectors

$$\{(1,0,1,1), (5,0,2,2), (-2,0,1,1), (3,0 0,0)\}$$

and T is the subspace of $\mathbb{R}^4$ spanned by the vectors

$$\{1,-1,0,1), (0,0,0,0), (0,1,1,0), (0,3,3,0)\}.$$

Give bases for the subspaces S, T, $S \cap T$, $S + T$.

Give also a basis for a subspace U of $\mathbb{R}^4$, which is such that $S \cap U = \{0,0,0,0)\}$ and $S + U = \mathbb{R}^4$. [C]

Examination questions 3: Miscellaneous

1 Let $\mathbf{A} = \begin{bmatrix} 1 & 1 & 2 \\ 0 & 1 & 2 \\ 2 & 2 & 5 \end{bmatrix}$, $\mathbf{B} = \begin{bmatrix} 1 & 1 & 2 \\ 0 & 1 & 2 \\ 0 & 0 & 1 \end{bmatrix}$, $\mathbf{C} = \begin{bmatrix} 1 & 0 & 0 \\ 0 & 1 & 2 \\ 0 & 0 & 1 \end{bmatrix}$.

Find elementary matrices $\mathbf{E}_1$, $\mathbf{E}_2$ and $\mathbf{E}_3$ such that

$$\mathbf{E}_1\mathbf{A} = \mathbf{B}, \quad \mathbf{E}_2\mathbf{B} = \mathbf{C} \quad \text{and} \quad \mathbf{E}_3\mathbf{C} = \mathbf{I},$$

where $\mathbf{I}$ is the unit matrix. Hence, or otherwise, find the inverse matrix of $\mathbf{A}$.

[SMP]

2 The linear transformation of the plane consisting of reflection in the line $y = 2x$ has matrix $\mathbf{M}$. Write down eigenvectors of $\mathbf{M}$ corresponding to the eigenvalues 1 and -1. Use your answers to calculate

$$\mathbf{M}\begin{bmatrix} 1 \\ 0 \end{bmatrix} \quad \text{and} \quad \mathbf{M}\begin{bmatrix} 0 \\ 1 \end{bmatrix}.$$

Hence determine $\mathbf{M}$. [SMP]

3 Evaluate the determinant of the matrix $\begin{bmatrix} 3 & 1 & 2 \\ 1 & 5 & 4 \\ 2 & 3 & 3 \end{bmatrix}$.

What can you deduce about the following set of planes?

$$\begin{aligned} 3x + y + 2z &= 0, \\ x + 5y + 4z &= 0, \\ 2x + 3y + 3z &= 0. \end{aligned}$$

[SMP]

4 The matrix $\mathbf{M}$ is given by $\mathbf{M} = \begin{bmatrix} a & b \\ c & d \end{bmatrix}$, where a, b, c, d are real numbers. Find $\mathbf{M}^2$.

Given that $\mathbf{M}^2 = \mathbf{M}$ and that b and c are non-zero, prove that $\mathbf{M}$ is singular. Prove also that in this case the transformation $\mathbf{T}$, defined by $\mathbf{T}: \begin{bmatrix} x \\ y \end{bmatrix} \mapsto \mathbf{M}\begin{bmatrix} x \\ y \end{bmatrix}$ maps all points of the plane to points of the line $(1 - a)x = by$. [C]

5 Find the values of l, m, n such that the product $\mathbf{BA}$ of the matrices

$$\mathbf{A} = \begin{bmatrix} 1 & 2 & 1 \\ 4 & 1 & 2 \\ -10 & 3 & 4 \end{bmatrix}, \quad \mathbf{B} = \begin{bmatrix} 1 & 0 & 0 \\ l & 1 & 0 \\ m & n & 1 \end{bmatrix}$$

is of the form
$$\mathbf{BA} = \begin{bmatrix} p_1 & q_1 & r_1 \\ 0 & q_2 & r_2 \\ 0 & 0 & r_3 \end{bmatrix}.$$

Hence, or otherwise, solve the set of equations
$$\mathbf{Ax} = \mathbf{y};$$
$$\text{where } \mathbf{x} = \begin{bmatrix} x_1 \\ x_2 \\ x_3 \end{bmatrix} \text{ and } \mathbf{y} = \begin{bmatrix} 0 \\ 8 \\ -4 \end{bmatrix}.$$
[L]

6 **M** denotes the matrix $\begin{bmatrix} 1.36 & 0.48 \\ 0.48 & 1.64 \end{bmatrix}$. A transformation **T** of points of the xy-plane is such that $\mathbf{T}: \begin{bmatrix} x \\ y \end{bmatrix} \mapsto \mathbf{M}\begin{bmatrix} x \\ y \end{bmatrix}$. Show that each point on the line $3x + 4y = 0$ is invariant under **T**.

Verify, showing your working, that $\mathbf{M} = \mathbf{R}^{-1}\mathbf{DR}$, where $\mathbf{D} = \begin{bmatrix} 2 & 0 \\ 0 & 1 \end{bmatrix}$ and $\mathbf{R} = \begin{bmatrix} 0.6 & 0.8 \\ -0.8 & 0.6 \end{bmatrix}$. By considering the effect on $\begin{bmatrix} 1 \\ 0 \end{bmatrix}$ and $\begin{bmatrix} 0 \\ 1 \end{bmatrix}$, or otherwise, describe the geometrical transformations which result when column vectors are multiplied by **D** and by **R**.

Hence, by considering **T** as a sequence of three transformations, or otherwise, find the equation of a line l which is such that **T** maps any point of l, other than the origin, to some different point of l. [C]

7 A transformation of the plane which takes the point (x, y) to the point (x^*, y^*) is given by
$$\begin{bmatrix} x^* \\ y^* \end{bmatrix} = \begin{bmatrix} \alpha & \beta \\ \gamma & \delta \end{bmatrix}\begin{bmatrix} x \\ y \end{bmatrix},$$
where $\alpha, \beta, \gamma, \delta$ are constants and $\alpha\delta \neq \beta\gamma$.

(*a*) Show that if the transformation maps $(1, 0)$ on itself and $(0, 1)$ on itself, then it maps every point of the plane on itself.

(*b*) Show that if the transformation maps P to Q and Q to R and the centroid of the triangle PQR is at the origin, then the transformation maps R to P.

(*c*) By taking P, Q as $(1, 0)$, $(0, 1)$ respectively and choosing R suitably, use part (*b*) to find a 2×2 matrix $\mathbf{A} \neq \mathbf{I}$ such that $\mathbf{A}^3 = \mathbf{I}$. [Oxford Entrance]

8 (*a*) The matrix **A** is square and non-singular, and there exists at least one value of λ for which the equation $\mathbf{Ax} = \lambda\mathbf{x}$ has a non-zero solution **x**. Find the value of the constant μ in each of the following cases:

(i) $\alpha\mathbf{Ax} = \mu\mathbf{x}$, where α is a real constant,

(ii) $\mathbf{A}^2\mathbf{x} = \mu\mathbf{x}$,

(iii) $\mathbf{A}^{-1}\mathbf{x} = \mu\mathbf{x}$,

(iv) $\mathbf{A}^n\mathbf{x} = \mu\mathbf{x}$, where n is a positive integer.

(*b*) Given that
$$\mathbf{A} = \begin{bmatrix} 2 & 0 & 1 \\ 0 & 2 & -1 \\ 1 & -5 & 1 \end{bmatrix},$$

find the values of λ for which

(i) $\mathbf{Ax} = \lambda\mathbf{x}$,
(ii) $\mathbf{A}^3\mathbf{x} = \lambda\mathbf{x}$,
(iii) $\mathbf{A}^{-2}\mathbf{x} = \lambda\mathbf{x}$. [Cambridge Entrance]

9 Find the principal axis of the ellipsoid

$$3x^2 + 6y^2 + 2z^2 - 2xy - 2yz - 2zx = 1$$

associated with the integer eigenvalues of the corresponding matrix. [SMP]

10 For each of the following assertions concerning 2×2 matrices $\mathbf{A}$ and $\mathbf{B}$, state whether it is true or false, justifying your answer:

(*a*) If $\mathbf{A}^2 = \mathbf{A}$, then $\mathbf{A}$ is a singular matrix.

(*b*) For all $\mathbf{A}$, $\mathbf{A}^2 - 5\mathbf{A} + 6\mathbf{I} = (\mathbf{A} - 3\mathbf{I})(\mathbf{A} - 2\mathbf{I})$, where $\mathbf{I}$ is the unit 2×2 matrix.

(*c*) For all $\mathbf{A}$ and $\mathbf{B}$, $\mathbf{A}^2 - 5\mathbf{AB} + 6\mathbf{B}^2 = (\mathbf{A} - 3\mathbf{B})(\mathbf{A} - 2\mathbf{B})$.

(*d*) If $\mathbf{A}$ and $\mathbf{B}$ are symmetric matrices then $\mathbf{AB}$ is also a symmetric matrix. (A symmetric matrix $\mathbf{A}$ satisfies $\mathbf{A}^{\mathrm{T}} = \mathbf{A}$.)

(*e*) If $\mathbf{A} = \begin{bmatrix} \cos\frac{1}{6}\pi & -\sin\frac{1}{6}\pi \\ \sin\frac{1}{6}\pi & \cos\frac{1}{6}\pi \end{bmatrix}$, then $\mathbf{A}^{12} = \mathbf{I}$. [C]

11 The matrix
$$\mathbf{M} = \begin{bmatrix} 1 & -1 & -1 \\ -1 & 3 & -1 \\ -1 & -1 & 3 \end{bmatrix}$$
is used to map all points
$$\mathbf{r} = \begin{bmatrix} x \\ y \\ z \end{bmatrix}$$
in space into points $\mathbf{r}' = \mathbf{Mr}$.

(*a*) Show that every point on the line L defined by $x = -y = -z$ maps into a point on L.

(*b*) Show that all points $\mathbf{r}$ are mapped into a plane Π, and find its equation.

(*c*) Find the line L' in Π which is perpendicular to L and passes through the origin, and show that every point on L' maps into a point on L'. [Oxford Entrance]

12 A 2×2 matrix $\mathbf{A} = \begin{bmatrix} a & b \\ c & d \end{bmatrix}$ has the property $\mathbf{A}^2 = \mathbf{A}$. Show that $a + d = 0$, 1 or 2. Find the matrix $\mathbf{A}$ in the case where $a + d = 2$. When $a + d = 1$ show that $ad - bc = 0$.

Consider the matrix transformation

$$\begin{bmatrix} x' \\ y' \end{bmatrix} = \begin{bmatrix} \frac{1}{2} & \frac{1}{4} \\ 1 & \frac{1}{2} \end{bmatrix} \begin{bmatrix} x \\ y \end{bmatrix}$$

of a point with coordinates (x, y) into a point with coordinates (x', y'). Find the images of the special points $(1, 2)$, $(2, 0)$, $(0, 4)$. Give a geometrical interpretation of the transformation. [Oxford Entrance]

13 When column vectors, representing points in a plane with the usual axes, are premultiplied by the matrix

$$\mathbf{M} = \begin{bmatrix} 3 & -2 \\ 6 & k \end{bmatrix},$$

a transformation of the plane results.

(*a*) If $k = 3$, find (i) the point whose image is $(8, 9)$, (ii) the image of the line $y = x$.
(*b*) If $k = -4$, find (i) the set of points which map onto the origin, (ii) the image of the line $y = \frac{3}{2}x - \frac{1}{2}$. [C]

14 (*a*) Show that the following system of equations is consistent for exactly one value of k. For this value of k find an expression for the most general solutions.

$$\left.\begin{aligned} 2x - 3y + z &= -1 \\ 3x + y - 5z &= 2 \\ x - 7y + 7z &= k \end{aligned}\right\}$$

(*b*) The matrix $\begin{bmatrix} -1 & 2 & -1 \\ 2 & 2 & -2 \\ -1 & -2 & -1 \end{bmatrix}$ has -2 as an eigenvalue. Find the set of real eigenvectors corresponding to this eigenvalue. [O]

15 (*a*) Prove that, when n is a positive integer,

$$\begin{bmatrix} 1 & 0 \\ a & 1 \end{bmatrix}^n = \begin{bmatrix} 1 & 0 \\ na & 1 \end{bmatrix}.$$

Prove that the result also holds when n is a negative integer.
(*b*) The transformation **T** of the xy-plane is defined by

$$\mathbf{T}: \begin{bmatrix} x \\ y \end{bmatrix} \mapsto \begin{bmatrix} a & b \\ c & d \end{bmatrix} \begin{bmatrix} x \\ y \end{bmatrix}.$$

Show that **T** leaves all lines through the origin invariant if and only if $b = c = 0$ and $a = d \neq 0$.
In this case, describe **T** geometrically. [C]

16 Calculate the eigenvalues of the matrix

$$\mathbf{A} = \begin{bmatrix} 1 & 0 & 1 \\ 0 & 2 & 0 \\ 1 & 0 & 3 \end{bmatrix},$$

and find three eigenvectors, $\mathbf{k}_1$, $\mathbf{k}_2$, $\mathbf{k}_3$, of unit length, one for each eigenvalue.
If **S** denotes the 3×3 matrix whose columns are the vectors $\mathbf{k}_1$, $\mathbf{k}_2$, $\mathbf{k}_3$ and $\mathbf{S}'$ denotes the transpose of **S**, verify that
(*a*) $\mathbf{S'S} = \mathbf{SS'} = \mathbf{I}$;
(*b*) $\mathbf{S'AS}$ is a diagonal matrix **D**;
and prove that for any integer $n \geqslant 1$, $\mathbf{A}^n = \mathbf{SD}^n\mathbf{S}'$. [MEI]

17 Prove that a square matrix **A** cannot have more than one inverse.
If **A** is 3×3 and **b** is a 3×1 vector, prove that the equation

$$\mathbf{Ax} = \mathbf{b}$$

has a unique solution for **x** if, and only if, **A** is non-singular.
Find the solution-set of the system of equations

$$\left.\begin{aligned} x + y - \lambda z &= 4 \\ \lambda x - y + z &= -1 \\ 8x - y - z &= 5 \end{aligned}\right\}$$

for those values of λ which do not yield a *unique* solution. [O & C]

18 Reflections in the x- and y-axes are denoted by **X**, **Y** respectively, while reflection in the line $y = x/\sqrt{3}$ is denoted by **M**. It is given that **M** may be represented by the matrix $\begin{bmatrix} \frac{1}{2} & \frac{1}{2}\sqrt{3} \\ \frac{1}{2}\sqrt{3} & -\frac{1}{2} \end{bmatrix}$.

Find the matrix that represents **YMX**. Show that its eigenvalues are ± 1, and find the corresponding eigenvectors. Hence describe geometrically a single transformation equivalent to **YMX**. [SMP]

19 (*a*) Show that if $\mathbf{A} = \begin{bmatrix} p & q \\ r & s \end{bmatrix}$, then

$$\mathbf{A}^2 - (p+s)\mathbf{A} + (ps - qr)\mathbf{I} = \mathbf{0},$$

where **I** is the identity matrix.

(*b*) Given that $\mathbf{X} = \begin{bmatrix} a & b \\ c & d \end{bmatrix}$ and that $\mathbf{X}^2 = \mathbf{0}$, show that **X** can be written either in terms of a and b only or in terms of c only, or of b only.

Show that when **X** is written in terms of c only, the solution can be written in the form

$$\mathbf{X} = c\begin{bmatrix} 0 & -1 \\ 1 & 0 \end{bmatrix}\begin{bmatrix} 1 & 0 \\ 0 & 0 \end{bmatrix}$$

and interpret this result in terms of transformations of the plane represented by these matrices, relating your answer to the fact that $\mathbf{X}^2 = \mathbf{0}$. [MEI]

20 (*a*) Find the eigenvalues and eigenvectors of $\begin{bmatrix} -1 & 2 & 2 \\ 2 & 2 & 2 \\ -3 & -6 & -6 \end{bmatrix}$.

(*b*) Matrices **A** and **B** are *similar* if there exists a non-singular matrix **P** such that

$$\mathbf{B} = \mathbf{P}^{-1}\mathbf{A}\mathbf{P}.$$

By considering the determinant of $\lambda\mathbf{I} - \mathbf{B}$, or otherwise, show that similar matrices have the same eigenvalues.

(*c*) Take the matrix **P** in part (*b*) as the matrix whose columns are the eigenvectors you found in part (*a*). Calculate the corresponding matrix **B**. [MEI]

21 (*a*) **A** is a matrix with eigenvalue λ and corresponding eigenvector **x**. Show that, for every positive integer n, $\mathbf{A}^n\mathbf{x} = \lambda^n\mathbf{x}$. Deduce that if $\mathbf{B} = a\mathbf{A}^2 + b\mathbf{A} + c\mathbf{I}$, then $a\lambda^2 + b\lambda + c$ is an eigenvalue of **B**.

(*b*) Let

$$\mathbf{A} = \begin{bmatrix} 1 & 0 & 0 \\ 1 & 0 & 1 \\ 0 & 1 & 0 \end{bmatrix}.$$

Show that for every integer $n \geqslant 3$,

$$\mathbf{A}^n = \mathbf{A}^{n-2} + \mathbf{A}^2 - \mathbf{I}.$$

Calculate $\mathbf{A}^{50}$. [MEI]

22 A square matrix **B** has an inverse $\mathbf{B}^{-1}$; **B** satisfies

$$\mathbf{B}\mathbf{X} = \lambda\mathbf{X} \qquad (1)$$

for some scalar λ and non-zero column vector **X**. Show that the inverse of **B** satisfies $\mathbf{B}^{-1}\mathbf{X} = \lambda^{-1}\mathbf{X}$.

For $\mathbf{B} = \begin{bmatrix} 3 & 1 \\ 1 & 3 \end{bmatrix}$ show there are exactly two values λ_1, λ_2 such that equation (1) has a solution for $\mathbf{X}$, and find corresponding normalised vectors $\mathbf{X}_1, \mathbf{X}_2$ (a column vector $\begin{bmatrix} x \\ y \end{bmatrix}$ is normalised if $x^2 + y^2 = 1$).

Show that $\lambda_1 \mathbf{X}_1 \mathbf{X}_1{}^{\mathrm{T}} + \lambda_2 \mathbf{X}_2 \mathbf{X}_2{}^{\mathrm{T}} = \mathbf{B}$, where $\mathbf{X}_i{}^{\mathrm{T}}$ is the row vector transpose of $\mathbf{X}_i$, $i = 1, 2$.

Assuming a similar representation for $\mathbf{B}^{-1}$, determine $\mathbf{B}^{-1}$.

[Cambridge Entrance]

23 The linear transformation $\sigma: \mathbb{R}^3 \to \mathbb{R}^3$ is represented by the matrix $\begin{bmatrix} 2 & 1 & 3 \\ 0 & 3 & -3 \\ -1 & 2 & -4 \end{bmatrix}$ with respect to the standard basis of $\mathbb{R}^3$.

(*a*) Show that the range of σ has dimension 2.

(*b*) Show that all points of the line

$$\mathbf{r} = \begin{bmatrix} 3 \\ 0 \\ -1 \end{bmatrix} + \lambda \begin{bmatrix} -2 \\ 1 \\ 1 \end{bmatrix}$$

are mapped to the same point by σ, and find the position vector of this point.

(*c*) Find the subset of $\mathbb{R}^3$ whose image under σ is the point with position vector $\begin{bmatrix} 5 \\ -3 \\ -5 \end{bmatrix}$.

[C]

24 (*a*) Show that the eigenvalues of the matrix $\mathbf{A}$, where

$$\mathbf{A} = \begin{bmatrix} 1 & 0 & -4 \\ 0 & 5 & 4 \\ -4 & 4 & 3 \end{bmatrix},$$

are 3, -3, 9 and find the corresponding eigenvectors, $\mathbf{e}_1$, $\mathbf{e}_2$ and $\mathbf{e}_3$.

Use these eigenvectors to construct a matrix $\mathbf{P}$ such that

$$\mathbf{P}^{\mathrm{T}}\mathbf{A}\mathbf{P} = \begin{bmatrix} 3 & 0 & 0 \\ 0 & -3 & 0 \\ 0 & 0 & 9 \end{bmatrix}.$$

(*b*) Find the quadratic polynomial $\mathbf{X}^{\mathrm{T}}\mathbf{A}\mathbf{X}$, where $\mathbf{X} = \begin{bmatrix} x \\ y \\ z \end{bmatrix}$.

(*c*) The vector $\mathbf{V} = \begin{bmatrix} u \\ v \\ w \end{bmatrix}$ is obtained from $\mathbf{X}$ by the transformation $\mathbf{V} = \mathbf{P}^{\mathrm{T}}\mathbf{X}$.

Express each of u, v and w in terms of x, y and z.

(*d*) Show that

$$\mathbf{X}^{\mathrm{T}}\mathbf{A}\mathbf{X} = \mathbf{V}^{\mathrm{T}}(\mathbf{P}^{\mathrm{T}}\mathbf{A}\mathbf{P})\mathbf{V}$$

and express $\mathbf{X}^{\mathrm{T}}\mathbf{A}\mathbf{X}$ in terms of u^2, v^2 and w^2.

[MEI]

25 Let **A**, **B** and **C** denote 2×2 matrices with entries from the real numbers; **O** denotes the zero matrix $\begin{bmatrix} 0 & 0 \\ 0 & 0 \end{bmatrix}$ and **I** denotes the identity matrix $\begin{bmatrix} 1 & 0 \\ 0 & 1 \end{bmatrix}$. Decide which of the following statements are true and which false. Give proofs of the true ones and examples to demonstrate the falsity of the remaining ones.

(*a*) If $\mathbf{AB} = \mathbf{O}$ then either $\mathbf{A} = \mathbf{O}$ or $\mathbf{B} = \mathbf{O}$.

(*b*) $\mathbf{A}(\mathbf{B} + \mathbf{C}) = \mathbf{AB} + \mathbf{AC}$.

(*c*) If $\det(\mathbf{A}) \neq 0$ then **A** has an inverse.

(*d*) If $\mathbf{AB} = \mathbf{B}$ and $\mathbf{B} \neq \mathbf{O}$, then $\mathbf{A} = \mathbf{I}$.

(*e*) If $\mathbf{AB} = \mathbf{BA}$ for every matrix **B**, then $\mathbf{A} = \begin{bmatrix} \lambda & 0 \\ 0 & \lambda \end{bmatrix}$ for some real number λ.

[Cambridge Entrance]

26 Prove that, in any field, the only solution of the equation $x^2 = 0$ is $x = 0$.

Give an example of each of

(*a*) a field in which the equation $x^2 = a$ has two distinct solutions for every non-zero element a of the field;

(*b*) a field in which the equation $x^2 = a$ has just one solution for each element a of the field. [SMP]

27 Use row operations to reduce the matrix

$$\mathbf{A} = \begin{bmatrix} 1 & 1 & 2 & 7 \\ 2 & 1 & 3 & 2 \\ 4 & 1 & 5 & -8 \end{bmatrix}$$

to a canonical form and hence find the rank of **A**. Find a basis for the kernel and a basis for the range of the transformation represented by **A**. [SMP]

28 Let $\mathbf{c}_1 = \begin{bmatrix} 1 \\ 1 \end{bmatrix}, \mathbf{c}_2 = \begin{bmatrix} -1 \\ 1 \end{bmatrix}, \mathbf{c}_3 = \begin{bmatrix} 2 \\ 1 \end{bmatrix}, \mathbf{c}_4 = \begin{bmatrix} 1 \\ 3 \end{bmatrix}$. Find linear relations between $\mathbf{c}_1, \mathbf{c}_2, \mathbf{c}_3$ and between $\mathbf{c}_2, \mathbf{c}_3, \mathbf{c}_4$. Hence or otherwise, find the kernel of the transformation

$$\begin{bmatrix} x \\ y \\ z \\ t \end{bmatrix} \mapsto \begin{bmatrix} 1 & -1 & 2 & 1 \\ 1 & 1 & 1 & 3 \end{bmatrix} \begin{bmatrix} x \\ y \\ z \\ t \end{bmatrix},$$

and solve the equations
$$\left.\begin{aligned} x - y + 2z + t &= 1 \\ x + y + z + 3t &= 5 \end{aligned}\right\}$$
[SMP]

29 (*a*) Show that the matrix **X**, where $\mathbf{X} = \begin{bmatrix} -2 & 3 \\ 5 & 4 \end{bmatrix}$, belongs to the linear space (over $\mathbb{R}$) spanned by the matrices **A**, **B**, **C**, where

$$\mathbf{A} = \begin{bmatrix} 1 & 0 \\ 2 & 1 \end{bmatrix}, \quad \mathbf{B} = \begin{bmatrix} 1 & -1 \\ 0 & 0 \end{bmatrix}, \quad \mathbf{C} = \begin{bmatrix} -1 & 0 \\ 1 & 2 \end{bmatrix}.$$

Find the dimension of this space.

(*b*) Find a relationship between x, y, z equivalent to the statement that (x, y, z) belongs to the subspace of $\mathbb{R}^3$ spanned by the vectors

$$\mathbf{a} = (1, 2, -1), \quad \mathbf{b} = (3, -1, 3), \quad \mathbf{c} = (1, -5, 5).$$

Find the dimension of this subspace.

(*c*) Determine the value of *a* given that the vectors $\begin{bmatrix}1\\2\\3\end{bmatrix}$, $\begin{bmatrix}-1\\3\\0\end{bmatrix}$, $\begin{bmatrix}a\\1\\2\end{bmatrix}$ do not form a spanning set of $\mathbb{R}^3$. [C]

30 The linear transformation $\sigma: \mathbb{R}^3 \to \mathbb{R}^4$ is represented by the matrix $\begin{bmatrix}1 & 2 & 1\\2 & 0 & 3\\1 & -6 & 3\\6 & -4 & 10\end{bmatrix}$ with respect to the standard bases of $\mathbb{R}^3$ and $\mathbb{R}^4$. Find bases for the null space of σ and for the range of σ.

Obtain the set of vectors in $\mathbb{R}^3$ which are mapped by σ to the vector $\begin{bmatrix}3\\0\\-9\\-6\end{bmatrix}$. [C]

31 The symmetry **S** of the regular octahedron *ABCDEF* shown in the figure takes *C* to *B*, *D* to *E* and *A* to *F*. By taking axes *Oxyz* as shown, find a matrix for **S** and hence decide whether **S** is direct or opposite.

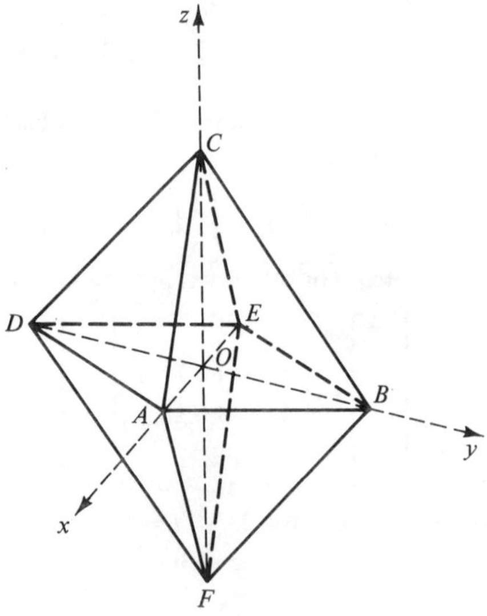

Figure 1 [SMP]

32 Explain what is meant by the statement that the m column vectors $\mathbf{x}_1, \mathbf{x}_2, \ldots, \mathbf{x}_m$, where each vector consists of n elements, are linearly independent.

Find the matrix **A**, where $\mathbf{y} = \mathbf{A}\mathbf{x}$ represents a linear transformation for which

$$\begin{bmatrix}3\\1\\2\end{bmatrix} = \mathbf{A}\begin{bmatrix}1\\0\\0\end{bmatrix}, \quad \begin{bmatrix}2\\3\\1\end{bmatrix} = \mathbf{A}\begin{bmatrix}0\\1\\0\end{bmatrix}, \quad \begin{bmatrix}3\\2\\1\end{bmatrix} = \mathbf{A}\begin{bmatrix}0\\0\\1\end{bmatrix}.$$

Find the images of $\mathbf{x}_1 = \begin{bmatrix} 1 \\ 1 \\ 1 \end{bmatrix}$, $\mathbf{x}_2 = \begin{bmatrix} 4 \\ 3 \\ -1 \end{bmatrix}$, and $\mathbf{x}_3 = \begin{bmatrix} 5 \\ 4 \\ 0 \end{bmatrix}$ under this transformation.

Show that

(*a*) $\mathbf{x}_1$ and $\mathbf{x}_2$ are linearly independent;

(*b*) $\mathbf{Ax}_1$ and $\mathbf{Ax}_2$ are linearly independent;

(*c*) $\mathbf{x}_1$, $\mathbf{x}_2$ and $\mathbf{x}_3$ are linearly dependent. [L]

33 A group, with identity e, is defined in terms of generators a and b by $a^4 = b^2 = e$, $ba = a^3b$. Part of the group table is given below. Copy and complete the table.

	e	a	a^2	a^3	b	ab	a^2b	a^3b
e					b	ab	a^2b	a^3b
a					ab	a^2b	a^3b	b
a^2					a^2b	a^3b	b	ab
a^3					a^3b	b	ab	a^2b
b	b	a^3b	a^2b	ab				
ab	ab	b	a^3b	a^2b				
a^2b	a^2b	ab	b	a^3b				
a^3b	a^3b	a^2b	ab	b				

State the order of each element and the number of subgroups of order 2.

Find

(*a*) a subgroup which is isomorphic to the group $(\{1, 2, 3, 4\}, \times \pmod 5)$,

(*b*) a subgroup which is isomorphic to the group of symmetries of the rectangle. [C]

34

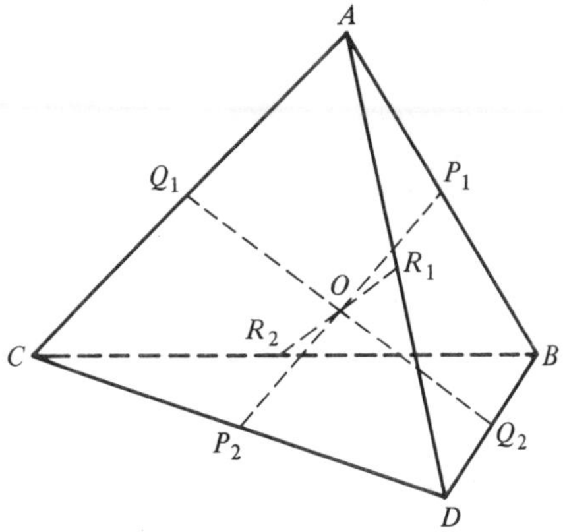

Figure 2

In Fig. 2 P_1, P_2, Q_1, Q_2, R_1, R_2 denote the mid-points of the sides of the regular tetrahedron $ABCD$ with P_1P_2, Q_1Q_2, R_1R_2 meeting at O. Describe geometrically the symmetry operation $\mathbf{T}$ corresponding to the permutation

$$\begin{pmatrix} A & B & C & D \\ D & C & B & A \end{pmatrix}.$$

Deduce the effect of $\mathbf{T}$ on the lines P_1P_2, Q_1Q_2, R_1R_2 and hence, or otherwise, prove that R_1R_2 is orthogonal to the plane containing P_1P_2 and Q_1Q_2. [SMP]

35 Consider the simultaneous differential equations

$$\dot{x} = 2x + 3y, \quad \dot{y} = 2x + y$$

(where x and y are functions of t and dots denote differentiation). These are written in the form

$$\begin{bmatrix} \dot{x} \\ \dot{y} \end{bmatrix} = \mathbf{A}\begin{bmatrix} x \\ y \end{bmatrix}, \quad \text{where } \mathbf{A} = \begin{bmatrix} 2 & 3 \\ 2 & 1 \end{bmatrix}.$$

Find a matrix $\mathbf{P}$ such that $\quad \mathbf{P}^{-1}\mathbf{AP} = \begin{bmatrix} 4 & 0 \\ 0 & -1 \end{bmatrix}.$

Deduce that $\quad \dot{u} = 4u, \quad \dot{v} = -v,$

where $\quad \begin{bmatrix} u \\ v \end{bmatrix} = \mathbf{P}^{-1}\begin{bmatrix} x \\ y \end{bmatrix}.$

Given that $x = 2$ and $y = 3$ when $t = 0$, find the values of u and v when $t = 0$. Express u and v as functions of t, and deduce that the solution of the equations for x and y is

$$x = 3e^{4t} - e^{-t}, \quad y = 2e^{4t} + e^{-t}.$$

[SMP]

36 **M** is the set of matrices of the form $\begin{bmatrix} x & x \\ x & x \end{bmatrix}$, where $x \in \mathbb{Q}$. Prove that **M**, together with the usual operations of matrix addition and multiplication, is a commutative ring with unity. (Associative and distributive properties may be assumed.)

Determine whether **M** is a field. [C]

37 A cube has $ABCD$ and $EFGH$ as parallel faces, and AE, BF, CG, DH as parallel edges (Fig. 3). State the number of rotational symmetries of the cube, giving reasons for your answer. List the possible angles of rotation. What is the number of opposite isometries of the cube?

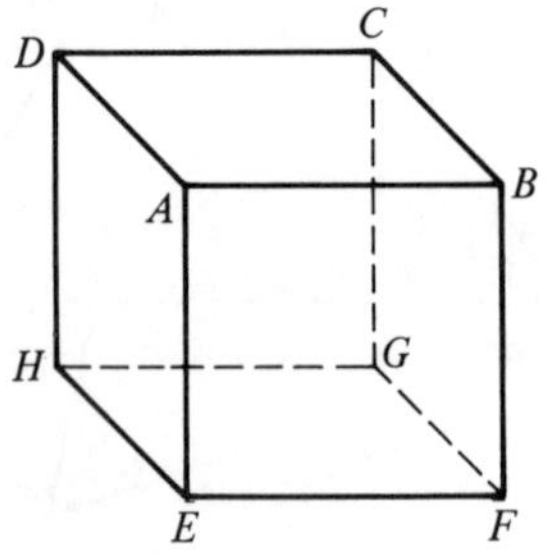

Figure 3

The midpoints of BC, CD, DH, HE, EF, FB are denoted by P, Q, R, S, T, U respectively. Prove that these six points are equidistant from A and G, and deduce that they are coplanar. Find a rotational symmetry of the cube of period 3 which maps $P \to R \to T \to P$, and $Q \to S \to U \to Q$; also find an opposite isometry of the cube of period 2 which maps $P \leftrightarrow S$, $Q \leftrightarrow T$ and $R \leftrightarrow U$. By combining these two isometries, find an opposite isometry of the cube which defines a rotational symmetry of $PQRSTU$. [SMP]

38 If $\mathbf{A} = \begin{bmatrix} j & 0 \\ 0 & -j \end{bmatrix}$ and $\mathbf{B} = \begin{bmatrix} 0 & -1 \\ 1 & 0 \end{bmatrix}$, show that $\mathbf{A}^4 = \mathbf{I}, \mathbf{B}^2 = \mathbf{A}^2, \mathbf{BA} = \mathbf{A}^3\mathbf{B}$ ($\mathbf{I}$ is the unit 2×2 matrix).

Find the order of the group G generated by $\mathbf{A}$ and $\mathbf{B}$, that is, the number of distinct matrices that can be formed by taking products of $\mathbf{A}$'s and $\mathbf{B}$'s in any order.

Find all the subgroups of G of order 4. [O]

39 Verify that the matrices

$$\mathbf{M} = \begin{bmatrix} 2 & 1 & 2 \\ 1 & 2 & -2 \\ -2 & 2 & 1 \end{bmatrix}, \quad \mathbf{L} = \frac{1}{9}\begin{bmatrix} 2 & 1 & -2 \\ 1 & 2 & 2 \\ 2 & -2 & 1 \end{bmatrix}$$

are inverses of each other.

Prove that lines OA, OB, OC drawn from the origin and represented by the vectors

$$\begin{bmatrix} 2 \\ 1 \\ -2 \end{bmatrix}, \quad \begin{bmatrix} 1 \\ 2 \\ 2 \end{bmatrix} \quad \text{and} \quad \begin{bmatrix} 2 \\ -2 \\ 1 \end{bmatrix}$$

respectively, form three edges of a cube. A rotation about the diagonal OD, represented by

$$\begin{bmatrix} x \\ y \\ z \end{bmatrix} \mapsto \mathbf{P}\begin{bmatrix} x \\ y \\ z \end{bmatrix},$$

maps A to B, B to C and C to A. Write down the matrix $\mathbf{PM}$, and deduce the matrix $\mathbf{P}$.

If

$$\mathbf{T} = \begin{bmatrix} 0 & 0 & 1 \\ 1 & 0 & 0 \\ 0 & 1 & 0 \end{bmatrix},$$

verify that $\mathbf{P} = \mathbf{MTM}^{-1}$, and give a geometric interpretation of this relationship. Give a geometrical reason why $\mathbf{P}$ and $\mathbf{T}$ have the same set of eigenvalues.

Calculate the eigenvalues of $\mathbf{T}$, and verify that one of them is equal to $\cos(\frac{2}{3}\pi) + j\sin(\frac{2}{3}\pi)$. Find corresponding eigenvectors, and deduce a set of eigenvectors for $\mathbf{P}$. [SMP]

40 For each of the following five assertions, relating to the given vectors $\mathbf{X}_1, \mathbf{X}_2, \mathbf{X}_3, \mathbf{X}_4$ (not necessarily distinct) in $\mathbb{R}^3$, state whether the assertion is false or true. Give a proof of each assertion you state to be true, and give a counter-example for each assertion you state to be false.

(*a*) Given that $\mathbf{X}_1 \neq \mathbf{0}$, then the set of vectors of the form $a\mathbf{X}_1$, where $a \in \mathbb{R}$, is a one-dimensional subspace of $\mathbb{R}^3$.

(*b*) Given that $\mathbf{X}_1, \mathbf{X}_2$ are linearly independent, then the set of all vectors of the form $a\mathbf{X}_1 + b\mathbf{X}_2$, where $a, b \in \mathbb{R}$, is a two-dimensional subspace of $\mathbb{R}^3$.

(*c*) Given that $\mathbf{X}_1, \mathbf{X}_2$ are linearly dependent, then the set of all vectors of the form $a\mathbf{X}_1 + b\mathbf{X}_2$, where $a, b \in \mathbb{R}$, is not a subspace of $\mathbb{R}^3$.

(*d*) Given that $\mathbf{X}_1, \mathbf{X}_2, \mathbf{X}_3$ are linearly dependent, then the set of all vectors of the form $a\mathbf{X}_1 + b\mathbf{X}_2 + c\mathbf{X}_3$, where $a, b, c \in \mathbb{R}$, is a two-dimensional subspace of $\mathbb{R}^3$.

(*e*) Given that $\mathbf{X}_1, \mathbf{X}_2, \mathbf{X}_3$ are linearly independent, then $\mathbf{X}_4$ can be expressed uniquely as a linear combination of $\mathbf{X}_1, \mathbf{X}_2, \mathbf{X}_3$. [C]

41 A matrix $\mathbf{A}$ is orthogonal if $\mathbf{A}^T\mathbf{A} = \mathbf{I}$, where $\mathbf{A}^T$ is the transpose of $\mathbf{A}$ and $\mathbf{I}$ is the identity matrix.

(*a*) Show that if $\mathbf{A}$ is a 3×3 orthogonal matrix, then

(i) $\det(\mathbf{A}) = \pm 1$,

(ii) the rows and the columns of $\mathbf{A}$ each form a set of orthogonal vectors of length unity.

(*b*) If $\mathbf{x} = \begin{bmatrix} x_1 \\ x_2 \\ x_3 \end{bmatrix}$, write down $\mathbf{x}^T\mathbf{x}$.

Show that a matrix $\mathbf{A}$ is orthogonal if, and only if, the transformation

$$\mathbf{y} = \mathbf{A}\mathbf{x}$$

is such that the length of the vector $\mathbf{y}$ is the same as the length of the vector $\mathbf{x}$.

Verify this result in the case when $\mathbf{A} = \begin{bmatrix} \frac{1}{\sqrt{2}} & \frac{-1}{\sqrt{2}} \\ \frac{1}{\sqrt{2}} & \frac{1}{\sqrt{2}} \end{bmatrix}$. [MEI]

42 Prove that, if a and b are distinct elements of a field, then

$$a^2 = b^2 \quad \Leftrightarrow \quad a + b = 0.$$

(You may assume that, if x and y are elements of a field, then

$$xy = 0 \quad \Leftrightarrow \quad \text{either } x = 0 \text{ or } y = 0.)$$

Deduce that, if p is an *odd* prime number, there are exactly $\frac{1}{2}(p + 1)$ perfect squares in the finite field $\mathbb{Z}_p$. What is the corresponding result when $p = 2$?

Prove further that, if a and b are distinct elements of a field, then

$$a^4 = b^4 \quad \Leftrightarrow \quad \text{either } a + b = 0 \text{ or } a^2 + b^2 = 0.$$

Show that, if there is an element q in $\mathbb{Z}_p$ such that $q^2 = -1$, then $a = \lambda$, $b = q\lambda$ satisfy $a^2 + b^2 = 0$ for all λ in $\mathbb{Z}_p$.

Verify that in $\mathbb{Z}_{29}$ the element $q = 12$ has the property $q^2 = -1$, and hence write down four elements in the field whose fourth powers are equal to 1. Without calculating any further powers, deduce six other sets of four elements in this field such that all the elements of each set have the same fourth power. How many different fourth powers are there in $\mathbb{Z}_{29}$? [SMP]

43 Let V and W be subspaces of $\mathbb{R}^n$. Show that $V \cap W$ is also a subspace of $\mathbb{R}^n$. Find a basis for $V \cap W$ in the following cases:

(*a*) $V = \{(x_1, x_2, x_3, x_4) \in \mathbb{R}^4 : x_1 = x_3 = 0\}$
$W = \{(x_1, x_2, x_3, x_4) \in \mathbb{R}^4 : x_4 = 2x_2\}$

(*b*) $V = \{(x_1, x_2, x_3, x_4) \in \mathbb{R}^4 : x_1 + 2x_2 = 0\}$
$W = \{(x_1, x_2, x_3, x_4) \in \mathbb{R}^4 : 7x_4 = 3x_2\}$

(*c*) $V = \left\{\mathbf{X} \in \mathbb{R}^3 : \mathbf{AX} = \mathbf{0}, \quad \text{where } \mathbf{A} = \begin{bmatrix} 1 & 2 & 1 \\ 0 & 1 & 3 \end{bmatrix}\right\}$

$W = \left\{\mathbf{X} \in \mathbb{R}^3 : \mathbf{BX} = \mathbf{0}, \quad \text{where } \mathbf{B} = \begin{bmatrix} 2 & 1 & -7 \\ -4 & -2 & 14 \end{bmatrix}\right\}$ [C]

44 The set of all 2×2 matrices is denoted by S. The relations $\rho_1, \rho_2, \rho_3, \rho_4$ are defined on S as follows:

$$\mathbf{A}\rho_1\mathbf{B} \Leftrightarrow \mathbf{A}^{\mathrm{T}} = \mathbf{B}$$

$$\mathbf{A}\rho_2\mathbf{B} \Leftrightarrow \mathbf{AB} = \mathbf{BA}$$

$$\mathbf{A}\rho_3\mathbf{B} \Leftrightarrow \mathbf{AB} = \mathbf{I} \quad \text{(where } \mathbf{I} \text{ is the } 2 \times 2 \text{ identity matrix)}$$

$$\mathbf{A}\rho_4\mathbf{B} \Leftrightarrow \text{non-singular } 2 \times 2 \text{ matrices } \mathbf{P} \text{ and } \mathbf{Q} \text{ can be found such that } \mathbf{B} = \mathbf{PAQ}.$$

Show, by counter-examples, that ρ_1, ρ_2 and ρ_3 are not equivalence relations.

Prove that ρ_4 is an equivalence relation and that all non-singular matrices in S belong to the same equivalence class. [C]

45 The set **S** consists of all matrices of the form $\begin{bmatrix} a & b \\ c & d \end{bmatrix}$, where $a, b, c, d \in \mathbb{Z}_5$. The operations $\otimes$ and $\oplus$, defined on S, denote matrix multiplication and matrix addition respectively, with the arithmetic performed modulo 5. The operation $\otimes$ is distributive over $\oplus$, and both operations are associative . Given that $\mathbf{J} = \begin{bmatrix} 1 & 3 \\ 4 & 2 \end{bmatrix}$, evaluate **K**, **L**, **M**, **N**, where $\mathbf{K} = \mathbf{J} \otimes \mathbf{J}$, $\mathbf{L} = \mathbf{K} \otimes \mathbf{J}$, $\mathbf{M} = \mathbf{L} \otimes \mathbf{J}$, $\mathbf{N} = \mathbf{M} \otimes \mathbf{J}$, and show that the set $\{\mathbf{J}, \mathbf{K}, \mathbf{L}, \mathbf{M}\}$ forms a cyclic group under the operation $\otimes$.

Evaluate $\mathbf{J} \oplus \mathbf{J}$, $\mathbf{K} \oplus \mathbf{J}$, $\mathbf{L} \oplus \mathbf{J}$, $\mathbf{M} \oplus \mathbf{J}$, $\mathbf{O} \oplus \mathbf{J}$, where $\mathbf{O} = \begin{bmatrix} 0 & 0 \\ 0 & 0 \end{bmatrix}$.

Show that $(T, \oplus, \otimes)$ is a field, where $T = \{\mathbf{O}, \mathbf{J}, \mathbf{K}, \mathbf{L}, \mathbf{M}\}$. [C]

46 A group G has exactly nine elements and is *not* cyclic. Prove that all the elements other than the identity i have the same period (order), and state its value.

Two elements of G other than the identity are denoted by x and y, and y is not equal to either x or x^2. Prove that y^2 is not equal to either x or x^2.

Prove further that xy is not equal to any of the elements x, x^2, y or y^2.

Prove that the assumption that $xy = yx^2$ leads to the conclusions $(xy)^2 = y^2$ and $(xy)^3 = x$; explain why this is false. Prove similarly that the assumptions (*a*) $xy = y^2x$ and (*b*) $xy = y^2x^2$ both lead to contradictions.

It can in fact be proved that the nine elements $i, x, x^2, y, y^2, yx, yx^2, y^2x$ and y^2x^2 are all different. Deduce that G is commutative, and hence that all groups having exactly nine elements are commutative. [SMP]

47 Explain why the set X of all 2×2 matrices (whose elements are real numbers) forms a vector space of dimension 4 (over the real numbers).

For a fixed 2×2 matrix **A**, define linear transformations $\mathbf{L}_{\mathrm{A}}$, $\mathbf{R}_{\mathrm{A}}$ from X to itself by

$$\mathbf{L}_{\mathrm{A}}(\mathbf{B}) = \mathbf{AB}, \quad \mathbf{R}_{\mathrm{A}}(\mathbf{B}) = \mathbf{BA}.$$

State a condition on **A** which determines whether or not $\mathbf{L}_{\mathrm{A}}$ is one-to-one.

Given that
$$\mathbf{A} = \begin{bmatrix} 1 & -2 \\ -3 & 6 \end{bmatrix},$$

find the dimension of the kernel of $\mathbf{L}_{\mathrm{A}}$. Show that the kernel of $\mathbf{L}_{\mathrm{A}}\mathbf{R}_{\mathrm{A}}$ consists of all matrices

$$\mathbf{B} = \begin{bmatrix} p & q \\ r & s \end{bmatrix}$$

in X which satisfy the condition

$$p - 3q - 2r + 6s = 0.$$

Find the range of $\mathbf{L}_{\mathrm{A}}\mathbf{R}_{\mathrm{A}}$. [SMP]

48 Two 2×2 matrices, $\mathbf{A}$ and $\mathbf{B}$, are said to be *similar* if there exists a non-singular matrix $\mathbf{P}$ such that $\mathbf{B} = \mathbf{P}^{-1}\mathbf{A}\mathbf{P}$. Prove the following assertions:

(*a*) Any matrix $\mathbf{A}$ is similar to itself.

(*b*) If $\mathbf{A}$ is similar to $\mathbf{B}$, and $\mathbf{B}$ is similar to $\mathbf{C}$, then $\mathbf{A}$ is similar to $\mathbf{C}$.

(*c*) If $\mathbf{A}$ is similar to $\mathbf{B}$, then $\mathbf{A}^k$ is similar to $\mathbf{B}^k$ for any positive integer k.

(*d*) If $\mathbf{A}$ is non-singular and similar to $\mathbf{B}$, then $\mathbf{B}$ is non-singular and $\mathbf{A}^{-1}$ is similar to $\mathbf{B}^{-1}$.

(*e*) If $\mathbf{A}$ is similar to $\mathbf{B}$, then $\mathbf{A}$ and $\mathbf{B}$ have the same eigenvalues.

(*f*) The matrix $\begin{bmatrix} 1 & \alpha \\ 0 & 1 \end{bmatrix}$ cannot be similar to a diagonal matrix if $\alpha \neq 0$. [O & C]

49 Denote by $\mathbf{L}$ the mapping which relates the function $f(x)$ to the function

$$x^2 f''(x) - (2x^2 - x)f'(x) + (x^2 - x - 1)f(x),$$

so that, for example, $\mathbf{L}(x^2) = x^4 - 5x^3 + 3x^2.$

Show that $\mathbf{L}$ satisfies the conditions for a linear mapping.

Determine the image under $\mathbf{L}$ of the functions (i) $f(x) = x^n$, (ii) $f(x) = e^x$, (iii) $f(x) = x^n e^x$. Use (ii) to find two linearly independent functions in the kernel of $\mathbf{L}$. Given that this kernel is two-dimensional, write down an expression for *any* function in the kernel of $\mathbf{L}$. Hence find the general solutions of the differential equations

(*a*) $x^2 \dfrac{d^2y}{dx^2} - (2x^2 - x)\dfrac{dy}{dx} + (x^2 - x - 1)y = e^x$

(*b*) $x^2 \dfrac{d^2y}{dx^2} - (2x^2 - x)\dfrac{dy}{dx} + (x^2 - x - 1)y = x^2 e^x$

(*c*) $x^2 \dfrac{d^2y}{dx^2} - (2x^2 - x)\dfrac{dy}{dx} + (x^2 - x - 1)y = x^3 - 3x^2$ [SMP]

50 Sketch, in two separate diagrams, the graphs of the periodic functions

$$y = f(x), \quad y = g(x),$$

where

$$f(x) = \sin \pi x, \quad 0 \leqslant x < 1$$

$$g(x) = \begin{cases} \cos \pi x, & 0 < x < 1 \\ 0, & x = 0, \end{cases}$$

and for all x, $f(x + 1) = f(x), \quad g(x + 1) = g(x).$

Two of the symmetries of the graph of $y = f(x)$ are the reflections $\mathbf{P}$ and $\mathbf{Q}$ in the lines $x = 0$ and $x = \frac{1}{2}$ respectively. What symmetries of the graph are represented by (*a*) $\mathbf{PP}$, (*b*) $\mathbf{QP}$, (*c*) $\mathbf{PQ}$, (*d*) $\mathbf{PQP}$, (*e*) $\mathbf{QPQP}$, (*f*) $\mathbf{QPQPQ}$? (Adopt the usual convention that the transformation written on the right is performed first.) Describe the complete set of symmetries of the graph of $y = f(x)$, and show that they can all be generated from $\mathbf{P}$ and $\mathbf{Q}$.

Find two symmetries $\mathbf{R}, \mathbf{S}$ of the graph of $y = g(x)$ such that $\mathbf{RR}, \mathbf{SS}, \mathbf{SR}$ represent the same transformations as $\mathbf{PP}, \mathbf{QQ}, \mathbf{QP}$ respectively. Are the symmetry groups of the two graphs isomorphic to each other? [SMP]

Projects 5–6

PROJECT 5 COMBINATIONS OF ISOMETRIES

As this project relies heavily on the result that 'every isometry of the plane can be expressed as a combination of a number of reflections' we begin by investigating what happens when two reflections and then three reflections are combined.

You might like to try to complete the following statements for yourself before working through the explanations that follow.

Two reflections

As reflection is an opposite isometry, two reflections will give a direct isometry, that is, either a translation or a rotation.

Notation: **L** and **M** are reflections in lines l and m.

With the isometry **ML** there are three cases to consider:

(1) If $l = m$, the isometry **ML** is . . . .

(2) If l is parallel to m, the isometry **ML** is . . . .

Choose a convenient coordinate system; for example, line l has equation $x = 0$ and line m has equation $x = d$.

If P is the point (x, y), then

$$\begin{aligned}\mathbf{ML}(P) &= \mathbf{ML}(x, y)\\ &= \mathbf{M}(-x, y)\\ &= (2d + x, y),\end{aligned}$$

so **ML** is a translation in the direction perpendicular to the lines, through twice the distance between them.

(3) If l and m meet in a point, the isometry **ML** is . . . .

Choose the point of intersection of l and m as the origin and use polar coordinates.

If l has polar equation $\theta = 0$, m has the polar equation $\theta = \alpha$ and P is the point (r, θ), then

$$\begin{aligned}\mathbf{ML}(P) &= \mathbf{ML}(r, \theta)\\ &= \mathbf{M}(r, -\theta)\\ &= (r, 2\alpha + \theta),\end{aligned}$$

so **ML** is a rotation about the point of intersection of the lines and through twice the angle between them.

So a translation can be replaced by two reflections in parallel lines, and a rotation by two reflections in intersecting lines.

Three reflections

Three reflections will give an opposite isometry, which is therefore a reflection or a glide-reflection. A glide-reflection is equivalent to a reflection in a line, followed by a translation parallel to the line. Since a translation can be replaced by two reflections, a glide reflection is equivalent to three reflections.

Notation: **L**, **M**, **N** are reflections in the lines l, m, n.

With the isometry **NML** there are four cases to consider:

(1) If l, m and n are all parallel, the isometry **NML** is . . . .

$$\begin{aligned} \mathbf{NML} &= \mathbf{NT}, && \text{where } \mathbf{T} \text{ is a translation,} \\ &= \mathbf{NNL}_1, && \text{where } \mathbf{T} = \mathbf{NL}_1,\ l \text{ being a line parallel to } n, \\ &= \mathbf{L}_1, \end{aligned}$$

so **NML** reduces to a single reflection in a line parallel to the three original lines.

(2) If l, m and n meet in a single point O, the isometry **NML** is . . . .

$$\begin{aligned} \mathbf{NML} &= \mathbf{NR}, && \text{where } \mathbf{R} \text{ is a rotation with centre } O, \\ &= \mathbf{NNL}_2, && \text{where } \mathbf{R} = \mathbf{NL}_2 \text{ for some reflection } \mathbf{L}_2, \\ &= \mathbf{L}_2, \end{aligned}$$

so **NML** reduces to a single reflection.

(3) If two, but not all three, of l, m, n are parallel, the isometry **NML** is . . . .
(*a*) If m and n are parallel, then

$$\begin{aligned} \mathbf{NML} &= \mathbf{TL}, && \text{where } \mathbf{T} \text{ is a translation,} \\ &= \mathbf{T}_{\parallel}\mathbf{T}_{\perp}\mathbf{L}, && \text{where } \mathbf{T} \text{ is replaced by its components } \mathbf{T}_{\parallel} \\ & && \text{and } \mathbf{T}_{\perp}, \text{ parallel and perpendicular to } l, \\ &= \mathbf{T}_{\parallel}\mathbf{PQL}, && \text{where } \mathbf{T}_{\perp} = \mathbf{PQ},\ p \text{ and } q \text{ being lines parallel to } l, \\ &= \mathbf{T}_{\parallel}\mathbf{L}, && \text{using result (1)} \end{aligned}$$

so **NML** reduces to a glide-reflection.

(*b*) If l and m are parallel, a similar case arises.

(*c*) If l and n are parallel, then $\mathbf{NML} = \mathbf{NLL}_3$,

where l and m are replaced by the lines l and l_3 which meet in the same point, which is the case (*a*) above.

(4) If the three lines form a triangle, the isometry **NML** is . . . .

Replace lines m and n by lines m_1 and n_1 meeting at the same point and containing the same angle. Also choose m_1 so that it is parallel to l.

So $\mathbf{NML} = \mathbf{N_1M_1L}$, which is the same as case (3);

that is, **NML** reduces to a glide-reflection.

Therefore reflections in three lines reduce to a glide-reflection unless the lines are parallel or concurrent, in which cases they reduce to a reflection.

Combinations of isometries

We have shown that

(1) A translation can be written as a combination of two reflections in parallel lines.

(2) A rotation can be written as a combination of two reflections in intersecting lines.

(3) A glide-reflection can be written as a combination of three reflections.

So any combination of isometries can be investigated as combinations of reflections.

Example

What is the combination of two rotations? (*Notation:* **R** is a rotation through angle θ with centre A; **S** is a rotation through angle ϕ with centre B.)

Solution

(1) If A and B are the same point, then **SR** is a rotation through angle $\theta + \phi$, with centre A.

(2) If A and B are different points and l is the line AB, then

$$\mathbf{R} = \mathbf{LM},$$

where the line m passes through A and the angle between m and l is $\frac{1}{2}\theta$

and $$\mathbf{S} = \mathbf{NL},$$

where the line n passes through B and the angle between l and n is $\frac{1}{2}\phi$,

so $$\mathbf{SR} = (\mathbf{NL})(\mathbf{LM})$$
$$= \mathbf{NM}.$$

The angle between m and n is $\frac{1}{2}(\theta + \phi)$, so **SR** is equivalent to a rotation through angle $(\theta + \phi)$ with centre the point of intersection of lines m and n. What happens if $\theta + \phi = 0°$ or $360°$? □

Exercise

Use this approach to investigate what happens with other combinations of isometries, for example:

(*a*) a rotation and a translation

(*b*) a reflection and a translation
(*c*) a rotation and a reflection
(*d*) a glide-reflection and a rotation
(*e*) a glide-reflection and a reflection
(*f*) two glide-reflections

PROJECT 6 PATTERNS

Geometric design is all around us: tiles on a floor, bricks in a wall, wallpaper patterns, fabric designs, iron work, etc. In this project we are going to look at the infinite patterns which arise as a result of the systematic repetition of a 'motif'. The aim is to generate the different patterns which can arise, and not to prove any results about them. The interested reader can consult some of the more specialised books, for example, *Introduction to Geometry* by H. S. M. Coxeter (Wiley, 1961).

'Frieze' (or strip) patterns

While there is no limit to the choice of 'motif', it is at first surprising to find that there are only seven distinct ways of combining isometries to generate an infinite strip pattern. Taking the motif as 'K', these are shown in Fig. 1.

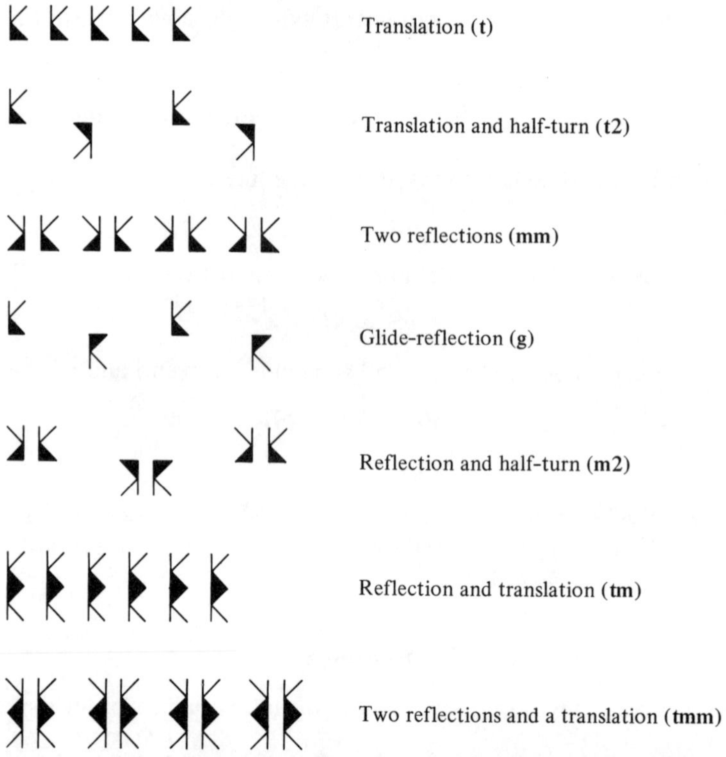

Figure 1

Notation

t: translation
m: reflection
g: glide-reflection
2: rotation of order 2, that is, a half-turn

Exercise A

1 Classify the following frieze patterns:

(*a*) ...H H H H... (*b*) ...T ⊥ T ⊥ T ⊥... (*c*) ...I I I I I...
(*d*) ...L L L L... (*e*) ...N N N N N... (*f*) ...V ∧ V ∧ V ∧...
(*g*) ...X X X X... (*h*) ...P P P P P... (*i*) ...P d P d P d...
(*j*) ...S S S S... (*k*) ...O O O O... (*l*) the sine curve

2 Construct examples of the seven frieze patterns using the flag motif .

3 Repeat question 2 with a motif of your own choice.

'Wallpaper' (or plane) patterns

In two dimensions there are 17 distinct patterns which can arise. Five of these patterns involve only direct isometries, while the other 12 patterns involve at least one opposite isometry. Taking the motif as , these are shown in Fig. 2.

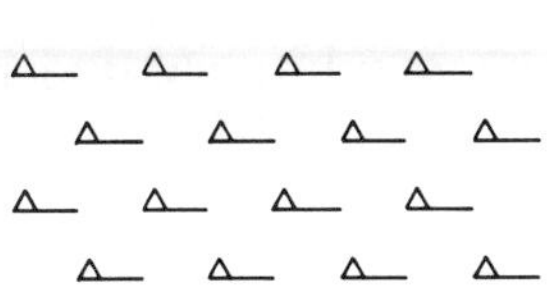

Two translations (**p1**)

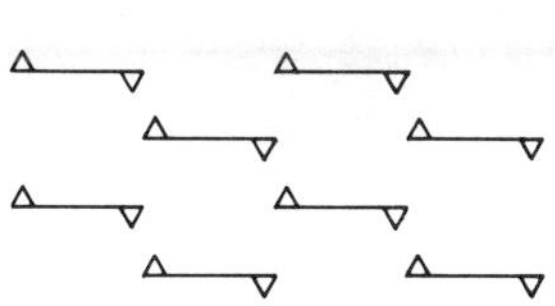

Half-turn and two translations (**p2**)

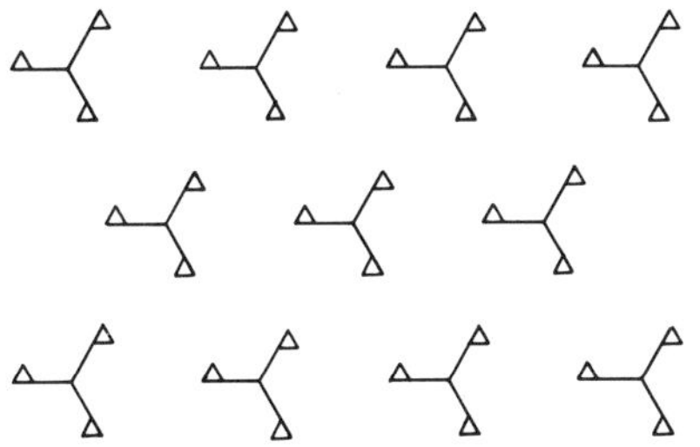

Rotation through 120° and translations (**p3**)

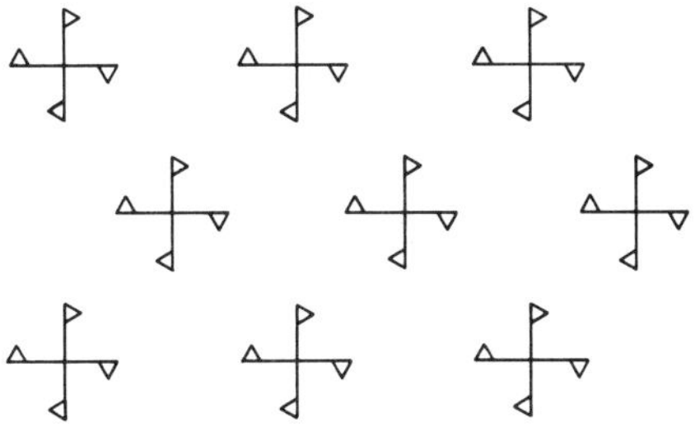

Rotation through 90° and translations (**p4**)

Figure 2

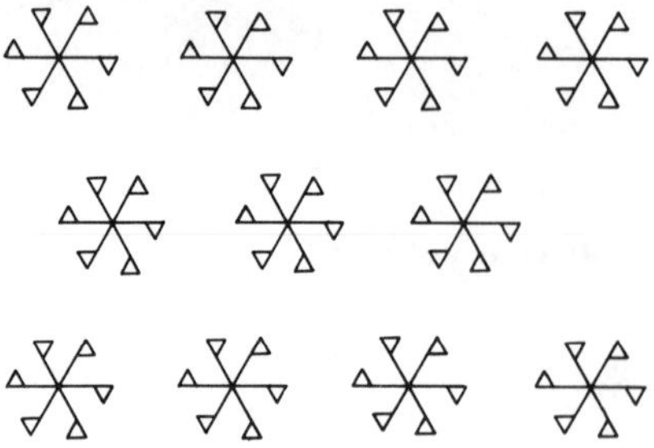

Rotation through 60° and translations (**p6**)

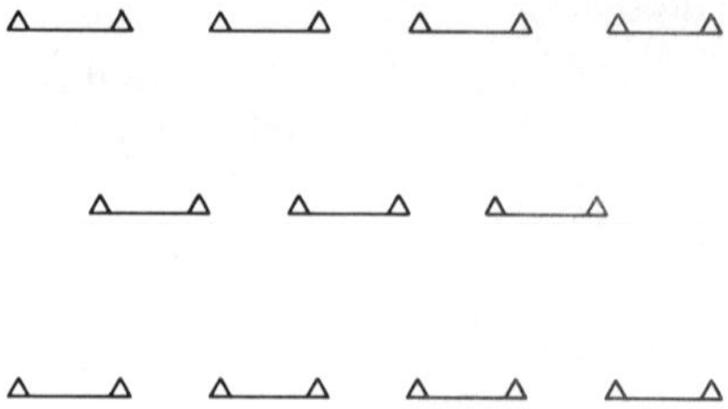

Reflection and translations (**pm**)

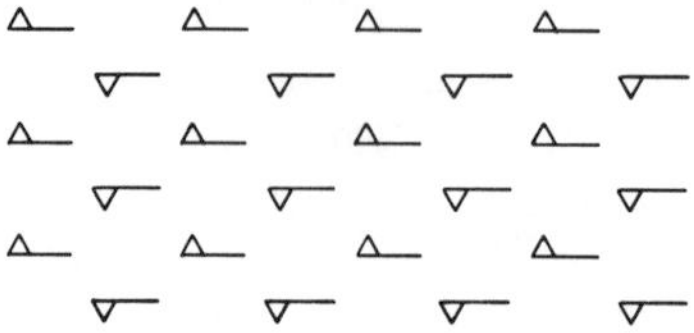

Glide-reflection and translations (**pg**)

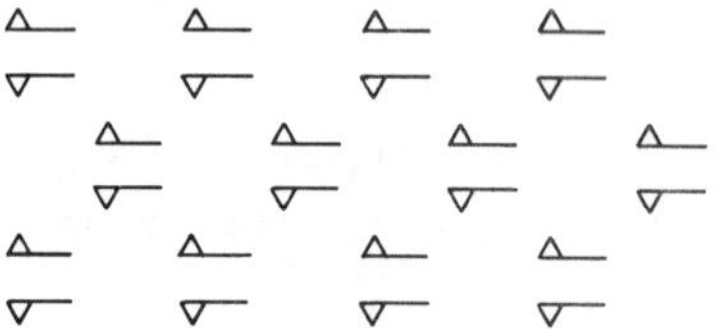

Reflection and parallel glide-reflection (**cm**)

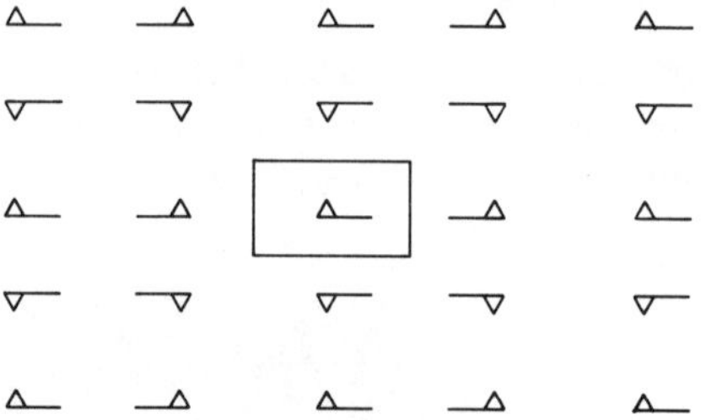

Reflections in four sides of a rectangle (**pmm**)

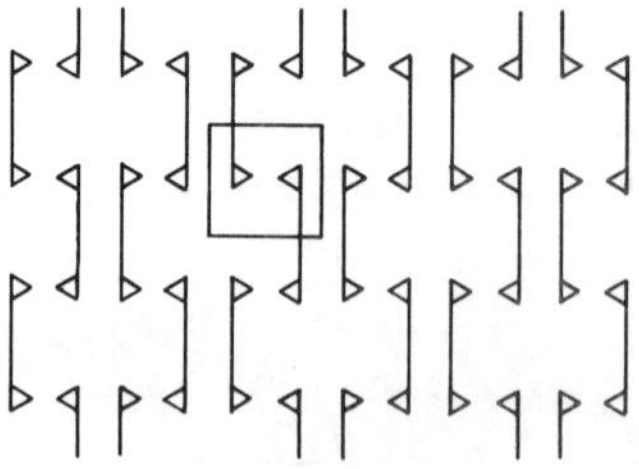

Reflections in two-perpendicular directions and a half-turn (**cmm**)

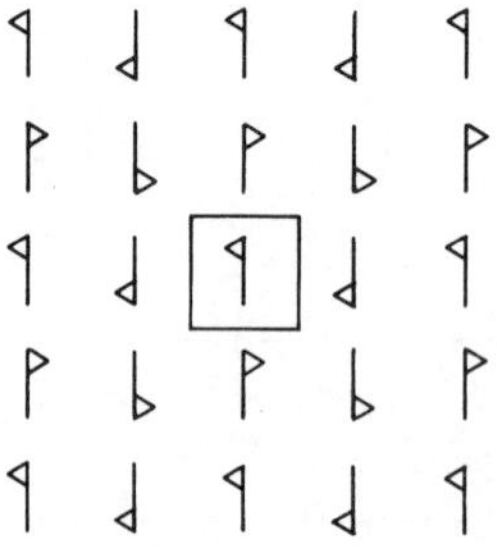

Glide-reflections in two perpendicular directions (**pgg**)

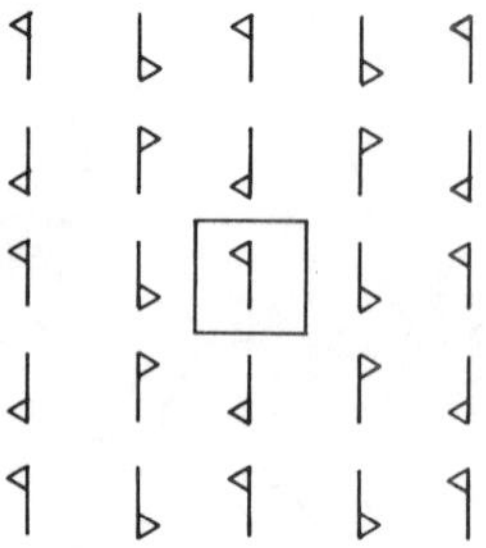

Reflection and glide-reflection in a perpendicular direction (**pmg**)

Figure 2 (*continued*)

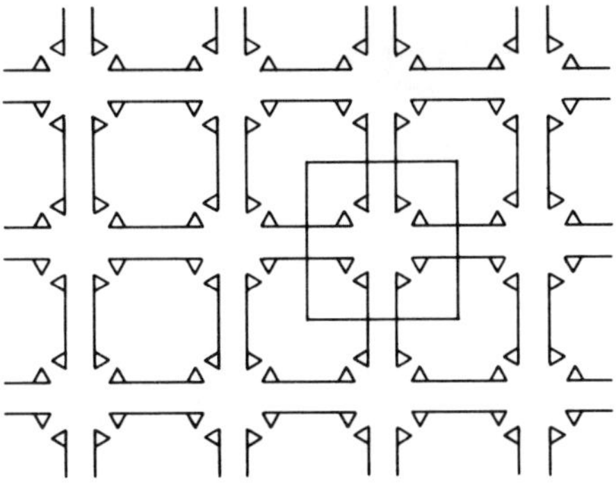

Quarter-turn and reflection (**p4m**)

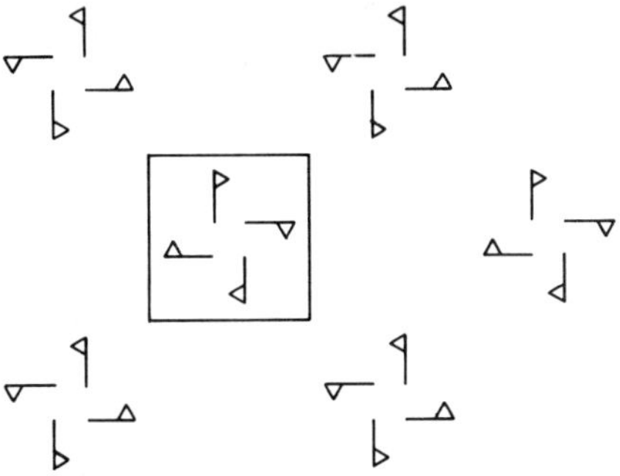

Quarter-turn and glide-reflection (**p4g**)

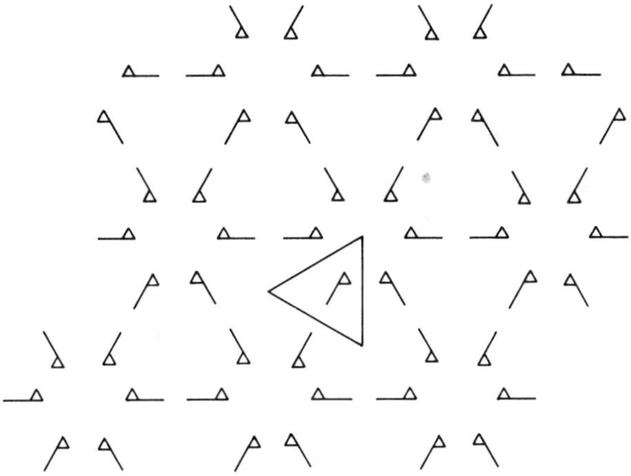

Reflections in the three sides of an equilateral triangle (**p31m**)

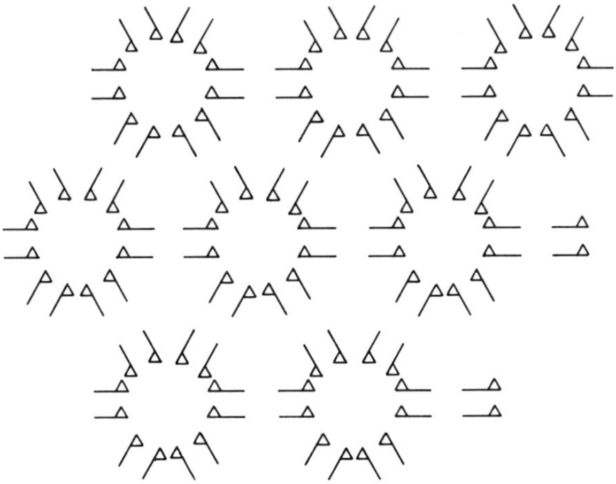

120° rotation and reflection (**p3m1**)

Figure 2 (*continued*)

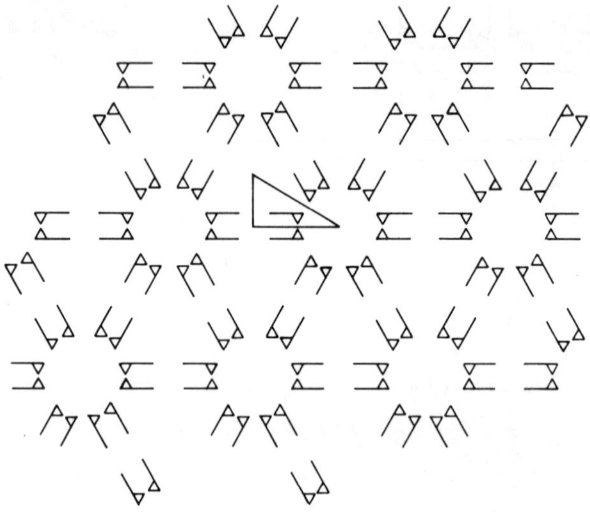

Reflections in the sides of a 30°, 60°, 90° triangle (**p6m**)

Figure 2 (*continued*)

Exercise B

1 **p2** could be described either as a half-turn and two translations or as three half-turns. Where are the centres of the half-turns? Try to give alternative descriptions of the other patterns.

2 With a different motif, construct your own wallpaper patterns.

Three dimensions

If the ideas of the previous sections are extended to three dimensions, there are 230 possible patterns which fill space.

Comments and solutions to questions in the text

Chapter 1

Q.6 Using Method (1):

$$\begin{bmatrix} 3 & 2 \\ 1 & 2 \end{bmatrix}\begin{bmatrix} -4 \\ 5 \end{bmatrix} = \begin{bmatrix} -2 \\ 6 \end{bmatrix}$$

$$\begin{bmatrix} 3 & 2 \\ 1 & 2 \end{bmatrix}\begin{bmatrix} p \\ q \end{bmatrix} = \begin{bmatrix} 3p + 2q \\ p + 2q \end{bmatrix}$$

Using Method (3):

Position vector of image of $(-4, 5)$ = 4 (position vector of image of **i**) + 5 (position vector of image of **j**)

$$= -4\begin{bmatrix} 3 \\ 1 \end{bmatrix} + 5\begin{bmatrix} 2 \\ 2 \end{bmatrix}$$

$$= \begin{bmatrix} -2 \\ 6 \end{bmatrix}$$

Similarly, position vector of image of $(p, q) = p\begin{bmatrix} 3 \\ 1 \end{bmatrix} + q\begin{bmatrix} 2 \\ 2 \end{bmatrix}$

$$= \begin{bmatrix} 3p + 2q \\ p + 2q \end{bmatrix}$$

Q.7 (*a*) $\mathbf{T}(k\mathbf{a}) = \begin{bmatrix} p & q \\ r & s \end{bmatrix}\begin{bmatrix} ke \\ kf \end{bmatrix} = \begin{bmatrix} pke + qkf \\ rke + skf \end{bmatrix}$

$$k\mathbf{T}(\mathbf{a}) = k\begin{bmatrix} p & q \\ r & s \end{bmatrix}\begin{bmatrix} e \\ f \end{bmatrix} = k\begin{bmatrix} pe + qf \\ re + sf \end{bmatrix}$$

$$= \begin{bmatrix} kpe + kqf \\ kre + ksf \end{bmatrix}$$

so $\mathbf{T}(k\mathbf{a}) = k\mathbf{T}(\mathbf{a})$.

(*b*) $\mathbf{T}(\mathbf{a} + \mathbf{b}) = \begin{bmatrix} p & q \\ r & s \end{bmatrix}\begin{bmatrix} e + g \\ f + h \end{bmatrix} = \begin{bmatrix} p(e + g) + q(f + h) \\ r(e + g) + s(f + h) \end{bmatrix}$

$$\mathbf{T}(\mathbf{a}) + \mathbf{T}(\mathbf{a}) = \begin{bmatrix} p & q \\ r & s \end{bmatrix}\begin{bmatrix} e \\ f \end{bmatrix} + \begin{bmatrix} p & q \\ r & s \end{bmatrix}\begin{bmatrix} g \\ h \end{bmatrix}$$

$$= \begin{bmatrix} pe + qf \\ re + sf \end{bmatrix} + \begin{bmatrix} pg + qh \\ rg + sh \end{bmatrix}$$

so, $\mathbf{T}(\mathbf{a} + \mathbf{b}) = \mathbf{T}(\mathbf{a}) + \mathbf{T}(\mathbf{b})$

Q.8 Using $\mathbf{r} = \mathbf{a} + t(\mathbf{b} - \mathbf{a})$:

(*a*) $\mathbf{r} = \begin{bmatrix} 4 \\ -1 \end{bmatrix} + t\begin{bmatrix} -2 \\ 7 \end{bmatrix}$

(*b*) $\mathbf{r} = \begin{bmatrix} 0 \\ 3 \end{bmatrix} + t\begin{bmatrix} 2 \\ -3 \end{bmatrix}$

(*c*) $\mathbf{r} = \begin{bmatrix} 3 \\ -1 \end{bmatrix} + t\begin{bmatrix} -1 \\ 1\frac{1}{2} \end{bmatrix}$

(*d*) $\mathbf{r} = \begin{bmatrix} -1 \\ -2 \end{bmatrix} + t\begin{bmatrix} 3 \\ 6 \end{bmatrix}$

Q.9 (*a*) At the point of intersection

$$\begin{bmatrix} 1 \\ 3 \end{bmatrix} + t\begin{bmatrix} -1 \\ 4 \end{bmatrix} = \begin{bmatrix} 2 \\ -1 \end{bmatrix} + s\begin{bmatrix} 3 \\ -1 \end{bmatrix}.$$

Equating components:
$$\left.\begin{aligned} 1 - t &= 2 + 3s \\ 3 + 4t &= -1 - s \end{aligned}\right\}$$

Solving for s and t gives $s = 0$, $t = -1$, so the position vector of the point of intersection is $\begin{bmatrix} 2 \\ -1 \end{bmatrix}$.

(*b*) At the point of intersection,

$$\begin{bmatrix} 0 \\ -4 \end{bmatrix} + t\begin{bmatrix} -1 \\ -1 \end{bmatrix} = \begin{bmatrix} 1 \\ -2 \end{bmatrix} + s\begin{bmatrix} 2 \\ 6 \end{bmatrix}.$$

Equating components:
$$\left.\begin{aligned} -t &= 1 + 2s \\ -4 - t &= -2 + 6s \end{aligned}\right\}$$

Solving for s and t gives $s = -\frac{1}{4}$, $t = -\frac{1}{2}$, so the position vector of intersection is $\begin{bmatrix} \frac{1}{2} \\ -3\frac{1}{2} \end{bmatrix}$.

Q.10 (*a*) Line AB is
$$\mathbf{r} = \begin{bmatrix} 1 \\ -4 \end{bmatrix} + t\begin{bmatrix} 2 \\ 9 \end{bmatrix}.$$

$$\begin{aligned} \mathbf{T}(\mathbf{r}) &= \mathbf{T}\begin{bmatrix} 1 \\ -4 \end{bmatrix} + t\mathbf{T}\begin{bmatrix} 2 \\ 9 \end{bmatrix} \\ &= \begin{bmatrix} 6 & -3 \\ 2 & -1 \end{bmatrix}\begin{bmatrix} 1 \\ -4 \end{bmatrix} + t\begin{bmatrix} 6 & -3 \\ 2 & -1 \end{bmatrix}\begin{bmatrix} 2 \\ 9 \end{bmatrix}. \end{aligned}$$

So equation of image is
$$\mathbf{r} = \begin{bmatrix} 18 \\ 6 \end{bmatrix} + t\begin{bmatrix} -15 \\ -5 \end{bmatrix},$$

which is a line through (18, 6) in the direction $\begin{bmatrix} -15 \\ -5 \end{bmatrix}$.

(*b*) Line AB is
$$\mathbf{r} = \begin{bmatrix} 4 \\ 3 \end{bmatrix} + t\begin{bmatrix} 2 \\ 4 \end{bmatrix}.$$

$$\mathbf{T}(\mathbf{r}) = \begin{bmatrix} 6 & -3 \\ 2 & -1 \end{bmatrix}\begin{bmatrix} 4 \\ 3 \end{bmatrix} + t\begin{bmatrix} 6 & -3 \\ 2 & -1 \end{bmatrix}\begin{bmatrix} 2 \\ 4 \end{bmatrix}$$
$$= \begin{bmatrix} 15 \\ 5 \end{bmatrix} + t\begin{bmatrix} 0 \\ 0 \end{bmatrix}$$
$$= \begin{bmatrix} 15 \\ 5 \end{bmatrix}.$$

So in this case the image of the line AB is a point – hence the words 'in general'.

Q.11 There are several different ways of proving this result. One way is:

$$\begin{aligned} \mathbf{T}(\mathbf{0}) &= \mathbf{T}(\mathbf{a} + -\mathbf{a}) \\ &= \mathbf{T}(\mathbf{a}) + \mathbf{T}(-\mathbf{a}), && \text{by property } (B) \\ &= \mathbf{T}(\mathbf{a}) + (-1)\mathbf{T}(\mathbf{a}), && \text{by property } (A) \\ &= \mathbf{0}. \end{aligned}$$

Q.12 We know that for a linear transformation the image of the origin is the origin. Is this true for a translation? (This is an example of a proof by contradiction.)

Q.13 $\mathbf{T}(\lambda\mathbf{a} + \mu\mathbf{b}) = \mathbf{T}(\lambda\mathbf{a}) + \mathbf{T}(\mu\mathbf{b})$ by property (B)

$= \lambda\mathbf{T}(\mathbf{a}) + \mu\mathbf{T}(\mathbf{b})$ by property (A).

Q.14 (*a*) $\begin{bmatrix} 2 \\ 5 \end{bmatrix} = p\begin{bmatrix} 4 \\ 6 \end{bmatrix} + q\begin{bmatrix} -2 \\ 1 \end{bmatrix}$; that is, $\left.\begin{aligned} 2 &= 4p - 2q \\ 5 &= 6p + q \end{aligned}\right\}$

Solving these equations, $p = \frac{3}{4}$, $q = \frac{1}{2}$, so $\begin{bmatrix} 2 \\ 5 \end{bmatrix} = \frac{3}{4}\begin{bmatrix} 4 \\ 6 \end{bmatrix} + \frac{1}{2}\begin{bmatrix} -2 \\ 1 \end{bmatrix}$.

Similarly, (*b*) $\begin{bmatrix} 2 \\ 5 \end{bmatrix} = 2\begin{bmatrix} 1 \\ 2 \end{bmatrix} + 1\begin{bmatrix} 0 \\ 1 \end{bmatrix}$

(*c*) $\begin{bmatrix} 2 \\ 5 \end{bmatrix} = 4\begin{bmatrix} 1 \\ 3 \end{bmatrix} - 1\begin{bmatrix} 2 \\ 7 \end{bmatrix}$

Q.15 If the base vectors were in the same direction then it would *not* be possible to express every point of the plane as a linear combination of them; for example, try expressing $\begin{bmatrix} 4 \\ 3 \end{bmatrix}$ as a linear combination of $\begin{bmatrix} 1 \\ 1 \end{bmatrix}$ and $\begin{bmatrix} 2 \\ 2 \end{bmatrix}$.

Q.16 See Fig. 1 (overleaf).

Q.17 There are many possible counter-examples; for example,

$$\mathbf{T}\begin{bmatrix} 2 \\ 2 \end{bmatrix} = \begin{bmatrix} 5 \\ -2 \end{bmatrix} \quad \text{and} \quad \mathbf{T}\begin{bmatrix} 1 \\ 4 \end{bmatrix} = \begin{bmatrix} 4 \\ 0 \end{bmatrix},$$

but

$$\mathbf{T}\begin{bmatrix} 2+1 \\ 2+4 \end{bmatrix} = \begin{bmatrix} 6 \\ 2 \end{bmatrix} \neq \begin{bmatrix} 5 \\ -2 \end{bmatrix} + \begin{bmatrix} 4 \\ 0 \end{bmatrix}.$$

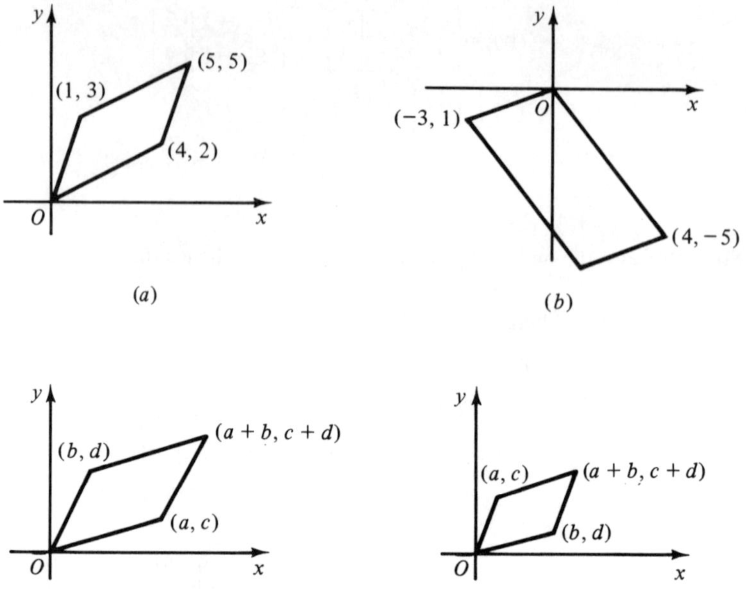

(c)

Figure 1

Chapter 2

Q.1 Stage 2: get a '1' in the top left corner.
Stage 3: get a '0' in the bottom left corner.
Stage 4: get a '1' in the bottom right corner.
Stage 5: get a '0' in the top right corner.

Q.2 (*a*) Multiplies the first row by 6: $\begin{bmatrix} 6a & 6b \\ c & d \end{bmatrix}$

(*b*) Multiplies the second row by $-\frac{1}{2}$: $\begin{bmatrix} a & b \\ -\frac{1}{2}c & -\frac{1}{2}d \end{bmatrix}$

(*c*) Adds 4 times the first row to the second row: $\begin{bmatrix} a & b \\ c+4a & d+4b \end{bmatrix}$

(*d*) Interchanges the two rows: $\begin{bmatrix} c & d \\ a & b \end{bmatrix}$

Q.3

$$\begin{bmatrix} 1 & 0 \\ -1 & 1 \end{bmatrix}\begin{bmatrix} 1 & \frac{3}{2} \\ 1 & -2 \end{bmatrix} = \begin{bmatrix} 1 & \frac{3}{2} \\ 0 & -\frac{7}{2} \end{bmatrix}$$

$$\begin{bmatrix} 1 & 0 \\ 0 & -\frac{2}{7} \end{bmatrix}\begin{bmatrix} 1 & \frac{3}{2} \\ 0 & -\frac{7}{2} \end{bmatrix} = \begin{bmatrix} 1 & \frac{3}{2} \\ 0 & 1 \end{bmatrix}$$

$$\begin{bmatrix} 1 & -\frac{3}{2} \\ 0 & 1 \end{bmatrix}\begin{bmatrix} 1 & \frac{3}{2} \\ 0 & 1 \end{bmatrix} = \begin{bmatrix} 1 & 0 \\ 0 & 1 \end{bmatrix}$$

Q.4 $E_4E_3E_2E_1 = \begin{bmatrix} \frac{2}{7} & \frac{3}{7} \\ \frac{1}{7} & -\frac{2}{7} \end{bmatrix}$, which is the inverse of $\begin{bmatrix} 2 & 3 \\ 1 & -2 \end{bmatrix}$.

Q.5 See discussion in the text.

Q.6 By multiplication, $\begin{bmatrix} 1 & 0 \\ 0 & 0 \end{bmatrix}\begin{bmatrix} 1 & c \\ 0 & 1 \end{bmatrix} = \begin{bmatrix} 1 & c \\ 0 & 0 \end{bmatrix}$.

Chapter 3

Q.1 You may well think of other properties as well as those listed below.

	Length	Angle	Ratio	Area	Sense	Parallelism	Invariant points
(*a*) rotation	✓	✓	✓	✓	✓	✓	centre of rotation
(*b*) reflection	✓	✓	✓	✓		✓	line of reflection
(*c*) shear	✓			✓	✓	✓	line
(*d*) enlargement		✓	✓		✓	✓	centre of enlargement
(*e*) two-way stretch						✓	point
(*f*) projection							line of projection

Q.2 Yes, as $\begin{bmatrix} a & b \\ c & d \end{bmatrix}\begin{bmatrix} 0 \\ 0 \end{bmatrix} = \begin{bmatrix} 0 \\ 0 \end{bmatrix}$.

Q.3 Divide up the surrounding rectangle as in Fig. 1.

Q.4 The ratio is independent of the figure chosen.

Q.5

	Ratio of areas	Determinant
(*a*) rotation	1	1
(*b*) reflection	1	-1
(*c*) shear	1	1
(*d*) enlargement	k^2	k^2, where k is the enlargement factor
(*e*) one-way stretch	$\lvert a \rvert$	a, where a is the factor
(*f*) two-way stretch	$\lvert ab \rvert$	ab, where a and b are the factors
(*g*) projection	0	0

Q.6 Consider the point (1, 0) and its image:

$$\begin{bmatrix} 0.6 & 0.8 \\ 0.8 & -0.6 \end{bmatrix}\begin{bmatrix} 1 \\ 0 \end{bmatrix} = \begin{bmatrix} -0.6 \\ 0.8 \end{bmatrix}$$

The angle of rotation is 126.9°.

Q.8 (*a*)

$$\begin{bmatrix} -0.8 & 0.6 \\ 0.6 & 0.8 \end{bmatrix}\begin{bmatrix} k \\ 3k \end{bmatrix} = \begin{bmatrix} k \\ 3k \end{bmatrix}$$

(*b*)

$$\begin{bmatrix} -0.8 & 0.6 \\ 0.6 & 0.8 \end{bmatrix}\begin{bmatrix} x \\ y \end{bmatrix} = -\begin{bmatrix} x \\ y \end{bmatrix}$$

$$\Rightarrow \quad \left.\begin{aligned} -0.8x + 0.6y &= -x \\ 0.6x + 0.8y &= -y \end{aligned}\right\}$$

$$\Rightarrow \quad \begin{aligned} 0.6y &= -0.2x; \quad \text{that is} \quad x = -3y \\ 0.6x &= -1.8y; \quad \text{that is} \quad x = -3y. \end{aligned}$$

So all points on the ine $x = -3y$ satisfy $\mathbf{M}\begin{bmatrix} x \\ y \end{bmatrix} = -\begin{bmatrix} x \\ y \end{bmatrix}$. This line is perpendicular to the line $y = 3x$.

Q.9 If the axis of reflection is l, then all points on l', the line through the origin perpendicular to l, satisfy $\mathbf{M}\begin{bmatrix} x \\ y \end{bmatrix} = -\begin{bmatrix} x \\ y \end{bmatrix}$ (Fig. 2).

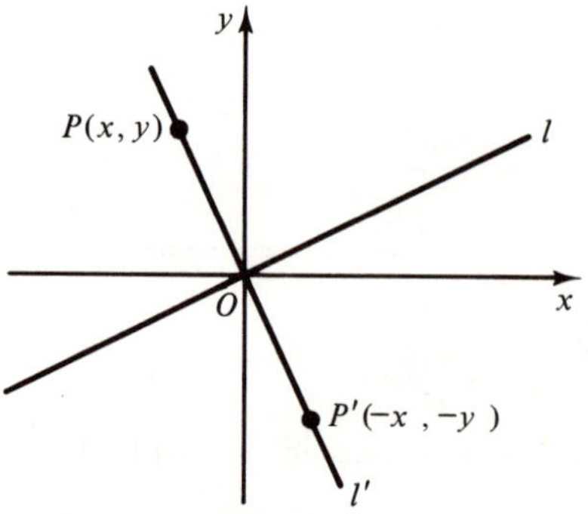

Figure 2

Chapter 4

Q.1

$$\begin{bmatrix} 1 & 1 \\ -2 & 4 \end{bmatrix}\begin{bmatrix} k \\ 2k \end{bmatrix} = \begin{bmatrix} 3k \\ 6k \end{bmatrix}$$

So the image point also lies on the line $y = 2x$.

Q.2

$$\mathbf{M} - \lambda\mathbf{I} = \begin{bmatrix} 1-\lambda & 2 \\ 3 & 2-\lambda \end{bmatrix},$$

so $\det(\mathbf{M} - \lambda\mathbf{I}) = (1-\lambda)(2-\lambda) - 6$.

The characteristic equation is $\lambda^2 - 3\lambda - 4 = 0$, so the eigenvalues are $\lambda = 4$ and -1. Substituting in $(\mathbf{M} - \lambda\mathbf{I})\mathbf{x} = \mathbf{0}$ gives the corresponding eigenvectors $\begin{bmatrix} 2 \\ 3 \end{bmatrix}$ and $\begin{bmatrix} 1 \\ -1 \end{bmatrix}$ (or any non-zero scalar multiple).

Q.3 $\mathbf{RSR}^{-1} = \begin{bmatrix} 1 & 1 \\ 1 & 2 \end{bmatrix}\begin{bmatrix} 2 & 0 \\ 0 & 3 \end{bmatrix}\begin{bmatrix} 2 & -1 \\ -1 & 1 \end{bmatrix} = \begin{bmatrix} 1 & 1 \\ -2 & 4 \end{bmatrix} = \mathbf{M}$

Q.4 $\mathbf{U} = \begin{bmatrix} 2 & 1 \\ 3 & -1 \end{bmatrix}, \quad \mathbf{\Lambda} = \begin{bmatrix} 4 & 0 \\ 0 & -1 \end{bmatrix}$

$$\mathbf{U\Lambda U}^{-1} = \begin{bmatrix} 2 & 1 \\ 3 & -1 \end{bmatrix}\begin{bmatrix} 4 & 0 \\ 0 & -1 \end{bmatrix}\begin{bmatrix} \frac{1}{5} & \frac{1}{5} \\ \frac{3}{5} & -\frac{2}{5} \end{bmatrix} = \begin{bmatrix} 1 & 2 \\ 3 & 2 \end{bmatrix}$$

Q.5 If we chose eigenvectors $\begin{bmatrix} 2 \\ -6 \end{bmatrix}$ and $\begin{bmatrix} 4 \\ 4 \end{bmatrix}$,

$$\mathbf{U} = \begin{bmatrix} 2 & 4 \\ -6 & 4 \end{bmatrix}$$

$$\mathbf{U\Lambda U}^{-1} = \begin{bmatrix} 2 & 4 \\ -6 & 4 \end{bmatrix}\begin{bmatrix} 2 & 0 \\ 0 & \frac{1}{3} \end{bmatrix}\left(\frac{1}{32}\begin{bmatrix} 4 & -4 \\ 6 & 2 \end{bmatrix}\right) = \begin{bmatrix} \frac{3}{4} & -\frac{5}{12} \\ -\frac{5}{4} & \frac{19}{12} \end{bmatrix}$$

Q.6

Eigenvalues	*Eigenvectors*
3	$\begin{bmatrix} 2 \\ 1 \end{bmatrix}$
2	$\begin{bmatrix} 1 \\ -1 \end{bmatrix}$

So $\mathbf{U} = \begin{bmatrix} 2 & 1 \\ 1 & -1 \end{bmatrix}$ and $\mathbf{\Lambda} = \begin{bmatrix} 3 & 0 \\ 0 & 2 \end{bmatrix}$,

so $\mathbf{M} = \mathbf{U\Lambda U}^{-1} = \begin{bmatrix} \frac{8}{3} & \frac{2}{3} \\ \frac{1}{3} & \frac{7}{3} \end{bmatrix}$.

Chapter 5

Q.1 As the question specifies the unit cube, the main assumptions are that lines are mapped to lines and planes are mapped to planes.

Q.2 Yes – the proof is the same as for Q.11 in Chapter 1.

Q.3 Use the same approach as for Q.7 in Chapter 1.

Q.4 Find a counter-example; for example, if $\mathbf{a} = \begin{bmatrix} 1 \\ 0 \\ 0 \end{bmatrix}$ and $\mathbf{b} = \begin{bmatrix} 0 \\ 1 \\ 0 \end{bmatrix}$,

$$\mathbf{S}(\mathbf{a}+\mathbf{b}) = \mathbf{S}\begin{bmatrix}1\\1\\0\end{bmatrix} = \begin{bmatrix}1\\12\\3\end{bmatrix}, \quad \mathbf{S}(\mathbf{a}) = \begin{bmatrix}1\\12\\3\end{bmatrix}, \quad \mathbf{S}(\mathbf{b}) = \begin{bmatrix}0\\12\\3\end{bmatrix}$$

so

$$\mathbf{S}(\mathbf{a}+\mathbf{b}) \neq \mathbf{S}(\mathbf{a}) + \mathbf{S}(\mathbf{b}).$$

Q.5
$$\mathbf{r} = \begin{bmatrix}1&4&3\\-2&0&1\\3&1&5\end{bmatrix}\begin{bmatrix}1\\2\\-2\end{bmatrix} + s\begin{bmatrix}1&4&3\\-2&0&1\\3&1&5\end{bmatrix}\begin{bmatrix}2\\0\\6\end{bmatrix} + t\begin{bmatrix}1&4&3\\-2&0&1\\3&1&5\end{bmatrix}\begin{bmatrix}3\\1\\1\end{bmatrix}$$
$$= \begin{bmatrix}3\\-4\\-5\end{bmatrix} + s\begin{bmatrix}20\\2\\36\end{bmatrix} + t\begin{bmatrix}10\\-5\\15\end{bmatrix}$$

Q.6 Result 1: Transformations represented by 3×3 matrices are linear.
Result 2: In general, lines are mapped onto lines, and in general, planes are mapped onto planes.
Result 3: For a linear transformation, $\mathbf{T}(\mathbf{0}) = (\mathbf{0})$.
Result 4: For a linear transformation, $\mathbf{T}(\lambda\mathbf{a} + \mu\mathbf{b}) = \lambda\mathbf{T}(\mathbf{a}) + \mu\mathbf{T}(\mathbf{b})$.
Result 5: If we know the image of three points in three-dimensional space (whose position vectors are not in the same plane), we can find the image of every point in space.
Result 6: Under a linear transformation, the image of the unit cube is a parallelepiped.

Q.7 See Fig. 3.

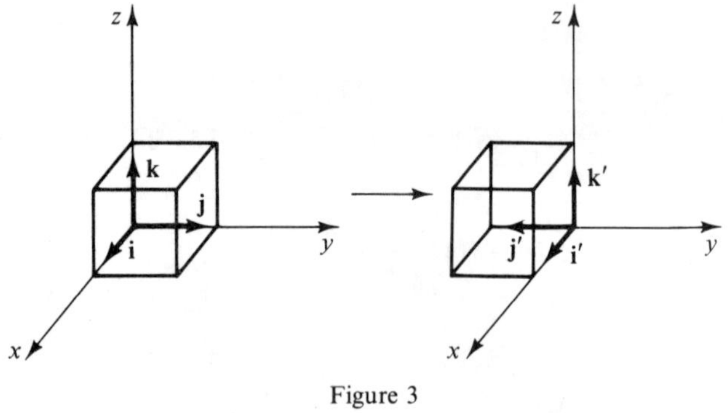

Figure 3

Chapter 6

Q.1 Two cases arise: (1) the three planes are the same; (2) two of the planes are the same and the third different. In (1), the three planes intersect in a plane. In (2), the three planes either meet in a line or are parallel (Fig. 4, opposite).

Q.2 (*a*) Multiplies the first row by 6.
(*b*) Subtracts 3 times the first row from the second row.
(*c*) Adds twice the third row to the second row.
(*d*) Interchanges the second and third rows.

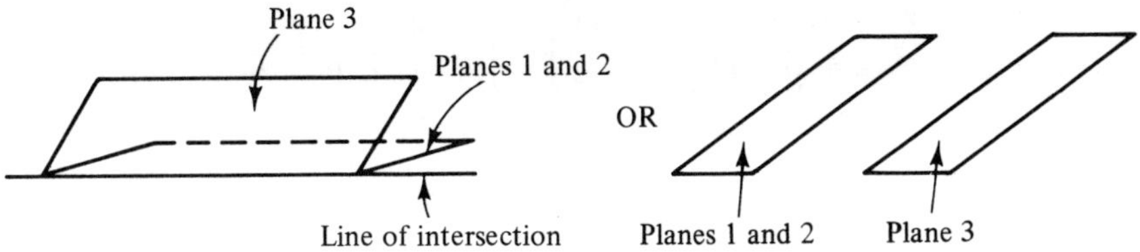

Figure 4

Q.3

$$\mathbf{E}_1\begin{bmatrix}1 & -2 & -1\\ 3 & 1 & 5\\ -4 & 2 & -3\end{bmatrix}=\begin{bmatrix}1 & 0 & 0\\ -3 & 1 & 0\\ 0 & 0 & 1\end{bmatrix}\begin{bmatrix}1 & -2 & -1\\ 3 & 1 & 5\\ -4 & 2 & -3\end{bmatrix}$$

$$=\begin{bmatrix}1 & -2 & -1\\ 0 & 7 & 8\\ -4 & 2 & -3\end{bmatrix}\text{, and so on.}$$

Q.4 $\mathbf{E}_8\mathbf{E}_7\mathbf{E}_6\mathbf{E}_5\mathbf{E}_4\mathbf{E}_3\mathbf{E}_2\mathbf{E}_1=\begin{bmatrix}13 & 8 & 9\\ 11 & 7 & 8\\ -10 & -6 & -7\end{bmatrix}$

Q.5 Both sides simplify to

$$a_1b_2c_3-a_1b_3c_2-a_2b_1c_3+a_2b_3c_1+a_3b_1c_2-a_3b_2c_1$$

Q.6 Right-hand side $=a_1(b_2c_3-b_3c_2)-a_2(b_1c_3-b_3c_1)+a_3(b_1c_2-b_2c_1)$

$$=\det(\mathbf{A})$$

Q.7 (*a*) $a_2A_2+b_2B_2+c_2C_2=a_2(b_1c_3-b_3c_1)+b_2(a_1c_3-a_3c_1)-c_2(a_1b_3-a_3b_1)$

$$=a_1(b_2c_3-b_3c_2)-a_2(b_1c_3-b_3c_1)+a_3(b_1c_2-b_2c_1)$$

$$=\det(\mathbf{M})$$

(*b*) $b_1B_1+b_2B_2+b_3B_3=-b_1(a_2c_3-a_3c_2)+b_2(a_1c_3-a_3c_1)-b_3(a_1c_2-a_2c_1)$

$$=a_1(b_2c_3-b_3c_2)-a_2(b_1c_3-b_3c_1)+a_3(b_1c_2-b_2c_1)$$

$$=\det(\mathbf{M})$$

(*c*) $a_3A_1+b_3B_1+c_3C_1=a_3(b_2c_3-b_3c_2)-b_3(a_2c_3-a_3c_2)+c_3(a_2b_3-a_3b_2)$

$$=0$$

Similar results are

(*a*) $\det(\mathbf{M})=a_iA_i+b_iB_i+c_iC_i$ for $i=1,2,3$

(*b*) $\det(\mathbf{M})=x_1X_1+x_2X_2+x_3X_3$ for $\left.\begin{matrix}x=a,b,c\\ X=A,B,C\end{matrix}\right\}$

(*c*) $a_iA_j+b_iB_j+c_iC_j=0$ for $i=1,2,3$; $j=1,2,3$; and $i\neq j$.

Q.8

$$\begin{bmatrix}a_1 & b_1 & c_1\\ a_2 & b_2 & c_2\\ a_3 & b_3 & c_3\end{bmatrix}\begin{bmatrix}A_1 & A_2 & A_3\\ B_1 & B_2 & B_3\\ C_1 & C_2 & C_3\end{bmatrix}=\begin{bmatrix}\det(\mathbf{M}) & 0 & 0\\ 0 & \det(\mathbf{M}) & 0\\ 0 & 0 & \det(\mathbf{M})\end{bmatrix}$$

Q.9 $$\begin{bmatrix} 13 & 8 & 9 \\ 11 & 7 & 8 \\ -10 & -6 & -7 \end{bmatrix}\begin{bmatrix} 1 & -2 & -1 \\ 3 & 1 & 5 \\ -4 & 2 & -3 \end{bmatrix} = \begin{bmatrix} 1 & 0 & 0 \\ 0 & 1 & 0 \\ 0 & 0 & 1 \end{bmatrix}$$

Premultiplying $$\begin{bmatrix} 1 & -2 & -1 \\ 3 & 1 & 5 \\ -4 & 2 & -3 \end{bmatrix}\begin{bmatrix} x \\ y \\ z \end{bmatrix} = \begin{bmatrix} 6 \\ -4 \\ 7 \end{bmatrix} \quad \text{by} \quad \begin{bmatrix} 13 & 8 & 9 \\ 11 & 7 & 8 \\ -10 & -6 & -7 \end{bmatrix}$$

we get $$\begin{bmatrix} 1 & 0 & 0 \\ 0 & 1 & 0 \\ 0 & 0 & 1 \end{bmatrix}\begin{bmatrix} x \\ y \\ z \end{bmatrix} = \begin{bmatrix} 13 & 8 & 9 \\ 11 & 7 & 8 \\ -10 & -6 & -7 \end{bmatrix}\begin{bmatrix} 6 \\ -4 \\ 7 \end{bmatrix}$$

$$\Rightarrow \qquad \begin{bmatrix} x \\ y \\ z \end{bmatrix} = \begin{bmatrix} 109 \\ 94 \\ -85 \end{bmatrix},$$

so $$x = 109, \quad y = 94, \quad z = -85.$$

Chapter 7

Q.1 Check using matrix multiplication.

Q.2 $\mathbf{M}^n = \mathbf{U}\boldsymbol{\Lambda}^n\mathbf{U}^{-1}$

$$= \begin{bmatrix} 3 & 1 & 1 \\ 9 & 6 & 5 \\ 1 & 1 & 1 \end{bmatrix}\begin{bmatrix} 1 & 0 & 0 \\ 0 & 16 & 0 \\ 0 & 0 & 81 \end{bmatrix}\begin{bmatrix} \frac{1}{2} & 0 & -\frac{1}{2} \\ -2 & 1 & -3 \\ \frac{3}{2} & -1 & \frac{9}{2} \end{bmatrix}$$

$$= \begin{bmatrix} 91 & -65 & 315 \\ 420 & -309 & 1530 \\ 90 & -65 & 316 \end{bmatrix}$$

Q.3 $$\mathbf{M}^3 - 6\mathbf{M}^2 + 11\mathbf{M} - 6\mathbf{I} = \begin{bmatrix} 26 & -19 & 96 \\ 111 & -87 & 459 \\ 25 & -19 & 97 \end{bmatrix} - 6\begin{bmatrix} 7 & -5 & 27 \\ 24 & -21 & 126 \\ 6 & -5 & 28 \end{bmatrix}$$

$$+ 11\begin{bmatrix} 2 & -1 & 6 \\ 3 & -3 & 27 \\ 1 & -1 & 7 \end{bmatrix} - 6\begin{bmatrix} 1 & 0 & 0 \\ 0 & 1 & 0 \\ 0 & 0 & 1 \end{bmatrix}$$

$$= \begin{bmatrix} 0 & 0 & 0 \\ 0 & 0 & 0 \\ 0 & 0 & 0 \end{bmatrix}.$$

Q.4 $\mathbf{M}^{-1} = \frac{1}{6}(\mathbf{M}^3 - 6\mathbf{M} + 11\mathbf{I})$

$$= \frac{1}{6}\begin{bmatrix} 7 & -5 & 27 \\ 24 & -21 & 126 \\ 6 & -5 & 28 \end{bmatrix} - 6\begin{bmatrix} 2 & -1 & 6 \\ 3 & -3 & 27 \\ 1 & -1 & 7 \end{bmatrix} + 11\begin{bmatrix} 1 & 0 & 0 \\ 0 & 1 & 0 \\ 0 & 0 & 1 \end{bmatrix}$$

$$= \frac{1}{6}\begin{bmatrix} 6 & 1 & -9 \\ 6 & 8 & -36 \\ 0 & 1 & -3 \end{bmatrix} = \begin{bmatrix} 1 & \frac{1}{6} & -\frac{3}{2} \\ 1 & \frac{4}{3} & -6 \\ 0 & \frac{1}{6} & -\frac{1}{2} \end{bmatrix}.$$

Chapter 8

Q.1 (i) $\mathbf{A}^{\mathrm{T}} = \begin{bmatrix} 2 & -4 \\ 3 & 1 \end{bmatrix}$; $\mathbf{B}^{\mathrm{T}} = \begin{bmatrix} 1 & -3 \\ 0 & 6 \end{bmatrix}$; $(\mathbf{AB})^{\mathrm{T}} = \mathbf{B}^{\mathrm{T}}\mathbf{A}^{\mathrm{T}} = \begin{bmatrix} -7 & -7 \\ 18 & 6 \end{bmatrix}$;

$$(\mathbf{BA})^{\mathrm{T}} = \mathbf{A}^{\mathrm{T}}\mathbf{B}^{\mathrm{T}} = \begin{bmatrix} 2 & -30 \\ 3 & -3 \end{bmatrix}.$$

(ii) $\mathbf{A}^{\mathrm{T}} = \begin{bmatrix} 1 & 3 & -1 \\ 2 & 0 & -3 \\ -5 & 4 & 2 \end{bmatrix}$; $\mathbf{B}^{\mathrm{T}} = \begin{bmatrix} 6 & 4 & -1 \\ -5 & -3 & 2 \\ 1 & 7 & 0 \end{bmatrix}$;

$$(\mathbf{AB})^{\mathrm{T}} = \mathbf{B}^{\mathrm{T}}\mathbf{A}^{\mathrm{T}} = \begin{bmatrix} 19 & 14 & -20 \\ -21 & -7 & 18 \\ 15 & 3 & -22 \end{bmatrix};$$

$$(\mathbf{BA})^{\mathrm{T}} = \mathbf{A}^{\mathrm{T}}\mathbf{B}^{\mathrm{T}} = \begin{bmatrix} -10 & -12 & 5 \\ 9 & -13 & -2 \\ -48 & -18 & 13 \end{bmatrix}.$$

Q.2 If $\mathbf{A}$ is a $p \times q$ matrix, then $\mathbf{A}^{\mathrm{T}}\mathbf{A}$ is a $q \times q$ matrix and $\mathbf{A}\mathbf{A}^{\mathrm{T}}$ is a $p \times p$ matrix, so $\mathbf{A}^{\mathrm{T}}\mathbf{A}$ and $\mathbf{A}\mathbf{A}^{\mathrm{T}}$ are always defined.

Q.3 If $\mathbf{A} = \begin{bmatrix} a & b \\ c & d \end{bmatrix}$, then $\mathbf{A}^{\mathrm{T}} = \begin{bmatrix} a & c \\ b & d \end{bmatrix}$

$$\Rightarrow \quad \det(\mathbf{A}) = ad - bc \quad \text{and} \quad \det(\mathbf{A}^{\mathrm{T}}) = ad - bc.$$

The result is also true if $\mathbf{A}$ is a 3×3 matrix – prove by direct expansion.

Q.4 Prove by direct expansion of both sides.

Q.5 $\mathbf{x}^{\mathrm{T}}\mathbf{y} = [a \quad b]\begin{bmatrix} c \\ d \end{bmatrix} = ac + bd = \mathbf{x}\,.\,\mathbf{y}$; that is, $\mathbf{x}^{\mathrm{T}}\mathbf{y}$ is the scalar product of $\mathbf{x}$ and $\mathbf{y}$.

Q.6 Isometries: (*b*) a rotation about O through $\tan^{-1}(\frac{4}{3})$; (*c*) a reflection in $y = -x$; (*f*) a rotation, with axis the x-axis, through $\tan^{-1}(-\frac{4}{3})$.
Not isometries: (*a*) a shear; (*d*) a rotation and enlargement; (*e*) a shear.

Q.7 (*a*) $\begin{bmatrix} 1 & -4 \\ -4 & -15 \end{bmatrix}$ (*b*) $\begin{bmatrix} 1 & 0 \\ 0 & 1 \end{bmatrix}$ (*c*) $\begin{bmatrix} 1 & 0 \\ 0 & 1 \end{bmatrix}$ (*d*) $\begin{bmatrix} 2 & 0 \\ 0 & 2 \end{bmatrix}$

(*e*) $\begin{bmatrix} 1 & 0 & 0 \\ 0 & 1 & 2 \\ 0 & 2 & 5 \end{bmatrix}$ (*f*) $\begin{bmatrix} 1 & 0 & 0 \\ 0 & 1 & 0 \\ 0 & 0 & 1 \end{bmatrix}$.

Q.8 For the isometries, $\mathbf{M}^T\mathbf{M} = \mathbf{I}$.

Q.9 $\begin{bmatrix} \cos\theta & \sin\theta \\ -\sin\theta & \cos\theta \end{bmatrix}\begin{bmatrix} \cos\theta & -\sin\theta \\ \sin\theta & \cos\theta \end{bmatrix} = \begin{bmatrix} 1 & 0 \\ 0 & 1 \end{bmatrix}$, as $\sin^2\theta + \cos^2\theta = 1$

$$\begin{bmatrix} \cos\theta & \sin\theta \\ \sin\theta & -\cos\theta \end{bmatrix}\begin{bmatrix} \cos\theta & \sin\theta \\ \sin\theta & -\cos\theta \end{bmatrix} = \begin{bmatrix} 1 & 0 \\ 0 & 1 \end{bmatrix}.$$

Q.10 If the columns of $\mathbf{M}$ are $\mathbf{x}_1$, $\mathbf{x}_2$ and $\mathbf{x}_3$,

then $\mathbf{M}^T\mathbf{M} = \begin{bmatrix} \mathbf{x}_1{}^T\mathbf{x}_1 & \mathbf{x}_1{}^T\mathbf{x}_2 & \mathbf{x}_1{}^T\mathbf{x}_3 \\ \mathbf{x}_2{}^T\mathbf{x}_1 & \mathbf{x}_2{}^T\mathbf{x}_2 & \mathbf{x}_2{}^T\mathbf{x}_3 \\ \mathbf{x}_3{}^T\mathbf{x}_1 & \mathbf{x}_3{}^T\mathbf{x}_2 & \mathbf{x}_3{}^T\mathbf{x}_3 \end{bmatrix} = \begin{bmatrix} 1 & 0 & 0 \\ 0 & 1 & 0 \\ 0 & 0 & 1 \end{bmatrix}$

$\Rightarrow \quad \mathbf{x}_1{}^T\mathbf{x}_1 = \mathbf{x}_2{}^T\mathbf{x}_2 = \mathbf{x}_3{}^T\mathbf{x}_3 = 1$ ($\mathbf{x}_1$, $\mathbf{x}_2$ and $\mathbf{x}_3$ are all unit vectors)

$\mathbf{x}_1{}^T\mathbf{x}_2 = \mathbf{x}_1{}^T\mathbf{x}_3 = \mathbf{x}_2{}^T\mathbf{x}_3 = 0$

$\Rightarrow \quad \mathbf{x}_1 \cdot \mathbf{x}_2 = \mathbf{x}_1 \cdot \mathbf{x}_3 = \mathbf{x}_2 \cdot \mathbf{x}_3 = \mathbf{0}$ ($\mathbf{x}_1$, $\mathbf{x}_2$ and $\mathbf{x}_3$ are mutually orthogonal vectors).

Q.11 Either check directly that $\mathbf{M}^{-1} = \mathbf{M}^T$ or think geometrically:

For $\mathbf{M} = \begin{bmatrix} \cos\theta & -\sin\theta \\ \cos\theta & \cos\theta \end{bmatrix}$, $\mathbf{M}^T = \begin{bmatrix} \cos\theta & \sin\theta \\ -\sin\theta & \cos\theta \end{bmatrix}$

$$= \begin{bmatrix} \cos(-\theta) & -\sin(-\theta) \\ \sin(-\theta) & \cos(-\theta) \end{bmatrix},$$

which is a rotation through $(-\theta)$;

and for $\mathbf{M} = \begin{bmatrix} \cos\theta & \sin\theta \\ \sin\theta & -\cos\theta \end{bmatrix}$, $\mathbf{M}^T = \mathbf{M}$; that is, both are reflections.

Q.12 Think of the geometrical cases which can arise:
(*a*) $\mathbf{Mx} = 1\mathbf{x}$ for all points in the plane, so $\mathbf{M}$ is an identity.
(*b*) All points in the direction $\mathbf{x}_1$ are fixed and $\mathbf{Mx}_2 = -\mathbf{x}_2$, so $\mathbf{M}$ is a reflection.
(*c*) $\mathbf{Mx} = -\mathbf{x}$ for all points in the plane, so $\mathbf{M}$ is a half-turn.
(*d*) There are no fixed directions, so the transformation is a rotation.

Q.13 $\det\left(\begin{bmatrix} 2-\lambda & -2 & 0 \\ -2 & 1-\lambda & 2 \\ 0 & 2 & -\lambda \end{bmatrix}\right) = 0.$

This simplifies to $\lambda^3 - 3\lambda^2 - 6\lambda + 8 = 0$

$$\Rightarrow \quad (\lambda - 1)(\lambda + 2)(\lambda - 4) = 0,$$

so the eigenvalues are 1, -2, 4.

The corresponding eigenvectors (of unit length) are:

$$\lambda = 1,\ \tfrac{1}{3}\begin{bmatrix} 2 \\ 1 \\ 2 \end{bmatrix}; \quad \lambda = -2,\ \tfrac{1}{3}\begin{bmatrix} 1 \\ 2 \\ -2 \end{bmatrix}; \quad \lambda = 4,\ \tfrac{1}{3}\begin{bmatrix} -2 \\ 2 \\ 1 \end{bmatrix}.$$

$$\Rightarrow \quad \mathbf{U} = \begin{bmatrix} \frac{2}{3} & \frac{1}{3} & -\frac{2}{3} \\ \frac{1}{3} & \frac{2}{3} & \frac{2}{3} \\ \frac{1}{3} & -\frac{2}{3} & \frac{1}{3} \end{bmatrix} \quad \text{and} \quad \mathbf{U}^{-1}\mathbf{M}\mathbf{U} = \begin{bmatrix} 1 & 0 & 0 \\ 0 & -2 & 0 \\ 0 & 0 & 4 \end{bmatrix}.$$

Q.14
$$\det\left(\begin{bmatrix} (a-\lambda) & h \\ h & (b-\lambda) \end{bmatrix}\right) = 0$$

$$\Rightarrow \quad (a-\lambda)(b-\lambda) - h^2 = 0$$

$$\Rightarrow \quad \lambda^2 - (a+b)\lambda + ab - h^2 = 0$$

$$\Rightarrow \quad \lambda = \frac{(a+b) \pm \sqrt{((a-b)^2 + 4h^2)}}{2}.$$

Now $(a-b)^2 + 4h^2 \geqslant 0$, so the eigenvalues are both real. If $a = b$ and $h = 0$, then the two eigenvalues are equal.

Chapter 9

Q.1 Multiply out $[x \quad y]\begin{bmatrix} 2 & 0 \\ 0 & -3 \end{bmatrix}\begin{bmatrix} x \\ y \end{bmatrix}$.

Q.2 Different pairs of axes of the ellipse are rotated onto the x- and y-axes to give the ellipses shown in Fig. 5.

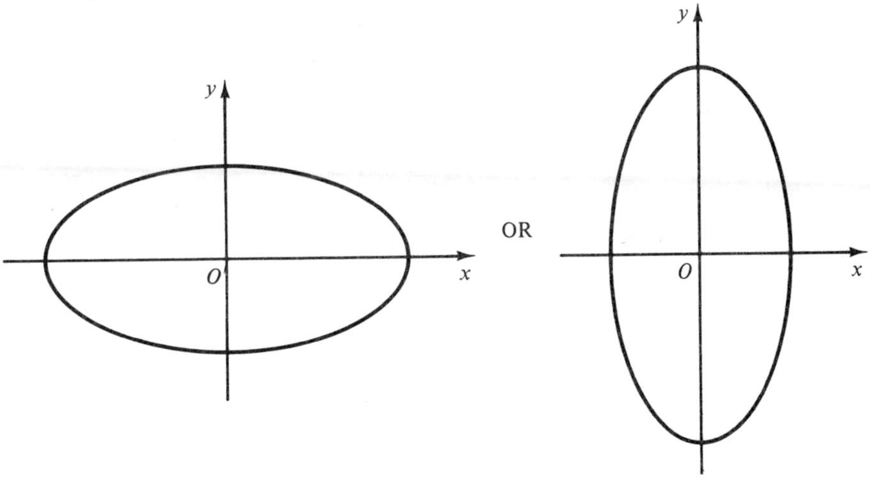

Figure 5

Q.3
$$\mathbf{M} = \begin{bmatrix} 3 & \frac{5}{2} & -3 \\ \frac{5}{2} & -4 & \frac{3}{2} \\ -3 & \frac{3}{2} & 2 \end{bmatrix}.$$

Q.4 If one of a', b', c' is zero, we have a cylinder with either an elliptical or a hyperbolic cross-section. For example, (i) $2x^2 + 3y^2 + 0z^2 = 1$ is a cylinder in the direction of the z-axis with an elliptical cross-section; (ii) $4y^2 - z^2 = 1$ is a cylinder in the direction of the x-axis with a hyperbolic cross-section.

If two of a', b', c' are zero we have two parallel planes, for example if $4y^2 = 1$, we have the planes $y = \pm\frac{1}{2}$.

Chapter 10

Q.1 If

$$\mathbf{a} = (u_1, u_2, u_3, \ldots), \quad \text{where } u_{n+2} = 3u_{n+1} - 2u_n$$

and

$$\mathbf{b} = (v_1, v_2, v_3, \ldots), \quad \text{where } v_{n+2} = 3v_{n+1} - 2v_n,$$

then

$$\begin{aligned} \mathbf{a} + \mathbf{b} &= (u_1 + v_1, u_2 + v_2, u_3 + v_3, \ldots) \\ &= (t_1, t_2, t_3, \ldots), \quad \text{where } t_n = u_n + v_n. \\ \Rightarrow \quad t_{n+2} &= u_{n+2} + v_{n+2} \\ &= (3u_n - 2u_{n+1}) + (3v_n - 2v_{n+1}) \\ \Rightarrow \quad t_{n+2} &= 3(u_n + v_n) - 2(u_{n+1} + v_{n+1}) \\ \Rightarrow \quad t_{n+2} &= 3t_n - 2t_{n+1}, \quad \text{and this satisfies relation } (A). \end{aligned}$$

Q.2 Define $k\mathbf{p} = (k, 0, 3k, -6k, 21k, -60k, \ldots)$.

As $\mathbf{p} \in S$,
$$u_{n+2} = 3u_n - 2u_{n+1},$$
so
$$(ku_{n+2}) = 3(ku_n) - 2(ku_{n+1});$$
that is, $k\mathbf{p} \in S$.

Q.3 $\mathbf{r} = 3\mathbf{p} - 2\mathbf{q}$.

Q.4 (*a*) $\mathbf{g} = -6\mathbf{p} + 3\mathbf{q}$
(*b*) $\mathbf{h} = a\mathbf{p} + b\mathbf{q}$; no.

Q.5 For example, $\mathbf{s} = \mathbf{p} + \mathbf{q} + \mathbf{r}$

or $\mathbf{s} = -2\mathbf{p} + 3\mathbf{q} + 2\mathbf{r}$

or $\mathbf{s} = 7\mathbf{p} - 3\mathbf{q} - \mathbf{r}$ and so on, so the answer is not unique.

Q.7 (*a*) $\begin{bmatrix} a & h \\ h & b \end{bmatrix} + \begin{bmatrix} c & k \\ k & d \end{bmatrix} = \begin{bmatrix} a+c & h+k \\ h+k & b+d \end{bmatrix} \in S \quad \Rightarrow \quad S$ is closed.

(*b*) $k\begin{bmatrix} a & h \\ h & b \end{bmatrix} = \begin{bmatrix} ak & kh \\ kh & kb \end{bmatrix} \in S \quad \Rightarrow \quad S$ is closed.

Q.8 (*a*) No, as $\lambda\mathbf{A} + \mu\mathbf{B} = \begin{bmatrix} \lambda & \mu \\ \mu & \lambda \end{bmatrix}$, so the entries in the leading diagonal are the same.
(*b*) $\mathbf{X} = 4\mathbf{A} + 4\mathbf{B} - \mathbf{C}$.
(*c*) $\mathbf{X} = 4\mathbf{A} + 4\mathbf{B} + 5\mathbf{C} + 6\mathbf{D}$ or $\mathbf{X} = 4\mathbf{A} + 4\mathbf{B} - 7\mathbf{C} - 6\mathbf{D}$, so the answer is not unique.
(*d*) $\{\mathbf{A}, \mathbf{B}, \mathbf{C}\}$ is a basis for S; the dimension is 3.
(*e*) For example, $\{\mathbf{A}, \mathbf{B}, \mathbf{D}\}$ is another basis.

Q.9 One possible basis is

$$\left\{\begin{bmatrix}1&0&0\\0&0&0\\0&0&0\end{bmatrix},\begin{bmatrix}0&0&0\\0&1&0\\0&0&0\end{bmatrix},\begin{bmatrix}0&0&0\\0&0&0\\0&0&1\end{bmatrix},\begin{bmatrix}0&1&0\\1&0&0\\0&0&0\end{bmatrix},\begin{bmatrix}0&0&1\\0&0&0\\1&0&0\end{bmatrix},\begin{bmatrix}0&0&0\\0&0&1\\0&1&0\end{bmatrix}\right\}.$$

Q.10 (*a*) If $\mathbf{M}$ and $\mathbf{N}$ are orthogonal matrices, then

$$\mathbf{M}^{\mathrm{T}}\mathbf{M}=\mathbf{I} \quad\text{and}\quad \mathbf{N}^{\mathrm{T}}\mathbf{N}=\mathbf{I}$$

$$\Rightarrow\quad (\mathbf{MN})^{\mathrm{T}}\mathbf{MN}=\mathbf{N}^{\mathrm{T}}\mathbf{M}^{\mathrm{T}}\mathbf{MN}=\mathbf{N}^{\mathrm{T}}\mathbf{IN}=\mathbf{I},$$

so $\mathbf{MN}$ is an orthogonal matrix. Similarly, $\mathbf{NM}$ is an orthogonal matrix.

(*b*) $\begin{bmatrix}1&0\\0&1\end{bmatrix}$ is an orthogonal matrix but $\begin{bmatrix}2&0\\0&2\end{bmatrix}$ is not orthogonal.

Q.11

$$\frac{d^2y_1}{dx^2}-5\frac{dy_1}{dx}+6y_1=0$$

and

$$\frac{d^2y_2}{dx^2}-5\frac{dy_2}{dx}+6y_2=0.$$

Therefore

$$\frac{d^2(y_1+y_2)}{dx^2}-5\frac{d(y_1+y_2)}{dx}+6(y_1+y_2)=0$$

and

$$\frac{d^2(ky_1)}{dx^2}-5\frac{d(ky_1)}{dx}+6(ky_1)=0.$$

Q.12 Differentiate and substitute. One possible set for the basis is $\{e^{2x}, e^{3x}\}$; the dimension is 2.

Q.13 Check by differentiation. It breaks down because of the non-zero constant term on the right-hand side of the differential equation.

Q.14 We are given that (x_1, y_1, z_1) and (x_2, y_2, z_2) are solutions,

so

$$\left.\begin{aligned}3x_1+4y_1-z_1&=0\\3x_2+4y_2-z_2&=0\end{aligned}\right\} \quad\text{and}\quad \left.\begin{aligned}2x_1-y_1+3z_1&=0\\2x_2-y_2+3z_2&=0\end{aligned}\right\}$$

By addition,

$$3(x_1+x_2)+4(y_1+y_2)-(z_1+z_2)=0$$

and

$$2(x_1+x_2)-(y_1+y_2)+3(z_1+z_2)=0,$$

so $(x_1+x_2, y_1+y_2, z_1+z_2)$ is a solution.

Similarly, (kx_1, ky_1, kz_1) is also a solution.

Q.15 $\begin{bmatrix}x\\y\\z\end{bmatrix}=k\begin{bmatrix}1\\-1\\-1\end{bmatrix}$ so $\left\{\begin{bmatrix}1\\-1\\1\end{bmatrix}\right\}$ is a basis; the dimension is 1.

If the equations are taken as the equations of planes, then they intersect in a line, therefore one-dimensional.

Q.16 The set of solutions is not closed under addition or multiplication by real numbers.

Q.17 Yes – for example,
$$\begin{bmatrix} x_1 \\ y_1 \end{bmatrix} + \begin{bmatrix} x_2 \\ y_2 \end{bmatrix} = \begin{bmatrix} x_1 + x_2 \\ y_1 + y_2 \end{bmatrix},$$
$$k\begin{bmatrix} x_1 \\ y_1 \end{bmatrix} = \begin{bmatrix} kx_1 \\ ky_1 \end{bmatrix}.$$

Chapter 11

Q.1 (*a*)
$$\begin{bmatrix} p \\ q \end{bmatrix} = \lambda_1\begin{bmatrix} 2 \\ 1 \end{bmatrix} + \lambda_2\begin{bmatrix} 1 \\ 3 \end{bmatrix};$$

that is,
$$\left.\begin{aligned} p &= 2\lambda_1 + \lambda_2 \\ q &= \lambda_1 + 3\lambda_2 \end{aligned}\right\}$$

which has the solution $\lambda_1 = \dfrac{3p - q}{5}, \quad \lambda_2 = \dfrac{2q - p}{5}.$

So
$$\begin{bmatrix} p \\ q \end{bmatrix} = \left(\frac{3p-q}{5}\right)\begin{bmatrix} 2 \\ 1 \end{bmatrix} + \left(\frac{2q-p}{5}\right)\begin{bmatrix} 1 \\ 3 \end{bmatrix}.$$

(*b*)
$$\begin{bmatrix} p \\ q \end{bmatrix} = \lambda_1\begin{bmatrix} 4 \\ -2 \end{bmatrix} + \lambda_2\begin{bmatrix} -2 \\ 1 \end{bmatrix};$$

that is,
$$\left.\begin{aligned} p &= 4\lambda_1 - 2\lambda_2 \\ q &= -2\lambda_1 + \lambda_2 \end{aligned}\right\}$$

These equations will have a solution only if $p + 2q = 0$.

(*c*)
$$\begin{bmatrix} p \\ q \end{bmatrix} = \lambda_1\begin{bmatrix} 1 \\ 0 \end{bmatrix} + \lambda_2\begin{bmatrix} 0 \\ 1 \end{bmatrix} + \lambda_3\begin{bmatrix} 3 \\ 2 \end{bmatrix};$$

that is,
$$\left.\begin{aligned} p &= \lambda_1 + 3\lambda_3 \\ q &= \lambda_2 + 2\lambda_3 \end{aligned}\right\}$$

Again, there are an infinite number of possible values for λ_1, λ_2 and λ_3. (Put λ_3 equal to any value you like, and this will determine λ_1 and λ_2.)

Q.2 *Necessary* (that is, if unique then linearly independent)

We use proof by contradiction:

Assume $\{\mathbf{a}_1, \mathbf{a}_2, \ldots, \mathbf{a}_n\}$ is a linearly dependent set and
$$\mathbf{v} = \lambda_1\mathbf{a}_1 + \lambda_2\mathbf{a}_2 + \ldots + \lambda_n\mathbf{a}_n \qquad (A)$$
is one expression for $\mathbf{v}$.

Now
$$\mathbf{0} = \mu_1\mathbf{a}_1 + \mu_2\mathbf{a}_2 + \ldots + \mu_n\mathbf{a}_n \qquad (B)$$
with some μ's not zero.

Adding (*A*) and (*B*) gives
$$\mathbf{v} = (\lambda_1 + \mu_1)\mathbf{a}_1 + \ldots + (\lambda_n + \mu_n)\mathbf{a}_n,$$
which is a different expression for $\mathbf{v}$.

As this contradicts the uniqueness of the expression for $\mathbf{v}$, our original assumption must have been wrong.

Sufficient (that is, if linearly independent then unique)
Assume two expressions for $\mathbf{v}$ are

$$\mathbf{v} = \lambda_1\mathbf{a}_1 + \ldots + \lambda_n\mathbf{a}_n$$

and
$$\mathbf{v} = \mu_1\mathbf{a}_1 + \ldots + \mu_n\mathbf{a}_n.$$

Then
$$\mathbf{0} = (\lambda_1 - \mu_1)\mathbf{a}_1 + \ldots + (\lambda_n - \mu_n)\mathbf{a}_n.$$

As $\{\mathbf{a}_1, \mathbf{a}_2, \ldots, \mathbf{a}_n\}$ are linearly independent, all the scalars $(\lambda_r - \mu_r) = 0$; that is, $\lambda_r = \mu_r$, so the expression for $\mathbf{v}$ is unique.

Q.3 $\mathbf{p}$ has coordinates $(1,0)$ and $\mathbf{q}$ has coordinates $(0, 1)$.

Q.4 The basis implied is the set of eigenvectors of the matrix.

Chapter 12

Q.1 $m \times n$.

Q.2 In general, if $k_1\mathbf{c} + k_2\mathbf{c} + k_3\mathbf{c} = \mathbf{0}$ is a linear combination of the columns of the matrix, then $\lambda \begin{bmatrix} k_1 \\ k_2 \\ k_3 \end{bmatrix}$ belongs to the kernel.

Chapter 13

Q.1 Check by substituting directly into the two equations.

Q.2 If $p(x)$ is a particular solution of

$$\mathbf{T}(y(x)) = f(x),$$

then
$$\mathbf{T}(p(x)) = f(x).$$

So
$$\mathbf{T}(y(x) - p(x)) = \mathbf{0}(x) \quad \text{(the function } x \mapsto 0\text{)}.$$

Therefore $y(x) - p(x)$ belongs to the kernel of the transformation $\mathbf{T}$;

that is,
$$y(x) - p(x) = k(x), \quad \text{where } k(x) \in \text{kernel}$$

or
$$y(x) = p(x) + k(x);$$

that is, the complete solution consists of a particular integral and the kernel (complementary function).

Chapter 14

Q.1 You will probably have listed some of the axioms of a vector space – see Definition 1.

Q.2

$$\mathbf{a} + (-\mathbf{a}) = \mathbf{0} \quad \text{(by axiom A4)}$$

$$\lambda(\mathbf{a} + (-\mathbf{a})) = \mathbf{0} \quad \text{(premultiplying by } \lambda)$$

$$\lambda\mathbf{a} + \lambda(-\mathbf{a}) = \lambda\mathbf{0} \quad \text{(by axiom M4)}$$

$$\lambda\mathbf{a} + \lambda(-\mathbf{a}) = \mathbf{0} \quad \text{(using the result of Example 2).}$$

Adding $-(\lambda\mathbf{a})$ to each side (it exists by axiom A4):

$$-(\lambda\mathbf{a}) + (\lambda\mathbf{a} + \lambda(-\mathbf{a})) = -(\lambda\mathbf{a}) + \mathbf{0}$$

$$(-(\lambda\mathbf{a}) + (\lambda\mathbf{a})) + \lambda(-\mathbf{a}) = -(\lambda\mathbf{a}) + \mathbf{0} \quad \text{(by axiom A3)}$$

$$\mathbf{0} + \lambda(-\mathbf{a}) = -(\lambda\mathbf{a}) + \mathbf{0} \quad \text{(by axiom A4)}$$

$$\lambda(-\mathbf{a}) = -(\lambda\mathbf{a}) \quad \text{(by axiom A2).}$$

$$(\lambda + -\lambda)\mathbf{a} = 0\mathbf{a} = \mathbf{0} \quad \text{(using the result of Example 1)}$$

$$\lambda\mathbf{a} + (-\lambda)\mathbf{a} = \mathbf{0} \quad \text{(by axiom M5)}$$

Adding $-(\lambda\mathbf{a})$ to each side (it exists by axiom A4):

$$-(\lambda\mathbf{a}) + (\lambda\mathbf{a} + (-\lambda)\mathbf{a}) = -(\lambda\mathbf{a}) + \mathbf{0}$$

$$(-(\lambda\mathbf{a}) + (\lambda\mathbf{a})) + (-\lambda)\mathbf{a} = -(\lambda\mathbf{a}) + \mathbf{0} \quad \text{(by axiom A3)}$$

$$\mathbf{0} + (-\lambda)\mathbf{a} = -(\lambda\mathbf{a}) + \mathbf{0} \quad \text{(by axiom A4)}$$

$$(-\lambda)\mathbf{a} = -(\lambda\mathbf{a}) \quad \text{(by axiom A2).}$$

So
$$(-\lambda)\mathbf{a} = \lambda(-\mathbf{a}) = -(\lambda\mathbf{a})$$

Q.3 (*a*) If $\lambda = 0$ the result is true.
(*b*) If $\lambda \neq 0$ then λ^{-1} exists, so

$$\lambda^{-1}(\lambda\mathbf{a}) = \lambda^{-1}\mathbf{0} \quad \text{(premultiplying by } \lambda^{-1})$$

$$(\lambda^{-1}\lambda)\mathbf{a} = \lambda^{-1}\mathbf{0} \quad \text{(by axiom M3)}$$

$$1\mathbf{a} = \lambda^{-1}\mathbf{0} \quad \text{(by properties of real numbers)}$$

$$\mathbf{a} = \lambda^{-1}\mathbf{0} \quad \text{(by axiom M2)}$$

$$\mathbf{a} = \mathbf{0} \quad \text{(using the result of Example 2).}$$

So either
$$\lambda = 0 \quad \text{or} \quad \mathbf{a} = \mathbf{0}.$$

Q.4 Axioms A1 and M1 are the only ones you need to check, because

(*a*) as axioms A3, A5, M2, M3, M5 hold for all vectors in V, they will hold for all vectors in the subset U;

(*b*) A2 follows from M1 by putting $\lambda = 0$ to give $0\mathbf{a}$; but, by Example 1, $0\mathbf{a} = \mathbf{0}$ for all $\mathbf{a} \in V$, so $\mathbf{0} \in U$.

(*c*) A4 follows from M1 by putting $\lambda = -1$ to give $(-1)\mathbf{a}$, but, by Q.2, $(-1)\mathbf{a} = -(1\mathbf{a}) = -\mathbf{a}$, so inverses exist in U.

Chapter 15

Q.1

*	I	X	Y	H
I	I	X	Y	H
X	X	I	H	Y
Y	Y	H	I	X
H	H	Y	X	I

Q.2 (*a*)

*	I	A	B	P	Q	R
I	I	A	B	P	Q	R
A	A	B	I	R	P	Q
B	B	I	A	Q	R	P
P	P	Q	R	I	A	B
Q	Q	R	P	B	I	A
R	R	P	Q	A	B	I

(*b*)

*	I	Q	H	T	X	Y	U	V
I	I	Q	H	T	X	Y	U	V
Q	Q	H	T	I	U	V	Y	X
H	H	T	I	Q	Y	X	V	U
T	T	I	Q	H	V	U	X	Y
X	X	V	Y	U	I	H	T	Q
Y	Y	U	X	V	H	I	Q	T
U	U	X	V	Y	Q	T	I	H
V	V	Y	U	X	T	Q	H	I

Q.3 (*a*) 4, (*b*) 6, (*c*) 8.

Q.4 Not associative; for example $b \circ (c \circ d) = b \circ a = d$

and $(b \circ c) \circ d = a \circ d = b.$

Q.5 If $x \circ a = y \circ a$

then $(x \circ a) \circ a^{-1} = (y \circ a) \circ a^{-1}$ (postmultiplying by a^{-1})

$\Rightarrow$ $x \circ (a \circ a^{-1}) = y \circ (a \circ a^{-1})$ (associativity)

$\Rightarrow$ $x \circ e = y \circ e$ (inverses)

$\Rightarrow$ $x = y$ (identity).

Q.6 (*a*) {**I**}, {**I**, **X**}, {**I**, **Y**}, {**I**, **Z**}, *G*
(*b*) {**I**}, {**I**, **A**, **B**}, {**I**, **A**}, {**I**, **B**}, {**I**, **C**}, *G*
(*c*) {**I**}, {**I**, **Q**, **H**, **T**}, {**I**, **H**}, {**I**, **X**}, {**I**, **Y**}, {**I**, **U**}, {**I**, **V**}, {**I**, **H**, **X**, **Y**}, {**I**, **H**, **U**, **V**}, *G*

Q.7 The order of a subgroup is a factor of the order of the group.

Chapter 16

Q.1 A one-to-one mapping is

$$\mathbf{I} \leftrightarrow i$$
$$\mathbf{H} \leftrightarrow a$$
$$\mathbf{X} \leftrightarrow b$$
$$\mathbf{Y} \leftrightarrow c$$

If we replace the elements in table (1) by the corresponding elements we get table (4), so the two groups are isomorphic.

Q.2 If we rewrite table (3) in the order 6, 8, 4, 2,

$\times_{10}$	6	8	4	2
6	6	8	4	2
8	8	4	2	6
4	4	2	6	8
2	2	6	8	4

and replace the elements of this table by the corresponding elements we get table (2), so the two groups are isomorphic.

Q.3 (*a*)

	Group $(G, *)$		*Group* $(H, \circ)$
Identity elements	e		h
If	a	$\leftrightarrow$	x
and	e	$\leftrightarrow$	p
then	$a * e$	$\leftrightarrow$	$x \circ p$

But $a * e = a$, so $x \circ p = x = x \circ h$; using the left cancellation law, this implies that $p = h$, that is, the identity elements correspond.

(*b*) If also $\quad a^{-1} \leftrightarrow y$

then $\quad a * a^{-1} \leftrightarrow x \circ y$

but $\quad a * a^{-1} = e$ and $e \leftrightarrow h$

$$\Rightarrow \quad x \circ y = h$$

so $\quad y = x^{-1}$;

that is, inverse elements correspond.

Q.4 **Q** and **X** will generate the symmetry group of the square. (See §15.1 for notation.)

Q.5 Two elements, for example, **X**, **Y** or **X**, **H** or **Y**, **H**. (See §15.1 for notation.)

Q.6 **T** would generate the subgroup, since $\mathbf{T}^2 = \mathbf{H}, \mathbf{T}^3 = \mathbf{Q}, \mathbf{T}^4 = \mathbf{I}$. **H** will not generate the subgroup, since $\mathbf{H}^2 = \mathbf{I}$.

Chapter 17

Q.1 As $a \neq 0$, the inverse of a exists under .

$$a^{-1}.(a.b) = a^{-1}.(a.c)$$

$$(a^{-1}.a).b = (a^{-1}.a).c \quad \text{(associativity under .)}$$

$$1.b = 1.c \quad \text{(inverses under .)}$$

$$b = c \quad \text{(identity under .)}$$

Q.2 (*a*) $\mu = 7$
(*b*) empty set
(*c*) $\mu = 6$
(*d*) $\mu = 4$
(*e*) empty set
(*f*) empty set

(g)

λ	1	2	3	4	5	6	7	8	9	10
μ	1	6	4	3	9	2	8	7	5	10

Q.3 (a) As we are considering the remainders on division by p, addition is closed.
(b) 0 is the identity element.
(c) $(p - a)$ is the inverse of a.
(d) Addition of ordinary numbers is associative, and as we are dealing with remainders on division by p, it will also be true for $\mathbb{Z}_p$.

Q.4 $A(1, 3)$, $B(3, 2)$, $C(1, 1)$, $D(2, 3)$

Q.5 Five points: $(0, 3)$, $(1, 0)$, $(2, 2)$, $(3, 4)$, $(4, 1)$

Q.6 It is relatively easy to check the first three axioms. For axiom 4: in (a) is the triangle inequality, and in (b) and (c) $|x_1 - x_2|$ and $|y_1 - y_2|$ are the distances between the projections of A and B on the x- and y-axes respectively. Consider the separate cases (i) the projection of C lies between the projections of A and B on the axes, and (ii) the projection of C does not lie between the projections of A and B on the axes.

Chapter 18

Q.1 See Fig. 6.

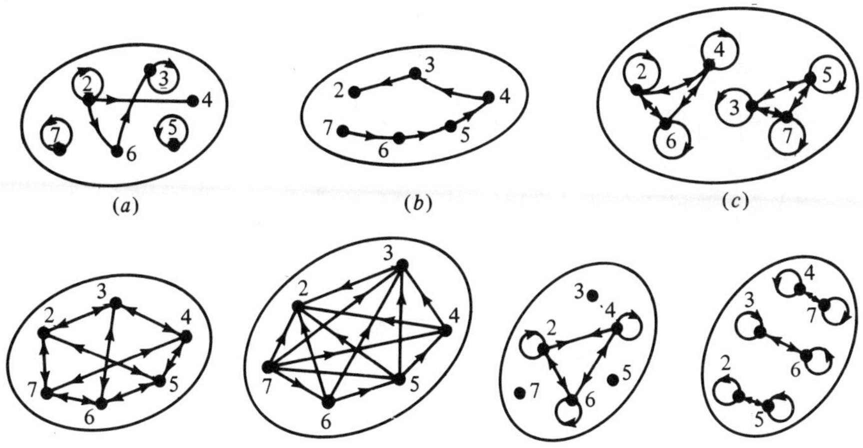

(a) (b) (c) (d) (e) (f) (g)

Figure 6

	(a)	(b)	(c)	(d)	(e)	(f)	(g)
Q.2	×	×	✓	×	×	×	✓
Q.3	×	×	✓	✓	×	✓	✓
Q.4	✓	×	✓	×	✓	✓	✓

Answers

Exercise 1A

1 (*a*) Shear, x-axis invariant, factor 3
(*b*) One-way stretch in y-direction, x-axis invariant, factor $1\frac{1}{2}$
(*c*) Shear, invariant line $y = x$, with $(1,0) \mapsto (2,1)$

2 (*a*) Only for $k = 1$ (*b*) No (*c*) No

3 (*a*) Yes, for all $k \in \mathbb{R}$ (*b*) Yes (*c*) Yes

4 (*a*) Only for $k = 1$ (*b*) No (*c*) No

5 $K(2,-3)$; $A'(-1,0)$, $B'(1,\frac{1}{2})$, $C'(5,0)$, $D'(10,5)$; $K'(7,2)$; yes; CD and $C'D'$ are the same line.

6 Yes

Exercise 1B

1 (*a*) $\mathbf{r} = \begin{bmatrix} 5 \\ 7 \end{bmatrix} + t\begin{bmatrix} 2 \\ 5 \end{bmatrix}$ (*b*) $\mathbf{r} = \begin{bmatrix} 1 \\ 3 \end{bmatrix} + t\begin{bmatrix} -2 \\ 8 \end{bmatrix}$

(*c*) $\mathbf{r} = \begin{bmatrix} 5 \\ -2 \end{bmatrix} + t\begin{bmatrix} -6 \\ 2 \end{bmatrix}$ (*d*) $\mathbf{r} = \begin{bmatrix} 2 \\ -2 \end{bmatrix} + t\begin{bmatrix} -5 \\ -5 \end{bmatrix}$

2 (*a*) $\begin{bmatrix} 10 \\ 6 \end{bmatrix}$ (*b*) $\begin{bmatrix} -7 \\ -6 \end{bmatrix}$ (*c*) $\begin{bmatrix} -6 \\ 21 \end{bmatrix}$ (*d*) $\begin{bmatrix} \frac{177}{29} \\ -\frac{68}{29} \end{bmatrix}$ (*e*) $\begin{bmatrix} -\frac{79}{11} \\ -\frac{93}{11} \end{bmatrix}$

3 (*a*) $\frac{10}{11}\begin{bmatrix} 3 \\ -1 \end{bmatrix} + \frac{18}{11}\begin{bmatrix} 2 \\ 3 \end{bmatrix}$ (*b*) $-6\begin{bmatrix} -1 \\ -\frac{2}{3} \end{bmatrix} + 0\begin{bmatrix} 1 \\ 1 \end{bmatrix}$ (*c*) $\frac{16}{11}\begin{bmatrix} 4 \\ 3 \end{bmatrix} - \frac{2}{11}\begin{bmatrix} -1 \\ 2 \end{bmatrix}$

4 $\mathbf{r} = \begin{bmatrix} 11 \\ 15 \end{bmatrix} + t\begin{bmatrix} 13 \\ 5 \end{bmatrix}$; $(-28,0)$, $(0, 10\frac{10}{13})$

5 $(2,-11)$, $(-5,-7)$, $(-7,27)$

6 $(-11,32)$

7 $8x + 3y + 42 = 0$

8 $y = x + 1$

Exercise 1C

1 (*a*) Yes (*b*) No (*c*) Yes (*d*) No (*e*) Yes
(*f*) Yes (*g*) No (*h*) No

2 (*a*) $\begin{bmatrix} x \\ y \end{bmatrix} \mapsto \begin{bmatrix} 0 & 1 \\ 1 & 0 \end{bmatrix}\begin{bmatrix} x \\ y \end{bmatrix}$ (*c*) $\begin{bmatrix} x \\ y \end{bmatrix} \mapsto \begin{bmatrix} 1 & 1 \\ 1 & -1 \end{bmatrix}\begin{bmatrix} x \\ y \end{bmatrix}$

(*e*) $\begin{bmatrix} x \\ y \end{bmatrix} \mapsto \begin{bmatrix} 0 & 1 \\ 0 & 3 \end{bmatrix}\begin{bmatrix} x \\ y \end{bmatrix}$ (*f*) $\begin{bmatrix} x \\ y \end{bmatrix} \mapsto \begin{bmatrix} 1 & -3 \\ 0 & 1 \end{bmatrix}\begin{bmatrix} x \\ y \end{bmatrix}$

3 $\begin{bmatrix} 1 & 4 \\ -3 & 2 \end{bmatrix}$

Miscellaneous exercise 1

1 For example, $\begin{bmatrix} 1 \\ 3 \end{bmatrix} + \frac{1}{3}\begin{bmatrix} -2 \\ 5 \end{bmatrix} + \frac{5}{3}\begin{bmatrix} 4 \\ -1 \end{bmatrix}$ or $\frac{1}{13}\begin{bmatrix} 1 \\ 3 \end{bmatrix} + \begin{bmatrix} -2 \\ 5 \end{bmatrix} + \frac{29}{13}\begin{bmatrix} 4 \\ -1 \end{bmatrix}$; one of the three vectors can be written as a linear combination of the other two.

2 In general, points inside a triangle map to points inside the image 'triangle'.

3 (*a*) $y = \left(\frac{x}{3}\right)^2$ (*b*) $x = -y^2$ (*c*) $y = -x^2$

4 (*a*) $x^2 + y^2 = 4$ (*b*) $x^2 + y^2 = 2$ (*c*) $5x^2 - 16xy + 13y^2 = 1$

6 The image is a point if $\frac{p}{r} = \frac{r}{s} = \frac{b-d}{c-a}$.

Exercise 2A

1 (*a*) (1,4) (*b*) (2, −3)
(*c*) Same line – infinite number of solutions
(d) Parallel lines – empty solution set

2 (*a*) $(\frac{1}{7}, \frac{10}{7})$ (*b*) $(\frac{47}{8}, \frac{51}{16})$ (*c*) Determinant = 0, so method not applicable

3 (*b*) (1.4,0.2)

4 (*b*) $(\frac{5}{3}, \frac{2}{3})$

Exercise 2B

1 (*a*) $\begin{bmatrix} 1 & 0 \\ 0 & 2 \end{bmatrix}$ (*b*) $\begin{bmatrix} 1 & -1 \\ 0 & 1 \end{bmatrix}$ (*c*) $\begin{bmatrix} 0 & 1 \\ 1 & 0 \end{bmatrix}$ (*d*) $\begin{bmatrix} 1 & 0 \\ 1 & 1 \end{bmatrix}$

2 (*a*) $\mathbf{E}_1 = \begin{bmatrix} 1 & 0 \\ -1 & 1 \end{bmatrix}$, $\mathbf{E}_2 = \begin{bmatrix} \frac{1}{2} & 0 \\ 0 & 1 \end{bmatrix}$, $\mathbf{E}_3 = \begin{bmatrix} 1 & -1 \\ 0 & 1 \end{bmatrix}$, $\mathbf{E}_4 = \begin{bmatrix} 1 & 0 \\ -1 & 1 \end{bmatrix}$

(*b*) $\begin{bmatrix} \frac{3}{2} & -1 \\ -\frac{5}{2} & 2 \end{bmatrix}$

(*c*) $\mathbf{E}_1^{-1} = \begin{bmatrix} 1 & 0 \\ 1 & 1 \end{bmatrix}$, $\mathbf{E}_2^{-1} = \begin{bmatrix} 2 & 0 \\ 0 & 1 \end{bmatrix}$, $\mathbf{E}_3^{-1} = \begin{bmatrix} 1 & 1 \\ 0 & 1 \end{bmatrix}$, $\mathbf{E}_4^{-1} = \begin{bmatrix} 1 & 0 \\ 1 & 1 \end{bmatrix}$

4 (*a*) $\begin{bmatrix} 2 & -1 \\ -1 & 1 \end{bmatrix}$ (*b*) $\begin{bmatrix} -1 & -2 \\ -\frac{2}{3} & -1 \end{bmatrix}$ (*c*) $\begin{bmatrix} 3 & 2 \\ \frac{10}{3} & \frac{7}{3} \end{bmatrix}$

5 Yes

Exercise 2C

1 (*a*) $\begin{bmatrix} 1 & 0 \\ 0 & -1 \end{bmatrix}$ (*b*) $\begin{bmatrix} \frac{1}{2} & -\frac{1}{2}\sqrt{3} \\ \frac{1}{2}\sqrt{3} & \frac{1}{2} \end{bmatrix}$ (*c*) $\begin{bmatrix} 1 & -3 \\ 0 & 1 \end{bmatrix}$ (*d*) $\begin{bmatrix} 1 & 0 \\ 0 & 3 \end{bmatrix}$

(e) $\begin{bmatrix} 5 & 0 \\ 0 & 5 \end{bmatrix}$ (f) $\begin{bmatrix} -\frac{1}{2}\sqrt{3} & \frac{1}{2} \\ \frac{1}{2} & \frac{1}{2}\sqrt{3} \end{bmatrix}$ (g) $\begin{bmatrix} 0 & 0 \\ 0 & 1 \end{bmatrix}$ (h) $\begin{bmatrix} -0.6 & 0.8 \\ 0.8 & 0.6 \end{bmatrix}$

2 (a) $\begin{bmatrix} \cos\theta & -\sin\theta \\ \sin\theta & \cos\theta \end{bmatrix}$ (b) $\begin{bmatrix} \cos 2\theta & \sin 2\theta \\ \sin 2\theta & -\cos 2\theta \end{bmatrix}$

3 (a) Shear with y-axis invariant, factor -2
(b) Two-way stretch, factors 3 and 2
(c) Reflection in the line $y = x$
(d) Rotation about the origin through $-\cos^{-1}(0.8) \simeq -36.9°$
(e) Enlargement, centre the origin, scale factor -3
(f) A projection parallel to the y-axis onto the x-axis
(g) Rotation about the origin through $-90°$
(h) Reflection in the y-axis

Exercise 2D
(*Note:* it is possible to describe a matrix transformation in a number of different ways, only one of which is given here.)

1 One-way stretch in x-direction, y-axis invariant, scale factor 2,
shear with invariant line the x-axis, factor 1,
shear with invariant line the y-axis, factor 2

2 Reflection in the x-axis,
reflection in the y-axis,
shear with invariant line the y-axis, factor -2,
shear with invariant line the x-axis, factor 2

3 One-way stretch in y-direction, x-axis invariant, scale factor -3,
shear with invariant line the x-axis, factor -1,
shear with invariant line the y-axis, factor 5

4 One-way stretch in y-direction, x-axis invariant, scale factor 2,
one-way stretch in x-direction, y-axis invariant, scale factor 3,
shear with invariant line the y-axis, factor $\frac{4}{3}$

5 Shear with invariant line the x-axis, factor -2,
projection parallel to the y-axis onto the x-axis,
shear with invariant line the y-axis, factor -3

6 Shear with invariant line the x-axis, factor -1,
projection parallel to the y-axis onto the x-axis,
one-way stretch in x-direction, y-axis invariant, scale factor -2,
shear with invariant line the y-axis, factor $-\frac{5}{2}$

7 Shear with invariant line the x-axis, factor 2,
one-way stretch in y-direction, x-axis invariant, scale factor 3,
one-way stretch in x-direction, y-axis invariant, scale factor 2,
reflection in the line $y = x$

8 Projection parallel to the x-axis onto the y-axis,
one-way stretch in y-direction, x-axis invariant, scale factor 4,
shear with invariant line the x-axis, factor $\frac{3}{4}$

9 Projection parallel to the x-axis onto the y-axis,

one-way stretch in y-direction, x-axis invariant, scale factor 2,
shear with invariant line the x-axis, factor 1,
shear with invariant line the y-axis, factor -1

Miscellaneous exercise 2

1 (*a*) (i) $p = -\frac{3}{2}$, q any value (coincident lines are also parallel)
(ii) $p = -\frac{3}{2}$, $q = -\frac{5}{2}$
(*b*) $\frac{7}{4}$, 3

2 $\left(\frac{2}{1-\alpha}, \frac{1+\alpha}{1-\alpha}\right)$; $x - y = 1$

3 (*a*) (2, 3) (*b*) $y = 3$

4 $\begin{bmatrix} a & b \\ c & d \end{bmatrix}$;
shear with invariant line the x-axis, factor $\frac{b}{a}$,
one-way stretch in y-direction, x-axis invariant, scale factor $\frac{(ad - bc)}{a}$,
shear with invariant line the y-axis, factor c,
one-way stretch in x-direction, y-axis invariant, scale factor a
(*a*) A different decomposition is needed: maybe start with $\begin{bmatrix} 0 & 1 \\ 1 & 0 \end{bmatrix}$.
(*b*) The scale factor for one of the one-way stretches will be 0, so we have a projection.

5 $1, \frac{5}{3}$; the equations are incompatible.

Exercise 3A

1 (*a*) Line $y = 0$ (*b*) 1 (*c*) Anticlockwise
(*d*) Shear with x-axis invariant, factor -2

2 (*a*) Line $y = 0$ (*b*) 1 (*c*) Clockwise
(*d*) Reflection in the x-axis

3 (*a*) Point (0, 0) (*b*) 1 (*c*) Anticlockwise
(*d*) Rotation about the origin through $\cos^{-1}(\frac{5}{13})$

4 (*a*) Point (0, 0) (*b*) 1 (*c*) Clockwise
(*d*) Two-way stretch, factors 3 and $-\frac{1}{3}$ in the directions of the x- and y-axes respectively

5 (*a*) Line $y = 0$ (*b*) 0 (*c*) —
(*d*) Projection parallel to the y-axis onto the x-axis

6 (*a*) Point (0, 0) (*b*) 6 (*c*) Clockwise
(*d*) Two-way stretch, factors 2 and -3 in the directions of the x- and y-axes respectively

7 (*a*) Line $2x + y = 0$ (*b*) 2 (*c*) Anticlockwise
(*d*) Shear with invariant line $y = -\frac{1}{2}x$ followed by a one-way stretch in direction $y = 2x$ with $y = -\frac{1}{2}x$ invariant

8 (*a*) Line $x + y = 0$ (*b*) 1 (*c*) Anticlockwise
(*d*) Shear with invariant line $y = -x$ in which $(1, 0) \mapsto (0, 1)$

The 'sense' changes if the determinant is negative.

Exercise 3B

1 (*a*) $\begin{bmatrix} -0.8 & 0.6 \\ 0.6 & 0.8 \end{bmatrix}$ (*b*) $\begin{bmatrix} 0 & 1 \\ -1 & 2 \end{bmatrix}$ (*c*) $\begin{bmatrix} 2 & -1 \\ -1 & 2 \end{bmatrix}$

(*d*) $\begin{bmatrix} 0.8 & 0.4 \\ 0.4 & 0.2 \end{bmatrix}$ (*e*) $\begin{bmatrix} 0.6 & -0.8 \\ -0.8 & -0.6 \end{bmatrix}$

2 (*a*) Reflection in the line $y = \frac{1}{2}x$
(*b*) Shear with invariant line $y = -x$, factor 2
(*c*) One-way stretch in the direction $y = \frac{1}{3}x$, factor 11, with invariant line $y = -3x$
(*d*) Projection parallel to $y = -\frac{2}{3}x$ onto the line $y = \frac{3}{2}x$
(*e*) Reflection in the line $y = -3x$

Miscellaneous exercise 3

1 If $\mathbf{A} = \begin{bmatrix} 4 & -1 \\ 3 & 5 \end{bmatrix}$ and $\mathbf{B} = \begin{bmatrix} 13 & -5 \\ 15 & -4 \end{bmatrix}$, one possible matrix $\mathbf{P}$ is $\begin{bmatrix} 1 & -1 \\ 6 & -3 \end{bmatrix}$.

3 Reflection in the line $x + y = 0$

4 $\begin{bmatrix} 3.5 & -0.5 \\ -0.5 & 3.5 \end{bmatrix}$

5 $\mathbf{x} = \lambda \begin{bmatrix} b \\ 1 - a \end{bmatrix}$: $\lambda \in \mathbb{R}$ and $\lambda \neq 0$

Exercise 4A

	Characteristic equation	Eigenvalues and corresponding eigenvectors
1	$\lambda^2 - \lambda - 6 = 0$	$3, \begin{bmatrix} 1 \\ 1 \end{bmatrix}$; $-2, \begin{bmatrix} 1 \\ -4 \end{bmatrix}$
2	$\lambda^2 - 5\lambda + 4 = 0$	$1, \begin{bmatrix} 1 \\ -1 \end{bmatrix}$; $4, \begin{bmatrix} 2 \\ 1 \end{bmatrix}$
3	$\lambda^2 + 3\lambda - 10 = 0$	$2, \begin{bmatrix} 3 \\ 1 \end{bmatrix}$; $-5, \begin{bmatrix} 1 \\ -2 \end{bmatrix}$
4	$\lambda^2 + 7\lambda + 12 = 0$	$-3, \begin{bmatrix} 2 \\ -1 \end{bmatrix}$; $-4, \begin{bmatrix} 1 \\ -1 \end{bmatrix}$
5	$\lambda^2 - 2\lambda - 35 = 0$	$7, \begin{bmatrix} 1 \\ 1 \end{bmatrix}$; $-5, \begin{bmatrix} 1 \\ -1 \end{bmatrix}$
6	$\lambda^2 - 8\lambda = 0$	$0, \begin{bmatrix} -3 \\ -2 \end{bmatrix}$; $8, \begin{bmatrix} -1 \\ 2 \end{bmatrix}$
7	$\lambda^2 - \frac{5}{6}\lambda + \frac{1}{6} = 0$	$\frac{1}{2}, \begin{bmatrix} 2 \\ 1 \end{bmatrix}$; $\frac{1}{3}, \begin{bmatrix} 3 \\ 2 \end{bmatrix}$
8	$\lambda^2 - \frac{1}{4}\lambda - \frac{1}{8} = 0$	$\frac{1}{2}, \begin{bmatrix} 2 \\ 1 \end{bmatrix}$; $-\frac{1}{4}, \begin{bmatrix} 1 \\ 2 \end{bmatrix}$
9	$\lambda^2 - \frac{1}{4}\lambda - \frac{3}{4} = 0$	$1, \begin{bmatrix} 5 \\ 2 \end{bmatrix}$; $-\frac{3}{4}, \begin{bmatrix} 1 \\ -1 \end{bmatrix}$

Exercise 4B

1 (*a*) (i) $\mathbf{U} = \begin{bmatrix} 1 & 1 \\ 1 & -4 \end{bmatrix}$, $\mathbf{\Lambda} = \begin{bmatrix} 3 & 0 \\ 0 & -2 \end{bmatrix}$

(ii) Two-way stretch in oblique directions $y = x$ and $y = -4x$, factors 3 and -2

(iii) $\begin{bmatrix} 188 & 55 \\ 220 & 23 \end{bmatrix}$ (iv) $\frac{1}{6}\begin{bmatrix} 1 & 1 \\ 4 & -2 \end{bmatrix}$ (v) $13\mathbf{M} + 42\mathbf{I}$

(*b*) (i) $\mathbf{U} = \begin{bmatrix} 1 & 2 \\ -1 & 1 \end{bmatrix}$, $\mathbf{\Lambda} = \begin{bmatrix} 1 & 0 \\ 0 & 4 \end{bmatrix}$

(ii) Two-way stretch in oblique directions $y = -x$ and $y = \frac{1}{2}x$, factors 1 and 4

(iii) $\begin{bmatrix} 683 & 682 \\ 341 & 342 \end{bmatrix}$ (iv) $\frac{1}{4}\begin{bmatrix} 2 & -2 \\ -1 & 3 \end{bmatrix}$ (v) $85\mathbf{M} - 84\mathbf{I}$

(*c*) (i) $\mathbf{U} = \begin{bmatrix} 3 & 1 \\ 1 & -2 \end{bmatrix}$, $\mathbf{\Lambda} = \begin{bmatrix} 2 & 0 \\ 0 & -5 \end{bmatrix}$

(ii) Two-way stretch in oblique directions $y = \frac{1}{3}x$ and $y = -2x$, factors 2 and -5

(iii) $\begin{bmatrix} -419 & 1353 \\ 902 & -2674 \end{bmatrix}$ (iv) $\frac{1}{10}\begin{bmatrix} 4 & 3 \\ 2 & -1 \end{bmatrix}$ (v) $-87\mathbf{M} + 190\mathbf{I}$

(*d*) (i) $\mathbf{U} = \begin{bmatrix} 2 & 1 \\ -1 & -1 \end{bmatrix}$, $\mathbf{\Lambda} = \begin{bmatrix} -3 & 0 \\ 0 & -4 \end{bmatrix}$

(ii) Two-way stretch in oblique directions $y = -\frac{1}{2}x$ and $y = -x$, factors -3 and -5

(iii) $\begin{bmatrix} 538 & 1562 \\ -781 & -1805 \end{bmatrix}$ (iv) $\frac{1}{12}\begin{bmatrix} -5 & -2 \\ 1 & -2 \end{bmatrix}$ (v) $-175\mathbf{M} - 444\mathbf{I}$

2 $\begin{bmatrix} -2 & 1 \\ 1 & -1 \end{bmatrix}$

3 $\begin{bmatrix} \frac{37}{21} & -\frac{10}{21} \\ -\frac{5}{7} & \frac{4}{7} \end{bmatrix}$

4 4, -1; the eigenvectors are the same.

Miscellaneous exercise 4

1 $\begin{bmatrix} 1 & 1 \\ -1 & 2 \end{bmatrix}$, $\begin{bmatrix} \frac{1}{4} & 0 \\ 0 & 1 \end{bmatrix}$; $\begin{bmatrix} \frac{3}{8} & \frac{5}{16} \\ \frac{5}{8} & \frac{11}{16} \end{bmatrix}$, $\begin{bmatrix} \frac{11}{32} & \frac{21}{64} \\ \frac{21}{32} & \frac{43}{64} \end{bmatrix}$, $\begin{bmatrix} \frac{1}{3} + \frac{2}{3}(\frac{1}{4})^n & \frac{1}{3} - \frac{1}{3}(\frac{1}{4})^n \\ \frac{2}{3} - \frac{2}{3}(\frac{1}{4})^n & \frac{2}{3} + \frac{1}{3}(\frac{1}{4})^n \end{bmatrix}$; $\begin{bmatrix} \frac{1}{3} & \frac{1}{3} \\ \frac{2}{3} & \frac{2}{3} \end{bmatrix}$.

3 (*a*) 90° (*b*) 90° (*c*) 90° (*d*) 90°
All the matrices are symmetric about the leading diagonal.

4 (*a*) 3 (twice); $\begin{bmatrix} 1 \\ -1 \end{bmatrix}$

(*b*) $\mathbf{U} = \begin{bmatrix} 1 & 1 \\ -1 & -1 \end{bmatrix}$, so $\mathbf{U}^{-1}$ does not exist.

5 (*a*) $2 \pm 3j$; $\left[\sqrt{13}, \cos^{-1}\left(\frac{2}{\sqrt{13}}\right)\right]$, $\left[\sqrt{13}, -\cos^{-1}\left(\frac{2}{\sqrt{13}}\right)\right]$

(*b*) Rotation about the origin through $-\cos^{-1}\left(\frac{2}{\sqrt{13}}\right) \simeq -56.3°$, and an enlargement, centre the origin, scale factor $\sqrt{13}$.

Revision exercise 1

A1 $\mathbf{r} = \begin{bmatrix} 5 \\ 1 \end{bmatrix} + t\begin{bmatrix} 2 \\ 2 \end{bmatrix}$

A2 $\begin{bmatrix} -32 & 19 \\ 2 & 0 \end{bmatrix}$

A3 $\begin{bmatrix} -6 \\ 1 \end{bmatrix} = 11\begin{bmatrix} 1 \\ -3 \end{bmatrix} + 17\begin{bmatrix} -1 \\ 2 \end{bmatrix}$

B1 (*a*) $(-46, 20)$ (*b*) $\begin{bmatrix} -5 & 8 \\ 3 & -1 \end{bmatrix}$ (*c*) $3y = 2x - 19$

B2 $7y = x - 25$; $11y + 2x = 0$; $(-1, 2)$; $(11, -2)$

B3 $5y + 6x + 7 = 0$

B4 $5y - x = 12$; $45°$

B5 (*a*) $y = -\dfrac{1}{x}$ (*b*) $y = \dfrac{1}{x}$ (*c*) $y = -\dfrac{1}{x}$ (*d*) $y = \dfrac{9}{x}$

Revision exercise 2

A1 $x = 5$, $y = 3$

A2 $\begin{bmatrix} 0.4 & 0.2 \\ -0.6 & -0.8 \end{bmatrix}$

A3 $\begin{bmatrix} -\frac{1}{2}\sqrt{3} & -\frac{1}{2} \\ \frac{1}{2} & -\frac{1}{2}\sqrt{3} \end{bmatrix}$

A4 (*a*) Unique (*b*) None (*c*) Infinite (*d*) None

A5 Reflection in $y = \frac{1}{2}x$

B1 (*b*) $(\frac{14}{11}, \frac{6}{11})$

B2 $\begin{bmatrix} 1 & 0 \\ 0 & 1 \end{bmatrix}$

B3 $(3.8, -7.4)$; multiply first row by $\frac{1}{3}$, subtract 7 times first row from second row, multiply second row by $\frac{3}{5}$, subtract a third of the second row from the first row; $\begin{bmatrix} 0.8 & -0.2 \\ -1.4 & 0.6 \end{bmatrix}$; inverse

B4 e.g. $\mathbf{M} = \begin{bmatrix} 1 & 2 \\ 0 & 1 \end{bmatrix}\begin{bmatrix} 1 & 0 \\ 0 & 2 \end{bmatrix}\begin{bmatrix} 1 & 0 \\ -3 & 1 \end{bmatrix}$

B5 Reflection in $y = x$; reflection in $y = 0$; $90°$ rotation about origin; $-90°$ rotation about origin.

(*a*) $\begin{bmatrix} \frac{1}{\sqrt{2}} & -\frac{1}{\sqrt{2}} \\ \frac{1}{\sqrt{2}} & \frac{1}{\sqrt{2}} \end{bmatrix}$ or $\begin{bmatrix} -\frac{1}{\sqrt{2}} & \frac{1}{\sqrt{2}} \\ -\frac{1}{\sqrt{2}} & -\frac{1}{\sqrt{2}} \end{bmatrix}$ (*b*) 4 (*c*) $\begin{bmatrix} -1 & 0 \\ 0 & 1 \end{bmatrix}$

Revision exercise 3

A1 (*a*) $y = x$ (*b*) $(0, 0)$

A2 $\frac{1}{10}$

A3 e.g. $\begin{bmatrix} 8 \\ 9 \end{bmatrix}$

A4 Choose any non-singular matrix **P** and calculate $\mathbf{P}^{-1}\mathbf{AP}$.

A5 $\begin{bmatrix} 2 & 1 \\ 1 & 2 \end{bmatrix}$

B1 $y = -x$; e.g. shear with invariant line $y = -x$, factor 2, followed by a one-way stretch, factor 7 parallel to $y = x$, invariant line $y = -x$

B2 (*a*) $\begin{bmatrix} 1 & 0 \\ 0 & 1 \end{bmatrix}$ (*b*) $\begin{bmatrix} 2 \\ 1 \end{bmatrix}, \begin{bmatrix} 1 \\ -2 \end{bmatrix}$ (*c*) Reflection in $y = \frac{1}{2}x$

B3 $\mathbf{S} = \begin{bmatrix} -0.6 & 0.8 \\ 0.8 & 0.6 \end{bmatrix}$, $\mathbf{T} = \begin{bmatrix} 0.6 & 0.8 \\ 0.8 & -0.6 \end{bmatrix}$, $\mathbf{ST} = \begin{bmatrix} 0.28 & -0.96 \\ 0.96 & 0.28 \end{bmatrix}$,

$\mathbf{TS} = \begin{bmatrix} 0.28 & 0.96 \\ -0.96 & 0.28 \end{bmatrix}$;

rotation about origin through $+\cos^{-1} 0.28 \approx 73.7°$,
rotation about origin through $-\cos^{-1} 0.28 \approx -73.7°$

B4 (*a*) $\left(\frac{-5a + 12b}{13}, \frac{12a + 5b}{13}\right)$ (*b*) $\left(\frac{4a + 6b}{13}, \frac{6a + 9b}{13}\right)$ (*c*) $\begin{bmatrix} \frac{4}{13} & \frac{6}{13} \\ \frac{6}{13} & \frac{9}{13} \end{bmatrix}$

B5 $\frac{1}{\sqrt{3}}$; 30°, 120°, 210°, 300°

Revision exercise 4

A1 3, 5, $\begin{bmatrix} 1 \\ -1 \end{bmatrix}, \begin{bmatrix} 2 \\ -1 \end{bmatrix}$

A3 Two-way stretch in oblique directions $y = -\frac{3}{2}x$ and $y = 2x$, factors 1 and 8

A4 $\begin{bmatrix} 1 & 3 \\ 2 & 1 \end{bmatrix}\begin{bmatrix} 4 & 0 \\ 0 & -1 \end{bmatrix}\begin{bmatrix} 1 & 3 \\ 2 & 1 \end{bmatrix}^{-1}$

A5 $\begin{bmatrix} \frac{10}{3} & -\frac{2}{3} \\ \frac{2}{3} & \frac{5}{3} \end{bmatrix}$

B1 $\begin{bmatrix} 470 & 254 \\ -127 & 89 \end{bmatrix}$

B2 2, 3; $\begin{bmatrix} 1 \\ 1 \end{bmatrix}, \begin{bmatrix} 1 \\ 2 \end{bmatrix}$

B3 $y = \left(\frac{6 + \sqrt{2}}{3 + 3\sqrt{2}}\right)x$; $-\sqrt{2}, \frac{1}{\sqrt{2}}$

B4 (*a*) $\begin{bmatrix}4\\2\end{bmatrix}, \begin{bmatrix}-3\\9\end{bmatrix}$

(*b*) $\frac{3}{7}\begin{bmatrix}2\\1\end{bmatrix}-\frac{1}{7}\begin{bmatrix}-1\\3\end{bmatrix},\ \frac{1}{7}\begin{bmatrix}2\\1\end{bmatrix}+\frac{2}{7}\begin{bmatrix}-1\\3\end{bmatrix};\quad -\frac{1}{7}\begin{bmatrix}15\\-3\end{bmatrix},\ \frac{1}{7}\begin{bmatrix}-2\\20\end{bmatrix}$

(*c*) $\begin{bmatrix}\frac{15}{7} & -\frac{2}{7}\\ -\frac{3}{7} & \frac{20}{7}\end{bmatrix}$

B5 $a+b-1;\quad \begin{bmatrix}b-1\\a-1\end{bmatrix}, \begin{bmatrix}1\\-1\end{bmatrix}$

Exercise 5A

1 (*a*) $\begin{bmatrix}2 & 4 & -1\\1 & 2 & 3\\4 & 0 & 2\end{bmatrix}$ (*b*) $\begin{bmatrix}2 & 0 & -\frac{2}{3}\\0 & 0 & \frac{1}{3}\\5 & \frac{1}{2} & 2\end{bmatrix}$ (*c*) $\begin{bmatrix}3 & 3 & -1\\1 & 1 & -1\\0 & 0 & 2\end{bmatrix}$

2 $\mathbf{r}=\begin{bmatrix}0\\0\\2\end{bmatrix}+t\begin{bmatrix}0\\1\\0\end{bmatrix}$; yes

3 (*a*) $\mathbf{r}=s\begin{bmatrix}1\\0\\0\end{bmatrix}+t\begin{bmatrix}0\\0\\1\end{bmatrix}$ (*b*) $\mathbf{r}=s\begin{bmatrix}0\\1\\0\end{bmatrix}+t\begin{bmatrix}0\\0\\1\end{bmatrix}$ (*c*) $\mathbf{r}=s\begin{bmatrix}0\\0\\1\end{bmatrix}+t\begin{bmatrix}1\\1\\0\end{bmatrix}$

(*a*) $\mathbf{r}=s\begin{bmatrix}\frac{1}{\sqrt{2}}\\ \frac{1}{\sqrt{2}}\\0\end{bmatrix}+t\begin{bmatrix}0\\0\\1\end{bmatrix}$ (*b*) $\mathbf{r}=s\begin{bmatrix}-\frac{1}{\sqrt{2}}\\ \frac{1}{\sqrt{2}}\\0\end{bmatrix}+t\begin{bmatrix}0\\0\\1\end{bmatrix}$

(*c*) $\mathbf{r}=s\begin{bmatrix}0\\0\\1\end{bmatrix}+t\begin{bmatrix}0\\\sqrt{2}\\0\end{bmatrix}$

Rotation of 45° about the z-axis

4 $\mathbf{r}=\begin{bmatrix}0\\1\\0\end{bmatrix}+t\begin{bmatrix}1\\1\\1\end{bmatrix}+s\begin{bmatrix}2\\-1\\-1\end{bmatrix}$

5 (*a*) Linear (*b*) Linear (*c*) Not linear (*d*) Not linear

6 (*a*) $\begin{bmatrix}3\\0\\2\end{bmatrix}$ (*b*) $\mathbf{r}=\begin{bmatrix}0\\1\\0\end{bmatrix}+t\begin{bmatrix}-1\\1\\-1\end{bmatrix}$ (*c*) $\mathbf{r}=\begin{bmatrix}0\\1\\0\end{bmatrix}+s\begin{bmatrix}4\\-1\\3\end{bmatrix}$

Yes; $\mathbf{r}=\begin{bmatrix}0\\1\\0\end{bmatrix}+t\begin{bmatrix}-1\\1\\-1\end{bmatrix}+s\begin{bmatrix}4\\-1\\3\end{bmatrix}$

Exercise 5B

1 (*a*) $\begin{bmatrix} 1 & 0 & 0 \\ 0 & 1 & 0 \\ 0 & 0 & -1 \end{bmatrix}$ (*b*) $\begin{bmatrix} 0 & 0 & 1 \\ 0 & 1 & 0 \\ -1 & 0 & 0 \end{bmatrix}$ (*c*) $\begin{bmatrix} 1 & \frac{4}{3} & 0 \\ 0 & 1 & 0 \\ 0 & 0 & 1 \end{bmatrix}$

(*d*) $\begin{bmatrix} 1 & 0 & 0 \\ -3 & 1 & 0 \\ -1 & 0 & 1 \end{bmatrix}$ (*e*) $\begin{bmatrix} 1 & 0 & 0 \\ 0 & 0 & 1 \\ 0 & 1 & 0 \end{bmatrix}$ (*f*) $\begin{bmatrix} -1 & 0 & 0 \\ 0 & -1 & 0 \\ 0 & 0 & 1 \end{bmatrix}$

2 (*a*) Three-way stretch in the directions of the x-, y- and z-axes, with factors 2, -2, 3
(*b*) Enlargement, centre of the origin, factor 4
(*c*) Rotation of 90° about the x-axis
(*d*) Shear, factor 3, in direction of z-axis, with plane $y = 0$ invariant
(*e*) Rotation of $-\cos^{-1} 0.8 \simeq -36.9°$ about the z-axis
(*f*) Shear, factor -2, in direction of y-axis, with plane $x = 0$ invariant
(*g*) Reflection in the plane $z = 0$
(*h*) Rotation of 180° about the y-axis
(*i*) Rotation of 45° about the y-axis

3 $\begin{bmatrix} 0 & 1 & 0 \\ 1 & 0 & 0 \\ 0 & 0 & 1 \end{bmatrix}, \begin{bmatrix} 0 & -1 & 0 \\ -1 & 0 & 0 \\ 0 & 0 & 1 \end{bmatrix}$;

reflection in the plane $y = 0$, rotation of $-90°$ about the z-axis, reflection in the plane $x = y$, reflection in the plane $x = -y$

4 (*a*) The line $\mathbf{r} = \lambda \begin{bmatrix} -2 \\ -7 \\ 1 \end{bmatrix}, \quad \lambda \in \mathbb{R}$ (*b*) The line $\mathbf{r} = \lambda \begin{bmatrix} -4 \\ 1 \\ 0 \end{bmatrix}, \quad \lambda \in \mathbb{R}$

(*c*) The plane $x + y + z = 0$ (*d*) The plane $x - y + z = 0$

Miscellaneous exercise 5

1 $\begin{bmatrix} -2 \\ 1 \\ 3 \end{bmatrix}$; $y = 0$

2 (*a*) $(0, 0, 0)$ (*b*) the plane $x - y + z = 0$ (*c*) the plane $x - y + z = 0$
Projection in the direction perpendicular to the plane $x - y + z = 0$ onto the plane $x - y + z = 0$

3 (*b*) $\begin{bmatrix} -1 \\ 20 \\ -22 \end{bmatrix}$ (*c*) The line $\mathbf{r} = \lambda \begin{bmatrix} 9 \\ 8 \\ -7 \end{bmatrix}, \lambda \in \mathbb{R}$

4 $\mathbf{R} = \begin{bmatrix} \cos\theta & -\sin\theta & 0 \\ \sin\theta & \cos\theta & 0 \\ 0 & 0 & 1 \end{bmatrix}, \quad \mathbf{S} = \begin{bmatrix} 1 & 0 & 0 \\ 0 & -1 & 0 \\ 0 & 0 & 1 \end{bmatrix}$

(*a*) $\begin{bmatrix} \cos\theta & \sin\theta & 0 \\ -\sin\theta & \cos\theta & 0 \\ 0 & 0 & 1 \end{bmatrix}$

(*b*) $\begin{bmatrix} \cos 2\theta & \sin 2\theta & 0 \\ \sin 2\theta & -\cos 2\theta & 0 \\ 0 & 0 & 1 \end{bmatrix}$; reflection in the plane $y = (\tan\theta)x$

5 $[x \quad y \quad z], \begin{bmatrix} 0 & 0 & a \\ b & 0 & 0 \\ 0 & c & 0 \end{bmatrix};$

$[x^2 + y^2 + z^2], \begin{bmatrix} by \\ cz \\ ax \end{bmatrix};$ $(OP)^2$; $(OP')^2 = (OP)^2$; each of $a, b, c = \pm 1$

Exercise 6A

1 $\{(1, 2, -3)\}$; unique point.

2 $\{(2 + 2\lambda, -1 + 17\lambda, 4 + 7\lambda): \lambda \in \mathbb{R}\}$; a line, as the planes form a sheaf.

3 Empty solution set; the planes form a prism.

4 $\{(1 + \lambda, 4 - 11\lambda, 3 - 7\lambda): \lambda \in \mathbb{R}\}$; a line, as two of the planes are coincident.

5 Empty solution set; two of the planes are parallel.

6 $\{(10 - \lambda, 7 + \lambda, \lambda): \lambda \in \mathbb{R}\}$; a line, as the planes form a sheaf.

7 Empty solution set; the planes form a prism.

8 $\{(-9 + 2\lambda, 6 - \lambda, \lambda): \lambda \in \mathbb{R}\}$; a line, as the planes form a sheaf.

9 $\{(-3, 4, 2)\}$; unique point.

10 $\{(x, y, z): 2x - 5y + 7z = 3\}$; all the same plane.

Exercise 6B

1 $(1, 2, 3)$

For example,

$$\mathbf{E}_1 = \begin{bmatrix} 1 & 0 & 0 \\ -2 & 1 & 0 \\ 0 & 0 & 1 \end{bmatrix}, \mathbf{E}_2 = \begin{bmatrix} 1 & 0 & 0 \\ 0 & 1 & 0 \\ -3 & 0 & 1 \end{bmatrix}, \mathbf{E}_3 = \begin{bmatrix} 1 & 0 & 0 \\ 0 & 1 & 0 \\ 0 & 5 & 1 \end{bmatrix},$$

$$\mathbf{E}_4 = \begin{bmatrix} 1 & 0 & 0 \\ 0 & 1 & 0 \\ 0 & 0 & -\frac{1}{37} \end{bmatrix}, \mathbf{E}_5 = \begin{bmatrix} 1 & 0 & 0 \\ 0 & 1 & 5 \\ 0 & 0 & 1 \end{bmatrix}, \mathbf{E}_6 = \begin{bmatrix} 1 & 0 & 0 \\ 0 & -1 & 0 \\ 0 & 0 & 1 \end{bmatrix},$$

$$\mathbf{E}_7 = \begin{bmatrix} 1 & 0 & -3 \\ 0 & 1 & 0 \\ 0 & 0 & 1 \end{bmatrix}, \mathbf{E}_8 = \begin{bmatrix} 1 & 1 & 0 \\ 0 & 1 & 0 \\ 0 & 0 & 1 \end{bmatrix};$$

$$\frac{1}{37}\begin{bmatrix} 7 & 3 & 8 \\ 9 & -12 & 5 \\ 13 & -5 & -1 \end{bmatrix}$$

2 $(\frac{3}{4}, -\frac{1}{2}, \frac{5}{4})$

For example,

$$\mathbf{E}_1 = \begin{bmatrix} 1 & -1 & 0 \\ 0 & 1 & 0 \\ 0 & 0 & 1 \end{bmatrix}, \mathbf{E}_2 = \begin{bmatrix} 1 & 0 & 0 \\ -1 & 1 & 0 \\ 0 & 0 & 1 \end{bmatrix}, \mathbf{E}_3 = \begin{bmatrix} 1 & 0 & 0 \\ 0 & 1 & 0 \\ 3 & 0 & 1 \end{bmatrix},$$

$$\mathbf{E}_4 = \begin{bmatrix} 1 & 0 & 0 \\ 0 & 1 & 0 \\ 0 & 1 & 1 \end{bmatrix}, \mathbf{E}_5 = \begin{bmatrix} 1 & 0 & 0 \\ 0 & 1 & 0 \\ 0 & 0 & \frac{1}{12} \end{bmatrix}, \mathbf{E}_6 = \begin{bmatrix} 1 & 0 & 0 \\ 0 & 1 & 2 \\ 0 & 0 & 1 \end{bmatrix},$$

$$\mathbf{E}_7 = \begin{bmatrix} 1 & 0 & 0 \\ 0 & \frac{1}{5} & 0 \\ 0 & 0 & 1 \end{bmatrix}, \mathbf{E}_8 = \begin{bmatrix} 1 & 0 & -3 \\ 0 & 1 & 0 \\ 0 & 0 & 1 \end{bmatrix}, \mathbf{E}_9 = \begin{bmatrix} 1 & 3 & 0 \\ 0 & 1 & 0 \\ 0 & 0 & 1 \end{bmatrix};$$

$$\frac{1}{60}\begin{bmatrix} 6 & 21 & -9 \\ -8 & 22 & 2 \\ 10 & -5 & 5 \end{bmatrix}$$

3 (*a*) $\begin{bmatrix} -\frac{5}{4} & -3 & -1 \\ \frac{1}{2} & 1 & 0 \\ \frac{3}{2} & 3 & 1 \end{bmatrix}$ (*b*) $\begin{bmatrix} -3 & -8 & 5 \\ -3 & -5 & 0 \\ -2 & -4 & 1 \end{bmatrix}$ (*c*) $\begin{bmatrix} 1 & 2 & 0 \\ 1 & 13 & -2 \\ 0 & -\frac{5}{2} & \frac{1}{2} \end{bmatrix}$

Exercise 6C

1 (*a*) 11 (*b*) 26

2 (*a*) (i) -31 (ii) -31
(*b*) (i) 21 (ii) 21
(*c*) (i) -2 (ii) -2
The determinant of a matrix is unaltered if rows and columns are interchanged.

3 (*a*) (i) -82 (ii) 82
(*b*) (i) -10 (ii) 10
(*c*) (i) 8 (ii) -8
If two rows of a matrix are interchanged, the determinant of the matrix changes sign.

4 (*a*) 0 (*b*) 0 (*c*) 0
(*d*) 0 (*e*) 0 (*f*) 0
If two rows or columns of a matrix are the same or a multiple of one another, then the determinant of the matrix is zero.

5 $\begin{bmatrix} -4 & -1 & -2 \\ -4 & 0 & -9 \\ -3 & 0 & 6 \end{bmatrix}, \begin{bmatrix} 0 & -1 & 0 \\ 10 & 1 & -1 \\ 0 & 0 & 5 \end{bmatrix};$ 17, -3, -51, 50;

$\det(\mathbf{AB}) = \det(\mathbf{A}) \times \det(\mathbf{B})$

6 $\begin{bmatrix} 3 & -1 & 1 \\ -1 & 2 & 1 \\ 2 & 0 & 2 \end{bmatrix};$ 4

7 19

8 (*a*) (i) 1 (ii) $\begin{bmatrix} 1 & 0 & -2 \\ 0 & 1 & 1 \\ 0 & 0 & 1 \end{bmatrix}$; 1 (*b*) (i) 1 (ii) $\begin{bmatrix} \frac{1}{2} & 0 & \frac{1}{2}\sqrt{3} \\ 0 & 1 & 0 \\ -\frac{1}{2}\sqrt{3} & 0 & \frac{1}{2} \end{bmatrix}$; 1

(*c*) (i) 1 (ii) $\begin{bmatrix} 1 & 0 & 0 \\ 0 & -1 & 0 \\ 0 & 0 & 1 \end{bmatrix}$; -1 (*d*) (i) 10 (ii) $\begin{bmatrix} 2 & 0 & 0 \\ 0 & 1 & 0 \\ 0 & 0 & 5 \end{bmatrix}$; 10

(*e*) (i) 27 (ii) $\begin{bmatrix} 0 & 0 & 0 \\ 0 & 1 & 0 \\ 0 & 0 & 1 \end{bmatrix}$; 0 (*f*) (i) 27 (ii) $\begin{bmatrix} 3 & 0 & 0 \\ 0 & 3 & 0 \\ 0 & 0 & 3 \end{bmatrix}$; 27

(*g*) (i) 1 (ii) $\begin{bmatrix} -1 & 0 & 0 \\ 0 & -1 & 0 \\ 0 & 0 & -1 \end{bmatrix}$; -1 (*h*) (i) 1 (ii) $\begin{bmatrix} 0 & 0 & 1 \\ 0 & 1 & 0 \\ 1 & 0 & 0 \end{bmatrix}$; -1

A minus sign indicates an 'opposite' transformation.

Exercise 6D

1 (*a*) 0 (*b*) 9 (*c*) 100 (*d*) 0 (*e*) 0 (*f*) 0

2 (*a*) $\frac{1}{9}\begin{bmatrix} 7 & 1 & 3 \\ -4 & 2 & -3 \\ -2 & 1 & 3 \end{bmatrix}$ (*b*) $\frac{1}{8}\begin{bmatrix} -2 & 6 & -4 \\ 3 & -1 & 2 \\ -5 & 15 & -14 \end{bmatrix}$

(*c*) $-\frac{1}{2}\begin{bmatrix} 6 & 10 & -18 \\ 14 & 24 & -42 \\ 12 & 20 & -35 \end{bmatrix}$ (*d*) $-\frac{1}{25}\begin{bmatrix} 15 & 20 & -5 \\ -22 & -31 & -1 \\ 6 & 13 & -2 \end{bmatrix}$

Exercise 6E

1 (*a*) $(\frac{22}{9}, -\frac{19}{9}, -\frac{5}{9})$ (*b*) $(\frac{22}{8}, -\frac{13}{8}, \frac{43}{8})$

(*c*) $(\frac{1}{2}, \frac{1}{2}, 1)$ (*d*) $(2, 1, 1)$

2 (*a*) (i) 0 (ii) $\{(-17\lambda, 19\lambda, 10\lambda): \lambda \in \mathbb{R}\}$
(*b*) (i) -149 (ii) $\{(0, 0, 0)\}$
(*c*) (i) 0 (ii) $\{(-160\lambda, 809\lambda, 378\lambda): \lambda \in \mathbb{R}\}$
(*d*) (i) 0 (ii) any point on the plane $32x - 25y + 34z = 0$

Miscellaneous exercise 6

1 (*b*) (i) 0 (ii) 12 (iii) 0

2 (*a*) $(b - a)(c - a)(c - b)$
(*b*) (i) $rst(r - s)(s - t)(t - r)$ (ii) $-(x - y)(y - z)(z - x)(x + y + z)$
(iii) $-(l - m)(m - n)(n - r)(l + m + n)$ (iv) $(a - b)(b - c)(c - a)$

4 (*a*) 2, 5 (*b*) -2, 3, 4 (*c*) 1, 2, 3

5 (*a*) $\lambda = 2$; empty solution set
(*b*) $\lambda = 11$; $\{(13\mu, 9\mu, 7\mu): \mu \in \mathbb{R}\}$

Exercise 7A

1 0, 10; -1, $\begin{bmatrix} 1 \\ -1 \\ 0 \end{bmatrix}$

2

Characteristic equation	Real eigenvalues and corresponding eigenvalues
(*a*) $\lambda^3 - 3\lambda^2 + 2\lambda = 0$	$0, \begin{bmatrix} 1 \\ 0 \\ -1 \end{bmatrix}$; $1, \begin{bmatrix} 0 \\ 1 \\ 0 \end{bmatrix}$; $2, \begin{bmatrix} 1 \\ 0 \\ 1 \end{bmatrix}$
(*b*) $\lambda^3 - 6\lambda^2 + 11\lambda - 6 = 0$	$1, \begin{bmatrix} 1 \\ 0 \\ -1 \end{bmatrix}$; $2, \begin{bmatrix} 2 \\ -1 \\ 0 \end{bmatrix}$; $3, \begin{bmatrix} 0 \\ 1 \\ -1 \end{bmatrix}$
(c) $\lambda^3 + 8\lambda^2 + 19\lambda + 12 = 0$	$-1, \begin{bmatrix} 0 \\ 1 \\ -1 \end{bmatrix}$; $-3, \begin{bmatrix} 2 \\ -1 \\ 0 \end{bmatrix}$; $-4, \begin{bmatrix} 1 \\ 0 \\ -1 \end{bmatrix}$
(*d*) $\lambda^3 - 9\lambda^2 + 6\lambda + 56 = 0$	$-2, \begin{bmatrix} 3 \\ -2 \\ 0 \end{bmatrix}$; $4, \begin{bmatrix} 1 \\ 0 \\ 0 \end{bmatrix}$; $7, \begin{bmatrix} 6 \\ 2 \\ 3 \end{bmatrix}$
(*e*) $\lambda^3 + 2\lambda^2 - \lambda - 14 = 0$	$2, \begin{bmatrix} 2 \\ 1 \\ 1 \end{bmatrix}$
(*f*) $\lambda^3 - \frac{1}{4}\lambda^2 - \frac{1}{4}\lambda - \frac{1}{2} = 0$	$1, \begin{bmatrix} 2 \\ 4 \\ 3 \end{bmatrix}$

3 (*a*) Repeated eigenvalue is 1; any vector in the plane $x - y + z = 0$ is an eigenvector; 4, $\begin{bmatrix} 1 \\ -1 \\ 1 \end{bmatrix}$.

(*b*) Repeated eigenvalue is 1, $\begin{bmatrix} 1 \\ 0 \\ 0 \end{bmatrix}$; 2, $\begin{bmatrix} 1 \\ 1 \\ -1 \end{bmatrix}$.

4 90° between any pair: -3, $\begin{bmatrix} -3 \\ -4 \\ 5 \end{bmatrix}$; 2, $\begin{bmatrix} 4 \\ -3 \\ 0 \end{bmatrix}$; 7, $\begin{bmatrix} 3 \\ 4 \\ 5 \end{bmatrix}$

Exercise 7B

1 (*a*) (i) $\mathbf{U} = \begin{bmatrix} 1 & 0 & 1 \\ 0 & 1 & 0 \\ -1 & 0 & 1 \end{bmatrix}$, $\mathbf{\Lambda} = \begin{bmatrix} 0 & 0 & 0 \\ 0 & 1 & 0 \\ 0 & 0 & 2 \end{bmatrix}$

(ii) Three-way stretch in oblique directions $\begin{bmatrix} 1 \\ 0 \\ -1 \end{bmatrix}, \begin{bmatrix} 0 \\ 1 \\ 0 \end{bmatrix}, \begin{bmatrix} 1 \\ 0 \\ 1 \end{bmatrix}$ with factors 0, 1, 2

(iii) $\begin{bmatrix} 16 & 0 & 16 \\ 0 & 1 & 0 \\ 16 & 0 & 16 \end{bmatrix}$ (iv) $\mathbf{M}^{-1}$ does not exist, as $\det(\mathbf{M}) = 0$

(*b*) (i) $\mathbf{U} = \begin{bmatrix} 1 & 2 & 0 \\ 0 & -1 & 1 \\ -1 & 0 & -1 \end{bmatrix}, \mathbf{\Lambda} = \begin{bmatrix} 1 & 0 & 0 \\ 0 & 2 & 0 \\ 0 & 0 & 3 \end{bmatrix}$

(ii) Three-way stretch in oblique directions $\begin{bmatrix} 1 \\ 0 \\ -1 \end{bmatrix}, \begin{bmatrix} 2 \\ -1 \\ 0 \end{bmatrix}, \begin{bmatrix} 0 \\ 1 \\ -1 \end{bmatrix}$ with factors 1, 2, 3

(iii) $\begin{bmatrix} 63 & 62 & 62 \\ 211 & 454 & 211 \\ -242 & -484 & -241 \end{bmatrix}$ (iv) $\frac{1}{6}\begin{bmatrix} 0 & -6 & -6 \\ -1 & 1 & -1 \\ 4 & 8 & 10 \end{bmatrix}$

(*c*) (i) $\mathbf{U} = \begin{bmatrix} 0 & 2 & 1 \\ 1 & -1 & 0 \\ -1 & 0 & -1 \end{bmatrix}, \mathbf{\Lambda} = \begin{bmatrix} -1 & 0 & 0 \\ 0 & -3 & 0 \\ 0 & 0 & -4 \end{bmatrix}$

(ii) Three-way stretch in oblique directions $\begin{bmatrix} 0 \\ 1 \\ -1 \end{bmatrix}, \begin{bmatrix} 2 \\ -1 \\ 0 \end{bmatrix}, \begin{bmatrix} 1 \\ 0 \\ -1 \end{bmatrix}$ with factors -1, -3, -4

(iii) $\begin{bmatrix} 538 & 1562 & 1562 \\ 242 & 241 & 242 \\ -1023 & -2046 & -2047 \end{bmatrix}$ (iv) $-\frac{1}{12}\begin{bmatrix} 5 & 2 & 2 \\ 8 & 20 & 8 \\ -9 & -18 & -6 \end{bmatrix}$

2 (*a*) $\mathbf{U} = \begin{bmatrix} 1 & 0 & 1 \\ 1 & 1 & -1 \\ 0 & 1 & 1 \end{bmatrix}, \mathbf{\Lambda} = \begin{bmatrix} 1 & 0 & 0 \\ 0 & 1 & 0 \\ 0 & 0 & 4 \end{bmatrix}$

(*b*) $\mathbf{U} = \begin{bmatrix} 1 & 1 & 1 \\ 0 & 0 & 1 \\ 0 & 0 & -1 \end{bmatrix}$ and as $\det(\mathbf{U}) = 0$, $\mathbf{U}^{-1}$ does not exist.

3 $\begin{bmatrix} 1 & -2 & 1 \\ 3 & -4 & 1 \\ 3 & -7 & 4 \end{bmatrix}$

4 $\begin{bmatrix} 1 & 2 & 0 \\ -1 & -1 & 1 \\ 0 & 1 & -1 \end{bmatrix}\begin{bmatrix} 0 & 0 & 0 \\ 0 & 1 & 0 \\ 0 & 0 & -3 \end{bmatrix}\begin{bmatrix} 0 & -1 & -1 \\ \frac{1}{2} & \frac{1}{2} & \frac{1}{2} \\ \frac{1}{2} & \frac{1}{2} & -\frac{1}{2} \end{bmatrix}$;

$$\begin{bmatrix} 1 & 1 & 1 \\ \dfrac{(-3)^n - 1}{2} & \dfrac{(-3)^n - 1}{2} & \dfrac{-(-3)^n - 1}{2} \\ \dfrac{1-(-3)^n}{2} & \dfrac{1-(-3)^n}{2} & \dfrac{1+(-3)^n}{2} \end{bmatrix}$$

5 $\begin{bmatrix} \frac{1}{4} & \frac{1}{4} & \frac{1}{4} \\ \frac{1}{2} & \frac{1}{2} & \frac{1}{2} \\ \frac{1}{4} & \frac{1}{4} & \frac{1}{4} \end{bmatrix}$

Miscellaneous exercise 7

1 $\mathbf{U} = \begin{bmatrix} 2 & 2 & 1 \\ 1 & 1 & -1 \\ 0 & 1 & 0 \end{bmatrix}, \mathbf{\Lambda} = \begin{bmatrix} 1 & 0 & 0 \\ 0 & 1 & 0 \\ 0 & 0 & -\frac{1}{2} \end{bmatrix}; \begin{bmatrix} \frac{2}{3} & \frac{2}{3} & 0 \\ \frac{1}{3} & \frac{1}{3} & 0 \\ 0 & 0 & 1 \end{bmatrix}$; no

2 The characteristic equations are the same. $\mathbf{D}$ and $\mathbf{P}^{-1}\mathbf{DP}$ are similar matrices (see question 3).

4 For example, $\mathbf{D} = \begin{bmatrix} 1 & 0 & 0 \\ 0 & -2 & 0 \\ 0 & 0 & 3 \end{bmatrix}$ and $\mathbf{P}^{-1}\mathbf{DP}$, where $\mathbf{P}$ is a non-singular matrix.

5 $\begin{bmatrix} \frac{1}{\sqrt{2}} & 0 & \frac{1}{\sqrt{2}} \\ 0 & 1 & 0 \\ \frac{1}{\sqrt{2}} & 0 & \frac{1}{\sqrt{2}} \end{bmatrix}$, $\begin{bmatrix} \frac{1}{\sqrt{2}} & 0 & \frac{1}{\sqrt{2}} \\ 0 & -1 & 0 \\ \frac{1}{\sqrt{2}} & 0 & \frac{1}{\sqrt{2}} \end{bmatrix}$, $\begin{bmatrix} -\frac{1}{\sqrt{2}} & 0 & -\frac{1}{\sqrt{2}} \\ 0 & 1 & 0 \\ -\frac{1}{\sqrt{2}} & 0 & -\frac{1}{\sqrt{2}} \end{bmatrix}$,

$\begin{bmatrix} -\frac{1}{\sqrt{2}} & 0 & -\frac{1}{\sqrt{2}} \\ 0 & -1 & 0 \\ -\frac{1}{\sqrt{2}} & 0 & -\frac{1}{\sqrt{2}} \end{bmatrix}$

Exercise 8A

1 (*a*) Reflection in the line $3x + 4y = 0$

(*b*) Rotation about the origin through $\cos^{-1}\frac{5}{13} \approx 67.4°$

(*c*) Rotation with axis $\begin{bmatrix} \sqrt{2}+1 \\ 1 \\ 1 \end{bmatrix}$ through $\cos^{-1}\left(\dfrac{1-\sqrt{2}}{2\sqrt{2}}\right) \approx 98.4°$

(*d*) Reflection in the plane $(1-\sqrt{2})x + y + z = 0$, followed by a rotation with axis $\begin{bmatrix} 1-\sqrt{2} \\ 1 \\ 1 \end{bmatrix}$ through $\cos^{-1}\left(\dfrac{1+\sqrt{2}}{2\sqrt{2}}\right) \approx 31.4°$

(*e*) Reflection in the plane $x + y + z = 0$

(*f*) Half-turn with axis $\begin{bmatrix} 1 \\ 2 \\ 2 \end{bmatrix}$

2 $\begin{bmatrix} \frac{1}{\sqrt{3}} & \frac{1}{\sqrt{3}} & \frac{1}{\sqrt{3}} \\ \frac{1}{\sqrt{3}} & \frac{-1-\sqrt{3}}{2\sqrt{3}} & \frac{-1+\sqrt{3}}{2\sqrt{3}} \\ \frac{1}{\sqrt{3}} & \frac{-1+\sqrt{3}}{2\sqrt{3}} & \frac{-1-\sqrt{3}}{2\sqrt{3}} \end{bmatrix}$

Exercise 8B

2 (*a*) $\begin{bmatrix} \frac{1}{\sqrt{5}} & \frac{2}{\sqrt{5}} \\ -\frac{2}{\sqrt{5}} & \frac{1}{\sqrt{5}} \end{bmatrix}$ (*b*) $\begin{bmatrix} \frac{2}{\sqrt{5}} & -\frac{1}{\sqrt{5}} \\ \frac{1}{\sqrt{5}} & \frac{2}{\sqrt{5}} \end{bmatrix}$ (*c*) $\begin{bmatrix} \frac{1}{\sqrt{2}} & -\frac{1}{\sqrt{2}} \\ \frac{1}{\sqrt{2}} & \frac{1}{\sqrt{2}} \end{bmatrix}$

(*d*) $\begin{bmatrix} \frac{1}{\sqrt{2}} & 0 & \frac{1}{\sqrt{2}} \\ 0 & 1 & 0 \\ -\frac{1}{\sqrt{2}} & 0 & \frac{1}{\sqrt{2}} \end{bmatrix}$ (*e*) $\begin{bmatrix} \frac{4}{5} & \frac{3}{5\sqrt{2}} & \frac{3}{5\sqrt{2}} \\ -\frac{3}{5} & \frac{4}{5\sqrt{2}} & \frac{4}{5\sqrt{2}} \\ 0 & \frac{1}{\sqrt{2}} & -\frac{1}{\sqrt{2}} \end{bmatrix}$ (*f*) $\begin{bmatrix} 0 & \frac{3}{5} & \frac{4}{5} \\ 1 & 0 & 0 \\ 0 & \frac{4}{5} & -\frac{3}{5} \end{bmatrix}$

4 $\mathbf{A} = \frac{1}{2}(\mathbf{A} + \mathbf{A}^{\mathrm{T}}) + \frac{1}{2}(\mathbf{A} - \mathbf{A}^{\mathrm{T}})$

Miscellaneous exercise 8

1 $\lambda\begin{bmatrix} 1 & 0 \\ 0 & 1 \end{bmatrix} + \mu\begin{bmatrix} 0 & 2 \\ -3 & -3 \end{bmatrix}$

2 $b = c = 0$, or $c = 0$ and $d = b - a$, or $b = 0$ and $d = c - a$

3 $\begin{bmatrix} 1 & 2 \\ 2 & 5 \end{bmatrix}, \begin{bmatrix} 2 & 5 \\ 5 & 12 \end{bmatrix}, \begin{bmatrix} 5 & 12 \\ 12 & 29 \end{bmatrix}, \begin{bmatrix} 12 & 29 \\ 29 & 70 \end{bmatrix}$; $\mathbf{A}^{n+1} - 2\mathbf{A}^n - \mathbf{A}^{n-1} = \mathbf{0}$

4 Possible forms are: $\begin{bmatrix} 1 & 0 \\ 0 & 1 \end{bmatrix}, \begin{bmatrix} -1 & 0 \\ 0 & -1 \end{bmatrix}, \begin{bmatrix} \cos 2\theta & \sin 2\theta \\ \sin 2\theta & -\cos 2\theta \end{bmatrix}, \begin{bmatrix} 1 & \lambda \\ 0 & -1 \end{bmatrix}, \begin{bmatrix} 1 & 0 \\ \lambda & -1 \end{bmatrix},$
$\begin{bmatrix} -1 & \lambda \\ 0 & 1 \end{bmatrix}, \begin{bmatrix} -1 & 0 \\ \lambda & 1 \end{bmatrix}$

6 $\begin{bmatrix} \lambda & 0 & 0 \\ 0 & \mu & \gamma \\ 0 & -\mu & \gamma \end{bmatrix}$

7 (*b*) 0, 1

8 (*b*) $\begin{bmatrix} 2 & 2 \\ -2 & -2 \end{bmatrix}$ (*c*) 0

9 $\begin{bmatrix} 0 & -2 \\ 2 & 0 \end{bmatrix}, \begin{bmatrix} 0 & -2j \\ 2j & 0 \end{bmatrix}, \begin{bmatrix} 2j & 0 \\ 0 & -2j \end{bmatrix}$; the commutator of any pair is a multiple of the third matrix.

12 $-1 + \sqrt{14}, \begin{bmatrix} j\sqrt{5} \\ \sqrt{14} - 3 \end{bmatrix}$; $-1 - \sqrt{14}, \begin{bmatrix} \sqrt{14} - 3 \\ j\sqrt{5} \end{bmatrix}$;
$\frac{1}{\sqrt{(18 - 6\sqrt{14})}}\begin{bmatrix} j\sqrt{5} & \sqrt{14} - 3 \\ \sqrt{14} - 3 & j\sqrt{5} \end{bmatrix}$

Exercise 9A

1 Ellipse

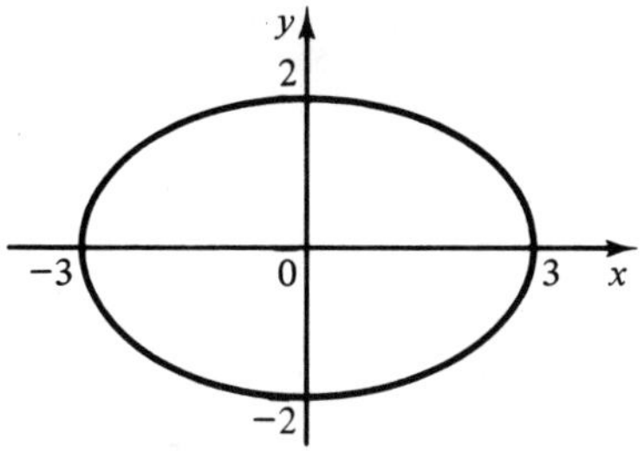

2 Parabola

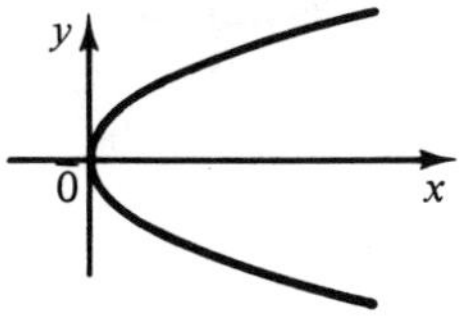

3 Hyperbola

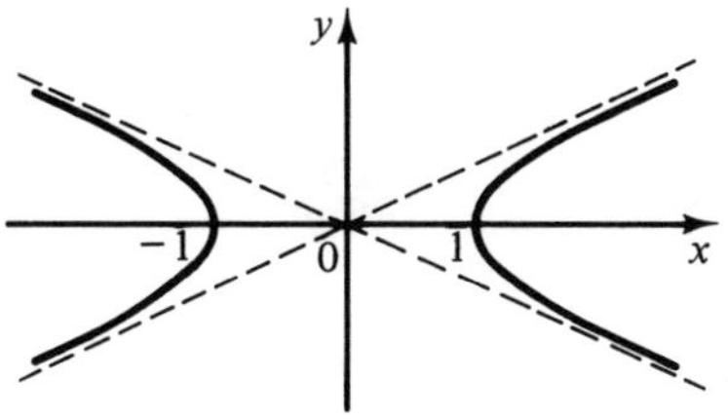

4 Ellipse

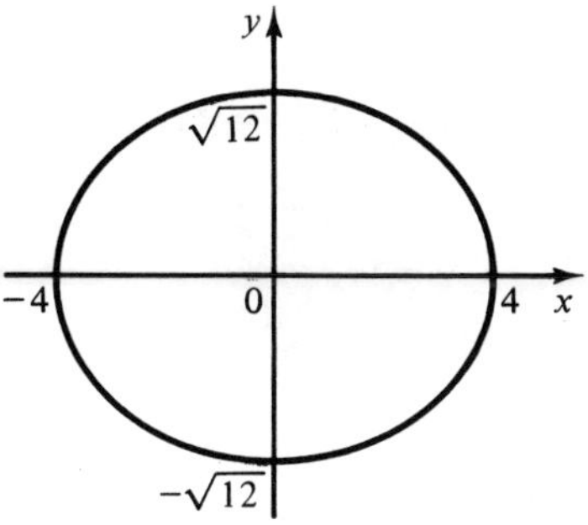

5 Hyperbola

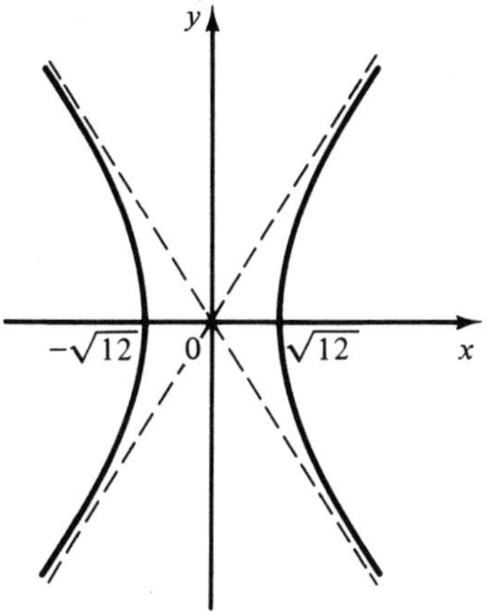

6 Circle

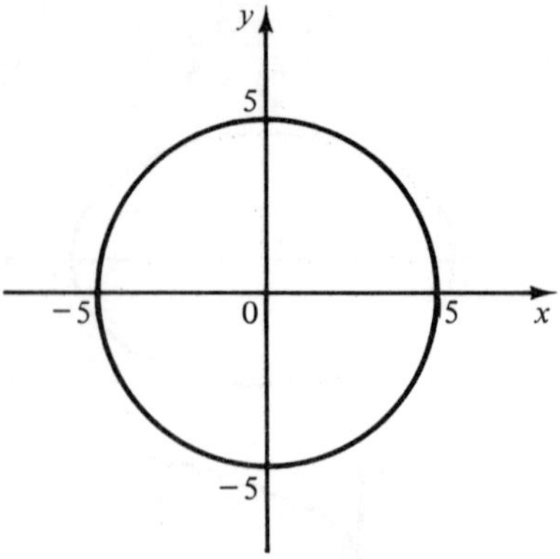

Exercise 9B

1 $32x^2 + 3y^2 = 16$

2 $xy = 2$

3 $16x^2 + y^2 = 144$

4 $\dfrac{x^2}{16} + \dfrac{y^2}{81} = 1$

5 $19x^2 + 24xy + y^2 = 25$

6 $x^2 + y^2 = 1$

Exercise 9C

1 Ellipse; $45x^2 + 20y^2 = 1$; $y = -\frac{3}{4}x$, $y = \frac{4}{3}x$

2 Hyperbola; $13x^2 - 26y^2 = 1$; $y = \frac{2}{3}x$, $y = -\frac{3}{2}x$

3 Ellipse; $3x^2 + 5y^2 = 1$; $y = -x$, $y = x$

4 Hyperbola; $3x^2 - 2y^2 = 1$; $y = -\frac{1}{2}x$, $y = 2x$

5 Hyperbola; $\frac{1}{2}x^2 - \frac{1}{2}y^2 = 8$; $y = x$, $y = -x$

6 Ellipse; $\frac{7}{2}x^2 + \frac{9}{2}y^2 = 10$; $y = x$, $y = -x$

7 Pair of straight lines through the origin; $8x^2 - 7y^2 = 0$; $y = \frac{1}{2}x$, $y = -2x$

8 Pair of parallel straight lines; $5x^2 = 125$; $y = 2x$, $y = -\frac{1}{2}x$

Exercise 9D

1 $2x^2 + 3y^2 - 3z^2 = 1$; hyperboloid of one sheet; $\begin{bmatrix} 1 \\ 0 \\ 0 \end{bmatrix}, \begin{bmatrix} 0 \\ 1 \\ -1 \end{bmatrix}, \begin{bmatrix} 0 \\ 1 \\ 1 \end{bmatrix}$

2 $3x^2 + 3y^2 = 1$; cylinder with circular cross-section; $\begin{bmatrix} 1 \\ 1 \\ 1 \end{bmatrix}$ and any two perpendicular vectors in the plane $x + y + z = 0$

3 $2x^2 + 5y^2 + 8z^2 = 1$; ellipsoid; $\begin{bmatrix} 2 \\ 2 \\ -1 \end{bmatrix}, \begin{bmatrix} 2 \\ -1 \\ 2 \end{bmatrix}, \begin{bmatrix} -1 \\ 2 \\ 2 \end{bmatrix}$

4 $2x^2 - y^2 - 4z^2 = 1$; hyperboloid of two sheets; $\begin{bmatrix} 1 \\ -2 \\ 2 \end{bmatrix}, \begin{bmatrix} -2 \\ 1 \\ 2 \end{bmatrix}, \begin{bmatrix} 2 \\ 2 \\ 1 \end{bmatrix}$

5 $2x^2 - y^2 - z^2 = 1$; hyperboloid of two sheets; $\begin{bmatrix} 1 \\ 1 \\ 1 \end{bmatrix}$ and any two perpendicular vectors in the plane $x + y + z = 0$

6 $\frac{1}{2}x^2 + \frac{1}{2}y^2 - z^2 = 1$; hyperboloid of one sheet; $\begin{bmatrix} 1 \\ 1 \\ 2 \end{bmatrix}$ and any two perpendicular vectors in the plane $x + y + 2z = 0$

7 $5x^2 - 5y^2 = 1$; cylinder with rectangular hyperbola as cross-section; $\begin{bmatrix} 0 \\ 4 \\ -3 \end{bmatrix}$, $\begin{bmatrix} 5 \\ 3 \\ 4 \end{bmatrix}, \begin{bmatrix} 5 \\ -3 \\ -4 \end{bmatrix}$

8 $x^2 = 1$; pair of parallel planes; $\begin{bmatrix} 2 \\ 1 \\ -2 \end{bmatrix}$ and any two perpendicular vectors in the plane $2x + y - 2z = 0$

Miscellaneous exercise 9

1 (*a*) $(-0.49, 0.18)$ (*b*) $(\frac{1}{6}, -\frac{19}{12})$; $ab - h^2 = 0$

2 (*a*) $(-3, -1, 4)$ (*b*) $(2, -1, -3)$

3 $ab - h^2 = 0$. No; however, conics of the form $ax^2 + 2hxy + by^2 = 0$ will in general be a pair of non-parallel straight lines through the origin.

Revision exercise 5

A1 $\mathbf{r} = \begin{bmatrix} -15 \\ 16 \\ -22 \end{bmatrix} + t\begin{bmatrix} 13 \\ -30 \\ 25 \end{bmatrix}$

A2 (*a*) Shear in the direction of the z-axis, factor -3, with the plane $x = 0$ invariant
(*b*) A rotation of $-90°$ about the z-axis

A3 $\begin{bmatrix} 1 & 0 & 0 \\ 0 & 0 & 1 \\ 0 & 1 & 0 \end{bmatrix}$

A4 (*a*) $\mathbf{M}^2 = \mathbf{M}^4 = \mathbf{I}$; $\mathbf{M}^3 = \mathbf{M}$
M represents a reflection in the plane $z = (\tan 22\frac{1}{2}°)y$.

(*b*) $\mathbf{M}^2 = \begin{bmatrix} 1 & 0 & 0 \\ 0 & 0 & -1 \\ 0 & 1 & 0 \end{bmatrix}$, $\mathbf{M}^3 = \begin{bmatrix} 1 & 0 & 0 \\ 0 & -\frac{1}{\sqrt{2}} & -\frac{1}{\sqrt{2}} \\ 0 & \frac{1}{\sqrt{2}} & -\frac{1}{\sqrt{2}} \end{bmatrix}$, $\mathbf{M}^4 = \begin{bmatrix} 1 & 0 & 0 \\ 0 & -1 & 0 \\ 0 & 0 & -1 \end{bmatrix}$

M represents a rotation through 45° about the x-axis.

B1 Projection parallel to the y-axis onto the plane $y = 0$; points $(3, \lambda, -1)$, $\lambda \in \mathbb{R}$.

B2 $2x - 2y + z = 0$; one-way stretch, factor 2, perpendicular to the plane $2x - 2y + z = 0$, with invariant plane $2x - 2y + z = 0$

B3 $\mathbf{S} = \begin{bmatrix} 1 & 0 & 0 \\ 0 & -1 & 0 \\ 0 & 0 & 1 \end{bmatrix}$, $\mathbf{T} = \begin{bmatrix} 0 & 0 & 1 \\ 0 & 1 & 0 \\ 1 & 0 & 0 \end{bmatrix}$, $\mathbf{U} = \begin{bmatrix} 1 & 0 & 0 \\ 0 & 0 & -1 \\ 0 & 1 & 0 \end{bmatrix}$; rotation of 180° about the line $r = \lambda \begin{bmatrix} 1 \\ 0 \\ 1 \end{bmatrix}$; reflection in the plane $y = z$

B4 $\begin{bmatrix} 0 & 0 & 1 \\ 0 & -1 & 0 \\ 1 & 0 & 0 \end{bmatrix}$

B5 $\mathbf{r} = \lambda \begin{bmatrix} 2 \\ -4 \\ -7 \end{bmatrix}$

Revision exercise 6

A1 The three planes meet in the unique point $(2, -1, 3)$

A2 (*a*) -48 (*b*) 267

A3 $\frac{1}{3} \begin{bmatrix} 18 & 1 & -11 \\ -33 & -1 & 20 \\ 24 & 1 & -14 \end{bmatrix}$

A4 $a, b, -(a + b)$

A5 The equations are inconsistent; the three planes represented by these equations form a prism.

B1 (*a*) $(1, -2, 1)$ (*b*) empty solution set (*c*) $(\lambda, -3\lambda, \frac{1}{2} + \lambda)$: $\lambda \in \mathbb{R}$ (*d*) 8 (*e*) 16

B2 (*b*) $\begin{bmatrix} 4 & 3 & -\frac{2}{3} \\ 1 & \frac{3}{2} & \frac{1}{3} \\ -2 & \frac{1}{2} & 1 \end{bmatrix}$; 12

B3 $\begin{bmatrix} 1 & 0 & 0 \\ 0 & 1 & -3 \\ 0 & 0 & 1 \end{bmatrix}$, $\begin{bmatrix} 1 & 0.4 & 0 \\ 0 & 1 & 0 \\ 0 & 0 & 1 \end{bmatrix}$; 46

B4 1, $\left\{ \lambda \begin{bmatrix} 1 \\ 1 \\ -1 \end{bmatrix} : \lambda \in \mathbb{R} \right\}$; 2, $\left\{ \lambda \begin{bmatrix} 4 \\ 2 \\ -5 \end{bmatrix} : \lambda \in \mathbb{R} \right\}$; -3, $\left\{ \begin{bmatrix} 3 \\ -1 \\ 5 \end{bmatrix} : \lambda \in \mathbb{R} \right\}$

B5 $\lambda \neq 1;\ \frac{1}{2}\begin{bmatrix} -2 & -1 & 5 \\ 2 & 1 & -3 \\ -4 & -1 & 7 \end{bmatrix};\ \begin{bmatrix} -5 \\ 4 \\ -8 \end{bmatrix}$

Revision exercise 7

A1 2, 3, −3

A2 $-2, \begin{bmatrix} 7 \\ 2 \\ -10 \end{bmatrix};\ 3, \begin{bmatrix} 1 \\ 1 \\ 0 \end{bmatrix};\ 4, \begin{bmatrix} 2 \\ 1 \\ 1 \end{bmatrix}$

A3 Three-way stretch in the oblique directions $\begin{bmatrix} 7 \\ 2 \\ -10 \end{bmatrix}, \begin{bmatrix} 1 \\ 1 \\ 0 \end{bmatrix}, \begin{bmatrix} 2 \\ 1 \\ 1 \end{bmatrix}$ with factors −2, 3, 4, respectively

A4 $\mathbf{U} = \begin{bmatrix} 7 & 1 & 2 \\ 2 & 1 & 1 \\ -10 & 0 & 1 \end{bmatrix}, \mathbf{\Lambda} = \begin{bmatrix} -2 & 0 & 0 \\ 0 & 3 & 0 \\ 0 & 0 & 4 \end{bmatrix}$

B1 $\begin{bmatrix} 3 & 4 & -4 \\ 4 & 5 & 0 \\ -4 & 0 & 1 \end{bmatrix}$

B2 $1, \begin{bmatrix} 1 \\ -1 \\ -1 \end{bmatrix};\ -2, \begin{bmatrix} 11 \\ 1 \\ -14 \end{bmatrix};\ 3, \begin{bmatrix} 1 \\ 1 \\ 1 \end{bmatrix}$

(*a*) The image points lie on the same line, but are three times as far from the origin.

(*b*) Three-way stretch in the oblique directions $\begin{bmatrix} 1 \\ 1 \\ 1 \end{bmatrix}, \begin{bmatrix} 1 \\ -1 \\ -1 \end{bmatrix}, \begin{bmatrix} 11 \\ 1 \\ -14 \end{bmatrix}$ with factors 0, −2, −5; the image points all lie on the plane $15x + 3y + 12z = 0$.

B3 $\begin{bmatrix} 0.4 & 0.4 & 0.4 \\ 0.45 & 0.45 & 0.45 \\ 0.15 & 0.15 & 0.15 \end{bmatrix}$; the columns are the eigenvector associated with eigenvalue 1.

B4 $2, \begin{bmatrix} 1 \\ 1 \\ 1 \end{bmatrix};$ −1 (twice), any vector in the plane $x + y + z = 0$;

$\mathbf{P} = \begin{bmatrix} 1 & 0 & 1 \\ -1 & 1 & 1 \\ 0 & -1 & 1 \end{bmatrix}$

B5 $\pm\begin{bmatrix} 1 & 0 & 2 \\ 0 & 3 & 1 \\ 0 & 0 & 2 \end{bmatrix}, \pm\begin{bmatrix} 1 & 0 & -6 \\ 0 & -3 & -1 \\ 0 & 0 & -2 \end{bmatrix}, \pm\begin{bmatrix} 1 & 0 & 2 \\ 0 & -3 & -5 \\ 0 & 0 & 2 \end{bmatrix}, \pm\begin{bmatrix} 1 & 0 & -6 \\ 0 & 3 & 5 \\ 0 & 0 & -2 \end{bmatrix}$

Revision exercise 8

A1 $\begin{bmatrix} \frac{2}{\sqrt{14}} & -\frac{1}{\sqrt{3}} & -\frac{4}{\sqrt{42}} \\ -\frac{1}{\sqrt{14}} & \frac{1}{\sqrt{3}} & -\frac{5}{\sqrt{42}} \\ \frac{3}{\sqrt{14}} & \frac{1}{\sqrt{3}} & \frac{1}{\sqrt{42}} \end{bmatrix}$

A2 $\begin{bmatrix} \frac{2}{\sqrt{5}} & -\frac{1}{\sqrt{5}} \\ \frac{1}{\sqrt{5}} & \frac{2}{\sqrt{5}} \end{bmatrix}$

A3 $\mathbf{A}^2$ is a symmetric matrix, but **AB** will only be symmetric if **A** and **B** commute.

A4 Rotation about the y-axis through $-\cos^{-1}(\frac{5}{13}) \approx -67.4°$

B1 Reflection in the plane $x - 2y + 2z = 0$

B2 $\begin{bmatrix} -\frac{2}{3} & \frac{1}{\sqrt{5}} & \frac{1}{\sqrt{2}} \\ \frac{1}{3} & \frac{2}{\sqrt{5}} & 0 \\ \frac{2}{3} & 0 & \frac{1}{\sqrt{2}} \end{bmatrix}$

B3 (*b*) $a = -\frac{1}{\sqrt{2}}, \quad b = \frac{1}{\sqrt{2}}, \quad c = \frac{1}{3\sqrt{2}}, \quad d = \frac{1}{3\sqrt{2}}, \quad e = \frac{2\sqrt{2}}{3}$

B4 (*b*) The same eigenvector

B5 $(-2, 14)$

Revision exercise 9

A1

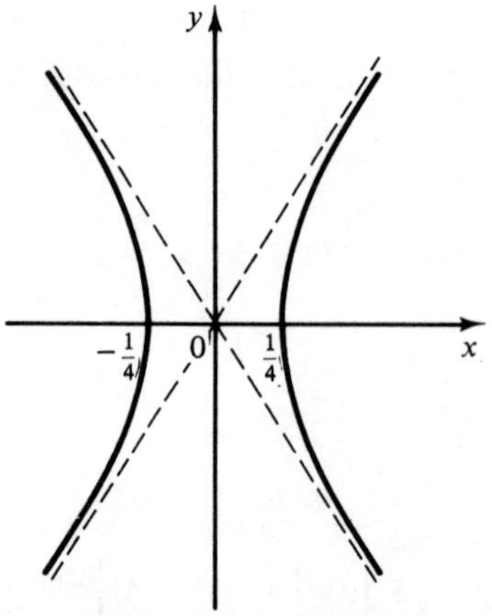

(*a*)

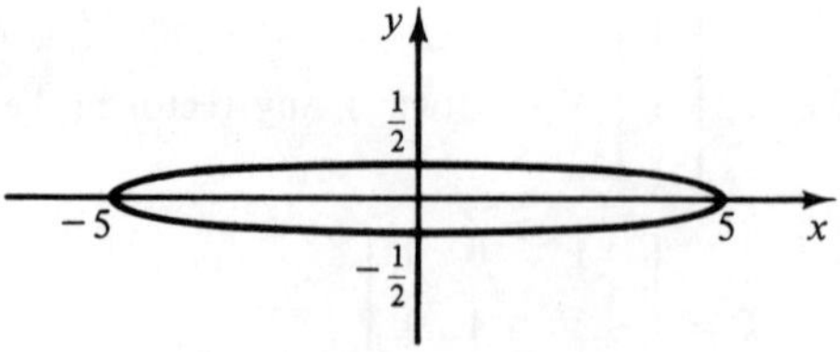

(*b*)

A2 $\frac{5}{2}x^2 - xy + \frac{5}{2}y^2 = 1$

A3 $\mathbf{M} = \begin{bmatrix} 3 & -3 & 0 \\ -3 & -4 & 2 \\ 0 & 2 & 2 \end{bmatrix}$

A4 $4xy = 5$ – a rectangular hyperbola

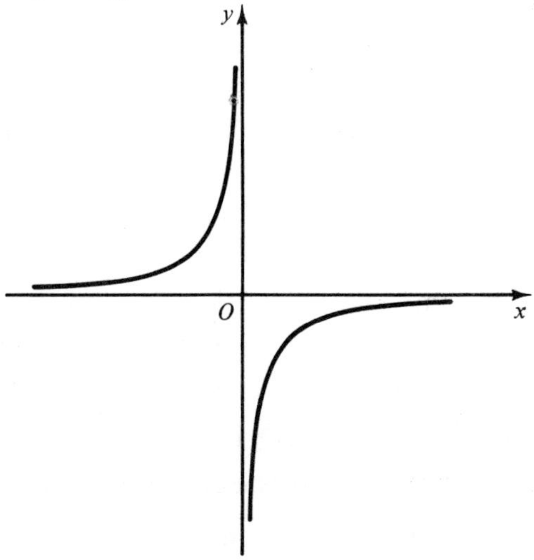

A5 $4\sqrt{3}$, $12\sqrt{2}$

B1 $\begin{bmatrix} 2 \\ 1 \\ 3 \end{bmatrix}$

B2 $9, \begin{bmatrix} 2 \\ 3 \end{bmatrix}$; $-4, \begin{bmatrix} 3 \\ -2 \end{bmatrix}$;

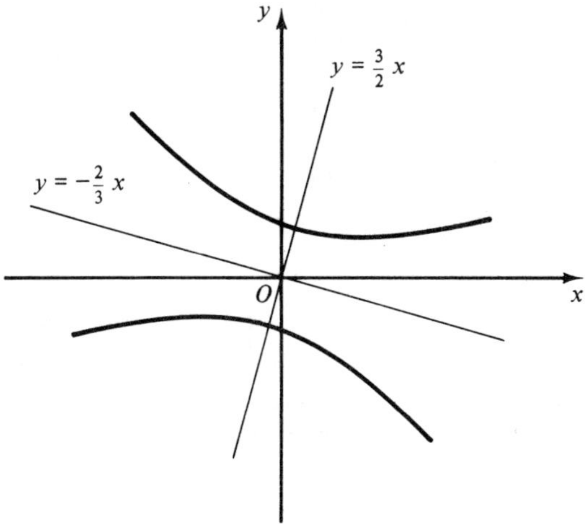

B3 $61x^2 + 126xy + 229y^2 = 1000$

B4 1, 1, −2; $\begin{bmatrix} \frac{1}{\sqrt{2}} & 0 & \frac{1}{\sqrt{3}} \\ \frac{1}{\sqrt{2}} & \frac{1}{\sqrt{2}} & -\frac{1}{\sqrt{3}} \\ 0 & \frac{1}{\sqrt{2}} & \frac{1}{\sqrt{3}} \end{bmatrix}$; $x^2 + y^2 - 2z^2 = 1$;

$\cos^{-1}\left(\frac{1}{\sqrt{3}}\right)$, $\cos^{-1}\left(-\frac{1}{\sqrt{3}}\right)$, $\cos^{-1}\left(\frac{1}{\sqrt{3}}\right)$

B5 (*a*) Pair of planes through the origin (*b*) Hyperboloid of two sheets
(*c*) Ellipsoid

Examination questions 1: Chapters 1–9

1 $\begin{bmatrix} 1 & 0 & 0 \\ -2 & 1 & 0 \\ 0 & 0 & 1 \end{bmatrix}, \begin{bmatrix} 1 & 0 & 0 \\ 0 & 1 & 0 \\ 0 & 1 & 1 \end{bmatrix}, \begin{bmatrix} 1 & 0 & -1 \\ 0 & 1 & 0 \\ 0 & 0 & 1 \end{bmatrix}; \begin{bmatrix} 3 & -1 & -1 \\ -2 & 1 & 0 \\ -2 & 1 & 1 \end{bmatrix}$

2 (*a*) $x = 0$ (*b*) $(3, -\frac{1}{2}, -1\frac{1}{2})$ (*c*) $y = z$

3 Reflection in the y-axis; rotation about the origin through $\frac{2}{3}\pi$; reflection in the y-axis rotated through $-\frac{2}{3}\pi$, that is, $y = -\frac{1}{\sqrt{3}}x$.

$\mathbf{R} = \begin{bmatrix} \frac{1}{2} & -\frac{1}{2}\sqrt{3} \\ -\frac{1}{2}\sqrt{3} & -\frac{1}{2} \end{bmatrix}$; eigenvalues ± 1; eigenvectors $\begin{bmatrix} -\sqrt{3} \\ 1 \end{bmatrix}, \begin{bmatrix} 1 \\ \sqrt{3} \end{bmatrix}$

4 $\begin{bmatrix} 1 \\ 1 \\ -1 \end{bmatrix}, \begin{bmatrix} 1 \\ 1 \\ -2 \end{bmatrix}, \begin{bmatrix} 0 \\ 1 \\ -1 \end{bmatrix}; \begin{bmatrix} 1 & 1 & 0 \\ 1 & 1 & 1 \\ -1 & -2 & -1 \end{bmatrix}, \begin{bmatrix} 1 & 1 & 1 \\ 0 & -1 & -1 \\ -1 & 1 & 0 \end{bmatrix}$;

one possibility is $\begin{bmatrix} 1 & -1 & -1 \\ -2 & 2 & -1 \\ 2 & 0 & 3 \end{bmatrix}$

5 $\begin{bmatrix} 1 \\ -2 \end{bmatrix}, \begin{bmatrix} 6 \\ 2 \end{bmatrix}; \begin{bmatrix} \frac{11}{7} \\ \frac{6}{7} \end{bmatrix}, \begin{bmatrix} \frac{9}{7} \\ -\frac{4}{7} \end{bmatrix}; \begin{bmatrix} \frac{11}{7} & \frac{9}{7} \\ \frac{6}{7} & -\frac{4}{7} \end{bmatrix}$

6 $\{(-3\lambda, 3 + 4\lambda, 2 + 5\lambda): \lambda \in \mathbb{R}\}$; a straight line

7 $x = 2y$

8 1, $1 + \sqrt{3}$, $1 - \sqrt{3}$; for $\lambda = 1$, $\mathbf{x} = \begin{bmatrix} 0 \\ 1 \\ 2 \end{bmatrix}$; points on the line $\mathbf{r} = \lambda\begin{bmatrix} 0 \\ 1 \\ 2 \end{bmatrix}$ are unchanged by the transformation represented by matrix **A**.

9 2, 7; $\begin{bmatrix} 2 \\ -1 \end{bmatrix}, \begin{bmatrix} 1 \\ 2 \end{bmatrix}$.

Semi-axis: $\dfrac{1}{\sqrt{2}}, \dfrac{1}{\sqrt{7}}$

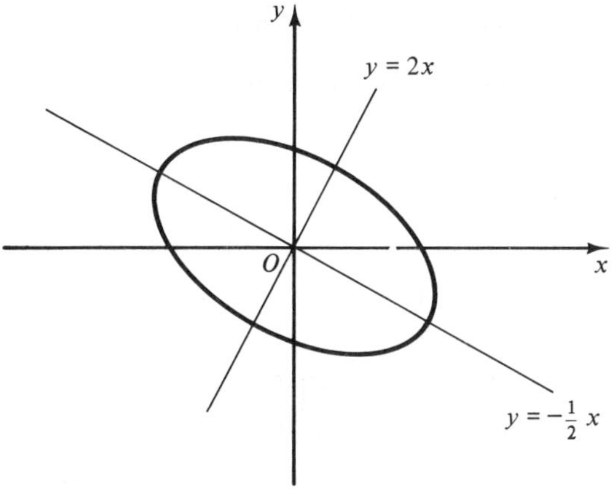

10 Hyperbola; $y = x$, $y = -x$

11 2; 0, 1; $\dfrac{1}{\lambda(\lambda-1)^2}\begin{bmatrix} (\lambda^2+1) & -2\lambda & -2\lambda^2 \\ 1 & \lambda(\lambda-2) & -\lambda \\ -\lambda & \lambda & \lambda^2 \end{bmatrix}$;

$\begin{bmatrix} 2 & 0 & 4 \\ 0 & 2 & 1 \\ 1 & -1 & 2 \end{bmatrix}, \frac{1}{2}\begin{bmatrix} 5 & -4 & -8 \\ 1 & 0 & -2 \\ -2 & 2 & 4 \end{bmatrix}$

12 $k = 1$: $(-1, 2, 3)$; the three planes intersect in a unique point.
$k = 2$: $\{(5-4\lambda, \lambda, -1+3\lambda): \lambda \in \mathbb{R}\}$; the three planes form a sheaf and intersect in a line.
$k = 3$: empty set; the three planes form a prism.

13 (*a*) $(\frac{7}{25}a + \frac{24}{25}b, \frac{24}{25}a - \frac{7}{25}b)$
(*b*) $(\frac{16}{25}a + \frac{12}{25}b, \frac{12}{25}a + \frac{9}{25}b)$

$\begin{bmatrix} \frac{16}{25} & \frac{12}{25} \\ \frac{12}{25} & \frac{9}{25} \end{bmatrix}$

14 (*a*) $\begin{bmatrix} -1 & 0 \\ 0 & 1 \end{bmatrix}$ (*b*) $y = 3x$

15 (*a*) $y = \frac{1}{5}(5-x)^2$; two-way stretch, factors -5 and 5 in the directions of the x- and y-axes respectively; or a reflection in the y-axis followed by an enlargement, centre the origin, scale factor 5.

(*b*) $\left(\dfrac{-a+b+c}{3}, \dfrac{2a-b}{3}, \dfrac{2a-c}{3}\right)$; $\frac{1}{3}\begin{bmatrix} -1 & 1 & 1 \\ 2 & -1 & 0 \\ 2 & 0 & -1 \end{bmatrix}$

16 2, 4; 30°

17 (*b*) 1, $\begin{bmatrix} 3 \\ 2 \\ 1 \end{bmatrix}$; -1, $\begin{bmatrix} 1 \\ 0 \\ 1 \end{bmatrix}$; 2, $\begin{bmatrix} 1 \\ 3 \\ 1 \end{bmatrix}$

18 (*a*) Determinant $= 1 + p^2 + q^2 + r^2 > 0$

(*b*) $\begin{bmatrix} 1 \\ -2 \end{bmatrix}$ and $\begin{bmatrix} 2 \\ -4 \end{bmatrix}$ both map to $\begin{bmatrix} 0 \\ 0 \end{bmatrix}$; $2x + y = 1$; $y = -4x$; a line parallel to L

19 $\begin{bmatrix} 1 \\ -1 \\ 1 \end{bmatrix}$; $12x - 5y + z = 0$; 0, $\begin{bmatrix} 1 \\ -1 \\ 1 \end{bmatrix}$; 3, $\begin{bmatrix} 1 \\ 2 \\ -2 \end{bmatrix}$; 6, $\begin{bmatrix} 1 \\ 5 \\ 13 \end{bmatrix}$

20 $\begin{bmatrix} 1 \\ -1 \end{bmatrix}, \begin{bmatrix} 2 \\ 3 \end{bmatrix}$; $\begin{bmatrix} 1 & 2 \\ -1 & 3 \end{bmatrix}$

21 $\begin{bmatrix} 0 & 1 \\ 2 & 1 \end{bmatrix}, \begin{bmatrix} 0 & -1 \\ -2 & -1 \end{bmatrix}, \begin{bmatrix} \frac{4}{3} & \frac{1}{3} \\ \frac{2}{3} & \frac{5}{3} \end{bmatrix}, \begin{bmatrix} -\frac{4}{3} & -\frac{1}{3} \\ -\frac{2}{3} & -\frac{5}{3} \end{bmatrix}$

22 $\frac{1}{2}$; $(0, -\frac{1}{2}, 1)$. 0; there is not a unique solution. $x = 1 - \lambda$, $y = -\frac{1}{2}\lambda$

23 2, 8; $\begin{bmatrix} \frac{1}{\sqrt{2}} & -\frac{1}{\sqrt{2}} \\ \frac{1}{\sqrt{2}} & \frac{1}{\sqrt{2}} \end{bmatrix}$

(*a*) Rotation about origin through $-45°$, two-way stretch with factors 2 and 8, rotation about origin through $45°$

24 5, -1; $x + y = 0$, $y = 2x$;
$\lambda = 5$: points on $x + y = 0$ map to the origin, line $y = 2x$ is invariant.
$\lambda = -1$: line $x + y = 0$ is invariant, points on $y = 2x$ map to the origin.

25 $\frac{1}{9}\begin{bmatrix} 10 & -4 & 1 \\ 7 & -1 & -2 \\ -8 & 5 & 1 \end{bmatrix}$; $(6, 2, -5)$.

Exercise 10A

1 (*a*) (i) Yes (ii) Yes
(*b*) (i) Yes (ii) No – $(0, 1, 1)$, multiply by -1
(*c*) (i) No – $(4,0,0) + (1,1,1)$ (ii) No – $(4,0,0)$, multiply by 2
(*d*) (i) Yes (ii) Yes
(*e*) (i) No – $(-1, -\frac{1}{2}) + (\frac{1}{2}, 1)$ (ii) Yes
(*f*) (i) Yes (ii) Yes
(*g*) (i) No – $(-x^2) + (x^2)$ (ii) No – multiply by 0
(*h*) (i) Yes (ii) Yes
(*i*) (i) Yes (ii) Yes

2 (*a*) $\{(-3, 1, 1), (1, 3, -3)\}$ (*d*) $\{(-3, 1, 1)\}$ (*f*) $\{x^3, x^2, x, 1\}$
(*h*) $\{\sin 2t, \cos 2t\}$ (*i*) $\left\{\begin{bmatrix} 0 & 1 \\ 1 & 0 \end{bmatrix}\right\}$

3 (*a*) $y = -\frac{3}{8}$, $z = -\frac{7}{8}$ (*b*) $y = \frac{1}{8}$, $z = -\frac{11}{8}$ (*c*) $y = 0$, $z = -10$

$\mathbf{d} = \begin{bmatrix} 1 \\ 0 \\ -\frac{3}{8} \\ -\frac{7}{8} \end{bmatrix}$ $\mathbf{e} = \begin{bmatrix} 0 \\ 1 \\ \frac{1}{8} \\ -\frac{11}{8} \end{bmatrix}$ $\mathbf{f} = \begin{bmatrix} 2 \\ 6 \\ 0 \\ -10 \end{bmatrix}$

$\mathbf{a} = 2\mathbf{d} - 2\mathbf{e}$, $\mathbf{b} = \mathbf{d} + 3\mathbf{e}$, $\mathbf{c} = 5\mathbf{d} - \mathbf{e}$,
$\mathbf{c} = 2\mathbf{a} + \mathbf{b}$, $\mathbf{d} = \frac{3}{8}\mathbf{a} + \frac{1}{4}\mathbf{b}$, $\mathbf{e} = -\frac{1}{8}\mathbf{a} + \frac{1}{4}\mathbf{b}$, $\mathbf{f} = 2\mathbf{b}$.
b and **f** do not form a basis.

Miscellaneous exercise 10

1 (*b*) $\begin{bmatrix} 1 & 2 & 3 \\ 4 & 2 & 0 \\ 1 & 2 & 3 \end{bmatrix}, \begin{bmatrix} 1 & 2 & 3 \\ 4 & 2 & 0 \\ 1 & 2 & 3 \end{bmatrix}, \begin{bmatrix} 1 & -4 & 3 \\ 2 & 0 & -2 \\ -3 & 4 & -1 \end{bmatrix}, \begin{bmatrix} 1 & -2 & 1 \\ -1 & -1 & 2 \\ 0 & 3 & -3 \end{bmatrix},$

$\begin{bmatrix} 1 & 2 & 3 \\ 4 & 2 & 0 \\ 1 & 2 & 3 \end{bmatrix}$, impossible

(*c*) The dimension is 4.

Basis: for example $\begin{bmatrix} 1 & 2 & 3 \\ 4 & 2 & 0 \\ 1 & 2 & 3 \end{bmatrix}, \begin{bmatrix} 1 & -4 & 3 \\ 2 & 0 & -2 \\ -3 & 4 & -1 \end{bmatrix}, \begin{bmatrix} 1 & -2 & 1 \\ -1 & -1 & 2 \\ 0 & 3 & -3 \end{bmatrix},$

(all from part (*b*)) and $\begin{bmatrix} 0 & 2 & 1 \\ 2 & 1 & 0 \\ 1 & 0 & 2 \end{bmatrix}$

(*d*) 2

Exercise 11A

1 (*a*) $\mathbf{a} = \mathbf{b} + \mathbf{c}$ (*b*) $\mathbf{a} = -\frac{3}{5}\mathbf{b} + \frac{2}{5}\mathbf{c}$ (*c*) $\mathbf{a} = \mathbf{b} - 2\mathbf{c}$

2 (*b*), (*c*)

3 (*a*) $2x - 1 = \frac{1}{2}(x + 1) + \frac{3}{2}(x - 1)$ (*b*) No (*c*) Yes
(*d*) $ax + b = (2a - b)(2x + 3) + (-3a + 2b)(x + 2)$ (*e*) $\{x, 1\}$; 2

4 (*a*) $3x^2 + 2x + 1 = -\frac{10}{3}(1) + \frac{2}{3}(2 + 3x) + 3(1 + x^2)$
(*b*) $px^2 + qx + r = (r - p - \frac{2}{3}q)(1) + \frac{1}{3}q(2 + 3x) + p(1 + x^2)$

5 (*b*)

6 (*a*) $\left\{\begin{bmatrix} 2 \\ 1 \end{bmatrix}, \begin{bmatrix} 3 \\ -1 \end{bmatrix}\right\}$ (*b*) $\left\{\begin{bmatrix} 3 \\ -1 \\ 4 \end{bmatrix}, \begin{bmatrix} 2 \\ -2 \\ 3 \end{bmatrix}\right\}$ (*c*) $\{1 + x, 2 - 3x\}$
(*d*) $\left\{\begin{bmatrix} 4 & 2 \\ 2 & -1 \end{bmatrix}, \begin{bmatrix} 1 & -3 \\ -3 & 5 \end{bmatrix}, \begin{bmatrix} -2 & 4 \\ 4 & -3 \end{bmatrix}\right\}$

Exercise 11B

1 (*a*) $2\begin{bmatrix} 4 \\ -1 \end{bmatrix} + 5\begin{bmatrix} -2 \\ 3 \end{bmatrix}$ (*b*) $\begin{bmatrix} 2 \\ 1 \\ -3 \end{bmatrix} - 2\begin{bmatrix} 4 \\ -1 \\ 0 \end{bmatrix} + 3\begin{bmatrix} 3 \\ 0 \\ 2 \end{bmatrix}$
(*c*) $3\begin{bmatrix} 1 & 1 \\ 0 & 0 \end{bmatrix} - 4\begin{bmatrix} 0 & 1 \\ 0 & 1 \end{bmatrix} + 2\begin{bmatrix} 0 & 0 \\ 1 & 1 \end{bmatrix}$ (*d*) $4(1) - 1(1 + t) + 3(1 + t)^2$

2 (*a*) $(\frac{13}{5}, -\frac{6}{5})$ (*b*) $(\frac{7}{2}, -3)$

3 (*a*) $(-12, 11)$ (*b*) $(-73, 124)$

4 (*a*) $\left\{\begin{bmatrix}1\\0\end{bmatrix}, \begin{bmatrix}-3\\-32\end{bmatrix}\right\}$ (*b*) $\left\{\begin{bmatrix}-2\\-32\end{bmatrix}, \begin{bmatrix}1\\0\end{bmatrix}\right\}$ (*c*) $\left\{\begin{bmatrix}1\\0\end{bmatrix}, \begin{bmatrix}-2\\-32\end{bmatrix}\right\}$

The answers are not unique.

Exercise 11C

1 (*a*) $\begin{bmatrix}32 & 19\\-46 & -27\end{bmatrix}$ (*b*) $\begin{bmatrix}6 & 4 & 3\\-1 & -3 & -1\\-1 & 2 & -2\end{bmatrix}$

2 $(\frac{7}{3}, \frac{1}{6}), (-\frac{8}{3}, \frac{5}{3})$; (a) $\begin{bmatrix}0 & -2\\2 & 0\end{bmatrix}$ (*b*) $\begin{bmatrix}-\frac{2}{3} & -\frac{20}{3}\\\frac{2}{3} & \frac{2}{3}\end{bmatrix}$

3 $(4, 1), (-4\frac{1}{2}, -1)$; (*a*) $\begin{bmatrix}-1 & 0\\-\frac{1}{2} & -1\end{bmatrix}$ (*b*) $\begin{bmatrix}-1 & -\frac{1}{2}\\0 & -1\end{bmatrix}$

4 $\lambda_1 = 5, \lambda_2 = -2$; $\mathbf{e}_1 = \begin{bmatrix}1\\-1\end{bmatrix}, \mathbf{e}_2 = \begin{bmatrix}4\\3\end{bmatrix}, (a, b) = (-\frac{16}{7}, \frac{11}{7})$.

$(-24, 2), (-\frac{80}{7}, -\frac{22}{7})$

5 (*a*) $x'^2 + 6y'^2 = 1, \left\{\begin{bmatrix}\frac{1}{\sqrt{5}}\\-\frac{2}{\sqrt{5}}\end{bmatrix}, \begin{bmatrix}\frac{2}{\sqrt{5}}\\\frac{1}{\sqrt{5}}\end{bmatrix}\right\}$ (*b*) $2x'^2 - 3y'^2 = 1, \left\{\begin{bmatrix}\frac{2}{\sqrt{5}}\\\frac{1}{\sqrt{5}}\end{bmatrix}, \begin{bmatrix}\frac{1}{\sqrt{5}}\\-\frac{2}{\sqrt{5}}\end{bmatrix}\right\}$

(*c*) $14x'^2 - 11y'^2 = 1, \left\{\begin{bmatrix}\frac{4}{5}\\-\frac{3}{5}\end{bmatrix}, \begin{bmatrix}\frac{3}{5}\\\frac{4}{5}\end{bmatrix}\right\}$ (*d*) $13x'^2 - 12y'^2 = 1, \left\{\begin{bmatrix}\frac{4}{5}\\\frac{3}{5}\end{bmatrix}, \begin{bmatrix}\frac{3}{5}\\-\frac{4}{5}\end{bmatrix}\right\}$

6 (*a*) $x = Ae^{6t} + Be^{t}$, $y = -\frac{1}{4}Ae^{6t} + Be^{t}$

(*b*) $x = Ae^{7t} + Be^{-6t}$, $y = 2Ae^{7t} - \frac{9}{2}Be^{-6t}$

(*c*) $x = A + Be^{13t}$, $y = -3A + \frac{4}{3}e^{13t}$

Miscellaneous exercise 11

1 Yes, two-dimensional vector space

2 $\begin{bmatrix}13 & 23\\-6 & -11\end{bmatrix}$

3 $(3x + 2y)^2 = 1$

4 $x = 2Ae^{3t} + Be^{-2t}$, $y = -Ae^{3t} + 2Be^{-2t}$

6 $(\frac{4}{7}, -\frac{13}{7}), (\frac{2}{7}, \frac{11}{7})$; no, yes, no, no

Exercise 12A

1 Domain basis $\{t^2, t, 1\}$, codomain basis $\{t^2, t, 1\}$, $\begin{bmatrix}1 & 0 & 0\\2 & 1 & 0\\1 & 1 & 1\end{bmatrix}$

2 Domain basis $\{t^2, t, 1\}$, codomain $\{1\}$, $\begin{bmatrix}\frac{x^3}{3}, \frac{x^2}{2}, x\end{bmatrix}$

3 Not linear

4 Domain basis $\{1, i\}$. (*a*) Not linear (*b*) Codomain basis $\{1, i\}$, $\begin{bmatrix} b & 0 \\ 0 & b \end{bmatrix}$

(*c*) Codomain basis $\{1, i\}$, $\begin{bmatrix} 1 & 0 \\ 0 & -1 \end{bmatrix}$ (*d*), (*e*) Not linear

(*f*) Codomain basis $\{1, i\}$, $\begin{bmatrix} -2 & 0 \\ 0 & 2 \end{bmatrix}$

5 Domain basis $\{x^2, e^x, xe^x, x^2e^x\}$

(*a*) Codomain basis $\{2x - x^2, e^x, xe^x\}$, $\begin{bmatrix} 1 & 0 & 0 & 0 \\ 0 & 0 & 1 & 0 \\ 0 & 0 & 0 & 2 \end{bmatrix}$

(*b*) Codomain basis $\{2 - 2x + x^2, 2e^x - 2x^2e^x\}$, $\begin{bmatrix} 1 & 0 & 0 & 0 \\ 0 & 0 & 0 & 1 \end{bmatrix}$

6 Domain basis $\left\{\begin{bmatrix} 1 & 0 & 0 \\ 0 & 0 & 0 \\ 0 & 0 & 0 \end{bmatrix}, \begin{bmatrix} 0 & 1 & 0 \\ 0 & 0 & 0 \\ 0 & 0 & 0 \end{bmatrix}, \begin{bmatrix} 0 & 0 & 1 \\ 0 & 0 & 0 \\ 0 & 0 & 0 \end{bmatrix}, \begin{bmatrix} 0 & 0 & 0 \\ 1 & 0 & 0 \\ 0 & 0 & 0 \end{bmatrix},\right.$

$\left.\begin{bmatrix} 0 & 0 & 0 \\ 0 & 1 & 0 \\ 0 & 0 & 0 \end{bmatrix}, \begin{bmatrix} 0 & 0 & 0 \\ 0 & 0 & 1 \\ 0 & 0 & 0 \end{bmatrix}, \begin{bmatrix} 0 & 0 & 0 \\ 0 & 0 & 0 \\ 1 & 0 & 0 \end{bmatrix}, \begin{bmatrix} 0 & 0 & 0 \\ 0 & 0 & 0 \\ 0 & 1 & 0 \end{bmatrix}, \begin{bmatrix} 0 & 0 & 0 \\ 0 & 0 & 0 \\ 0 & 0 & 1 \end{bmatrix}\right\}$,

codomain basis $\{1\}$, $[1 \quad 0 \quad 0 \quad 0 \quad 1 \quad 0 \quad 0 \quad 0 \quad 1]$

7 Domain basis $\{x^2, x, 1\}$, codomain basis $\{x^2, x, 1\}$, $\begin{bmatrix} 1 & 0 & 0 \\ -4 & -1 & 0 \\ 4 & 2 & 1 \end{bmatrix}$

Exercise 12B

1 $\begin{bmatrix} 1 & 0 & -\frac{3}{4} \\ 0 & 1 & -4\frac{3}{4} \\ 0 & 0 & 0 \end{bmatrix}$ **2** $\begin{bmatrix} 1 & 0 & \frac{1}{2} \\ 0 & 1 & -\frac{1}{4} \\ 0 & 0 & 0 \\ 0 & 0 & 0 \\ 0 & 0 & 0 \\ 0 & 0 & 0 \end{bmatrix}$ **3** $\begin{bmatrix} 1 & 0 & 1\frac{1}{2} & \frac{1}{2} \\ 0 & 1 & 1\frac{1}{2} & -\frac{1}{2} \end{bmatrix}$

4 $\begin{bmatrix} 1 & 0 & 0 & 6\frac{1}{2} & 2\frac{1}{2} \\ 0 & 1 & 0 & -3\frac{1}{4} & -\frac{3}{4} \\ 0 & 0 & 1 & -3 & -1 \end{bmatrix}$ **5** $\begin{bmatrix} 1 & 0 & 0 & 0 \\ 0 & 1 & 0 & 0 \\ 0 & 0 & 1 & 0 \\ 0 & 0 & 0 & 1 \end{bmatrix}$ **6** $\begin{bmatrix} 1 & 0 & 0 & 3 & 1 \\ 0 & 1 & 0 & 0 & \frac{1}{2} \\ 0 & 0 & 1 & 0 & 0 \\ 0 & 0 & 0 & 0 & 0 \end{bmatrix}$

Exercise 12C

1 (*a*) Kernel basis $\left\{\begin{bmatrix} 0 \\ 5 \\ -3 \end{bmatrix}, \begin{bmatrix} -5 \\ 0 \\ 1 \end{bmatrix}\right\}$, image space basis $\left\{\begin{bmatrix} 1 \\ 2 \end{bmatrix}\right\}$

(*b*) $\left\{\begin{bmatrix} 1 \\ 1 \\ -1 \end{bmatrix}\right\}$, $\left\{\begin{bmatrix} 4 \\ 1 \\ 5 \end{bmatrix}, \begin{bmatrix} 2 \\ 3 \\ 0 \end{bmatrix}\right\}$ (*c*) $\varnothing$, $\left\{\begin{bmatrix} 2 \\ -1 \\ 4 \\ 7 \end{bmatrix}, \begin{bmatrix} 0 \\ 3 \\ -2 \\ 7 \end{bmatrix}\right\}$

(*d*) $\varnothing$, $\left\{\begin{bmatrix}-3\\4\\1\end{bmatrix}, \begin{bmatrix}2\\9\\-2\end{bmatrix}\right\}$ (*e*) $\varnothing$, $\left\{\begin{bmatrix}2\\3\\2\end{bmatrix}, \begin{bmatrix}4\\1\\0\end{bmatrix}, \begin{bmatrix}4\\-1\\4\end{bmatrix}\right\}$

(*f*) $\left\{\begin{bmatrix}1\\-5\\3\end{bmatrix}\right\}, \left\{\begin{bmatrix}0\\-1\\2\end{bmatrix}, \begin{bmatrix}-1\\-1\\3\end{bmatrix}\right\}$

2 $\mathbf{M} = \begin{bmatrix}4 & -5\\12 & -15\end{bmatrix}$; image space of $\mathbf{M}^2 = \left\{\lambda\begin{bmatrix}1\\3\end{bmatrix}\right\}$, kernel of $\mathbf{M}^2 = \left\{\mu\begin{bmatrix}5\\4\end{bmatrix}\right\}$

3 $\begin{bmatrix}1 & 0 & 1\\2 & 2 & 4\\-3 & 1 & -2\\4 & 5 & 9\end{bmatrix}$

4 $\begin{bmatrix}1 & -5 & 1\\1 & -5 & 1\end{bmatrix}$

5 (*a*) $2\begin{bmatrix}2\\3\\-1\end{bmatrix} - 3\begin{bmatrix}1\\4\\2\end{bmatrix} + \begin{bmatrix}-1\\6\\8\end{bmatrix} = \mathbf{0}, \ -5\begin{bmatrix}1\\4\\2\end{bmatrix} + 3\begin{bmatrix}-1\\6\\8\end{bmatrix} + 2\begin{bmatrix}4\\1\\-7\end{bmatrix} = \mathbf{0}$

(*b*) $\begin{bmatrix}2\\-3\\1\\0\end{bmatrix}, \begin{bmatrix}0\\-5\\3\\2\end{bmatrix}$; yes

(*c*) Dimension 2; basis $\left\{\begin{bmatrix}1\\4\\2\end{bmatrix}, \begin{bmatrix}-1\\6\\8\end{bmatrix}\right\}$

(*d*) $2[2 \ \ 1 \ \ -1 \ \ 4] + [-1 \ \ 2 \ \ 8 \ \ -7] = [3 \ \ 4 \ \ 6 \ \ 1]$, $2x - y + z = 0$

6 $\left\{\begin{bmatrix}2\\-1\\1\end{bmatrix}\right\}, \left\{\begin{bmatrix}2\\1\\-1\\4\end{bmatrix}, \begin{bmatrix}3\\4\\6\\1\end{bmatrix}\right\}$

Miscellaneous exercise 12

1 $\mathbf{N} = \begin{bmatrix}1 & -1\\1 & -1\end{bmatrix}, \mathbf{N}^2 = \begin{bmatrix}0 & 0\\0 & 0\end{bmatrix}$

2 (*b*) $r(\mathbf{CD}) \leqslant r(\mathbf{C})$ and $\leqslant r(\mathbf{D})$ (*c*) Yes

3 No

4 $\begin{bmatrix}-\sqrt{3} & \sqrt{3} & 0\\-1 & -1 & 2\end{bmatrix}, \begin{bmatrix}\lambda\\\lambda\\\lambda\end{bmatrix}$

5 $(\sqrt{(\frac{2}{3})}, \sqrt{(\frac{1}{3})})$, $\begin{bmatrix} 1 & \sqrt{(\frac{2}{3})} & 0 \\ 0 & \sqrt{(\frac{1}{3})} & 1 \end{bmatrix}$; $(\sqrt{2}, -\sqrt{3}, 1)$

6 $(0,0)$, $(2,0)$, $(\sqrt{2},\sqrt{2})$, $(0,2)$, $(-\sqrt{2},\sqrt{2})$, $(2+\sqrt{2},\sqrt{2})$, $(2,2)$, $(2-\sqrt{2},\sqrt{2})$, $(\sqrt{2},\sqrt{2}+2)$, $(0,2\sqrt{2})$, $(-\sqrt{2},2+\sqrt{2})$, $(2+\sqrt{2},\sqrt{2})$, $(2,2\sqrt{2})$, $(2-\sqrt{2},2+\sqrt{2})$, $(0,2+2\sqrt{2})$, $(2,2+2\sqrt{2})$;

$$\left\{\lambda\begin{bmatrix} 1 \\ -\sqrt{2} \\ 1 \\ 0 \end{bmatrix} + \mu\begin{bmatrix} 1 \\ 0 \\ -1 \\ \sqrt{2} \end{bmatrix}\right\}$$

Exercise 13A

1 (*a*) $\begin{bmatrix} x \\ y \\ z \end{bmatrix} = \lambda\begin{bmatrix} -1 \\ 10 \\ 7 \end{bmatrix}$ (*b*) $\begin{bmatrix} x \\ y \\ z \\ t \end{bmatrix} = \lambda\begin{bmatrix} 1 \\ 0 \\ -12 \\ 7 \end{bmatrix} + \mu\begin{bmatrix} -7 \\ 12 \\ 0 \\ 11 \end{bmatrix}$

(*c*) $\begin{bmatrix} x \\ y \\ z \\ t \end{bmatrix} = \lambda\begin{bmatrix} 1 \\ -1 \\ 0 \\ 0 \end{bmatrix} + \mu\begin{bmatrix} 3 \\ 0 \\ 0 \\ -1 \end{bmatrix} + v\begin{bmatrix} 2 \\ 0 \\ 1 \\ 0 \end{bmatrix}$ (*d*) $\begin{bmatrix} x \\ y \\ z \end{bmatrix} = \lambda\begin{bmatrix} -8 \\ 5 \\ 7 \end{bmatrix}$

2 $\begin{bmatrix} x \\ y \\ z \end{bmatrix} = \lambda\begin{bmatrix} 0 \\ 2 \\ -1 \end{bmatrix} + \mu\begin{bmatrix} 4 \\ 0 \\ -1 \end{bmatrix}$, $\mu = 0$ if $p \neq -\frac{1}{2}$

3 $\left\{\lambda\begin{bmatrix} 2 \\ 1 \\ 3 \end{bmatrix}\right\}$, $\begin{bmatrix} x \\ y \\ z \end{bmatrix} = \lambda\begin{bmatrix} 2 \\ 1 \\ 3 \end{bmatrix}$

4 $\lambda = 1$ or $\lambda = 2$

Exercise 13B

1 (*a*) 9 (*b*) 27 (*c*) $\frac{2}{5}$

2 $a = 15$, $b =$ anything

3 (*a*) $\begin{bmatrix} x \\ y \\ z \end{bmatrix} = \lambda\begin{bmatrix} -1 \\ 10 \\ 7 \end{bmatrix} + \begin{bmatrix} 1 \\ 2 \\ 1 \end{bmatrix}$ (*b*) No solution

(*c*) $\begin{bmatrix} x \\ y \\ z \\ t \end{bmatrix} = \begin{bmatrix} 17 \\ 0 \\ 0 \\ 0 \end{bmatrix} + \lambda\begin{bmatrix} 1 \\ -1 \\ 0 \\ 0 \end{bmatrix} + \mu\begin{bmatrix} 3 \\ 0 \\ 0 \\ -1 \end{bmatrix} + v\begin{bmatrix} 2 \\ 0 \\ 1 \\ 0 \end{bmatrix}$

(*d*) $\begin{bmatrix} x \\ y \\ z \end{bmatrix} = \begin{bmatrix} 0 \\ 3 \\ 1 \end{bmatrix} + \lambda\begin{bmatrix} -8 \\ 5 \\ 7 \end{bmatrix}$

4 $\left\{\lambda\begin{bmatrix}1\\2\\-5\\2\end{bmatrix}+\mu\begin{bmatrix}0\\2\\-3\\1\end{bmatrix}\right\}$, $\begin{bmatrix}x\\y\\z\\t\end{bmatrix}=\lambda\begin{bmatrix}1\\2\\-5\\2\end{bmatrix}+\mu\begin{bmatrix}0\\2\\-3\\1\end{bmatrix}+\begin{bmatrix}0\\1\\3\\-2\end{bmatrix}$

5 (*a*) No solution (*b*) $\begin{bmatrix}x\\y\\z\\t\end{bmatrix}=\begin{bmatrix}11\\0\\-8\\-13\end{bmatrix}+\lambda\begin{bmatrix}-1\\1\\0\\2\end{bmatrix}$

Miscellaneous exercise 13

4 $\begin{bmatrix}a_0 & -a_1 & -a_2 & -a_3\\a_1 & a_0 & -a_3 & a_2\\a_2 & a_3 & a_0 & -a_1\\a_3 & -a_2 & a_1 & a_0\end{bmatrix}$

(*c*) $1+0i+0j+0k$; $\frac{1}{4}-\frac{1}{4}i-\frac{1}{4}j-\frac{1}{4}k$; yes

(*d*) Determinant is $(a_0^2+a_1^2+a_2^2+a_3^2)^2 \neq 0$, so inverse exists

Exercise 14A

1 Yes **2** No: A1, A2, A4, M1 **3** No: M1 **4** Yes
5 Yes **6** No: A4, M1 **7** No: A1, A2, A4, M1 **8** Yes
9 No: A1 **10** No: A1, A2, A4, M1 **11** Yes **12** No: A1
13 Yes **14** Yes **15** No: A1, A2, A4, M1 **16** Yes
17 No: M1 **18** No: A1, A2, A4, M1 **19** Yes **20** Yes
21 Yes **22** No: M2

Exercise 14B

2 (*a*) Yes (*b*) No (*c*) No (*d*) Yes (*e*) No (*f*) Yes

4 (*b*) $\left\{\begin{bmatrix}1\\0\\-1\\0\end{bmatrix},\begin{bmatrix}0\\1\\0\\-1\end{bmatrix}\right\}$ (*c*) $\left\{\begin{bmatrix}1\\0\\-1\\0\end{bmatrix},\begin{bmatrix}0\\1\\0\\-1\end{bmatrix},\begin{bmatrix}1\\0\\0\\0\end{bmatrix},\begin{bmatrix}0\\1\\0\\0\end{bmatrix}\right\}$

5 For example, $\left\{\begin{bmatrix}1\\1\end{bmatrix},\begin{bmatrix}2\\0\end{bmatrix},\begin{bmatrix}1\\0\end{bmatrix}\right\}$.

If a set of vectors is linearly dependent, then one vector can be expressed as a linear combination of the others.

8 (*a*) Yes, $\{\mathbf{a}_2,\mathbf{a}_3,\mathbf{a}_4\}$ (*b*) No (*c*) No

Exercise 14C

1 For example: $(\mathbf{x}_1,\mathbf{x}_2)=\left(\begin{bmatrix}1\\0\end{bmatrix},\begin{bmatrix}0\\1\end{bmatrix}\right)$, matrix of transformation $=\begin{bmatrix}1 & 0\\0 & 0\end{bmatrix}$

6 W_1 is the xy-plane; W_2 is generated by $\begin{bmatrix}0\\1\\2\end{bmatrix}$.

Miscellaneous exercise 14

1 Yes, yes, $\{(r, 0)\}$

2 $\dim(U \cap V) \leqslant \min\{\dim(U), \dim(V)\}$

3 (*b*) $\dim(U) + \dim(V) = \dim(U \cap V) + \dim(U + V)$

5 (*b*) $U \cap V = \{f\colon f(x) = 0 \quad \text{for all } x \in \mathbb{R}\}$

Revision exercise 11

A1 $\begin{bmatrix} 5 \\ -2 \end{bmatrix} = \frac{11}{3}\mathbf{u} + \frac{4}{3}\mathbf{v}, \begin{bmatrix} 3 \\ -1 \end{bmatrix} = \frac{13}{6}\mathbf{u} + \frac{5}{6}\mathbf{v}$

A2 $\left\{\begin{bmatrix} 1 & 0 \\ 0 & 0 \end{bmatrix}, \begin{bmatrix} 0 & 1 \\ 0 & 0 \end{bmatrix}, \begin{bmatrix} 0 & 0 \\ 1 & 0 \end{bmatrix}, \begin{bmatrix} 0 & 0 \\ 0 & 1 \end{bmatrix}\right\}$

A3 $(\frac{9}{43}, -\frac{22}{43})$

A4 $\begin{bmatrix} 3 & 4 \\ -1 & -1 \end{bmatrix}$

B1 (*a*) $p = 3$ or $p = -1$ (*b*) $p = 1$ or $p = 4$ or $p = 2$

B2 $7x'^2 - 6y'^2 = 1, \left\{\frac{1}{\sqrt{13}}\begin{bmatrix} 3 \\ -2 \end{bmatrix}, \frac{1}{\sqrt{13}}\begin{bmatrix} 2 \\ 3 \end{bmatrix}\right\}$

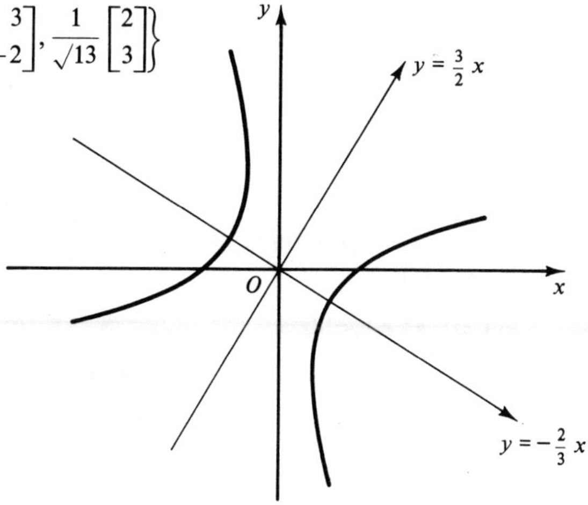

B3 $(0, -1), (-3, -1)$; (*a*) $\begin{bmatrix} 0 & -1 \\ -1 & 0 \end{bmatrix}$ (*b*) $\begin{bmatrix} -1 & 3 \\ 0 & 1 \end{bmatrix}$

B4 $x = Ae^{3t} + Be^{5t}, y = -Ae^{3t} - \frac{1}{2}Be^{5t}$

Revision exercise 12

A1 Yes

A2 With usual bases, matrix is $\begin{bmatrix} 3 & 0 & 1 & 0 \\ 0 & -4 & 0 & 1 \\ 1 & 1 & 1 & 0 \end{bmatrix}$

A3 $\begin{bmatrix} 1 & 0 & -\frac{1}{11} & -\frac{7}{11} \\ 0 & 1 & -\frac{2}{11} & \frac{8}{11} \\ 0 & 0 & 0 & 0 \end{bmatrix}$

A4 Kernel basis $\left\{\begin{bmatrix} 8 \\ -7 \\ -3 \end{bmatrix}\right\}$, image space basis $\left\{\begin{bmatrix} 5 \\ 2 \\ 1 \end{bmatrix}, \begin{bmatrix} 7 \\ 1 \\ 2 \end{bmatrix}\right\}$

A5 1

B1 Kernel is $\left\{\begin{bmatrix} 2\lambda & 2\mu \\ \lambda & \mu \end{bmatrix} : \lambda, \mu \in \mathbb{R}\right\}$, image space is $\left\{\begin{bmatrix} 2\nu & 2\xi \\ -3\nu & -3\xi \end{bmatrix} : \nu, \xi \in \mathbb{R}\right\}$

B3 $\{e^{-2x}, xe^{-2x}, x^2e^{-2x}\}$; $\begin{bmatrix} -2 & 1 & 0 \\ 0 & -2 & 2 \\ 0 & 0 & -2 \end{bmatrix}$; $\{0\}$

B5 $\mathbf{P} = \begin{bmatrix} 1 & 0 & 0 \\ \frac{1}{5} & \frac{1}{10} & 0 \\ -\frac{1}{5} & \frac{2}{5} & 0 \end{bmatrix}$, $\mathbf{Q} = \begin{bmatrix} 1 & -7 & \frac{1}{2} & \frac{3}{2} \\ 0 & 1 & \frac{1}{2} & -\frac{1}{2} \\ 0 & 0 & 1 & 0 \\ 0 & 0 & 0 & 1 \end{bmatrix}$; $\mathbf{x}' = \mathbf{Q}^{-1}\mathbf{x}$, $\mathbf{y}' = \mathbf{P}\mathbf{y}$;

$\mathbf{x}' = [0 \quad 0 \quad \lambda \quad \mu]^{\mathrm{T}}$, $\mathbf{x} = [\frac{1}{2}(\lambda + 3\mu) \quad \frac{1}{2}(\lambda - \mu) \quad \lambda \quad \mu]^{\mathrm{T}}$

Revision exercise 13

A1 (*a*) 2 (*b*) 1 **A2** $c = 2b - a$ **A3** $\mathbf{x} = \begin{bmatrix} \lambda + 6 \\ \lambda + 3 \\ \lambda + 2 \\ \lambda \end{bmatrix}$

A4 (*a*) $\lambda \begin{bmatrix} -3 \\ 2 \\ 1 \end{bmatrix}$ (*b*) No solution (*c*) $\begin{bmatrix} -2 \\ 4 \\ 0 \end{bmatrix} + \lambda \begin{bmatrix} -3 \\ 2 \\ 1 \end{bmatrix}$

A5 2 and 3; $r(\mathbf{A}) \neq r(\mathbf{A}|\mathbf{d})$

B1 42, $(x, y, z) = (1, 4, -5)$. Find the point on the line of intersection of the planes $\left.\begin{aligned} 2x + 3y - 5z &= 39 \\ 4x - 6y + 2z &= -30 \end{aligned}\right\}$ which is closest to the origin.

B2 $\mathbf{c}_1 + \mathbf{c}_2 - \mathbf{c}_3 = \mathbf{0}$, $\mathbf{c}_2 - 2\mathbf{c}_3 + \mathbf{c}_4 = \mathbf{0}$;

$$\left\{\lambda \begin{bmatrix} 1 \\ 1 \\ -1 \\ 0 \end{bmatrix} + \mu \begin{bmatrix} 0 \\ 1 \\ -2 \\ 1 \end{bmatrix}\right\}, \begin{bmatrix} x \\ y \\ z \\ t \end{bmatrix} = \begin{bmatrix} 3 \\ -2 \\ 0 \\ 0 \end{bmatrix} + \lambda \begin{bmatrix} 1 \\ 1 \\ -1 \\ 0 \end{bmatrix} + \mu \begin{bmatrix} 0 \\ 1 \\ -2 \\ 1 \end{bmatrix}$$

B3 (*a*) $\lambda(2x^2 - x - 2)$ (*b*) $(-x^2 + 3) + \lambda(2x^2 - x - 2)$

B4 (*b*) $\begin{bmatrix} 0 & 3 & 1 \\ -3 & 0 & -2 \\ -1 & 2 & 0 \end{bmatrix}$ (*c*) $\left\{\lambda \begin{bmatrix} 2 \\ 1 \\ -3 \end{bmatrix}\right\}$; $\left\{\mu \begin{bmatrix} 3 \\ 0 \\ 2 \end{bmatrix} + \nu \begin{bmatrix} 1 \\ -2 \\ 0 \end{bmatrix}\right\}$

(*d*) (i) No solution (ii) $\mathbf{v} = \begin{bmatrix} -2 \\ 6 \\ -4 \end{bmatrix} + \lambda \begin{bmatrix} 2 \\ 1 \\ -3 \end{bmatrix}$

B5 $b = 4 - a \ (a \neq -\frac{1}{7})$; $(9\lambda, 10\lambda + \frac{2}{3}, -7\lambda + \frac{1}{3}), \lambda = \dfrac{a-5}{21a+3}$

Revision exercise 14

A4 (*a*) Yes (*b*) No (*c*) Yes

B2 Vectors of the form $\begin{bmatrix} 3\lambda \\ 6\lambda \\ 5\lambda \\ 10\lambda \end{bmatrix}, \lambda \in \mathbb{R}$

B3 $\mathbf{k} = (0, 0, 1)$, for example

B5 Not all zero

Exercise 15A

1 (*a*)

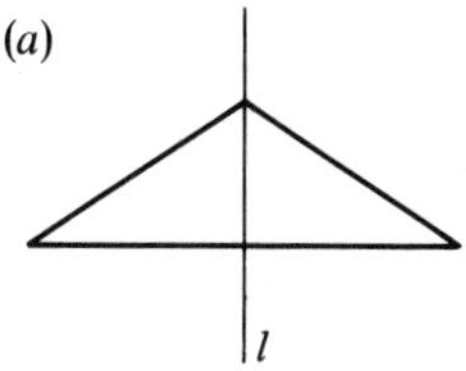

I: identity
L: reflection in axis l

*	I	L
I	I	L
L	L	I

(*b*)

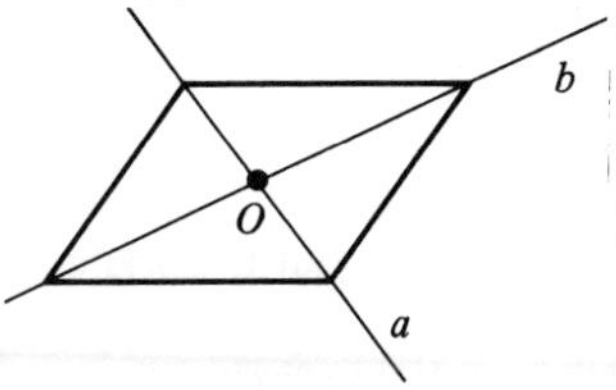

I: identity
A: reflection in axis a
B: reflection in axis b
H: 180° rotation about centre O

*	I	A	B	H
I	I	A	B	H
A	A	I	H	B
B	B	H	I	A
H	H	B	A	I

(*c*)

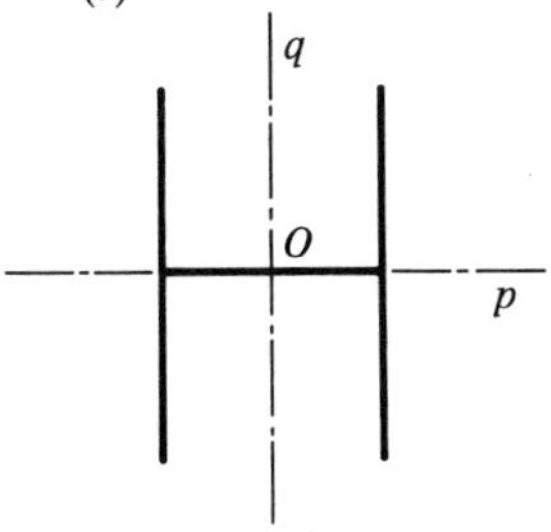

I: identity
P: reflection in axis p
Q: reflection in axis q
R: 180° rotation about point O

*	I	P	Q	R
I	I	P	Q	R
P	P	I	R	Q
Q	Q	R	I	P
R	R	Q	P	I

(*d*)

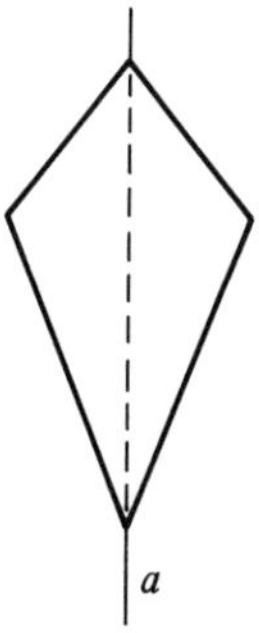

I: identity
A: reflection in axis a

*	I	A
I	I	A
A	A	I

(*e*) shape

I: identity
R: 90° rotation about centre
S: 180° rotation about centre
T: 180° rotation about centre

*	I	R	S	T
I	I	R	S	T
R	R	S	T	I
S	S	T	I	R
T	T	I	R	S

(*f*) ellipse

I: identity
F: reflection in the major axis
G: reflection in the minor axis
H: 180° rotation about the centre

*	I	F	G	H
I	I	F	G	H
F	F	I	H	G
G	G	H	I	F
H	H	G	F	I

2 Two symmetries: T, isosceles triangle, kite
Three symmetries:

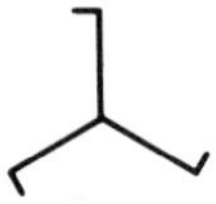

Five symmetries:

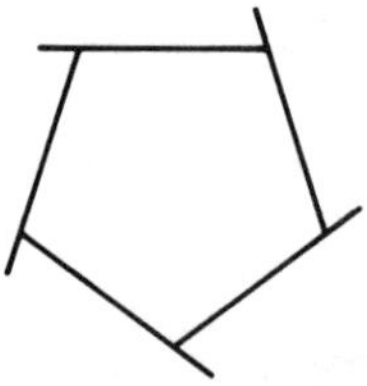

3 (*a*) Identity, reflections in x- and y-axes, half-turn about the origin
(*b*) Identity, reflections in $y = x$ and $y = -x$, half-turn about the origin
(*c*) Identity, reflections in $x = 0$, $y = 0$, $y = x$, $y = -x$, rotations about the origin through 90°, 180°, 270°
(*d*) Identity, reflection in any axis passing through the origin, rotation through any angle about the origin
(*e*) Identity, reflections in $x = 0$, $y = 0$, $y = x$, $y = -x$, rotations about the origin through 90°, 180°, 270°

4 (*a*) Reflections in lines joining vertex to mid-point of opposite side; rotations through multiples of 72° about centre
(*b*) Reflections in lines joining opposite vertices, and lines joining mid-points of opposite sides; rotations through multiples of 60° about centre

5 (*a*) $\begin{pmatrix}1 & 2 & 3 & 4\\ 3 & 2 & 1 & 4\end{pmatrix}$ (*b*) $\begin{pmatrix}1 & 2 & 3 & 4\\ 2 & 1 & 4 & 3\end{pmatrix}$ (*c*) $\begin{pmatrix}1 & 2 & 3 & 4\\ 2 & 3 & 4 & 1\end{pmatrix}$ (*d*) $\begin{pmatrix}1 & 2 & 3 & 4\\ 1 & 3 & 2 & 4\end{pmatrix}$

6 (*a*) $\begin{pmatrix}1 & 2 & 3 & 4 & 5\\ 2 & 1 & 3 & 5 & 4\end{pmatrix}$ (*b*) $\begin{pmatrix}1 & 2 & 3 & 4 & 5\\ 5 & 1 & 4 & 2 & 3\end{pmatrix}$

(*c*) $\begin{pmatrix}1 & 2 & 3 & 4 & 5\\ 3 & 2 & 5 & 1 & 4\end{pmatrix}$ (*d*) $\begin{pmatrix}1 & 2 & 3 & 4 & 5\\ 1 & 2 & 3 & 4 & 5\end{pmatrix}$

7 n is a multiple of 6

8 (*a*) No (*b*) Yes (*c*) $i = 4$, $j = 3$

Exercise 15B

1

	Closed	Associative	Commutative	Identity	Inverse
(*a*)	✓	✓	✓	✓	✓
(*b*)	✓	✓	×	✓	×
(*c*)	×	×	✓	×	—
(*d*)	×	×	✓	×	—
(*e*)	✓	×	✓	×	—
(*f*)	✓	✓	✓	✓	×
(*g*)	✓	✓	✓	✓	×
(*h*)	✓	✓	✓	✓	×
(*i*)	✓	✓	✓	✓	✓
(*j*)	✓	✓	✓	✓	✓

3 (*a*) $\{10\}$, $\{8, 10\}$, $\{4, 10, 16\}$, $\{2, 4, 8, 10, 14, 16\}$
(*b*) $\{6\}$, $\{6, 9\}$, $\{3, 6, 9, 12\}$
(*c*) $\{8\}$, $\{6, 8\}$, $\{2, 4, 8\}$, $\{2, 4, 6, 8, 10, 12\}$
(*d*) $\{0\}$, $\{0, 3\}$, $\{0, 2, 4\}$, $\{0, 1, 2, 3, 4, 5\}$
(*e*) {A}, {A, B}, {A, C}, {A, D}, {A, B, C, D}
(*f*) {A}, {A, B}, {A, B, C, D}
(*g*) {A}, {A, C}, {A, E}, {A, F}, {A, G}, {A, H}, {A, B, C, D}, {A, C, E, G}, {A, C, F, H}, {A, B, C, D, E, F, G, H}
(*h*) {A}, {A, B, C}, {A, D}, {A, E}, {A, F}, {A, B, C, D, E, F}
(*i*) $\{f\}$, $\{f, g, h\}$
(*j*) $\{p\}$, $\{p, r\}$, $\{p, q, r, s\}$
(*k*) $\{s\}$, $\{s, u\}$, $\{s, t, u, v\}$
(*l*) $\{i\}$, $\{i, f\}$, $\{i, g\}$, $\{i, r\}$, $\{i, p, q\}$, $\{i, f, g, p, q, r\}$

4 (*a*) $\begin{bmatrix} a & b \\ b & a \end{bmatrix}, \begin{bmatrix} b & a \\ a & b \end{bmatrix}$; both represent groups.

(*b*) $\begin{bmatrix} a & b & c \\ b & c & a \\ c & a & b \end{bmatrix}$ and permutations of $\{a, b, c\}$ represent a group.

$\begin{bmatrix} a & b & c \\ c & a & b \\ b & c & a \end{bmatrix}$ and permutations of $\{a, b, c\}$ do not represent a group.

5 (*a*) Not a group: axioms (2), (3) and (4) fail.
(*c*) Not a group: axiom (2) fails.

9 Symmetric about main diagonal; even number of lines

10 $\left\{\begin{bmatrix} 1 & 0 \\ 0 & 1 \end{bmatrix}, \begin{bmatrix} 2 & 7 \\ -1 & -3 \end{bmatrix}, \begin{bmatrix} -3 & -7 \\ 1 & 2 \end{bmatrix}\right\}$

Exercise 16A

1 (*a*), (*c*), (*d*) and (*e*) are isomorphic.

2 (*a*) and (*b*), (*c*) and (*d*) are isomorphic.

3 (*a*) Rotations of a square (*b*) Symmetries of a rectangle
(*c*) Rotations of a hexagon (*d*) Rotations of an equilateral triangle

5 6

Exercise 16B

1 (*a*) $\{e, q, r, s\}$ (*b*) $\{e, a\}$ (*c*) $\{e\}$, $\{e, a\}$, $\{e, b\}$, $\{e, c\}$, $\{e, p\}$, $\{e, r\}$, $\{e, q, r, s\}$
(*d*) $\{e, a, c, r\}$ (*e*) $\{e, a, b, c, p, q, r, s\}$ (*f*) $\{e, q, r, s\}$, $\{b, a, p, c\}$
(*g*) $\{e, a\}$, $\{b, q\}$, $\{c, r\}$, $\{p, s\}$

2 (*a*) $\left\{\begin{bmatrix}1 & 0\\0 & 1\end{bmatrix}, \begin{bmatrix}4 & -7\\3 & -5\end{bmatrix}, \begin{bmatrix}-5 & 7\\-3 & 4\end{bmatrix}\right\}$

(*b*) $\left\{\begin{bmatrix}1 & 0\\0 & 1\end{bmatrix}, \begin{bmatrix}3 & -1\\7 & -2\end{bmatrix}, \begin{bmatrix}2 & -1\\7 & -3\end{bmatrix}, \begin{bmatrix}-1 & 0\\0 & -1\end{bmatrix}, \begin{bmatrix}-3 & 1\\-7 & 2\end{bmatrix}, \begin{bmatrix}-2 & 1\\-7 & 3\end{bmatrix}\right\}$

(*c*) $\left\{\begin{bmatrix}1 & 0\\0 & 1\end{bmatrix}, \begin{bmatrix}5 & 13\\-2 & -5\end{bmatrix}, \begin{bmatrix}-1 & 0\\0 & -1\end{bmatrix}, \begin{bmatrix}-5 & -13\\2 & 5\end{bmatrix}\right\}$

3 $\left\{x \mapsto x, x \mapsto \dfrac{3x-1}{7x-2}, x \mapsto \dfrac{2x-1}{7x-3}\right\}$

$\left\{x \mapsto x, x \mapsto \dfrac{3x-1}{7x-2}, x \mapsto \dfrac{2x-1}{7x-3}, x \mapsto \dfrac{2x-1}{3x-2}, x \mapsto \dfrac{3x-1}{8x-3}, x \mapsto \dfrac{x}{5x-1}\right\}$

5 (*a*) 2 (*b*) 4 (*c*) 2 (*d*) 8

12 No

Exercise 16C

2 (*a*) Rotations of an equilateral triangle

	e	a	a^2
e	e	a	a^2
a	a	a^2	e
a^2	a^2	e	a

(*b*) Symmetries of a rectangle

	e	a	b	ab
e	e	a	b	ab
a	a	e	ab	b
b	b	ab	e	a
ab	ab	b	a	e

(*c*) A prism with rotational symmetry of order 4 about a central axis, and reflection symmetry in the plane midway between the ends

	e	b	b^2	b^3	a	ab	ab^2	ab^3
e	e	b	b^2	b^3	a	ab	ab^2	ab^3
b	b	b^2	b^3	e	ab	ab^2	ab^3	a
b^2	b^2	b^3	e	b	ab^2	ab^3	a	ab
b^3	b^3	e	b	b^2	ab^3	a	ab	ab^2
a	a	ab	ab^2	ab^3	e	b	b^2	b^3
ab	ab	ab^2	ab^3	a	b	b^2	b^3	e
ab^2	ab^2	ab^3	a	ab	b^2	b^3	e	b
ab^3	ab^3	a	ab	ab^2	b^3	e	b	b^2

(*d*) Rotations of a regular hexagon

	e	a	a^2	b	ab	a^2b
e	e	a	a^2	b	ab	a^2b
a	a	a^2	e	ab	a^2b	b
a^2	a^2	e	a	a^2b	b	ab
b	b	ab	a^2b	e	a	a^2
ab	ab	a^2b	b	a	a^2	e
a^2b	a^2b	b	ab	a^2	e	a

4

	e	a	b	c	ab	bc	ca	abc
e	e	a	b	c	ab	bc	ca	abc
a	a	e	ab	ac	b	abc	c	bc
b	b	ab	c	bc	a	c	abc	ac
c	c	ac	bc	e	abc	b	a	ab
ab	ab	b	a	abc	e	ac	bc	c
bc	bc	abc	c	b	ac	e	ab	a
ca	ca	c	abc	a	bc	ab	e	b
abc	abc	bc	ac	ab	c	a	b	e

5 (*a*) 2, 11; $2^4 = 11^2 = 1, 2.11 = 11.2$
(*b*) 2, 13; $2^6 = 13^2 = 1, 2.13 = 13.2$

Exercise 16D

1 No

4 When l, m, n are concurrent or parallel

6 (*a*) $\mathbf{P}_1$ = rotation of 120° about line through 1 and mid-point of 234 in anticlockwise direction as viewed looking down on 1; $\mathbf{P}_2$ = opposite rotation to $\mathbf{P}_1$; $\mathbf{X}$ = rotation of 180° about line through mid-points of 14 and 23.

(*b*) $\pi_{q_1} = \begin{pmatrix} 1 & 2 & 3 & 4 \\ 3 & 2 & 4 & 1 \end{pmatrix}, \pi_{q_2} = \begin{pmatrix} 1 & 2 & 3 & 4 \\ 4 & 2 & 1 & 3 \end{pmatrix}$

$\pi_{r_1} = \begin{pmatrix} 1 & 2 & 3 & 4 \\ 2 & 4 & 3 & 1 \end{pmatrix}, \pi_{r_2} = \begin{pmatrix} 1 & 2 & 3 & 4 \\ 4 & 1 & 3 & 2 \end{pmatrix}$

$\pi_{s_1} = \begin{pmatrix} 1 & 2 & 3 & 4 \\ 2 & 3 & 1 & 4 \end{pmatrix}, \pi_{s_2} = \begin{pmatrix} 1 & 2 & 3 & 4 \\ 3 & 1 & 2 & 4 \end{pmatrix}$

$\pi_y = \begin{pmatrix} 1 & 2 & 3 & 4 \\ 3 & 4 & 1 & 2 \end{pmatrix}, \pi_z = \begin{pmatrix} 1 & 2 & 3 & 4 \\ 2 & 1 & 4 & 3 \end{pmatrix}$

$\pi_i = \begin{pmatrix} 1 & 2 & 3 & 4 \\ 1 & 2 & 3 & 4 \end{pmatrix}$

(*c*) $\{\pi_i\}$, $\{\pi_i, \pi_x\}$, $\{\pi_i, \pi_y\}$, $\{\pi_i, \pi_z\}$, $\{\pi_i, \pi_{p_1}, \pi_{p_2}\}$, $\{\pi_i, \pi_{q_1}, \pi_{q_2}\}$, $\{\pi_i, \pi_{r_1}, \pi_{r_2}\}$, $\{\pi_i, \pi_{s_1}, \pi_{s_2}\}$, $\{\pi_i, \pi_x, \pi_y, \pi_z\}$, $\{\pi_i, \pi_x, \pi_y, \pi_z, \pi_{p_1}, \pi_{p_2}, \pi_{q_1}, \pi_{q_2}, \pi_{r_1}, \pi_{r_2}, \pi_{s_1}, \pi_{s_2}\}$

Miscellaneous exercise 16

1 (*b*) The product of the orders of groups G and H
(*d*) No

(e)

	(0,0)	(0,1)	(1,0)	(1,1)
(0,0)	(0,0)	(0,1)	(1,0)	(1,1)
(0,1)	(0,1)	(0,0)	(1,1)	(1,0)
(1,0)	(1,0)	(1,1)	(0,0)	(0,1)
(1,1)	(1,1)	(1,0)	(0,1)	(0,0)

Isomorphic to $\{1, 3, 5, 7\}$ under multiplication mod 8; 16

3 (a) $\begin{pmatrix} 1 & 2 & 3 \\ 1 & 3 & 2 \end{pmatrix} \circ \begin{pmatrix} 1 & 2 & 3 \\ 2 & 1 & 3 \end{pmatrix}$; no

(b) $\begin{pmatrix} 1 & 2 & 3 \\ 1 & 2 & 3 \end{pmatrix}, \begin{pmatrix} 1 & 2 & 3 \\ 2 & 3 & 1 \end{pmatrix}, \begin{pmatrix} 1 & 2 & 3 \\ 3 & 1 & 2 \end{pmatrix}$; yes

(c) No

4 (a) (i) Through mid-points of opposite faces, 3 (ii) through opposite vertices, 4 (iii) through mid-points of opposite edges, 6
(b) All possible permutations
(c) (i) 6 (ii) 8 (iii) 9
(d) No
(e) (i) {permutations fixing a certain diagonal}; (ii) {symmetries fixing or interchanging a certain pair of opposite faces}; (iii) {even permutations}

Exercise 17A

1 (a) $x = 4$ (b) No solution (c) $x = 1$ or 5
(d) $x = 3$ (e) $x = 0$ (f) $x = 7$

2 (b) $a = q$; 0 or 2 if $a \neq 0$, 1 if $a = 0$

3 (a) $x = 1$ or 6 (b) No solution (c) $x = 1, 2, 4$ or 5

4 (a) $\begin{bmatrix} 3 \\ 2 \end{bmatrix}$ (b) $\begin{bmatrix} 3 \\ 5 \end{bmatrix}$

Exercise 17B

1

	Commutative group under +	Group under . (if zero is excluded)	Multiplication commutative	Distributive laws hold	$a.b = a.c$ and $a \neq 0$ $\Rightarrow b = c$
(a)	✓	×	✓	✓	✓
(b)	✓	✓	✓	✓	✓
(c)	✓	×	✓	✓	×
(d)	✓	×	✓	✓	✓
(e)	✓	✓	✓	✓	✓
(f)	✓	✓	✓	✓	✓
(g)	✓	✓	✓	✓	✓
(h)	✓	✓	✓	✓	✓
(i)	✓	×	✓	✓	✓
(j)	×	✓	×	×	✓
(k)	✓	×	×	✓	×
(l)	✓	×	×	×	×

2 (*b*) Ring (*c*) Integral domain (*e*) Integral domain
(*f*) Field (*g*) Ring (*j*) Ring (*k*) Integral domain (*l*) Ring

3 $(\mathbb{Z}, \otimes, \oplus)$ is a ring, but not a field

Exercise 17D

1 (*a*) $(0, 2)$ (*b*) $(2, 1)$ (*c*) Parallel

2 $(0,3)$, $(1,0)$, $(2,2)$, $(3,4)$, $(4,1)$, $(0,0)$, $(1,2)$, $(2,4)$, $(3,1)$, $(4,3)$; no, the lines are parallel

3 $(4,3)$, $(0,0)$, $(1,2)$; $x + 2y = 0$

4 $x = 1$, $y = 3$, $x + y = 4$, $2x + y = 0$, $x + 2y = 2$, $x + 4y = 3$

5 Yes (5 points), 6; 30

6 $[4, 1, 3]$, $[3, 2, 1]$; five do not represent lines; 30

8 p^2, $p(p + 1)$

Miscellaneous exercise 17

1 Yes

4 (*a*) 3, 4, 6 (*b*) $\dfrac{p+1}{2}$ if $p \neq 2$, 2 if $p = 2$

5 Yes

Exercise 18A

1 (*a*) F T F	(*b*) F F F	(*c*) F T F	(*d*) T T T	(*e*) T T T
(*f*) T T T	(*g*) F T T	(*h*) T T T	(*i*) T T T	(*j*) F T F
(*k*) T T F	(*l*) F F T	(*m*) T F T	(*n*) T F F	(*o*) T T T
(*p*) T T T	(*q*) T F T			

2 (*d*) Parallel lines
(*e*) Similar triangles
(*f*) Congruent triangles
(*h*) {odd integers}, {even integers}
(*i*) {odd integers}, {even integers}
(*o*) Congruent classes mod 5
(*p*) Numbers of same length

3 (*a*) Any non-empty set with a void relation
(*b*) Non-zero elements of $\mathbb{Z}$ with $xRy \Leftrightarrow x$ and y have same sign or same parity
(*c*) $\mathbb{R}$ with $xRy \Leftrightarrow x \leqslant y$
(*d*) $\mathbb{C}$ with $z_1 R z_1 \Leftrightarrow |z_1| = |z_2|$

5 (*a*) $\mathbf{A} = \begin{bmatrix} \frac{1}{2} & 1 \\ \frac{7}{2} & -3 \end{bmatrix}$, $\mathbf{B} = \begin{bmatrix} \frac{3}{5} & \frac{1}{5} \\ \frac{7}{10} & -\frac{1}{10} \end{bmatrix}$ (*b*) Yes

6 (*b*) $\begin{bmatrix} 0 \\ 3 \end{bmatrix}, \begin{bmatrix} 1 \\ 3 \end{bmatrix}, \begin{bmatrix} 2 \\ 3 \end{bmatrix}$ (*c*) $\left\{\begin{bmatrix} \mu \\ 3 \end{bmatrix}\right\}$, $\mu \in \mathbb{R}$

7 (*b*) The line $x + y = 2$

8 5

Exercise 18B

1 (*a*) $x \equiv 7 \pmod 9$ (*b*) $x \equiv 6 \pmod 7$ (*c*) $x \equiv 10 \pmod{11}$
(*d*) $x \equiv 1 \pmod 3$ (*e*) $x \equiv 2 \pmod 3$ (*f*) No solution
(*g*) $x \equiv \pmod 6$ (*h*) No solution (*i*) No solution
(*j*) $x \equiv 4$ or $6 \pmod{10}$

2 (*a*) $x \equiv 4,\ y \equiv 1$ (*b*) $x \equiv 0, 1, 2, 3, 4, 5, 6$ and $y \equiv 4, 1, 5, 2, 6, 3, 0$, respectively
(*c*) No solution

3 (*a*) 40

6 $a = 0,\ p = 4$

Miscellaneous exercise 18

1 (*d*) {identity}, {non-identity rotations}, {reflections}
(*e*) {identity}, {180° rotation}, {±90° rotations},
{reflections in diagonals}, {reflections in other lines}

3 (*a*) Yes; new equivalence classes are intersections of old equivalence classes.
(*b*) No. For example, see Exercise 18A, question 1(*k*).

4 $\mathbf{P}^{-1} = \begin{bmatrix} 4 & 6 \\ 6 & 1 \end{bmatrix}, \mathbf{D} = \begin{bmatrix} 5 & 0 \\ 0 & 1 \end{bmatrix}, \mathbf{P} = \begin{bmatrix} 5 & 5 \\ 5 & 6 \end{bmatrix}$

$\mathbf{A}^{10} = \begin{bmatrix} 0 & 2 \\ 6 & 3 \end{bmatrix}$

5 (*a*) 49 (*b*) 119

Revision exercise 15

A1

	Closed	Associative	Identity	Inverses
(*a*)	✓	✓	✓	✓
(*b*)	✓	✓	✓	✓
(*c*)	×	✓	×	—
(*d*)	✓	✓	✓	✓

A2 (*a*, (*c*)

A3 (*a*) $\begin{pmatrix} 1 & 2 & 3 & 4 \\ 2 & 1 & 3 & 4 \end{pmatrix}$ (*b*) $\begin{pmatrix} 1 & 2 & 3 & 4 \\ 1 & 4 & 3 & 2 \end{pmatrix}$ (*c*) $\begin{pmatrix} 1 & 2 & 3 & 4 \\ 2 & 4 & 1 & 3 \end{pmatrix}$

A4 (*a*)

	e	*a*
e	*e*	*a*
a	*a*	*e*

where *a* is the reflection in the vertical line

(*b*)

	e	*a*	*b*	*c*
e	*e*	*a*	*b*	*c*
a	*a*	*e*	*c*	*b*
b	*b*	*c*	*e*	*a*
c	*c*	*b*	*a*	*e*

where *a* is reflection in the *x*-axis,
b is reflection in the *y*-axis
c is 180° rotation about *O*

B1 (*a*) No

B2 T is non-Abelian, U Abelian.

B3 $\varnothing$, $\{X\}$, $\{Y\}$, $\{Z\}$, $\{X,Y\}$, $\{Y,Z\}$, $\{Z,X\}$, $\{X,Y,Z\}$
Subgroups
$\{\varnothing\}$
$\{\varnothing,\{X\}\}$, $\{\varnothing,\{Y\}\}$, $\{\varnothing,\{Z\}\}$
$\{\varnothing,\{X,Y\}\}$, $\{\varnothing,\{X,Z\}\}$, $\{\varnothing,\{Y,Z\}\}$
$\{\varnothing,\{X,Y,Z\}\}$
$\{\varnothing,\{X\},\{Y\},\{X,Y\}\}$, $\{\varnothing,\{X\},\{Z\},\{X,Z\}\}$, $\{\varnothing,\{Y\},\{Z\},\{Y,Z\}\}$
$\{\varnothing,\{X\},\{Y,Z\},\{X,Y,Z\}\}$, $\{\varnothing,\{Y\},\{X,Z\},\{X,Y,Z\}\}$,
$\{\varnothing,\{Z\},\{X,Y\},\{X,Y,Z\}\}$
$\{\varnothing,\{X,Y\},\{X,Z\},\{Y,Z\}\}$
$\{\varnothing,\{X\},\{Y\},\{Z\},\{X,Y\},\{X,Z\},\{Y,Z\},\{X,Y,Z\}\}$

B4 (*b*) $fg: x \to 1 - \dfrac{1}{x}$ (*d*) e

	f	g	h
g	r^2	e	r
h	r	r^2	e
r		f	g

Subgroups of order 2: $\{e, f\}$, $\{e, g\}$, $\{e, h\}$
Subgroup of order 3: $\{e, r, r^2\}$
4 is not a factor of 6.

Revision exercise 16

A1 Rotations of a square

A2 $\begin{bmatrix}1 & 0\\0 & 1\end{bmatrix}$, $\begin{bmatrix}0 & 1\\-1 & 0\end{bmatrix}$, $\begin{bmatrix}-1 & 0\\0 & -1\end{bmatrix}$, $\begin{bmatrix}0 & -1\\1 & 0\end{bmatrix}$, $\begin{bmatrix}-j & 0\\0 & j\end{bmatrix}$, $\begin{bmatrix}j & 0\\0 & -j\end{bmatrix}$, $\begin{bmatrix}0 & j\\j & 0\end{bmatrix}$, $\begin{bmatrix}0 & -j\\-j & 0\end{bmatrix}$

A3 4, 5, 9

A5 (*b*) a

B1 $e = 1, b = -1, a = i, c = -i$, or $e = 1, b = -1, a = -i, c = i$

B3 k^{-1}, inverse $s_1 = k^{-1} \circ s_1^{-1} \circ k$

B4 8: order of a, a^3, b, ba, ba^2, $ba^3 = 4$, order of $a^2 = 2$, order of $e = 1$

B5 $\left\{\begin{bmatrix}1 & 0 & q\\0 & 1 & 0\\0 & 0 & 1\end{bmatrix} : q \in \mathbb{Q}\right\}$

Revision exercise 17

A2 (*a*) $x = 5$ (*b*) empty set (*c*) $\begin{bmatrix}x\\y\end{bmatrix} = \begin{bmatrix}6\\4\end{bmatrix}$

A3 No

A4 (*a*) (0, 1), (1, 5), (2, 2), (3, 6), (4, 3), (5, 0), (6, 4).
(0, 2), (1, 1), (2, 0), (3, 6), (4, 5), (5, 4), (6, 3).
The lines intersect at (3, 6).
(*b*) $x + y + 2 = 0$, not unique

A5 Yes

B1 (*a*) Yes (*b*) No

B2 (*a*) $\{A, -A, (0,0)\}$ for $A \neq (0,0)$ (*b*) $\{A, (2,1), -A, (1,2)\}$ for $A \neq (1,2)$
(*c*) 24, 5

B3 (*a*) False (*b*) False (*c*) True: $\{(0,n): n \in \mathbb{Z}\}$; yes

Revision exercise 18

A1

	Reflexive	Symmetric	Transitive
(*a*)	✓	✓	×
(*b*)	✓	✓	✓
(*c*)	✓	✓	✓
(*d*)	✓	✓	✓

A3 Positive rationals

A4 (*a*) $x \equiv 1 \pmod 7$ (*b*) empty set (*c*) $x \equiv 1$ or $2 \pmod 3$ (*d*) empty set

A5 m square-free

B1 (*a*) Yes (*b*) No (*c*) Yes (*d*) Yes

B4 (*b*) The line $x + 2y = 4$

B5 (*a*) (i) No (ii) Yes (iii) No (*b*) (i) Yes (ii) Yes (iii) Yes
(*c*) (i) No (ii) Yes (iii) No (*d*) (i) Yes (ii) Yes (iii) Yes
(*e*) (i) Yes (ii) Yes (iii) Yes
Equivalence classes: (*b*) odd natural numbers and even numbers, (*d*) for each $n \in \mathbb{N}$, the equivalence class is $\left\{\frac{a}{n}: a \in \mathbb{Z} \text{ and } a, n \text{ having no common factor}\right\}$, (*e*) $\{a, c\}$, $\{b, d, e\}$, $\{f\}$.

Examination questions 2: Chapters 10–19

1 $7, \begin{bmatrix} 1 \\ 1 \end{bmatrix}$; $-1, \begin{bmatrix} 1 \\ -1 \end{bmatrix}$; $\frac{1}{\sqrt{2}}\begin{bmatrix} 1 & 1 \\ -1 & 1 \end{bmatrix}$

2 $\left\{\begin{bmatrix} 2 \\ -3 \\ 0 \\ 1 \end{bmatrix}, \begin{bmatrix} 1 \\ -1 \\ 1 \\ 0 \end{bmatrix}\right\}$

3 $k = 1$; $\left\{\lambda \begin{bmatrix} -1 \\ 1 \\ 1 \\ 0 \end{bmatrix} + \mu \begin{bmatrix} -1 \\ 2 \\ 0 \\ 1 \end{bmatrix} : \lambda, \mu \in \mathbb{R}\right\}$

4 $2r_1 + r_2 + 5r_3 = 0$; rank $= 2$; dimension of kernel $= 2$;
$\left\{\begin{bmatrix} 1 \\ -2 \\ 0 \end{bmatrix}, \begin{bmatrix} 2 \\ 1 \\ -1 \end{bmatrix}\right\}$

5 (*a*) Yes (axioms of a ring) (*b*) Yes (axioms of a field)
In $\mathbb{Z}_{11}$, $x = 7$ or 10; in $\mathbb{Z}_9$, $x = 2$, 5 or 8

8 $\mathbf{a} = \begin{bmatrix} -1 \\ 2 \\ 0 \end{bmatrix}, \mathbf{u} = \begin{bmatrix} 2 \\ 1 \\ -1 \end{bmatrix}.$

9 $\begin{bmatrix} x \\ y \\ z \end{bmatrix} \mapsto \begin{bmatrix} y \\ 0 \\ 0 \end{bmatrix}$

10 (*a*) (i) No – not symmetric (ii) Yes (iii) Yes
(*b*) $x = 1$ or 2

11 (*b*) rank = 2; basis $\left\{ \begin{bmatrix} -3 \\ 4 \\ 1 \end{bmatrix} \right\}$

13 (*b*) (i) $\left\{ \begin{bmatrix} 1 \\ 2 \\ -1 \end{bmatrix} \right\}$ is the basis of the null space of L; the dimension is 1.

(ii) $L\begin{bmatrix} 0 \\ -1 \\ 0 \end{bmatrix} = 1\begin{bmatrix} 1 \\ 0 \\ 1 \end{bmatrix} + \tfrac{1}{2}\begin{bmatrix} 0 \\ -1 \\ 0 \end{bmatrix} + \tfrac{1}{2}\begin{bmatrix} 0 \\ 1 \\ 2 \end{bmatrix}$

$L\begin{bmatrix} 0 \\ 1 \\ 2 \end{bmatrix} = -1\begin{bmatrix} 1 \\ 0 \\ 1 \end{bmatrix} - \tfrac{7}{2}\begin{bmatrix} 0 \\ -1 \\ 0 \end{bmatrix} - \tfrac{3}{2}\begin{bmatrix} 0 \\ 1 \\ 2 \end{bmatrix}$

14 4; $\left\{ \begin{bmatrix} 1 & 0 \\ 0 & 0 \end{bmatrix}, \begin{bmatrix} 0 & 1 \\ 0 & 0 \end{bmatrix}, \begin{bmatrix} 0 & 0 \\ 1 & 0 \end{bmatrix}, \begin{bmatrix} 0 & 0 \\ 0 & 1 \end{bmatrix} \right\}$

(*a*) Yes; $\left\{ \begin{bmatrix} 1 & 0 \\ 0 & 1 \end{bmatrix} \right\}$

(*b*) Yes; $\left\{ \begin{bmatrix} 1 & 0 \\ 0 & 0 \end{bmatrix}, \begin{bmatrix} 0 & 1 \\ 1 & 0 \end{bmatrix}, \begin{bmatrix} 0 & 0 \\ 0 & 1 \end{bmatrix} \right\}$

(*c*) No (not closed under addition)

15 $\left\{ \begin{bmatrix} 1 & 0 \\ 0 & 1 \end{bmatrix} \right\}$; no (eigenvalues are not the same)

16 2, 3

17

*	0	1	2	3
0	1	2	3	0
1	2	3	0	1
2	3	0	1	2
3	0	1	2	3

∘	0	1	2	3
0	0	1	2	3
1	1	3	1	3
2	2	1	0	3
3	3	3	3	3

Yes, 0 is the unity element; not a field as the 'non-zero' elements do not form a group under ∘.

18 (*a*) Yes; $\{x^2, x\}$
(*b*) No (not closed under addition)
(*c*) Yes; $\{x^2, -1, x-1\}$
(*d*) Yes; $\{x^2, 1\}$

19 (*d*) G is cyclic.

20 (*a*) $\mathbf{C} = \begin{bmatrix} 1 & 0 \\ 0 & 1 \end{bmatrix}, \mathbf{D} = \begin{bmatrix} -1 & 0 \\ 0 & -1 \end{bmatrix}$;

	A	B	C	D
A	C	D	A	B
B	D	C	B	A
C	A	B	C	D
D	B	A	D	C

(*b*) (i) Both S and T are rings.
(ii) T is a field but S is not (inverse property).

21 (*a*) (i) 'Stay-put' transformation (ii) self-inverse
(*b*) (i) **A** (ii) (**B**, **D**), (**C**, **C**), (**D**, **B**)
Not isomorphic, as (*a*) is a Klein group and (*b*) is a cyclic group.

22 (*a*) $\mathbf{u} = \begin{bmatrix} 5 \\ 8 \\ 11 \end{bmatrix}$ (*b*) $\mathbf{v} = \begin{bmatrix} 6 \\ 8 \\ 11 \end{bmatrix}$

$z = 30$; basis of $V' = \left\{ \begin{bmatrix} 1 \\ 3 \\ 4 \end{bmatrix}, \begin{bmatrix} 1 \\ 1 \\ 2 \end{bmatrix} \right\}$; the dimension is 2

23 (*a*) (i) True (ii) True (iii) $e = -1$ (iv) Only true if $a \neq -2$
(*b*) $*$ is not associative; 0 is the identity element; elements $< -\frac{1}{2}$ do not have an inverse but elements $\geqslant -\frac{1}{2}$ always have an inverse (not necessarily unique).

24 Subgroups with exactly two elements: $\{I, K\}$, $\{I, P\}$, $\{I, Q\}$, $\{I, R\}$, $\{I, S\}$
Subgroups with exactly four elements: $\{I, J, K, L\}$, $\{I, P, Q, K\}$, $\{I, R, S, K\}$

25 (*b*) S: $\{(1, 0, 1, 1), (5, 0, 2, 2)\}$
T: $\{(1, -1, 0, 1), (0, 1, 1, 0)\}$
$S \cap T$: $\{(1, 0, 1, 1)\}$
$T + S$: $\{(1, 0, 1, 1), (5, 0, 2, 2), (1, -1, 0, 1)\}$
U: $\{(0, 1, 0, 0), (0, 0, 0, 1)\}$.

Examination questions 3: miscellaneous

1 $\begin{bmatrix} 1 & 0 & 0 \\ 0 & 1 & 0 \\ -2 & 0 & 1 \end{bmatrix}, \begin{bmatrix} 1 & -1 & 0 \\ 0 & 1 & 0 \\ 0 & 0 & 1 \end{bmatrix}, \begin{bmatrix} 1 & 0 & 0 \\ 0 & 1 & -2 \\ 0 & 0 & 1 \end{bmatrix}; \begin{bmatrix} 1 & -1 & 0 \\ 4 & 1 & -2 \\ -2 & 0 & 1 \end{bmatrix}$

2 $\begin{bmatrix} 1 \\ 2 \end{bmatrix}, \begin{bmatrix} 2 \\ -1 \end{bmatrix}; \frac{1}{5}\begin{bmatrix} -3 \\ 4 \end{bmatrix}, \frac{1}{5}\begin{bmatrix} 4 \\ 3 \end{bmatrix}; \frac{1}{5}\begin{bmatrix} -3 & 4 \\ 4 & 3 \end{bmatrix}$

3 0; the three planes meet in a line through the origin (a sheaf).

5 $l = -4, m = -\frac{22}{7}, n = \frac{23}{7}$; $\mathbf{x} = \begin{bmatrix} 1 \\ -2 \\ 3 \end{bmatrix}$

6 **D** represents a one-way stretch in the direction of the x-axis, factor 2; **R** represents a rotation about the origin through $-\cos^{-1}(0.6)$; $3y = 4x$

7 (*c*) $\begin{bmatrix} 0 & -1 \\ 1 & -1 \end{bmatrix}$

8 (*a*) (i) $\alpha\lambda$ (ii) λ^2 (iii) $\dfrac{1}{\lambda}$ (iv) λ^n

(*b*) (i) $-1, 2, 4$ (ii) $1, 4, 16$ (iii) $1, \frac{1}{4}, \frac{1}{16}$

9 $\begin{bmatrix} 2 \\ 1 \\ 3 \end{bmatrix}$

10 (*a*) No, $\mathbf{A} = \mathbf{I}$ is not singular
(*b*) Yes
(*c*) No, only if **A** and **B** commute
(*d*) No
(*e*) Yes

11 (*b*) $2x + y + z = 0$

(*c*) $\mathbf{r} = \lambda \begin{bmatrix} 0 \\ 1 \\ -1 \end{bmatrix}$

12 $\begin{bmatrix} 1 & 0 \\ 0 & 1 \end{bmatrix}$; $(1,2), (1,2), (1,2)$; projection onto the line $y = 2x$, parallel to $2x + y = 0$

13 (*a*) (i) $(2, -1)$ (ii) $y = 9x$
(*b*) (i) The line $3x - 2y = 0$ (ii) $(1, 2)$

14 (*a*) $k = -4$; $\{(\frac{5}{11} + 14\lambda, \frac{7}{11} + 13\lambda, 11\lambda) : \lambda \in \mathbb{R}\}$

(*b*) $\left\{ \lambda \begin{bmatrix} 1 \\ 0 \\ 1 \end{bmatrix} + \mu \begin{bmatrix} 0 \\ 1 \\ 2 \end{bmatrix} : \lambda, \mu \in \mathbb{R} \right\}$

15 Enlargement, centre the origin, scale factor a

16 $2, \begin{bmatrix} 0 \\ 1 \\ 0 \end{bmatrix}$; $2 + \sqrt{2}, \begin{bmatrix} \dfrac{1}{\sqrt{(4+2\sqrt{2})}} \\ 0 \\ \dfrac{1+\sqrt{2}}{\sqrt{(4+2\sqrt{2})}} \end{bmatrix}$; $2 - \sqrt{2}, \begin{bmatrix} \dfrac{1}{\sqrt{(4-2\sqrt{2})}} \\ 0 \\ \dfrac{1-\sqrt{2}}{\sqrt{(4-2\sqrt{2})}} \end{bmatrix}$

17 $\lambda = 2, \left\{ \begin{bmatrix} 1 \\ 3 \\ 0 \end{bmatrix} + \lambda \begin{bmatrix} 1 \\ 5 \\ 3 \end{bmatrix} \right\}$; $\lambda = 5$, empty solution set

18 $\begin{bmatrix} -\frac{1}{2} & \frac{1}{2}\sqrt{3} \\ \frac{1}{2}\sqrt{3} & \frac{1}{2} \end{bmatrix}$; $\begin{bmatrix} 1 \\ \sqrt{3} \end{bmatrix}, \begin{bmatrix} -\sqrt{3} \\ 1 \end{bmatrix}$; reflection in the line $y = \sqrt{3}x$

19 (*b*) Projection onto the x-axis parallel to the y-axis, followed by a 90° rotation, centre the origin, followed by an enlargement, centre the origin, scale factor c

20 (*a*) $0, \begin{bmatrix} 0 \\ 1 \\ -1 \end{bmatrix}$; $-2, \begin{bmatrix} -2 \\ 1 \\ 0 \end{bmatrix}$; $-3, \begin{bmatrix} 1 \\ 0 \\ -1 \end{bmatrix}$

(*c*) $\begin{bmatrix} 0 & 0 & 0 \\ 0 & -2 & 0 \\ 0 & 0 & -3 \end{bmatrix}$

21 $\begin{bmatrix} 24 & 0 & 0 \\ 25 & 24 & 0 \\ 25 & 0 & 24 \end{bmatrix}$

22 $2, \begin{bmatrix} \frac{1}{\sqrt{2}} \\ -\frac{1}{\sqrt{2}} \end{bmatrix}$; $4, \begin{bmatrix} \frac{1}{\sqrt{2}} \\ \frac{1}{\sqrt{2}} \end{bmatrix}$; $\mathbf{B}^{-1} = \frac{1}{2}\mathbf{X}_1\mathbf{X}_1^{\mathrm{T}} + \frac{1}{4}\mathbf{X}_2\mathbf{X}_2^{\mathrm{T}}$

23 (*b*) $\begin{bmatrix} 3 \\ 3 \\ 1 \end{bmatrix}$ (*c*) The line $\mathbf{r} = \begin{bmatrix} 3 \\ -1 \\ 0 \end{bmatrix} + \lambda \begin{bmatrix} -2 \\ 1 \\ 1 \end{bmatrix} : \lambda \in \mathbb{R}$

24 (*a*) $\begin{bmatrix} 2 \\ 2 \\ -1 \end{bmatrix}, \begin{bmatrix} 2 \\ -1 \\ 2 \end{bmatrix}, \begin{bmatrix} -1 \\ 2 \\ 2 \end{bmatrix}$; $\mathbf{P} = \begin{bmatrix} 2 & 2 & -1 \\ 2 & -1 & 2 \\ -1 & 2 & 2 \end{bmatrix}$

(*b*) $x^2 + 5y^2 + 3z^2 - 8xz + 8yz$

$$\begin{aligned} u &= 2x + 2y - z \\ v &= 2x - y + 2z \\ w &= -x + 2y + 2z \end{aligned}$$

(*d*) $3u^2 - 3v^2 + 9w^2$

25 (*a*) False – for example, $\begin{bmatrix} 1 & 0 \\ 0 & 0 \end{bmatrix}\begin{bmatrix} 0 & 0 \\ 0 & 1 \end{bmatrix} = \begin{bmatrix} 0 & 0 \\ 0 & 0 \end{bmatrix}$

(*b*) True

(*c*) True

(*d*) False – for example, $\begin{bmatrix} 0 & 1 \\ 1 & 0 \end{bmatrix}\begin{bmatrix} 1 & 1 \\ 1 & 1 \end{bmatrix} = \begin{bmatrix} 1 & 1 \\ 1 & 1 \end{bmatrix}$

(*e*) True

26 (*a*) The field of complex numbers

(*b*) The field $\mathbb{Z}_2$

27 $\begin{bmatrix} 1 & 0 & 1 & -5 \\ 0 & 1 & 1 & 12 \\ 0 & 0 & 0 & 0 \end{bmatrix}$; rank is 2;

kernel basis $\left\{ \begin{bmatrix} 1 \\ 1 \\ -1 \\ 0 \end{bmatrix}, \begin{bmatrix} 5 \\ -12 \\ 0 \\ 1 \end{bmatrix} \right\}$;

range basis $\left\{\begin{bmatrix}1\\2\\4\end{bmatrix}, \begin{bmatrix}1\\1\\1\end{bmatrix}\right\}$

28 $3\mathbf{c} - \mathbf{c}_2 - 2\mathbf{c}_3 = \mathbf{0}$
$5\mathbf{c}_2 + 4\mathbf{c}_3 - 3\mathbf{c}_4 = \mathbf{0}$

The kernel is $\left\{\lambda\begin{bmatrix}3\\-1\\-2\\0\end{bmatrix} + \mu\begin{bmatrix}0\\5\\4\\-3\end{bmatrix} : \lambda, \mu \in \mathbb{R}\right\}$

$$\begin{bmatrix}x\\y\\z\\t\end{bmatrix} = \begin{bmatrix}3\\2\\0\\0\end{bmatrix} + \lambda\begin{bmatrix}3\\-1\\-2\\0\end{bmatrix} + \mu\begin{bmatrix}0\\5\\4\\-3\end{bmatrix} : \lambda, \mu \in \mathbb{R}$$

29 (*a*) $\mathbf{X} = 2\mathbf{A} - 3\mathbf{B} + \mathbf{C}$; the dimension is 3
(*b*) $5x - 6y - 7z = 0$; the dimension is 2
(*c*) $a = \frac{7}{9}$

30 null space $\left\{\begin{bmatrix}-6\\1\\4\end{bmatrix}\right\}$, range $\left\{\begin{bmatrix}1\\2\\1\\6\end{bmatrix}, \begin{bmatrix}2\\0\\-6\\-4\end{bmatrix}\right\}$;

$$\left\{\begin{bmatrix}9\\0\\-6\end{bmatrix} + \lambda\begin{bmatrix}-6\\1\\4\end{bmatrix} : \lambda \in \mathbb{R}\right\}$$

31 $\begin{bmatrix}0 & 1 & 0\\0 & 0 & 1\\-1 & 0 & 0\end{bmatrix}$; opposite

32 $\begin{bmatrix}3 & 2 & 3\\1 & 3 & 2\\2 & 1 & 1\end{bmatrix}$; $\begin{bmatrix}8\\6\\4\end{bmatrix}, \begin{bmatrix}15\\11\\10\end{bmatrix}, \begin{bmatrix}23\\17\\14\end{bmatrix}$

33 Top left corner:

$$\begin{matrix}e & a & a^2 & a^3\\a & a^2 & a^3 & e\\a^2 & a^3 & e & a\\a^3 & e & a & a^2\end{matrix}$$

Bottom right corner:

$$\begin{matrix}e & a^3 & a^2 & a\\a & e & a^3 & a^2\\a^2 & a & e & a^3\\a^3 & a^2 & a & e\end{matrix}$$

Element:	e	a	a^2	a^3	b	ab	a^2b	a^3b
Order:	1	4	2	4	2	2	2	2

(*a*) $\{e, a, a^2, a^3\}$
(*b*) $\{e, a^2, b, a^2b\}$

34 Half-turn about R_1R_2

35 $\mathbf{P} = \begin{bmatrix} 3 & 1 \\ 2 & -1 \end{bmatrix}$; $u = e^{4t}$, $v = -e^{-t}$

36 Not a field, as no inverses under multiplication

37 24 rotation symmetries: $\frac{1}{2}\pi$, π, $\frac{3}{2}\pi$ about three face-centred axes; $\frac{2}{3}\pi$, $\frac{4}{3}\pi$ about four diagonal axes; π about six edge-centred axes; 24 opposite isometries.

Rotation through $\frac{2}{3}\pi$ about AG; central inversion; composition is a rotational symmetry of $PQRSTU$.

38 8; $\{\mathbf{I}, \mathbf{A}, \mathbf{A}^2, \mathbf{A}^3\}$, $\{\mathbf{I}, \mathbf{B}, \mathbf{A}^2, \mathbf{A}^2\mathbf{B}\}$, $\{\mathbf{I}, \mathbf{A}^2, \mathbf{AB}, \mathbf{A}^3\mathbf{B}\}$

39 $\mathbf{PM} = \begin{bmatrix} 1 & 2 & 2 \\ 2 & -2 & 1 \\ 2 & 1 & -2 \end{bmatrix}$; $\mathbf{P} = \frac{1}{9}\begin{bmatrix} 8 & 1 & 4 \\ 4 & -4 & -7 \\ 1 & 8 & 4 \end{bmatrix}$

$(OABC) \xrightarrow{\mathbf{M}^{-1}} (Oxyz) \xrightarrow{\mathbf{T}} (Oyzx) \xrightarrow{\mathbf{M}} (OBCA)$

P and **T** represent transformations of the same type 1, w, w^2 (where $w = e^{\frac{2}{3}\pi j}$).

Eigenvectors of **T**: $\begin{bmatrix} 1 \\ 1 \\ 1 \end{bmatrix}, \begin{bmatrix} 1 \\ w^2 \\ w^3 \end{bmatrix}, \begin{bmatrix} 1 \\ w \\ w^2 \end{bmatrix}$

Eigenvectors of **P**: $\begin{bmatrix} 5 \\ 1 \\ 1 \end{bmatrix}, \begin{bmatrix} \frac{1}{2} + \frac{1}{2}\sqrt{3}j \\ 1 - 2\sqrt{3}j \\ -\frac{7}{2} - \frac{1}{2}\sqrt{3}j \end{bmatrix}, \begin{bmatrix} \frac{1}{2} - \frac{1}{2}\sqrt{3}j \\ 1 + 2\sqrt{3}j \\ -\frac{7}{2} + \frac{1}{2}\sqrt{3}j \end{bmatrix}$

40 (*a*) True
(*b*) True
(*c*) False – for example, if $\mathbf{X}_1 = \mathbf{X}_2 \neq \mathbf{0}$, then they form a one-dimensional subspace of $\mathbb{R}^3$.
(*d*) False – for example, if $\mathbf{X}_1 = \mathbf{X}_2 = \mathbf{X}_3 \neq \mathbf{0}$, then they form a one-dimensional subspace of $\mathbb{R}^3$.
(*e*) True

41 ${x_1}^2 + {x_2}^2 + {x_3}^2$

42 When $p = 2$ there are two perfect squares, 0^2 and 1^2. In $\mathbb{Z}_{29}$,

$1^4 = 28^4 = 12^4 = 17^4 = 1$

$2^4 = 27^4 = 24^4 = 5^4 = 16$

$3^4 = 26^4 = 7^4 = 22^4 = 23$

$4^4 = 25^4 = 19^4 = 10^4 = 24$

$6^4 = 23^4 = 14^4 = 15^4 = 20$

$8^4 = 21^4 = 9^4 = 20^4 = 14$

$11^4 = 18^4 = 16^4 = 13^4 = 25$

$\mathbb{Z}_{29}$ has eight different fourth powers, 0 and the above seven.

43 (*a*) $\left\{\begin{bmatrix}0\\1\\0\\2\end{bmatrix}\right\}$ (*b*) $\left\{\begin{bmatrix}-14\\7\\0\\3\end{bmatrix}\begin{bmatrix}0\\0\\1\\0\end{bmatrix}\right\}$ (*c*) $\left\{\begin{bmatrix}5\\-3\\1\end{bmatrix}\right\}$

44 (i) ρ_1 not reflexive, as $\mathbf{A}^{\mathrm{T}} \neq \mathbf{A}$ for all $\mathbf{A}$

(ii) ρ_2 not transitive, for example $\mathbf{A} = \begin{bmatrix}2 & 4\\4 & 3\end{bmatrix}$, $\mathbf{B} = \begin{bmatrix}1 & 1\\1 & 1\end{bmatrix}$, $\mathbf{C} = \begin{bmatrix}5 & 3\\3 & 5\end{bmatrix}$

(iii) ρ_3 not transitive as $\mathbf{A}\rho_3\mathbf{B}$ and $\mathbf{B}\rho_3\mathbf{A} \not\Rightarrow \mathbf{A}\rho_3\mathbf{A}$ unless $\mathbf{A}^2 = \mathbf{I}$.

45 $\begin{bmatrix}3 & 4\\2 & 1\end{bmatrix}, \begin{bmatrix}4 & 2\\1 & 3\end{bmatrix}, \begin{bmatrix}2 & 1\\3 & 4\end{bmatrix}, \begin{bmatrix}1 & 3\\4 & 2\end{bmatrix}; \begin{bmatrix}2 & 1\\3 & 4\end{bmatrix}, \begin{bmatrix}4 & 2\\1 & 3\end{bmatrix}, \begin{bmatrix}0 & 0\\0 & 0\end{bmatrix}, \begin{bmatrix}3 & 4\\2 & 1\end{bmatrix}, \begin{bmatrix}1 & 3\\4 & 2\end{bmatrix},$
that is, **M**, **L**, **O**, **K**, **J**.

46 The period is 3.

47 **A** is invertible, or $\det(\mathbf{A}) \neq 0$; $\dim(\ker(\mathbf{L}_\mathrm{A})) = 2$; range of $\mathbf{L}_\mathrm{A}\mathbf{R}_\mathrm{A} = \{\lambda\mathbf{A} : \lambda \in \mathbb{R}\}$

49 (i) $\mathbf{L}(x^n) = (n^2 - 1)x^n - (2n + 1)x^{n+1} + x^{n+2}$

(ii) $\mathbf{L}(e^x) = -e^x$

(iii) $\mathbf{L}(x^n e^x) = (n^2 - 1)x^n e^x$

$$\left(Ax + \frac{B}{x}\right)e^x$$

(*a*) $\left(Ax + \frac{B}{x} - 1\right)e^x$

(*b*) $\left(Ax + \frac{B}{x} + \tfrac{1}{3}x^2\right)e^x$

(*c*) $\left(Ax + \frac{B}{x}\right)e^x + x$

50

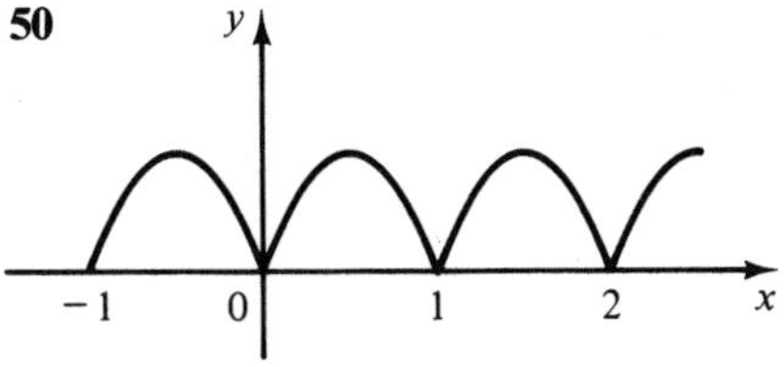

$f(x)$

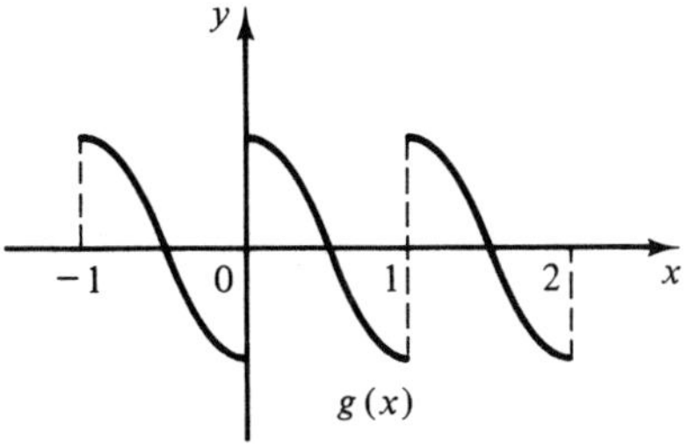

$g(x)$

(*a*) Identity (*b*) Translation +1 (*c*) Translation −1
(*d*) Reflection in $x = -\tfrac{1}{2}$ (*e*) Translation +2 (*f*) Translation in $x = \tfrac{3}{2}$
Symmetries of $f(x)$ are translation through $\pm n \equiv (\mathbf{QP})^n$ or $(\mathbf{PQ})^n$, and reflection in $x = \pm\frac{n}{2} \equiv (\mathbf{QP})^n\mathbf{P}$ or $(\mathbf{PQ})^n\mathbf{P}$.

R is a half-turn about (0, 0); **S** is a half-turn about $(\tfrac{1}{2}, 0)$; yes.

Index